COUNTERREVOLUTION

Counterrevolution: Extravagance and Austerity in Public Finance

Melinda Cooper

ZONE BOOKS

near futures

ZONE BOOKS
633 Vanderbilt Street, Brooklyn, New York 11218

Printed in the United States of America.
Distributed by Princeton University Press,
Princeton, New Jersey, and Woodstock, United Kingdom

Library of Congress Cataloging-in-Publication Data
Names: Cooper, Melinda, author.
Title: Counterrevolution : extravagance and austerity in public finance /
    Melinda Cooper.
Description: New York : Zone Books, [2024] | Series: Near futures | Includes
    bibliographical references and index. | Summary: "This book seeks to
    explain the combination of austerity and extravagance that characterizes
    government spending and central bank monetary policy in our times."
    — Provided by publisher.
Identifiers: LCCN 2023040951 (print) | LCCN 2023040952 (ebook) |
    ISBN 9781942130932 (hardcover) | ISBN 9781942130949 (ebook)
Subjects: LCSH: United States — Economic policy — 1971-1981. | Finance,
    public — United States — History — 20th century. | Neoliberalism —
    United States. | Supply-side economics — United States. | BISAC:
    POLITICAL SCIENCE / History & Theory | PHILOSOPHY / Political
    Classification: LCC HC106.7 .C678 2024 (print) | LCC HC106.7 (ebook) |
    DDC 338.973 — dc23/eng/20231017
LC record available at https://lccn.loc.gov/2023040951
LC ebook record available at https://lccn.loc.gov/2023040952

CONTENTS

Fiscal and Monetary Counterrevolution

Could things have turned out differently? Looking back on the free market counterrevolution of the last half century, it is hard to avoid a sense of historical fatalism. There can be little doubt that Keynesian capitalism in the 1970s was overwhelmed by a series of problems that eluded its usual methods of crisis management. With increasing strain on its fiscal and monetary limits, the Keynesian welfare state was forced to fight on all fronts against a perfect storm of threats, from foreign trade competition to third-world nationalism, oil price shocks, and rising wage and social demands at home. To observers on both the left and right, it seemed obvious that the fiscal and monetary crisis of the postwar state could not be resolved without a self-administered euthanasia of Keynesianism itself.[1] But what was to follow?

The shock therapy unleashed by Ronald Reagan and Margaret Thatcher in the early 1980s followed the hardline script of market deregulation, welfare retrenchment, and monetary deflation advocated by neoliberal thinkers of the Mont Pelerin Society. Yet social democratic governments around the world, from Australia to France, pursued their own softer versions of neoliberal transition and thus paved the way to a new consensus. By the 1990s the debate was seemingly over. While the political right and left fought over the precise form of free market transition, the neoliberal solution to the crisis of Keynesianism was embraced by all. With the collapse of the Soviet Union, only the most utopian of leftists would cling to the belief that things could have turned out otherwise.

This sense of inevitability has become so engrained on both the left and right that it comes as a shock to realize that the neoliberal resolution to the capitalist crisis of the 1970s was by no means self-evident to those we now consider the victors. For many of the major characters in this book, the real story of the 1970s was a fight to the death between labor and capital, the outcome of which was far from preordained. As much as they steeled themselves for battle, their overwhelming mood was melancholic—even apocalyptic—rather than triumphant.

The Virginia school economist James M. Buchanan blamed the fiscal and monetary pathologies of the decade on a wider "behavioral revolution."[2] The same zeitgeist that had produced runaway inflation was also responsible, he thought, for a "generalized erosion in public and private manners, increasingly liberalized attitudes toward sexual activities, a declining vitality of the Puritan work ethic, deterioration in product quality, explosion of the welfare rolls, widespread corruption in both the private and the governmental sector, and, finally, observed increases in the alienation of voters from the political process."[3] Buchanan had witnessed the first stirrings of this revolution on campus, when student activists and Black militants took aim at the nexus between the university, the petrochemical industry, and U.S. imperialism. He "had sensed an urge to stand and fight, to do battle in the quads," as he "saw rules and conventions that embodied capital value fall undefended before the new barbarians."[4] Instead, he purchased a farmhouse in the Appalachian foothills, where he could retreat whenever the "wider disruption of social order"[5] became too much.

For Arthur Laffer, the Chicago school economics graduate who was then working in Gerald Ford's Department of Treasury, the parlous state of financial markets at mid-decade evoked the doomsday prophecies of the first millennium, when traders in church indulgences came face to face with the prospect of eternal damnation. "As we stand poised on the verge of the dawning of the third millennium after the birth of Christ," he told a gathering of financial analysts in New York, "I feel it is far more than just interesting—perhaps even imperative—to analyze the behavior of our current markets in the perspective of the historical precedents set during the twilight of the first millennium."[6] Dwindling returns on financial assets and ever-expanding social budgets convinced Laffer that the future of capitalism was relentlessly bleak. The expansion of social insurance programs buffering wage earners from the market had destroyed the work ethic and would soon condemn financial asset holders to an eternity of extortionate taxes, interest rates, and inflation. There was, he thought, no easy way out. "Perhaps the solution to our doomsday problem is the exact opposite of the solution found at the end of the first millennium," Laffer concluded; "We need the appearance of God."

For all their hyperbole, these dispatches from the 1970s are a helpful reminder of the despair that gripped right-wing economists at the time. In their eyes, at least, the battle was still in progress and victory by no means assured.

On the left, by contrast, we are just as likely to find a guarded sense of optimism. The Marxist economist James O'Connor fully appreciated the promise and perils of the moment. Writing at the beginning of the decade, O'Connor understood that the burgeoning "fiscal crisis of the state" reflected an intensified struggle between wage workers, industrialists, and asset holders on the one hand and different sectors of the working and "surplus" classes on the other.[7] The struggle resulted from the fact that growing portions of the private industrial sector had been de facto socialized as a result of permanent government contracts and soaring public investment, while the corporations that benefited from this arrangement jealously guarded their profits from social redistribution. The conflict had been containable as long as the New Deal social compact was reserved for the white, male, industrial worker. But the expanding welfare state had itself created new classes of public-sector workers (disproportionately female and African American) and state dependents (students, welfare recipients, patients, and detainees) who no longer accepted their status as social surplus. The resulting conflict pitted not only private-sector workers against industrialists but also public-sector workers and state dependents against the paternalist administration of social services by the state.[8] Yet the fiscal and monetary methods of the Keynesian social consensus were premised on the fact that redistribution was limited to a small portion of the wage-earning class. Any challenge to these limits would result in a fiscal (and monetary) crisis of the Keynesian state. Without in any way downplaying the internal divisions of the left, O'Connor saw a very different future from the one that history has bequeathed us. The conflict, he claimed, could be resolved only by socialism, that is, by the suppression of private profit, the full redistribution of social wealth, and a participatory administration of welfare, health care, and education by its beneficiaries.[9]

With this provocation, O'Connor was popping a thought bubble first blown by the Austrian economist Joseph Alois Schumpeter at a time when welfare state capitalism was still in its infancy. In an essay published in 1918,

Schumpeter suggested that the rising importance of the fiscal state—a state armed with historically unprecedented powers to tax, spend, create money, and issue debt—had fundamentally shifted the terrain on which class struggle was played out.[10] Written in response to postwar fears of overhanging debt and rising tax burdens, the essay offered a novel perspective on the question of fiscal crisis. While others warned of intractable budgetary problems thrown up by the costs of war, Schumpeter dismissed the idea that the state was in any real danger of becoming insolvent or going bankrupt. Much more ominous than the economic burden of rising war debt, he countered, was the political threat of "rising social expenditures"—for it was "from that side" that the capitalist state might "be conquered."[11]

In other words, what the capitalist state had run up against were political limits to its own modus operandi, not absolute economic limits to fiscal and monetary policy. The rise of the modern fiscal state—by which Schumpeter meant the nascent social state of the early twentieth century—placed elected legislators in a quandary when it came to the management of private wealth. Capitalist states had long resorted to debt finance and taxation to fund their imperial and commercial pursuits. But the expansion of the democratic franchise had placed qualitatively new demands on the state that threatened its capacity to maintain social order. The growing portion of spending, actuarial, and redistributive functions foisted on government by an increasingly enfranchised polity had brought class struggle into the heart of the state and turned its budget into a ledger of conflict. As advocates of the gold standard well knew, working-class insurgency could be defeated from above by the imposition of sound finance and balanced budgets. But fiscal crisis could also be resolved in another fashion. If the poor continued to extract resources from the state, then the private economy might eventually be overwhelmed from below by the clamor of democratic demands.[12] At some point, Schumpeter warned, fiscal and monetary *redistribution* would tilt into fiscal and monetary *revolution*—a complete takeover of the state's powers to create money, issue debt, and distribute wealth.

What Schumpeter was contemplating here was a very different style of revolution to the one we commonly associate with classical Marxism.[13] Yet it was Schumpeter who correctly foresaw the kinds of struggle that would emerge in the 1960s and 1970s as welfare state capitalism entered another period of fiscal and monetary crisis. The "hour has not yet struck" for fiscal revolt, he wrote in the conclusion to his 1918 essay.[14] Yet the hour would come some five decades later. And when it did, Schumpeter's articulation of elite fears proved uncannily clairvoyant.

For much of the twentieth century, the Keynesian consensus between labor unions, industrialists, and the state provided an answer to Schumpeter's fears. As political theorist Geoff Mann has argued, Keynesianism is best understood as a project of Hegelian mediation applied to the social sphere and enacted as a bulwark against communism.[15] By fostering a constant growth in national income, welfare-state capitalism found a way to divide the spoils between capitalists and workers while containing redistribution within tolerable limits. Yet while this may have forestalled the danger of fiscal and monetary revolution, it did not eliminate it. The Polish economist Michał Kalecki was one of the first to offer an unflinching appraisal of the political limits of Keynesianism as a project of mediation. As early as the 1940s, at a time when large corporations were settling into a working relationship with organized labor and the big spending state, Kalecki sought to understand why business leaders were still so suspicious of the prospect of full employment.[16] If the activist use of the deficit and monetary policy could deliver a reliable workforce and steadily rising profits while simultaneously tempering the volatilities of the business cycle, why were so many corporate leaders still so loath to see a full implementation of the Keynesian social state?

Like Schumpeter, Kalecki understood that the limits of the Keynesian consensus were political, not technical. Efforts by government to subsidize public services, welfare, and the wage might be beneficial in stimulating profits in the short term. But by releasing workers from the fear of unemployment and welfare dependents from poverty, they threatened the raison d'être of capitalism itself. Absent the discipline of the market, there was nothing to stop workers from pushing up wages or politicians from redistributing wealth to win their votes. If pushed too far, it was possible that the institutions of the social state—from public schools and hospitals to health care, old age, and unemployment insurance—would be seized from below, turning state dependents into agents of a new kind of social revolution. It was for this reason, Kalecki foresaw, that business elites would allow only limited and temporary implementation of Keynesian policies: spending on physical infrastructure or defense would be favored over long-term investments in education, health care, and welfare, while boom-bust cycles would be tolerated as an economically disruptive but politically safe alternative to permanent deficit spending. Instinctively, industrialists and asset holders understood that labor discipline was more important to the survival of capitalism than nominal profit rates or the stability of economic growth. After all, any sustained rollout of Keynesian social investment policies would inevitably lead to chronic wage and consumer price inflation—with a corresponding erosion of real profits and the ever-present risk of a wage-price spiral. As soon as asset holders in particular were threatened by rising wages and prices, Kalecki warned, a "powerful block is likely to be formed between big business and the rentier interests, and they would probably find more than one economist to declare that the situation was manifestly unsound."[17]

This was a remarkably prescient account of the political turmoil of the 1970s, when wages effectively outran the power of corporations to collect profits and the resulting consumer price inflation eroded the wealth of financial asset holders. Even Kalecki, however, did not envisage the full scope of the social revolt of the 1970s, which brought into question the racial and gendered foundations of the Keynesian social contract as much as its class order. The era's spirit of insurgency extended well beyond the ranks of unionized, industrial workers. It also mobilized those who had been excluded from the New Deal contract: African American factory and domestic workers, public-sector employees, migrant farm laborers, welfare mothers, students, and dependents of the family wage. A resurgent feminism challenged the very structure of the male breadwinner family that undergirded the Keynesian social order and thus provoked the ire of social conservatives as much as free market liberals. If this was not quite a revolution, it came close enough to trigger a monumental backlash.

What we have experienced since then is one long counterrevolution.

EXTRAVAGANCE AND AUSTERITY

By counterrevolution, I do not mean a return to the world of honest money and limited government dreamed of by the purest of free market radicals. The libertarian credo that calls for the abolition of the Federal Reserve, an end to fiat money, and the repeal of the income tax continues to play an important role in U.S. politics, but it has had little impact on the reshaping of institutions. Indeed, as libertarians themselves lament, state budgets are bigger than ever, public debt grows beyond all measure, and the Federal Reserve has assumed powers of money creation unimaginable in earlier decades.[18] If institutional size and firepower are anything to go by, we are very far from the reign of sound finance that libertarian gold bugs would like to see. Why then do so many of us live in a world of unremitting fiscal and monetary austerity, as if ruled over by the hard money constraint of gold?

To make sense of this paradox, we need to understand how the neoliberal counterrevolution assigned an unofficial dual mandate to fiscal and monetary authorities, on the one hand setting them free from the traditional constraints on public money and debt creation while on the other instructing them to use these powers for the narrowest of ends.[19] We do not lack the means to collectivize public debt issuance, to monetize that debt, to channel that money into collective spending on education, health care, welfare, and the transition to renewable energy, or to redistribute the ensuing social wealth. What we lack is the political will. The challenge for neoliberal technocrats has been to turn these institutional possibilities into political dead ends while doing all in their power to accommodate the interests of private asset holders.

The challenge first presented itself in 1971, when President Nixon made the fateful decision to close the gold window that allowed currency traders to exchange their U.S. dollars for hard money. The decision bought precious time. Its immediate effect was to release the United States from the blackmail of foreign trade partners, who could always force the country to put its fiscal and monetary house in order by threatening to withdraw their dollars for gold. As non-fiat money in limited supply, gold was an enforcer of monetary and fiscal austerity. It was the hard monetary medium that limited the ability of the United States to run budget deficits or lower interest rates. The suspension of the gold window released the U.S. government from this discipline, allowing it to deal with its growing trade deficit and rising domestic inflation on its own terms.[20] But in so doing, it also removed a convenient external constraint on U.S. domestic politics. In the absence of a hard technical limit to budget deficits and inflation, could elected legislators be trusted to enforce social spending austerity of their own accord?

To business leaders and financial investors alike, the transition to floating exchange rates appeared like a mixed blessing that could ease balance-of-payment pressures in the short term while throwing up worse problems down the road. Uppermost in their mind was the growing power of trade unions, which in the early 1970s were regularly winning wage settlements in excess of the consumer price level. The specter of "wage push inflation"—a general inflation of consumer prices that was catalyzed by oil price shocks but driven forward by the bargaining power of organized labor—haunted the business and political elites of the period.[21] Economists invoked the threat of "hyperinflation": without the discipline of fixed exchange rates, they warned, there was a real danger that weak-willed legislators would keep expanding the social budget and prevail on the Federal Reserve to accommodate their spending with wanton "money printing." For many, the fact that the Federal Reserve had the power to directly purchase Treasury debt (a process known variously as debt monetization, monetary finance, or more pejoratively "money printing") and thus allow the government to spend at zero or low cost was a fatal institutional weakness. Because of this they thought that any solution to the conundrum of floating exchange rates would have to include a radical overhaul of the central bank's charter and sphere of influence.

The scope of the problem was clearly appreciated by Chicago school neoliberal Milton Friedman, who repeated Irving Fisher's warning that "irredeemable money had almost invariably proved a curse to the country employing it."[22] While Friedman was personally in favor of floating exchange rates, the success of the regime, he averred, would depend on whether "we find a substitute for convertibility into specie that will serve the same function: maintaining pressure on the government to refrain from its resort to inflation as a source of revenue."[23] The Federal Reserve could not be allowed to accommodate rising wage settlements and social demands by monetizing (and thus inflating away) government debt. It was imperative that it "find a nominal anchor for the price level to replace the physical limit on a monetary commodity."[24] In the absence of gold, an alternative form of monetary discipline would have to be found.

While Friedman had set out the terms of the challenge, it fell to Paul Volcker, President Carter's appointee as chair of the Federal Reserve in 1979, to find a workable solution. By refusing to accommodate incoming President

Reagan's big-spending military and tax cut budget of 1981 and letting interest rates soar, Volcker established the new expectation of central bank impassivity in the face of government desperation. The stance—soon to be formalized in the norm of "central bank independence"—established a strict institutional separation between the Treasury and the central bank and forbade the latter from accommodating government spending by resorting to "money printing." [25] Between 1980 and 2008 central banks around the world massively off-loaded their public bond holdings, determined to wean governments off the drug of cheap money and rein in their spending. [26] Henceforth, treasuries would be forced to issue tradable securities and finance their spending in the bond markets, where they would be subject to the unsentimental appraisal of bond vigilantes. Bruised by the trauma of the 1970s, bond traders were phobic of any form of government spending that might empower labor or push up the social wage: as such, they could be expected to punish weak-willed governments with exorbitant interest rates.

By the early 1980s, then, the U.S. government's release from the monetary discipline of gold was replaced by a new kind of institutional constraint. In the words of his biographer William Silber, Volcker showed that a "determined central banker could act like a surrogate for gold" and thus "rescued the experiment in fiat currency from failure." [27] Neoliberal monetary orthodoxy would transmute Volcker's personal determination into a steely institutional animus against (wage-push) inflation. The U.S., and world, economy would henceforth operate on an institutional ersatz for gold—"a gold standard without gold." [28]

The advantage of this arrangement was that it allowed the Federal Reserve to deploy monetary austerity in the most targeted of ways, while at the same time holding all its powers of monetary accommodation in reserve for special occasions. There was good reason why a youthful gold bug such as Alan Greenspan did not hesitate to enter the temple of fiat money in the wake of Paul Volcker. [29] Greenspan understood much earlier than most that if the Federal Reserve could be disciplined to suppress the slightest hint of wage inflation, its powers of money creation could nevertheless be selectively unleashed to foster the inflation of asset-based wealth. [30] Neoliberal monetary orthodoxy could do everything that gold was meant to do—and more. The key variable here was government fiscal policy, which had to be austere enough to keep the (social) wage in check yet simultaneously generous enough to reward investment in financial assets.

The most obvious feature of neoliberal fiscal policy has been its fierce will to retrenchment. With the neoliberal turn of the 1980s, the fiscal crisis of the state was resolved in favor of social spending cuts as opposed to tax increases (at least of the visible or direct kind), and welfare states since then have operated under a regime of permanent fiscal austerity.[31] Social spending decisions, we are told, must bend to the constraints of demographic aging, declining growth rates, and the international bond market. There is only so much money to go around, and since almost everyone agrees that defense outlays are off the table, what we are left with is a competition between different items in the social welfare budget.

We should not underestimate the political endgame here: Republicans have never hidden their desire to fully privatize Social Security and Medicare. In the meantime, however, the timeline of retrenchment has followed the reverse order of priorities laid out in the New Deal welfare state, winning its first outright victories with stigmatized public assistance programs associated with impoverished African American and Latina women, and proceeding from here to the more secure entitlement programs that were designed to protect the male breadwinner wage.

The will to retrenchment, moreover, goes far beyond the sphere of social insurance to encompass the whole gamut of social spending programs associated with the postwar emancipation of women and racial minorities. Just as decisive as the fiscal conservative rationale behind these attacks was the social conservative agenda to "defund the left."[32] Following the student revolts of the 1960s and 1970s, higher education was a prime target for retrenchment: the slow attrition of federal funding from the Reagan administration onward shifted its fortunes to the states, where it had to compete with a rapidly growing prison and corrections budget.[33] Public schools too came under fire in the 1970s not only as hotbeds of left-wing teacher unionism but also as purveyors of state-subsidized sex education and racial tolerance. They remain on the front line of the culture wars to this day, as conservatives call for a reassertion of parental rights in the face of rampant gender and racial indoctrination.[34] Perhaps the most enduring alliance between fiscal and religious conservatives, however, was the long campaign to defund Planned Parenthood, to introduce religious exemptions in public hospital settings, and to make abortion unaffordable to poor women. Long before the judicial counterrevolution of the Trump era made it possible to overturn *Roe v. Wade* outright, the religious right did all in its power to outlaw abortion by fiscal means. In this and other cases, fiscal austerity and moral discipline went hand in hand.

Yet we misunderstand the scope of neoliberal fiscal policy if we assume austerity to be its sole setting. Beyond the zero-sum game of competing claims on direct expenditure lies a whole realm of *indirect* government spending that escapes the naked eye. To grasp the complexity of neoliberal fiscalism fully, we need to look at the large and growing portion of government outlays that takes the paradoxical form of indirect spending through the tax code.[35] Tax deductions, exclusions, preferences, exemptions, deferrals, and credits are all deliberate departures from a baseline rate of income taxation that are designed to facilitate certain kinds of investment choice in the private economy. There is general recognition among public finance economists that tax provisions of this kind are functionally equivalent to traditional public spending. For this reason, they are referred to as "tax expenditures" and counted as such in annual reports issued by the Treasury Department and Joint Committee on Taxation.[36]

As functional subtractions from the federal budget, tax expenditures have the same effect on Treasury accounts as direct government spending. Yet they are commonly perceived as both tax *and* spending cuts by the public and are rarely singled out as contributions to the budget deficit.[37] Social tax expenditures such as the Earned Income Tax Credit (EITC) have proven useful to New Democrats, who want to pursue a minimal social spending agenda while avoiding the charge of fiscal profligacy. But it is Republicans who have made the most extravagant use of the tax expenditure option to enact massive spending programs on behalf of the well-off, in the process creating a shadow welfare state that should be unaffordable by their own metrics.[38] Tax expenditures are one reason why Republicans in power regularly leave massive budget deficits and debt burdens in their wake while seemingly pursuing the most austere of social spending agendas.

As a ratio of government spending, tax expenditures have grown dramatically over the past four decades. At last estimate, the U.S. Treasury currently foregoes $1.5 trillion in annual revenue through its income-related tax expenditures—higher than the Social Security budget or more than one-third of direct government spending.[39] Their overall impact is highly regressive. At the same time that Republican legislators in particular resist any increase in direct social spending, they actively reward citizens for channeling their savings into "private" alternatives to "public" welfare, thus offering a permanent subsidy to asset-based wealth accumulation.[40] This is most obviously the case when it comes to the suite of tax expenditures relating to dividends and capital gains, which overwhelmingly benefit households in the top 1 percent of the income distribution. But it also applies to tax expenditures on private housing, which in a low-interest-rate environment have contributed to the transformation of the home into a financial asset and sharpened the class divisions between the homeowner and the renter. As tax expenditures have grown with respect to direct social spending, the United States is left with a divided welfare state of threadbare income transfers and outrageously generous subsidies to private wealth. Fiscal austerity, then, is only one side of the neoliberal tax and spending agenda.

The same dynamic is at work in industrial and urban policy, which relies increasingly on tax incentives to would-be private investors rather than direct public investment.[41] The dwindling of federal support for lower levels of government has forced cash-strapped state and local governments to lavish resources on private investors, corporations, and real estate developers in the hope that some of the resulting gains will come trickling back down at some point in the future. The municipal debt market that holds legislators in its grip demands that public outlays reward private investors before all others.[42] Thus, while cities and states outdo each other in indirect spending on private asset holders, their direct commitment to public services grows hopelessly thin.

The increasingly regressive profile of fiscal policy explains why the inveterate monetary hawk Alan Greenspan turned dovish in the late 1990s and why his Federal Reserve successors felt free to break that last taboo of central bank independence—the prohibition against monetizing the federal debt—in the wake of two global financial crises. It helps us to understand, also, why the massive exercise in debt monetization pursued under the guise of quantitative easing (QE) led to asset price (not wage) inflation, in apparent defiance of orthodox monetary logic.[43] It turns out that monetary and fiscal policy cannot be understood independently: one monetary action can produce vastly different effects depending on the fiscal environment it is operating in. Thus, while central bank "money printing" may have looked like a slippery slope to the hyperinflation of wages in the early 1970s, at a time when a Republican President Nixon was expanding the social budget and the trade union movement still had clout, it no longer presented the same threat in the 2000s, when so much of government social spending was sustaining the wealth of private asset holders. During the past four decades, the steady buildup of tax expenditures serving to subsidize the value of financial assets—from capital gains preferences to estate tax deductions—has created a situation in which low interest rates and cheap debt will automatically feed into asset price inflation and a further concentration of wealth in the hands of the already rich. These fiscal buffers work on the downside as well as the upside, helping to explain why at least some asset classes remain surprisingly resilient to any reversal in the Federal Reserve's low-interest-rate policy. When financial asset holders begin to suffer real losses, they have recourse to special tax provisions not available to the average wage earner that allow them to write off income taxes into the far future. For those with enough money to qualify, failure is never absolute.

At this point it should be clear why "neofeudalism" is not an adequate descriptor of our current conjuncture.[44] What we have witnessed during the last four decades of counterrevolution is not a dismantling of the modern Treasury or central bank much less the self-abolition of capitalism, but an extraordinary intensification of fiscal and monetary capacities in the service of a dual mandate. For all its airs of haughty asceticism, the Federal Reserve has relinquished none of its powers to create money or sustain wealth. Indeed, in the last few decades, it has acquired extraordinary new powers to deal with the threat of asset price deflation, extending its lender-of-last-resort function from government-chartered to shadow banks and from U.S. to world capital markets.[45] Yet it has jealously guarded these powers from democratic or redistributive intent, deploying them only when it was sure that financial asset holders would be the primary beneficiaries. The fiscal state, too, has lost none of its powers of debt issuance and redistribution, despite the oft-repeated diagnoses of terminal impotence. Even while it vaunts its commitment to spending restraint, the neoliberal state indulges in orgies of tax expenditure that reliably violate its own rules of budget balance. The combined effect has been to re-create the austere conditions of classical sound finance for mere wage earners and welfare beneficiaries while furnishing a world of unimaginable abundance for asset holders.

PUBLIC CHOICE AUSTERITY AND SUPPLY-SIDE EXTRAVAGANCE

This book investigates the key moments and actors in this long counterrevolution, focusing in particular on the role of Virginia school public choice theory and supply-side economics in reshaping the budgetary politics of American government. As members of the wider "neoliberal thought collective," these movements produced distinct but ultimately complementary responses to the capitalist crisis of the 1970s.[46]

With its intellectual roots in the conservative southern Democratic tradition, Virginia school public choice theory calls for constitutional limits to the tax and spending powers of the state at every level of government. Its policy agenda of tax cuts and balanced budgets is a recipe for austerity, much more severe than the balanced budget regime of the postwar Republican mainstream. This agenda originated in the Solid South of one-party Democratic states, which practiced an extreme form of public spending austerity as a way of disciplining Black agricultural and domestic workers and the poorest of whites. It was upheld as budgetary gospel by the conservative southern Democrats who ruled the Senate until the civil rights era and was subsequently transmuted into an elaborate philosophy of constitutional economics by the father of Virginia school neoliberalism, James M. Buchanan. As southern Democrats passed the baton of budget austerity to Sunbelt Republicans in the 1970s, Buchanan's prescriptions for budgetary restraint would be embraced wholesale by the ascendant right wing of the Republican Party.

With its blueprints for tax and spending limits, supermajority voting rules, and a federal balanced budget amendment, the political legacy of Virginia school neoliberalism is much more significant than is commonly assumed. It was the intellectual driving force behind the long wave of tax and expenditure limitations that forced austerity on state and local government in the late 1970s and 1980s. It continues to fuel the interminable campaign for a federal balanced budget amendment. And it has left its imprint in the now familiar spectacles of Republican debt ceiling showdowns, the routine abuse of the

Senate filibuster, and threatened defaults on U.S. sovereign debt. The Virginia school style of zealous austerity has become so entrenched in Republican Party politics that it is difficult to appreciate how drastically it departed from the Republican mainstream of the postwar period. The so-called Eisenhower Republicans of this era were certainly committed to the principle of balanced budgets. Yet they had also made their peace with the expanded government budget bequeathed by the New Deal, World War II, and America's role as an emerging imperial power. Hence, they were prepared to increase taxes if extra revenue was needed to cover public spending. As children of the anti–New Deal South, Virginia school neoliberals espoused a much bleaker fiscal politics that insisted on balanced budgets while ruling out the possibility of direct tax increases. With all other options off the table, the tightening of the fiscal screw could only ever lead to spending cuts.

The supply-side movement, by contrast, advocated tax cuts without spending restraint or debt limits, in an apparent repudiation of fiscal austerity. With their close ties to the U.S. Treasury Department, itself intimately enmeshed in the world of Wall Street bond traders, supply-side economists had a more sophisticated analysis of the realities of government finance. In the immediate aftermath of Nixon's floating of the dollar, they were quick to recognize the newly pivotal role played by U.S. Treasury debt in global financial markets and sought to consolidate its hegemony to the advantage of U.S. asset holders. The Columbia University economist and future Nobel Prize winner Robert Mundell was among the first to understand how the United States, in a new environment of floating exchange rates, could leverage its position as issuer of the world's reserve currency to escape the zero-sum constraints binding other economies. As long as the government maintained the right domestic budgetary priorities, he argued, the global demand for U.S. Treasury debt and other dollar-denominated assets would ensure a constant inflow of cheap credit to the United States, thus freeing its government from spending constraints and allowing it to finance an extravaganza of tax cuts.[47]

At first blush, supply-side economists seemed to be preaching the exact opposite to public choice theory. Tax cuts need not be balanced by spending restraint, they counseled, as long as investors could be found to purchase the resulting government debt at low cost. Where Virginia school economists intoned the mantra of balanced budgets and fiscal austerity, supply-side economists celebrated a non-Keynesian version of the "free lunch." They, too, proclaimed their difference from Eisenhower Republicans. But where Virginia school neoliberals wanted to salvage balanced budgets with spending cuts, supply-siders at their most populist dismissed the logic of austerity altogether. In their frequent media tirades, prominent movement figures such as Jude Wanniski lambasted public choice theorists for their outdated allegiance to the "household budget" theory of public finance, with its phobia of government deficits and naive perspective on the workings of public debt.[48] The GOP, they argued, could reinvent itself as the party of abundance.[49]

Yet the supply-siders, too, recognized that fiscal and monetary abundance had its own constraints. It was obvious, for example, that U.S. Treasury debt would remain attractive to investors only as long as the dollar's value was protected from the threat of (wage and consumer price) inflation. The 1978 flight from the dollar demonstrated how easily the United States could lose its newly hegemonic position if the government failed to rein in the power of trade unions and radical social movements. For supply-siders, fiscal extravagance was possible then, but only in one direction. Tax incentives to private wealth creation could be pushed without remorse because they posed no risk of inflating wages or consumer prices. By contrast, any public spending that might empower labor or lift the social wage would repel global investors and thus compromise the hegemonic role of the dollar. The upshot was that the United States could free itself from the normal constraints of balanced budgets only if it enacted a selective form of austerity.

Thus, public choice and supply-side economists found an uneasy point of convergence around the need to contain *certain kinds* of public spending. While they might never agree on the fundamentals, representatives of both schools found common ground in a shared animosity toward Eisenhower Republicanism. As is so often the case, moreover, political actors barely paused to contemplate the logical conflict. Thus, Newt Gingrich and almost all his followers on the insurgent Republican right embraced a syncretic faith of balanced budget piousness and supply-side indulgence. At the same time that Virginia school balanced budget rules demanded continuous assaults on "unaffordable" social services, supply-side tax expenditures (dubbed "incentives") authorized a guilt-free transfer of public money into the coffers of personal wealth holders, real estate developers, and corporations. The logical contradictions could never be perfectly resolved, of course, since supply-side tax expenditures would always violate the Virginia school prohibition against budget deficits. Yet this itself imparted a self-reinforcing momentum to the whole cycle, allowing legislators to invoke the soaring federal debt as proof of fiscal sinfulness each time they inflicted a new round of cutbacks.

What we are left with is the paradox of increasingly austere social spending budgets alongside ever-expanding volumes of federal debt. As public finance economists have long noted, even when constitutionally enforced, tax and spending limits or balanced budget rules rarely if ever end up reducing the volume of public debt issuance. Instead, as the recent history of state and local government has made clear, they remove public-debt finance from the realm of democratic decision making and revenue collection from the general tax fund, favoring the use of so-called revenue bonds that support private infrastructure investment and nakedly regressive types of collateral such as user fees. At the federal level, it hardly needs pointing out that the national debt has surpassed the worst fears of debt millenarians, even while the profile of public spending and taxation has grown increasingly mean and regressive. The combined message of public choice and supply-side fiscalism was clear. Public debt (municipal, state, and federal) could be issued ad infinitum, as long as it channeled most of its benefits toward the private accumulation of wealth. The government spending spigot could keep flowing, as long as the resulting social wealth was distributed upward. What the alliance between supply-side and public choice economics delivered in practice was the precise mixture of fiscal austerity and extravagance demanded by neoliberal monetary orthodoxy.

DYNASTIC CAPITALISM

The counterrevolution in public finance has brought with it levels of wealth concentration not seen since the Gilded Age and has profoundly reshaped the organizational form of capitalism itself. The publicly traded, vertically integrated corporation that dominated the landscape of mid-twentieth-century capitalism and drew ever greater numbers of workers into its orbit of long-term secure employment is no longer the institution it once was.[50] Private, family-owned corporations have assumed a new prominence in American and global capitalism. New businesses are avoiding the lure of public markets for as long as they can, growing to massive size before they launch an IPO. And even when they go public, they are finding ingenious ways to install new forms of elite, patrimonial control behind the façade of the shareholder-owned corporations. The organizational priorities of corporations are increasingly dictated by private, unincorporated entities such as private equity firms, hedge funds, and venture capitalists, with their ruthless disregard for anything but capital gains in share prices. These alternative investment funds are playing an ever more important role in the direct provision of finance to new companies that wish to avoid the public share markets for as long as possible. Among the most aggressive of the new alternative investment funds are so-called family offices—kin-based wealth investment funds that have multiplied as a result of the decade-long surge in wealth concentration.

As historian Steve Fraser observes, "family capitalism has experienced a renaissance."[51] Few would have predicted this outcome in the 1970s heyday of business revanchism. The tax and regulatory reforms that were meant to revive investment in fixed capital assets, expand employment, and reinvigorate industrial profits instead incentivized firms to divest from their internal workforces and to outsource fixed capital costs. The governance reforms that were meant to realign the incentives of the corporation in favor of the mass shareholder public simply exchanged the old managerial elite for a new owner-investor elite that ruthlessly concentrated power in its own hands. And instead of reviving the profit and growth rates of Fordism's glory days, the shareholder revolution changed the profit form itself, reorienting corporations away from industrial profits (derived from retained earnings) toward capital gains (asset price appreciation) and dividends (income from assets).[52]

While it would be easy to conclude that we have regressed to a state of feudalism, the fact is that the family dynasts of our time enjoy a level of organized public support that medieval lords could only dream of. We live in an age of paradoxes where nominally private, non-state-chartered (or shadow) money is permanently backstopped by the world's most powerful central bank and private family wealth soars in value with the full collusion of fiscal and monetary authorities. In the meantime, the same state institutions see wage inflation as a mortal threat to the value of financial assets and demand that consumers pay for nominally public services in the form of crippling personal debt.

It might be objected of course that private wealth has always been subsidized to some degree by the modern fiscal state. The distributive remit of central banks and treasuries has been a matter of fierce contestation since at least the early twentieth century. But while there have been moments when fiscal and monetary policy shifted in favor of wage workers (during the New Deal and more ambiguously, in the late 1960s and early 1970s) and others where it flipped back in favor of asset holders (the 1980s and beyond), what we have experienced since the Global Financial Crisis of 2008 is without precedent. By taking whole chunks of the private and public debt market onto its books and assuming a preemptive role in the defense of asset prices, the Federal Reserve has socialized the risks of private wealth as never before, while exposing mere wage earners to the full violence of the free market. It is significant, in this regard, that the only situation in which the Federal Reserve is prepared to change course is when it believes (wrongly or rightly) that its asset-stimulating policies may have inadvertently triggered an inflation in wages. It was the fear of wage rises among the lowest-paid service workers, not the vertiginous wealth gains of the 1 percent or coordinated profit hikes by large corporations, that prompted Fed chairman Jerome Powell to begin unwinding QE in mid-2022.[53] Yet even for would-be monetary hawks, there can be no easy exit from the central bank regime of asset price accommodation. As long as fiscal incentives continue to channel wealth into financial assets, and as long as capital gains outperform industrial profits as a return on investment, the Federal Reserve appears locked into a pledge of permanent crisis response, where it has little choice but to come to the rescue when asset markets fail. Interest rate rises create policy space for central banks to act in the future, but by themselves they cannot release it from its role in validating a fiscal regime that overwhelmingly promotes the value of financial assets.

If there is any virtue in this regime, it lies in the fact that the powers of public finance to create wealth and socialize risk are visible as never before, even as they are deployed in the most unequal of ways. We know that fiscal and monetary extravagance is technically possible. We have yet to fully embrace this knowledge as the starting point for a more expansive vision of revolutionary change. If pseudoscientific laws of price stability and balanced budgets can be transgressed at will to socialize the risks of the wealthiest asset holders, why would we not deploy the same powers in service of the many? If wage inflation is the biggest threat to asset price and profit-driven inflation, why would we not pursue this insight as a pathway to radical wealth redistribution from below? To be sure, such propositions are bound to appear utopian in a context where the left is very far from possessing the organizational power to act on them in any systematic way. Yet merely to articulate them as the horizon of communist politics can concentrate the mind and clarify strategic priorities. The notion that social redistribution might be pursued beyond the limits tolerable to the capitalist state has long haunted the most perceptive observers of capitalist class politics. During the 1970s, the strategy was embraced by elements of the anarcho-communist left who consciously worked "in and against the state" to release the social wage from the conditionalities of the Keynesian welfare apparatus.[54] Today, left-wing Keynesians (or so-called post-Keynesians) are the most lucid analysts of the hidden possibilities of public finance and central bank money creation.[55] Yet as advocates of class consensus, exponents of Modern Monetary Theory (MMT) are duty bound to pull back from the edge when redistribution is pushed too far.

Are we prepared to go over the edge in pursuit of revolutionary extravagance?

CHAPTER ONE

Capital Gains: Supply-Side Economics and the Return of Dynastic Capitalism

How do we explain the election of Donald Trump, the Republican outsider whose fortunes were built on the vertiginous appreciation of asset prices and esoteric tax dodges? Why did so many small business owners choose to vote for a candidate who consolidated his inherited wealth with the help of tax-free capital gains while systematically defrauding his many business partners and contractors? And lest we focus too exclusively on Trump's populist appeal, why have so many in the financial and political world bailed him out each time he spectacularly failed? Trump played to multiple audiences during his presidential campaign, sometimes presenting as a champion of the blue-collar worker and drainer of swamps, other times as the consummate dealmaker. Yet any doubts about his real political colors were dispelled upon his arrival in office, where one of his first moves was to push through a shamelessly plutocratic tax cut.

The 2017 Tax Cuts and Jobs Act was designed by five veteran supply-siders, all fellow travelers of the Tea Party movement and alumni of the Reagan administration.[1] Their names were Arthur Laffer, for many the mascot of supply-side economics; Stephen Moore, Heritage Foundation fellow and founding president of the Club for Growth; Steve Forbes, editor-in-chief of *Forbes* business magazine and board member of FreedomWorks; Lawrence Kudlow, financial news services host at CNBC and Fox; and David Malpass, former chief economist at Bear Stearns in the years leading up to its collapse. This close-knit group of advisors enjoyed remarkable staying power within the president's high-turnover inner circle, outlasting many of his more celebrated mentors, despite their continuing reservations with regard to his trade protectionist tendencies. In the last year of Trump's tenure, they were still there, urging the president to avoid lockdowns in the face of the coronavirus pandemic.[2] They had been by Trump's side from the earliest days of his presidential campaign, when he first invited them to devise a tax plan that was "bigger and more beautiful" than Reagan's supply-side tax cuts of 1981.[3]

Trump's nostalgia for Reagan's Economic Recovery Tax Act (ERTA) of 1981 makes sense when we look back at his early career. Drafted by a group of supply-side economists installed in the Department of Treasury, Reagan's first-year tax cuts set commercial real estate values on fire for much of the decade, luring investor funds into newly tax-protected assets in midtown New York and business districts across the country. As a young real estate developer, Trump had been among the chief beneficiaries of these cuts. Now that he was installed in the Oval Office, he had good reason to expect "bigger and more beautiful" rewards from the same school of economists who had served him so well in the past.

As it turns out, Trump's supply-side advisors delivered him a $1.5 trillion tax cut that was outrageously advantageous to the joint family interests of the clans of Trump and his son-in-law Jared Kushner. The 2017 Tax Cuts and Jobs Act doubled the individual estate tax exemption to $11.2 million and introduced a record-breaking cut to the marginal corporate tax rate, triggering another of the many rounds of share buybacks, stock price surges, and windfall capital gains that have followed the Global Financial Crisis.[4] But while most businesses had to give up industry-specific breaks in exchange for these cuts, the commercial real estate sector received fortified protections for its existing tax shelters, including more generous depreciation allowances and a reduction in the tax rate on rental and mortgage-interest income.[5] Shareholders in real estate investment trusts, or REITs—among them Trump and Kushner—were granted a further reduction in the marginal tax rate owed on their income. Trump's tax reform also revived the old idea of the enterprise zone—once championed by the supply-side populist Jack Kemp—to incentivize private capital investment in impoverished communities. A forerunner to the cross-sector tax cut on capital gains that Trump postponed until his hoped-for second term, the rebaptized "opportunity zone" program allowed real estate developers to defer and potentially avoid the capital gains tax altogether, as long as they invested their money in designated census tracts. Among its first beneficiaries were several Trump family members and associates.

The supply-side movement in economics was (and continues to be) a powerful player in the reshaping of American and global capitalism. It counts among the several currents of neoliberal economics that came into their own in the 1970s, as a self-conscious weaponization of classical free market ideals against the big spending liberal state.[6] The widespread use of the term "supply-side economics" to refer to this specific current in anti-Keynesian thought is somewhat misleading. It sets up a false dichotomy between supply-side interventions focused on investment and production and demand-side policies focused on consumption, as if neoliberals favored the former and Keynesians the latter. Keynes was always attentive to both: what distinguishes the supply-side movement from Keynesian or supply-side liberalism is its foundational opposition to progressive taxation.[7] Tax incentives are an instrument utilized by Keynesians and neoliberals alike. Yet only neoliberal supply-siders see the progressive tax system as an outright disincentive to growth.

Roused into action by the crisis conditions of the 1970s, a first generation of supply-siders identified inflation and an increasingly progressive tax system as twin threats to the interests of capital. As industrialists fought to protect their profit margins and investors struggled to make good on flagging financial assets, the supply-side movement called for the reduction of taxes on capital gains, preferential treatment for investor income, and the introduction of accelerated depreciation allowances on fixed capital assets. At a time when most assumed that monetary restraint implied a scarcity of credit, the supply-side economist Robert Mundell correctly predicted that the suppression of wage and price inflation would pivot investors back into U.S. financial markets, freeing up an abundance of credit for leveraged investment in dollar-denominated assets.[8] The supply-siders never abandoned their dream of a pure gold standard but settled for the anti-inflationary activism introduced by Federal Reserve Chairman Paul Volcker in the late 1970s.[9] When brought into force by President Reagan's first-year tax legislation, the supply-side formula for economic recovery oversaw the precipitous rise of an urban real estate sector joined at the hip with Wall Street and built on the back of increasingly precarious construction labor. Donald Trump was truly a child of the supply-side revolution.

Yet supply-siders themselves have often misunderstood (or misrepresented) the nature of their project. Tracing a direct line of descent from President Kennedy, who advocated tax cuts as an instrument of economic stimulus during the 1960s recession, supply-siders sometimes present themselves as non-Keynesian growth economists, intent on expanding the pie by pressing on the supply-side levers of production and investment rather than the demand side of consumption.[10] With each round of tax cuts they have promised a return to the elusive growth rates of the Fordist era, where workers and owners could share in an expanding national product without setting off inflation. Except for a brief period during the Clinton administration, none of this has materialized.[11]

But if the supply-siders have failed by their own account, by another set of metrics they have been singularly triumphant. With the help of an ever-vigilant Federal Reserve, always ready to pounce on the slightest sign of wage and consumer price inflation, the supply-siders who populated the Reagan administration helped usher in a new organization of economic life in which asset price appreciation through debt leverage came to replace growth in the national product as the catalyst of wealth creation. Although this is sometimes adduced as evidence of a long slowdown (a thesis advanced most famously by Robert Brenner), it would be better understood as a shift in the operational logic of capitalism, rendering growth rates and industrial profits a weak measure of dominant economic trends.[12]

In confirmation of this thesis, the economist Jacob A. Robbins observes that since the 1980s, the bulk of wealth creation has arisen from appreciating asset prices rather than investment from savings.[13] Working with a comprehensive measure of income, which includes both realized (hence, taxed) and unrealized returns on investment, Robbins calculates that between 1980 and 2017 capital gains comprised a third of total capital income, even when volatility across specific asset classes was taken into account.[14] This stands in stark contrast to the period between the end of World War II and 1980, when asset price fluctuations were relatively subdued and capital gains represented a negligible component of capital income. As Greta Krippner has shown, the historical shift that occurred around 1981 saw returns on financial investment—in the form of rents, interest, yield, royalties, and capital gains—overtake profits, defined as retained earnings from investment in capital stock. Crucially, this shift was not confined to the financial services, insurance, and real estate sectors but extended to manufacturing too, where financial returns for the first time became more important than industrial profits.[15] The transition that is perhaps too crudely referred to as "financialization" is one that turned asset price movements into the chief determinant of income and wealth shares across the economy.

Yet this shift in the operating logic of capital remains stubbornly illegible to our current system of national accounts, which focuses on income deriving from the production of goods and services to the exclusion of capital gains. The mid-twentieth-century econometrician Simon Kuznets, perhaps the foremost influence on our current system of accounts, saw asset price movements as peripheral to the real work of economic production. Capital gains and losses, he reasoned, "are not increments to or drafts upon the heap of good produced by the economic system for consumption or for stock destined for future use," and for this reason they should be "excluded from measures of real income and output."[16] While this made a certain sense within the regulatory structure of New Deal capitalism, which was designed to rein in the stock market excesses of the 1920s, the continuing exclusion of capital gains renders us blind to the most consequential economic trends of our times. In the absence of a more comprehensive set of indicators, statisticians can only tell us how woefully our current economic outcomes fall short by the standards of mid-twentieth-century econometrics. Average rates of growth, capital stock investment, and industrial profits have all performed dismally since 1973, as Robert Brenner reminds us.[17] But what if the real action were happening elsewhere, invisible to these metrics?

Perhaps the best illustration of this dilemma can be found in Thomas Piketty's landmark *Capital in the Twenty-First Century*, which ultimately attributes increasing wealth concentration to a declining growth rate combined with the tendency of inherited wealth to accumulate value over time.[18] But even in those studies where Piketty and his colleagues do measure the effect of asset prices, the tax records they rely upon only register the capital gains that are made when an asset is sold or realized—an always limited segment of overall gains, much of which is never realized within the lifetime of the asset holder.[19] This is no small oversight, since appreciating asset prices, even if never realized or subject to sale, add value to collateral and can therefore be used to leverage greater volumes of credit at lower interest rates than would otherwise be possible. If sustained by the right combination of tax shelters and accommodative monetary policy, the wealth generated through asset price appreciation is liable to become self-reinforcing, all the while remaining completely invisible to the IRS and national income accounts. Drawing on a much wider array of sources than those available in the tax records, Jacob Robbins comes to the sobering conclusion that Piketty and his colleagues have in fact underestimated the true extent of inequality in our times, by overlooking the place of unrealized capital gains in the wealth portfolios of the ultrarich.[20]

With prevailing economic winds pointing to asset price inflation, on the one hand, and wage disinflation, on the other, it was inexorable that the family would acquire a new and formidable salience in the reproduction of elite power. It has always been the case, of course, that financial assets and their associated income flows can be transmitted from generation to generation in a way that a stream of wages cannot.[21] But when income from financial assets is climbing much faster than income from labor, the family becomes an all-important conduit in the process of class stratification, ensuring as it does that wealth is reserved for kin into the foreseeable future. Both tax and inheritance law consolidate this role, endowing the legal institution of the family with unique powers to shield capital gains from taxation. It is no coincidence that supply-side economists have always seen estate tax reform and cuts to the capital gains tax as working hand in hand toward the revival of entrepreneurial spirits. There is no better instrument for the long-term hoarding of wealth than the legal haven of the family.

Four decades of supply-side common sense have created the conditions under which dynastic wealth has flourished. With the Trump presidency behind us, we now know what this means for the American political system. As the son of a real estate developer with close ties to the New York Democratic machine, Donald Trump always moved in a world where the boundaries between business, family, and political patronage were difficult to discern. The supply-side revolution of the 1970s elevated the Trump family business model to a new level, allowing the young Donald Trump to transcend his provincial origins in Queens and emerge as a global real estate impresario. If Trump's father was his first enabler, supply-side economics was his second and more enduring one. Few, however, could have imagined that several decades after his New York debut, Trump as president would end up annexing the supply-side movement within his own family retinue, forcing it to serve his interests in particular. In a supremely ironic turn of events, the movement that did so much to elevate dynastic wealth became a servant to one of its more monstrous creations.

SUPPLY-SIDE ECONOMICS, ELITE AND POPULAR

Few of the anti-Keynesian movements spawned in the 1970s have exerted a more enduring influence on American political life than supply-side economics. Embraced by Republican presidents from Ronald Reagan to Donald Trump, with ever-diminishing resistance from party moderates, the supply-side prescription of marginal tax cuts on everything from corporate profits to personal and investment income has established itself as the party's default economic doctrine. It is now axiomatic among Republicans that the road to economic prosperity is paved with tax cuts. Yet the critical literature rarely accords supply-side economics the same intellectual coherence as the other economic movements that evolved alongside it. As if still bearing the taint of "voodoo economics"—a charge laid by George H. W. Bush—supply-side economics is typically dismissed as a media-created movement whose fortunes petered out some time in the late 1980s.[22] According to this narrative, the key players in the supply-side movement were Arthur Laffer, author of the infamous "Laffer Curve" predicting ever-increasing budget receipts from ever-decreasing taxes; Robert Bartley, the *Wall Street Journal* editor who turned the paper into a tabloid for this message; Jude Wanniski, the journal's associate editor; the Republican congressman Jack Kemp; the economist Paul Craig Roberts, who advised Jack Kemp on his first tax cut bills and succeeded Wanniski as associate editor at the *Journal*; and Bruce Bartlett, another staff economist to Jack Kemp. Robert Mundell, a professor in economics at Columbia University and future recipient of the Nobel Memorial Prize, was the one respectable academic among them.

The durability of this popular image owes everything to the representations of the actors involved.[23] Under the editorial influence of Robert Bartley, the *Wall Street Journal* of the late 1970s became the unlikely venue for a brand of tax cut populism designed to lure working-class Democrats into the arms of the Republican Party. Muting any reference to public spending austerity, estate tax repeal, and upward redistribution, populist supply-siders such as Jude Wanniski, Jack Kemp, and Arthur Laffer peddled across-the-board cuts to personal income as a Republican riposte to the Democrats' promises of full employment. The idea that tax cuts would "pay for themselves" was an essential ingredient in their message. All too conscious of the Republican Party's reputation as bearer of economic pain, the Lafferite supply-siders of the *Wall Street Journal* needed to assure the public that tax cuts could be enacted without any corresponding loss in popular social programs. It is these actors who have most openly claimed the "supply-side" appellation as their own. Accordingly, it is their very partial account of the movement that has come to serve as official history.

Yet it is unlikely that the populist supply-side movement would have made much legislative headway had it not shared key assumptions with a handful of elite economists closely associated with the Treasury Department under Presidents Nixon and Ford. More cautious in their rhetoric than Laffer and friends, this group of political insiders worried that American "capital formation" was coming under threat from the inflationary wage demands of organized labor and openly advocated the use of regressive tax cuts to counteract this trend.[24] The elite supply-siders—among them the economists Martin Feldstein and Michael J. Boskin, the tax consultant Norman B. Ture, and Treasury official William E. Simon—enjoyed a level of insider credibility that was never extended to the likes of Arthur Laffer.[25]

In a candid reflection on his relationship to the wider movement, published in the wake of the Reagan experiment, Martin Feldstein made a point of distinguishing between "traditional supply-siders" such as himself and the "new supply-siders" with their "extravagant claims."[26] Although he was clearly at pains to distance himself from less respectable economists such as Arthur Laffer, Feldstein nevertheless observed that what differentiated the "new from the traditional supply-siders" was not the economic assumptions they mobilized nor the policy changes they advocated "but the claims that they made" on their behalf. All exponents of supply-side economics subscribed to the view that progressive taxation was a drag on investment and marginal tax cuts a necessary spur to economic renewal. Feldstein, however, did not believe that supply-side prescriptions could be enacted without fiscal pain. Nor did he anticipate that supply-side tax cuts would pay for themselves. Elite supply-siders such as Feldstein were not afraid to preach spending restraint alongside tax cuts and openly defended inherited wealth as an incentive to "capital formation" (taboo admissions in Laffer's circles). Yet what they sacrificed in terms of populist appeal, they more than offset with insider access, thereby ensuring the wider supply-side movement its long-term stranglehold over Republican Party politics.

SUPPLY-SIDE ECONOMICS AND THE BUSINESS REVOLT

With their unparalleled access to the nerve centers of political and academic power, the elite supply-siders played an all-important role in legitimating the grievances of American business during the 1970s. As corporate managers woke to the multiple threats of oil embargoes, rising inflation, and wave upon wave of strike action, they developed a new esprit de corps. Trade associations that may have acted alone or in competition with one another in earlier decades now coalesced around the idea that their collective survival required a much more assertive posture on the part of business elites and a much more deliberate attitude toward the work of policy formation.[27] Even among former business partners of the New Deal state, the idea was taking hold that foreign competition and a more militant third world were not the only factors threatening their profit rates. For many, it seemed that business was under attack from the state itself, which had become much too responsive to the demands of public interest organizations and labor unions. In the space of a decade, the number of corporate public relations offices in Washington, DC, increased fivefold, while the scale and professionalism of these operations changed beyond recognition.[28]

If wage-push inflation was a challenge for industrial capitalists, the latter's efforts to retain their profit margins by pushing up consumer prices was equally devastating to financial asset holders. Inflating consumer prices seriously eroded the wealth of the top decile and centile of households—those whose wealth was invested in financial assets such as stocks, bonds, or Treasury bills, and whose income derived primarily from interests, dividends, rents, and capital gains rather than wages. As prices roared upward, wealth holders struggled to find avenues of investment that could protect their assets from long-term depreciation. Wage and consumer price inflation translated into financial asset disinflation and therefore posed an ongoing challenge to the wealth-building strategies of the rich.[31] "If times [had] been bad for investors generally," warned one legal scholar, they had "been worse for trust beneficiaries" who saw their once secure trust funds whittled away by a combination of the estate tax and rising prices.[32]

The problem was compounded by the dearth of diversification options that might allow investors to offset losses in one asset class with gains in another. The stock market performed so poorly throughout the decade that *BusinessWeek* published a feature issue on the "death of equities."[33] An investor who had purchased a portfolio of Dow Jones industrial stocks in 1968 would have seen its value appreciate by an annual rate of about 3 percent—and would have lost twice as much through the effects of inflation. Yet little relief was to be found in the normally safe bond market, where investors were collecting low and intermittently negative returns despite steadily rising coupon rates.[34] As inflation reached a crescendo in the closing years of the decade, it seemed that no interest rate premium was high enough to protect investors from losses. Traditionally considered the safest of assets, Treasury bonds were now dismissed as "certificates of confiscation."[35]

These conditions created a new, if fleeting sense of class unity among different sectors of the business world. The large industrial corporations that had sealed an uneasy truce with unionized labor under the New Deal consensus now joined forces with the small business associations that had long opposed the expansion of labor rights.[36] Ironically, the success of public interest organizations in implementing cross-sector legislation now turned back to bite, as all firms, big and small, came under the purview of the same consumer and environmental protections.[37] Perhaps most decisive in the formation of the business revolt was the cross-section of interests affected by the wage demands of the late 1960s. As explained by Gerald Epstein, the rise of wage-push inflation afflicted the industrial and financial sectors in different but ultimately galvanizing ways. Unable to stem the rising wage demands of workers through direct confrontation, manufacturers tried to retain their profit margins by ratcheting up consumer prices, but this only transferred the problem to financial asset holders, who were now faced with diminishing returns on securities and shares. Instead of turning against each other, financial and industrial capitalists joined forces in a generalized war against unionized labor.[38]

This new unity of purpose was reflected in the broad cross-section of business associations that stepped up their political presence during this period. The business revolt included the venerable U.S. Chamber of Commerce and the National Association of Manufacturers, which had long fought against the New Deal consensus from the hard Republican right, as well as the newly formed Business Roundtable, a close relative to the moderate Business Council that had once served as a broker between large corporations, labor unions, and the state. It also extended to wholly new ventures such as the American Council for Capital Formation, a brain trust of former Treasury Department officials who lobbied Congress on behalf of corporate clients.[39] Tensions remained just beneath the surface, but business interests were learning to work together as never before.

As spokesmen for the business revolt, the elite supply-siders were especially concerned that recent moves to enhance the progressivity of the tax code were interacting in perverse ways with inflation to completely extinguish the gains from investment. What motivated their concern, they insisted, was not the plight of the wealth holder as such but the generalized malaise of the U.S. economy, which they saw as sacrificing its capacity to save, invest, and produce in exchange for a surfeit of consumption. With dwindling returns on investment, business was saving and spending less on new capital stock; without the spur of new investment, labor productivity was bound to slow down too. For these business world Cassandras, the root cause of economic distress was wage (and thus consumer price) inflation, which worked against investment by rewarding the immediate pleasures of consumption and penalizing the deferred use of money. But government fiscal policy deserved its share of the blame, too: after all, at a time when inflation demanded urgent action, the state was actively worsening things by pursuing ever higher rates of taxation.

The push for progressive tax reform had been gaining momentum since the late 1960s, when President Johnson belatedly increased the marginal rates on long-term capital gains and curtailed the use of accelerated depreciation schedules for aging assets. Hoping to push things further, the left-wing Democratic candidate George McGovern campaigned against Nixon by promising a radical redistribution of wealth, with significant increases to the capital gains and estate taxes.[40] McGovern lost disastrously to Nixon in the 1972 elections. But as conservative commentators were quick to note, many of the same ideas were taken up by the centrist Jimmy Carter later in the decade, when inflation was much more of a threat.[41] During his 1976 campaign for the presidential elections, Carter promised to eliminate tax preferences for asset holders by bringing depreciation schedules "more closely into line with...actual economic decline" and equalizing the taxation of capital gains and ordinary income.[42] The overarching objective of these reforms was to shift the tax burden from low- and middle-income earners, who received few of the advantages of such tax shelters, to high-income earners, who were the overwhelming beneficiaries of asset price gains.

Supply-side economists met this challenge head on. Arrayed across the most powerful institutions of academia, business, and government, they spent the decade of the 1970s building up a formidable case against progressive tax reform. Often working in concert with elite trade associations such as the Business Roundtable, they testified before countless congressional hearings and wrote dozens of academic articles and reports, all driving home the point that American "capital formation" could not withstand any further increase in marginal rates of taxation.

The tax specialist Norman B. Ture was ubiquitous in the congressional debates around capital formation during the 1970s. Having pursued his graduate studies under Milton Friedman, Ture went on to work for Wilbur Mills at the House Ways and Means Committee, where he helped shape the Kennedy/Johnson tax cut of 1964.[43] This interlude earned Ture a name as the key mediator between the Kennedy and Reagan tax cuts, but by all accounts, at this time Ture belonged very much within the mainstream liberal tax reform tradition. Later in the 1960s, Ture joined the National Bureau of Economic Research (NBER), where he wrote what came to be recognized as the definitive study on tax depreciation—a specialty that would hold him in good stead in the years ahead, when depreciation allowances would become an all-important tax write-off for real estate developers such as Donald Trump.[44] By this time, Ture's politics had moved sufficiently to the right that he was invited to sit on a Nixon-appointed task force on business taxes. In 1971, Ture set up a private consulting firm and sold his research services to the many newly militant business associations now fighting on the front line of the tax war. In a series of widely disseminated reports commissioned by the National Association of

Manufacturers and the U.S. Chamber of Commerce throughout the 1970s, Ture catalogued the travails of the manufacturing sector in the face of inflation. It was not simply the case that businesses were making less profits than before, Ture charged; in many industries, business owners could now expect zero or negative returns on investment as a progressive tax code compounded the corrosive effects of inflation.[45]

Ture was particularly nonplussed by the impact of ungenerous depreciation schedules and the capital gains tax on would-be investors. Under a so-called straight line depreciation system, for instance, a new auto plant with an estimated useful life of ten years could take one-tenth of its original value in tax deductions every year. But under the impact of inflation, the market value of the plant was rising every year, such that any deduction calculated on the original price was soon rendered worthless. The same distortionary effect could be imputed to the capital gains tax, when the bookkeeping value of an asset was recorded in nominal as opposed to real (inflation-adjusted) terms and thus assigned to a higher tax bracket. The problem might have been solved through the simple mechanism of adjusting prices for inflation. But Ture was convinced that part of the blame resided in the progressivity of the tax code itself, which he saw as actively discouraging investment and savings in favor of consumption. The point, he insisted, was not to reverse these incentives but to "neutralize" a tax system that was now openly biased against the investor. Thus, Ture framed his case against tax progressivity as a move toward "neutral" treatment of consumers and producers. To establish this purportedly "neutral" baseline, he called for cuts to the capital gains tax and accelerated depreciation schedules, allowing investors to claim tax write-offs up front and thus reinvest their money as quickly as possible.

According to the progressive tax specialist Stanley S. Surrey, who had worked alongside Norman B. Ture during the Kennedy years, supply-side tax incentives such as these were the functional equivalents of direct government spending.[46] What supply-side economists defined as tax cuts and neutral prompts to market freedom, Stanley Surrey repositioned as tax *expenditures*. Although he was not opposed to the use of such expenditures as instruments of industrial or social policy, he thought it important to recognize their inherently regressive nature and their potential misuse as tax shelters for the wealthy. Surrey's theory of tax expenditures was based on a pragmatic interpretation of the so-called Haig-Simons concept of income, developed by economists Robert Murray Haig and Henry C. Simons, which recognized that the changing market value of an asset could confer real economic power and should therefore be included within the tax base.[47]

In fact, Surrey's 1973 primer on tax expenditures had singled out Ture's favorite methods—accelerated depreciation and the preferential treatment of capital gains—as especially prone to abuse by investors in real estate and other financial assets.[48] Not surprisingly, Ture was a vociferous opponent of the tax expenditure concept.[49] His own views were influenced by the economist Irving Fisher, who argued, contra Haig and Simons, that asset appreciation did not count as income and should therefore remain immune from taxation. Like Fisher, Ture believed that income should only be taxed at the point of consumption. In this view, any levy on nonconsumed income was a disincentive to savings and investment: far from privileging the already wealthy, so-called tax expenditures merely restored a little balance to a tax code that relentlessly punished the would-be investor.[50]

The up-and-coming Harvard economist Martin Feldstein lent scholarly gravitas to such arguments. In the early 1970s, Feldstein was the youngest-ever professor in the history of Harvard University and a rising star in academic economics. His work on the "perverse incentives" of social insurance had already attracted interest from the political right: after a postdoctoral stint in Britain, where he studied the alleged failures of the National Health Service, Feldstein would go on to critique the U.S. system of unemployment insurance as a disincentive to work and Social Security as a fatal diversion of national savings from private investment toward consumption.[51] Elected president of the National Bureau for Economic Research in 1977, Feldstein relocated the organization from New York to Cambridge, Massachusetts, and turned it into the most powerful source of economic scholarship in the nation. Under Feldstein's celebrated direction, observes Robert Collins, the NBER served as an effective "outpost of supply-side emphasis, if not doctrine."[52]

Feldstein's own studies on economic incentives were eloquent testimonials to the business-led tax revolt of the period. While most of Ture's consulting work at this time was concerned with incentives to tangible investment in the manufacturing sector, Feldstein offered a parallel set of arguments with respect to financial assets. In a series of studies published throughout the 1970s, Feldstein sought to demonstrate how the capital gains tax stifled new business investment, diminished government revenues, and froze up asset markets by locking investors into existing positions.[53] In other articles, he attributed a similar depressive effect to the whole range of taxes on capital income: dividends, rents, interest, and yields.[54] The most urgent problem to be addressed was the corrosive effect of (wage and consumer) price inflation on the value of financial assets: in a context of generally rising prices, Feldstein observed, the nominal value of assets was just as likely to reflect the phantasmatic gains of inflation as any real capital gains, yet investors were taxed as if there were no difference. As inflation soared into the double digits, investors would end up paying taxes on capital losses rather than gains.[55] It was no wonder that Americans saved too little and consumed too much, Feldstein concluded: an overly generous Social Security system and high taxes on capital income reduced the rewards that savers received for postponing consumption. To remedy this situation, he recommended reducing (if not eliminating) taxes on capital gains and dividends and making up the difference with sales taxes that would fall on citizens at the moment of consumption.[56] That such a proposal amounted to the most regressive of taxation systems was dismissed as the price to pay for greater savings and investment.

While populist supply-siders such as Arthur Laffer avoided direct references to inherited wealth, their elite counterparts did not hesitate to identify the bequest motive as the most primordial of economic incentives. In an article spelling out this logic, Michael J. Boskin argued that by penalizing the transfer of wealth from one generation to the next, the taxation of estates, gifts, and capital gains ultimately disincentivized capital formation itself.[57] As the marginal cost of leaving assets to one's children rose, so too did the propensity to consume wealth during one's lifetime—to the detriment of the nation's capital stock. Just as an "increase in the price of beer will lead to an increase in the amount of wine consumed," explained Boskin, "so will the estate-tax induced increase in the price of bequests lead to an increase in *lifetime* consumption by the wealthy."[58] Although Boskin conceded that "the estate tax probably partially accomplishes the goal of limiting intergenerational transfers of extremely large fortunes," he downplayed its potential to equalize the broader distribution of wealth.[59] Ultimately, he claimed, it was workers who lost out from the taxation of bequests, since any diminution of the incentive to invest would lessen the productivity of labor and hence wages (at least if one accepted the neoclassical theory of marginal productivity).

Throughout the Ford years, the elite supply-siders could count on the good will of Treasury Secretary William E. Simon, who never lost an opportunity to lament the parlous state of U.S. capital formation.[60] In the depths of the 1975 recession, with unemployment nearing 10 percent, Simon argued in the face of a chastened but still conventional economic wisdom that the problem was not flagging demand but a failure of the work ethic and entrepreneurial drive. What the economy needed was a permanent tax cut to incentivize savings and investment, not more public spending on the unemployed.[61] Simon was favorable to permanent cuts on all sources of income taxation—whether that income was personal, corporate, or investment-based—and saw flat-rate consumption taxes as a congenial alternative. Like Feldstein and Ture, however, he was particularly concerned that a punitive capital gains tax had fatally discouraged risk-taking and so condemned the U.S. economy to a seemingly permanent state of low growth.[62]

For much of the 1970s, a Republican-controlled Department of Treasury served as the incubator of supply-side ideas and personnel. As treasury secretary during the Ford administration, Simon was single-handedly responsible for forcing the theme of "capital formation" onto the legislative agenda.[63] Simon's immediate predecessor as deputy secretary of the treasury under Nixon was Texan business consultant Charls E. Walker, who soon distinguished himself as the most ruthless one-person lobbying machine in Washington. During his time at the Treasury Department, Walker had urged the largest U.S. corporations to set up the Business Roundtable and then went on to serve as tax consultant and congressional lobbyist for the same organization.[64] In 1975, Walker was nominated chairman of the newly formed American Council for Capital Formation (ACCF), an outfit that would help curate President Reagan's tax cuts of 1981.[65] By the time Norman B. Ture joined its Board of Directors in 1977, the ACCF's legislative program already reflected his influence: accelerated depreciation schedules, cuts to the capital gains tax, and generous estate tax exemptions were all on the agenda.[66]

In spite of Simon's best efforts at the Department of Treasury, however, the elite supply-siders faced a Democratic majority in Congress and could make no significant headway during the Ford administration. Instead, their first federal legislative breakthrough arrived during the Carter years, when businesses reformers rode the wave of popular tax revolts across the country to push through an astonishingly regressive change to the capital gains tax. Charls E. Walker of the American Council for Capital Formation led the charge on this campaign, springing into action as soon as Carter expressed his desire to enact a more progressive tax code.[67] When a growing number of Democrats started parroting the capital formation argument, it seemed that the battle was half won. This at any rate was what Carter appeared to acknowledge when in January 1978 he delivered a considerably diluted draft bill.[68] Yet instead of backing off, the American Council for Capital Formation upped the ante, prevailing on Republican Representative William Steiger to introduce an alternative bill that would roll back the maximum capital gains rate to 28 percent. The so-called Steiger Amendment—otherwise known as the Revenue Act of 1978—was blatantly regressive. But the legislation received a popular sanction of sorts from middle-income homeowners in California who were busy fighting their own battle against the taxation of their rising housing wealth. Tax revolt was in the air, and although the driving forces behind the elite and popular revolt were very different, congressional Democrats were reluctant to be cast as enemies of the white homeowner.[69] Thus, they turned against Carter en masse and helped inaugurate a new era of supply-side ascendancy in federal tax legislation.

NEW YORK CITY—SUPPLY-SIDE GROUND ZERO

The last federal tax bill of the decade, the Steiger Amendment is widely held up as the first milestone in the supply-side crusade against progressive taxation.[70] But before they claimed ascendance on the federal stage, the supply-siders achieved a less celebrated but no less significant breakthrough at the city and state government level, when near-bankrupt New York City came begging for a federal bailout in 1975 and was condemned to a brutal restructuring program by Treasury Secretary William Simon.[71] By the end of the decade, New York's Democratic leaders would be convinced that supply-side prescriptions offered the only way out of enduring austerity and set about implementing them on their own initiative.[72] By accident rather than design, New York City turned out to be the supply-siders' first urban laboratory—all the more important because its agents were not card-carrying supply-siders but pragmatic, sometimes historically liberal public officials.

New York City's fiscal crisis announced itself to the world in early 1975, when the city found it could no rely on long-standing banking partners to roll over its short-term debt and finance its current expenditure.[73] The city's exclusion from the municipal bond markets was sudden and brutal. But New York City's fiscal predicament was far from unique. Most of the old industrial cities of the Northeast and Midwest were feeling the pinch during this period, as a decade-long loss of tax revenue was compounded by the gradual tapering off of federal antipoverty dollars under Nixon and the exodus of investment funds out of American bond markets. But for several reasons New York City was exceptional: its position as the financial and banking capital of the United States, consolidated after World War II, made it uniquely vulnerable to the vicissitudes of the global economy, increasingly so as investors found novel ways to circumvent New Deal banking regulations and world financial markets became more integrated during the 1970s.[74] At the same time, the city's long history of social and labor activism, nourished by generations of political refugees, an enduring commitment to rent control, its unique network of local hospitals, its City University offering free tuition to residents, and an initially militant public sector singled it out for a special kind of venom on the part of business reformers.[75] When the city was forced to the brink of default in the spring of 1975, President Ford and his advisors (among them, Alan Greenspan, Donald Rumsfeld, and William Simon) were determined to make an example of it. Treasury Secretary William Simon, who had previously headed the municipal bond desk at Salomon Brothers New York, proved especially intransigent when it came to meting out punishment. The city, he wrote, was a victim of a fiscal Ponzi scheme that had relied on the taxes of its productive, private-sector workers to subsidize the salaries of municipal workers and their welfare clientele—eventually driving the productive out of town. "Liberal politics, endlessly glorifying its own 'humanism,' has, in fact, been annihilating the very conditions for human survival."[76]

The business revolt of the 1970s left more than ideological debris in its wake. Its material aftermath was everywhere to be seen in the deserted central cities of the industrial Northeast and Midwest, which for over a decade now had been losing manufacturing capacity to the outer boroughs and Sunbelt cities, where land, tax, and often labor came cheaper.[77] In the 1960s, New York City was in a state of transition: breweries, garment makers, and food processors were moving out, taking with them their contingent of skilled workers and draining the city of its solid revenue base of income and sales taxes.[78] New York was to remain an export city, but the kinds of commodities it traded were changing: white-collar services were overtaking processed food and garments as the city's major export, and utilities were gradually replacing the docks as the city's infrastructural nerve center. The mostly white workers who held professional and management positions within the new office sector were now more likely to live in the suburbs, where they had been lured by federal mortgage subsidies. As they moved out, they also took the bulk of the city's income tax revenue with them, leaving behind the many African Americans and Latinos who had migrated to the city in search of better work opportunities.

Many of these urban migrants did find new employment in an expanding and newly militant public sector, albeit at the lower rungs of the wage scale.[79] But many were also dependent on the welfare and free public services that central cities were now struggling to finance out of their existing revenue base. For a time, Johnson's War on Poverty made up the shortfall, injecting much-needed public service funds into the central cities, and crucially also acting as a stimulus to public-sector employment for racial minorities. But the problem of catering to the welfare needs of these low-wage residents became acute when Nixon began restricting the flow of funds to local government.[80] Again, New York City's social democratic history exacerbated its fiscal woes. By the 1970s, New York was not the only city to be financing a growing portion of its current expenditure with short-term debt, but relative to cities of comparable size, New York had assumed an unusually large share of welfare costs, and for this reason it was particularly hard hit by the simultaneous withdrawal of federal funds and an industrial tax base.[81]

But it was not only industrial capital that had fled the city in search of cheaper factors of production. Inspired by the example of the offshore Eurodollar market, New York bankers who had for many years been willing partners in the city's bond issues were now beginning to explore more lucrative investment options elsewhere. Markets in all kinds of fixed-income securities—corporate bonds, U.S. Treasury debt, and municipal paper—were in trouble at the beginning of the 1970s as price inflation cast a long shadow over future yields.[82] Relative to corporate paper, municipal bonds had long been considered a particularly safe and lucrative investment: the interest they earned was tax exempt, and the credibility of city governments was considered practically unassailable after World War II, based as it was on the power to tax a growing manufacturing base. But as the high inflation rates of the 1970s eroded the real return on city bonds, the investors who had once earned a reliable income from underwriting and trading them became fickle, demanding shorter maturities and higher interest rates to recoup their losses.

William Simon proposed the concept of a "capital shortage" to account for problems in the bond market: the core issue, he thought, was voracious overspending on the part of the federal government, which was simply eating up all the available credit and crowding out both private borrowers and smaller units of government.[83] But as a former specialist in municipal bonds, Simon would have known that if anything New York banks were facing the very different conundrum of overabundance at that time.[84] Flush with liquidity after the oil price hikes of the early 1970s, Arab oil producers had deposited the bulk of their surplus petroleum dollars in New York banks, who were then entrusted with finding the best investment opportunities for their clients. New York bankers feared that the U.S. inflation rate would compromise returns on investment and so redirected the bulk of these funds to capital-hungry developing nations.[85] Bankers' newfound ability to pick and choose between domestic and offshore investment opportunities gave them enormous bargaining power over municipal governments at a time when many among the business elite were beginning to look askance at the alleged excesses of the public sector. Objectively speaking, capital was not scarce; it had simply found a way to make itself scarce. Having pressed home the point that they could always find better opportunities elsewhere, bond investors were now in a position to bring cities to their knees and dictate the terms on which they would lend.

In the first phase of the crisis, city and state leaders sought to prove their fiscal bona fides by following the traditional script of balanced budget conservatism: spending cuts combined with selective tax increases. New York City mayors had been steadily pushing up the property tax since the late 1960s to pay off the interest on their short-term debt.[86] In the summer of 1975, Mayor

Abraham Beame raised it by a further 11.3 percent, the highest annual hike ever.[87] Meanwhile, the city enacted a brutal program of public service cutbacks, first under the tutelage of the Municipal Assistance Corporation, then under the enhanced powers of the Emergency Finance Control Board: public-sector wages were frozen; local hospitals, fire stations, and public library branches were closed; 400,000 permanent city workers were laid off, some of them then hired back as trainees under the federal Comprehensive Employment and Training Act (CETA); promised wage increases were abandoned, and labor unions were persuaded to allocate much of their pension savings to the purchase of municipal bonds, making their future retirement security dependent on the health of the bond markets.[88] Treasury Secretary William Simon urged the city to increase its sales tax and extend it to food and medicine.[89] The city didn't follow this advice to the letter, but it did introduce an alternative set of regressive consumption taxes. Transit fees were hiked, and new tuition charges were introduced at the City University of New York—regressive levies in everything but name.[90]

By the mayoral elections of 1977, however, Treasury was pushing the city to wean itself of federal loans, and city officials now turned their attention to the project of restructuring the city's finances on a long-term basis.[91] Mass layoffs and public service cuts may have averted the immediate danger of default, but an entire new model of public finances was needed if the city was to reenter the private credit markets. One document in particular proved decisive in reshaping policy aspirations. Released in June 1977, the final report of the Temporary Commission on City Finances, a team of advisors appointed under Mayor Abraham Beame, reflected an emerging consensus among public officials that urban recovery would come from the supply side.[92] Written under the research direction of Raymond Horton, a public finance economist at the Columbia Graduate School of Business, the report urged the city to awaken its wealth of dormant investment opportunities through an onslaught of targeted tax incentives. Continuing austerity was necessary (the report called for an immediate end to rent control) but cutbacks alone would never rouse the city out of its current state of stagnation unless a new engine of prosperity were found. If tax cuts were the obvious answer, the report emphasized that it was not the breadth but the choice and durability of such incentives that made all the difference. Wherever possible, long-term selective tax incentives, targeted at the most productive forms of investment, were to be favored over short-term across-the-board tax cuts.[93]

Unclear as to the source of urban renewal, the report identified everything from the corporate income tax, incentives to manufacturing investment, the sales tax, and the assessment of commercial real estate values as ripe for relief, but the overall message was clear: New York City's recovery would come from public incentives to private investment in the form of sustained tax expenditures rather than continuing concessions to the public service sector.[94] Unless the city acted now to moderate its overly progressive tax structure, productive capital would continue to flee in search of lower-tax environments in neighboring counties and states.[95] Although the lead author of the report, Raymond Horton, described himself as a "social democrat," he conceded that the solution expressed a "classic, trickle down" approach.[96]

Other public agencies followed suit. Around the same time that the Temporary Commission published its final report, the General Accounting Office released its own assessment of the city's long-term financial outlook: adopting the counterfactual method typical of supply-side fiscalism, it warned that the city could not continue to raise taxes on investment without actively undermining its future tax base. In case the supply-side provenance of this public finance paradox wasn't clear enough, GAO rammed home the argument with a characteristic supply-side flourish: misaligned incentives might actually lead to weaker revenues than would otherwise be the case.[97] In the meantime, the Special Task Force on Taxation, appointed by Governor Hugh Carey in 1976, was concerned that the tax burden on middle and upper management was encouraging businesses to move to the South and paradoxically increasing the burden on the low-wage workers who were left behind in the city.[98] A less progressive income tax structure, it was implied, would be good not only for managers but also for the lower-income workers who relied on them for creating new employment opportunities.

Few of these policy advisors considered themselves to be supply-siders. Indeed, most thought that some kind of public investment was needed to revive New York City's finances. Yet finding themselves with a hopelessly narrow menu of public financing options, they independently reached the conclusion that liberal objectives required supply-side methods. With the city still in a state of fiscal tutelage, it was clear that a return to the social spending priorities of the past was off the table. In the midterm, the city could only really spend in the deferred form of the so-called tax expenditure, that is, by selectively forgoing future tax revenues. Moreover, it could only wean itself off federal loans and return to the commercial credit market if it allocated these tax exemptions in a way that was congenial to bond traders. Accordingly, the Temporary Commission on City Finances advised the city to increase its public spending commitments on transport and communications infrastructure, that is, the kind of project that would best prop up commercial investment.[99] If the city's leaders wanted to pursue other, more redistributive projects such as renewed spending on health, education, and affordable housing, this could best be accomplished by recapturing a small portion of the capital gains accruing to private interests. The model was one that would come to dominate urban planning in the years ahead, as municipal and state governments came to accept the premise that social services could only be maintained by collecting the "trickle down" benefits of publicly subsidized private investment.

The Temporary Commission was agnostic about which forms of investment to target. Indeed, it still clung to the idea that New York City's manufacturing could be revived via the targeted use of tax breaks. But as Mayor Ed Koch took up his position in City Hall, it rapidly became clear that one sector in particular—Manhattan real estate—was set to gain most from the new supply-side agenda.[100] This was something of a foregone conclusion. Manufacturers had been steadily departing the city for several decades now, sometimes with the help of city incentives. Supply-side prescriptions for urban renewal gave the impression that incentives to industrial and real estate investment were interchangeable, but this was far from the case. The Fordist model of accumulation treated land as a so-called factor of production—a necessary component in the production of commodities and accumulation of surplus value, land was not supposed to generate profits in and of itself. According to this model, the value of industrial real estate, like that of machinery, was expected to depreciate with time—hence the kernel of common sense in the accounting norm that taxes on investment must make allowance for depreciation or wear and tear. As Samuel Stein observes, the status of land as a "sunk cost" for industrial production created at least one point of commonality among urban wage workers and manufacturers during the Fordist era: both had a vested interest in low land values.[101] But as soon as tax incentives are directed toward the value of land as such, the whole point of investment is to bid up the locational value of real estate, thereby pricing out both manufacturers and wage workers. In the long run, incentives to manufacturing and real estate investment cannot coexist in peace, given the very different value they impart to land.

Released in the midst of the mayoral election campaign of 1977, the final report of the Temporary Commission on City Finances served as a kind of blueprint for Koch's urban development agenda.[102] In his first term alone, Koch presided over a cornucopia of special tax abatements for high-rent real estate investment. The Industrial and Commercial Incentive Board, or ICIB, was established in 1977 with a mandate to revive New York's manufacturing base through the discretionary use of tax incentives. Under Koch, it ended up bestowing most of its largesse on midtown office construction.[103] Koch also expanded on incentives to residential real estate: chief among these were the J-51 program, which rewarded landlords with generous property tax exemptions for renovations, and the 421-a-421b, which encouraged developers to build new market-rate residential housing on vacant or abandoned land.[104] Neither of these programs included any provision for affordable housing. Indeed, most of the conversions carried out under the J-51 program came at the cost of SRO hotels for low-income single residents in midtown and downtown Manhattan. Even landlords who were still nominally subject to the full property tax saw the relative burden of that tax dwindle as property assessors regularly underestimated the market value of real estate. By the end of Koch's first term, the effects of these multiple tax abatements were obvious—the value of Manhattan real estate, which had plummeted in 1975, was now climbing higher by the year, as developers rushed to capitalize on vacant land and the prospect of tax write-offs stretching into the distant future.[105]

The person who has profited more than any other from New York City's tax incentive program is Donald Trump. Astonishingly, the young Trump's first tax abatement was brokered in the depths of the fiscal crisis of 1975.[106] At forty years in duration, it remains the longest-lasting in the city's history. The tax write-off allowed Trump to turn the dilapidated Commodore Hotel on Forty-Second Street and Lexington Ave into the luxury Grand Hyatt. Since Donald Trump, at twenty-nine years old, was still an unknown quantity, negotiations were overseen by his father, Fred, whose history of lucrative government housing contracts afforded him a direct line to city officials. In addition to the hundreds of millions of dollars in gifts he received from his father, much of it artfully protected from the estate tax, a young Donald Trump also inherited the trust fund of political favors in waiting that his father had built up over many years as one of the biggest donors to the New York Democratic Party.[107] New York Democrats were so beholden to the family that they granted the young Trump an extraordinary number of concessions and were prepared to overlook his already negligent, if not fraudulent, business practices to expedite his first major real estate deal. Today, the city's finance department calculates that the annual loss in tax revenues from the Grand Hyatt deal alone has been colossal, rising from $6.3 million in 1983 to $17.8 million in 2016.[108] But the Grand Hyatt was only the first of the fifteen Manhattan construction projects that Trump would pursue over the following years, each time exploiting the full range of tax exemptions on offer and never hesitating to turn to hardball litigation when the city tried to thwart him. Trump's appetite for tax-abated real estate investment was so voracious that even pro-development Mayor Ed Koch took exception to his methods.[109] All up, city tax records indicate that Trump has reaped at least $885 million in tax breaks to construct his real estate empire of luxury apartments, hotels, and office buildings.[110]

By the end of the 1970s, the *Wall Street Journal* was jubilant. As incoming president Ronald Reagan prepared to unveil the first comprehensive tax bill openly inspired by supply-side economics, the *Journal*'s opinion page advised naysayers to look to the wonders achieved in New York City. The anonymous op-ed congratulated Mayor Koch, Governor Carey, and their many advisors for setting aside ideological force of habit to pursue what was a de facto supply-side politics. "None of these men are supply-side theorists," it noted, "but they all had the common sense to see that taxes were killing their people."[111]

Between them, Koch and Carey had indeed carried out an impressive program of supply-side tax reform. Aside from his orgy of real estate tax cuts, exemptions, and assessment holidays, Koch also lowered the local corporate income tax and halted the annual rise in the personal income tax—all within his first term.[112] Such actions were hardly surprising coming from Koch, who had won the city election with a pledge to bring revenue producers back to the city.[113] What was more surprising was the apparent supply-side conversion of Governor Carey, visible to even his closest advisors.[114] By 1977, Governor Carey's formula for economic revival consisted of continuing rollbacks to welfare and Medicaid coupled with business-friendly tax cuts. It was, he said, the "year of the taxpayer."[115] Working in concert with the state legislature, Governor Carey eliminated the three highest brackets of the personal income tax, bringing the top marginal rate down to 10 percent by 1982.[116] He also let the corporation and bank tax surcharge expire and bowed to the wishes of bankers by phasing out the stock transfer tax.[117] The last move demonstrated just how constrained the state's fiscal choices had become: the stock transfer tax had been in place since 1903 and had been commandeered to back up state emergency bonds in the first years of the crisis regime, yet Wall Street firms now threatened to decamp to New Jersey unless the tax was revoked, and Carey succumbed to their blackmail.

But the "real ace in the hole," according to the *Wall Street Journal*, was New York real estate.[118] The op-ed noted approvingly that despite the rapid appreciation in New York property values and an absolute rise in city tax revenues, the relative burden of property taxes on landlords had actually plunged since Koch was in power.[119] The newly buoyant state of New York City finances was held up as proof that declining per-unit taxes on real estate investment could coexist with and even lead to a bonanza in public revenues as long as prices kept going up.[120] Nowhere was it mentioned that soaring real estate values were steadily pricing low-income renters out of the city and pushing tens of thousands of residents onto the streets.

This was just a foretaste of the commercial real estate boom that would grip New York City in the 1980s, when Reagan's federal tax cuts, high interest rates, and low inflation would bring global investment funds back to the United States. But to those who had long championed the idea that economic prosperity could be engineered through tax cuts, New York's soaring real estate values were proof enough that supply-side urbanism could offer an enduring alternative to New York's much-maligned social democratic polity. Even with the limited fiscal levers available to them as leaders of state and local government, Koch and Carey had succeeded in depreciating public-sector wages and appreciating asset values—a model that would redefine federal spending priorities in the years ahead.

In *A Time for Truth*, the free market manifesto which he published at the end of the decade, William Simon reflected back on his role in the New York City crisis and sounded a warning: if Americans didn't draw the right lessons from New York, "then New York's present must inevitably become America's future."[121] Like New York at the municipal level, the United States was sinking into an "abyss of debt piled on debt," inflicting "arbitrary assaults" on business and steadily growing the tax burden so as to redistribute wealth "to a combined clientele of the acutely needy and a growing portion of the middle class."[122] Admittedly, the federal government had unique monetary and fiscal instruments at its disposal that could delay the moment of reckoning. While "New York [could] not print and inflate money to escape, deceptively, from its debts; the federal government can."[123] Investors and producers could "flee from New York; they cannot flee from the United States." Nevertheless, the "national Ponzi game" could not go on forever. New York was the United States in microcosm—a warning of what was to come.

By the end of the decade, New York's fiscal crisis did indeed seem to be playing itself out on a grand scale, although in both cases the crisis was less a spontaneous correction to monetary and fiscal hubris than a deliberately concocted solution to plummeting asset values. The first signs of trouble appeared in late 1977, when the value of the dollar began to slide against other major currencies. It soon became clear that investors were dumping their dollar-denominated assets in expectation of growing inflation, thereby driving down the value of the dollar in international markets.[124] What began as an orderly exit in 1977 turned into a stampede the following year, as the dollar fell to around half its value against the West German mark, the Swiss franc, and the Japanese yen. The flight from the dollar was widely interpreted as a vote of no confidence in the Carter administration, which had entered office hoping to lead a joint reflationary effort with its major trading partners, Germany and Japan, but ended up going it alone when Japan refused to cooperate.[125]

As Carter's advisors no doubt recognized, a depreciated dollar was not without its benefits. If left to run its course, dollar depreciation would shrink the enormous U.S. trade deficit; by making U.S. exports cheaper and more attractive to overseas consumers, it could serve as a much-needed stimulus to manufacturing and agriculture. A cheaper dollar also offered a welcome reprieve to U.S. households and third world countries whose dollar-denominated debts were becoming easier to pay off by the day.[126] But if dollar depreciation was good news for some, it was a serious threat to the domestic and international banks who were heavily exposed to dollar-denominated assets and could only watch in horror as inflation wore down their value. Even as they rushed to offload their assets as quickly as they could, financial institutions quietly urged the U.S. government to protect the "integrity" of the dollar or risk sacrificing its role as reserve currency in international trade.[127]

Carter's irresolution reflected the difficulty of governing from the center at a time when the partners of the New Deal consensus were no longer walking in lockstep. He had entered office intent on powering the United States out of its mid-decade recession with a mixture of fiscal and monetary stimulus. What he had not bargained for was the new belligerence of financial asset holders in the face of inflation. Carter finally chose his side in August of 1979, when he nominated the staunchly anti-inflationary Paul Volcker as chair of the Federal Reserve. Testifying before Congress, Volcker made it clear that his tenure would mark a radical departure from the postwar norm of (relatively) accommodative monetary policy. "The traditional response throughout the postwar period to any prospect of declining production and rising unemployment has been a sharp shift in monetary and fiscal policy toward expansion and the enhancement of aggregate demand—even at the risk of adding to inflation," he observed. "A decade or two ago, with prices historically fairly stable, that risk was discounted. But now we have to face squarely the adverse consequences of prematurely or unduly large moves to stimulate the economy.... Ultimately, the perceived trade-off between unemployment and inflation would only be worsened. That is the lesson of the 1970s, not just in the United States but elsewhere."[128]

In his efforts to reverse the upward trajectory of inflation, Volcker eschewed the conventional central bank method of tinkering with the federal funds rate (the rate at which banks lend to each other overnight) and instead chose to limit new money creation via the direct control of bank reserves. The choice of targets was a nod to Milton Friedman's monetarism, although in private Volcker confessed that he was never a true believer.[129] The important thing was not the instrument but the outcome: the deliberate creation of a recession that would throw hundreds of thousands of workers into unemployment and lastingly quash the power of labor. If Carter and Volcker were secretly united in this aim, they were both attempting to deflect the blame onto others. Ultimately, it was Carter who paid the price when in 1980 he lost the presidency by a landslide.

For all his rhetorical deference to the ideas of Milton Friedman, who argued that inflation was always and everywhere a monetary phenomenon, Volcker shared the conventional view among Federal Open Market Committee members that rising prices were a result of excessive union power and overly generous wages. In a speech before the Committee on Banking, Finance and Urban Affairs delivered in July 1981, Volcker explained that "wages respond to higher prices" but "in the economy as a whole, labor accounts for the bulk of all costs, and those rising costs in turn maintain the momentum of the inflationary process." With unemployment now in the double digits, Volcker nevertheless complained that "only small and inconclusive signs of a moderation in wage pressures have appeared."[130] In January the following year, he told the Joint Economic Committee of the U.S. Congress that the "general indexes in worker compensation still show relatively little improvement." Although consumer price inflation had been dropping steadily since 1980, "growth in nominal wages" would need to be stopped in its tracks before victory could be declared.[131]

Whatever their other reservations about Volcker's ruthlessness, both Carter and Reagan were more than willing to help out when it came to thwarting unions. It was Carter who first signaled the change in tone with regard to labor negotiations: the federal bailout of Chrysler in 1979 came at the price of serious wage and benefit concessions for unionized workers. With the Volcker recession in full swing, the task of disciplining labor was much easier for Reagan, who had double-digit unemployment to back him up when he sacked public-sector air-traffic controllers in 1981. By 1982, union membership was in precipitous decline and wage negotiations were more likely than ever to result in worker concessions.[132] The White House and Federal Reserve were now acting in unison to crush the power of labor.

Such cooperation notwithstanding, fiscal and monetary authorities were at loggerheads on the question of the deficit. Many, including Volcker, thought that Reagan's extravagant tax and spending decisions risked squandering the

Federal Reserve's efforts at monetary austerity. Reagan's determination to enact supply-side tax cuts as a matter of priority, along with his lavish military spending, led to record deficits within his first year of government. Ironically, also, Volcker's success in stabilizing the price level added to the scale of Reagan's budgetary woes: the Federal Reserve–induced recession had cost the government dearly in terms of unemployment benefits, yet thanks to Volcker the resulting debt could no longer be conveniently inflated away.[133]

Reagan's fiscal indiscipline was a source of tension in his early administration: it pitted fiscal conservatives against supply-side tax cutters and opened up a rift within the supply-side movement itself, as former sympathizers balked at the impending costs of excessive government deficits.[134] The voice of elite supply-side economics, William E. Simon turned to a time-honored axiom of sound finance doctrine—which held that excessive government debt "crowded out" private borrowers—to denounce Reagan's economic policy.[135] As would-be public and private investors competed against each other for scarce resources, Simon warned, interest rates would keep climbing upward until they completely starved the private economy of all funding.

The argument was inconvenient to the more populist supply-siders within the early Reagan administration (among them Arthur Laffer, Jack Kemp, Paul Craig Roberts, and Norman B. Ture), who thought that tax cuts should always be prioritized over compensatory spending cuts.[136] In public, Arthur Laffer and friends had made a name for themselves by blithely insisting that tax cuts would pay for themselves, thanks to the expected increase in economic activity. Although often interpreted as a mark of extraordinary recklessness or naivety, there was method to the madness. As Jude Wanniski explained in a 1976 article, fiscal conservatism had turned Republicans into the dupes of big-spending Democrats, forcing them to hike taxes every time their opponents overindulged in public spending.[137] Democrats were thus able to present themselves as the bearers of free gifts while Republicans had to clean up after the party. To break out of this role once and for all, Wanniski urged Republicans to abandon their respect for balanced budgets and embrace the idea that tax cuts should come first, whatever the immediate damage in terms of budget deficits. This way, Democrats would be forced to clean up after *them*.

Others developed a more sophisticated explanation as to why supply-side deficits didn't matter. As early as 1972, Robert Mundell argued that the crowding-out thesis made little sense in a world where private asset holders could cross borders in search of the most lucrative investment opportunities. As long as the United States was prepared to follow the right "policy mix" of high interest rates, low inflation, and marginal tax cuts, however, international capital flows could be expected to gravitate back into dollar-denominated assets.[138] Mundell's analysis suggested that the so-called shortage of capital experienced by New York city in 1975 and U.S. borrowers as a whole in the late 1970s had little to do with public deficit spending per se: rather, it reflected investors' aversion to high inflation and high taxes on capital income. This meant that the political meaning of "the deficit" needed to be nuanced as a function of the fiscal decisions it reflected. The kind of public borrowing induced by supply-side tax cuts was unlikely to lead to wage and consumer price inflation, since most of its benefits went to financial asset holders. As long as the Federal Reserve kept a lid on inflation, Mundell reassured his followers, foreign investors would be more than willing to finance Reagan's deficits. The problem was not the deficit per se, explained Paul Craig Roberts, but the kind of spending that generated it: Keynesian or non-Keynesian, inflationary or noninflationary.[139] Investors hated the former and loved the latter.

To the surprise of many in the Reagan administration, Mundell's reassuring forecasts turned out to be prescient. With consumer price inflation down to 2.5 percent in mid-1983, investors who had dumped their dollar-denominated assets in the 1970s now couldn't get enough of them. The capital outflow of the Carter years reversed direction as investors rushed back into U.S. financial instruments, and the price of the dollar surged back upward.[140] The process was accentuated by the fact that countries like Japan were simultaneously deregulating their financial markets such that investors were now free to roam the world in search of the safest, inflation-proof assets. As the U.S. Treasury slowly became accustomed to the idea that "crowding out" was not a law of nature, it too took deliberate steps to make U.S. financial markets more welcoming to foreign investors.[141]

In a statement delivered before Congress in October 1983, Treasury Undersecretary Beryl Sprinkel took stock of the new economic environment in which the United States found itself. Sprinkel credited the Federal Reserve's "resolute determination to control inflation" with restoring the financial fortunes of the United States.[142] By signaling his resolve to suppress wage and consumer price inflation at any cost, Volcker had restored the reputation of the dollar as a "safe haven" for financial asset holders worldwide.[143] Admittedly, the high dollar had dealt a serious blow to commodity producers, who now found themselves competing against cheap imported products from Japan. But this, to Sprinkel's mind, was more than offset by the phenomenal rise in foreign direct investment flows, which for the first time in U.S. postwar history now exceeded outflows.[144] The turnaround was already visible in financial asset markets, which embarked on a secular price surge at precisely the point when wage and consumer price inflation were coming to a standstill. Importantly, Sprinkel recognized that the Federal Reserve's anti-inflation agenda was not the sole factor involved in restoring the fortunes of asset holders: Reagan's tax legislation of 1981, with its sweeping enactment of supply-side tax cuts, also deserved credit. Supply-side tax cuts played the all-important role of channeling investment funds into specific tax-preferred asset classes: in this way, they guided and protected the process of asset price inflation that had first been enabled by the Federal Reserve's monetary policy and the deregulation of financial markets.

REAGAN'S SUPPLY-SIDE REVOLUTION

In August 1981, Reagan signed into law the Economic Recovery Tax Act (ERTA), a triumph of supply-side doctrine that catered to both the elitist and populist factions of the tax-cut movement.[145] This was the first major legislative breakthrough of the Reagan administration and the largest cut to the corporate and personal income tax in U.S. history. The bill met with surprisingly little resistance from Democrats, who, despite their control of the House of Representatives, were reluctant to oppose tax cuts that would ease the pocketbooks of workers also.[146] Reagan's messaging was pitch perfect when he reassured the public that this newfangled thing called "supply-side economics" was simple "common sense."[147] The 1981 tax cuts were, in his words, "the greatest political win in half a century."[148]

Driving the ERTA's investment tax cuts was the same coalition of business interests that had ushered in the Steiger Amendment.[149] Once elected, Reagan convened a transition team of specialist advisors and chose Charls E. Walker, chairman of the American Council for Capital Formation, as head of his tax policy taskforce.[150] Another alumnus of the ACCF, Norman B. Ture, was appointed undersecretary for tax and economic affairs in the Treasury Department.[151] Here he was joined by Paul Craig Roberts, with whom he had worked at Jack Kemp's congressional office.[152] Together, the two men bridged the elitist and populist divide within the tax-cut movement: with his legacy of specialist consulting work on business tax cuts, Ture was the perfect advocate for accelerated depreciation schedules, capital gains cuts, and estate tax exemptions; Roberts too had always championed tax cuts for business, but as advisor to Kemp, he had also drafted the Kemp-Roth bill of across-the-board tax cuts for individuals (about which we will hear more in the following chapter). At last, the supply-siders had established a Treasury Department stronghold under a president who was passionately committed to their cause.

The passage of the ERTA of 1981 was a stunning vindication of the supply-side credo. In addition to the across-the-board income tax cuts that Jack Kemp and his populist associates had called for, the act also implemented the precise agenda of investment incentives laid out by Feldstein, Ture, and Walker in the previous decade. By themselves, the personal tax cuts were more regressive than most members of the public would have realized: when introduced into a progressive tax code, across-the-board tax cuts automatically deliver their greatest benefits to those in the highest brackets. It was Reagan's business tax cuts, however, that truly skewed the benefits in favor of the highest income earners.[153] At the same time that it raised the estate tax exemption, allowing wealthy households to bequeath a larger proportion of their fortunes to their heirs, the ERTA lowered the capital gains tax once again, from 28 to 20 percent, and implemented a strikingly generous version of Ture's long-wished-for accelerated depreciation schedule.[154] For those who had spent the 1970s lamenting the demise of American "capital formation," the legislation was a cornucopia of gifts.

The passage of the ERTA in the first six months of Reagan's presidency ensured that when the Volcker shock started to show results, investors in financial assets were rewarded with a combination of low inflation and lavish tax incentives. The Federal Reserve and the White House were far from united in their views on the deficit, but they accomplished what was essential in the eyes of business elites, enduringly reversing the relationship between wage and asset prices in favor of financial investors. The wages of all but the highest income earners now entered a long period of stagnation, while financial asset prices surged upward, fueled by the expectation of low inflation, supply-side tax expenditures, and, as the decade progressed, declining real interest rates. The immediate trigger to the market turnaround came from the notoriously pessimistic Henry Kaufman, chief economist at Salomon Brothers, who in his morning memo of August 17, 1982, predicted that inflation expectations would "erode gradually" over the following year.[155] The surprise announcement from such a respected prophet of gloom was enough to push up the Dow Jones Industrial Average by a record 38.81 points in one day. Throughout the rest of the decade, the Standard and Poor's index of five hundred stocks would continue to outperform its historical average, posting annual increases of 17.4 percent versus the 9.7 percent annual average of the past.[156] The bond market too awoke from the slumber of the 1970s, as fixed-income investors were rewarded with historically exceptional returns (comparable to stocks). With interest rates falling, bond traders who had purchased long-term treasuries with sky-high coupon rates in the early 1980s earned an annualized total return (comprising interest plus appreciation) of more than 14 percent.[157] "The ascendancy of financial assets in the 1980s has been dramatic and unassailable," observed a Salomon Brothers investment report at decade's end.[158]

The low inflation environment of the 1980s allowed the federal government to sustain record levels of public debt and opened up hitherto unimaginable borrowing opportunities for households and corporations, which now found ready access to credit whatever their current or projected savings. Helped along by the Reagan administration's lax enforcement of antitrust rules and cuts to the capital gains tax in 1978 and 1981, a new kind of business strategy—the so-called leveraged buyout, or LBO—exploded onto the scene with the end of the Volcker recession, just as the stock market took off and credit started flowing.[159] The buyout pioneers of the 1970s—veteran practitioners such as Kohlberg, Kravis, and Roberts—had started out acquiring private companies in their sunset years and the smaller subdivisions of large corporations.[160] In 1979, they made their first acquisition of an entire publicly traded corporation, Houdaille, for what in retrospect would look like the paltry sum of $370 million.[161] The new credit conditions of the 1980s turned buyouts into a decidedly more grandiose affair. Would-be corporate raiders soon learned they did not need to rely on ever-vigilant investment banks and insurance companies to fund their deals: instead, they could finance things "in house" by borrowing against the assets of the target company and selling on these high-risk high-yield securities in the newly liquid junk bond market. The leveraged buyout, or LBO, worked as follows. A small group of activist investors would buy out the existing shareholders of a public corporation with the help of high-powered debt, using the company's own assets as collateral. This debt would then be transferred onto the books of the target company, whose cash flows for the next few years would be diverted to the task of paying back the money owed.[162] The sponsors of leveraged buyouts sought out established companies with steady cash flows, low initial debt levels, and little need for long-term capital investment. Uneventful and stolid companies like these were least likely to interrupt the real purpose of the buyout: the rebirth of the corporation as a tax-protected vehicle for generating capital gains.

If corporate raiders and junk bond dealers were depicted as folk devils in the popular business literature, the apostles of "shareholder value" welcomed them as the harbingers of a new, investor-oriented style of business. In their 1976 article "Theory of the Firm," the Chicago-trained economists Michael C. Jensen and William H. Meckling advanced the idea that the primary objective of the public corporation should be to maximize shareholder value by distributing all available cash flows to public owners (in the form of dividends or appreciated stock prices).[163] The messianic role of the leveraged buyout was to force all corporations to recognize this truth—or risk a hostile takeover.

Jensen saw all this organizational change as the natural consequence of a "third industrial revolution" in which digital innovation played a commanding role.[164] But if shareholder value ideology entailed innovation, it was above all in the arena of tax accounting. By taking a company private and loading it up with debt, the buyout sponsors exempted the company from the corporate income tax for the duration of the agreement and simultaneously made it eligible for tax deductions on interest.[165] While a solvent publicly traded company was expected to pay the corporate income tax on its annual earnings and dole out regular dividends to its shareholders, the debt-laden private company had no such obligations and could also claim back its interest payments as tax write-offs.[166] Another tax workaround was offered by the accelerated depreciation rules in Reagan's 1981 tax cuts, which covered used as well as new assets: under these rules, investors were able to "step up" the tax value of the company's assets to the price they had acquired them for, so they could now claim correspondingly higher deductions for depreciation.[167] If all went well, the debt would be paid down within a few years and the corporation sold back to a bull market, where investors could expect to reap phenomenal gains on their shares. As capital gains, these returns would be taxed at much lower rates than ordinary income, if they were taxed at all (buyout firms often used shell companies known as "mirror subsidiaries" to avoid capital gains taxes altogether).[168]

The first buyout deal to attract widespread public attention was one engineered by none other than former treasury secretary William E. Simon and his business partner, the tax specialist Raymond Chambers. In January 1982, Simon and Chambers (operating under the business name of Wesray) had acquired the Gibson Greeting Card Company from a larger conglomerate at a purchase price of $81 million, investing roughly $330,000 each of their own money and making up the rest with bank loans and real estate leasebacks.[169] A mere eighteen months later, with the stock market in full swing, they sold the company back to the public, who were prepared to fork out $27 each for shares originally purchased at 14 cents. All told, the exit deal had generated $75 million worth of capital gains for each of the two general partners—a two-hundredfold return on the money they had invested. Observers were astonished that Simon and Chambers had accomplished this feat "without really doing much but buy and sell."[170] In the years ahead, corporate raiders would have to wreak considerably more havoc to merit such spectacular capital gains, as shareholders demanded brutal restructurings and mass layoffs as proof that a company's asset values had been truly enhanced. In 1983, however, there was enough of a margin between the depressed asset valuations of the 1970s and the hyperbolic expectations of a newly buoyant stock market to ensure that corporate raiders merely had to wait a little while to reap the rewards from appreciating asset prices.

If this is what Simon had meant all along by "capital formation," then it was something very different from the investment in fixed and human capital stock that had generated rising profits and wages during the heyday of postwar Fordism. Leveraged buyouts paved the way for corporate restructurings which treated internal labor forces—especially when unionized—and in-house R&D units as wasteful excess. For all the talk of business-led innovation, the period from 1980 onward saw a steep decline in business investment in employment-generating assets such as plant, equipment, and software, and a steady divestiture from internal R&D.[171] And despite supply-siders' conviction that vigorous "capital formation" could only flow from retained earnings, savings reached a thirty-year low during the Reagan years and continued to trend downward over the following decades.[172]

The influx of foreign investors into U.S. financial markets, along with fierce competition among newly deregulated banking institutions, had unleashed a new style of investment in which collateralized debt took precedence over savings and debt was collateralized by the expectation of market-based price gains in financial asset values (stocks, bonds, real estate, or intellectual property). If the Fordist model of accumulation was mediated by production (making the ratio between fixed and variable capital, automation, and human labor a central point of conflict), this new model of investment treated the production process as an outsourceable component and focused all its energies on the appreciation of stock prices. Managers and workers alike were ruthlessly subject to this one overriding objective.

There was nothing that predestined one particular commodity class or capital stock to assume a new life as a financial asset. Nor was it a case of intangible assets taking the place of tangible commodities, as some have suggested.[173] Rather, one and the same "substance" could acquire vastly different mathematical powers of self-appreciation by virtue of the market- and tax-based valuation process it was caught up in. Whether one looked to the merger and acquisition market or commercial real estate, the same logic of debt-leveraged asset price appreciation was at work. The component assets of a corporation that had delivered dwindling productivity and lackluster profits during the high inflation years of the 1970s could now inspire the wildest of shareholder expectations. Real estate that had served as a simple "factor of production," peripheral to the accumulation process, at the height of Fordist industrialism, could be resuscitated as a source of appreciating value in and of itself (hence the sudden "gentrification" of old industrial tracts and the rehabilitation of the warehouse as luxury dwelling). The economic indicators that had defined and measured output since midcentury could not make sense of this alternative cycle of capital and so gave the impression that investment and savings were at historic lows. But while it is certainly true that savings rates had plummeted, another kind of investment—one fueled by debt leverage and the expectation of future price appreciation—was rampant.[174] Its dynamics could only have been revealed by a system of national accounts that measured capital gains.

To understand why the fortunes of wage earners and financial asset holders diverged so radically during this period, there was no better object lesson than the hostile takeover, which offered a firm-level diorama of the wider macroeconomic trends of the decade. The disciplinarians of "shareholder value" saw internal workforces as disposable assets and punished any board of managers that wasted their earnings on them. Activist investors resented even the limited public-private welfare state that had been created by the largest public corporations during the postwar era and blackmailed managers into shedding or reclassifying long-term employees. It was ironic, then, that some of the earliest (and it turns out some of the longest-lasting) institutional investors in leveraged buyout pools were employee pension funds.[175] The fact that pension fund managers were investing in the stock market was not in itself new: U.S. pension funds had diversified from government bonds into corporate stocks as early as the 1950s.[176] But during this time, the public corporation operated within the framework of managerial capitalism, which privileged the long-term expansion of the firm (and hence, the long-term growth prospects of employment) over the demands of stock price appreciation. In the 1980s, by contrast, pension fund managers were investing in a business form—the leveraged buyout—that called for the slashing of workforces and the active suppression of wages. Thus, while pension fund lobbying groups such as the Council of Institutional Investors made real strides in amplifying the voice of worker shareholders in the 1990s, their complicity with the ideology of shareholder value could only work against them in the long run, since it leveraged workers' savings to finance their own obsolescence.[177]

It was during this period, also, that the professional manager assumed the new identity of the financial asset holder. In 1981, Reagan resuscitated the stock option as an attractive form of executive compensation by restoring its tax status as investor income (hence liable to the preferential capital gains tax).[178] As share prices took off at the end of 1983, so too did the proportion of manager pay composed of stock options: between 1980 and 1994, the mean value of stock options granted to the chief executives of the top corporations increased by 683 percent while their salary and bonus income rose by 95 percent—spectacular gains in a period when the wages of most workers were barely holding their own.[179] During the high-tech boom of the late 1990s, the use of stock options would be extended to scientist entrepreneurs (in exchange for patented innovations) and high-tech employees in Silicon Valley.[180] The move was applauded by Michael C. Jensen and William H. Meckling, who saw the substitution of investor (capital) income for salaried (labor) income as the best means of aligning the interests of managers and shareholder owners.[181] The generalization of stock options and other kinds of stock-based remuneration ensured that the new managerial science involved more than a cultural shift: at stake was the legal and economic redefinition of the manager as an asset holder and beneficiary of capital gains.

The shift helps explain why incomes stagnated for most workers during this period, except for a small proportion at the top of the income spectrum who seemed to be traveling away from the mean at breakneck speed. The difference reflected the fact that most managers and some employees were being compensated in the form of tax-protected, stock-market-aligned capital income, at the time when the divergence between income from capital and income from labor was becoming extreme. There *was* class mobility during this period, but for the most part it was enjoyed by a select group of corporate managers, entrepreneurs, and Silicon Valley employees.

Apart from this group of ultra-high-income earners, the households that benefited most from the asset price boom of the 1980s were those already in possession of financial assets. During this period, the asset-rich experienced extraordinary virtual or unrealized gains in their bequeathable wealth as the ambient run-up in asset prices drove up their market value by the millions. In their ongoing study of wealth and income trends, Lawrence Mishel and Jared Bernstein found that the wealthiest households received both more capital gains and more interest income during the 1980s.[182] As wages stagnated and public assistance benefits were slashed, the bottom fifth of households experienced a net decline in income, while the top 1 percent saw dramatic increases in both their labor income (wages and benefits) and capital income (that is, income deriving from interest, rents, dividends, and capital gains).[183] The growing chasm between rich and poor was even starker when it came to wealth shares: at the same time that the net worth of the upper 0.5 percent of households swelled by a full 47.2 percent, the bottom 40 percent of households saw their wealth holdings shrink.[184] Most of this spike in wealth inequality could be attributed to the asset price boom unleashed by the Volcker shock and Reagan's tax cuts: given that the wealthiest households hold the greatest share of financial assets (stocks, bonds, and real estate), any significant surge in asset prices is bound to inflate their existing wealth holdings without any need for savings out of income.[185] Trump was only the most garish symptom of a new economic dispensation that inflated the fortunes of trust-fund sons, however dubious their business acumen.

APPRECIATING DEPRECIATION

The centerpiece of Reagan's business tax cuts was a system of accelerated depreciation schedules allowing investors to claim sweeping deductions on their assets within a foreshortened time period. These paper investment losses could then be used to offset taxes owed on other income, thus serving as a legally sanctioned tax shelter.[186] In the past, such deductions were based on the investor's estimate of the depreciable life of an asset, but such estimates were always open to contestation by the IRS. Reagan's 1981 tax reforms not only put an end to this ad-hoc system of depreciation claims and counterclaims but also established a set of depreciation schedules that were so generous they allowed some investors to avoid all forms of taxation for several years on end.

If supply-side tax reformers had sincerely wanted to correct for the distortions of inflation, they could have simply mandated the use of real (inflation-adjusted) as opposed to nominal asset values in the estimation of depreciation write-offs.[187] Instead, they introduced a fixed set of schedules that were calculated to deliver a negative tax, that is, a net gain after taxation. The cost of a piece of machinery or equipment could now be written off over a period of three to five years, and a production plant over ten years, even when the useful life of these assets extended much longer. The depreciation on a commercial property could be claimed in fifteen years as opposed to the previously established forty years.

The tax shelter opportunities created by Reagan's tax reforms were especially lucrative for real estate investors, since property assets also qualified for the preferential capital gains tax (which the ERTA had slashed from 28 to 20 percent) at the moment of sale. As soon as the depreciable life of a real estate investment came to a legal end, the owner could now sell off the asset at a sharply reduced rate of taxation and pocket the gains.[188] In the meantime, the building's actual market value may not have depreciated at all: indeed, given the experience of the late 1970s, savvy investors looking for tax shelter opportunities would likely have expected property prices to keep rising. And so they did. When the legal fiction of asset depreciation was applied in a policy context that actively favored asset price appreciation, what had begun as an extraordinary tax shelter gave way to something much more extreme: the active instigation of private capital gains on the part of government.

For all his pledges of renewed economic prosperity, Reagan had never promised a manufacturing revival. The Republican Party as a whole eschewed the kind of interventionist reindustrialization policies bandied about by Democrats during the Carter years.[189] The Reagan tax cuts, it was claimed, would simply "neutralize" the tax code and cut regulation so as to release the spontaneous forces of private investment and capital formation from the dead weight of government. The important point was that economic prosperity of some kind would materialize, whatever form it took. Still, most observers expected the business tax cuts of 1981 to encourage reinvestment in manufacturing plants and machinery.[190] Even Norman B. Ture, the intellectual father of Reagan's accelerated depreciation schedules, thought that the ERTA would ultimately catalyze a new golden age of industrialization. There was little doubt in his mind that "if we are to achieve a sustained and vigorous resurgence of economic growth, the prime mover will have to be the manufacturing sector."[191]

But the conditions created by the Volcker recession only hastened the deindustrialization of the U.S. economy. The high dollar brought commodity exports to a near standstill and steered investors away from domestic manufacturing toward more reliable sources of return. Instead of reinvesting in new capital stock and upgrading their aging production facilities, U.S. manufacturers used their depreciation allowances to subsidize their ongoing disinvestment from the industrial workforce. It was not that they had no excess profits to invest: they simply chose to diversify these funds into mergers and acquisitions, financial investments, and real estate, where they could reap consistently high rates of return without having to encounter the restive industrial worker.[192] The commercial real estate sector had already proven its capacity to generate spectacular capital gains in late 1970s New York. Following the passage of Reagan's accelerated depreciation allowances, investors flooded into the sector as quickly as they had fled manufacturing.

As urban geographers have long noted, it was during this period that real estate assumed a newly central role in the dynamics of U.S. and global capital. Samuel Stein summarizes decades of dialogue with the early work of David Harvey when he notes that real estate in the early 1980s "went from being a secondary to a primary source of urban capital accumulation."[193] In more precise terms, I would argue, real estate emerged as a primary investment class at the point where capital itself switched from a *regime of accumulation*, organized around production and measurable in terms of growth, to a *regime of asset price appreciation*, pivoting around capital gains. As Stein explains, real estate represented a sunk cost in the eyes of the industrial capitalist, whose primary interest lay in the mass production of commodities and the metric profit gains to be made from cheaper inputs, wage moderation, and accelerated productivity: if the price of land could be held down, then the value of industrial profits would rise accordingly.[194] For much of the postwar period, this calculus underwrote both the dynamism of U.S. capitalism and the imperatives of municipal finance: closely integrated with the industrial growth machine, central cities relied on a massified base of industrial property taxes along with the buoyant sales and income tax receipts afforded by industrial wages to fulfill their basic functions.

But as industrial wage workers moved to the suburbs and one manufacturer after another fled the central city in search of cheaper sites of production, the vacant land and crumbling warehouses they left behind were made available to a very different logic of investment. No longer an external factor in the service of industrial production, real estate now emerged, along with the "shareholder value" of the newly restructured corporation, as a seemingly autonomous vehicle of capitalist "self-valorization"—that is, as a direct source of capital gains.[195] When this occurred, it had as much to do with the exigencies of municipal revenue generation as it did with financial deregulation and the investment appetites of global capital. Cities were already in dire fiscal straits when they were confronted with Reagan's drastic cuts to federal aid and a wave of popular tax and spending limitations: property, sales, and income taxes had all begun to fall in the 1970s as a result of deindustrialization and suburban flight.[196] It was little wonder, then, that they greeted commercial real estate developers and middle-class gentrifiers with open arms. The wager was simple enough: as cities lost their industrial tax base and were forced to accept *percentage-wise* limits on the amount of property tax they could collect, they discovered that the *per-unit* appreciation of property values could make up for the loss. Gentrified brownstones, converted lofts, and shiny new office towers represented a bonanza in future property taxes. They also lured back the kind of high-end earners who could enduringly replenish city income and sales taxes. In this way, property price appreciation became the last hope of the postindustrial city.

In the decades ahead, the supply-side solution to the fiscal crisis of New York City became a model for urban revenue generation across the country. In a quest to escape the all-too-immediate limits on their powers of revenue generation, cities plunged headlong into an always frenzied, often futile game of supply-side revenue recapture: while rising real estate values and their attendant wealth effects held out the promise of buoyant tax collections sometime in the future, cities had to cut taxes to lure such investments in the first place.[197] They hoped to recoup in the future the fiscal powers they surrendered in the present. But this made cities permanently hostage to the interests of real estate developers such as Donald Trump. In the absence of a vigorous industrial base, rising property values became the collateral of choice for municipal bond issuance, making any public investment initiative contingent on the good fortunes of real estate.[198] This shift in urban revenue generation helps explain why investors responded to Ronald Reagan's first-year tax cuts by rushing into commercial real estate. By the time Reagan introduced his accelerated depreciation allowances, city planners had all but given up on their industrial tax base and were determined to lure real estate developers by any means possible.

For the commercial banks and thrifts that had recently been liberated from New Deal banking regulations, commercial real estate turned out to be the ideal investment vehicle. The abolition of interest rate ceilings meant that domestic banking institutions were now able to lure back depositors with globally competitive returns on deposits.[199] Yet in order to honor their interest obligations to depositors, banks and thrifts needed to seek out high-risk investment opportunities with commensurately high returns.[200] For reasons that had more to do with the intricacies of Reagan's tax reforms than the inherent qualities of the asset itself, investors, developers, and banks all turned to commercial real estate as the most lucrative option.[201] In their eagerness to make the most of the high interest rates of the early 1980s, commercial banks and thrifts were willing to finance most—sometimes all—of the purchasing price of a property up front. Investors, for their part, found they could buy into real estate with next to no down payment and still benefit from the tremendous tax shelters afforded by accelerated depreciation schedules.[202] The combination of interest rate deregulation and supply-side tax incentives created a virtuous circle of abundant leverage and appreciating asset prices: as more and more investors rushed to take part in the real estate bonanza, asset prices soared upward; as the market value of real estate rose, so too did the value of collateral, making it easier for borrowers to secure and pay off high-interest loans.

As real estate boomed in the business districts of Manhattan, Houston, and Los Angeles, it became hard to ignore the true extent of the wealth transfer that Reagan had legislated into existence. In New York alone, land values were inflating at an average of 23.5 percent per year in the mid-1980s.[203] The ERTA had made it possible for real estate developers to use borrowed money to generate previously unthinkable capital gains, most of which would either be exempted from taxation at the point of sale or completely overridden if the investor used the windfall to purchase a new property. In the meantime, the legal fiction of depreciation—which purports to compensate for the declining value of an asset—would generate paper losses great enough to exempt the investor from paying taxes on all his other sources of income. Mortgage interest payments too could be used to offset taxable income as long as the investment in question was operating at a loss.[204] The upshot was that an investor, without paying a cent of his own, could be actively making money from fictional losses on an asset that all the while was appreciating in value at a vertiginous rate, showering him with capital gains that would likely never be taxed at all.

With his growing portfolio of real estate, much of it located in midtown Manhattan, Trump was among those who profited handsomely from the commercial construction boom of the 1980s. His full tax returns from this period have yet to be released. But documents made public during a later court case suggest that Trump, among many others, made abundant use of Reagan's accelerated depreciation rules to shelter himself from income tax during this period. Like most real estate developers, it is likely that Trump operated his projects under the legal form of the "pass-through" partnership, that is, a business that allows the owner to transfer income and losses onto his personal income tax return. In 1984, the year in which Trump Tower was completed and its Fifth Avenue apartments put up for sale, Trump claimed $624,000 in deductions and paid zero income taxes.[205] "I appreciate depreciation," Trump wrote in his 1987 business memoir *The Art of the Deal*.[206] For the normally hyperbolic Trump, this reads as something of an understatement, as if he were professing a simple fondness for this particular bookkeeping procedure. But the phrase can also be understood as a literal account of the relationship between asset price appreciation, debt leverage, and regressive tax expenditures. Without the promise of future tax write-offs and preferential capital gains treatment, the banks that financed Trump's mortgages would have had no incentive to offer such generous leverage, while the real estate he invested in would have been worth much less. The effect of supply-side tax incentives was to actively subsidize and thus bid up the asset values they claimed to be simply protecting. In other words, it was tax depreciation that turned real estate into an appreciable asset, so that Trump in good faith could claim that he "appreciated depreciation."

Trump's modus operandi of the 1980s was so singular that it briefly attracted the attention of the heterodox economist Hyman Minsky, who compared his real estate deals to the decade's multiple "bubbles" in everything from baseball cards to third world debt and Japanese real estate. "One of the puzzles of the 1980s was the rapid rise in the financial wealth of Donald Trump," Minsky wrote. "Trump's fortune was made in real estate. Many large fortunes have been made in real estate, since real estate is highly leveraged," but two factors "made Trump somewhat unique—one was that he developed a fortune in a time of high real interest rates, and the second was that the cash flows on most of Trump's properties were negative."[207] Trump's real estate fortune was a perfect example of what Minsky called Ponzi finance, where investment is collateralized purely on the basis of its projected price appreciation or capital gains. Commercial banks and savings and loan associations were willing to keep lending to real estate developers like Trump because they expected the value of New York real estate to rise faster than the debt-service payments they owed on their loans. And as long as the market value of his real estate projects kept going up, Trump could continue to refinance his debt, even if he was earning little or no current rental income from the property in question (in fact, Trump's mortgage interest was deductible as long as he was losing current income). In Minsky's words, "Trump's wealth surged because the market value of his properties—or at least the appraised value—was increasing faster than the interest rate.... The efficiency with which Trump managed these properties was more or less irrelevant.... Trump was golden—he had a magic touch—as long as property prices were increasing at a more rapid rate than the interest rate on the borrowed funds."[208]

For Minsky, the tendency of investors to gravitate from hedge to speculative to Ponzi finance during periods of financial stability was an inherent feature of capitalist markets—something close to a law of dynamics, albeit one guided by the psychology of animal spirits.[209] As such, Minsky saw the process of debt-leveraged asset price appreciation—or Ponzi finance—as both the expression of capitalism's greatest creativity and the source of its chronic breakdowns. Minsky's quasi-physical understanding of the laws of debt finance led him to the conclusion that asset price appreciation is always in the long run unsustainable, destined at some point to collapse under the strain of its own overreach. The puzzle, in Trump's case, Minsky thought, was "that the lenders failed to recognize that the arithmetic of his cash flows was virtually identical with that of the developing countries; in effect, Trump was Brazil in drag. In the short run, Trump could make his interest payments with funds from new loans—but when the increase in property prices declined to a value below the interest rate, Trump would become short of the cash necessary to pay the interest on the outstanding loan."[210]

Both in this brief text and his larger body of work, Minsky has little to say about the role of tax legislation in enabling or disabling the process of asset price appreciation and leveraged investment. Minsky's reflections on the role of taxation are few and far between—and when they appear, somewhat underwhelming.[211] More generally, it can be argued that Minsky tends to cast the institutional and legal environment of market interactions in an exclusively exogenous and repressive role, so that tax laws are imagined to regulate or constrain a set of market dynamics whose natural tendency is to bridle under and ultimately destabilize such limits. Yet it is doubtful that the commercial real estate boom of the 1980s would have existed had it not been for the multiple tax incentives afforded by Reagan's 1981 tax legislation. As noted by the tax scholar Tim Edgar, supply-side tax incentives such as accelerated depreciation, the mortgage interest rate deduction, and the capital gains preference are hardly exogenous factors in the shaping of asset markets: as indirect expenditures, they guarantee a base level of capital gains to the investor and thus actively subsidize certain investment decisions. In an important sense, Edgar writes, the tax expenditure is itself "an asset that adds value to an [investment] and induces the issue of more debt than would otherwise occur in a world without taxes."[212] It was not the investor's primal appetite for risk nor the blind seduction of animal spirits that drove up real estate prices in the 1980s but rather a calculated exploitation of tax-subsidized capital gains.

WINNING BY LOSING

If anyone had doubted the link between Reagan's tax legislation of 1981 and the commercial real estate boom, Reagan's second significant round of tax reform would have disabused them. By the mid-1980s, the ERTA was coming under increasing attack not only from those who decried its bias toward the wealthy but also from business interests who had not enjoyed the special tax shelters offered to real estate.[213] In many ways the Tax Reform Act of 1986 doubled down on the supply-side dictum that tax rates must be cut at the margin, but it did so in a more populist and deficit-conscious spirit that was calculated to placate both blue-collar Reagan Democrats and disgruntled Republican insiders. The act lowered all federal income tax rates, both personal and corporate, reduced the number of tax brackets, and slashed the top rate from 50 percent to 28 percent.[214] This time, however, Reagan was determined that tax cuts would be "revenue neutral," their inevitable impact on the federal deficit offset by the closure of tax loopholes, shelters, and deductions for the wealthy.[215] Accordingly, the act mandated that tax rates on capital gains and ordinary income should be equalized and raised the maximum rate on long-term capital gains from 20 to 28 percent.[216] This was bad enough for real estate investors and developers. But many of the specific incentives available to the sector were also phased out. The 1986 Tax Reform Act eliminated the tax shelter value of real estate by stretching out the statutory depreciation period from 15–19 years to 27.5 years. And it also excluded the sector from lucrative loss deduction rules by singling out real estate as a "passive" investment, even when a real-estate professional might be engaged full time in managing property.[217] Under these new rules, a developer such as Trump could no longer use rental income losses to offset taxes on his other sources of income.

With this three-strike assault on their tax shelters, the Tax Reform Act of 1986 wiped out the incentives that had lured so many investors and lenders into real estate in the first place.[218] The virtuous circle of appreciating collateral and generous leverage established by Reagan's first round of tax cuts now gave way to fire sales, plummeting collateral values, and unrenewable debt. Investors rushed to offload their newly acquired assets at precisely the moment it was becoming difficult to sell, leaving many not only with poorly collateralized debt burdens but with a portfolio of other business ventures that were now fully liable for taxation. The precipitous drop in commercial real estate values—the largest since the Great Depression—was catastrophic also for the newly deregulated thrifts that had staked so much on this one sector.[219] By the end of the decade, a third of all savings and loan associations had failed nationwide, and the industry's own deposit insurance fund went bankrupt trying to bail them out.[220] In the end, taxpayers funded the lion's share of the bailout. The largest tax-funded rescue package in U.S. history until this point, the savings and loan debacle demonstrated just how far the state was prepared to go to cover the financial risks it had itself enabled—not simply by lifting interest rate ceilings but by failing to reassess the sector's deposit insurance requirements in line with its new exposure to risk. As such, it set the stage for the multiple bank bailouts of the following decades.

A 2019 *New York Times* report based on leaked IRS documents revealed that in 1987, the year when he published *The Art of the Deal*, Donald Trump was losing tens of millions of dollars on new and old business deals.[221] Although he was still making use of the less generous depreciation write-offs available under the new tax law, most of Trump's losses at this time could no longer be explained as deliberately concocted tax shelters. Instead, it appears that in the inhospitable new tax environment established in 1986, Trump was struggling to break even on his existing commercial real estate ventures in hotels, apartment blocks, and retail space. In the meantime, he had launched himself into a new series of hotel developments in Atlantic City, New Jersey, where he hoped to reinvent himself as a casino operator. Trump was now amassing millions of dollars in actual losses by the year, briefly posing as a bond raider to postpone the damage. But by the summer of 1990, he could no longer meet the interest payments on his core businesses, and banks were threatening to foreclose on his loans.[222]

In the normal course of things, this should have led to a devastating personal bankruptcy. Trump had unwisely posted a personal guarantee on the loans he had taken out, leaving his own assets vulnerable to liquidation.[223] Yet one of the four bankers who had the largest exposures to Trump's casinos persuaded the others that Trump was "too big to fail." This banker was none other than Wilbur Ross, who would later reappear by Trump's side in the White House, as United States Secretary of Commerce. Noting the crowds of fans that continued to mob Trump in the streets, Ross explained to reporters that one of the "assets of the casino, albeit one we don't have a mortgage on," was Donald Trump himself.[224] If Trump went down, so too did the business's chief drawing card and with it any hope of recuperating the full return on their investments. Despite the reprieve, Trump ended up filing for bankruptcy twice within the next few years. Yet the Chapter 11 bankruptcy provisions he now invoked—an option reserved for the wealthiest legal clients—kept his personal assets off-limits and slated his business assets for reorganization rather than liquidation. Trump did remarkably well from the arrangement: in addition to the 50 percent ownership share he retained in the Taj Mahal, he was now guaranteed a minimum annual management fee of $500,000. As one biographer noted, "this was only one of the many ways that losing money had changed over the course of the twentieth century." From the New Deal until the 1970s, business bankruptcy "had been a black hole from which few were able to emerge."[225] In 1978, however, Congress passed a sweeping new Bankruptcy Code that made life easier for corporate and other business debtors and authorized them to retain possession of assets in the wake of reorganization. By the 1990s, corporations, private firms, and LLCs had learned how to make strategic use of this new code to write off losses and emerge phoenix-like from the conflagration of failure.[226] Trump was among those who exploited this new legal dispensation to the full. Making profits from losses was his trademark business style.

In the meantime, however, the 1986 tax reform had deprived Trump of one of his favorite methods for doing this. By redefining real estate investment as a form of passive income generation, the act prevented Trump and his peers from turning their real estate investment losses into lucrative tax write-offs. This outrage prompted him to make a rare congressional appearance on behalf of the industry.[227] Testifying before the House Budget Committee in late 1991, Trump denounced Reagan's Tax Reform Act of 1986 as "an absolute catastrophe for our country."[228] The real estate industry was in an "absolute depression," and this, he thought, translated as a depression for the whole country.[229] "I bought things that were great deals in the middle 1980s and even the later 1980s but when the tax law kicked in," Trump reported with some candor, "all of a sudden those deals…were no longer good economic deals because they changed the game on me."[230] Restoring real estate tax shelters, he argued, would be a much cheaper option than bailing out the banks who had financed them, as had happened during the savings and loan crisis.[231]

The real estate industry didn't get all the reforms it wanted—it was not successful in reinstating the enormous fictional losses introduced by the ERTA's accelerated depreciation rules—but it did convince Congress to reverse the "passive loss" provisions of the 1986 tax law. The Revenue Reconciliation Act of 1993, passed with the overwhelming support of House Democrats, made it possible once again for real estate professionals to use their operating losses to claim unlimited deductions on all other sources of income—for example, wages, portfolio income, or consulting fees.[232] These losses could be redeployed into the future to offset income earned in any of the following twenty years, thanks to a law dating from 1918 that allows business owners but not ordinary wage earners to distribute their tax deductions over time.[233]

Trump no doubt continued to use the depreciation rules that had served him so well in the early 1980s. But under the less generous terms established by Reagan in 1986, depreciation no longer offered the extraordinary tax shelter opportunities it once had. And in any case, by this time most of Trump's losses were involuntary rather than deliberate. *New York Times* reporters found that in 1990 and 1991, Trump's business losses amounted to more than $250 million each year—dwarfing the losses of the nearest taxpayers at the time.[234] In 1995, a year after the new deduction rules came into effect, Trump declared close to a billion in losses. Under the new rules that he himself had helped to introduce, this would have granted him a tax deduction large enough to liberate him from all federal income tax for almost two decades.[235] Thanks to the respite offered by his creditors and his own interventions into the tax legislation process, Trump had found a way to leverage his losses into a bailout. He could now convert the business losses he had made using his creditors' money into a personal tax shelter (the fact that these losses were made with borrowed money made little difference in the eyes of the tax code).[236] Loss deductions are one of the several ways in which financial asset holders are able to protect themselves from outright failure, even when faced with unexpected and involuntary losses.

Trump was now free to appreciate himself—the one asset that had survived his casino debacles intact.[237] He would spend the next few decades selling his services as a reality television star and licensing his name to branded apartment buildings, golf courses, and menswear lines. "I was able to use the tax laws in this country and my business acumen to dig out of the real estate mess," Trump declared during his 2016 presidential campaign.[238] What he failed to mention was his own role in helping push these new tax laws through. In little more than a decade, Trump went from being a local beneficiary of supply-side tax legislation to an active participant in the long supply-side campaign for asset-enhancing tax reform.

GEORGE W. BUSH'S SUPPLY-SIDE PRESIDENCY

Following their tumultuous moment of glory in the early days of the Reagan administration, supply-siders would have to wait another two decades before they regained untrammeled access to the White House. Supply-side economics returned in force during the George W. Bush administration, this time under the uncontested leadership of "traditional" supply-sider Martin Feldstein and several generations of his students.[239] A feature article in *Fortune* magazine aptly described Feldstein as the "economic Merlin" of the Bush White House.[240] Although he held no official position, his influence on Bush's economic policy was unmistakable. After a first meeting at the governor's mansion in Austin at the height of the 2000 election campaign, Feldstein continued to guide the president's economic policies well into his second term, when Bush tried unsuccessfully to implement the economist's long-cherished dream of privatizing Social Security.

Another key advisor was Lawrence B. Lindsey, a former PhD student of Feldstein's who had worked for him at the Council of Economic Advisers in the early Reagan years. At a time when supply-side economics had fallen into disrepute, Lindsey's 1990 book *The Growth Experiment* argued that the Reagan revolution had failed only insofar as it was left unfinished. The final chapters of the book outlined an agenda for completing the revolution: like Trump and many other beneficiaries of Reagan's first round of tax cuts, Lindsey wished to reverse the moderating impact of Reagan's 1986 tax reform, particularly when it came to taxation of investment income. High on his agenda was a program of investor-friendly cuts to the taxation of capital gains and dividends, almost identical to those that Feldstein had been advocating since the 1970s.[241] Following confirmation of the contested election results of 2000, Lindsey was appointed director of the National Economic Council, where he served as Bush's top economic advisor. He was by no means alone in preaching the "capital formation" gospel of tax cuts for investors: the Bush administration was populated by a small legion of Feldstein protégés, including such heavyweights as R. Glenn Hubbard, chairman of the White House Council of Economic Advisers, and Richard H. Clarida, head of the economic policy division of the Treasury Department.[242]

These self-confessed "traditional" supply-siders did not cultivate the same kind of media attention as Arthur Laffer and other populist supply-siders of the early 1980s.[243] Yet under their guidance, Bush accomplished a far more radical experiment in supply-side economics than Reagan had. For much of his first term, Reagan was torn between the warring factions of the Republican party, as fiscal conservatives and elite supply-siders (including Martin Feldstein) balked at the excesses of Lafferism and counselled prudence in the face of spiraling deficits. George W. Bush encountered far less pushback.

In the years between Reagan and Bush Jr., something had shifted in the Republican fiscal imagination. After Newt Gingrich and other Republican radicals skewered Bush Sr. for raising taxes in the early 1990s, moderate Republicans were on notice that higher taxes spelled political death. The message was driven home by Grover Norquist, founder of Americans for Tax Reform, who in the following years persuaded (or shamed) almost every Republican in Congress to pledge their opposition to future tax increases. Clinton's surrender to fiscal conservatism was the final death blow to Eisenhower Republicanism: with the Democrats now rebranded as the party of balanced budgets, Republicans could stop worrying about the deficit when it came to their own policy actions.[244]

The difference between George H. W. Bush and his son speaks volumes about the shift in Republican Party sentiment. As vice president to Reagan, Bush Sr. had been notoriously contemptuous of "voodoo economics" and pushed back against Reagan's income tax cuts; the younger Bush, by contrast, was surrounded by enablers, including Vice President Dick Cheney, who opined that "deficits don't matter."[245] Even Feldstein, who had resigned from Reagan's Council of Economic Advisers in protest against the deficit, was now arguing that Clinton's surplus needed to be returned to the people in the form of tax cuts. "The reason I don't sound like the Marty of 1984," he told a reporter, "is that we've got a different situation today."[246] With interest rates at historic lows, Feldstein predicted (incorrectly) that Bush's deficits would sort themselves out as the economy grew.

As the chaotic events of the early millennium unfolded, and Bush chopped and changed his arguments for tax cuts to suit them, it became clear just how thoroughly Republicans had learned to work the budget issue to their advantage. Bush spent much of the election campaign of 2000 telling voters that Clinton's balanced budgets were a sign of Democratic avarice. The surplus belonged to the people, Bush argued, and should be returned to them as soon as possible, lest Democrats have the gall to spend it. The story changed within a few months of Bush's inauguration, when the dot-com market collapsed and the economy teetered on the verge of recession. With the help of Lawrence Lindsey, Bush now repackaged his tax-cut agenda as an alternative, non-Keynesian form of stimulus—one that would revive the economy from the supply-side of work, savings, and investment rather than the demand side of consumption.[247] The new narrative was consolidated with the World Trade Center attacks of September 11, 2001, when markets were plunged into a further state of turmoil. For the incoming Bush administration, it seemed there was no problem that tax cuts could not solve.

With both houses of Congress in the hands of the Republicans, the first of Bush's tax cuts was approved in early 2001, barely a few months into his presidency. This was a program of income tax reductions, ranging from a 35 percent cut to the highest income bracket to a 10 percent cut to the lowest, to be phased in over a period of five years.[248] The bill was intended to evoke the populist spirit of the 1981 income tax cuts. Yet even the nominal percentage cuts to the lowest and highest income brackets were wildly misaligned and the real difference was much greater (the break was worth almost sixty times as much for the person earning $50,000 as compared to the person earning $10,000).[249] A further provision—applauded by Martin Feldstein as a boost to savings and investment—raised the exemption rate on the federal estate tax to $3.5 million per person, with a provision for total elimination by 2010.[250]

A final round of cuts, enacted in 2003, bore the unmistakable imprint of Martin Feldstein and the elite program in supply-side economics. Heeding advice that Feldstein had been giving since the 1970s, the Jobs and Growth Tax Relief Reconciliation Act of 2003 slashed the top marginal tax rates on dividends and long-term capital gains and increased depreciation allowances.[251] Bush tried but failed to win a permanent repeal of the federal estate tax. This was not quite the complete elimination of taxation on capital income that antitax cheerleaders such as Grover Norquist and Stephen Moore had hoped for. But it came close enough. As tax scholar W. Elliot Brownlee observes, the Bush cuts significantly weakened both the progressivity of the tax system and the expenditures it financed. "These fiscal shifts stood as the most important since the 1920s in increasing economic inequality. They established a bold line of demarcation between the World War II regime and [a new] retro-liberal tax regime."[252]

Among the major beneficiaries of the Bush tax cuts were private equity firms, the newly respectable descendants of the corporate raiders of the 1980s.[253] Private equity players encountered an unusually favorable set of circumstances at the beginning of the new millennium. Bush had slashed the tax burden on capital gains and thus sweetened the deal for investors at the very moment that interest rates were reaching historic lows. The rewards were particularly seductive for the general partners in a private equity deal, whose earnings were defined as investment income (so-called carried interest) and therefore taxed at the preferential capital gains rate.[254] Under Bush's new tax rules, it would have been irrational for general partners not to "risk all" on acquisition deals. In truth, they were incurring very little risk at all, since the legal liability for the debt that financed the acquisition was borne by the target corporation.[255]

Regulatory pressures also played a role in reviving the fortunes of the private equity firm. A spate of corporate scandals from Enron to WorldCom had discredited the image of public corporations at a time when the ravages of the old leveraged buyout firms were fading from memory. In response to these scandals, the Public Company Accounting Reform and Investor Protection

Act of 2002, otherwise known as the Sarbanes-Oxley Act, had imposed heavy new reporting requirements on publicly traded corporations.[256] In contrast to the 1980s, then, when takeovers were often hostile, the private equity firms of the early millennium found many willing victims among companies that were all too happy to be taken private under the auspices of an acquisition deal.

Most companies did not wait for a private equity offer, however, before adopting their own strategies to profit from the Bush tax cuts. Beginning in 2003, share buybacks surged, as corporate executives looked to maximize the capital gains to be made from rising stock prices and falling taxes.[257] Given that the mere announcement of a share repurchase program can be enough to raise the price of stocks, it is unsurprising that firms would resort to this method as a way of amplifying and locking in the advantages of lower capital gains rates.[258] Ironically, however, the 2003 tax cut was supposed to have minimized this form of cash distribution. By the early millennium, there was growing concern that firms were indulging in stock buybacks at the expense of long-term investment in R&D or human capital: to many observers, the popularity of stock repurchases was a sign that asset price appreciation, not innovation or new employment, had become the overriding concern of corporate executives.[259] The 2003 tax cut was designed to counter this trend by reducing capital gains and dividends to the same low rate.[260] But while dividend payouts did indeed increase following the 2003 tax cut, stock buybacks climbed even higher, reaching a historic peak in 2005, when Bush offered a one-off tax holiday for multinational corporations repatriating capital to the United States.[261] It is estimated that 92 percent of these repatriated profits went into buybacks rather than employment-generating capital investment.

The corporate fixation on stock price appreciation begins to makes sense when we look at the incentives built into executive pay since the early 1990s, when Clinton limited the amounts that could be paid out in bonuses and inadvertently encouraged corporations to look for alternative forms of executive compensation.[262] The use of stock options as a component of executive pay exploded in the years following Clinton's change to the tax code, to the point that they now constitute the bulk of executive pay. As a type of derivative contract, the stock option yields a gain for the holder only if the value of a share rises above a certain "strike price" stipulated at the moment of issue. In other words, it directly ties pay to company stock values, giving executives a personal incentive to stimulate price appreciation. The fact that dividends do not have the same tonic effect on stock prices as share buybacks do explains why CEOs are increasingly inclined to favor the latter over the former.[263]

If Bush's tax cuts were a powerful spur to investment in financial assets, the incentive became irresistible under the impact of Greenspan's newly accommodative monetary policy. Greenspan's reinvention in the late 1990s as chief orchestrator of asset price inflation came as a surprise to many who had known him since his first years at the Federal Reserve, where he had earned a reputation as an overzealous corrector of market frothiness, always ready to crank up interest rates when credit looked too easy and wage inflation imminent.[264] But from his earliest studies in market dynamics, Greenspan had been alert to the peculiar dynamics of asset price appreciation, which he understood as providing an alternative, non-Keynesian route to economic growth. Greenspan had studied the impact of stock price inflation in the 1950s and house price inflation in Southern California in the 1970s and was convinced, despite the reigning academic orthodoxy, that speculative or virtual gains of this kind had a real effect on economic behavior.[265] In fact, Greenspan was one of the few central bank practitioners to understand the importance of unrealized capital gains in stimulating consumption and had for many years advocated the development of a more refined set of national economic indicators that would take such asset price dynamics into account.[266]

During his first period of tenure at the Federal Reserve beginning in the late 1980s, when the specter of wage inflation still loomed large, Greenspan feared that asset price appreciation could not be encouraged without also triggering wage and consumer price inflation. But by the time of Clinton's second administration, the Federal Reserve and Treasury under such deficit hawks as Robert Rubin had so browbeaten the New Democrats into fiscal submission that Greenspan no longer had anything to fear in the way of wage growth. At this point, Greenspan seems to have convinced himself that the central bank could use loose monetary policy to stimulate asset price inflation while relying on the Treasury to suppress any redistributive public spending that might contribute to the inflation of the social wage. Better still, under a Republican president such as George W. Bush, the central bank could slash interest rates to near zero while allowing the Treasury to cut taxes on wealth and spend lavishly on defense (as long as fiscal stimulus was confined to marginal tax cuts and military outlays, there was no danger that government spending would empower labor). If even Democrats could be relied upon to suppress wage growth, then there was no reason to accept the idea that asset price surges were dangerous bubbles in need of deflating; the whole point of monetary policy was to make sure that such "bubbles" never ended.

During the late 1990s, Greenspan made this philosophy explicit when he declared that price inflation in asset markets was impossible to predict or preempt; all the central bank could do was intervene after the fact to buy up toxic assets, in the hope of triggering a new round of price inflation in another asset class.[267] As it became clear that the Fed was routinely intervening to thwart the downward slide of asset prices, market actors began to refer to this philosophy as a kind of central bank "put" initiated on behalf of all asset holders.[268] The put option is a type of derivative contract that grants investors the right, but not the obligation, to sell a share at a set price should its value fall in the future. It is regularly used by portfolio holders as a hedge against stock price falls and a safeguard against short sellers looking to gain from these same price fluctuations. But while individual traders purchase put options to protect their own privately assumed risks, with the so-called "Greenspan put," the Federal Reserve told the same traders it would hedge downside risk on their behalf. With this public safety net in place, financial asset holders were assured that they could only ever *fail up*, safe in the knowledge that any act of excessive risk taking would be retroactively validated and rewarded by a permissive central bank. In an interview given to CNBC after his retirement from the Federal Reserve, Greenspan expressed his support for the continuation of this policy under Ben Bernanke: it was "capital gains throughout the system" that had helped markets recover from the Global Financial Crisis, Greenspan remarked.[269] Far from representing a failure of monetary policy, permanent asset price appreciation now represented the ideal horizon of Federal Reserve crisis management.

CENTRAL-BANK-INDUCED WEALTH CONCENTRATION

Until the Global Financial Crisis of 2008, Greenspan's efforts to push up asset prices seemed destined to meet a natural end. The Federal Reserve could only cut interest rates to zero; beyond this point, it disposed of no obvious tools for honoring the "Greenspan put." Yet Greenspan's successors turned out to be more committed to the cause of asset price inflation than they were to the conventions of monetary policy. So when the "shadow" investment bank Lehman Brothers went under in 2008 and the collapse of the world's largest insurer, AIG, threatened to bring down the entire interbank lending system, the new chairman of the Federal Reserve, Ben Bernanke, resorted to unconventional monetary measures on a grand scale. Under his watch, the Federal Reserve embarked on a massive program of asset purchases, otherwise known as quantitative easing (QE), involving the transfer of long-term securities from the books of primary dealer banks onto the balance sheet of the Fed. What financial institutions received in return were liquid bank reserves that could be lent back into the economy at low-interest rates.

The scope of the intervention was unprecedented. Between the Global Financial Crisis of 2008 and the aftermath of the 2020 pandemic, the Federal Reserve stepped far beyond its normal sphere of action and broke all its self-imposed rules against the practice of "money printing" (the purchase of government debt by the central bank) to ensure the health of asset markets. In the depths of the Great Recession, Bernanke's Federal Reserve purchased over $1 trillion in Treasury and other debt over a period of eighteen months. The pandemic response went much further. When turmoil gripped the U.S. Treasury market in March 2020, the Federal Reserve, under Jerome Powell, stepped in and bought $100 billion in bonds *per day*. Within a matter of weeks, it had transferred $1.5 trillion in securities onto its balance sheet and restored calm to financial markets.[270] Bernanke and his successors never abandoned the "Greenspan put" then: they simply took it to the next level, pulling out all the stops to ensure that asset holders were buffered from the risk of falling prices. By monetizing Treasury and other debt en masse, extending its credit backstop from government-chartered banks to the shadow banking sector, and making dollar swap lines available to overseas central banks, the Federal Reserve reinvented itself as market-maker of last resort and de facto central bank to the world.[271]

In its traditional form, monetary policy seeks to influence the so-called federal funds rate—the price at which banks lend to each other overnight—by buying and selling short-maturity Treasury debt from primary dealer banks. The goal is to influence short-term interest rates, nudging them up when the economy is overheated and pushing them back down when it is sluggish. By contrast, QE targeted long-term government bonds and broadened the central bank's portfolio of asset purchases from treasuries to other instruments—mortgage-backed securities in the wake of the 2007 housing meltdown, and corporate bonds during the coronavirus pandemic. The theory was that QE, by ensuring ultra-low long-term interest rates, would stimulate leverage across the economy, encouraging corporations to increase their capital investment and households to step up their spending with the help of cheap credit. In what has been aptly described as a form of "trickle down" monetary policy, rising asset prices, diminishing yields, and cheap credit were expected to deliver higher employment and growth levels.[272] Yet in the absence of a homeowners' bailout or a coherent federal investment policy, QE simply funneled leverage into stock prices and dizzying capital gains. As government bonds were drained from the market and returns on remaining treasuries plunged to historic lows, investors went hunting in corporate debt markets, accepting ever higher risk ratings in return for yield. With so much investor appetite for their debt, publicly traded companies made extravagant use of leverage to drive up their stock market valuations, often borrowing more than their net worth to indulge in lavish dividend payouts and stock buybacks.[273] Private equity firms too made a triumphant comeback: acquisitions may have been harder to come by, thanks to a shrinking pool of unrestructured and plausibly undervalued companies, but those who managed to clinch a deal were now exiting with record-breaking capital gains.[274]

The distributional consequences were shocking, if entirely predictable. In the absence of any countervailing trend toward sustained fiscal stimulus, QE was bound to exacerbate wealth inequality, not only because it drove up asset prices across the board but also because it favored a particular class of assets (stocks) that were disproportionately to be found in the portfolios of the already wealthy.[275] The decade following the Global Financial Crisis witnessed the largest spike in wealth concentration in postwar America, most of it the result of asset price gains.[276] During the peak months of the pandemic, between 2020 and mid-2021, surging asset prices catapulted almost one hundred new billionaires onto the Forbes list of richest Americans and inflated the wealth of all American billionaires combined by more than a trillion dollars.[277]

Just as significant as the scale of this wealth was its distinct organizational profile—private, often unincorporated, and family-based as opposed to corporate, publicly owned, and managerial. The postmillennial wealth surge released the richest Americans from the grip of outside investors, turning personal and family wealth holders into standalone economic forces, at least as powerful (if not more so) than the old elite of corporate CEOs, investment bankers, and party factions. We are just beginning to grasp the consequences of this shift, both in the political and economic arena.

It could be argued, of course, that the very largest family enterprises have always enjoyed a certain operational freedom when compared to publicly traded corporations. Most of them are either privately owned (Cargill, Mars, and Koch Industries, for example) or controlled by family members holding majority ownership stakes (Walmart and the Waltons), affording them a unique power to disregard stakeholder noise. But in recent years, the political and economic clout of these companies, along with their asset valuations, has grown beyond all measure. During the pandemic years alone, the top ten families in the Forbes 400 saw their net worth increase by the billions. The wealth of the Lauder family almost doubled, growing by almost $22 billion in the space of two years. The Koch family gained $17 billion, the Waltons an astonishing $30 billion.[278]

Alongside these Forbes 400 regulars—first-, second-, and third-generation beneficiaries of inherited wealth—we have also seen the rise of a new class of billionaires, most of whom made their money in platform start-ups such as Uber or Airbnb or alternative investments (hedge funds, private equity, or venture capital).[279] As newcomers to the billionaire list, men such as Uber's ex-CEO Travis Kalanick or Palantir's Peter Thiel are hailed as self-made entrepreneurs and proffered as evidence that American capitalism has not yet turned completely oligarchic. If the American economy is still capable of churning out Schumpeterian heroes such as these, the story goes, then surely meritocracy lives on and will eventually outpace the slow sedimentation of inherited wealth.[280] Yet the same billionaire entrepreneurs who pulled themselves up by the upper-middle-class bootstraps typically go on to found dynasties of their own. When they cash out their stakes in a private tech start-up or close a private equity fund, they invariably channel their fortune into a family wealth fund, and so lay the foundation for a new lineage of twenty-first-century Rockefellers and Vanderbilts.

Until recently, the large family enterprise was considered a marginal player in American capitalism, long since made redundant by the modern "democratic" structures of managerial capitalism. Economic historians such as Alfred Chandler routinely dismissed the familial form of business management as an archaism and impediment to industrial progress—better served, it was thought, by the separation of powers and distributed ownership of the publicly traded corporation.[281] And for most of the twentieth century, this analysis was borne out by the evolution of American business, which progressively absorbed the family dynasties of the Gilded Age into the anonymous shareholder crowd and confined family enterprise to the small business sector. A handful of classic family dynasties, among them the Morgans and the Rockefellers, have endured since the nineteenth century. But most family businesses rapidly lost their distinct institutional form in the early twentieth century when they were forced to compete with and adapt to the presence of rising industrial conglomerates, with their much greater sources of capital.[282] As more and more companies followed the "Berle and Means" model of industrial organization and resorted to the stock market to fund their large-scale operations, most family owners became minority investors in businesses they had founded.[283]

Viewed within a longer time horizon, the resurgence of the large, privately held family enterprise can be understood as one of the many unforeseen side effects of the shareholder revolution and its reshaping of corporate power.[284] Once valued for the economies of scale it offered to large industrial ventures and the liquidity it afforded to investors, the publicly traded corporation was the undisputed focal point of American business for much of the twentieth century. It has long been associated with a particular style of capitalism—dubbed "managerial" by Alfred Chandler—and was challenged in the 1980s by the ideology of "shareholder capitalism," with its overriding concern with maximizing investor returns.

In hindsight, it appears that the shareholder revolution, an ideology meant to shift the balance of power from the professional manager to the owner-investor, also ended up undermining the raison d'être of large-scale ownership itself, as a generation of corporate raiders discovered they could best maximize "shareholder value" by limiting the number of shareholders to a handful of private activists.[285] Michael C. Jensen, one of the fathers of shareholder value theory, foresaw as much in the late 1980s when he noted that the leveraged buyout craze would signal the death of the public corporation as it had existed throughout the twentieth century.[286] Although the obituary was premature, time has tended to confirm Jensen's insight.

It would take a series of key tax and regulatory reforms to turn the hostile takeovers of the 1980s into the respectable form of the mutually agreed-upon private equity deal. But by the first decade of the millennium, more and more firms were going private, while start-up ventures were waiting much longer to launch an IPO, if they chose to do so at all.[287] Private investment funds have grown precipitously since the Global Financial Crisis and now command so much capital that they offer a serious alternative to public securities markets. As recently as the early 2000s, the only real options for companies that wanted to expand was an IPO for start-ups or the corporate bond market for more established firms. Today it is no longer necessary for a company to go public when it wants to scale up operations; it has only to find a congenial investment fund to shepherd it through the transition phase.

Today, small start-up and growing companies can reach colossal size on the strength of private capital alone, and as long as they remain in this state, they are shielded from the public disclosure rules that come with public listing.[288] In recent years, we have seen a precipitous fall in newly listed public corporations and a corresponding rise in the numbers of so-called unicorns—private companies with valuations of one billion or more. Large-scale privately held companies such as Koch Industries were once rare enough to warrant their reputation as near-mythical creatures. Today, unicorns are an increasingly common sighting, especially among tech start-ups that would once have followed the trajectory of the early IPO (think Uber, Airbnb, PayPal, and Dropbox, all of which were valued at well over a billion dollars before they floated their shares).[289] When companies such as these choose to go public, it is generally to allow early investors and employees to cash out their illiquid shares, not because they need to access the capital available in public share markets.[290]

Public corporations are in no danger of disappearing, of course—in fact, the most prominent among them are getting larger and more monopolistic by the day—but many of the newest entrants are publicly owned in name only. Especially when it comes to big tech, some of the largest corporations by market capitalization rely on "dual-class" share structures and other byzantine voting rules that allow the company's founder to override other institutional or individual shareholders.[291] The owners of Facebook, Google, and Tesla shares are powerless to enforce organizational change because the companies' founders dispose of more votes per share than the ordinary stockholder. Many of the newest companies to enter the share market have adopted such rules in perpetuity. As noted by former SEC commissioner Robert J. Jackson Jr., perpetual dual-class shares "don't just ask investors to trust a visionary founder. It asks them to trust that founder's kids. And their kids' kids. And their *grandkid's* kids; they raise the prospect that control over our public companies...will be forever held by a small, elite group of corporate insiders—who will pass that power down to their heirs."[292] Thus the platform companies that monopolize our digital media infrastructure lie in the hands of an increasingly autocratic, patrimonial elite. Shareholder democracy hits a brick wall when business founders find new ways to establish dynastic strongholds within the legal structures of the publicly traded corporation.

Just as newly listed public corporations are beginning to act more like private, dynastic enterprises under the tight control of a small inner core, families are also becoming more prominent in the world of alternative investment and private capital provision. Once the preserve of private equity firms, the market in direct private finance has seen a recent influx of family offices, a sign of the extreme wealth that is now concentrated in the hands of personal investors and their kin. In the past decade or so, it has become a commonplace for the very rich—of new and old extraction—to channel their personal and family assets into a private wealth management fund.[293] Whether they are heirs to an established business dynasty such as the Waltons or the Cargills, unicorn founders, or alternative asset managers, twenty-first-century billionaires are almost always beneficiaries of a family office. Thus, whatever their differences on other issues, they share a common class interest in the appreciation of family assets.

The so-called single family office was originally conceived as a vehicle for managing the administrative, legal, and investment needs of ultrawealthy clans across generations.[294] John D. Rockefeller is thought to have created the prototype when in 1893 he hired a dedicated team of professional staff to manage his sprawling investments and philanthropic ventures in house.[295] A relic of the Gilded Age, the Rockefeller family office survives to this day, having trained generations of heirs in the fine art of wealth preservation, and now sells its advisory services to family investors worldwide. Family offices reappeared in the 1980s, and their numbers have continued to creep up since then. But the real explosion took place after 2010 as a result of the surging asset prices brought about by the Federal Reserve's unconventional monetary policy.[296]

While family offices continue to perform the traditional work of wealth preservation, overseeing everything from tax avoidance to succession planning on behalf of their members, they are also increasingly active players in the world of alternative investment.[297] High-net-worth households typically have many years of experience working in partnership with private investment firms, for the most part passively investing in deals sponsored by outside general partners. But now that they find themselves with sufficient resources to rival standalone private investment firms, a growing number of them are employing private equity or hedge fund professionals in-house and taking active charge of acquisition deals.[298] Family offices have become a "disruptive force" in the private capital markets, notes the *Wall Street Journal*, so busy are they pursuing deals that were once reserved for their more established rivals.[299]

In their strategic acumen and appetite for bold maneuvers, the new generation of family offices look very much like hedge funds and private equity firms, except for the fact that they are only authorized to serve kin (and kin-like) clients and can only draw on family assets to make their investments.[300] But the influence cuts both ways, and family offices are also leaving their imprint on the wider world of private investment, most notably in the recent trend toward "permanent capital" holdings in sectors such as rental housing or infrastructure. The classic private equity firm was notoriously short-sighted in its investment horizons, typically wiping its hands of a deal after five to seven years. By contrast, the family wealth fund doesn't come with a fixed expiration date. So-called permanent or long-dated capital is a natural fit for family offices thinking in terms of multigenerational wealth management, and increasingly this is a quality that target companies are looking for in private equity, too.[301] Although it may not be the solution that critics of corporate myopia were looking for, the family office is steadily replacing the accelerated horizons of the classic private equity firm with the long vistas of dynastic wealth expansion.

For a decade or so, family offices have enjoyed a distinct legal advantage over other private investment funds. Following the global market meltdown of 2008, Congress brought private fund advisors under regulatory oversight by requiring them to register with the Securities and Exchange Commission and publish quarterly reports on their activities. Until this point, hedge funds and private equity firms had operated under the "private advisor exemption" absolving them from public disclosure. The exemption meant they could act on specialized knowledge without tipping off other market investors and stake out high-risk positions without fear of litigation. At worst, it allowed them to hide behind a veil of secrecy when they took undue risks with other people's money. The Dodd-Frank Act ended the exemption for most hedge funds and private equity firms on the grounds that their activities could pose a systemic threat to markets. Family offices emerged unscathed, however, thanks to a concerted lobbying drive by a group of family office executives called the Private Investor Coalition.[302] This gave family offices an edge over other private investment firms at the very moment they were coming into extreme wealth. Despite commanding volumes of capital rivaling those of the largest hedge funds and private equity firms, family offices alone could operate in complete secrecy and were thus afforded a unique strategic advantage. The exemption was so coveted that several hedge fund managers, among them George Soros, promptly reimbursed their outside investors and registered as family offices.

In addition to its privileged status under federal securities regulation, the family office occupies an enviable tax position: it enjoys all the tax advantages of private equity (chief among them the carried interest loophole, which allows its income to be taxed at the preferential capital gains rate), while also falling under the special tax protections of the family. In its current form, U.S. tax law allows wealth holders to build up vast asset portfolios without ever incurring the capital gains tax, so long as they transfer these assets to their children and grandchildren rather than selling them to outside parties. Even if inheritors choose to sell up assets, moreover, they will only be taxed for the gains made *after* the moment of inheritance, leaving the wealth accrued during the lifetime of the testator untouched.[303] The family is thus ideally positioned to consolidate the wealth derived from appreciating asset prices.[304]

The scope of the family tax shelter becomes palpable when we consider the growing proportion of family wealth that derives solely from asset price appreciation. As of 1997, 36 percent of the total value of all estates was held in the form of unrealized capital gains—wealth that passively accrued to the owner as a simple consequence of rising market values.[305] Two decades later, this percentage stood at 32 percent for estates worth between $5 and $10 million and as high as 55 percent for estates worth more than $100 million.[306] In theory, some of this wealth will be subject to the estate tax. But by 2017, successive supply-side tax cuts had elevated the tax-free threshold on estates to $22.8 million for married couples—and in any case, the savviest of clans routinely make use of trust arrangements to escape the burden altogether.[307] We do not usually think of the family as part of the tax-shelter industry. But there is good reason why the same investors who hide their wealth in distant tropical islands and dream of permanent sea steads off the coast of California are also those who make regular use of the family as a form of "inshore" tax protection.

The family is truly a tax haven in a heartless world.

PALACE WARS

The historian Steve Fraser remarks that the "resurgence of what might be called dynastic or family capitalism, as opposed to the more impersonal managerial capitalism many of us grew up with, is changing the nation's political chemistry" along with its economic structures.[308] In the last decade or so, America's wealthiest families have become political kingmakers, exerting an influence at least equal to traditional party factions. In the wake of the 2010 *Citizens United* decision, many feared that the floodgates would open to a deluge of corporate money. As it turns out, however, blue-chip corporations have shied away from super PACs for fear of the backlash they might suffer at the hands of activist investors and social media campaigns. In 2012, the first year in which outside groups played a significant role in funding elections, publicly listed corporations contributed less than 0.5 percent of the money raised by the most active super PACs.[309] Six years later, during the 2018 midterms, they still accounted for less than 5 percent.[310] Most of these were fossil fuel companies that had nothing to lose from backing conservative causes. For the average listed company, however, the reputational risks of overt political preference are just too high. S&P 500 corporations are not so much "woke" as legally accountable to shareholders and constantly vulnerable to the risk of consumer backlash. Private, unlisted companies and their general partners are far less constrained, and it is these actors that contribute the vast majority of super PAC money.

A *New York Times* investigation into the political donations fueling the 2016 presidential primaries found that ultrawealthy families had supplied almost half of the money for Republican and Democratic contenders in the early stages of the election cycle, most of it through channels opened up by *Citizens United*.[311] The profile of these donors, the *Times* noted, reflected the changing composition of the American elite and the growing importance of private, family-based investment funds in the high spheres of financial capitalism. Very few of the donors belonged to the "old" world of investment banking, institutional investment, or corporate management. And relatively few were heirs to old money. Most of them had amassed their fortunes in private asset management and had ridden the postmillennial wave of surging asset prices to amass gargantuan personal wealth. These were the founders of new dynasties, not heirs to the old. Among the superdonors of 2016, the largest single faction made their fortunes in private equity, hedge funds, and venture capital. The next two largest groups were concentrated in real estate and construction and oil and gas.

In another context, the political theorists Marlène Benquet and Théo Bourgeron point to the profound political shifts we are seeing as a result of the ascendance of alternative asset management (private equity, hedge funds, venture capital, and real estate investment funds) since the turn of the millennium. Benquet and Bourgeron distinguish between two waves of financialization: the first wave, driven by the passive investment strategies of institutional investors, pension funds, and investment banks had a dominant influence on political life from the late 1970s to the 1990s; and the second wave, centered on the active investment strategies of private equity, hedge funds, and real estate investment funds, has in recent years become increasingly assertive in defending its own class interests, sometimes placing them in outright opposition to the forces of first-wave finance.[312] Benquet and Bourgeron, for instance, argue that Brexit was less a popular protest vote against the neoliberal constitutionalism of the European Union than the symptom of an infraclass war among London's financial elites. This thesis can be helpful in explaining some of the more shocking political realignments of the last decade or so, from the rise of Jair Bolsonaro in Brazil to Trump's unexpected hijacking of the Republican Party.

Without a doubt, the U.S. presidential elections of 2016 were a show of force for the new billionaire donor class. Investors who hailed from the world of private equity and hedge funds were angered by provisions in the Dodd-Frank Act that subjected them to new public disclosure requirements and were fearful that the Democrats, under Hillary Clinton, would hold good on their threat to abolish the carried interest loophole. Republicans, especially those veering to the hard right, thus became the chief beneficiaries of super-PAC spending in the early stages of the campaign. The families who made the largest and earliest donations to the Republican campaign (among them the Mercers) favored Tea Party candidate Ted Cruz, who railed against "woke" corporations and presented himself as a friend to the "small" unincorporated business.[313] By contrast, Trump, who also threatened to abolish the carried interest loophole, started out with relatively few backers from the world of private investment. The handful that gathered around him had either bailed him out in the past or were hoping to be bailed out by him in the near future.[314] Many more Republican donors kept their distance from a candidate who looked too erratic to work with. It was only when Trump emerged as the presumptive nominee, in mid-2016, that megadonors such as hedge fund billionaire Robert Mercer rallied behind him.

Although Trump was not their first choice then, private investment donors were clearly rooting for Republicans in the 2016 campaign.[315] Early observers of super-PAC money took this to mean that the new billionaire donor class would inexorably skew right.[316] But things have not turned out that way. The Democrats have their own dynastic consorts, most prominent among them George Soros and Henry Laufer as well as individual members of the Pritzker, Walton, and Lauder clans.[317] The class composition of the Democrats' billionaire donor base is indistinguishable from that of the Republicans, except for the greater concentration of its private investor faction in the West Coast tech sector and relatively slim presence in real estate, construction, and fossil fuels.[318] Many of the hedge fund men who supported Trump in 2016 stood on the sidelines in 2020, coughing up a mere $3.6 million for his campaign and its allied super PACs. In the same election cycle, private equity and hedge fund managers channeled a massive $21 million into the Biden campaign, despite the fact that Biden was threatening to tax investor income at the ordinary rate rather than the capital gains rate.[319] The assurance of political stability, it seems, was more important than tax preferences (which in any case the Biden administration has thus far failed to abolish).

The billionaire class is not captured by one party or the other, then, and individual donors may hedge their bets by donating to both sides. But whether they lean Democratic or Republican, America's billionaires are remarkably united when it comes to the economic issues of taxation and public spending. In their 2018 study on the political preferences of ultrawealthy donors, political scientists Benjamin I. Page, Jason Seawright, and Matthew J. Lacombe found that billionaires overwhelmingly favor low taxes on capital gains and inherited wealth and look askance on public programs such as Social Security.[320] Although the media pronouncements of figures such as Warren Buffett, Bill Gates, or George Soros, seem to indicate the existence of a broad billionaire "center" pushing for a greater taxation of wealth, the fact is that most billionaires don't express their political views in public and very few share positions as progressive as these. The few "centrist" billionaires who have openly called for a higher estate tax, moreover, have conveniently spent very little money to ensure that such changes are implemented.[321]

As Doug Henwood notes, one clear point of distinction between Democrat- and Republican-leaning billionaires is the fact that the latter are much more energetic organizers and institution builders.[322] Business dynasties such as the Kochs, the Mercers, and the Uihleins have spent many years pushing the Republican Party further to the right, thanks to the network of policy institutions they have built up and their ever-tighter hold on party policy. In office, moreover, Republican Party members of Congress are much more representative of the new billionaire class. The fourteen-member George W. Bush cabinet, in its time the wealthiest in U.S. history, included ten multimillionaires.[323] The Trump cabinet of twenty-three staff members far surpassed this record: it counted seventeen multimillionaires, two centimillionaires, and one billionaire, with most of their wealth drawn from private equity investments, stock-based compensation, and share portfolios.[324]

As Republican members of Congress have become wealthier, they have left behind their connections to the corporate boardroom or investment bank and moved closer to the world of alternative investment. The George W. Bush cabinet still included many advisors who had served on the boards of S&P 500 corporations such as Alcoa, Lockheed Martin, and Enron.[325] Several of them, however, went on to work for private equity firms, among them former vice president Dan Quayle and former treasury secretary John Snow, both of whom went on to chair Cerberus Capital Management; Bush's campaign manager Ken Mehlman, who became head of public affairs at the veteran private equity firm Kohlberg Kravis Roberts (KKR); and former U.S. general and director of the CIA David Petraeus, who is now a partner at KKR and director of its Global Institute.[326] This is not to mention George H. W. Bush and the several other members of his cabinet who went on to pursue successful careers with the private equity firm the Carlyle Group,[327] or current Federal Reserve Chairman Jerome Powell, who also became a partner at the Carlyle Group after working for the Treasury under the first President Bush.[328] The revolving door between the Treasury Department, leading private equity firms, and the Federal Reserve is evidence enough of the growing symbiotic relationship between private investment and the state.

Yet the symbiosis between the Trump administration and the world of alternative investment was without precedent.[329] For all his campaign threats to overturn the carried interest deduction, once in office, Trump surrounded himself with private equity and hedge fund managers. As *Financial Times* editor Gillian Tett noted, a striking number of them were specialists in "distressed debt," and almost all owed financial favors to Trump (or were owed favors by him).[330] His incoming presidential cabinet included such figures as Secretary of Commerce Wilbur Ross, founder of an eponymous private equity firm dealing in distressed debt, who had once convinced creditors to keep Trump's casinos afloat; advisor on regulation Carl Icahn, among the wealthiest hedge fund managers in the country, who had recently purchased the distressed debt of the Trump Taj Mahal; Treasury Secretary Steven Mnuchin, founder of the private equity firm Liberty Strategic Capital, who had made a fortune by buying up distressed subprime debt in the wake of the housing crisis; economic advisor Stephen Schwarzman, cofounder and CEO of Blackstone and at the time the wealthiest man in private equity; Stephen Feinberg of Cerberus Capital Management, the hedge fund that drove Chrysler into bankruptcy in 2009;

John Paulson, whose failing hedge fund Trump had recently invested in; and Thomas Barrack, who in 1990 founded Colony Capital, a real estate buyout firm specialized in distressed property loans.[331] The dominance of private family wealth within Trump's inner sanctum is key to understanding his unique style of governing. As the political journalist Adele Stan stresses, "private companies play by a different set of rules than those governing firms that trade their shares on stock exchanges. Unlike their publicly traded counterparts, private companies don't have to worry about facing irate shareholders. That's because a private company's principals have chosen those shareholders, who are often drawn from a founder's family. No proxy fights or hostile takeovers to worry about; no bending to the will of big institutional investors."[332] These "are people who have thrived in a culture of unaccountability and self-dealing," and they have every incentive to import this same culture into office.

FAILING UP

In her masterful memoir of the Trump family, *Too Much and Never Enough*, Donald Trump's niece Mary recounts her horror at learning of the election results of 2016. "I began to feel as though I were watching my family history, and Donald's central role in it, playing out on a grand scale," she writes.[333] Mary Trump traces her uncle's idiosyncratic style of governing to the pathological relationship he established with his father, Fred Trump, during his childhood. It was not Donald, the memoir reminds us, but his older brother, Freddie, who had been chosen at birth to continue the family business. But as Donald grew up and watched his older brother wither beneath Fred Trump's astringent gaze, he learned that his father was not looking for genuine intelligence in his heir apparent, a quality he interpreted as a form of disrespect.[334] Instead, Fred Trump turned increasingly to his younger son, who had no visible talents of his own and scorned all authority except that of his father. Donald may have looked like a loser to the outside world. But for this same reason his father had nothing to fear from him, and he himself had nothing to lose in becoming a vessel for his father's grandiosity. So Donald slowly replaced his older brother as the Trump business heir, eventually taking up residence in the Trump family office while his brother lapsed into alcoholism and an early death.

For some time now, Trump's biographers and journalists have cast doubt on the idea that he was ever the "self-made man" he claimed to be. But before the publication of this memoir, few could have imagined how little Trump ever achieved on his own or how completely his father controlled the lives of his offspring. Each of Fred Trump's children were gifted part of his estate during their lifetime, thanks to a legal workaround that allowed them to avoid the gift tax.[335] But whether they were unaware of their rights or too afraid to assert them, Mary Trump recalls, none of them had free access to the use of their trust funds.[336] Instead, all except Donald Trump lived a semi-institutionalized life in one of their father's many apartment buildings, often relegated to the darkest and most rundown units in the block. The Trump children and grandchildren wanted for nothing—they were provided with free health care and private school educations—but remained dependent on their father's consent for every adult decision they made. Mary Trump notes the strange mixture of privilege and austerity that characterized the lives of her and her relatives.[337] Only Donald was exempted from this economy of scarcity. "Honest work was never demanded of him, and no matter how badly he failed, he was rewarded in ways that are almost unfathomable." With the help of his father's negligent validation, Trump had learned that he could only ever "fail up."[338]

From the mid-1970s to mid-1980s, when Donald Trump was making a name for himself as a real estate wunderkind, it appears that his father was bankrolling his every move and bailing out his every misstep. Fred Trump not only used his dense networks of Democratic Party political contacts to orchestrate deals and negotiate bespoke tax exemptions on his son's behalf but also clandestinely funneled millions of dollars into his accounts.[339] It was on the strength of these vicarious successes in Manhattan that Trump managed to persuade first the New York media and then the banks that he was worth investing in.[340] And so he was, as long as his father was surreptitiously acting as a lender of last resort. We might describe Trump father and son as a mutual self-appreciation machine: with the father offering the collateral of the family trust fund and an endless supply of debt leverage behind the scenes, Donald was free to talk up his worth as if it were entirely self-made. Donald Trump's reputation was thereby sufficiently embellished to draw in unsuspecting private creditors, who would soon be on the hook for his inevitable business failures.

The illusion first began to falter, Mary Trump observes, when her uncle ventured beyond the realm of his father's business expertise and tried his hand at becoming a casino operator in Atlantic City.[341] Released from his father's close tutelage, Trump made the simple business mistake of setting up three casinos in competition with each other. Even then, however, Fred Trump was in the wings trying to bail his son out, at one point sending his chauffeur to buy up millions of dollars in gambling chips from the Trump Castle Hotel Casino. In the last few decades, corporate CEOs have learned to profit from government bailouts and interest rate cuts by buying back shares in their own companies and thus pushing up their value; when Trump's casino threatened to fail, his own father bought back his gambling chips.

Mary Trump offers a rare glimpse into the power dynamics of that most secretive of institutions—the private family enterprise. As a trained psychologist, she brings a clinician's eye to the subject of Trump's personal idiosyncrasies. While there have been many other attempts to diagnose the former president's peculiar personality disorder, her account offers unique insight into the *political economy* of the Trump family psychodrama.[342] Mary Trump shows what can happen when great wealth is made available as an instrument for channeling psychic investment, when children are elevated and disinvested at will, disinherited or dangerously inflated, and when a father's power reaches out into the larger political arena.

As someone who watched the evolution of her uncle's business career from the corner of the room, Trump's estranged niece was surely right to fear that a Trump victory in the 2016 elections would project the family drama onto the national stage. But while it is true that Donald Trump, during his long career, has replicated the family dynamic of filial self-appreciation on a progressively grander scale, enlisting city officials, the New York press, the national business media, Fox News, the Republican Party and finally the American people into the game, the enabling has worked in the other direction too. The growing influence of supply-side economics in shaping the tax policy decisions of both major parties has created an environment in which someone like Trump could thrive.

Trump, after all, would surely have remained a local con artist without the help of supply-side tax incentives, which, at the very moment he was embarking on his first Manhattan deals, were actively encouraging trust-fund kids such as himself to leverage up on the basis of their family assets. Fred Trump was never the only enabler of his son's exploits. By the time of Reagan's tax reform of 1981, supply-side tax policies at the city, state, and federal level confirmed what Trump had learned in his childhood—that he could win by losing, or appreciate by depreciating, with other people ultimately shouldering the losses. The capital gains that entrepreneurs such as Trump made from tax write-offs in the 1980s would later be magnified by a Federal Reserve intent on cranking up asset values. In the late 1990s, Greenspan turned asset inflation into the be-all and end-all of monetary policy, while his successors (up until Powell's about-face on interest rates in mid-2022) supercharged the upward trend in asset prices via the use of unconventional monetary policy.

What elevates Trump's story from family psychodrama to economic parable of our times is the fact that his position as the son who could never fail—despite all his obvious failings—has become that of financial asset holders in general, thanks to the evolution of monetary and fiscal policy in the early twenty-first century. The Federal Reserve's two-decade-long policy of monetary accommodation, combined with successive rounds of supply-side tax cuts, has created a world in which asset holders like the young Trump can only ever fail up. The larger fiscal and regulatory environment has become so friendly to financial asset holders that even when interest rate policy is reversed, they can turn to a whole host of guardrails from special bankruptcy provisions to business loss deductions to cushion their fall and save them from the indignity of ordinary failure. Financial asset holders are multiply protected on the upside and the downside. This aspect of the story is absent from Mary Trump's account. Yet it is key to understanding the resurgence of the dynastic form in contemporary American capitalism.

THE PRESIDENTIAL FAMILY OFFICE

Thanks to Donald Trump, we now know how readily the U.S. presidency can fall under the spell of a ruling family elite. The story of his time in the White House—memorably described by one former volunteer as "family office meets organized crime, melded with 'Lord of the Flies'"—reveals an extraordinary breakdown of the barriers between private investment interests, family affairs, and presidential office.[343] Immediately after his inauguration, Trump placed relatives, family retinue, and former business partners (and often their kin) in strategic executive positions.[344] Over the next few months, he purged some of the most qualified officeholders from federal agencies and deliberately neglected to replace the many others who resigned in silent protest. It appears that most of these vacant positions were then filled by "acting" officeholders, under a provision that avoided the usual process of Senate scrutiny and confirmation—an adroitly formal use of the law that kept officeholders tightly dependent on Trump's favor and always conscious they could be dismissed on a whim.[345] If agency staff were not already personally aligned with Trump, they soon learned that tribute and flattery were the only ways of getting things done.

The same kind of deference was demanded of outside negotiators and Republican Party apparatchiks. Corporate lobbyists and foreign states alike appear to have rapidly absorbed the lesson that direct tribute was to be paid to the president in the form of services purchased at the Trump International Hotel in Washington, DC, or a visit to Mar-a-Lago in Florida.[346] And instead of facing off against each other, Republican Party factions were now reduced to the same status of supplicants whose disputes could only be adjudicated by Trump and his close family associates.

For all his talk of a deep state, Trump demonstrated just how frail the much-fabled "checks and balances" of the American system have become in the face of political corruption. The Emoluments Clause should have prevented the president from receiving gifts without the consent of Congress. Trump flouted it several times without consequence and routinely pushed the limits of legality when shuffling funds between his political campaign and family business. His nonchalance was abetted by a hard-right Supreme Court that, in the wake of the *Citizens United* decision of 2010, has shown little initiative in enforcing conflict of interest or campaign finance laws.[347]

Crucially, Trump accelerated the gutting of the Internal Revenue Service that was begun by Republicans in 2011. During his administration, the agency struggled to pursue routine checks and was rarely able to finance the resource-intensive audits required to uncover the complex shell companies and other shelters deployed by the ultrawealthy.[348] As political theorist Jeffrey Broxmeyer observes, the Republican Party under Trump came closer than ever to realizing the New Right's dream of deconstructing the administrative state—but in doing so, it sacrificed its own power to that of the Trump family.[349]

Trump was, not surprisingly, one of the first to benefit from his 2017 tax cuts. In 2019, the value of Trump Tower increased by 27 percent to $445 million. A Trump-owned office tower at 40 Wall Street shot up to $480 million, up by 13 percent over the previous year. Meanwhile, Trump's stake in two Vornado Realty properties, one in Manhattan and the other in the financial district of San Francisco, surged to $765 million, a 33 percent increase from the previous year.[350] Shareholders in real estate investment trusts (REITs), including both the Trump Organization and Kushner Companies, were now eligible for tax deductions of 20 percent on their dividends.[351] With his own coterie of supply-side advisors installed in-house, Trump had re-created the halcyon days of the early 1980s, when Reagan's tax cuts delivered vertiginous gains to Manhattan real estate developers.

Beyond the circles of the Trump-Kushner clan, the Republican congressmen who voted for Trump's tax legislation also benefited personally from these tax cuts. Trump's record cut to the corporate tax rate, from 35 percent to 21 percent, was a boon to the many Republican Party insiders who held large share portfolios. In what is now a familiar denouement to supply-side interventions, corporate capital investment slumped in the year following the tax cuts, while windfall profits were plowed back into stock buybacks and returned to investors in the form of capital gains and dividends.[352] And while tax cuts were automatically elevating the capital gains to be made on leveraged investment, Trump kept up a steady harassment campaign against Federal Reserve chairman Jerome Powell, who could not cut interest rates fast enough to satisfy the president's demand for cheaper and more abundant credit.[353] In the year following Trump's tax cut bill, the total volume of stock buybacks exceeded $1 trillion for the first time ever. Not only was this a gift to the most privileged Americans, but it also personally enriched the ten wealthiest Republicans in Congress, who at the time the bill was passed held two-thirds of their net worth in stocks, bonds, mutual funds, and real estate investment trusts.[354] Republican acquiescence to Trumpian rule makes more sense when we recognize the full scale of economic and political rewards it came with. In the wake of Trump's defeat in late 2020, it is not clear that the Republican Party will soon recover its ability to act autonomously without the centripetal direction of a ruling family elite.

As a heuristic for understanding the Trump presidency, it is hard to beat Max Weber's account of patrimonial power in *Economy and Society*.[355] Here

Weber distinguishes between the bureaucratic style of government, where the "(office) is separated from the household" and "business assets from private wealth," and the patrimonial form of power, which draws no boundaries between politics, economics, and the household.[356] The modern state and publicly traded corporation rely on the impersonal mediation of bureaucrats to perform their functions. The patrimonial ruler, by contrast, treats "political administration" as a "purely personal affair" and considers "political power" to be "part of his personal property, which can be exploited by means of contributions and fees."[357] In the patrimonial state, kinship relations serve as a privileged instrument of power: marriage is strategically deployed to seal commercial ties, and business relations themselves take a kinlike form in which partners become quasi-brothers and employees are absorbed into the family as permanent retinue. Beholden to no other authority outside his own circles, the "patrimonial master," like Trump, "wields power without constraint, at his own discretion and, above all, unencumbered by rules."[358]

At first glance, Weber's account of patrimonial power suggests a stageist view of history, in which successively more rational, impersonal, and bureaucratic forms of power evolve out of and shed their primitive selves with implacable momentum. The term "patrimonialism" is thus understood as referring to precapitalist forms of power; its apparent resurgence in the present could only indicate a return of the premodern or the end of capitalism as such. Weber was more nuanced than this: a typologist of power rather than an evolutionary thinker, he acknowledged that patrimonial power could coexist with and facilitate forms of wealth creation that were recognizably capitalist, albeit distinct from the managerial style of capitalism that was rapidly gaining ground at the time he wrote.[359] In fact, the proximate model for Weber's writings on patrimonialism was not Pharaonic Egypt or the pre-Columbian Inca empire but his own very claustrophobic extended family, a Gilded Age dynasty of merchants with commercial interests stretching from Manchester to Cuba and Argentina.[360]

In their attempts to capture the strangeness of our contemporary moment, several theorists have evoked a historically vague "feudalism" as precedent to our current moment.[361] We need not look so far. The long Gilded Age, stretching through and beyond the late nineteenth century, saw levels of wealth concentration equal to our own.[362] Its economy was dominated by family-owned and managed companies that had few obligations to outside investors and relied heavily on the resources of private financiers such as J. P. Morgan. By forging horizontal alliances among themselves, these ultrawealthy family enterprises grew into vast industrial "trusts" monopolizing entire sectors of the economy.[363] Their tireless efforts to capture the political process culminated in the election of the plutocrat-friendly President William McKinley in 1896 and a Senate so heavily populated by the ultrarich it was nicknamed the Millionaires' Club.[364] Gilded Age clans like the Rockefellers, the Vanderbilts, and the Mellons continued to flourish during the Republican-dominated 1920s. Their share of national household wealth reached a peak in 1929—fittingly enough, under the watch of Treasury Secretary Andrew Mellon of the eponymous banking dynasty—before succumbing to the redistributive agenda of the New Deal.[365]

During the 1930s, President Franklin D. Roosevelt, with the cooperation of the Treasury, seized the powers of the fledgling U.S. tax system to enact a broad redistribution of wealth. The Revenue Act of 1935 raised the capital gains tax to its highest level yet, pushed up the estate tax rate to 70 percent, and increased overall taxation of the wealthy by nearly 50 percent.[366] The Federal Reserve, too, entered a new phase in the 1930s, when it temporarily freed itself from the constraints of gold to become an active enabler of Treasury spending.[367] Turn-of-the-century populists and progressives had fought for the establishment of an American central bank because they thought it would free the country from the crushing austerity of hard money.[368] But it was only under Roosevelt that the Federal Reserve (established in 1913) made good on this promise by lending its full weight to the expansionist agenda of the New Deal. When this compact between monetary and fiscal policy was sealed, the great fortunes of the Gilded Age were finally deflated.

What distinguishes today's emergent ruling families from their Gilded Age forerunners is the fact that their wealth is actively fostered now by the fiscal and monetary authorities that once reined them in. In recent years, the Federal Reserve has acquired powers of national and international market intervention that were unimaginable in the 1970s, let alone the 1930s. It has broken all the conventions of monetary restraint to engage in massive open market operations and manipulate the price of securities. Yet it has consistently used these powers to inflate asset values while doing everything possible to block any greater distribution of social wealth. By the same token, the American fiscal regime, which once taxed marginal incomes and inherited wealth at higher levels than any other industrial nation, has become so regressive it must be considered an instrument of wealth generation in the hands of the rich.[369] The resurgence of dynastic wealth is the most visible symptom of a counterrevolution that has annexed the full powers of the central bank and Treasury. What would it take for us to reclaim these formidable powers of wealth creation and unleash them for the many?

CHAPTER TWO

Wage Losses: Supply-Side Populism and the Blue-Collar Producer

Amid all the confusion thrown up by the 2016 presidential elections, there was almost unanimous agreement that Donald Trump was brought to power by the white working class. Trump himself did his best to establish this narrative. In a speech delivered in Michigan in August 2016, he claimed to speak for the forgotten victims of deindustrialization: "It's going to be a victory for the people, a victory for the wage-earner, the factory worker. Remember this, a big, big victory for the factory worker. They haven't had those victories for a long time."[1] On the eve of his election win, he announced, "Today the American working class is going to strike back, finally."[2]

From the earliest days of Trump's campaign, a broad spectrum of media outlets, from the *New York Times* to Fox News, corroborated the narrative. In an influential opinion piece published during the primaries, Thomas Frank reported that the "bulk of Trump's fan base" was made up of "working class white people" and castigated the liberal press for representing "demographic categories of nearly every kind" except that of the "blue-collar" worker.[3] But if a liberal masthead like the *New York Times* could justifiably be accused of marginalizing the politics of class, it lost no time in endorsing Frank's assessment of Trump's political base, declaring after the election that Trump had come to power "by riding an enormous wave of support among white working-class voters," a demographic that was assumed to overlap with that of "white voters without a degree."[4] Not to be outdone, the *Washington Post* compared Trump's base to the so-called Reagan Democrats, who defected to the Republican Party in 1980. Trump's "campaign strategy was to lure working-class Democrats to his cause, just the way Reagan did"; as evidence, the article pointed to "the white, non-college educated men who made up a significant part of Trump's base."[5] Despite its surprisingly flimsy empirical foundations, the media interpretation of Trump's success soon gave rise to a distinctive genre of secondary literature heralding the return of class in American political life. With minor shifts of emphasis depending on the political affiliation of the author, this literature was united in its assessment that whatever his personal faults, Trump had at long last forced the Democrats—and the liberal elite as a whole—into a long-overdue reckoning with class.

In much of this analysis, the categories of blue-collar, non-college-educated, and working class are woven so closely together that they are difficult to pry apart. In his commentary on the Trump election, Thomas Frank pits the neglected blue-collar worker against the white-collar professional, whose interests, he claims, have come to dominate the modern Democratic Party.[6] Michael Lind elevates this distinction to the level of a "new class war," claiming that the true fault line no longer runs between labor and capital but between the "professional-managerial overclass" and the uneducated masses.[7] In the meantime, Fox News pundits defend the uneducated private-sector blue-collar worker against an educated elite composed of high-ranking Democrats, Hollywood insiders, deep state technocrats—and white-collar public-sector workers.[8] It seems there is something so intuitive about the correlation between working-class status and low educational achievement that both pollsters and commentators assume it as given, making it difficult to disentangle the limitations of empirical data collection from analytical bias.[9]

Yet the idea that the majority of lower-income wage earners are blue-collar private-sector workers with little or no college education is also deeply anachronistic. This picture still made sense at the time Arthur Wolfe published his classic study of union voters in 1969, when blue-collar workers formed the core of the private-sector unionized workforce, but, according to Wolfe himself, was already beginning to morph by the end of the 1960s.[10] In the two decades of Fordist prosperity that followed World War II, unionized households headed by blue-collar workers pulled away from their nonunionized counterparts, becoming significantly more likely to own their own homes and draw in higher wages. And as blue-collar heads of households moved into the middle class, their loyalty to the Democrats also weakened.[11] In an ethnographic study of class published a decade later, David Halle made the astute observation that blue-collar workers had developed a divided class consciousness: men who considered themselves working-class on the factory floor increasingly identified as middle- or lower middle-class when it came to their status as homeowners.[12] Yet even as they moved into the homeowning middle class, these workers often retained a distinctive understanding of class mobility: if they aspired to move on from the factory, it was by becoming a small business owner, independent truck driver, or tradesman rather than by pursuing college education.[13]

As the private-sector union movement lost steam in the mid-1970s, this sense of double class consciousness proved decisive in drawing one group of unionized blue-collar workers toward the Republican right. It was the newly ascendant public-sector movement that emerged triumphant from the crisis of the 1970s and continued to thrive under adverse conditions, while private-sector unions bled membership and succumbed to the multiple blows of plant relocations, job loss, and regressive labor law reform. Today, the class composition of the American workforce has changed beyond all recognition. If we limit our attention to jobs that require no college education, it becomes clear that blue-collar manual work (manufacturing, mining, construction) has steadily lost ground to the booming low-wage service sector, which comprises everything from retail and sales to food service, nursing assistance, and home health care.[14] This sector employs a disproportionate number of female and minority workers. But even within the category of blue-collar work, the once dominant manufacturing sector has receded in importance, declining as a share of total employment from around 20 percent in 1980 to 8 percent today.[15] And whereas assembly-line work was once the archetype of manual labor, in recent years, workers have steadily migrated from the factory floor to new sites of blue-collar employment in logistics warehouses, recycling depots, and cargo docks.[16] White men continue to dominate in the burgeoning logistics sector, but to a much lesser extent than they did in the Fordist factory.[17]

As for traditional blue-collar but nonindustrial sectors such as construction, which maintain an enduring if cyclical presence in the labor market, here too we have seen significant changes. The steady expansion of nonunion contractors has led to a growing segregation of the workforce, as white workers have largely abandoned the nonunionized residential sector to undocumented migrants. In 1980, only 6 percent of construction workers (unionized or not) were Latinx; by 2000 that number had more than doubled, to 15 percent; in 2020, Latinx workers represented 30 percent of the construction workforce.[18] Even if we restrict our focus to blue-collar employment then, we can no longer assume that the average worker is industrial, unionized, male, or white.

Nor is it the case that white-collar work or public-sector employment signifies class ascension in the same way it did in the 1970s. Despite the pervasive assumption that white-collar workers are automatic members of an ill-defined "professional managerial" elite, it is not hard to find white- or pink-collar workers with secondary degrees who earn far less than workers with similar levels of education.[19] Public schoolteachers—earning almost 20 percent less than similarly qualified workers—have come to symbolize this predicament.[20] But their situation points to a wider trend in the low-wage workforce: between 1979 and 2011, the share of low-wage workers with some college education rose precipitously, from about one in five to one in three.[21] With more and more jobs demanding a college degree as an entry-level requirement, a new dividing line has emerged *among* college graduates, a full third of whom end up underemployed or relegated to low-wage retail and hospitality work. The persistence of the college wage premium can be attributed to the portion of college graduates who go on to earn outsized salaries, often in select fields such as finance, economics, and computer science.[22] Even for the best-paid college-educated workers, family wealth (or its absence) is a significant variable in calculating real wages. Differential student debt burdens significantly alter the real income of college graduates working in the same position. A college degree entirely paid for by parents is considerably more valuable than the same degree paid off with interest by the indebted graduate.

As a distinct demographic within the private-sector workforce, the white, male, blue-collar working class is diminishing in size and importance. Yet the figure of the blue-collar worker remains frozen in time, suspended at some point in the decade of the 1970s, and continues to wield an extraordinary power over the political imagination, as if he alone were capable of making and breaking elections. In fact, as the political scientists Nicholas Carnes and Noam Lupu remind us, exit polling data for the 2016 presidential elections indicate that Trump supporters were for the most part affluent Republicans belonging to the upper half of the income distribution. And while it is true that more than 70 percent of Trump supporters did not have college degrees, it turns out that this also applies to Republican voters as a whole.[23] The idea that low educational attainment serves as a reliable proxy for working-class status ignores the many small business owners, self-employed owner-managers, and trade contractors who rarely complete a college degree.[24] By all indications, small business owners were particularly fervent supporters of Trump.[25]

This is not to say that there was no Democratic swing toward Trump. Undeniably, Hillary Clinton's failure to replicate Obama's 2012 performance in key midwestern counties proved fatal to her election chances. Yet if blue-collar realignment was at play here, the phenomenon was primarily limited to a dozen or so Rust Belt counties in Ohio and Pennsylvania that had recently seen a wave of plant closures. Here, too, Trump's margin seems to be better explained by a drop in voter turnout for Clinton rather than a crowd movement toward Trump. Many of the other local counties that were hailed as blue-collar converts to Trump had long since transferred their allegiance to the Republicans.[26] As Mike Davis points out, election pundits have consistently conflated blue-collar votes long captured by Republican presidential candidates with Trump's more modest and localized conversion events. Davis concludes that "several hundred thousand white, blue-collar Obama voters, at most, voted for Trump's vision of fair trade and reindustrialization, not the millions usually invoked."[27]

The most important—and worrying—lesson to be drawn from the 2016 election is the fact that Republicans were able to translate such local, razor-thin margins into stunning political wins. Here Republican efforts to manipulate the voting process have converged with the Democrats' neglect of nonmetropolitan, industrial counties to amplify the smallest of voter defections.[28] In the wake of the Tea Party landslide of 2010, the Republicans have made full use of their near-dominance of state legislatures to suppress inconvenient votes and redraw electoral districts to maximum effect, helping them to magnify microscopic movements into an apparent "blue-collar wave."

It remains to be understood why the narrative of the "blue-collar wave" is so impervious to empirical critique. In his study of contemporary right-wing populism, Reece Peck unpacks the rhetorical process by which Fox News has come to define itself as the voice of the blue-collar working-class man, even as it subtly blurs the lines between the wage worker and owner-manager.[29] During the presidential campaign of 2008, the figure of Joe the Plumber—in real life, a tradesman from Ohio called Samuel Wurzelbacher—was celebrated by Fox News as the face of the aspiring blue-collar business owner and made to do symbolic battle with presidential candidate Barack Obama, who was widely vilified as a former "community organizer" and child of public-sector excess. In Peck's words, "Joe the Plumber was a useful political symbol because he—a tall, white, brawny tradesman—at least residually embodied the manly image of the industrial working class, an image that stood in contrast to the feminized labor of service sector workers, which is the sector that actually employs the majority of the present-day working class."[30]

What Peck rightly identifies as the "residual" quality of this image is worth pondering. It is as if, in the grammar of right-wing populism, the predicate "blue-collar" had come unstuck from the "wage earner" subject. Much like the ubiquitous hard hat in an election photo shoot, the "blue-collar" epithet can be worn haphazardly by a person of any occupational status or income and wealth level, as long as he is male, white, and not too conspicuously educated. As a color code for manual labor, the signifier "blue collar" retains its aura as a marker of real economic value—its self-evident productive status standing in contrast to the always contested value of pink- and white-collar service work[31]—but obscures the boundaries between the business owner and the wage earner. Indeed, right-wing populism almost invariably treats the blue-collar worker as an aspirational business owner and willfully ignores the distinction between the small and large business, the independent contractor as de facto gig worker and the independent contractor as owner-manager. Fox News could hail Trump as a blue-collar billionaire for the same reason it identified Samuel Wurzelbacher the would-be business owner as a working-class icon.[32] By forcibly uniting labor and capital under the corporatist banner of "blue-collar" production, right-wing populism cultivates an imagined alliance of interests between the blue-collar taxpayer and the billionaire businessman.

The origins of this symbolic alliance can be traced back to the mid-1970s, when a small group of business-friendly economists and politicians came to the realization that the Republicans would never secure a winning coalition unless they extended their tax-cut agenda from the corporate elite to the "little man"—both wage earners and small business owners. The key players here were Republican congressman Jack Kemp, *Wall Street Journal* associate editor Jude Wanniski, and the renegade economist Arthur Laffer, then based at the

University of Southern California. I refer to these figures as "supply-side populists," in contrast to the coalition of elite supply-side economists and powerful trade associations who propelled a first wave of investment tax cuts in the mid-1970s.

The elite and populist supply-side economists had at first worked in unison. For a few years, Kemp, Wanniski, and Laffer had been among the most vocal champions of the elite "trickle down" message in the public and media spheres. But at some point during the recession of 1975, they broke with their elite counterparts by shifting the focus of tax reform from the large corporation to the individual wage earner and proposing across-the-board personal tax cuts as a central plank of Republican Party policy. Unless the GOP made some kind of overture to ordinary workers, they thought, it would be forever relegated to political minority status.[33] At a time when the private-sector union movement was on the defensive and blue-collar wages were entering a long period of stagnation, supply-side populists reached out to the blue-collar worker as a taxpayer and asset owner rather than a wage earner, urging him to take up arms against the inflationary wage demands of other workers. By exploiting the divided class consciousness of the blue-collar man, they found a way to turn workers in the unionized private sector against another class of workers—in particular, those employed in the newly militant public sector—and in so doing, established the now familiar gendered and racial fault lines of right-wing populism. The figure of the construction worker was singled out to play a leading role in this morality tale. In the wake of deindustrialization, builders had become the most visible face of blue-collar employment, since the place-bound construction sector had not experienced the same dramatic decline in workforce numbers as manufacturing. The building trades contractor, moreover, had long straddled the divide between unionized wage worker and small business owner. As Joe the Plumber would prove, he was thus ripe for symbolic recuperation by a populist right that had always defended the small-time producer against unproductive elites—from below and above.

WAGE-PUSH INFLATION AND THE CONSTRUCTION WORKER

Among the many theatrical gestures he lavished on blue-collar workers during his presidential campaign, Trump reserved special attention for those in the building trades. When he was not posing in front of the cameras wearing a hard hat or holding a shovel, Trump was reminiscing about his years working on construction sites, untroubled by the fact he was a real estate developer, not a builder.[34] "I've spent my professional life among construction workers, bricklayers, electricians, and plumbers," he announced on the campaign trail. "I feel more comfortable around blue-collar workers than Wall Street executives."[35] A few days after his inauguration, President Trump met with a delegation of leaders from the building trades unions to confirm the political compact.[36] "America's building trades and its President are very much united," he told them, before reiterating his promise to oversee a grand infrastructure bill that would keep them employed into the far future.[37]

As political theater, the meeting recalled a much earlier moment, when Nixon had invited the building trades to the White House to seal a hoped-for new alliance between the Republican Party and blue-collar workers. The sense of déjà vu was so uncanny that several political commentators described Trump's populism as a reenactment of Nixon's.[38]

The comparison was misleading, however. Nixon had briefly contemplated the prospect of a reinvigorated welfare state, founded on conservative family values and a corporatist pact between white blue-collar working men and business. Government-subsidized construction was to be the driver of Nixon's hard-hat welfare state. By contrast, Trump served up the same mix of nativism and family values but combined it with tax expenditures rather than direct spending. His much-vaunted infrastructure plan (which never materialized) would have relied entirely on tax incentives to construction companies and real estate developers like himself. For all the attention Trump bestowed on them, moreover, the so-called hard hats held much less bargaining power in the 2010s than they did in the early 1970s. Construction workers lost more than most in the four decades of wage stagnation that commenced in the 1980s. Today they are far from representing the political threat they once did. The building trades unions had once been so formidable that when economists first identified the problem of wage-push inflation they singled out construction workers as the prime culprits.[39] At the beginning of the 1970s, the building trades were flying high on the long postwar boom in public and private capital investment. From the national highway system and Cold War defense installations of the 1950s to the public housing projects of the Great Society,

COUNTERREVOLUTION

114

federal and state contracts generated a seemingly endless source of heavy construction work for building tradesmen and provided a longer-than-usual buffer against the boom-and-bust cycles that ordinarily plagued the industry.[40]

By the late 1960s, public construction projects accounted for one-third of all building work, turning many supposed private-sector workers into de facto beneficiaries of state job creation. Under the terms of the Davis-Bacon Act of 1931, moreover, contractors were required to pay workers at "local prevailing wages," effectively preventing them from importing cheaper nonunion labor onto building sites.[41] The end of the recession in 1965 led to a further surge in construction, this time as a result of private-sector factory and plant expansion. The result was a sharp uptick in wages that business observers saw as a sign of trouble ahead. Between June 1968 and June 1969, wages and benefits for nonresidential construction workers rose by 10 percent—faster than the prevailing rate of consumer price inflation.[42] With numerous urban renewal projects on the horizon and an anticipated boom in residential construction, business elites feared that wage hikes such as these would continue into the next decade. An early and ever-watchful observer of the phenomenon of wage-push inflation, *Fortune* magazine warned in 1970 that this "kind of wage trajectory is a grave and growing menace to the economic and social health of the United States. It is shaping up as the most important obstacle in the way of subduing inflation. It threatens to tear apart the intricate functional distinctions in incentives and rewards that make an economy dynamic and help it use its resources efficiently."[43]

The problem, as seen by the business media, was that wage gains for skilled craftsmen in the building trades were now setting the standard for wage demands in the nonunion construction sector and beyond.[44] Fewer than half of builders in residential housing were unionized, yet their rates were rising in step with the construction workers who toiled on large public works and industrial building projects. If the contagion spread to the nonunion South and Southwest, there was no telling where it would end.[45] There were growing fears, moreover, that factory workers were taking their cues from the building trades.[46] Unionized construction workers were frequently called upon to complete plumbing or electrical projects in factories, where they rubbed shoulders with in-house maintenance workers on lower wages. The contrast between construction wages and those of factory workers performing similar or equivalent tasks seemed to be encouraging industrial unions to push for more ambitious wage settlements.

The business media regularly depicted construction unions as a kind of ancien régime resistant to the democratizing forces of the free market. A *Fortune* magazine feature from 1968 spoke of the aristocratic families that ruled the various craft associations and intimated that they were governed by unwritten laws of succession and primogeniture comparable to a feudal elite. "The line of succession in some of the most powerful building-trade unions is determined by such naked nepotism. Sons of labor barons, like the progeny of royal families, are groomed for succession with careful ritual."[47] The article deplored the hierarchical, gerontocratic structure of the trade brotherhoods, where the average age of members hovered around forty. Construction, it alleged, was fast becoming an "old man's trade" thanks to the union's stranglehold over the training and hiring of workers.[48] Many of these problems were blamed on a basic lack of democracy at the local union level, where only delegates, not rank-and-file members, had the power to elect national representatives. At the last convention of the carpenters union, it was reported, "a delegate complained plaintively that the union had cheered the one-man one-vote decision at the Supreme Court but refused to extend that privilege to its own members."[49]

The cynicism of the business media's concern with rank-and-file democracy hardly needs pointing out. Yet historians confirm the picture of the building trades as a tightly protected domain in which familial and ethnic allegiances played an unusually important role in distributing work and determining career prospects. The building trades were exclusively masculine, dominated in many regions by "white ethnic" men of Irish, Italian, and Polish descent. New apprentices almost always needed to be sponsored by a father or uncle before they were accepted into an apprenticeship program—a system of masculine lineage that Peter Brennan, president of New York City's Building and Construction Trades Council, candidly referred to as the "father-son deal."[50] The labor historian Joshua Freeman notes that the building trades unions frequently expressed contempt toward "unskilled" factory workers and "unproductive" white-collar workers and sometimes stood in opposition to their wage demands.[51] It was not just the union hiring hall and apprenticeship system that ensured the industry's impermeability to outsiders; it was a whole system of socialization. New apprentices were regularly subject to hazing and humiliation as a rite of passage into construction site manhood, and the collective harassment of women—both on and off the job—was practically a way of life.[52] Most building trades unions practiced a policy of stubborn inaction when it came to government directives to include African American workers in their apprenticeship programs. When ad hoc efforts at affirmative action were first implemented in the late 1960s, the unions' impassivity was replaced by overt malice. Building trades workers met Black Power actions on construction sites with violence and harassed African American apprentices until they quit of their own accord.[53] Beneficiaries of an industry that was hostile to Blacks and off-limits to women, construction workers cultivated a white masculinist image that became steadily more exaggerated in the 1960s and 1970s as their status came under threat from organized business, minority workers, and the wider forces of social change.[54]

THE CONSTRUCTION USERS ANTI-INFLATION ROUNDTABLE

As we saw in the previous chapter, the powerful new coalition of trade associations that instigated the business revolt of the 1970s announced themselves to the world as defenders of American "capital formation." Yet it was the labor issue of wage inflation in the building trades unions that first spurred them into action. A first expression of this revolt, the Construction Users Anti-Inflation Roundtable, or CUAIR—established in 1969 as a precursor to the Business Roundtable—brought together the largest building contractors and their industrial clients with the aim of creating a bulwark against the unions.[55] The leader of the group, former chairman of U.S. Steel Roger Blough, complained that the general contractors who oversaw large construction projects on behalf of industrial "users" such as General Motors, Monsanto, Dow, and DuPont had become way too lax in their relations with local unions, letting them get away with extortionate wage demands and overtime allowances in exchange for the timely completion of projects.

For a long time, it had been in the interest of both the large contractors and the building trades unions to maintain tight union control over the training and supply of workers: the role of the unions in organizing apprenticeships and in dispatching workers onto construction sites via the hiring hall process ensured a reliable supply of high-skilled workers and minimized time lost to jurisdictional disputes.[56] The collusion reached as far back as the 1940s, when general contractors had joined forces with unions in opposing the Taft-Hartley Act and subsequently helped them circumvent its rules against closed shops.[57] But according to Blough, this once mutually beneficial relationship no longer made sense when construction workers were spreading the wildfire of wage inflation to the entire industrial workforce.[58] The large construction "users" who had intensified their building and plant construction works in recent years risked fanning the flames of insurrection among their own workers if they ceded too readily to the building trades.

To curb this threat, the Construction Users Anti-Inflation Roundtable called for a united front among contractors and their industrial clients, urging them to break their long-established ties with unionized labor and step up the pressure on state and federal government to roll back protective labor laws.[59] The government should be just as concerned as business elites, it argued: not only were construction wages cutting into the profits of large corporations, but they were also driving up the price of federal highways, public housing, and defense projects.[60] The CUAIR at first found a sympathetic ear in President Nixon, who six months into his first term in 1968 announced a 75 percent reduction in federal building contracts until such time as unionized tradesmen and general contractors found a way to curb costs.[61] Two years later he ordered the temporary suspension of the Davis-Bacon Act, citing "excessive and accelerating wage settlements in the construction industry" and their contribution to "inflation in the overall economy."[62]

From its earliest meetings, the Construction Users Anti-Inflation Roundtable discussed the possibility of using civil rights law to weaken the union stranglehold over apprenticeships and hiring. The general public, it figured, was unlikely to sympathize with the profit doldrums of the likes of U.S. Steel, but civil rights violations could easily be wielded to tarnish the image of the powerful construction unions. From the beginning of the century, African American men in construction had been confined to the unskilled "trowel trades" of bricklaying and plastering and were only rarely granted access to the more lucrative craft trades such as plumbing or electrical work. Federal construction contracts had included antidiscrimination clauses since the 1940s. Yet local unions had little trouble circumventing them.[63] Civil rights groups were still picketing all-white construction crews in the 1960s when

Presidents Kennedy and Johnson enacted more robust legislation. And even then, it took the direct-action tactics of the more militant Black Power movement—an often overlooked player in the labor politics of the late 1960s—to enforce union compliance on the ground.[64]

The Construction Users Anti-Inflation Roundtable was an unlikely and no doubt opportunistic supporter of these developments. Nevertheless, it applied great pressure on the Nixon government to enforce antidiscrimination laws in the construction sector and widely publicized its message in the business press. In 1968, *Fortune* magazine dedicated a long feature article to the problem of racism in the construction industry, carefully cataloguing the many complaints that had been lodged against the unions by civil rights groups. Casting itself as the benevolent mediator between the warring parties of the New Deal consensus, the magazine called on the government to ensure stricter compliance with antidiscrimination laws but also recommended changes (such as elimination of the hiring hall system) designed to undermine the strength of organized labor itself. This it framed as a necessary move to introduce greater rank-and-file democracy within the union movement. "All of these recommendations, of course, would change the character of the labor movement dramatically," *Fortune* magazine conceded; "but labor needs to be reformed. The last barriers to the caste system in American society are failing and labor, like other institutions, must be prepared to make sacrifices to make the democratic ideal of equality become reality."[65]

Nixon's first response to the combined pressure of business elites and the civil rights movement was to implement a federal affirmative action program for construction, replete with minority hiring quotas.[66] Although the program achieved moderate success, however, Nixon soon lost interest in affirmative action, along with the entire "reserve army" strategy of using surplus workers to undermine construction unions. Inspired by an unexpected demonstration of support from hard-hat workers, who rallied behind his military actions in Cambodia, Nixon was soon convinced that the threat of wage inflation would be better countered by "law and order" populism, based on a corporatist alliance between blue-collar workers and the state. To this end, he spent the last few years of his presidency cultivating the most reactionary elements within the blue-collar union movement, hoping to enlist them as partners in his crusade to deconstruct the New Deal labor-liberal consensus.

When a group of hard-hat workers unleashed their fury on student antiwar demonstrators in New York City in May of 1970, the ever-resourceful Nixon immediately understood the political opportunity that had opened up to him. The City of New York had organized a day of public school and college walk-outs following the slaying of four students during antiwar demonstrations at Kent State the previous week. The memorial event was trashed by construc-tion workers, who descended into the streets at lunch time to wreak havoc on a group of largely peaceful protestors.[67] Incensed by what they saw as acts of flag desecration and senseless antipatriotism in the streets below them, the hard-hat rioters stormed city hall and beat up any protestors or suspiciously long-haired passersby they could get their hands on. This initial act of fury soon morphed into an extended display of support for Nixon's invasion of Cambo-dia. The hard-hat counterprotests continued over the following few weeks as construction workers took to the streets of New York in regular, flag-waving lunchtime marches. The events culminated in a mass demonstration on May 20, when Peter Brennan, president of the Building and Construction Trades Council of New York, led a contingent of more than twenty thousand con-struction workers through the streets to express their support for Nixon and rail against antiwar "faggots" like Mayor John Lindsay.[68]

The hard-hat riots notwithstanding, polling data consistently showed that blue-collar workers were more opposed to the war than the college-educated middle class—after all, their sons were more likely to be serving there.[69] Even as the general public and dissident trade unions turned increasingly against the war, however, the AFL-CIO (The American Federation of Labor and Congress of Industrial Organizations) remained steadfast in its commitment to Cold War foreign policy.[70] And few members of the AFL-CIO were more passionate in their support of the war than the Building and Construction Trade Councils. Their hostility toward student activists was motivated by more than Cold War patriotism: barely a year earlier, hard-hat workers had attacked protestors call-ing for the desegregation of worksites in Chicago and Pittsburgh, and it seems that many observers sensed a connection between these incidents and the New York City riot.[71] In their public statements on events in New York, Black trade union leaders described the riots as the "deed of a racist union which has now turned to repressive violence against students and blacks."[72] After all, few union locals had been more resistant toward integration efforts than Peter Brennan's Building and Construction Trades Council of New York.[73]

The hard-hat riot took place just one month after the Department of Labor had distributed a report on "The Problem of the Blue-Collar Worker" to internal officials in the Nixon administration.[74] Commonly referred to as the Rosow Report, after the name of its author, Assistant Secretary of Labor Jerome M. Rosow, the document painted a much more sympathetic picture of the blue-collar worker and his economic plight than that which circulated in the business press at the time.

The report found fault with the New Deal social compact for failing to take account of the full economic responsibilities of the blue-collar worker as breadwinner. Despite the growing power of American unions, Rosow found American wages wanting when compared with those of European workers, whose welfare states provided child allowances and universal health care over and above the formal wage.[75] In his telling, the wage-push inflation of the late 1960s was an understandable and rather desperate response to the economic squeeze that confronted male workers once they transitioned from the life of a single man to the status of husband and father. Any breadwinner who wanted to give his dependants the same standard of living he himself had enjoyed as a single man had no option but to moonlight on a second job, "have his wife work," or keep up the pressure for wage increases.[76] Insult was added to injury when blue-collar workers felt that government policy was paying more attention to the needs of African Americans and the welfare poor, whose economic status was just one step below theirs. "Many of these workers," Rosow noted, "are immigrants or sons of immigrants; they feel unsure about their place in the 'mainstream' of American society. Some live in mixed neighborhoods—feeling the pressure of constant succession by lower-income groups, especially minorities."[77] These were "the real forgotten people," Rosow claimed, since they are "most exposed to the poor and welfare recipients. Often their wages are only a notch or so above the liberal states' welfare payments. Yet they are excluded from social programs targeted at the disadvantaged."[78]

If Nixon was serious about curbing wage inflation, Rosow advised, his best option would be to consolidate the family wage once and for all, in effect exchanging a more robust social wage for constant battles around the formal wage. To this end, Rosow urged Nixon to ease the tax burden on low-wage workers, subsidize childcare for blue-collar workers, strengthen the federal grant system for college students, and include blue-collar workers within federal manpower programs. Last but not least, Rosow called on the federal government to act as a "model employer" of blue-collar workers when implementing public construction projects.[79]

The Rosow Report brought much-needed specifics to the seductive idea of Republican party realignment first proposed by Nixon staffer Kevin Phillips. In his influential study, *The Emerging Republican Majority*, Phillips had urged Republicans to cultivate the "silent majority" of wavering Democrats who had voted for George Wallace in the 1968 elections—the southern white Protestants who resented the Democrats' embrace of civil rights, of course, but also the blue-collar workers of the North and Midwest, in particular the many "white ethnic" Catholics among them who were troubled in some way by the Democratic Party's lurch to the socially liberal left.[80] For Phillips, this realignment could be achieved only if the Republican Party abandoned its attachment to small government and embraced the cause of conservative welfarism.

The Rosow report offered precious detail on how this could work in practice. But it took the further intervention of the hard-hat riots to make the proposal look feasible. This unexpected show of strength from building trades workers was a gift to Nixon: not only did it vouch for his increasingly unpopular incursions in Southeast Asia, but it also opened up a real and hitherto elusive line of communication between the Republicans and the union movement as a whole. Up until this point, Kevin Phillips's vision of a blue-collar Republican bloc referred to vague cultural affinities: here at last was a concrete point of connection and a chance to dislodge organized labor from the New Deal coalition.

Nixon lost no time in consummating the alliance. Shortly after the final hard-hat march, he invited New York's Peter Brennan, along with a delegation of twenty-two other union leaders, to the White House, in a carefully orchestrated display of unity between the Republican Party and organized labor.[81] He would spend the next few years cultivating the union vote, a wager that paid off when the AFL-CIO conspicuously refused to endorse either candidate in the 1972 electoral standoff between Nixon and McGovern.

The election was a Republican landslide, with some of the most significant swings in their favor coming from blue-collar workers: Nixon that year

COUNTERREVOLUTION

122

won 62 percent of the popular vote, all but one state in the Electoral College, 57 percent of the manual worker vote, and 54 percent of the union vote in what looked like a resounding validation of his populist outreach.[82] Upon his return to office, Nixon appointed Peter Brennan secretary of labor in gratitude for his endorsement of Nixon's presidency. From this position, Brennan did all in his power to slow down the process of affirmative action on the construction site, the very policy that Nixon had tried to maneuver against the trade unions a few years earlier.[83] Nixon was apparently planning to appoint unionists to high-level positions within every department when the oil price shock of 1973 then the Watergate scandal interrupted his plans.[84] Whether or not Nixon genuinely intended to take meaningful action on Rosow's recommendations we will never know.[85] In any event, the sense of political possibility was sufficiently blunted by the ensuing recession that such a project would soon appear impossibly ambitious to both major parties. By the end of the decade, the experiment in blue-collar populism would reappear in a very different guise, stripped of all welfarist intent and recombined with the message of working-class tax relief.

THE LABOR COUNTERCULTURE

But no sooner had business elites identified the threat of the construction worker "medieval guild" than another, very different kind of challenge arose from within the rank and file of the old industrial unions. Union membership was undergoing a rapid generational shift in the 1970s: at the turn of the decade, one-quarter of all members were under the age of thirty, and many of them had two or three years more schooling than their fathers.[86] As children of the postwar boom, this new generation of workers bridled under the mind-numbing monotony of Taylorist production methods and had little patience for the accommodationist politics of the trade union leadership.[87]

A long wave of strikes, work stoppages, and slowdowns kicked off in 1970, a year in which an unusual number of contracts were fortuitously set to expire. In that year alone, U.S. postal workers launched a wildcat action against the federal government, rubber workers called a national strike against Goodyear, Teamsters stopped work across the country, and 400,000 workers walked off the job at GM Detroit. The mood was so intense that *Time* magazine hailed

1970 as the "year of the strike."[88] All up, the Bureau of Labor Statistics counted 5,716 strikes involving more than three million workers—the highest number ever recorded until then.[89]

The wage gains were real enough, although rapidly offset by employers' efforts to push up consumer prices. Industrial unions that went to the bargaining table in 1970 won wage and benefit increases of 10 percent or more.[90] But more alarming to business leaders was the fact that these workers were striking for something other than wage increases: they were "also in revolt against the numbing prospect of spending all their years until old age on the assembly lines."[91] Almost everywhere, workers seemed to be engaged in some form of passive resistance against the spirit of productivism: while senior workers bargained for retirement in their fifties, younger workers facing three decades or more on the assembly line found other means of escape.[92] Turnover rates, sick leave, and absenteeism increased dramatically in the early 1970s. As *BusinessWeek* soberly reported, "union leadership is faced with the same 'crisis of authority' that threatens other institutions, notably the universities."[93]

A sign of this repudiation of the old bargaining consensus, wildcat strikes accounted for a full third of all actions in the late 1960s and early 1970s.[94] Right-wing pundits who had called for a rank-and-file insurrection against the authoritarian structures of the building trades unions recoiled in horror when they got more than they bargained for: a generation of union members who didn't hesitate to reject contracts negotiated by their leaders. In a curious inversion of *Fortune* magazine's appeals to union democratization barely a year earlier, *BusinessWeek* complained ruefully that "laws passed to assure democracy within unions give a guaranteed opportunity to malcontents and minority groups to challenge union authority and perhaps upset agreements negotiated by the officers."[95] In the space of a few years, the diagnosis and etiology of wage inflation had shifted irretrievably. Where most business media had attributed the power of hard-hat unions to their intensely hierarchical, conservative structures of authority, the same observers began to see wage inflation as the product of rampant anti-authoritarianism, an intensification of the threat posed by the campus New Left.

In hindsight, it was the 1972 strike at a new GM plant in Lordstown, Ohio, that came to symbolize the new wave of labor unrest. The plant in question, built especially to compete with the cheaper Japanese and German car models flooding the American market, was supposed to churn out an unprecedented one hundred new Vega cars an hour. Instead, according to an editorial in the *New York Times*, a "kind of guerrilla warfare between workers and management...developed out of employee frustrations that differ[ed] only in intensity from those Charlie Chaplin immortalized in 'Modern Times' thirty-five years ago."[96] When the Lordstown site merged with a neighboring plant and a few hundred workers were laid off, the remaining workers—with an average age of twenty-five—had to pick up the slack under the watchful eye of a specialized work discipline team. Often they were expected to work six-hour shifts repeating the same task at speed, with a few seconds' distraction sufficing to bring the whole production line to a halt. Reported defects multiplied over the following months: whether the result of worker fatigue or sabotage, car after car rolled off the production line with slit upholstery, dented chassis, severed ignition wires, and loose bolts.[97] As some of the United Auto Workers' youngest members, the Lordstown saboteurs were not susceptible to the usual threats of dismissal and were left unmoved by promises of wage rises. Taking note of the situation, the UAW nominated boredom as a professional hazard in its 1972 bargaining round at Chrysler, the first time such an issue had been included in contract negotiations.[98]

This new generation of workers could not so easily be bought off with the kind of conservative welfarism that Nixon had manufactured for blue-collar construction workers. After all, they looked less like the hard-hat rioters than like the students whom those rioters had beaten up. Nor could they be readily neutralized by the reserve army strategy advocated by Roger Blough's Business Roundtable. As one reporter for *Fortune* magazine observed, the new attitudes cut across racial lines, making it difficult to set one group against another: both "young blacks and young whites have higher expectations of the jobs they fill and the wages they receive.... They are restless, changeable, mobile, demanding, all traits that make for impermanence...and for difficult adjustment to an assembly line."[99] It was no longer just the core workforce of white male wage earners who were imbued with inflationary expectations; so too were the surplus workers who were supposed to depress their wages. From the League of Revolutionary Black Workers, who refused to take orders from the ostensibly progressive United Auto Workers, to flight attendants, secretaries, and domestic workers, this was an era of unprecedented organizing on the part of those who had been relegated to the margins of the Fordist labor contract.[100] Industrial unions were even beginning to form promising new alliances with the New Left student movement, despite the inauspicious experience of the 1970 hard-hat riots.[101]

As noted in the *Wall Street Journal* editorial pages, the push for wage increases had become so widely shared that it seemed to be generating its own weather system, sweeping up traditionally lower-paid, unorganized, and recently unionized sectors in its upward spiral. The article went on to propose that the real driving logic here was no longer the conflict between labor and capital (wage-price inflation) but competitive emulation between differently situated sectors of the workforce, who were egging each other on in a process of generalized "wage-wage inflation."[102] Such fears may have been exaggerated: even when wage settlements were outpacing price inflation, the gains were small and always threatened by industry's efforts to claw back profit margins.[103] Yet the *Wall Street Journal* no doubt captured the increasing difficulty of maneuvering one set of workers against another at a time when all were becoming more militant. In a context of generalized wage inflation and omnipresent strike action, competition among workers became cumulative rather than subtractive and so led to a temporary neutralization of the reserve army strategy.

As if to confirm this sense of impotence among business elites, the evolving economic conditions of the 1970s seemed to impart a new inertia to the dynamic of wage-push inflation. With unemployment rates on the rise at the beginning of the decade, then spiking sharply following the oil price shock of 1973, the United States seemed to have contracted the British disease of "stagflation," a term that referred to the puzzling coexistence of high inflation, rising unemployment, and slow growth.[104] The mystery was how workers could continue to push for wage increases despite the growth in unemployment rolls, a phenomenon that defied the rules of postwar macroeconomics. The reigning consensus among mainstream (neoclassical synthesis) Keynesians was that the business cycle could be reliably managed through the controlled use of unemployment: when wage inflation got out of hand, a small number of workers could be pushed out of the workforce; when unemployment became socially unmanageable, a certain level of inflation would be tolerated.[105] A distillation of this consensus, the so-called Phillips curve, named after the British economist A. W. Phillips, posited a stable inverse relationship between unemployment and inflation such that a government could trade the one for the other with scientific precision. As early as 1968, Milton Friedman had developed a theoretical critique of the Phillips curve in which he invoked the concept of a mysterious "natural" rate of unemployment conducive to low inflation.[106] But as the United States plunged into recession after the oil price shock of 1973, without seriously slowing the momentum of wage inflation, a growing number of economists began to investigate the concrete conditions under which wages could rise despite the threat of unemployment.

THE KALECKI OF THE MASTER CLASS

Among the most influential analyses of this predicament came from Martin Feldstein, who in a report first delivered to the Joint Economic Committee of Congress in 1973 set out a supply-side perspective on the incentives to "voluntary unemployment" in the era of stagflation.[107] Feldstein began by questioning the gravity of the unemployment crisis as indicated by labor statistics: the numbers, he claimed, were artificially bloated by the inclusion in the unemployment statistics of new demographics with only a casual and non-compelling attachment to the workforce (married women, Black men, college students, and teenagers).[108] If these "peripheral" categories of worker were edited out, what was left was a much smaller number of long-term unemployed—and even this, Feldstein contended, was hardly comparable to the obdurate kernel of the unemployed encountered by Keynes at the height of the Depression.[109] Keynesian economists were mistaken in thinking that the unemployment of the mid-1970s could be compared to and managed like that of the 1930s: the problem, Feldstein argued, was one of fiscal overabundance rather than inadequate demand, and this problem stemmed from the fact that Keynesian policies of "full employment" had been pursued too far. Unemployment insurance and sundry other forms of public assistance had become so generous that unionized workers knew they could drop out of the workforce and indulge in long spells of unemployment before feeling compelled to take up work again.[110] Workers were now so insulated from the pangs of want that they retained the power to withdraw their labor and make exorbitant wage and benefit claims in the midst of a recession. Even non-core workers had been released from the discipline of hunger thanks to the minimum wage and the various forms of public assistance available to them.[111] Feldstein did not need to mention the fact that in a handful of states, striking workers were eligible for food stamps and unemployment insurance; this outrage had already been turned into a cause célèbre by the right-wing media and denounced as an outright subsidy to antiwork revolt.[112]

In keeping with the core supply-side insight that taxes now played an increasingly important role in economic incentives, Feldstein located the problem in the interaction between inflation, the social wage (in this case, unemployment benefits), and marginal tax rates on the formal wage. While unemployment insurance had become more generous in recent years, it was not subject to taxation; in the meantime, Feldstein observed, marginal tax rates on labor had grown at an alarming rate and under the impact of inflation were pushing workers up into higher tax brackets, a process that was commonly referred to as "bracket creep." This was not a problem that could have been foreseen by Keynes, who was writing at a time when economies were more threatened by deflation rather than inflation and a much lower percentage of the population was subject to income taxation.[113] But in the economic context of the 1970s, Feldstein thought, the interaction between taxes, unemployment insurance, and the wage structure was creating perverse incentives to nonwork. As the marginal benefit of working as compared to not working was taxed away, workers had less incentive to get off the unemployment rolls and return to work.[114] Unemployment insurance had the perverse effect of generating more unemployment.[115]

The arrangement was one that suited employers, too, since the ready availability of unemployment insurance meant they could hire and fire workers on a seasonal basis without losing access to manpower when it was urgently needed.[116] The practice of dropping in and out of the workforce, Feldstein observed, was particularly widespread among younger workers, who in this respect were becoming difficult to distinguish from "the student population of the same age."[117] Unlike the many industrial psychologists who pondered the issue, however, Feldstein thought that the shift in attitudes was shaped in an entirely rational way by the minimum wage and overly generous public assistance, all of which encouraged an "increased demand for leisure."[118]

The Feldstein report could have been a right-wing gloss on the work of Polish economist Michał Kalecki, so precisely did it confirm the latter's prognosis of the political limits of Keynesianism. Already in the early 1940s, Kalecki foresaw that business elites could reject the Keynesian consensus as soon as it threatened the compulsion to work.[119] By releasing workers from the fear of unemployment, efforts by government to subsidize public services, welfare, and the wage would inevitably weaken labor discipline and businesses' ability to protect their profit margins from union wage demands. This could lead in the worst scenario to a wage-price spiral in which businesses and unions tried to one-up each other with relentless wage and profit hikes. As soon as asset holders in particular were threatened by rising wages and prices, Kalecki had warned, a "powerful block is likely to be formed between big business and the rentier interests, and they would probably find more than one economist to declare that the situation was manifestly unsound."[120] With his alarmist writings on the indolence of over-insured workers and the crisis of American "capital formation," Feldstein was one such economist.

His report on the perverse incentives of unemployment insurance would be duly featured in the *Wall Street Journal* op-ed page, where it was illustrated by the case of "one Ray Evanoski, a Pennsylvania laborer" who complained that "his employer did *not* lay him off."[121] "The workers know…that a little layoff is nice work," the op-ed reflected, "even though they must realize the system that arranges incentives in this fashion is out of whack, and ultimately destructive." The piece concluded with a plea to President Ford to slash unemployment benefits while reducing tax rates on labor and capital alike. For the moment at least, social spending austerity and tax cuts were the standard supply-side response to worker stagflation.

STAGFLATION AND THE FEMINIZED MAN

Prescient as it was, however, contemporary observers added a nuance to the analysis of Keynesian limits that had eluded Kalecki in the 1940s. The Fordist/Keynesian labor consensus was built on the foundation of the male breadwinner wage, which assigned white men the role of provider for a dependent wife and children. It followed that any threat to this wage structure could also have disastrous effects on the gendered and racial organization of the family. After all, if a man could provide for his wife and children without having to engage in productive work, where would this leave his social worth as a man?

Just as the Keynesian abundance of long-term unemployment insurance had loosened the discipline of waged work, many feared that it would also weaken the obligations of the husband and father as breadwinner.

In a follow-up study to the Rosow Report released by the Department of Health, Education and Welfare in 1972, this fear was front and center.[122] Although inspired by the same desire to get to the root cause of wage-push inflation, the two reports delivered very different verdicts on the problems afflicting the average blue-collar worker. Most important, perhaps, where Rosow saw wage inflation as driven by the worker's frustrated desire to provide for his family against the headwinds of rising prices, the HEW report was more concerned that a flagging male work drive signaled a generalized flight from the responsibilities of breadwinner masculinity. As the report pointed out, full-time productive employment was not only critical to the economic position of the worker; it also guaranteed "family stability" and the well-being of women and children within it.[123] "In industrial America, the father's occupation has been the major determinant of status, which in turn has determined the family's class standing, where they lived, where the children went to school, and with whom the family associated—in short, the lifestyle and life chances of all the family members."[124] Any defection from this role would have "severe repercussions" in "other parts of the social system"[125]

A 1977 article in *BusinessWeek*, evocatively titled "The Great Male Cop Out," reported on the growing numbers of married men who (it was alleged) relied on unemployment benefits, food stamps, disability payments, and working wives to withdraw from the workforce and eschew the traditional duties of masculinity. The article observed with alarm that 2.2 million men of prime working age were without a job and no longer actively seeking employment. This flight from waged work was understood in gendered terms, as a retreat into domesticity and its unproductive pursuits: "Increasing numbers" of men, it reported, "have apparently discovered that contemporary society offers new government and corporate-financed alternatives to working for a living or that...their place is in the home."[126] As anecdotal evidence of this phenomenon, the article cited the case of a "former Philadelphian executive who dropped out of the labor force, read books on male liberation...and became a house husband supported by his wife's earnings." The problem, as construed by *BusinessWeek*, was less the fact of unemployment than its willful, actively chosen character. These were men who continued to collect the wages of masculinity without performing the productive labor that once went along with it. Alongside the growing workforce participation of women, the phenomenon of mass male unemployment was understood as a process of collective feminization—all the more troubling because it was assumed to be voluntary.

One person who systematically explored the relationship between stagflation and masculinity was George Gilder, a journalist and social commentator who had made a name for himself as a specialist in modern sex roles. It was Gilder more than anyone else who brought the supply-side ideas of Feldstein, Laffer, and Wanniski to a wider reading public while combining them with his own maverick perspective on cultural anthropology. Gilder's contribution was to show that the supply-side analysis of economic incentives was grounded, at a deeper level, in an elaborate system of sexual incentives, with the male libido playing the role of currency in both economies.[127] Gilder saw male sexual desire as an elemental force that was likely to wreak havoc if it was not contained within the generational horizons provided by wives and mothers. Women's sexuality was naturally disciplined by the fact of pregnancy and childbirth. Male desire, by contrast, was fundamentally protean and antisocial. It needed to be converted into a stable reproductive force by women, just as it needed to be disciplined into productive work by the laws of capitalism. Indeed, the former was the condition of the latter. Should either of these incentives fail, then men were liable to become both hypermasculinized and socially emasculated, urban predators for whom society could find no useful role.[128] In his earlier work, Gilder had explored this problem with respect to African American men, who (he claimed) had been rendered superfluous by the payment of welfare benefits to mothers and children.[129] By the end of the 1970s, he was convinced that white men too were suffering from a similar set of sexual and economic disincentives.[130] Where supply-side economists had shown that the combination of inflation and progressive taxation encouraged workers to choose leisure over work, Gilder went further and pointed to the deleterious effects of male indolence on masculinity.[131] What incentive did men have to adopt the male breadwinner role if they were always being rewarded for slacking off? And how could these incentives be restored when married women were simultaneously being pulled into the workforce by the need to supplement a floundering male wage?[132] What Gilder saw around him was a flourishing economy of feminized service work alongside a dwindling world of blue-collar male employment. "The man unable to perform his role as breadwinner," he lamented, "is being slowly unmanned."[133]

THE PUBLIC-SECTOR WORKER AND THE FEMINIZATION OF WAGE INFLATION

Fears of male feminization were exacerbated by the actual feminization of labor militancy that went along with the rising influence of the public-sector unions. Relative newcomers to organized labor, public-sector unions had multiplied and become increasingly combative in the 1960s, along with the easing of statutory constraints on their collective bargaining powers. At the beginning of the 1970s, it was blue-collar public-sector workers—dockworkers, postal workers, janitors, gravediggers, and garbage collectors—who commanded attention as they undertook a series of spectacular wildcat actions alongside their private-sector peers. A second wave of strike action followed soon after, this time led by white-collar, disproportionately African American public administrators, only to be succeeded later in the decade by a third wave of militancy from public-sector women, primarily teachers and clerical workers.[134]

The increasing visibility of public-sector workers in the 1960s and 1970s was an artefact of their long marginalization from the postwar consensus between big business and labor. Public-sector workers had been excluded from the National Labor Relations Act of 1935 on the grounds that the very nature of their employment—in the service of the public at large rather than a private employer—would be fatally compromised by the right to strike.[135] The NLRA, or Wagner Act, guaranteed the right of private-sector workers to elect their own unions, to bargain with employers, and to take strike action. It also outlawed egregious antiunion practices on the part of employers and obliged them to bargain in good faith with the unions that had been chosen by workers.[136] By standardizing private-sector labor law and bringing it under the central jurisdiction of the federal government, the Wagner Act served as a powerful impetus to the private-sector union movement, which went from strength to strength in the following decades. By contrast, public-sector unions were left at the mercy of state and local governments, which could choose to negotiate with workers on whatever terms they pleased. Thanks to their exclusion from the foundational act of modern labor law, public-sector unionism was "artificially repressed" at a time when the public-sector work-force was growing by leaps and bounds.[137] Public employment as a percentage of the labor force more than doubled between 1929 and 1952, at which time it encompassed nearly 17 percent of the workforce.[138] Yet prior to 1960, laws in every American state prohibited strike action on the part of public-sector employees and severely restricted their ability to collectively bargain.[139]

It was only in 1962, when President Kennedy issued Executive Order 10988, that the deadlock broke: Kennedy's decision, which granted federal employees the formal right to collectively bargain, was replicated by twenty-two states within the next decade, imparting a new and belated momentum to the long-repressed aspirations of public-sector workers.[140] While most of these statutes still outlawed strikes, public-sector workers lost no time in exploiting the small degree of freedom that had been granted them. After decades of legal repression, postal workers, garbage collectors, and teachers entered a period of explosive militancy as one occupation after another staged wildcat actions to secure their position at the bargaining table.[141]

In demographic terms alone, public-sector and private-sector unions looked very different. After all, the public sector had been employing women and African Americans for many years before the big private-sector industrial unions were forced to open their doors. The federal public sector in particular had long provided African American women and men with a haven from the brutal discrimination that reigned in the private sector, while working women were heavily employed as public schoolteachers in the decades following World War II.[142] Under the impetus of Johnson's Great Society, public employment opportunities for women and minorities expanded in the 1960s and continued to grow during the Republican administrations of Nixon and Ford. Between 1960 and 1970, African Americans went from representing 13.3 percent to 21.4 percent of the public-sector workforce, while women's share continued to increase well after the recession of 1975, rising from 43.8 to 48.2 between 1973 and 1981.[143] The growth of public-sector employment was a boon to African American women in particular, who made up more than one-quarter of the public-sector workforce by 1981.[144] Given this historical trajectory, it is not surprising that public-sector unions were always much closer to the New Left social movements than was the case with private-sector unions.[145]

For a brief moment in the early 1970s, it seemed that the pathways of public-sector and private-sector unions were aligning: relative newcomers to the picket line, public employees were just beginning to win rights that had long been taken for granted in the organized private sector, while the more countercultural elements within the private-sector union movement were breaking away from the political control of the AFL-CIO and making overtures to the New Left. It is significant in this regard that the tremendous strike wave of 1970 was kicked off by federal postal workers—many of them African American—heralding what looked like a long wave of convergent action on the part of America's divided labor movement.[146] In hindsight, however, it is clear that the optimism was misplaced. As Alexis Walker remarks, "rather than presaging a decade of coordinated public and private sector union militancy, 1970 and 1971 can be seen as a brief moment when public-sector labor's ascendance overlapped with a still relevant and powerful private-sector labor movement. Through the rest of the decade, the fortunes of the public and private sector unions would not overlap in the same way again."[147]

The once feared building trades were the first to succumb to the changing economic conditions of the 1970s, as the recession dried up housing construction, suspended activity in commercial real estate, and all but obliterated public contracts for new highways and energy infrastructure. By mid-decade, the unemployment rate in construction stood at 22 percent.[148] Although contract lock-ins ensured that industrial workers were able to maintain the pace of wage inflation for a few more years, the recession ultimately empowered employers to turn the table on unions, as factory after factory was closed or relocated.[149] Notwithstanding the fears of economists such as Martin Feldstein then, mass unemployment and deindustrialization were sufficient to dim the flame of industrial wage inflation. In the meantime, however, public-sector workers charged ahead, seemingly energized rather than defeated by the fiscal crises facing local and state governments. As private-sector industrial activity dwindled to a trickle, public-sector workers kept up the momentum, emerging as the new face of labor militancy at the end of the decade.

The pathways of private- and public-sector workers now diverged in more ways than one. Public-sector workers were on the front line of the urban fiscal crisis, which forced state and local governments to make invidious choices between public spending cuts and tax increases. In their dual roles as employees and administrators of public services such as health care, welfare, and education, public-sector workers fought tooth and nail for the maintenance of spending commitments in the face of dwindling government support and a punitive municipal bond market. But as long as the federal government refused to loosen the purse strings and ease the strain on state and local budgets, public-sector wage demands would almost inevitably translate into an increase in taxes.[150] This zero-sum game exposed a growing rift between public-sector workers and their private-sector counterparts, whose hopes of entering the wage inflation game were waning by the day. The dividing lines were no doubt already there, a product of both the nonsynchronous evolution of private- and public-sector unions and the vastly different demographic profiles of their rank and file. But these differences were amplified by the peculiar economic conditions of the late 1970s, which saw public-sector workers surge to the fore at precisely the moment private-sector blue-collar workers plunged into a long period of stagnant wage growth. Now that they were no longer the agents of wage-push inflation, now especially that the battle had been taken up by Fordism's marginal workers, blue-collar workers were more likely to see themselves as the victims of tax increases rather than the beneficiaries of a rising social wage.

The *Wall Street Journal*, which had been keeping a watchful eye on public-sector unions since the New York City fiscal crisis of 1975, studiously exploited the potential fault line.[151] Noting that the "wage rates of state and local employees [had] risen faster than those of any other major worker group over the last twenty years," the *Journal's* editorial page warned public-sector workers "they were being unrealistic if they [felt] that the mood of rebellion among voters and taxpayers applies only to the federal government and [would] not eventually touch them as well."[152]

In the course of the 1970s, the business media's perspective on wage-push inflation underwent a dramatic shift. Business observers who had begun the decade obsessing over the authoritarianism of blue-collar private-sector unions were now wringing their hands over white-collar militancy in the public sector. An article in the *Wall Street Journal* pitted public employees against the "ordinary, average American families"—"those who earn their incomes on assembly lines, behind store counters, at desks, on tractors, driving trucks"—and bemoaned the fact that their wages were being taxed away to subsidize the nonworking poor and those who catered to them—welfare workers, teachers, nurses.[153] Although relations between public-sector workers and their clients were far from straightforward, this nuance was lost on right-wing commentators, who willfully blurred the lines between the unearned income of the welfare rentier (or "queen") and the so-called sinecures of public employees.[154] In much of this commentary, the private sector was equated with blue-collar work, while the public sector was imagined as the preserve of the educated, white-collar employee. This color-coded division of labor offered a distorted picture of union membership: after all, the American Federation of State, County and Municipal Employees, or AFSCME (the largest public-sector union in the country), represented more blue-collar than white-collar workers, while private-sector unions were signing up a growing number of white-collar clerical and service workers.[155] But the imagined opposition reflected the growing realization that white-collar workers were now the most active element in public-sector militancy and implicitly referred to the fact that a disproportionate number of them were women.[156] During this period, the discussion of public-sector unionism became subtly gendered, as if the division between private and public sector could be mapped onto that between blue-collar men and white-collar women. As the historian John Shelton points out, public and media responses to teachers' strikes routinely counterposed the interests of privileged, white-collar female teachers and beleaguered blue-collar men, whose obligations as breadwinners were seen as compromised by women's rising wages.[157]

For much of the business media, wage inflation was beginning to look like a distinctly feminine malaise, driven not only by the belated dynamism of public-sector unions but also by a growing institutional receptiveness to women's equal wage claims. Of particular concern to business observers was the new direction taken by the Equal Employment Opportunity Commission, or EEOC, which in the late 1970s was moving beyond its initial focus on equal pay for equal work toward a new concept of "comparable worth": whereas the earlier concept reserved equal pay claims for identical job categories, the newer criterion sought to challenge the systemic undervaluation of traditional women's work and therefore posed a much more formidable threat to profit margins. In 1977, public-sector nurses lodged a sex discrimination case before the U.S. District Court in Denver on the grounds that the city paid them less than plumbers for work of "comparable worth." Although the nurses lost, *Fortune* magazine warned of the dire consequences that would attend any serious expansion of the EEOC's role in determining public-sector pay scales. "Even if only partly successful," it claimed, comparable worth cases "would have an enormous inflationary effect."[158] The article predicted a new wave of competitive wage inflation between blue-collar men and white-collar women, because no male worker would stand to see his gendered wage premium permanently eroded by institutional fiat. If anything, the assessment was optimistic. By the end of the 1970s, the prospect of so-called wage-wage inflation looked increasingly unlikely as workers turned against each other in a fight for seemingly scarce resources.

THE RISE OF SUPPLY-SIDE POPULISM

It was in this atmosphere of heightened tension among workers that the supply-side movement spawned a populist wing, one that we now commonly associate with the movement as a whole. Under the influence of Robert Bartley and Jude Wanniski, the *Wall Street Journal* had for several years served as a reliable mouthpiece for the elite supply-side economics of the "capital formation" school. It regularly publicized the work of the self-proclaimed "traditional" supply-sider Martin Feldstein (whom Wanniski implausibly claimed to have discovered) and was closely aligned with the views of the Treasury Department under Nixon and Ford.[159] But as the Ford administration rolled out its response to the recession, Wanniski was increasingly troubled by the failure of the Republican Party to offer any positive alternative to austerity. During the 1976 presidential campaign, the Democratic contender Jimmy Carter sang the praises of the proposed Humphrey-Hawkins bill, which promised public job creation and a renewed commitment to full employment.[160] Yet Ford refused to budge from his single-minded focus on "whipping inflation" and repeatedly vetoed the Democrats' job creation bills, proposing in their stead an austere remedy of public spending restraint and business tax cuts.[161] The Republican president never strayed from this "trickle down" formula, even when unemployment rates crept back up toward the 8 percent mark in the midst of the presidential race.[162] In an article published in the *Wall Street Journal* the week after the Republican National Convention of 1976, Wanniski noted with alarm that the "contestants to the Oval Office think they can confront Jimmy Carter without an employment strategy."[163]

Although Wanniski had until this point been a champion of the "capital formation" school of supply-side economics (differing only on the Mundellian fine point of deficits), he was now increasingly nervous about its strategic limits. With the GOP already tainted by the Watergate scandal, it was just not credible that the Republicans could ever secure a congressional majority by selling public spending austerity on the one hand and tax cuts for the rich on the other. Nixon had been right that the Republicans needed to reach out to the disaffected blue-collar worker, but Wanniski thought he had a better way to do it.

As we saw in the previous chapter, Wanniski berated Republicans for their slavish devotion to balanced budgets: as a student of Mundell, he had imbibed the lesson that budget deficits could always be financed by domestic or foreign investors, as long as inflation was also kept to a minimum.[164] But most Republicans had been educated in the Eisenhower tradition of fiscal conservatism, which insisted that balanced budgets must take priority over tax cuts. This cast Republicans in the unenviable role of political misers who rushed in after every Democratic spending spree with a round of tax hikes.[165] The Democrats had even seized the initiative on tax cuts: during the Johnson administration, they enacted both spending increases *and* tax cuts in the face of opposition from congressional Republicans. There was only one way to escape this deadlock, Wanniski thought: Republicans needed to abandon their preoccupation with responsibility and charge ahead with tax cuts, whatever their impact on the budget.[166] This, he thought, would force Democrats into the same defensive position that Republicans had played for so long.

Beyond this first epiphany, however, Wanniski soon came to the realization that the supply-siders' exclusive focus on the "trickle down" benefits of investment tax cuts was itself part of the problem. For the Republicans to have any hope of countering the Democrats' Humphrey-Hawkins bill, they needed to have a recognizable employment policy of their own. To this end, Wanniski urged them to embrace an agenda of across-the-board tax cuts extending to all levels of the income scale. This would not replace but supplement the investment-stimulating promise of elite tax cuts, at long last equipping Republicans with a positive message to broadcast to unemployed workers. The trick was to convince traditional Democrat voters that inflation was just as harmful to them as unemployment, and that tax cuts and not direct public spending were the fastest route to noninflationary job creation.

Wanniski had arrived at this position in the course of his conversations with Republican congressman Jack Kemp in the early months of 1976.[167] Kemp represented a traditionally Democrat-voting, blue-collar district in the environs of Buffalo, New York, where unemployment stood well above the national average. As such, he was keenly attuned to the weakness of Ford's austerity politics. The congressman had traveled a similar intellectual journey to Wanniski's. An early reader of the work of Mundell, he was a zealous convert to the idea that taxes were a drag on American growth.[168] Yet, by his own admission, he "was still having trouble seeing the whole picture": he "still thought that the only way to increase the nation's productivity was to lower business taxes as an inducement to greater profits and production."[169] Kemp was also an ardent believer in balanced budgets. In December 1975, just one month before his encounter with Wanniski, he was still preaching that tax cuts had to be counterbalanced by spending restraint—precisely the scrooge agenda that Wanniski denounced as fatal to Republican fortunes.[170]

But after meeting with Wanniski in January 1976, Kemp changed his tune entirely. The birth of supply-side populism seems to have been a case of mutual influence.[171] It was Wanniski who persuaded Kemp that across-the-board tax cuts were economically feasible, and Kemp who assured Wanniski that the project had some chance of political success.[172] With the charismatic and popular Kemp on board, Wanniski had not only a direct conduit into the Republican Party but also a credible mediator between the *Wall Street Journal* and the blue-collar working class. Kemp, for his part, had been disabused of his faith in balanced budgets and was now convinced that Republicans should make use of their objective fiscal freedom to extend income tax cuts to the average wage worker. Now that he had something more than trickle-down pieties to offer his blue-collar constituents, Kemp joined Wanniski and Laffer as a fervent apostle of supply-side populism.

In early 1977, Kemp called on his new economic advisor, Bruce Bartlett, to come up with a bill modeled on the Kennedy-Johnson tax cut of 1964.[173] After consulting with Arthur Laffer and Norman B. Ture, Bartlett delivered a bill calling for a 30 percent reduction in personal income rates, to be phased in over three years.[174] With Republican senator William Roth of Delaware as its cosponsor, the Kemp-Roth Tax Reduction Act was first put to the vote in July 1977. It was defeated two years in a row and an amended version quashed by presidential veto.[175] But Kemp-Roth picked up momentum each time it came to the vote, so that by the time of Carter's veto it had the support of most House Republicans and thirty-seven Democrats.[176]

Taking their cue from Norman B. Ture's estimates of the bill's revenue impact, Wanniski, Laffer, and Kemp spread the word that tax cuts would pay for themselves, a supply-side inversion of the Keynesian multiplier effect.[177] Other participants in the Kemp-Roth story distanced themselves from such extremes while nevertheless acknowledging that across-the-board tax cuts made serious political sense.[178] Significantly, Kemp-Roth was beginning to pick up endorsements from a growing number of conservative economists who were not otherwise associated with the supply-side movement: these included Alan Greenspan, Herbert Stein, Milton Friedman, and David Stockman (who would soon be a convert).[179] The tax cuts would not pay for themselves, Friedman observed, but would nevertheless play the useful role of restraining public spending (a calculation that became known, in colloquial terms, as "starving the beast").[180] Bruce Bartlett was surely right in seeing the Kemp-Roth bill as a turning point for the Republican Party. After abandoning the short-lived welfare populism of President Nixon, Republicans had struggled to rid themselves of their elitist patrician image. "Kemp gave Republicans something to *be for* and helped the party shed some of its negative image."[181]
The idea that across-the-board tax cuts could be safely enacted without balancing the budget had no clear precedent in the Republican tradition. The tax cuts implemented by President Calvin Coolidge and Treasury Secretary Andrew Mellon in the 1920s, which Wanniski sometimes cited as a precursor, were accompanied by a rigorous plan to balance the budget.[182] In fact, the most obvious precedent to the populist supply-side program was the tax-cut stimulus called for by President Kennedy and implemented in 1964 after his death. The populist supply-siders ruthlessly exploited this genealogy: it allowed them to adorn themselves in the garlands of postwar growth economics, to paint themselves as the messengers of prosperity and full employment, even as their associates in the business elite prepared a radical assault on the powers of labor.[183] But while Kemp-Roth was almost identical in form to the

Kennedy-Johnson Tax Reduction Act, the spirit of the 1964 tax cut was very different. The Keynesian economists of the Council of Economic Advisers (CEA) who had designed the Kennedy-Johnson tax cuts saw them as a stimulus to demand rather than supply.[184] And they had endorsed them as a second best to public spending increases in the understanding that they would be easier to push through Congress.[185] The most progressive of Kennedy's economic advisors, John Kenneth Galbraith, for instance, worried that resorting to tax cuts would give Republicans a weapon with which to attack public spending outlays in the future.[186] His fears were premature when it came to the Kennedy tax cuts, which when implemented under Johnson were paired with dramatic increases in public spending. But Galbraith was proven right when it came to the supply-siders, who saw their reactivation of the Kennedy tax cuts as an alternative to and dampener on redistributive public spending even as they repudiated the shibboleth of balanced budgets.

It was serendipitous that at the very moment Kemp was preaching the message of tax cuts without budgetary expiation, President Carter was beginning to have doubts about his own expansionary agenda. At the party's midterm conference of December 1978, Carter delivered a sobering message to his fellow Democrats: in the face of rising inflation and an international investor flight from the dollar, the party would have to accept the medicine of selective budget cuts as the price of its social programs.[187] This unexpected admission of defeat allowed Kemp to turn the tables on the "Keynesian" Democrats. In what proved to be a deft rhetorical maneuver, Kemp pilfered shamelessly from the lexicon of the Kennedy CEA economists to paint the Republicans as the bearers of noninflationary job creation and endlessly growing pies. In a speech delivered before the International Longshoremen's Association, AFL-CIO in July 1979, Kemp contrasted the Carter administration's zero-sum horizons with the expansive vistas of growth opened up by supply-side tax cuts. "With economic growth," he rhapsodized, "there is room for everyone to get ahead. Without it, the country tears itself apart, competing for pieces of a smaller and smaller pie."[188] Kemp concluded with this admonition to the Democrats: "It is time for Congress and the Carter Administration to stop haggling over how much to increase unemployment, how far to hold down wages, how to ration scarcity, and how far around the corner to push prosperity."[189] When he later looked back on the Republicans' rebranding under Reagan, Kemp ventured that "our victory was a direct result of our becoming more democratic.... We said that austerity is the problem not the solution." This, he averred, was the secret to a politically successful "conservative populism."[190]

By teaching that deficits were not to be feared, Robert Mundell had liberated the populist supply-siders from the straitjacket of fiscal responsibility.[191] But there was ambivalence in their repudiation of austerity. After all, if deficits weren't an issue in themselves, it mattered what kind of fiscal action had produced them. Public spending could be problematic because it generated (wage push) inflation or incentivized leisure over work.[192] In this case, the deficit, though indifferent in itself, was a symptom of pathological public spending and as such called for restraint. Paul Craig Roberts elegantly explained the nuance by distinguishing between Keynesian and non-Keynesian deficits: "a deficit caused by a spending increase and one caused by a tax rate reduction...do not have equal effects."[193] A deficit instigated by public spending could be inflationary, even without the direct monetization of Treasury debt, because it shifted incentives from investment to consumption and leisure. By contrast, "a deficit caused by tax rate reduction [would] not negatively impact on private investment, economic growth, employment, and the price level. The Kennedy tax rate reduction had, for non-Keynesian reasons, a fundamentally different impact on the economy than the spending deficits of later years."[194] If Mundell had authorized the supply-siders to implement deficit-generating tax cuts, he had certainly not sanctioned redistributive expenditures or real wage gains.

THE TAX REVOLT: PRIVATE- VERSUS PUBLIC-SECTOR WAGES

At the same time Kemp-Roth was building up momentum in Congress, the populist supply-side strategy received an unexpected boost from another direction. The California tax revolt of 1978 put serious strain on the already tenuous solidarity between public- and private-sector unions and thereby confirmed what supply-siders had always suspected: that one group of workers could be maneuvered against the other in the fight against taxes and inflation. Proposition 13 asked voters to support an amendment to the state constitution that would permanently cap local property taxes and thwart the ability of legislators to increase existing taxes in the future. The local property tax was both the major source of funding for schools and the bane of suburban homeowners; any effort to reduce it was thus bound to sharpen the dividing lines between female teachers and blue-collar heads of household. After all, white blue-collar working-class men had been among the chief beneficiaries of government incentives to private housing creation in the postwar era. Now that their wages were stagnating and house prices rising, they understandably resented the growing burden of local property taxes on their household incomes.[195] Yet any vote against the property tax would have a negative impact on female and Black public-sector workers, who as a result of their exclusion from postwar housing programs were less likely to be homeowners themselves. The result was that rank-and-file private- and public-sector workers often stood on opposite sides of the debate when it came to Prop 13, even when their trade unions took a united position against it.

As the official voice of supply-side populism, the *Wall Street Journal* exploited these tensions to the full, ostentatiously taking up the cause of the overtaxed blue-collar worker in his struggles against an overindulged public sector. At the height of the tax revolt, an anonymous editorial writer gloated that the "most serious problem facing labor" was "the divergence of interests between private versus public sector unionists."[196] At a time when private-sector militancy was in retreat, the *Wall Street Journal* discovered a newfound affection for the Cold War business unionism of the AFL-CIO and cast itself as the unlikely comrade of the private-sector blue-collar worker, who it now saw as the victim rather than the agent of inflation. By this time, the argument that consumer price inflation surreptitiously increased the federal tax burden on ordinary Americans by pushing up their nominal wages into higher tax brackets—so-called bracket creep—was ubiquitous in the mainstream media.[197] The argument was fallacious: in fact, the federal income-tax system had become significantly more progressive during the 1970s thanks to the efforts of legislators to offset consumer price inflation via the Earned Income Tax Credit (introduced in 1975) and increased personal exemptions for low-income earners.[198] But right-wing rhetoric fudged the issue by blurring the difference between the federal income-tax burden on wage workers and the local property-tax burden on blue-collar homeowners, where there was genuine cause for complaint. The *Wall Street Journal* added a further divisive twist to the bracket-creep narrative by accusing public-sector workers of powering the inflationary wage spiral that was ultimately felt in the pocketbooks of their

private-sector peers. "Workers in the private sector are suffering from inflation," it announced; "a major cause of inflation, and the direct cause of rising
taxation, is expansion of the public sector. Should the AFL-CIO push for more
public-sector jobs and benefits at the expense of private sector employees? Or
should it try to restrain the public sector on behalf of private employees?"[199]

Much more was at stake in the property tax revolt than the immediate conflict between private- and public-sector wages. In the course of the 1960s and
1970s, the public school had become a lightning rod for suburban anxieties
around the scope of public-sector redistribution and the role of property taxes
in funding it. In short order, the racial integration of schools, the introduction
of bilingual Spanish and English classes, and explicit sex education had all
sparked intense controversy over the jurisdictional boundaries between the
family home and the public school.[200] The fact that local schools were funded
in large part via a tax on the family home heightened the sense of injustice felt
by some parents, many of whom were outraged that their family wealth should
be diverted to pay for services they saw as trespassing on closely guarded property lines.

As Natalia Mehlman Petrzela observes, it is often difficult to disentangle
the role of economic and family values as driving forces of the tax revolt.[201] Parents' associations and taxpayers' groups frequently collaborated in asserting
the rights of homeowners to control the way in which family wealth was spent
and children educated.[202] As administrators and beneficiaries of public monies,
schoolteachers were cast as tax-funded usurpers of the rights of parents and
agents of the liberal elite. If the suburban home was the domain of the blue-
collar family man and his wife, the public school was reviled as the fiefdom of
the overly powerful white-collar woman, whose wages posed a direct threat to
the authority of husbands and fathers. The fact that such gendered divisions
of labor frequently coexisted within the one household—since the working
wives of blue-collar union men were often employed as schoolteachers—only
served to intensify the stakes.[203] The tax revolt was more than a contest between
private-sector and public-sector workers: it was also an attempt to restore the
household authority of men in the face of a declining male industrial wage. If
men could no longer secure their prerogatives on the foundation of the Fordist breadwinner wage, then that power could perhaps be reasserted by other
means, via a claim to private property rights or small business owner status.

Blue-collar working class homeowners, many with a union background, had been among the most active organizers in the early days of the tax revolt, when the movement was still heavily inflected by a spirit of insurrection against business and corporate tax breaks.[204] Well into the 1970s, the movement's political composition was still in flux: a number of homeowner groups formed temporary coalitions with left-wing and trade union activists to call for greater relief to homeowners and proportionally heavier property taxes for business. But the coalition that eventually prevailed saw these original activists throw in their lot with small business owners against the combined forces of big business, big government, and big labor.

Blue-collar workers continued to be important players in the final coalition behind Prop 13, even though the ballot fine print ensured that wealthy homeowners and small businesses stood to gain the most. Conscious that these workers gave the movement its populist imprimatur, the tax revolt impresario Howard Jarvis astutely framed the movement as a form of revanchist industrial action—a strike of the blue-collar taxpayer against the white-collar public-sector worker. "We the taxpayers are constantly burdened with strikes by public employees, and as all the people are presumed to enjoy equal rights in this nation, we taxpayers who pay the salaries, fringe benefits, and pensions of all public employees have the same right to strike as do the public employees."[205] That private-sector blue-collar workers were indeed willing to "strike" against the wages of other workers in order to reduce their own taxes was confirmed by pre-ballot polling data, which found that private-sector union members were the demographic most likely to support the ballot: nearly 63 percent of them intended to vote in favor, compared to 54 percent of the general public. Predictably, public-sector workers were the least favorable to the ballot.[206]

The supply-side populists could not have hoped for a more serendipitous endorsement of their tax-cut strategy.[207] Not only did the California tax revolt incite blue-collar working men to vote against the interests of a feminized, minoritized public sector, it also proved that the same blue-collar workers could be persuaded to cast their vote with business interests, as long as these interests were coded as small and antiestablishment. As homeowners, after all, blue-collar workers were also small property owners whose allegiances, depending on the context, could oscillate between other wage workers and other proprietors. When faced with a direct threat to their own wages and a united front from big government and big public-sector labor, it turned out that blue-collar homeowners were prepared to act in solidarity with small business owners.

This electoral alliance between blue-collar homeowners and small business was foundational to the supply-side populist strategy and critical to Reagan's electoral victory in 1980. Although most of Kemp's rhetoric at this time was designed to appeal to blue-collar workers, the Kemp-Roth income tax cuts were carefully calculated to help both wage earners and small business owners. Most small businesses were (and are) organized as "pass through" entities, which are subject to the individual rather than corporate income tax.[208] As such, their owners stood to gain as much from supply-side income tax cuts as wage earners. For the time being at least, they did not need to be cultivated with the same care as unionized blue-collar workers; they were, after all, solidly won over to the Republican camp. By contrast, antitax populists worked overtime to convince blue-collar wage earners that their interests were aligned with those of small business owners.

While the tax revolt had stressed the common property interests of blue-collar homeowners and small businesses, another strategy was to exploit the ambivalent employment status of workers in nonindustrial blue-collar sectors such as transport or construction. After all, many workers in these sectors were familiar with the experience of seasonal contract work, even if they were securely waged and unionized. The figure of the blue-collar owner operator became increasingly prominent in the 1970s, as sole proprietors engaged in their own struggles against consumer price inflation and corporations deployed deliberate strategies of worker reclassification to offload costs. Independent truck drivers became visible to the public as never before in the 1970s, as they staged a series of road blockages across the country in protest against rising fuel costs. Although many of them had benefited from union representation and negotiated pay rises in the past, their activism took on a distinct antigovernment and antiunion flavor as the decade progressed and served as a powerful catalyst to the deregulation of the entire sector under Carter.[209] The taxi industry too had its own contingent of independent "medallion owning" drivers, who operated alongside fleet drivers and for many years were considered the labor aristocrats of the sector.[210]

It was in the construction sector, however, that the dividing lines between traditional employment and small business ownership were truly blurred. For much of the twentieth century it was common practice among specialized trades workers and journeymen to alternate between unionized employment on large construction sites and off-season work as sole traders on small residential projects. This resulted in an ambiguous class position very different from that of the industrial wage worker. Labor historians note that "in large enterprises, the distinction between owner-manager and employee worker became ever clearer as the rift between them widened. But for carpenters these distinctions remained blurred, for decades longer. Unlike an industrial worker, a carpenter often owned the tools of his trade. There was considerable fluidity between working as an employee and becoming the owner of a small construction business. In some ways, many construction workers were more like small businessmen than industrial laborers."[211]

Ironically, it was this hybrid class status that had conferred on the building trades their unique bargaining power throughout much of the twentieth century. As holders of a specialized skill set who could readily withdraw their labor by setting up shop on their own, tradesmen were able to demand consistently better working conditions than industrial workers.[212] This helps explain both their exemplary position within the midcentury union movement and their recurrent tendency to eschew solidarity with other workers. As unionized workers, building tradesmen had the power to extract wage concessions that other workers could only dream of, yet their part-time status as small owner-managers also created a sense of distance from the rest of the working class. Ultimately, the ambivalent class position of building trades workers would be used against them in particular, as it was in the construction sector that the instrument of legal misclassification would be wielded most ruthlessly as a tool of wage suppression.

THE CHAMBER OF COMMERCE AND SMALL BUSINESS POPULISM

The tax revolt exposed fault lines in the business community as much as it sharpened tensions among workers.[213] By the end of the decade, what had at first appeared as a united bloc among trade associations was beginning to show signs of strain, as each organization positioned itself differently with respect to the rising antiestablishment wing of the Republican Party. The Business Roundtable had certainly grown more outspoken in its opposition to government regulation, labor unions, and progressive taxation during the 1970s. Yet as an organization it had evolved out of the New Deal alliance between large corporations and the state, and as such it continued to see insider suasion and nonpartisan lobbying as the best means of achieving its ends. By contrast, the Chamber of Commerce looked to the Republican right to advance its agenda and developed an increasingly populist voice and modus operandi as the decade progressed.[214] The Chamber's new leader, Richard Lesher—himself the son of a union plasterer—aggressively scouted for new subscribers in the world of small business and doubled the organization's membership within the space of a few years.[215] Most of its members, including the many new subscribers recruited by Lesher, were small businesses with fifty employees or less, although Fortune 500 executives continued to dominate the board. Lesher foregrounded the policy interests of the former over the latter, a move that created serious tensions both within the leadership of the Chamber and with other business associations.

Both in style and policy substance, Lesher's Chamber of Commerce hearkened back to the antigovernment libertarianism of the New Deal era, which saw small business as the embodiment of free enterprise and demonized the modern shareholder-owned corporation as an agent of the totalitarian state.[216] Unlike the Business Roundtable, which stood firmly against California's Prop 13 (fearing that the budgetary fallout would lead to higher corporate taxes), the Chamber celebrated the tax revolt as a movement of the "people."[217] And where most of the corporate managerial class shunned the populist supply-side ideas of Laffer, Kemp, and Wanniski, Richard Lesher distinguished himself as an early and enthusiastic advocate. "We want an across-the-board tax cut; one that benefits everybody. And it has to be a whopper," he told a local Chamber of Commerce meeting in early 1978.[218] Lesher was described by some as a "right wing extremist," a charge he turned against his accusers by denouncing them as out-of-touch elitists who disdained the commonsense wisdom of the little man. The "experts save their bitterest barbs for a relatively new and highly dangerous group of extremists who call themselves supply siders," he quipped. "These people actually believe individual behavior is influenced by incentives. Imagine that!... Perhaps many of you have already been thinking: 'Hey, wait a minute. I want to cut government spending, and reduce tax rates, and eliminate inequities favoring government employees, but that doesn't make me an extremist. I'm a sensible person.' Indeed, you are, and you have lots of company."[219]

Building on the organization's grassroots in hundreds of state and local Chambers of Commerce, Lesher helped consolidate a vast empire of print and visual media with maximum powers to shape public opinion. By the early 1980s, its monthly magazine, *Nation's Business*, had more paid subscribers than any other business publication in the country.[220] More so than the *Wall Street Journal*, it was *Nation's Business* that brought the populist message of supply-side economics into the offices and workshops of small business owners around the country.[221] But it transmitted this message in its own unique way, lacing Kemp's sunny entrepreneurial outlook with a strident social conservatism. The magazine published lurid denunciations of public-sector workers, welfare scroungers, feminists, and migrant workers.[222] The southern segregationist James J. Kilpatrick was a regular op-ed writer. Lesher himself was a frequent contributor to the ultraconservative *Human Events*. Under his helm, the U.S. Chamber of Commerce created an effective hybrid between supply-side populism and hard-right social conservatism.

The Chamber's increasingly broad appeal, under Lesher, rested on its ability to exploit the blurred lines between the actual and the aspirational sole trader. By addressing all workers—even and especially blue-collar workers—as self-employed business owners in waiting, *Nation's Business* sought to attract an audience well beyond the traditional base of the local Chamber of Commerce. The magazine featured articles on tradesmen doing battle with federal health and safety regulators, on long-haul truckers who had freed themselves from union oversight to build their own fleet, and on door-to-door salesmen who had escaped the drudgery of nine-to-five employment.[223] Its adversaries were the Occupational Safety and Health Administration, the Environmental Protection Agency, and the Internal Revenue Service—all government agencies that were accused of waging a merciless war of attrition against the "little man" and his efforts to make a living.[224]

Not incidentally, the U.S. Chamber of Commerce had close links with Amway, the direct sales company cofounded by board member Jay Van Andel and his childhood friend Richard DeVos in 1958.[225] In an interview with *Nation's Business*, Van Andel explained that the company's name Amway was an abbreviation of the "American Way": "We decided to use the idea of free enterprise—of the small businessman being able to go off on his own. We believed then, and we still do, that this is the heart and soul of the American ideal—to make your own way. You can start your own business, whether a fruit stand, a farm or whatever, and you can do your own thing in life."[226] The son of a car dealer and an electrical contractor, respectively, Van Andel and DeVos claimed to be orchestrating a free association of small business owners. In reality, Amway perfected a unique way of organizing business around a network of self-replicating contractual relationships in which all except the leaders of the company assumed the hybrid identity of exploiter and exploited. In 1979, *Fortune* magazine included Richard DeVos and Jay Van Andel in a list of the top fifty "invisible rich"—invisible because they had amassed fortunes in privately held companies as opposed to the then more common practice of ownership shares in a public corporation (the richest of all was Charles Koch, chairman and chief executive of the family company Koch Industries).[227] Given their extreme wealth, DeVos and Van Andel could hardly be described as small business men. Yet they saw themselves as belonging to a distinct class of private, family-based entrepreneurs whose personal and economic values were at odds with the S&P 500 corporation. Publicly traded companies were bureaucratic behemoths in league with the big state. Private business owners such as the DeVoses, the Van Andels, and the Kochs styled themselves as authentic entrepreneurs who refused to see their vision diluted by mass shareholder ownership or dependence on government contracts.

As leaders of Amway, DeVos and Van Andel's self-conception as small business owners in spirit allowed them to claim a special affinity with the many contractors who worked under them. The direct sales industry was unique in that it had been defining its workers as "independent contractors" since the 1930s, at a time when the standard contract of employment was becoming hegemonic.[228] From the moment it was established in 1958, Amway referred to its salespeople as "independent business owners" and thus eluded the reach of New Deal labor law.[229] Yet these so-called business owners enjoyed all the responsibilities and none of the advantages of sole proprietorship. Amway distributors were expected to acquire their own sales packs, prepurchase products in bulk, and pay for attendance at seminars while bearing all the insurance costs that would normally be covered by an employer. At about the same time that DeVos and Van Andel were listed in *Fortune* magazine, their distributors were making an average of $76 per month.[230] Amway's entire marketing strategy rested on its ability to present such vast disparities of wealth as differences of degree, not kind.

Familial ties were central to Amway's organizational structure at every level of the contractual chain.[231] Not only were Amway distributors encouraged to sell to their immediate social circles, but they were also instructed to enroll family members within the work of distribution, with husband and wife assigned to gender-appropriate roles inside and outside the home. The arrangement conferred considerable tax advantages on the 75 percent of Amway small business units made up of husband and wife: Amway functions were designed to double as family vacations and dinner dates, and as such could be deducted as business expenses.[232] But beyond its value as a tax shelter, DeVos and Van Andel were interested in the unique capacity of the family to exploit unpaid labor and recruit new "generations" of distributors.[233] Less fungible than the commercial contract, the ties of kinship allowed the Amway sales distributor (at that time, almost always a man) to conscript the labor of his wife and children without immediate recompense. The family constituted the cellular unit of the Amway business model, and as such the durability of its ties was of direct economic importance. "We do not recruit men alone or women alone to sell our products when we can recruit the whole family," DeVos proclaimed. "It is time in America for the family concept to be reaffirmed, time for us to be prodded back to our basic responsibilities as parents, time for us to believe in the family so strongly that we will be willing to make whatever rearrangements of priorities are necessary to make our own homes the incubators of the American dream."[234] Thus, the Amway "business owner" and his dependants were plunged back into a pre–New Deal world of household production.

THE RISE OF THE BLUE-COLLAR INDEPENDENT CONTRACTOR

For many years, the peculiar employment arrangements of the direct sales industry were of little relevance to the wider world of work, for the simple reason that the overwhelming trend was toward greater expansion of the standard contract of employment.[235] After the New Deal, full-time work in a large, unionized manufacturing firm became the standard model of employment for white, blue-collar men and a common point of reference in disputes over labor law. This model was so hegemonic that even the itinerant or project-based workers we would assume to be independent contractors today were commonly recognized as standard employees with rights to the full array of New Deal labor protections. During this period, for instance, building trades workers, long-haul truckers, and more briefly taxi drivers all attained wages and conditions comparable to or better than those of unionized industrial workers, despite the mobile and fluctuating nature of their work.[236]

This all changed in the 1970s, however, when employers in the construction, trucking, and taxi industries began to experiment with worker misclassification as a way of combating rising wages and prices. The calculus was straightforward: if employers could find a legitimate way to treat dependent workers as independent contractors, then they could divest themselves of the whole panoply of collective bargaining, minimum wage, and social insurance rights mandated under the New Deal, thus clawing back some of the competitive edge lost to inflation. As the decade progressed, business owners were encouraged by the fact that appellate court judges seemed increasingly ready to endorse their departures from New Deal labor law.[237] The remaining administrative hurdles were overcome in 1978, when Congress enacted section 530 of the Revenue Act, an income tax provision that promised lenience to employers who felt they were being unfairly pursued for misclassification.[238] Section 530 granted employers "safe harbor" to treat their employees as independent contractors, so long as this was a "longstanding recognized practice" of the industry in question.[239] With so much room for interpretation, the clause was ripe for abuse, especially in a sector such as construction where independent contract work was indeed a familiar if seasonal component of the average tradesman's experience. Intended as a form of interim relief, section 530 of the Revenue Act was extended indefinitely in 1982 and has since become a formidable legislative warrant to systemic worker misclassification.

One person who appreciated the full significance of the IRS classification debate was Ronald Reagan, who was at that point preparing to launch his second presidential campaign. In the radio addresses he delivered during this period, Reagan made a concerted appeal to the blue-collar worker, whose plight he identified with that of the blue-collar entrepreneur and small business man. At a time when Congress was debating the alleged excesses of the

IRS in policing worker classification, Reagan hoped to convince his audience that federal regulation, unions, and taxes were more of a threat to blue-collar workers than the immediate exploiter of their labor. In a radio address that aired in January 1978, Reagan took up the cause of a small business man in the Vermont logging industry who, he alleged, was being harassed by the IRS for misclassifying his employees as independent contractors.[240] The business-man in question had hired a whole host of contract workers to fell trees, haul them to the lumberyard, cut them to pulpwood size, and transport them to the paper mill, all using their own tools, machines, and trucks. By classify-ing these workers as independent contractors like himself, the small busi-ness man was able to escape the considerable Social Security, unemployment insurance, and other state and federal taxes he would otherwise have had to pay had he hired them as employees. But any acknowledgment of the very real differences of authority and income that distinguished the genuine indepen-dent contractor from his subcontractors was nowhere to be found in Reagan's address. "New England's loggers are not the only victims of the IRS attack," he proclaimed. "Independent contractors of all kinds—artisans, truckers, taxicab operators, repairmen and fishermen are under the same gun.... It's time that Congress told the IRS loud and clear that the independent small contractor is a vital part of America. They cannot survive if, in addition to the risks of the economy, they are harassed into insolvency by an IRS determined to make them pay the taxes of others with whom they contract, as well as their own."[241]

Reagan's rhetoric was crafted to flatter and disarm. By symbolically ele-vating the dependent contract worker to the rank of business owner, he pre-empted any more careful inquiry into the actual power relations between the genuine independent contractor and the misclassified worker and simultane-ously diverted the grievances of both parties toward the federal government and the IRS. This sleight of hand would prove decisive in Reagan's efforts to cleave blue-collar workers from the New Deal Democratic coalition in the presidential elections of 1980.

REAGAN'S SMALL BUSINESS REVOLUTION

As presidential candidate for the Republicans, Reagan was not the first choice of corporate elites. This was John Connally, a close ally of the Treasury

Department supply-siders who had built his primary campaign around an agenda of accelerated depreciation schedules and public spending restraint in everything but defense.[242] Reagan hit a very different note. Although he was by no means a stranger to big business (he had served, after all, as public relations envoy for General Electric for eight years), his early experience in Hollywood had made him especially sensitive to the interests of the sole trader and professional freelancer.[243] Throughout his tenure as president of the Screen Actors Guild in the late 1940s and 1950s, Reagan had complained of the unfair burdens placed on the professional actor, who on account of his uncertain legal position as both a freelancer and full-time dependant of the large production studios had all the obligations and none of the tax advantages of the sole trader.[244] Decades after he had left Hollywood, he recalled bitterly that at the height of his career he had been forced to pay marginal tax rates of 94 percent on his individual income while large capital-intensive corporations could slash their tax burdens with the help of depreciation allowances.[245] He asked: Why were professional entertainers and athletes not allowed to write off their tax in the same way as corporations? As president of the Screen Actors Guild, Reagan had called on Congress to approve a "human depreciation allowance" for actors and athletes on the grounds that their shelf life was surely more limited than that of the average oil well.[246] The suggestion went nowhere. Yet the experience instilled in Reagan a lifelong respect for the small business owner and sole trader while stoking his mistrust of the Fortune 500 "organization man" and his big government enablers.[247]

Reagan's small business rhetoric did little to reassure the corporate executives associated with the Business Roundtable. But it did endear him to Wanniski, Laffer, and Kemp, who, after initial reservations, were soon convinced that Reagan would make the perfect candidate for the populist supply-side cause. As the presidential primaries kicked off in early 1980, Wanniski noted approvingly that "Reagan began the campaign well ahead of the other candidates in the public-opinion polls, although he had almost no support from the Republican elitists. Reagan came on as a Western populist, with talk of radical change, and the Eastern establishment of businessmen and bankers lined up with George Bush or John Connally."[248] In January of that year, the Reagan team held an intensive three-day consultation with the populist supply-siders in Los Angeles. Here, Reagan announced that he would leave the "Fortune 500" to the other candidates: he would be the "candidate of the farmer, the small businessman, the independent, the entrepreneur."[249]

Reagan had to tread carefully during the presidential campaign of 1980. Despite his rising popularity among the union rank and file, blue-collar attachment to the trade union movement remained strong and it would have been dangerous for him to expose his radically libertarian views so early in the game. Although in previous years he had pledged to abolish the OSHA (Occupational Safety and Health Administration), repeal the Davis-Bacon Act, and implement right-to-work laws, Reagan now took every occasion to remind blue-collar workers he was the only former union leader to run for president.[250] When a New York reporter asked Reagan if he really expected a conservative Republican to make a dent in the city's blue-collar voting bloc, Reagan replied that "maybe a conservative Republican who also goes back to Roosevelt's New Deal" could do it. "I was a New Deal Democrat," he reminded his audience, but "I found in recent years that the leadership of the Democratic Party doesn't have anything in common with the Democratic Party I grew up in, and that's why I switched."[251] In Reagan's telling, it was the Democrats who had betrayed the spirit of the New Deal and abandoned its original beneficiaries—white, blue-collar workers—in favor of unproductive welfare dependents, feminized public-sector workers, and white-collar professionals. With Reagan as president, the Republicans would restore blue-collar men to their rightful place in the "Great Coalition . . . of the producers of America."[252]

Yet Reagan planned to achieve this proclaimed New Deal restoration through a complete inversion of Roosevelt's fiscal and legislative agenda: instead of activist public spending, protective labor laws, and an expanding, steeply progressive tax base, what Reagan offered his blue-collar voters was an essentially subtractive agenda of tax cuts and deregulation. In his campaign addresses to unionized workers, he unfailingly drew attention to the ways in which environmental protection laws, excessive government regulation, and rising taxes eroded wages, while ignoring the mounting right-wing assault on organized labor. In a campaign visit to New York City, construction workers applauded the presidential candidate when he pledged to overturn EPA opposition to a new, heavily polluting highway project.[253] In reaching out to blue-collar workers, Reagan addressed them first and foremost as taxpayers and made every effort to downplay their connections with other wage workers.

With government spending now coded as inflationary and biased toward the "unproductive" public-sector employee, Reagan sought to persuade his audience that tax cuts, not direct spending, were the best way to restore the blue-collar wage.

In fact, Reagan was more attuned to the interests of corporate capitalism than his election rhetoric let on. When he emerged as the Republican contender for president, corporate and financial leaders swiftly lined up behind him and set to work schooling him in the intricacies of "capital formation."[254] His signature first-year legislation, the Economic Recovery Tax Act (ERTA) of 1981, combined the tax reforms demanded by large capital-intensive industries with across-the-board tax cuts for individuals and small business.[255] Reagan had insisted on implementing both the elitist and populist tax-cut agendas despite the dire warnings of fiscal cataclysm from his closest advisers. Kemp, Laffer, and Wanniski put their weight behind both sets of tax cuts, but the favor was not returned. Instead, most of the elite advocates of "capital formation" saw individual income tax cuts as a dangerous descent into fiscal populism and feared (rightly, as it turned out) that they would lead to soaring budget deficits. Only one of the major trade associations, the small-business-oriented U.S. Chamber of Commerce, broke ranks on the issue and came out fighting for Reagan's income tax cuts, which after all were a gift to small business as much as wage workers.[256] Reagan himself—and Republicans thereafter—remained steadfast in their resolve to protect the ERTA income tax cuts from fiscal conservatives. While almost all of the ERTA's elite supply-side cuts were pruned in 1982 and many eliminated in 1986, the individual income tax cuts were left in place.[257] Reagan understood better than most that the Republican Party was doomed to perpetual minority status unless it could break the New Deal coalition between organized labor and the Democrats. Fiscal "irresponsibility" was the price to pay for electoral populism, and supply-siders such as Kemp, Wanniski, and Laffer assured him that the United States could afford it.

The wager paid off. Reagan in 1980 won a full 54 percent of the white working-class vote and 47 percent of the union vote; 22 percent of traditional Democrat voters defected to the Republicans.[258] Admittedly, Nixon had scored higher with each of these demographics in his 1972 campaign against the New Left favorite George McGovern.[259] But the blue-collar swing of 1980 proved more momentous in the long run because Reagan had arrived at a time when unionized labor was on the defensive. Few would pay a higher price for this defection than blue-collar workers themselves.

As a solution to stagnant wages, Reagan's tax cut agenda was an elaborate feint. Introduced into a progressive tax code, across-the-board personal tax cuts automatically delivered their greatest benefits to those in the highest brackets, who at the same time saw an even more dramatic reduction in taxes owed on their investment income. What little tax gains accrued to the lower half of the income distribution were soon to be eroded by a steady rise in regressive payroll taxes, the consequence of a bipartisan deal to shore up Social Security at workers' expense.[260] There can be no doubt that blue-collar workers were hit hard by the economic turmoil of the 1970s, but contrary to the arguments of right-wing populists, this was not the effect of bracket creep. The federal income tax system had become more, not less, progressive during the 1970s. For all its populist pretensions, Reagan's tax-cut agenda of 1981 abruptly reversed this egalitarian trend, dramatically shrinking the net tax burden of the wealthiest of Americans while simultaneously performing a bait and switch on wage workers, in the public and private sectors alike.[261]

REAGAN'S WAR ON LABOR

It was hardly coincidental that when Reagan launched his first open assault on the trade union movement, he singled out a public-sector union, the Professional Air Traffic Controllers Organization (PATCO), as his sacrificial victim. Although most airline workers, including pilots, machinists, and flight attendants, belonged to private-sector unions, professional air traffic controllers operated under the jurisdiction of the Federal Aviation Administration (FAA) and were therefore classified as public-sector employees. Having registered as a public-sector union in 1969, PATCO did not have the legal authority to declare strike action, although its members had engaged in several slowdowns and other kinds of gray-zone industrial action since its establishment. On August 3, 1981, about thirteen thousand air traffic controllers walked off the job in protest against failed wage negotiations. Ironically, PATCO organizers were emboldened by the fact that they had endorsed Reagan as president after a series of slights from President Carter and had received a written promise from the incoming president that he would work with them "in a spirit of cooperation."[262] Reagan would turn this act against them, using it to accentuate the divide between public-sector workers and the rest of the union movement. Only a few hours after PATCO members went on strike, Reagan served them with a forty-eight-hour ultimatum to return to work or lose their jobs. In a speech delivered in the White House Rose Garden, he reiterated his sympathy for private-sector unions, reminding them once again of his proud service as a president of the Screen Actors Guild, but carefully exempted public-sector workers from this expression of worker solidarity. "Let me make one thing plain: I respect the right of workers in the private sector to strike," Reagan explained. "Indeed, as president of my own union I led the first strike ever called by that union. I guess I'm the first one to ever hold this office who is a lifetime member of an A.F.L.-C.I.O. union. But we cannot compare labor management relations in the private sector with Government. Government cannot close down the assembly line, it has to provide without interruption the protective services which are Government's reason for being."[263]

In serving the PATCO strikers with an ultimatum, Reagan was relying on the fact that PATCO had distanced itself from the rest of the union movement by failing to support the legal walkouts of other airline unions during his first months in power. The air traffic controllers had struck out on their own, wrongly convinced that the FAA would not risk public safety by replacing them with less experienced workers. It was only at the last minute that they reached out to other airline workers for support. By this time, however, private-sector airline workers were reluctant to risk their own jobs for a union that had shown little appetite for solidarity in the past.[264] With no threat of joint action, Reagan called PATCO's bluff and summarily fired the remaining 11,345 striking workers.

More harmful in the long run than the loss of thousands of PATCO worker jobs was the highly visible failure of the trade union movement to unite in the face of Reagan's aggression. The lapse in solidarity sent a clear message to employers, who in the months and years following the PATCO strike stepped up their attacks on the union movement as a whole. Although striking private-sector employees, unlike their public-sector counterparts, were protected from dismissal under the terms of the NLRA, employers now turned increasingly to an obscure legal workaround as a way of shedding workers during industrial action. A hitherto little-known clause contained in a 1938 Supreme

Court decision *NLRB v. Mackay Radio & Telegraph Co.* permitted employers to "continue operations" if they permanently replaced rather than fired striking workers.[265] In principle, the replaced workers were still on the payroll, and employers would need to start paying them again as soon as a new position became available. But this was not likely to occur at a time when companies were trying to downsize. In the years that followed the PATCO strike, some of the largest U.S. corporations mobilized this clause to evade the reach of the NLRA and dismiss workers who had the nominal right to strike. It is estimated that some 300,000 workers lost their jobs in this way in the 1980s alone.

Although its immediate targets were public-sector workers, it was the private-sector union movement that in the long run suffered most from the PATCO debacle. The fortunes of public- and private-sector unions diverged sharply during the 1980s: while public-sector unions regrouped and expanded their ranks, private-sector unions never recovered from the onslaught.[266] Under Reagan, factories relocated en masse and private-sector unions hemorrhaged members, while blue-collar and industrial wages flatlined.[267]

Among the hardest-hit industries were the building trades. The Volcker recession had brought construction to a near standstill, resulting in unemployment rates of close to 90 percent in New York and other cities.[268] With unionized workers forced to accept employment in whatever form it came, the Business Roundtable's "construction users" were given free rein to pursue their long-planned attack on union hiring halls. According to the Business Roundtable's own calculations, union membership in the construction workforce fell from a high point of between 75 to 80 percent in the early 1970s to between 25 and 30 percent two decades later.[269] The same unions that had spent the late 1960s and early 1970s disrupting the terms of the Keynesian consensus with their inflationary wage demands were now reduced to haggling over the terms of defeat. In a third of all wage negotiations settled in the early 1980s, construction unions were forced to accept wage freezes or outright cuts as part of their settlements.[270] These losses would never be made up for. At the height of the housing boom of 2006, for instance, real construction wages were 17 percent below their 1973 level. The same workers who propelled the formidable wage-push inflation of the early 1970s were now earning less than the average wage for all industries.[271]

The legislative environment turned sharply in favor of employers, too, as governors across the country moved to repeal the state prevailing wage laws that set a floor under construction wages. Between 1981 and 1989, Alabama, Arizona, Colorado, Florida, Idaho, New Hampshire, Kansas, Louisiana, and Utah all repealed their prevailing wage laws, while fourteen other states introduced but failed to pass repeal bills.[272] The repeal (threatened or actual) of these so-called mini Davis-Bacon Acts was comparable in effect to deregulation in the trucking and airline industries. It opened the door to competitive price-cutting in the once protected sector of government-sponsored construction and put workers on notice that any attempt to negotiate conditions could leave them worse off. As the union hiring hall lost its once central position in vetting workers and contractors were released from the enormous countervailing power of the building trades unions, the practice of legal misclassification spread like wildfire from small-scale residential construction sites into multi-million dollar commercial and industrial projects.[273] With the legislative sanction of the 1978 Revenue Act, employers across the construction sector were able to divest themselves of workers' compensation and other social insurance costs at the stroke of a pen, simply by reclassifying their employees as sole traders.[274] The so-called gig economy practice of systemic legal misclassification was a reality in the construction sector long before it was adopted by digital platform–based companies such as Uber, Lyft, and Deliveroo in the twenty-first century. The sector remains a hotbed of worker misclassification to this day, accounting for 20 percent of all independent contractors across the American workforce in 2018.[275]

SMALL BUSINESS AND THE FISSURED CORPORATION

There can be no doubt that Reagan's paeans to small-scale entrepreneurial freedom played to the real aspirations of blue-collar wage workers. Yet the more he insisted on the effective identity between the worker and the small business owner, the more elusive the transition became for those who started out as waged dependants. The long-term effect of the Republican war on labor was to multiply the number of workers toiling under the direct authority of small business owners and to sharpen the class divide between them, making it increasingly difficult for misclassified workers to assert their bargaining powers qua wage workers, let alone accede to the position of owner-manager.

This was particularly obvious in the construction sector, where the dream had for many years been more accessible than elsewhere.

For much of the twentieth century, the peculiarity of the construction industry was its unique combination of pervasive subcontracting relations, small business ownership, and unusually strong labor protections.[276] In an industry that has never conformed to the corporate model of organization, "bigger builders" have always operated "like a federation of small independent companies rather than a single entity."[277] Today, it has become commonplace to see subcontracting arrangements like these as a byword for labor insecurity. Yet in the world of the building trades, the presence of the union hiring hall and collective bargaining rights once ensured a close alignment between the interests of the general contractor, the small owner-manager, and the worker, such that an ambitious apprentice could aspire to serve as both unionized employee and seasonal sole trader when he had completed his training. Up until the 1980s, specialized tradesmen and the small business subcontractors who hired them often belonged to the same union and thus had good reason to see themselves as members of the same craft fraternity. This was a particular sore point for the Construction Users Anti-Inflation Roundtable, which complained that even the general contractors who hired subcontractors on a project-by-project basis had such loyalty to the union that they routinely transmitted cost blowouts upward to the sponsor of a project rather than downward to the small business owner or worker.[278] Despite the predominance of subcontracting relations, then, unionized construction workers enjoyed at least the same level of security as the long-term employee of a corporation.

Today, however, only a small percentage of construction workers are unionized, leaving the project-based worker at the bottom of a contractual chain that ruthlessly transmits costs downward. The Business Roundtable of the 1970s encouraged corporate sponsors to go "double-breasted," that is, to set up nonunion building subsidiaries in competition with unionized operators, making it increasingly difficult for the latter to stay in business without also compromising on wages and conditions. The point was to make the general contractor directly answerable to the "construction user" who sponsored a building project and thus to destroy the old unwritten pact between general contractors, subcontractors, and workers.[279] As general contractors realigned their interests with real estate developers and other project sponsors, they transferred cost pressures downward onto the shoulders of subcontractors, who now had every incentive to compress wages and misclassify workers. With no shared allegiance to the union, the once complicit relationship between the small business owner and the worker turned antagonistic, while the distance between them became harder to bridge. Thus, at the very moment they found themselves reclassified en masse as "independent contractors" and de jure small business owners, construction workers were thrust back into a pre–New Deal world of brutal labor exploitation. Today, nonunionized construction workers who toil under the unmediated authority of the small owner-manager are in the same legal situation as the subordinate in the classic master-servant relationship. In a sector still dominated by family-based firms, the construction company begins to look like a descendant of the "precapitalist" household unit of production, in which the worker was subject to the same kinds of paternalist authority as next of kin.[280]

While these trends are unusually pronounced in the enduringly noncorporate construction sector, they have spread far beyond here to reshape the corporate sector, too. It used to be in the interest of the largest American corporations to perform the bulk of their administrative, retail, and manufacturing tasks in-house, a goal that could best be achieved by anchoring workers in place with a long-term contract of employment, generous benefits, and seniority rights. As the classic Fordist corporation succumbs to the challenges of shareholder activism and offshore competition, however, CEOs are increasingly adopting the kind of elaborate subcontracting relationships that were once largely confined to the noncorporate sector. Today it is common for corporations to contract out their core functions to an army of smaller businesses operating as specialist service providers or third-party sellers.[281] These subcontractors in turn are often obliged to outsource some of their own functions to other small businesses. In many ways, then, the construction industry norm—in which "bigger builders operate more like a federation of small independent companies rather than a single entity"[282]—is beginning to hold true of the Fortune 500 company also. As the vertically integrated corporation disassembles into a network of private contractual arrangements, a growing number of workers fall under the de facto jurisdiction of a small business, even when they are wearing the logos or fronting the desks of the largest of corporate brands.[283] Since most small businesses escape the oversight of the

Fair Labor Standards Act, this fact alone is sufficient to plunge workers back into a pre–New Deal world of unprotected labor relations.[284] In this and many other respects, the organizational form pioneered by Amway looks less like a cultish outlier than a precursor to wider changes across the workforce.

WAGE LOSSES AND CAPITAL GAINS

Working-class disunity was critical to Reagan's winning coalition of 1980. But how long could private-sector workers continue to be played off against the public sector, when their own working conditions were under relentless attack? And for how long would income tax cuts compensate for the chronic stagnation of blue-collar wages? The Republicans needed to offer some alternative prospect of class mobility if they wanted to permanently undermine the Democratic voting bloc. Jack Kemp was one of the few members of the Reagan administration to sense the limits of a pure antilabor strategy. He saw a solution to this problem in the idea that personal investment, driven by easy credit conditions and subsidized by government tax expenditures, could serve as an enduring alternative to traditional forms of welfare.

The tax revolt had demonstrated that under the right circumstances, wage workers could be persuaded to vote as homeowners in the interests of protecting their property rights from the tax impositions of public-sector workers. But this calculus had pitted homeowners against renters, taxpayers against so-called tax consumers, in an invidious logic of resentment and exclusion that merely exacerbated the gender- and race-based dividing lines of the New Deal consensus. With the end of the Volcker recession in 1982, however, the influx of global investment funds into the United States and the consequent relaxation of credit conditions suggested a way in which these dividing lines might be overcome. Accordingly, Kemp seized upon the possibilities of credit democratization as a way of embracing all constituents—suburban homeowner and inner city dweller, mortgagee and renter alike—in the promise of asset-owning democracy. If capital gains could replace wages as the vector of social mobility, then the whole fractious issue of stagnant wages and industrial job loss could be sidelined altogether.

One obvious policy model was provided by Martin Feldstein, who had long championed the use of personal investment accounts as an alternative to the pay-as-you-go system of Social Security (the former contributed to "capital formation," Feldstein argued, while the latter encouraged consumption and disincentivized savings and investment).[285] Kemp liked the basic idea but balked at its obvious bias toward the most secure wage earners and the already well-off. His own crusade was to extend the personal investment model to those at the bottom of the income and wealth scale—to those, in other words, who could only aspire to "own" assets on credit but lacked the collateral or steady income stream to do so without government intervention.

At the end of the decade, Kemp would describe his agenda as a form of "asset-based welfare"—a term coined by the social policy scholar Michael Sherraden.[286] But the basic idea was already at work in his earliest policy initiatives within the Reagan administration. Drawing on the translational work of the British scholar Stuart Butler, then based at the Heritage Foundation, Kemp worked tirelessly to import the ideas of British social reformers from Thatcher's Britain into the American context. As Reagan hacked away at urban poverty programs, Kemp launched bill after bill to promote the idea of small property ownership and micro-entrepreneurialism among low-income workers.[287] Kemp was the first congressman of either party to argue that "enterprise zones" could be deployed to bring back economic prosperity to America's blighted inner cities. The "enterprise zone" was the brainchild of another British scholar, Sir Peter Hall, an erstwhile Fabian socialist who had come up with the idea of turning inner city districts into "free trade zones," replete with tax incentives and exemptions to labor law.[288] As Stuart Butler acknowledged, it was the centerpiece of "a supply-side program to save the inner cities...the urban complement to the general conservative strategy of cutting taxes and regulation to stimulate economic growth."[289] But it was also, in Kemp's hands, a populist supply-side program, designed to help the cash-strapped micro-entrepreneur and the welfare mother. At a time when cities such as New York were lavishing tax incentives on wealthy real estate developers such as Donald Trump, the designation of impoverished inner cities as "enterprise zones" offered a seemingly more democratic vision of urban development, in which the smallest of businesses would be given access to tax incentives of their own. In his promotion of the "enterprise zone" approach to urban development, Kemp took inspiration from MIT economist David Birch, whose widely publicized (although soon contested) work suggested that 80 percent of new jobs were created by small business.[290] If Birch's findings were anything to go by, the federal urban renewal programs that cleared slums and poured federal money into public job creation schemes were going about things in exactly the wrong way: such programs would be much more effective, Birch seemed to suggest, if governments simply eliminated land-use regulations and lavished tax incentives on would-be entrepreneurs.

For the time being, Kemp found himself continually blocked by skeptics in his own party, who had little appetite for the populist agenda of property-owning democracy. During the Reagan years at least, it was at the state level that Kemp found most success, thanks to the intercession of the newly created American Legislative Exchange Council (ALEC).[291] Acting on ALEC's counsel, thirty-eight states and the District of Columbia created a total of 2,840 enterprise zones between 1981 and 1991.[292] Very few of these zones were created in poverty-stricken areas, however, and it was large manufacturing firms, not small business, that reaped the bulk of the tax incentives.[293] In practice, the creation of state and local "enterprise zones" simply formalized a series of ad hoc solutions that lower levels of government had come up with as a result of dwindling federal transfers and an increasingly uncertain revenue base. As the New York fiscal crisis of the 1970s had demonstrated, state and city governments that could no longer afford to stimulate growth through direct public spending could at least "spend" by subtraction, that is, by deliberately forgoing future tax revenues from a proposed business venture or infrastructure project.[294] Local mayors and state governors had seized upon the tax expenditure option as a makeshift response to fiscal straits. By the 1990s, it had become an all-purpose alternative to urban planning. Instead of engaging in direct subsidies to job creation, states and localities now competed with each other to lure manufacturing plants, logistics warehouses, and big-box retailers with a cornucopia of tax incentives. The supply-side solution to fiscal constraint rested on the counterfactual proposition that the long-term increment in tax revenues to be derived from a given project would compensate for the state's initial sacrifice of tax dollars.

In reality, state governors had next to no control over exchange rates and export markets, so any success in slowing the seemingly inevitable slide toward deindustrialization could only come at the expense of other states. As far as manufacturing jobs were concerned, tax competition was a zero-sum game. One industry that escaped this zero-sum logic, however, was real estate—a source of blue-collar job creation that could not be offshored. During the Reagan years, Kemp was one of the few congressmen of either party to perceive how the logics of real estate appreciation could be harnessed toward populist ends. Throughout his career, he held up the commercial real estate boom of the 1980s as a near-perfect confirmation of supply-side economic wisdom. In his telling, successive cuts to the capital gains tax in 1978 and 1981, Reagan's tax incentives to real estate investment and falling real interest rates had delivered a growth cycle founded on appreciating asset values and stagnant wages, thus proving that "noninflationary economic growth" was possible.[295] Kemp thought that the same formula could be applied to residential real estate, thus opening up the benefits of capital gains to the average homeowner while simultaneously creating blue-collar jobs in construction.

As Reagan slashed funds to cities and froze public housing budgets, Representative Jack Kemp came up with ever more ingenious ways to turn public housing tenants into mortgagees and prospective homeowners. Here again he turned to the example of Thatcher's Britain, where a whole generation of public housing tenants had been given the opportunity to purchase their housing units.[296] In 1982, the President's Commission on Housing gave the go-ahead to public housing sales in the United States. Following this, Kemp drafted legislation that would have allowed tenants to purchase their publicly owned homes at 25 percent of market value, with the help of government-backed mortgages at 70 percent of current interest rates. Although the resulting bill—the Urban Homestead Act of 1984—died in committee, the Department of Housing and Urban Development (HUD) used its existing authority to launch a series of pilot programs across the country.[297] Ultimately, very few units were sold off to their residents: public housing tenants in the United States were much poorer than their counterparts in Britain and could hardly service a mortgage on welfare benefits. Kemp's enthusiasm was not dinted, however, and over the following decade, he would initiate or inspire dozens of initiatives to implement the dream of property-owning democracy on American soil.[298]

When Reagan solicited blueprints for a second major round of tax reform in 1984, Kemp and his fellow Republican congressman Robert Kasten framed their proposal around the wealth-generating capacities of the family home.[299] Reaching out to his combined base of blue-collar workers and immigrant

Catholics, Kemp presented the bill as "first and foremost a 'pro-family' tax reform."[300] "In many important respects," he explained, "we have been guided by considering the impact of the tax code on the traditional one earner family of modest means with children.... There is, if you will, a natural-law basis for our bill, though one which sees the family rather than the individual considered in the abstract as the basic unit of society."[301] In a nod to religious conservatives, who in the 1980s had become increasingly concerned with the interactions between the tax code and the family, the Kemp-Kasten bill proposed first of all to increase the personal tax exemption for parents with dependent children.[302]

For Kemp, however, it was not enough to protect the family from excessive taxation; it was also necessary to facilitate the appreciation of wealth within the family. Kemp and Kasten were "unabashed in believing that homeownership ought to be encouraged." And while they thought that families should be incentivized "to be property owners in general, because it increases their economic independence and self-reliance," they also believed that "homeownership [was] especially important." In their words, "every family needs a piece of property that represents its special zone of freedom and even self-expression."[303] To this end, the Kemp-Kasten bill retained the already existing tax incentives to homeownership (the mortgage interest deduction and property tax rebate) while raising their value for low, and middle-income earners. It also proposed to extend interest deductions to any form of household credit that could be reinvested in the future of children—for instance, student debt.[304] In the populist supply-side imaginary, equity in the private home was reimagined as a bedrock of collateral that could secure parents' investments in the future of their children.

At first blush, the Kemp-Kasten bill looked like it bestowed most of its gifts on the "average" homeowner—the working male head of household of modest means. Yet a critical element in Kemp's vision was a proposed reduction of the marginal tax on long-term capital gains to a new low of 17 percent—a provision which Kemp described as "fair both to the ordinary investor and to the entrepreneur or venture capitalist."[305] As would soon become clear, a reduced capital gains tax was key to Kemp's vision of a homeowner economy simultaneously fueled by household credit, the residential construction sector, real estate, and financial services. Rising home values would bring prosperity to asset holders of all kinds—small business owners, real estate developers, financial investors, existing homeowners, and mortgagors—while simultaneously extending cheap credit to those previously excluded from the housing market. The differences were of degree, not kind.

Kemp got some of what he wanted with Reagan's second major tax bill. In keeping with his vision, the Tax Reform Act of 1986 almost doubled the personal income tax exemption and immediately removed thousands of lower-income Americans from the tax rolls. Reagan celebrated this as the most "pro-family measure" to come out of Congress ever. "It's in our families that America's most important work gets done: raising our next generation," he explained in terms reminiscent of George Gilder; "but over the last forty years, as inflation has shrunk the personal exemption, families with children have had to shoulder more and more of the tax burden. With inflation and bracket creep also eroding incomes, many spouses who would rather stay home with their children have been forced to go looking for jobs." A more generous personal exemption would "make it economical to raise children again."[306] Beyond this, Reagan had sought to placate the populist and elite supply-siders alike by bringing the marginal income and corporate rates down to a uniform 28 percent. Instead, he managed to enrage both constituencies by eliminating the special treatment of long-term capital gains (thus raising the marginal rate from 20 to 28 percent) and retiring special incentives to real estate investment.[307]

Kemp was bitterly disappointed by the Tax Reform Act of 1986. Like Trump, he blamed this legislation for "eroding the value of real estate and other assets" and triggering the end-of-decade recession.[308] Nevertheless, he clung to the idea that house price appreciation, if fostered by the right mix of tax and monetary incentives, could deliver the benefits of supply-side prosperity to a wider segment of the population. In a meeting with the National Association of Home Builders in 1991, Kemp extolled the commercial real estate boom of the 1980s as an object lesson in supply-side teaching and conveyed his hope that the same kind of asset-based business cycle could be replicated in the residential construction sector.[309] For this to occur, however, Congress would need to approve Bush Sr.'s proposal to restore the special tax treatment of capital gains. The "dynamic consequences of cutting capital gains taxes," Kemp told his audience, went "beyond the short-term unlocking" of investment funds. "There is also a boost to asset values and a permanent boost to the economy" that stems from increasing "demand for stocks and bonds, farms, factories, real estate, and other investments." Rising real estate values, he explained, would deliver "higher asset values" across the board, yield "stronger tax collections" for local, state, and federal government, and "unlock...trillions of dollars in unrealized capital gains."[310]

Kemp was to be disappointed yet again, as Bush's repeated attempts to lower the capital gains tax were blocked at every turn by congressional Democrats. The person that Kemp held most responsible for stagnant real estate values, however, was Alan Greenspan, who was still so haunted by the threat of inflation he repeatedly raised interest rates in the midst of the late 1980s recession.[311] In one of his many addresses to home builders, Kemp singled out Greenspan as the most significant roadblock in the way of supply-side prosperity. "I want Alan Greenspan to read my lips," he said: "Building housing is not inflationary."[312] Kemp would spend the next decade pleading with Greenspan to lower interest rates and unleash the power of cheap housing credit.

Although Greenspan for the time being remained impervious to these pleas, he was more of a kindred spirit than Kemp realized. It was Greenspan, after all, who first clearly identified the potential of asset ownership in general, and housing in particular, to serve as a source of capital gains and an alternative, non-Keynesian stimulus to aggregate demand. As a young economist in the 1950s, Greenspan turned conventional economic wisdom on its head when he suggested that stock price fluctuations drove the "real" economic process of fixed capital investment, not the other way around.[313] In 1977, Greenspan was intrigued when an analyst in his private consulting firm detected a similar process of asset-price-driven consumption in the regional economic data. This time, however, it was soaring house prices in Southern California, not stocks, that were driving the spending boom. After examining the data, Greenspan surmised that existing owners were taking advantage of vertiginous house prices to take out second and third mortgages, which they were then using to finance their household consumption.[314] The process seemed to be driving a non-Keynesian multiplier effect in which asset-backed household debt rather than direct government spending delivered a net growth in GDP.

In 1978, Greenspan presented a summary of these findings before the Congressional Joint Economic Committee, where he observed that "housing capital gains, whether realized or unrealized," had created a "wealth effect" by underwriting cheap consumer credit.[315] The text is noteworthy because it represents the first instance in which Greenspan deploys the term "wealth effect" to describe the stimulus impact of capital gains—a term he would help make ubiquitous as chair of the Federal Reserve in the 1990s and 2000s.[316] While the economic mainstream dismissed such "speculative" dynamics as peripheral to the fundamentals, Greenspan was so convinced of the real economic impact of asset price movements that he urged a change in the national accounts to include measures of capital gains, both realized and unrealized.[317] Greenspan needed no convincing then that the supply-side proposition of non-inflationary stimulus was technically possible. For a long time, however, he could see no way of fostering this alternative route to GDP growth without also fanning the flames of wage-price inflation. After all, Greenspan had been an active participant in the debate around construction wages during the 1970s and had seen how easily wage inflation could be stoked by easy credit conditions, booming property prices, and powerful building trades unions.[318] As long as workers retained an ounce of bargaining power, this threat remained uppermost in his mind, earning him his early reputation as an extreme monetary hawk. By the late 1990s, however, even Greenspan thought that the risk of wage inflation had receded, thanks in no small part to the dramatic shift in Democratic fiscal and trade policy under Clinton.

In the long run, it was Clinton who brought Kemp's asset-based policy agenda to fruition. The third-way Democratic Leadership Council had embraced Michael Sherraden's "asset-based welfare" at the same time as Kemp.[319] But whereas the Republican congressman struggled to find support beyond the Department of Housing and Urban Development, Clinton's enthusiasm for asset-based social policy was widely shared among New Democrats. It was Kemp's fate to be perpetually ten years ahead of his time. As secretary of HUD, his efforts to enact enterprise zone legislation failed repeatedly.[320] And although his long-cherished project to sell off public housing to residents was enshrined in federal legislation under the optimistic banner of Homeownership for People Everywhere (HOPE), the program ultimately floundered due to inadequate funding.[321] It was during the Clinton years that federal legislation to create enterprise zones—now known as empowerment zones—would finally be implemented.[322] It was Clinton also who inherited Kemp's HOPE program when Kemp departed HUD.[323]

Hailed by one HUD official as the "end of public housing as we know it," Clinton's HOPE VI sanctioned the continued erosion of direct public spending on housing, while experimenting with new ways to subsidize the private real estate market for nominally social ends.[324] Under its auspices, HUD set about demolishing the modernist high-rises that had become synonymous with urban ghettoization and provided former residents with rental vouchers to use in the private housing market. Later, suitably qualified residents were given the chance to repurpose their rental vouchers as a down payment—a revival of Kemp's rent-to-buy scheme that failed just as miserably.[325] While Democrats temporarily halted the free fall in HUD funding—increasing appropriations to $13 billion in 1995, up from its nadir of $9 billion in 1988 and 1989 but dramatically lower than the 1978 high point of $32 billion—most of this increase went toward rental vouchers for private landlords. The funding reprieve was short-lived, moreover, succumbing soon after to the balanced-budget zeal of the Gingrich Republicans, who seized the House in the 1994 midterm elections. Between 1995 and 1997, HUD lost 25 percent of its budget, public housing funds were slashed by 20 percent, and appropriations for homelessness declined almost as much.[326]

By contrast, Clinton lavished public subsidies on private homeowners. In 1997, he surprised even the real estate industry when he introduced an outrageously generous capital gains tax exemption on the sale of a primary residence. A married couple could now sell their home and keep $500,000 of its appreciated value tax-free, as long as they had lived in the home for two out of the previous five years (singles could claim $250,000 in tax-exempt capital gains).[327] George H. W. Bush—on Kemp's advice—had proposed but never managed to pass a similar bill.[328] The exemption went one step further than an already existing provision for deferring the capital gains tax (when a homeowner exchanged a property for one of equal or greater value) and supplemented a long list of other tax expenditures on private housing, including the mortgage-interest deduction and property tax write-offs. The contrast between Clinton's direct spending budget on public housing and his indirect expenditure on private homeownership could not have been starker. The National Coalition for the Homeless calculated that in 1997, $28 billion in federal spending would go toward low-income housing assistance while tax expenditures would cost a total of $101.8 billion.[329] Applicable to residential property alone, the tax break created an enormous incentive for the already well-off to buy and sell real estate in search of maximum returns. The year after its introduction, home sales increased by 13 percent.[330] Along with Greenspan's ultra-low interest rates of the turn of the millennium, the exemption would prove irresistible as a conduit to tax-enabled asset accumulation.

In the meantime, Clinton's direct spending record turned out to be unusually austere, despite his election promises of universal health insurance and ongoing public investment in infrastructure, research, and education. With Fed chairman Greenspan and hawkish Treasury advisors such as Robert Rubin, Lawrence Summers, and Alice Rivlin breathing down his neck, Clinton abandoned every one of his more expansive public spending ambitions within his first year in office and pursued a downsizing of the state that no Republican would have tolerated.[331] Clinton's first-term fiscal conservatism was supposed to earn him the right to spend as he pleased upon reelection. But despite balancing the budget ahead of schedule in 1996 and subsequently delivering three years of fiscal surplus in a row, he never revisited his first-year promises. Instead, he splurged on a supply-side wish list of tax cuts that owed as much to Jack Kemp as it did to Martin Feldstein. The Taxpayer Relief Act of 1997 shifted the marginal tax rate on long-term capital gains from 28 back to 20 percent (thus reversing the part of Reagan's 1986 tax reform that supply-siders hated the most), introduced the aforementioned capital gains tax exemption for homeowners, raised the federal gift and estate tax exemption from $600,000 to $1 million, and created an entirely new exemption worth $700,000 for small businesses and farms. The act also expanded the scope of the traditional individual retirement account (IRA) so beloved by Feldstein and introduced an alternative tax-advantaged account, the-so-called Roth IRA, named after Kemp's longtime associate, Senator William Roth of Delaware.[332]

The Clinton administration would have hurtled further down the road to supply-side nirvana had it not been halted in its tracks by the president's impeachment. By the late 1990s, the administration was engaged in secret discussions around the fate of Social Security. The special task force, led by Feldstein's protégé Lawrence Summers, contemplated several options for reform, including the partial diversion of existing obligations toward self-administered investment accounts and the direct investment of a major part of the Social Security fund in the stock market.[333] While Feldstein quibbled over the continuing role of government in these plans, the more striking fact was how completely the Democrats had made the supply-side agenda their own.[334] After the defeat of his first-year plan for universal health insurance, it seems that Clinton had permanently lowered his expectations: the role of government was to subsidize the personal pursuit of capital gains, not the collective provision of social insurance. All that socially conscious Democrats could expect in return was an expansion in social tax expenditures for the working poor.

Greenspan had approached the incoming Clinton administration with trepidation, fearful that a Democratic president would revive the fortunes of organized labor. Clinton was different, however. His signature trade policy—the North American Free Trade Agreement (NAFTA) of 1994—brought cheap imports flooding into the United States and exposed its auto and steel sector workers to the full brunt of global competition.[335] For more than a decade, mainstream economists had been arguing that the optimal rate of inflation could only be achieved at the price of high unemployment (the so-called nonaccelerating inflation rate of unemployment, or NAIRU). Yet in apparent defiance of this law, trade unions were oddly subdued in the tight labor market of the late 1990s, and wages barely kept up with productivity.[336]

All of this was reassuring to Greenspan, who now felt he could unleash the winds of asset price inflation without also awakening the threat of labor militancy. In private, he reflected that the omnipresent threat of job relocation had so "traumatized" the American worker that the economic laws of the 1970s no longer held.[337] Workers were simply too insecure to challenge the status quo. It had taken the fiscal surrender of the New Democrat Clinton to convince Greenspan that organized labor was definitively vanquished. But once he was assured of this, he rarely tightened monetary policy again. Between February 1995 and June 1999 Greenspan raised interest rates only once, and that by a timid one-quarter point. After the dot-com crash of the year 2000, he cut interest rates a further thirteen times, down to a low of 1 percent in 2003.[338] As someone who had always mistrusted the utopianism of supply-side economics, Greenspan now became a willing enabler of the kind of asset-based business cycle long espoused by Jack Kemp.

THE BLUE-COLLAR BUSINESS BOOM

The so-called wealth effect of rising asset prices was already visible during the stock price run-up of the late 1990s, when households in the upper income quintile (who disproportionately own stocks) significantly increased their consumer spending.[339] But Greenspan predicted an even greater stimulus from the house price boom of the 2000s, thanks to the much wider distribution of homeownership in the American population.[340] While generalized labor insecurity had emboldened Greenspan to lower interest rates and stimulate asset prices, the same policy also offered a form of redress to workers struggling with stagnant and insecure wages. Falling interest rates made it cheaper for consumers to borrow, especially if they held equity in their homes. As wages flatlined, asset prices went up, and so too did the value of collateral that underwrote household credit. For those workers who were already homeowners or mortgagors, rising asset prices served as a fount of cheap credit and an alternative, nonwage source of consumer purchasing power. For those who had poor credit histories or had never owned a home, so-called subprime mortgages could offset the risk of credit default with higher interest rates.

In this brave new world of exuberant asset owners and traumatized workers, it seemed that capital gains could replace wage gains as the motor of economic growth, thus consigning the labor question to the dustbin of history. From the media sidelines, a new generation of populist supply-siders such as Larry Kudlow and Stephen Moore celebrated the housing boom as a vindication of George W. Bush's "ownership society."[341] In reality, the boom was a bipartisan achievement, as much the child of Clinton as it was of Kemp, Greenspan, and Bush. For incoming President Bush, who had succeeded Clinton in 2001, the political rewards did not need to be spelled out. In addition to its role as a non-wage-based driver of household consumption, house price inflation also offered a way of incentivizing new production and investment while requiring no direct outlay of public money. Few industries gained more from the millennial turn to ultra-low interest rates than "blue-collar" construction—the populists' favorite sector.

In 2005, a financial analyst working for Northern Trust found that more than 40 percent of new private-sector job creation between November 2001 and April 2005 occurred in residential construction and the adjacent sectors of real estate, mortgage brokering, and home renovation retail.[342] The home building industry had undergone a wave of consolidations since the 1990s, with a dozen or so large home builders cornering the market for new land development in the most fevered regional markets. But these large companies employed few nonmanagerial workers.[343] Instead, they delegated the task of employing trades specialists and laborers to their subcontractors—small home builder firms that could provide carpenters, bricklayers, masons, electricians, plumbers, and a growing number of multipurpose day laborers according to the task at hand. Thus, most of the new employment generated by the housing boom came from small construction firms.[344]

The millennial real estate boom created a virtuous circle for the small business sector: while opening up an expansive vista of new construction contracts, it also inflated the personal asset positions of small-scale entrepreneurs (many of whom used their own homes as collateral), allowing them to scale up at speed and increase hiring to meet demand.[345] Home builders were only the most direct beneficiaries of housing price gains. Around them emerged a whole constellation of blue- and white-collar small business owners, from self-employed real estate agents, mortgage brokers, and accountants to landscape gardeners—all held aloft by the appreciating value of the private home.[346] Only one segment of the building industry failed to extract any benefits: the mostly nonunion laborers who toiled on residential construction sites. Demand for their services was voracious. Yet in defiance of conventional economic laws, they experienced stagnant (indeed by some estimates negative) wage growth between 2000 and the peak of the boom in 2005.[347]

For those who had watched the evolution of the residential construction sector over the previous decades, this would hardly have come as a surprise. The housing sector had been neglected by the building trades unions during the construction boom years of the 1960s and early 1970s, when much more lucrative work was to be found on commercial and public infrastructure projects. And it was the first to be abandoned when Reagan intensified his assault on trade unions in the 1980s. As a result, wages fell precipitously and U.S.-born workers fled in droves, either giving up construction altogether or confining their job searches to the more protected commercial and industrial sites. Today, residential remodeling—the lowest-waged, most deskilled sector in the building trades—is dominated by non-U.S.-born workers, most of them undocumented migrants from Latin America.[348] As small business owners themselves come under increasing pressure from large construction companies to squeeze budgets and accelerate project timelines, the easiest option for them is to transfer costs downward to nonunionized, legally insecure workers.[349] Thus, while almost everyone else benefited from the residential construction boom of the 2000s, blue-collar wage workers did not.

SMALL BUSINESS FAILURE AND THE RISE OF THE TEA PARTY

When the housing boom came crashing down at the end of 2007, many on the left assumed that subprime borrowers and laid-off workers would be the first to man the barricades. Surely this would be the catalyst for a popular revolt against neoliberalism and the pervasive economic insecurity it had wrought? Instead, it was small business owners and older homeowners who staged a latter-day Tea Party revolt, convinced that the crisis had been brought on by big corporations, public-sector employees, and subprime debtors themselves. While others railed against the excesses of the free market, Tea Partiers impugned big government and accused it of lavishing corporate and public welfare on undeserving claimants—at taxpayers' expense.

It was not only outside observers who were confused by the class status of the Tea Party grassroots. When sociologists Theda Skocpol and Vanessa Williamson asked grassroots Tea Partiers to describe their background, many of them proffered up the categories of "worker" or "working class." Upon further interrogation, it turned out that a plurality were or had been self-employed small business owners, albeit concentrated in sectors of the economy such as real estate, construction, remodeling, or repair that are commonly construed as "blue collar."[350] Few of them were wage workers, and even fewer were public-sector workers, with the notable exception of retired veterans. Surveys conducted by the Cato Institute and Politico confirmed that the percentage of small business owners among active Tea Partiers was almost four times higher than in the general population.[351] But raw demographic data hardly do justice to the peculiar mystique of small-scale entrepreneurialism in the movement: as noted by sociologist Nils Kumkar, who conducted his own observational research among Tea Partiers, small business ownership was "the common point of reference in all of their biographical trajectories—be it as their aspired to, their past, or their present socioeconomic status."[352] Although it was commonly assumed that Tea Partiers hailed from the lower middle or working class, all available surveys point to their overrepresentation in the highest third of the income distribution.[353] Indeed, the Cato survey, focusing on the most active Tea Party supporters, found that a full 41 percent belonged to the highest income quintile.[354] These were not misclassified employees, then, but genuine independent contractors: sole traders or small-scale entrepreneurs who worked under their own direction and on occasion employed others.[355] The pervasive misperception of Tea Partiers as "working class" seems to derive from the mismatch between their cultural and economic capital: while Tea Partiers are slightly more educated than the general population, their educational levels stand well below those of their overall income cohort, even when age is controlled for.[356] Here we find clear confirmation of the limits to standard electoral data, which routinely take the absence of college education as a simple proxy for working class.

The demographics of the Tea Party movement belie the assumption that popular insurgency, whether of the right or left, can be understood as a simple, mechanical response to economic insecurity. It is not necessary to posit a proportional relationship between absolute poverty and revolutionary zeal, however, to recognize the ways in which felt economic insecurity has fed into the right-wing insurrection of the last decade or so. Revolutions are rarely predictable on the basis of hard economic data alone. Right-wing counterrevolutions in particular are driven less by the experience of absolute than relative loss: the sense that rightful gains have been confiscated and hitherto unquestioned social contracts nullified without warning.[357] In the infamous rant he delivered on the floor of the Chicago Stock Exchange in early 2009—an event reputed to have sparked the Tea Party movement—CNBC business reporter Rick Santelli spoke of his rage at the idea of having to "subsidize the losers' mortgages" and thus catalyzed a movement that was as much a response to the underserved (and largely imagined) gains of others as it was an expression of personal loss.[358]

For those small business owners who had gained so much from the turn-of-the-century appreciation in housing values, the damage inflicted by the 2007 financial crash was real enough. As the residential real estate sector imploded and credit lines dried up, losses were particularly severe for the many small firms and sole traders that had scaled up at the height of the boom—the home builders, trade contractors, real estate brokers, home deco retail operators, accountants, mortgage brokers, and lawyers who made up the bulk of the Tea Party base.[359] As house prices plummeted, tens of thousands of small businesses were forced to downsize, restructure, file for bankruptcy, foreclose on investment or business properties, or in the worst-case scenario, abandon their primary residences to the banks. The crash was particularly ill timed for the older Americans on the verge of retirement who dominated Tea Party ranks.[360]

Yet for most Tea Partiers, these losses were relative, not absolute.[361] Although they may have seen the value of their housing assets collapse overnight, and along with it an expanding vista of business and credit opportunities, in all but a few cases, the Tea Party demographic of white, older, higher-income small business owners remained in possession of their homes. Theirs was the insecurity of asset owners on the verge of bankruptcy, not that of wage earners in free fall or subprime mortgagors dispossessed of their only equity. The millennial wealth gains of white homeowners and collateralized real estate investors were an artifact of intense government intervention: from Greenspan's accommodative monetary policy to tax expenditures such as the mortgage interest deduction and Clinton's expanded capital gains tax exemption on the family home. Further back than this, most middle-class white homeowners could thank a panoply of federal mortgage and insurance facilities for their acquisition of a family residence. Yet this kind of credit-based or tax code–enabled expenditure is rarely perceived as a form of government subsidy by its recipients and almost never suffers from the same withering public scrutiny as direct outlays on public housing or welfare.[362]

Even in the face of failure, moreover, the self-employed entrepreneurs and homeowners who made up the Tea Party base could draw on a host of legal liability protections and debt discharge laws that were not available to the noncollateralized debtor. The Chapter 7 and 13 bankruptcy options that are most frequently used by small business owners are specifically designed to limit absolute loss in the event of default. They too are an important element of the hidden welfare state that channels tax and credit protections toward the already well-off.[363] These debt discharge options are increasingly out of reach to low-income asset owners and the indebted poor. For the mostly white, higher-income debtors who can afford to file for bankruptcy, however, failure is rarely absolute, since debt discharge law is designed to sequester the filer's

most important assets from the claims of creditors. As a result of the multiple credit-based and legal protections they enjoy, white homeowners suffered
comparatively lower rates of foreclosure in the wake of the housing crisis, were
afforded more opportunities to protect their incomes and homes from foreclosure, and among overall foreclosure cases were much likelier than others
to be defaulting on investment properties (often strategically so) rather than
a primary residence.[364] In other words, it was asset *depreciation*, not historical or recent asset *dispossession*, that spurred the Tea Party into action. This
nuance helps explain the often-noted tension in Tea Party members' accounts
of their economic situation: the CBS/*New York Times* Poll, for instance, found
that "Tea Party supporters overall are more likely than the general public to
say their personal financial situation is fairly good or very good," while at the
same time "more than two thirds say the recession has been difficult or caused
hardship and major life changes."[365]

With its intense hostility toward investment banks and corporate giants,
the Tea Party revolt was met with confusion from the left. Progressives were
disconcerted by a movement that railed against big business even as it waged
war on subprime debtors, undocumented migrants, and public-sector unions.
The visible tensions between the Tea Party and older, more established trade
associations such as the Business Roundtable and the Chamber of Commerce
only underscored the movement's singularity.[366] Tea Party rhetoric looks more
familiar, however, if we place it in the long lineage of small business conservatism, which has always seen the administrative state and large corporation as
partners in crime. In the words of Dick Armey, chair of the Tea Party–aligned
FreedomWorks, "Big Business is sitting there on fat, pushy duffs looking for
government to keep them in business." Only "incompetent companies need
bailouts. People who run corporations are basically taking care of themselves.
They're not very reliable people and they're very comfortable with Big Government that greases the skids for them."[367]

In keeping with the tradition of anti–New Deal libertarianism, Tea Partiers denounced any visible form of government dependence, corporate or personal, as contrary to the spirit of the free market, while remaining blind to the
multiple ways in which their own wealth had been publicly subsidized through
the tax code.[368] They were vociferously opposed to government-sponsored
health insurance, arguing that small businesses stood to lose more from the

Affordable Care Act than large corporations. (In fact, small business employees have enjoyed unprecedented coverage following passage of the ACA, and insurance premiums have stabilized for the first time in years.)[369] In contrast to most established business associations, moreover, Tea Partiers were distrustful of free trade, from which they claimed small business had much less to gain than large corporations, and were opposed to the naturalization of undocumented migrants, who have long furnished them with a reliable source of cheap labor by virtue of their precarious legal status. Even the movement's notoriously contradictory stance on Medicare reflected the ambivalent position of small business owners, who may see themselves as deserving of government-funded insurance while also resenting the costs of payroll taxes on behalf of employees.

It was not just business, but the small family business that the Tea Party celebrated as the epitome of free enterprise—reflecting the reality that many so-called sole proprietorships rely on the hidden labor of spouses and other family members.[370] When President Obama prepared to restore the estate tax that George W. Bush had repealed a few years earlier, the Tea Party–linked Family Research Council condemned the move as a targeted attack on family businesses (which it conveniently assumed to be small). "Large, publicly traded corporations pay no death tax at all," it complained. "Family businesses undergo repeated trauma as they are passed from one generation of employers to the next, while their publicly traded competitors continue through generations unscathed."[371] Finally, the Tea Party was more interested in cuts to the individual as opposed to the corporate income tax, reflecting the fact that the vast majority of small businesses are pass-through entities, the earnings of which are reported on (or "passed through") the owner's individual income tax returns. For all its anticorporate rhetoric, then, the Tea Party was anything but anticapitalist. Indeed, what it claimed to be defending was the true spirit of free enterprise—private, unincorporated, and often family-based—against the bureaucratic capitalism of the state-dependent corporation.

THE RETURN OF SUPPLY-SIDE POPULISM

Utopias of financial democracy wax and wane along with credit cycles, reaching ecstasies of generosity as credit expands and collapsing back into invidious property-line disputes as soon as credit becomes scarce. The real estate boom of the early 2000s was no exception. As housing values plummeted and credit disappeared, so too did Kemp's (and Clinton's) expansive vision of asset-based democracy. The Tea Party electoral wave of 2010 brought Arthur Laffer back into the political limelight, along with younger acolytes such as Heritage Foundation fellow Stephen Moore and Fox News host Larry Kudlow. Although still committed to the populist rhetoric of tax cuts for the "little man," this new generation of supply-siders no longer had to contend with the powerful private-sector unions of the 1970s and instead were faced with an increasingly militant public sector. As such, they doubled down on their symbolic overtures to the (presumptively white, male) blue-collar worker, taxpayer, and small business owner while launching an all-out war on public-sector employees. With no pressing need to placate the labor movement anymore, Laffer and his allies abandoned Kemp's prevarications and outed themselves as unapologetic advocates of selective spending austerity (in the areas of health, housing, and education) alongside regressive tax expenditures.

This time around, the supply-side populists had a whole battalion of lobbying organizations at their disposal. Alongside old stalwarts such as the Chamber of Commerce and its rival, the National Federation of Independent Business, they could now rely on the increasingly powerful American Legislative Exchange Council to advance their cause at the state level and the more recently created Club for Growth to overcome any residual ideological resistance within the GOP. The Club for Growth had been cofounded in 1999 by Stephen Moore, with the purpose of promoting a more rigorous adoption of supply-side principles by Republican congressmen.[372] The board of directors included Moore's close associate Arthur Laffer.[373] Flush with donations from hedge fund and private equity managers such as Robert Mercer, the group fielded a series of primary challengers against moderate Republican incumbents during the 2000 election cycle and thus inaugurated the strategy of intraparty purging that has since become pervasive in Republican Party primaries.[374] By 2010, the group had emerged as the biggest spender among business PACs seeking to translate the Tea Party insurgency into electoral wins.[375] The club's focus was on ideological wedge politics and party realignment more than quantitative results: if a primary challenger from the hard right could force a centrist incumbent to follow a Tea Party script, then this was victory enough. The point was to force the GOP to the right by whatever means possible.

By the time of the Tea Party electoral wave of 2010, prominent supply-siders were also active in the American Legislative Exchange Council, which had served as an early conduit for Kemp's "enterprise zone" agenda. After leaving the Club for Growth in 2005, Moore and Laffer were appointed associate scholars at ALEC, where they began publishing an annual report on state business competition.[376] The so-called "ALEC-Laffer Economic Outlook" ranks states according to an index of tax competitiveness, as defined by supply-side criteria, and uses this data to predict future growth prospects. High marks are awarded to states that slash the income tax, keep property taxes to a minimum, and substitute sales taxes for taxes on production and investment. The index is informed by an overarching vision of tax and budget reform at the state level: Laffer and Moore would like to see existing (moderately progressive) state corporate and personal income taxes repealed entirely and replaced by a flat or single-rate tax. Failing this, they recommend that states substitute a sales tax for all other revenue sources, a proposal that would ensure much higher relative tax burdens on low- and moderate-income earners.[377] Marking their distance from the "third way" populism of Kemp, who always maintained a diplomatic silence when it came to public-sector spending and wages, Laffer and Moore openly rate public-sector pension obligations as a net loss to state competitiveness and advocate right-to-work laws as a way of breaking unions. They eschew even Kemp's support for such bipartisan compromise measures as the Earned Income Tax Credit (EITC), which has long allowed centrists to help the working poor by spending off-budget.

Following the midterm elections of 2010, when Tea Party candidates ousted establishment Republicans in key primaries across the country, incoming legislators turned to the ALEC–Laffer index as a guidebook for downsizing the state once and for all.[378] Suddenly Arthur Laffer was everywhere again, advising governors in Missouri, Oklahoma, Florida, Kansas, Indiana, Tennessee, North Carolina, and several other states on how to slash state income taxes, incentivize "small business" formation, and implement right-to-work laws.[379] Laffer, it seemed, had returned to complete the unfinished work of the early Reagan administration. This time, however, the supply-side experiment was playing out at the state level, with considerably less pushback from Republican Party fiscal conservatives.

In the state of Wisconsin, the supply-side movement found a ruthless envoy in Governor Scott Walker, a former member of ALEC who also worked in close partnership with the Wisconsin chapter of the Club for Growth.[380] A little more than a month into his governorship, having already passed a volley of tax cuts, Walker announced that the state was facing a crippling budget shortfall. This he attributed to the exorbitant costs of public-sector benefits and the unreasonable demands of the teachers' unions. In response, he unveiled a sweeping Budget Repair bill comprising $1.7 billion in budget cuts and the virtual elimination of public-sector bargaining rights.[381] The bill proposed to pay for the manufactured hole in pension and health insurance benefits by drawing down on public employee wages (an individual wage loss of between $400 and $600 per month was predicted, depending on the employee's plan). On top of these cuts, the bill dealt a crippling blow to the organizing power of public-sector unions. Instead of collecting member dues through automatic payroll deductions, unions were now obliged to recertify annually—a time-consuming and expensive process that was designed to utterly exhaust union resources.[382] The effect of the bill was to eliminate collective bargaining on anything but wages, which in any case were to be capped at the rate of consumer price inflation.[383] Workers could now only bargain to keep their wages stagnant.

In his attempts to crush the state's public-sector unions, Walker styled himself as a latter-day Reagan: in a prank phone conversation with an imposter David Koch, he confessed that he wanted to "change the course of history," just as Reagan had done when he fired PATCO strikers in 1981.[384] In reality, Walker's program was considerably more radical. Reagan, after all, had never contested the right of public-sector workers to engage in collective bargaining, only their right to strike. And where Walker had launched a preemptive strike against public-sector unions, on the pretext that they were the cause of the state's post-financial-crisis budgetary woes, Reagan had endorsed a wage rise offer to PATCO workers shortly before their strike.[385]

What Governor Walker retained from early supply-side rhetoric, however, was the promise that tax cuts would generate so much extra economic growth they would ultimately compensate for public-sector austerity. Thus, Walker rationalized his draconian budget agenda as a stimulus to private-sector job creation, even coming up with a new iteration of the Laffer curve (renamed the "Kohl curve" after the price-cutting retail chain Kohl's) to press home the point that tax cuts would ultimately deliver a greater overall volume of tax-able economic activity.[386] During his campaign for governor in 2009, Walker vowed to replace taxpayer-funded jobs in the public sector with 250,000 new private-sector jobs, to be paid for in the form of tax incentives to "job creators."[387] Walker's first-year budget alone included an estimated $135 million in tax breaks, including capital gains concessions and generous loss offset provisions for any new business investment in Wisconsin.[388] In late 2013, Walker flagged the idea (borrowed directly from Laffer and Moore) of eliminating the state's income tax and replacing it with an expanded set of sales taxes. He could not get legislators to agree to such a radical assault on the state's revenue base, but he did get close enough, ultimately forcing through two rounds of income tax cuts and a property tax reduction that delivered outsized benefits to the state's highest income earners.[389]

Scott Walker was an expert practitioner of the divide-and-conquer strategy first weaponized by populist supply-siders in the 1970s.[390] Even as he waged a merciless war against public schoolteachers and other municipal workers, he conspicuously exempted the blue-collar police, firefighter, and building trades unions from this attack. During his first campaign for governor, Walker had cast himself as a valiant defender of the rights of the taxpayer against the assaults of an unproductive public sector. "We cannot and should not maintain a system where public employees are the 'haves' and the taxpayers footing the bill are the 'have-nots,'" he proclaimed, repeating a script set out by supply-siders in the midst of the 1970s tax revolt.[391] A few days after Walker introduced his 2011 Budget Repair bill, a television ad sponsored by the Wisconsin Club for Growth compared the sacrifices made by private-sector workers at Harley-Davidson, Mercury Marine, and Sub-Zero, all of whom had recently suffered wage and benefit cuts, with the privileges enjoyed by public-sector workers: "State workers haven't had to sacrifice," the voiceover intoned. "It's not fair. Tell them to pay for their fair share, just like the rest of us."[392] As Walker's showdown with public-sector workers turned into a test case for Tea Party state legislators across the country, others chimed in with unlikely professions of solidarity with the blue-collar private-sector worker. Ohio governor-elect John Kasich, who was preparing to pass an antiunion law even broader than Wisconsin's, told the *Los Angeles Times* that he would always "sit down with" the "unions that make things," while professing his deep antipathy toward the "public-employee unions, particularly the teachers union."[393] On Fox News' *Hannity* program, Ann Coulter distinguished between "steelworkers, who should have unions" and "public sector workers, who shouldn't."[394] Meanwhile, the Koch-backed Americans for Prosperity organized a bus tour in support of Walker's Budget Repair bill and wheeled out Samuel "Joe the Plumber" Wurzelbacher to transmit their antiunion message.[395]

National Tea Party attacks against public-sector unions revived all the folklore of 1970s producerism: public employees, particularly schoolteachers, were represented as overprivileged, self-indulgent state-dependants, and were often presumed to be female, Black, and morbidly obese.[396] They were, in short, the new welfare queens of the radical right: collectors of unearned income who combined the features of the government-dependent underclass and the idle aristocracy. Even in a state such as Wisconsin, where most public-sector workers were white and male, Walker only had to invoke the distinction between the "haves" and the "have-nots" to call this half-unsaid iconography into being.

Among the mass of private-sector blue-collar workers he singled out for praise, Walker paid special attention to the building trades unions, whom he referred to as "his partners in economic development."[397] By framing his fiscal and regulatory agenda as a program not just in job creation but in blue-collar job creation specifically, Walker managed to win over several construction and mining unions during his first-term election campaign. In the lead-up to the gubernatorial elections of 2010, Local 139, a statewide union of heavy machine operators, endorsed Walker in exchange for his promise to increase highway construction.[398] The pipefitters and carpenters unions refrained from endorsing him but did make contributions to his campaign. In 2012, Milwaukee Ironworkers Local 8 backed Walker's efforts to enact new mining legislation designed to circumvent state environmental laws and pave the way for a $1.5 billion iron ore mine in the far northwest corner of Wisconsin.[399] Walker's most celebrated overture to blue-collar workers, however, was his deal with the Taiwanese electronics manufacturer Foxconn, which he convinced to set up a plant in Wisconsin.[400] Walker boasted that the deal would deliver thirteen thousand blue-collar jobs paying above $30,000 a year. In exchange, the state of Wisconsin pledged to grant Foxconn four billion dollars in tax credits and other incentives, effectively depriving itself of tax revenues from the project for the next quarter century.[401]

The Wisconsin Foxconn deal gave the lie to the idea that private-sector jobs, in contrast to public-sector employment, cost the state no money: the projected jobs were effectively state-funded, yet no share of the profits would return to public coffers. By 2019, it was clear that Foxconn would not be building a manufacturing facility in Wisconsin but rather an almost completely automated research site employing white-collar workers from the neighboring state of Illinois.[402] Since Wisconsin had already paid for job training, granted a series of sales tax exemptions, and built new roads and other infrastructure, the entire project amounted to a lavish act of public investment in one of the largest corporations in the world. Almost nothing was delivered in return.

By the time this failure was made public, Walker had long since dropped any pretense that private-sector workers were to be spared from the supply-side experiment. In March 2015, having consistently denied his intention to do so, Walker pushed an ALEC-inspired right-to-work law through the Wisconsin legislature.[403] A few months later, he repealed the state's prevailing wage (or mini-Davis-Bacon) laws, effectively removing the floor under construction wages on publicly funded projects.[404] Two years later, the average annual wage for Wisconsin construction workers had fallen by over 5 percent.[405] As more astute observers in the private-sector union movement had predicted, Walker's "partners in economic development" were ultimately abandoned to the same fate as public-sector workers.[406]

In Kansas, Tea Party governor Sam Brownback took a different lesson from the supply-side populist playbook. Instead of pitting blue-collar private-sector workers against the public-sector unions—an approach that made sense in Wisconsin, with its proud history of trade unionism—Brownback cast himself as a friend to the small business owner. Vowing to defend the "little guy" against the large corporate interests allegedly aligned with President Obama, Brownback marketed his supply-side tax-cut plan as an incentive to the small entrepreneur and predicted a cornucopia of new jobs as a result.[407] Kansas, he asserted, would become the "best place in America to start and grow a small business."[408]

True enough, most of Brownback's business backers were not corporations, but neither could they be described as uniformly small. Instead, they came from the world of private, unincorporated business and alternative private investment represented by the likes of the billionaire Koch brothers and the Mercers, respectively. Indeed, even among Tea Party governors, Brownback was unusually well connected to Koch Industries, which was headquartered in his state. The Kansas chapter of the Mercer-backed Club for Growth (headed by Governor Brownback's chief of staff), the Koch-funded Kansas Policy Institute (headed by a former aide to Charles Koch), and Americans for Prosperity all played an important role in shepherding Brownback to victory and pushing his "small business" agenda once in office.[409] Even the Kansas Chamber of Commerce, the venerable small business association, was chaired by a former advisor to the not-so-small Koch brothers.[410]

Brownback was one of several incoming Tea Party Republicans to take counsel from Arthur Laffer in preparing their assault on public revenues. After assuming office in early 2011, he personally invited Laffer to work with the Kansas Department of Revenue on a supply-side tax-cut plan.[411] Released in January 2012, the final draft followed the example of Reagan's individual income tax cuts of 1981, which Laffer and a first generation of supply-side populists had especially designed to appeal to both wage earners and small business owners. The bill proposed to cut the highest income tax rate by 25 percent while offering smaller rate reductions to those on lower incomes. Brownback went beyond Reagan, however, by calling for the complete elimination of all nonwage income on pass-through businesses such as sole proprietorships, limited liability companies, and Subchapter S corporations. The entire marketing exercise rested on the premise that any enterprise organized in pass-through form (and therefore subject to the individual rather than the corporate income tax) was equivalent to a small business—an equation that made some sense in the early 1980s but was wildly off base in the 2010s, when many more large businesses were operating in the unincorporated form of the pass-through.[412] Although the bill did eliminate state income taxes for hundreds of genuine small businesses, it inevitably delivered much greater numerical returns to the largest limited liability companies. Astonishingly, this included the many LLCs operating under the Koch umbrella.[413]

Brownback's radical supply-side experiment wreaked havoc on the state's budget and failed to deliver the free lunch promised by Laffer and his acolytes. The so-called small business tax exemption simply incentivized businesses and high-income earners to reclassify their earnings as pass-through nonwage income, resulting in a much deeper budget loss than anticipated.[414] For a state that had previously collected 40 percent of its revenue from income taxes, the solution of making up the difference with sales taxes (as Laffer and Moore prescribed) was easier said than done. By Laffer and Moore's own measures, the Kansas experiment failed miserably. Between early 2013, when the tax cuts took effect, and mid-2017, when they were repealed over Brownback's veto, Kansas's private-sector job creation lagged behind all states except Oklahoma. During the same period, the state's economic growth rate was lower than that of its five neighbors.[415] In early 2014, both Standard and Poor's and Moody's downgraded the state's bond ratings, citing the tax cuts as well as a Supreme Court ruling ordering the Kansas legislature to restore funding to public schools as confirmation of budgetary woes ahead.[416] The Kansas supply-side experiment was so counterproductive that it incited a rebellion among small business owners, many of whom had supported Brownback when he first came into office.[417]

Even the most conservative construction associations—natural allies of the early Brownback administration—were burned by his budgetary ineptitude. Antiunion trade organizations such as the Associated Builders and Contractors (ABC) and the Associated General Contractors of America (AGC) have long called for lower taxes on pass-through business income, reflecting the fact that the vast majority of their members are organized as sole proprietorships, limited liability companies, or S corporations.[418] Both organizations applauded when Brownback and a dozen other Tea Party legislators put an end to Project Labor Agreements, or PLAs—collectively bargained contracts that apply to union and nonunion contractors alike.[419] When Brownback appointed the owner of a family construction business as the head of the Kansas Department of Transport, it seemed that his political pact with building contractors was unbreakable.[420] The same business owners were less impressed, however, when the state was forced to divert more than $2 billion in funds from the Kansas Department of Transport to make up for budgetary shortfalls in the state's general fund.[421] Two years after Brownback's tax cuts went into effect, the Kansas Contractors Association complained that the state's raiding of public highway funds was costing them jobs, not creating them.[422] Brownback's tax cuts had served as a crash course in public finance, alerting small business owners to the fact that much of their "private-sector" profit-making was indirectly dependent on public money.

By the time of Trump's presidential campaign in 2016, supply-side experiments in Wisconsin and Kansas looked like a resounding failure. Not only were

Walker and Brownback's closest business allies questioning the wisdom of a radical tax cut agenda that dried up contracts and paralyzed job creation, but state-level Republican Parties were also splitting apart as moderates attempted to clean up the damage. But rather than take these failures as a warning sign, the Republican administration under Trump took inspiration from them.[423] Despite early speculation that Trump represented a radical break with the neoliberal status quo, it was these state-level experiments in supply-side economics that served as a model for his tax cut legislation of 2017.

TRUMP, THE TEA PARTY, AND THE "SMALL BUSINESS" INSURRECTION

For much of the 2016 presidential campaign, progressive commentators struggled to comprehend the foundations of Trump's popular support. Many simply assumed that the passion he unleashed was a long-overdue reaction to the decades of wage stagnation endured by the industrial working class; an ugly, perhaps misguided, but ultimately understandable response to the neoliberal era of endless free trade agreements and deindustrialization. According to this analysis, it was only natural that Trump would find a major support base among the white manufacturing workers of the rural Midwest and Northeast. After all, he had assiduously targeted this demographic during his campaign. For a year or so, under the guidance of Steve Bannon, Trump seemed to be championing the kind of protectionist "blue-collar" welfarism once entertained by Nixon—erstwhile friend of the hard-hat worker—and later embodied by former Nixon advisor Patrick Buchanan.[424] It was this persona (one of several adopted by Trump in 2016) that explains much of the early confusion regarding his real political intentions.

But while Trump's pandering to Rust Belt Democrats won him critical margins in Ohio and Pennsylvania, the few hundred thousand industrial workers who voted for him were hardly sufficient to constitute a long-term advantage.[425] Nor were they representative of Trump crusaders as a whole, the most zealous of whom were first politicized by the Tea Party movement. By all indications, Tea Partiers transferred their allegiance to Trump en masse during the 2016 elections, and small business owners have remained his most loyal acolytes.[426] Their long insurgency was catalyzed by the collapse of business and housing wealth at the end of the millennial property boom. Their rage intensified when a mixed-race president enacted a moderately ambitious federal stimulus program and attempted to expand health care for low-income Americans. It reached a fever pitch with the arrival of the coronavirus pandemic and the threat of state-mandated public health measures. And it exploded into direct action when their chosen president failed to receive a second term in office. More than one-third of those who stormed the Capitol on January 6, 2021, were small business owners and self-employed professionals.[427] The two militias that were most active in the riots—the Oath Keepers and the Proud Boys—had a history of defending white landowners and small businesses against federal law enforcement, petty criminals, and left-wing rioters.[428] Proud Boys leader Henry "Enrique" Tarrio, who was later convicted of seditious conspiracy charges for his role in the riot, was himself the owner of a small private security company in Miami. He was first drawn to the Proud Boys because of its "small business values." Most members of his Miami chapter were also small business owners who embraced the fraternity's motto of "Glorifying the Entrepreneur."[429] What all of this makes clear is the relatively insignificant role of the industrial working class in the Trump insurgency. It was the political convulsions of the small business sector—not the long saga of deindustrialization—that gave birth to the current cycle of far-right populism.

Although the original Tea Party favorite was Ted Cruz, who told the *Wall Street Journal* that "Republicans are and should be the party of small business and entrepreneurs,"[430] it quickly became clear that Trump personified the spirit of the movement much more convincingly than his rival. More than any other Republican candidate, Trump projected the image of the no-nonsense businessman who had started off "small" and made it "big" in the world of "blue-collar" production. Rewriting his biography to obscure his considerable dependence on family wealth, he presented himself to the world as the quintessential self-made man who had risen from a "relatively small real estate company based in Brooklyn" to make his fortune in the "best block of real estate anywhere in the world," New York City.[431] For all his billions, Trump was fluent in the language of small business resentment. "I've never had the 'security' of being on the government payroll," he boasted, "I was the guy who made the payroll."[432] Addressing a crowd of small business owners invited to the White House in the first months of his presidency, he told them: "I understand you. I have been there."[433]

Trump's presentation as a friend to small business proved critical in his efforts to sell his 2017 tax-cut bill to a broader public. Although the bill included shameless concessions to the wealthiest of corporations and individual taxpayers, it was the small business component that Trump and his supply-side advisors relentlessly publicized. In their primer on "Trumponomics," Arthur Laffer and Stephen Moore praised Trump for sticking to his guns when it came to protecting the interests of small business. Trump's integrity on this matter, they wrote, "only intensified our appreciation for his uncanny political sixth sense about voters."[434] "Corporations are not popular with voters," they noted. "Americans tend to think that corporations are faceless and greedy behemoths." On the other hand, "most Americans love small business and the little guy taking on the corporate raiders. It's in America's DNA to admire and cheer for those who risk everything, put out the shingle, and start a small business based on a few thousand dollars, lots of sweat equity and a good idea."[435] In particular, Laffer and Moore congratulated Trump for his proposal of massive cuts to income on pass-through businesses. No other candidate had suggested a tax cut that deep for "small business," they claimed.[436]

The claim rested on the premise that only small businesses filed pass-through income tax returns. Yet while supply-siders could plausibly sell personal tax cuts as a boon to small business in the early 1980s, when most pass-through entities and non-C corporations were effectively small, things are no longer so simple today. In 1981, when Reagan implemented his individual tax cuts for small business and wage workers, the bulk of business income was generated by large publicly traded C-corporations and as such was subject to the corporate income tax.[437] At this time, most pass-through entities were genuine small businesses, the majority of them organized as sole proprietorships. Subsequent changes to state and federal tax law, however, have significantly increased the incentives to organizing one's business as a pass-through entity and as a consequence, the size and scale of the typical pass-through has changed beyond recognition. The first of these reforms was Reagan's second-term tax legislation of 1986, which lowered the marginal rate on individual income tax to a level below that of the top corporate income rate. The second change occurred gradually, as states introduced new legal structures such as the limited liability company, or LLC, which allowed owners to claim corporate-like protections from personal responsibility for debts while filing for taxes on a pass-through basis.[438] As a result, a growing number of companies chose to unincorporate and adopt the alternative pass-through structure, once almost exclusively reserved for small businesses. Today, some of the largest, most successful, and asset-rich companies are registered as private, non-C corporations, and the bulk of all business income is derived from pass-through entities, a reversal of the hierarchy that prevailed in the 1980s.[439] And while it is true that the majority of genuine small businesses continue to be structured in the pass-through form of the sole proprietorship, most pass-through *income* is now being produced by a small sliver of hedge funds, private equity firms, and real estate partnerships.[440] Increasingly, big business "masquerades" as small business for tax purposes.[441] The privately held Trump Organization—a holding company for more than five hundred LLCs and other pass-through entities—is just one of the many vast business conglomerates that have learned to deploy this masquerade to maximum effect. Yet Trump and his supply-side advisors continue to act as if his pass-through tax cuts were a concession to the "little man" and the small business owner. As if translating Trump's own performance of underdog pluck into the language of tax law, the pass-through structure allows the asset-rich conglomerate to hide behind the legal structure of the small business and to reap all the benefits that populist politicians send its way.

When Trump took to the road to sell his tax-cut plan in the autumn of 2017, it was only natural that he would turn to a group of workers who have long played the role of the aspirational blue-collar businessman in the Republican imaginary. Standing against a backdrop of rigs adorned with the banner "Truckers for Tax Cuts," Trump told the invitation-only crowd of independent drivers that he would bring "lower taxes, bigger paychecks, and more jobs" for small family-owned businesses.[442] "For the many American truckers who file taxes as sole-proprietors, S corporations or partnerships," he announced, "we will cap your top tax rate at a maximum of 25 percent—substantially lower than what you're paying now. The more than 30 million Americans who have small businesses will see—listen to this—a 40 percent cut in their marginal tax rate."[443] This, he claimed, would be the biggest tax cut for small business in eight decades. In fact, it is doubtful that anyone in the crowd would have benefited from these cuts.[444] The 40 percent reduction in the marginal tax rate that Trump bragged about would apply only to the wealthiest of pass-through business owners, including himself. The same could be said for his promised repeal of the estate tax.[445]

At this point we need to ask whether the growing militancy of the Republican right can be adequately explained as the triumph of small over big business, as Tea Party candidates and Trump himself would have us believe. Even the most sophisticated of commentators have taken the Tea Party at its word on this point.[446] But as Trump's example should remind us, this is less an alliance of the small against the big than an insurrection of one form of capitalism (the private, the closely held or unincorporated, and often family-based) against another (the corporate, the publicly traded, and shareholder-owned). If it is true that most family enterprise was confined to the small business sector in the 1980s, while listed corporations accounted for the bulk of big business, this shorthand no longer applies today, as more and more large companies go private and high-powered hedge funds or private equity firms operate in the unincorporated form of the limited liability company.

The constituency of the insurrectionist right that brought Trump to power stretches from the smallest of businesses to the most rambling of dynasties and crucially depends on the alliance between the two. Without its radiating network of subcontractors, the dynastic enterprise would collapse as a political and economic force, while the many small business owners that gravitate toward a figure such as Trump are convinced that their own fortunes rise and fall along with his. In industries such as construction, real estate, and trucking, closely held or outright private, often family-owned companies dominate at every level of the subcontracting chain and businesses that preside over vastly different asset holdings are tightly implicated in each other's fortunes.[447] A small construction firm is dependent on the contract-generating capacities of the largest of real estate dynasties in much the same way that the smallest of Amway business units is structurally enmeshed in the expansion of the DeVos and Van Andel clans. While the relationship between these differently sized businesses is by its nature hierarchical (and in the case of the Trump organization very often abusive), as genuine owner-managers the smallest and largest of companies share a common set of interests that does not extend to the dependent worker or misclassified independent contractor.[448] As one small business owner explained when interrogated on his passion for Trump: "In all my years in business, I've never been paid by a poor man. I am paid by someone who is rich."[449]

It is surely no accident that the most significant donors to the Tea Party and Trump hail from the same world of privately held, family-controlled capitalism that produced Trump himself.[450] In 2020, Forbes named Koch Industries as the largest privately held company in the United States. The Mercer family, which did so much to facilitate Trump's road to power, owes its wealth to Renaissance Technologies, a privately held hedge fund that as an LLC was subject to the so-called "small business" tax on pass-through income. Trump's education secretary, Betsy DeVos, née Elizabeth Prince, was born into a business dynasty that made its fortune through the privately held Prince Corporation.[451] When she married Dick DeVos, son of Richard, in 1979, she consummated an alliance between the Prince family fortune and Amway, one of the largest private companies in the country. According to a 2018 investigation, most of Betsy DeVos's personal income derives from pass-through entities such as LLCs and limited partnerships, which means that the Trump "small business" tax cut would have saved her tens of millions of dollars. Amway itself is structured as an S-corporation, a type of pass-through that would also have qualified for Trump's 40 percent marginal tax cut to "small business."[452]

As noted by Doug Henwood, among the ranks of the top 1 to 0.1 percent we also find a whole cast of regional capitalists that we do not often associate with the commanding heights of American capitalism. This local gentry, the owners of privately held companies or holders of majority shares in a family-founded corporation, make up a significant but often overlooked component of Trump's support base.[453] Alongside celebrated hedge fund managers such as Robert Mercer and Stephen Feinberg, the largest donors to Trump's election campaigns included a handful of real-estate LLCs; the CEO of a family-founded and controlled wrestling corporation; the second-generation director of a large, privately owned poultry company based in Arkansas; and the Wisconsin billionaire Diane Hendricks, cofounder of a privately owned building supplies company.[454] These private family capitalists are less diversified than hedge fund and private equity billionaires, but they preside over vast networks of business subcontractors and as such wield significant power in their local communities.

As the scions of private, dynastic capital have seized the halls of power, they have elevated a new set of political associations as rivals to the old. The Koch-founded Citizens for a Sound Economy and the New Right's

American Legislative Exchange Council and its theocratic cousin the Council for National Policy (with close links to the DeVos and Prince families) once existed on the insurgent fringes of the American right.[455] Today their progeny of war machines, from Americans for Prosperity to FreedomWorks and the Family Research Council, dictate the form of Republican Party politics, while the once all-powerful Business Roundtable watches from the sidelines.[456] These newly dominant organizations would have us believe that theirs is the voice of small family business ranged against the vested power of the corporate and bureaucratic elite. More plausibly, they represent a shift in the center of gravity of American capitalism, which has appointed the once marginal form of the family-owned business to a newly central position in economic life at every scale. If the large publicly listed corporation was still the uncontested reference point for American business at the turn of the millennium, it is now increasingly being challenged by a style of private family-based capitalism whose reach extends from the smallest to the most grandiose of household production units.

CHAPTER THREE

Infinite Regress: Virginia School Neoliberalism and the Tax Revolt

I now turn from supply-side economics to Virginia school neoliberalism and the role it played in the fiscal counterrevolution of the last half century. The focal point of this and the following chapter is James McGill Buchanan, the founding figure of Virginia school "public choice" neoliberalism, who dedicated his life's work to the task of limiting public spending and decrying the abuses of public debt. Despite his intellectual stature, Buchanan's political interventions are less well known than those of the supply-siders. A prolific writer whose work seemed to bear on the more abstruse questions of constitutional economics, Buchanan was coy about his forays into public affairs. Although his ongoing preoccupations with majority rule, deficit finance, and "intergroup" redistribution were identical to those of conservative southern Democrats at midcentury, he only rarely and tangentially made explicit the link between his scholarly reflections and contemporary political events. As a philosopher of constitutional order, Buchanan defended his neutrality vis-à-vis specific tax and spending decisions: he was, he insisted, only interested in establishing the rules of the game; let the players themselves determine within-game choices and outcomes.[1] Richard E. Wagner, a former student and collaborator, contends that Buchanan eschewed the kind of engagement with legislatures or executive agencies common among other prominent economists and instead "spent his career almost exclusively as a thinker."[2] The widespread perception of Buchanan as primarily an intellectual authority encounters surprisingly little pushback from the critical literature.[3]

In fact, Buchanan's political engagements were far more consequential than is commonly supposed. As this chapter will show, not only was he personally involved in drafting the first tax and spending initiative in California in the early 1970s, but his ideas on constitutional tax and spending limits, the supermajority vote, and political strategy were also actively adopted by the political entrepreneurs who drove the tax revolt of the late 1970s and 1980s. Nor was Buchanan's political impact limited to local and state government. Buchanan was a key player in efforts to draft and enact a federal balanced budget amendment in the 1970s. He would remain closely involved in this campaign as the movement itself passed from the hands of bespoke antitax outfits in the 1970s to Charles Koch's Citizens for a Sound Economy in the 1990s and its later Tea Party offshoots. There can be no doubt that Buchanan performed active service in the long constitutional counterrevolution that he called for in much of his work.

James McGill Buchanan was born on a farm in rural Tennessee in 1919. He grew up in a family of modest means but considerable standing in the local community. Buchanan's grandfather had been a member of the Farmers' Alliance Party—one of many parties that emerged out of the late nineteenth-century Populist movement—and on this ticket was elected governor of the state of Tennessee in 1891.[4] From early on, Buchanan was expected to follow in his grandfather's footsteps and pursue legal studies at Vanderbilt University. The Great Depression upset these plans, however, and instead he enrolled in Middle Tennessee State Teachers College, paying his own way through school by milking cows morning and night. Five years of military service in Pearl Harbor and Guam would follow before Buchanan, with the help of the GI bill, was offered a scholarship to undertake a PhD at the University of Chicago in late 1945.[5] Within a few weeks at the bastion of "Chicago school" neoliberalism, Buchanan by his own telling underwent a "conversion" under the tutelage of first-generation Chicago school economist Frank Knight, who taught him that economic "institutionalism" need not lead to the market-skeptical views of American institutionalists such as John R. Commons, Thorsten Veblen, or Clarence Ayres.[6] Until this point, Buchanan avers, he, like many other students of the postwar years, was a "socialist," albeit one imbued with the libertarian and populist inclinations of the American South. "We were always libertarians first, socialists second," he reflects. "And we tended to be grossly naïve in our thinking about political alternatives. To us, the idealized attractions of populist democracy seemed preferable to those of the establishment-controlled economy. It was this sort of young socialist, in particular, who was

COUNTERREVOLUTION

especially ready for immediate conversion upon exposure to teachings that transmitted the principle of market coordination."[7] Thus, Buchanan held on to the antiestablishment impulses of his famous grandfather while replacing the egalitarian and redistributive outlook of the American Populists with the free market libertarianism of the right.

In 1957, Buchanan joined another University of Chicago alumnus, G. Warren Nutter, in setting up the Thomas Jefferson Center for Studies in Political Economy and Social Philosophy at the University of Virginia in Charlottesville. With financial help from the Volker Fund and appointments of such key neoliberal thinkers as Gordon Tullock, Ronald Coase, and Leland B. Yeager, the Center quickly established itself alongside the University of Chicago and UCLA economics departments as a key American outpost for the "neoliberal thought collective."[8] It was during these years that Buchanan earned his name as the founding father of "Virginia school" neoliberalism, more commonly known as the Virginia school of political economy to its proponents. What distinguished the Virginia school economists from their Chicago school, Austrian, or German ordoliberal peers was their special attention to the political process: Buchanan and his colleagues sought to extend the rules of market decision-making to nonmarket activities, with a particular focus on elections, public policymaking, and the emergence of constitutions.

Buchanan was happy to accept the "Virginia school" label.[9] But he also helped popularize another more ecumenical descriptor of the kind of work he was doing when he and Tullock set up the Public Choice Society (originally named the Committee for the Study of Non-Market Decision Making) in 1963.[10] While the Jefferson Center had trouble hiding its right-wing sectarianism, Buchanan and Tullock made a concerted effort to establish the newly named field of "public choice theory" as a broad church.[11] The first meetings of the committee assembled such scholars as Mancur Olson, Anthony Downs, Vincent Ostrom, and John Rawls, who shared little in common with Buchanan and Tullock on the political terrain.[12] There was good reason why Buchanan and Tullock might have wanted to reach out beyond their own circles. The Jefferson Center's authoritarian reign over the department of economics at the University of Virginia had attracted negative attention from other university staff.[13] In June 1963, the university administration hired a consultant to investigate things further. His final report confirmed that the center was "rigidly committed to a single point of view": the "'Virginia School,' an outlook described by its friends as 'Neo-Liberalism' and its critics as 'Nineteenth-Century Ultra-Conservatism.'"[14]

With the writing on the wall, Buchanan and Nutter disbanded the Jefferson Center in 1967 and transferred its funds to a private foundation.[15] When Buchanan's collaborator Gordon Tullock was denied a second request for promotion, Buchanan "exercised the academic exit option" and turned his back on the University of Virginia in 1968.[16] A one-year stint as a regular faculty member in the economics department at UCLA, where student activism had reached a fever pitch, only confirmed his feeling that something was seriously amiss with the academic world.[17] The entire experience marked a turning point in his intellectual as well as institutional life.[18] At the University of Virginia, Buchanan and Tullock had produced the first major work of Virginia school neoliberalism, *The Calculus of Consent*, untouched by the wider turmoil that was engulfing universities across the country. "We lived through a different sixties from the chaos that was developing in other academies," Buchanan noted in retrospect.[19] And it was this seclusion that he thought accounted for the book's misguided optimism regarding the state of American democracy. After Buchanan's exit from the University of Virginia and year of outrage at UCLA, the tenor of his work would shift dramatically. Adopting a tone that was at once more pessimistic and more activist, he warned all who would listen that American democracy was in mortal danger and urgently needed constitutional intervention to survive.[20]

Buchanan returned to Virginia bruised by his recent experiences. In 1969, he joined his old friend Tullock at Virginia Polytechnic Institute, at the time a second-tier state university that was only too happy to welcome a scholar of Buchanan's stature.[21] The move to Virginia Polytechnic, situated in the town of Blacksburg was, in Buchanan's words, a "self-acknowledged 'hunkering-down,' an attempt to salvage a personal tranquility of sorts, isolated maximally from turmoil in an industry that seemed bent on self-destruction."[22] As if to separate himself as far as possible from the urban chaos he had encountered in Los Angeles, Buchanan purchased a small farm in the nearby countryside and took pride in his ability to live off grid. "In that turbulent decade" of the 1960s, he recalled, "and for the first time in my life, there were riots in American cities; there were acts of terrorism against citizens; there were threats of even wider disruption in social order. Think, then, what it did mean, personally, to me to be able to live, and to live well, without direct dependence on an electricity distribution system.... Who could possibly challenge my claim to a level of well-being that is, quite simply, beyond the reach of anyone who must, perforce remain dependent on others for even the basic rudiments of living?"[23] While recognizing the necessary complexity of the modern free market order, Buchanan had come to appreciate the "valuational content in Jefferson's ideal polity of yeoman farmers, latterly put forth by the Southern Agrarians of the 1930s," where small government and nativist sentiments could comfortably coexist.[24]

Buchanan's southern agrarian idyll was hardly a retreat from political life, however. In fact, it was in these years that Buchanan began to exercise a real influence on the constitutional processes he studied, as a new generation of political entrepreneurs called on his help in fighting for tax and spending limits at all levels of government. Buchanan had fled California in disgust. But it was the then governor of California, Ronald Reagan, who would give him his first opportunity to translate his thought experiments in constitutional change into political reality. It was thanks to Reagan that Buchanan was adopted as movement thinker by the National Tax Limitation Committee, the driving force behind the local and state tax and expenditure limits of the late 1970s and 1980s. As Buchanan's intellectual stature grew, first as president of the Mont Pelerin Society between 1984 and 1986 and subsequently as recipient of the 1986 Nobel Memorial Prize in Economic Sciences, he became the darling of far more powerful actors with ample means to bring his constitutional agenda to fruition at the federal level.[25] Buchanan's final move to George Mason University in 1983 ushered in a close if somewhat fractious collaboration with Charles Koch and his Citizens for a Sound Economy.[26] With Buchanan's blueprints in hand, the evolving Koch network would help drive the intensified Republican counterrevolution of the 2010s, when Tea Party extremists resorted to the radical brinkmanship of threatened debt default to enforce the sober rule of balanced budgets.

REVOLUTION AND COUNTERREVOLUTION

As an interpreter of the American constitution, Buchanan aligned himself with the states' rights tradition of Thomas Jefferson and James Madison against the fiscal centralism of Alexander Hamilton, contrasting the former's "genuine" federalism with the latter's profligate use of public debt as an instrument of central government power.[27] According to Buchanan's narrative of decline, the American economy had prospered only as long as it followed the Jeffersonian model of federalism. For most of its antebellum history, he claimed, federal government had adhered to an implicit "fiscal constitution" that prohibited budget deficits and debt finance, except for the exceptional circumstances of war and capital works, and placed a tight lid on governmental powers to spend and redistribute wealth.[28] This constitutional architecture had been progressively dismantled, however, first with the "horrible civil war of the 1860s," which put an end to "viable federalism" and saw the federal government impose its will on recalcitrant Southern states, and second, with the "constitutional revolution" of 1936, when the Supreme Court lent its imprimatur to Franklin Roosevelt's New Deal and effectively "rewrote the political economic constitution" along Keynesian lines.[29] Buchanan understood this "constitutional revolution" as an egregious violation of Jeffersonian federalism.[30] With this decision, the Supreme Court found that the general welfare clause of the Constitution—Article 1, Section 8, Clause 1—authorized the federal government to levy taxes and expend funds for a range of new welfare programs that were evidently not enumerated in the original text: Social Security, welfare, workers' compensation, and unemployment benefits. In so doing, it trod all over the autonomous police power of states, forcibly enrolling them in a federal welfare structure they had not agreed to and dictating the terms on which benefits were to be financed and disbursed.

But if the New Deal amounted to a "revolution by default," the same could not be said of the "post–New Deal follies" that ensued.[31] With the generalization of the progressive income tax during World War II, Democratic and Republican administrations from that of Harry S. Truman onward steadily increased the federal government's taxing and spending powers to pay for everything from national infrastructure to expanded social welfare programs and national defense.[32] Buchanan feared that the seemingly unstoppable momentum of the federal power of taxation was forcing productive citizens to pay for public services that other "unproductive and essentially parasitic members of society" benefited most from.[33] As southern Blacks and poor whites threatened to emerge as a numerical electoral majority, Buchanan became increasingly alert to the dangers of majority rule itself, especially in the context of expanding fiscal transfers.[34] What could be expected when the unproductive, nontaxpaying poor got to decide on the disposition of an ever more generous federal budget? What would stop the voting majority from sucking up all the wealth of the taxpaying minority? His fears were intensified by the rulings of the Supreme Court on matters relating to the disposition of public and private property and the widening of the franchise.

Buchanan and Tullock's *Calculus of Consent*, a founding text of Virginia school public choice theory, published in 1962, was written against the background of mounting federal court challenges to the prerogatives of white property owners. In 1948, for instance, the Supreme Court ruled that states could no longer enforce racial covenants in real estate, a move it had previously hesitated to make because such covenants were included in private contracts. Without mentioning the *Shelley v. Kraemer* case by name, Buchanan and Tullock intimated that "municipal zoning" decisions of this kind threatened the basic rules of freedom of contract and amounted to the forcible confiscation and redistribution of private wealth at the hands of a distant elite.[35]

Subsequent judicial decisions regarding the electoral divisions employed by southern states made the threat more immediate. The landmark 1962 Supreme Court ruling in *Baker v. Carr* arose from a lawsuit against Buchanan's home state of Tennessee, which had not reviewed the composition of its voting districts since 1901. This posture of benign neglect with regard to electoral districts was one of the most significant methods by which conservative southern Democrats maintained their power over state lawmaking.[36] By failing to reapportion districts as people moved to the cities for work, conservative legislators ensured that the rural white property owners who habitually supported them were massively overrepresented at the expense of urban dwellers.

The *Baker v. Carr* case was wending its way through the federal courts at the time Buchanan and Tullock were drafting *The Calculus of Consent*. By Tullock's own admission, the case and its potential outcome were what drove the book's obsessive concern with the redistributive consequences of majority rule.[37] "Let us suppose that a constitution is adopted which openly and explicitly states that net income transfers among individuals and groups will be carried out by simple majority voting," they wrote, before predicting that "in this situation, it seems clear that the maximum possible departure from rational behavior in choosing the amount of redistribution could be present. The individuals in a successful majority coalition could impose net taxes on the minority and receive subsidies for themselves.... It seems certain that 'redistribution'...will be carried relatively 'too far' under these conditions."[38] With its final ruling on the *Baker v. Carr* case, released in March 1962, the Supreme Court held that state redistricting was indeed a justiciable question that could be legitimately monitored by the federal courts. The decision opened the door to a quick succession of test cases that would establish the "one person, one vote" standard for state electoral practices, ultimately paving the way to the Voting Rights Act of 1965.

Readers of *The Calculus of Consent* could be forgiven for failing to pick up these undercurrents. Despite the oblique references to the *Baker v. Carr* case peppered throughout the text, Buchanan and Tullock framed the book as a work of positivist political science and adopted a posture of scrupulous neutrality when it came to moral a priori.[39] The book set out to understand the foundations of constitutional democracy by deducing its emergence from the internal logic of voluntary exchange. Drawing on the tools of game theory, modern welfare economics, and Pareto efficiency, their thought experiment sought to identify the kind of political constitution that self-interested individuals would be most likely to choose, if they were unaware at the outset what resources they would dispose of once the constitution was up and running.[40]

Although the object of analysis was collective political order, Buchanan and Tullock were adamant that methodological individualism was the most appropriate framework for arriving there.[41] In his earlier work, Buchanan had established that the process of market exchange was the most efficient form of collective decision-making because it allowed each individual to express his will without sacrificing anything to the "organicist" fantasy of social welfare.[42] If we are to credit the axioms of rational choice economics, after all, market transactions are by definition consensual, and all parties are left better off after entering a contract. With this ideal in mind, Buchanan and Tullock sought to imagine a voting process that would approximate market logic as closely as possible: each individual vote, in this framework, would deliver an equivalent result in terms of interests represented, and no individual casting his vote would expect to suffer net harm at the hands of other voters. If extended to tax and spending decisions, this would mean that voters would receive only the goods they had chosen to pay for in the form of taxes. Individual voters would thus agree to taxation on a quid pro quo basis, consenting to taxes only in proportion to their consumption of public goods.

While it was easy to conjure up such an ideal outcome through thought experiment, it had to be acknowledged that the political process would not so readily yield this kind of quid pro quo consensus. After all, individual voters could have equal voice in the voting process and still be subjected to collective outcomes that went counter to their interests. Indeed, when a vote was determined by simple majority rule, Buchanan and Tullock pointed out, it was inevitable that the minority would at times suffer net losses at the hands of the collective.[43] This, they argued, was especially the case in an environment where poorer voters were increasingly called upon to vote on tax and spending decisions that could involve significant benefits to themselves (as consumers) and considerable harm to others (as taxpayers). "Majority rule allows members of the decisive coalition to impose external costs on other individuals in the group, costs that are not adequately taken into account in the effective decisions," they wrote.[44] "*Any* project yielding general benefits, quite independently of cost considerations, will be supported by the dominating majority if they are successful in imposing the full tax of the project on the shoulders of the minority."[45] The result would be "serious resource wastage" and overinvestment in public goods that would be better produced in the private sector.[46]

Buchanan and Tullock's efforts to model the voting process on voluntary market exchange led to a paradox: after all, the only case in which a collective vote could do justice to individual voters in the same way as the market was one where the outcome was pure consensus.[47] On this point, they deferred to the Swedish political philosopher Knut Wicksell, who in a different context had proposed the unanimity vote as the ideal horizon of democratic decision-making.[48] It was unlikely, however, that Wicksell's unanimity rule would work in anything but the smallest groups, since the costs involved in reaching consensus with each political decision would quickly outweigh the benefits. Like Wicksell, then, Buchanan and Tullock conceded that a compromise had to be reached, but one that was more respectful of individual dissent than the default majority rule. And like Wicksell, they concluded that some species of supermajority vote was the best alternative to outright consensus.[49] This, they argued, was precisely the outcome that the self-interested individuals in their imagined constitutional convention would reach if asked to come up with a minimal set of rules for some future political order. Acting under a veil of ignorance and unaware of whether they would end up rich or poor, rational individuals would inevitably turn to the supermajority vote as a way of protecting their possible future wealth from the envious designs of the minority. The supermajority vote, Buchanan and Tullock insisted, was not the same thing as simple minority rule, since its power to affect the collective decision-making process was wholly obstructive. As a veto mechanism, the supermajority vote was designed to prevent the majority from harming the minority, but it was not equipped with any positive resource-extractive powers of its own. As such, it did not merit the charge of minority tyranny that was sometimes laid against it.[50]

Looking back on his intellectual trajectory some years later, Buchanan drew attention to the chasm that separated *The Calculus of Consent* from his later work. In writing *The Calculus of Consent*, he reflected, "we were optimistic." The book "conveyed the positive, if also normative, message: 'Democracy works, if organized along the lines of the American constitutional republic.'"[51] Yet "the manuscript had scarcely been mailed off to the press when, to some of us, American democracy seemed demonstrably to fail." Buchanan was convinced that the newly elected president, John F. Kennedy, a representative of the liberal elite, had leveraged the power of dynastic wealth to purchase this position. Closer to home, at the University of Virginia, Buchanan faced increasing pressure as colleagues accused him and his associates of being "fascists." But it was President Lyndon B. Johnson's War on Poverty and Great Society programs that, for Buchanan, represented the most egregious sign of American degeneracy. "The Johnson landslide, the Great Society, the escalation of Vietnam, the draft dodgers, the generalized erosion of academic order, the breakdown in manners, morals and social convention, the emerging generational gap, the commencement of a drug culture, Woodstock, the follow-on assassinations of 1968, the Chicago convention, the Nixon agonies, the Cambodian spring, Kent State"—all served to weaken the fiscal and moral constitution that had hitherto dominated American government and restrained the ambition of New Deal social reformers.[52]

Although Johnson's social programs were hardly as generous in the short term as detractors like Buchanan imagined, they did represent a concerted attempt to remedy some of the shortcomings of the New Deal. By introducing major new initiatives in education and health care and opening up existing New Deal programs to all citizens, American legislation had for the first time embraced the nonunionized, nonindustrial, African American poor within a generalized vision of social welfare. To circumvent obstruction by state legislatures, the federal government very often channeled funds directly to the local level and coupled grants-in-aid with federal mandates designed to prevent local administrators from diverting funds to other purposes.[53] Its efforts to overcome state resistance were aided by the Warren Court, which studiously struck down state defenses for noncompliance and introduced hitherto unheard-of privacy protections for people on public assistance.[54] In Buchanan's eyes, such maneuvers on the part of the executive and judiciary amounted to outright constitutional confabulation: they "assume the authority to rewrite the basic constitutional contract, to change 'the law' at their own will," he complained—an outrage that, in his eyes, justified an equally insurrectionary response on the part of the "people."[55]

The expansion of federal spending under Johnson—and even more so Nixon—was on a different scale than the kinds of government overreach Buchanan and Tullock had critiqued in *The Calculus of Consent*. Debates about the proper scope of federal intervention were no longer restricted to the matter of legally demarcating private from public property, segregated from desegregated space, or the scope of the franchise, as they had been up until the early 1960s. Social expenditures doubled between 1963 and 1969, for the first time increasing faster than defense spending, while state and local governments received huge infusions of federal money allowing them to administer a host of new poverty programs.[56] Buchanan now perceived the threat of a wholesale redistribution of wealth to those who had been newly, if only precariously, welcomed into public space—specifically, the African American urban poor. This, in his eyes, presaged the arrival of Leviathan government. Soon, he predicted, there would be no more private enterprise left to speak of, and private wealth would be under constant threat of expropriation.[57]

Buchanan saw the political events of the 1960s as symptomatic of a deep moral and fiscal "sickness."[58] As the decade progressed, the willingness of the federal government to continue financing the welfare state despite rising inflation and budget deficits confirmed Buchanan's fears that the moral and fiscal constitution of the United States was in mortal danger.[59] Although he had been willing to tolerate the limited Keynesianism of the New Deal, whose economic benefits were restricted to working white men, he felt that the Great Society had gone one step too far by funding groups of people—in particular, the welfare poor, Black Power militants, and student activists—who had no respect for the basic institutions of family, property, and nation.[60] The diagnosis of crisis was a familiar one, but Buchanan was unique among the American neoliberals in thinking that it demanded a *constitutional* solution above and beyond the specific monetary and fiscal salves proposed by his peers.[61]

The social and political turmoil of the late 1960s led Buchanan to rethink the premises of *The Calculus of Consent*. The book's claim to novelty resided in its refusal of moral and normative a priori. The entire exercise rested on the notion that constitutional order could be expected to emerge by pure consent, assuming only the free will of self-interested individuals at the outset. In fact, as noted by Jacob Jensen, the project was hardly free of normative a priori.[62] In elevating market choice above all other values, Buchanan very deliberately delinked the question of economic freedom from that of economic power. The "inequalities present in market choice are inequalities in individual power and not in individual freedom," he asserted, thus implying that inequalities in power were beyond debate—a matter of universal consensus.[63] Yet nothing in Buchanan's work thus far could explain how such consensus was justified or enforced. Indeed, economic freedom, as he then understood it, implied a complete absence of coercion.[64] And if there was no coercion in market choice, then there was no need to explain how individuals came to accept the inviolability of property rights and the unequal distribution of wealth. Universal consent to economic inequality could be assumed as an anthropological a priori. Soon after the publication of *The Calculus of Consent*, Buchanan would begin to question this assumption. In the *Limits of Liberty: Between Anarchy and Leviathan*, published in 1975, he found fault with his own earlier work and that of other libertarians for espousing a kind of romantic anarchism.[65] In positing freedom of contract among individuals already endowed with property, he charged, what libertarians had failed to account for was the necessary role of nonconsensual state violence in enforcing property rights in the first place. It was easy enough to overlook this problem in the 1960s, Buchanan reflected, when a general social consensus still prevailed regarding the inviolability of basic property rights. But with the militant left-wing movements of the 1970s, it could no longer be assumed that all actors subscribed to these foundational premises, and the need to impose them by force became intellectually and politically unavoidable.[66] Thus, Buchanan abandoned the immanentist contractarianism of *The Calculus of Consent* in favor of a theory of social contract embedded in external, deliberately enforced, and not necessarily consensual obligations. "When he recognizes that there are limits to the other-regardingness of men, and that personal conflict would be ubiquitous in anarchy," Buchanan wrote, "the extreme individualist is forced to acknowledge the necessity of some enforcing agent, some institutionalized means of resolving interpersonal disputes."[67] While losing none of his faith in market freedom, Buchanan at this point discovered a newfound respect for the foundational moral values of family and community. The modern free market order, he now contended, had "evolved in application to the extended family in its role as the relevant tribal unit." As long as this implicit moral structure was in place, ostensibly free market actors had been unconsciously subservient to the "family interests" of wealth preservation and a "communitarian sense of loyalty to fellow members of the tribe."[68] The erosion of this moral order in 1960s America threatened the very survival of the capitalist economy and demanded some external intervention—this time on the part of the state. Marking his distance from both the spontaneist market order of Hayek and the free market rationalism of the Chicago school, Buchanan now argued that freedom of contract could not flourish without some stable anchoring in non-contractual foundations. In extreme circumstances, these foundations might need to be asserted by constitutional force.

The new speaking voice adopted by Buchanan in *The Limits of Liberty* was peremptory and urgent. *The Calculus of Consent*, he lamented, had provided "no agenda for state or collective action, in either procedural or operational terms."[69] Buchanan was now openly calling for a new constitutional revolution powerful enough to undo the cumulative damage first unleashed by the New Deal judicial revolution of 1936.[70] By "constitutional revolution," he wrote, "I refer to basic, non-incremental changes ... in the complex set of rules that enable men to live with one another, changes that are sufficiently dramatic to warrant the label 'revolutionary.'"[71] Impatient with his earlier work, he reflected that it was "time for the social scientist or social philosopher to go beyond the manipulation of elegant but ultimately irrelevant models." The time had come "to think about and to make an attempt at reconstruction of the basic constitutional order itself."[72] While others awaited an "attitudinal revolution," more conducive to the free market, Buchanan urged his readers to consider the need for constitutional limits on the tax and spending process.[73] At the time Buchanan was writing *The Limits of Liberty*, this project was already under way at the local and state government level, as political entrepreneurs fanned the flames of popular tax revolt across the United States.

PHILOSOPHY OF THE TAX REVOLT

For many years, Buchanan had been contemplating the prospect of a taxpayers' revolt. In *The Calculus of Consent*, he and Tullock predicted that the growing willingness of the federal government to confiscate and redistribute private wealth through its tax and spending powers would eventually incite a backlash from rational individuals.[74] By the late 1960s, Buchanan felt sure that a "taxpayers' revolt" was in the offing, thanks to the widespread resentment caused by the War on Poverty and Great Society programs.[75] Here, Buchanan mused that something had shifted in the cost-benefit calculus of the average taxpayer—something that might well persuade him to revise his previous support for the New Deal welfare state. "By a dramatic shift in the prevailing mythology," Buchanan reflected, "the willing taxpayer may become a part of the taxpayer revolution. Whereas he may have previously considered himself to be receiving a flow of benefits from the program as valuable at the margin as his dollar of tax, he may come to feel that the flow of benefits has diminished below expectations."[76] This shift in calculus, Buchanan observed, had to do with the very "publicness" of public services—which, unlike private goods, were liable to become less enjoyable depending on the kind of person they had to be shared with.[77] As the average taxpayer saw the benefits of his taxes flow further and further beyond his family or local community, the less likely he was to feel any personal satisfaction in the redistribution of his taxes. "A shift in the interpersonal, interfamilial, intergroup distributional mix away from that initially anticipated will tend to reduce the overall marginal desirability of the spending program," he noted. "Hence, budgetary reallocations aimed at making public services more fully available to those 'in need' may cause taxpayers not qualifying under the selective criteria adopted to man the barricades."[78]

By the mid-1970s, as we have seen, Buchanan was convinced that only a constitutional revolution could undo the cumulative damage wrought by the New Deal and subsequent affronts to fundamental law. Given the widespread distrust of organized politics evident on both the left and the right, he reasoned, this revolution would necessarily be "popular" in form: it would need to eschew the constraints of representative democracy and bureaucratic party structures and instead avail itself of the methods of direct democracy championed by the likes of a George Wallace on the right and a George McGovern on the left.[79] Further, it would need to impose *constitutional* limits on the government's power to tax and spend so as to insulate such safeguards from the vicissitudes of electoral politics and the temptations of professional politicians.[80] And it would have to introduce specific changes at the level of voting procedure in order to protect the taxpaying minority from the excesses of majority rule.[81] The two mechanisms that Buchanan defended in *The Limits of Liberty*—tax and spending limits and supermajority requirements for changes to tax legislation—would hereafter serve as key planks in his vision of constitutional counterrevolution.

Studiously neutral in his choice of references, Buchanan almost always turned to progressive thinkers when looking for historical precedents for his ideas. Much of his language ventriloquized the American tradition of populist and progressive reform, even when he arrived at diametrically opposing positions on tax and spending. Buchanan's use of the distinction between producers and nonproducers, for instance, drew directly from the rhetoric of late nineteenth-century agrarian populism, while identifying the welfare poor and public-sector workers (rather than bankers, land speculators, lawyers, liquor dealers, and gamblers) as the unproductive parasites.[82] His complaint that the state had been captured by "special interests" was indistinguishable from that of American Progressives, except for the fact that Buchanan's rent-seekers had morphed from railroad monopolists into government bureaucrats and welfare state dependents.[83] With no apparent sense of irony, Buchanan placed himself in the lineage of the American populist tradition to which his grandfather had belonged: "I had grown up on a reading diet from my grandfather's attic piled high with the radical pamphlets of the 1890s. The robber barons were very real to me."[84] It is hardly surprising, then, that Buchanan would follow the Populist and Progressive movements in identifying direct democracy as the best way of countering the power of the new special interests. Casting himself as a heroic defender of the popular will against antidemocratic elites, Buchanan lamented that the "residual fear of demos…combined with adherence to electoral democracy restricted to the selection of rulers, is a highly dangerous mixture" and mused that this "widespread attitude [was] perhaps instrumental in opposing reforms that allow for either direct or indirect democracy to become more influential in politics."[85]

If Buchanan nevertheless recognized that direct democracy was just as liable to majoritarian abuse as government by representation, here again he looked for an alternative in the work of the progressive economist Knut Wicksell, rather than the many American critics of New Deal progressivism who could have served the same purpose.[86] Buchanan's argument in favor of the supermajority vote was formally identical to Wicksell's defense of the unanimity rule.[87] Yet their political motivations were poles apart. Wicksell, who had campaigned for universal suffrage for women and the poor, worried that the votes of the newly enfranchised could all too easily be canceled out by the formation of voting blocs among propertied men. His near-unanimity rule was designed to ensure the redistribution of social wealth in the form of free public services, while protecting the poor from the burden of indirect consumption taxes.[88] Buchanan, by contrast, was concerned that the achievement of democratic voice by southern Blacks and impoverished whites would threaten the hard-earned tax dollars of propertied whites. Hewing to the letter rather than the spirit of Wicksell's thought, Buchanan repurposed the near-unanimity rule as a way of insulating wealth-holding taxpayers from the dangers of redistribution. With the American and European progressive traditions apparently on his side, Buchanan could present himself as a champion of unmediated democracy while nevertheless calling for a "democracy within limits."[89]

THE CALIFORNIA TAX REVOLT

By the end of the 1970s, Buchanan's call to constitutional revolution was seemingly answered in the form of California's Proposition 13. Approved by an overwhelming margin of 65 percent of voters, the so-called Jarvis-Gann Amendment of 1978 responded to widespread concern among suburban homeowners who had seen their property tax assessments ratcheted up under the influence of house price inflation. The amendment introduced constitutional limits on the taxing powers of state and local government. It lowered local property taxes to 1 percent of assessed market value and restricted annual increases in tax assessments to 2 percent per year for as long as homeowners continued to occupy the same home. It also instituted significant procedural limits on the power of government to introduce new taxes or raise existing ones. From this point on, a two-thirds supermajority vote from each house of the legislature was required for any increase in state taxes. At the local government level, cities, councils, and special districts were prohibited from introducing any new taxes or raising rates unless they secured the approval of two-thirds of voters at a local referendum.[90] One year later, Proposition 4, known as the Gann initiative, placed annual limits on state and local government appropriations and forced government to reimburse taxpayers for any spending in excess of these limits.[91] A further constitutional amendment, Proposition 58, was passed in 1986, exempting houses bequeathed from parents to children from market-value reappraisal at the moment of transfer. The message could not have been clearer. In a context of diminished social spending, the family home was to be treated as a protected class of wealth and a convenient alternative to public services—at least for those who were set to inherit. With its trio of tax limits, spending ceilings, and supermajority votes, California's experiment in constitutional reform would soon be reproduced in tax revolts across the country.

In hindsight, it is obvious that the formula has played perfectly into the hands of budget conservatives, imparting a permanent regressive bias to government revenue decisions, whatever the intentions of the government in power. Perhaps more important in the long run than the specific tax and spending limits introduced by these initiatives was the fact that a small legislative minority was now empowered to block any attempt to break loose from these constraints. In the state of California, one-third plus one member of either house of the legislature now wields sufficient power to block a budget, while a much more improbable supermajority is required to loosen the strings on government spending or enact more progressive tax rules. Republicans have been in the minority in both houses of state government for all but two years since Prop 13 passed, and yet during that time they have held continuous veto power over government revenue decisions, with predictable consequences for education, infrastructure, and welfare spending.[92]

How were so many Californians persuaded to vote for an amendment that has crippled the state's governing process and appears in many ways to have worked against the interests of its supporters? And why, after a series of failed initiatives in the 1960s and early 1970s, did the tax revolt garner so much support when it began to focus on property taxes in particular, the mainstay of local government revenue? Although it is no doubt true that the tax revolt could have been avoided if state political leaders had taken more timely and vigorous action to address real concerns on the part of low-income home-owners, this failure alone cannot account for the sheer scale of popular support for Prop 13, which extended far beyond the bounds of the low-income and elderly.[93] At least part of the answer seems to lie in the new role accorded to local government in the implementation of President Johnson's antipoverty agenda and the symbolic importance accorded to local property taxes as a result of this.

One of the effects of Johnson's Great Society programs was to dramatically increase the amount of federal money pouring into large cities and, in so doing, to bring local government decisions under federal oversight. Between 1962 and 1972, cities such as Los Angeles became dependent on federal aid for large parts of their social budget and almost tripled their per capita spending.[94] The opening of a direct line of communication between federal and local levels of government was a deliberate strategy on Johnson's part: by detouring around state governments, he hoped to neutralize the resistance that had often greeted federal welfare initiatives in the past and to directly address the issue of racial inequality at the urban level.[95] But this meant that local governments were now burdened with federal spending initiatives that were unpopular among middle-class white voters. These initiatives—ranging from public housing construction to legal aid offices, welfare support services, local health centers, preschool aid, and employment support for low-income youth—were perceived as radical, even subversive, by a broad swathe of the voting public and were frequently resented by the local government officials who had to implement them. To prevent any misuse of funds, the federal government disbursed resources to local government authorities in the form of "categorical grants" whose spending objectives were assigned by mandate and could not be diverted to other uses. In their first phase of implementation, most federal grants were allocated on a matching basis, meaning that an equal amount of local tax revenue had to be spent for every dollar provided by the federal government.[96] The more federal money poured into these programs, the more local tax revenue went to them also, adding to the perception that private wealth was being diverted to fund the irresponsible and idle lifestyles of the nonwhite welfare poor. By infusing federal money into the local community, Johnson inadvertently transformed the suburban backyard into a battleground over the national distribution of resources.

The topography of conflict had been laid down many years earlier, when federal housing programs were initiated during the New Deal and scaled up after World War II. These programs led to a growing segregation of metropolitan space, as the white middle class was encouraged to flee the inner cities and set up house in the sprawling suburban hinterland. During the 1950s and 1960s, homeownership rates soared among white, male industrial workers and their families thanks to a gamut of federal mortgage protections and tax subsidies, while African Americans and other racial minorities were largely cut off from federal assistance to private homeownership and relegated to the high-rent inner cities.[97] By the time of the tax revolt, several decades of invisible, asset-based welfare had allowed the white middle class to accumulate substantial wealth holdings that they could plausibly attribute to their own hard work and financial acumen. But this same wealth also exposed them to inflated home prices and higher property taxes. When suburban homeowners looked toward the inner city, they could all too easily be persuaded that its residents were profiting unjustly from their confiscated wealth—after all, taxes on inner-city properties were negligible given their low assessments, and most inner-city residents were renters anyway.[98] The fact that most of Johnson's antipoverty programs were directed toward those who had historically been excluded from private housing wealth only underscored the apparent injustice.

These, then, were the larger reasons why the question of property taxes became so inflamed and why a sudden increase in assessments led to a full-scale tax revolt, garnering support far beyond the bounds of those who feared the eventual loss of their homes. Quite simply, local government taxation had come to materialize the difference between property owners and the nonpropertied poor at a time when federal welfare programs were beginning to attend to the latter. As a marker of the dividing lines between those who paid taxes on private wealth and those who were, for the first time, becoming the recipients of redistributed public wealth, the local property levy became a flashpoint for much wider anxieties around the racial and sexual politics of redistribution.

Tax conservatives were quick to hail Prop 13 as a popular insurrection against public spending in general and against "welfare" in particular. Yet surveys conducted immediately before and after the vote revealed a great deal of confusion about the role of public spending in maintaining services that were taken for granted by everyone and even greater confusion about the precise boundary lines between general public spending and this thing called "welfare." Basing their analysis on survey data collected between 1977 and 1980, David O. Sears and Jack Citrin found that when Californians were asked whether or not spending should be increased on a series of specific budget items (as opposed to government spending in general), respondents consistently supported either a continuation of the status quo or, more often, an actual increase in resources.[99] Those surveyed were almost unanimously in support of greater spending on public services that, at least in principle, were available to everyone—the police, the fire department, public transportation, parks, and schools. The one item that was repeatedly singled out for cuts was "welfare"—public assistance programs for the noncontributing poor (the aged, the disabled, and children). Yet even here there was considerable ambivalence. As noted by Sears and Citrin, the word "welfare" was so negatively weighted that when its constituent programs for the elderly and disabled were singled out and presented separately, they received much stronger support.[100] The one exception was Aid to Families with Dependent Children (AFDC), the welfare program for single mothers and their children that was most heavily stigmatized in the popular imagination.

The irony here is that, in most cities and certainly in Los Angeles, AFDC was not funded from local taxes at all but rather from a combination of state and federal budgets. Yet, because this one particular welfare program had come to represent all that was wrong with the welfare state—its alleged corruption of racial, sexual, and economic norms—it came to serve as a symbolic lightning rod for organizers of the tax revolt.[101] The largely unmarked nature of asset-based subsidies to white homeowners flattered them into thinking that their lifestyles were sustained only by private initiative and the intergenerational transmission of familial wealth. By contrast, the welfare disbursed to inner-city renters was heavily marked as unearned and widely stigmatized as subsidizing the familial dysfunction of the urban Black poor.[102]

As Buchanan had predicted, the tax revolt was catalyzed less by a general animus against public spending than a parochial and communitarian desire to reserve hard-earned tax dollars for one's own kind.[103] Convinced of the causal connections between public spending, racial redistribution, and family dysfunction, tax resisters called for the repatriation of tax funds within the confines of the property-owning family. The tax funds that were now being redistributed from homeowners to renters, from whites to Blacks, and from working fathers and their families to fatherless nonworking families would thus be reclaimed for those whom the taxpayer recognized as neighbors, not strangers.

VIRGINIA SCHOOL NEOLIBERALISM AND THE TAX REVOLT

The California tax revolt seemed to confirm Buchanan's intuition that there existed a deep groundswell of popular support for constitutional limits on government overreach. In a long retrospective commentary on the referendum vote, Buchanan and his coauthor, the Australian political scientist Geoffrey Brennan, noted approvingly how closely the results hewed to Buchanan's longstanding prescriptions for constitutional counterrevolution. The tax revolt had "emerged not from within normal 'parliamentary' process and interparty competition, but from *outside* the system" and had availed itself of the instruments of voter initiative and referendum that were peculiar to California's distinct tradition of direct democracy.[104] "The enormous success of Prop 13 in California in the face of indifference and even opposition from most of the political establishment," they remarked, "must surely raise some doubts about the extent to which normal political processes reflect the popular will."

Buchanan and Brennan also commended the amendment for eschewing one-off tax and spending cuts in favor of "explicit constitutional constraints designed to be operative over an indefinite future."[105] In addition to limiting property taxes to 1 percent of market value, Prop 13 stipulated that any future increase in state taxes would need to be approved by two-thirds of the state legislature and allowed local governments to introduce new taxes or raise existing taxes only if they could secure two-thirds of electoral votes in a local referendum. Although the use of supermajority rules was not entirely new in California, these requirements were of a much more extensive and constraining kind than anything that had gone before.[106] Interestingly—and, it turns out, not coincidentally—they seemed to very precisely enact a version of the Wicksellian near-unanimity rule for tax decisions that Buchanan had been advocating in his writing for more than a decade now.

There is a distinctly disingenuous tone to Buchanan and Brennan's commentary on the tax revolt, as if popular insurgency had arisen out of nowhere to dictate the terms of a new "fiscal constitution." Buchanan and Brennan were merely delivering to the world what the popular will was telling them. But the role of Virginia school neoliberals in shaping the tax revolt was much more direct and long-standing than this text suggests. In 1972, Governor Ronald Reagan convened a Tax Reduction Task Force under the leadership of Lewis K. Uhler and assigned him the task of drafting the text of Prop 1, a first ballot to introduce tax and spending limits that was defeated by referendum in 1973 but successfully reprised in 1979. Uhler, a former member of the John Birch Society and a veteran of Reagan's state-led attacks on welfare, insisted on conscripting a number of leading economists to the task force. These included James Buchanan himself; his former doctoral student, William Craig Stubblebine of Claremont Men's College; his colleague and coauthor Gordon Tullock; future chairman of the Cato Institute William A. Niskanen; the Chicago school economist Milton Friedman; future Supreme Court Justice Anthony Kennedy; and Norman B. Ture, soon to emerge as a leading proponent of supply-side economics.[107]

Buchanan was enthusiastic from the start: in response to Uhler's invitation, he wrote, "I can attest that, in my view, this is the single most important domestic policy issue that confronts us, and indeed I think it overrides almost all others. Furthermore, it transcends any party or group affiliation."[108] Buchanan confessed his "near-despair and resignation" at the "apparent failure of small-scale attempts to get a taxpayer revolution off the ground" in the past but noted that if "someone of the national scale of Governor Reagan could take the lead," there would be "genuine prospects of success."

Uhler, for his part, was won over by Buchanan's proposals for constitutional revolution and was largely responsible for communicating these ideas to a broader public.[109] Buchanan's work appears to have convinced Uhler that constitutional tax and spending limits, as opposed to legislative action or court challenges, were the most promising way to undo the welfare state.[110] In correspondence with Ronald Reagan, Uhler shared a speech delivered by Buchanan on the eve of the Prop 1 ballot, which reflected on the strategic challenges of enacting constitutional tax limits. "Can the man-on-the-street, the middle American, the member of the silent majority, change his behavior vis-a-vis politics and politicians?" Buchanan asked. "Can he succeed in making articulate his intuitive sense that the time has come to do something about Leviathan? Is he willing to forego the immediate and apparent gratification that he seems to secure from government handouts in exchange for the additional freedom that he might gain in the Third Century?"[111] While Buchanan elsewhere presented tax resistance as an unproblematic expression of the popular will, the speech was unusual in acknowledging the "gratifications" that would inevitably be sacrificed in exchange for economic freedom. Despairing of the progovernment bias of the academic elite and the unreliability of voters, Buchanan suggested that a "counter-intelligentsia" needed to be "carefully and constructively" mobilized to channel the amorphous desires of the people.[112] Uhler underscored the point in his letter to Reagan: "Of special importance," he wrote, "are Jim's comments with respect to the wedding of academia and political leadership into a potent force for our side in the future."[113]

Put to the test in the spring of 1973, Prop 1 combined the principles of budget balance and tax limitation in the one measure. The ballot proposed that state spending could only increase in strict proportion to state income taxes, which would be fixed at 7 percent of annual state income. Added to this was a requirement that any future attempt to increase state taxes would need to muster a two-thirds supermajority vote in both houses of the legislature. It was "this provision, more than any other," Reagan averred, that "generated the greatest alarm in the bureaucracy which knew full well that if the people ever get veto power on excessive spending, the days of spendthrift government [were] over."[114] Although Reagan did everything possible to sell the ballot to "the transplanted southerners, Okies, and blue-collar workers of the San Joaquin Valley and the Los Angeles basin," his populist outreach fell short.[115] The ballot statement itself was impossibly complex, running to six pages of fine print which even Reagan confessed to not reading.[116] But ultimately it was the fear—expertly stoked by opponents—that a permanent limit to state income taxes would mean a corresponding hike in local property taxes that doomed the measure among the blue-collar homeowners Reagan was trying to reach.[117]

Prop 1 was defeated by 54 to 46 percent. But its failure contained lessons for other political entrepreneurs, who successfully seized on the property tax issue to formulate the Prop 13 ballot of 1978. As a result, it was political outsiders Howard Jarvis and Paul Gann, dismissed as cranks by Reagan's task force of expert advisors, who oversaw the first real victory of the tax revolt. After this breakthrough, however, Lewis Uhler's National Tax Limitation Committee, filled with veterans of the Prop 1 campaign such as Buchanan, Stubblebine, Friedman, and Niskanen, went on to establish itself as the principal driving force behind the national campaign to limit state and federal taxes.[118] Especially active in this campaign was Buchanan's former student, Stubblebine, who helped draft the successful Gann Amendment of 1979—a simplified version of Prop 1—and went on to consult on similar tax and spending referenda in other states.[119] All members of the National Tax Limitation Committee, including Buchanan, were later involved in the campaign to introduce a balanced budget amendment at the federal level, a campaign that I will explore in the following chapter. Buchanan's call to constitutional arms was the intellectual inspiration behind each of these initiatives.

DEMOCRACY TURNED AGAINST ITSELF

The California tax revolt must be counted as the first truly significant, because undeniably popular and democratic, insurrection against the welfare state. At a time when business conservatives were launching their own elite attacks on the injustices of the progressive tax system, the referendum vote was an unhoped-for gift to the right, not only because it elicited resounding support from a large cross-section of the white voting public but also because it took place outside the usual channels of representative party politics, availing itself of California's long and vigorous tradition of direct democracy to force change on an apathetic legislature.[120] To those who suspected that the tax revolt was mere cover for elitist designs against progressive taxation, the right had only to respond that the will of the people had finally prevailed against those who would silence them.

The choice of methods was by no means self-evident. After all, the turn-of-the-century Populists and Progressives who first championed direct democracy did so in a spirit that was fundamentally at odds with the 1970s tax revolt.[121] With little hope of being heard through the usual channels of political representation, the Populist and Progressive movements embraced the initiative, the referendum, and the recall as alternative modes of democratic expression that might elevate the voice of the marginalized against the "special interests" of established political parties and corporate elites. And they did so with the precise aim of ensuring a greater redistribution of wealth. Arguably elements in both of these movements were tainted from the beginning: their producerism (which designated certain kinds of workers as truly deserving), their nativism (materialized in antimigration and later eugenic policies), and their familialism (conveyed through the maternalist vision of women social reformers) added up to a very restricted understanding of social welfare.[122] Yet as advocates of popular constitutionalism, these movements were decisive in forcing the Democrats to introduce progressive taxation and income redistribution in modern America.[123] And they were directly responsible for building up the modern welfare state that later tax-revolt militants found so burdensome.

In what was surely a strategic move, the architects of the tax revolt revived the preferred methods of American Populists and Progressives with the express intention of reversing their accumulated achievements.[124] Much like Buchanan, they recuperated Populist and Progressive language for very different ends, designating taxpayers and homeowners as the true producers and denouncing their exploitation at the hands of the rentiers—an alliance of parasitic welfare queens and government "rent-seekers" intent on expropriating hard-earned wealth. As Uhler explained:

> The "general interest" is best defined as the citizens wearing their taxpayers' "hats." The term "special interest" historically has conjured up visions of cigar-smoking lobbyists representing oil, railroads, financial and other business interests. In recent years, there has been a proliferation of special interests. But these are very special interests—welfare rights organizations, associations of grantees of government funds, etc. While the classical special interests sought their "piece" of the public pie, their overriding interest

was protection of their existing wealth positions and curtailment of government interference with their ability to make a profit. The new special interests are largely oriented to obtaining government funds and increasing the size of the public sector as a means of improving their wealth positions. In light of the complexion of many legislative bodies today, the new special-interest groups, largely oriented to redistribution of wealth, are more potent political forces than the traditional special interests.[125]

Buchanan, too, was keenly attuned to the strategic value of the initiative and referendum process. While noting that constitutional reform of the kind attempted by Reagan's Tax Reduction Task Force required the "efforts of political entrepreneurs," he also thought it was in the interests of such campaigns to present themselves as expressions of the will of the demos—that is, to adopt the form of direct democracy.[126] Enacted in this way, he noted, the "opponents of such proposals can be challenged as if they are furthering the interests of establishment elites, who remain fearful of demos."[127] It was Gordon Tullock, in fact, who first recommended this strategy to Buchanan in 1965 when, in private correspondence, he suggested that "instead of trying to develop a quasi-market [to oppose social welfare measures] it might be better to become advocates of initiatives and referendums." Such a proposal "really would give the dirigiste a shock," he wrote, since "they would find it very difficult to oppose.... We would be on their left by their own definition of 'left.'"[128]

As cynical as these arguments no doubt are, they do raise serious questions about the relationship between neoliberalism and democratic process. The fact that the American neoliberal counterrevolution began with a popular tax revolt, achieved through the initiative and referendum process, complicates the idea that this was exclusively a "revolution from above" or that neoliberalism harbors an intrinsic animus toward democracy.[129] The argument is easy to sustain in hindsight, of course, as we enter an era of unabashed attacks on voting rights and blatant plutocratic rule. But it makes less sense as an explanation of the tax revolt, which was the first true political victory of the neoliberal counterrevolution. The undeniably popular success of the tax revolt seems to suggest the rather more troubling conclusion that the long-standing racial divide between whites and Blacks was so potent that it was able to convince a good portion of the white working and middle classes to vote against public

COUNTERREVOLUTION

222

spending *in general*, and hence against their own apparent interests as recipients of public services, in order to disenfranchise Blacks *in particular*.[130] This racial divide, along with the notion that welfare should be reserved for those in normative family relationships, appears to have galvanized a resoundingly democratic vote against the very idea of the welfare state.

Here we are reminded of the dangers that attend any attempt to cast claims to greater wealth redistribution in the language of producerism. As Michael Kazin's analysis of the American Populists suggests, any political movement that begins by distinguishing between the productive worker and the unproductive rentier runs the risk of scapegoating those who, through a history of dispossession, have always been relegated outside the sphere of formal waged labor—Native Americans, enslaved or bonded African Americans, noncitizens, and women.[131] The Populist and Progressive movements were internally riven, containing both overtly nativist currents and historically unprecedented instances of cross-racial organizing. But from the very start, their producerist idiom contained within it the seeds of division. When the figure of the "producer" shifted imperceptibly from the wage worker to the taxpayer and homeowner, as it did after World War II, the discursive and political chain of association between the rentier and the welfare recipient or public-sector worker proved all too seductive.

Political strategists such as Buchanan and Tullock had only to suggest the method of direct democracy to translate this popular resentment into a formidable force for change. What was no doubt less perceptible to suburban tax resisters was the fact that their groundswell of anger was about to be locked in time—its consequences rendered almost irreversible—thanks to the supermajority voting rule that was now attached to routine tax and spending decisions. This was the strategic tour de force accomplished by Buchanan and his followers. By yoking the racial and gendered resentments of white homeowners to the constitutional form of the supermajority vote, they made sure that historically specific and targeted grievances would be set in stone for the foreseeable future. Once the supermajority vote was ratified, its tendency to squeeze public spending would become self-reinforcing, so that middle-class tax resisters would soon discover that they too were consumers of public services and that their services were next in the line of fire, after the first round of attacks on the welfare poor.

Although Buchanan's style of formalistic thought experiment tended to obscure historical precedent, the constitutional solutions he developed were far from novel in the American context. Tax limits and supermajority provisions have a very long history in the American South, where they have commonly served the interests of propertied white citizens against the perceived depredations of northeastern elites, former slaves, and impoverished whites. During the constitutional convention of 1787, antifederalists in Virginia argued against the inclusion of a general welfare clause in the new American Constitution, fearing that it would impose onerous taxes on the states without any assurance of equal representation in Congress.[132] To forestall this threat, they called for the introduction of a supermajority vote to ratify the passage of federal tax bills. Delegates from slaveholder states also called for a supermajority provision to pass any law governing interstate commerce and navigation, both issues of prime importance to the southern export economy.[133] In the end, however, the framers reserved the supermajority vote for matters of national security only—foreign treaties, impeachment, and amendments to the Constitution. Ultimately, they did not want to repeat the mistakes of the Articles of Confederation—the nation's first short-lived framework of government—which had been completely hamstrung by a broad minority veto on tax, spending, and military legislation.[134]

The fears of southern property owners grew more intense in the first decades of the nineteenth century, as northern states became steadily more urbanized and populous than the still largely agricultural South (where slaves were not counted as citizens) and threatened to form a permanent majority in Congress. The introduction of an exceptionally high tariff in 1828 was designed to protect northern industry from cheap British imports, but cotton-producing southern states feared that the tariff would raise the price of the imported goods they relied upon and undercut their export markets by weakening British purchasing power. The unexpected passage of the bill, at a time when the abolition movement was just getting off the ground, awoke southern slaveholders to the fact that their regional privileges could soon be overpowered by a protectionist majority.[135] The resulting standoff led the United States to the brink of civil war, as John C. Calhoun of South Carolina, the then vice president, anonymously urged state legislators to declare the law "null and void" within the state's boundaries. Although the constitutional legitimacy of the move was uncertain, the threat was very real. Ultimately, secession was avoided at the eleventh hour when a compromise tariff was agreed upon in 1833. But Calhoun, having resigned from the vice presidency and returned to Congress as a senator, would spend the rest of his life perfecting an argument for the constitutional legitimacy of state nullification.

While Calhoun contemplated multiple techniques for exercising veto power over federal law—from a dual presidency to an early version of the Senate filibuster—it was the so-called concurrent majority that he considered the most promising.[136] Under Calhoun's proposal, the failure of one state to muster a "concurrent" majority in support of a majority decision in the federal legislature would suffice to block that law within its borders. The outlier state was thus armed with a minority veto power—what Calhoun called a "negative against all measures"—allowing it to ignore specific federal laws it deemed unconstitutional.[137] Calhoun's posthumously published *Disquisition on Government* (1853) framed the question of states' rights in terms of a searing critique of majority rule, where southern slave owners were imagined as a beleaguered minority ranged against the overweening power of northern elites.[138] The nullification of federal law and, failing this, secession from the union were proposed as the southern state's weapons against federal despotism.

A number of commentators from both the left and the right, most recently the historian Nancy MacLean, have highlighted the resonance between Buchanan's constitutional critique of majority rule and the political thought of John C. Calhoun.[139] The conceptual affiliation appears irrefutable, and less damning than might be assumed. It should be recalled here that Calhoun's thinking on majority tyranny was appreciated by liberal philosophers from across the political spectrum, including the English barrister Thomas Hare and, following him, John Stuart Mill.[140] Both writers relied on the formal logic of Calhoun's critique of majority rule in their efforts to imagine forms of democratic representation (proportional rather than majoritarian and district-based, for instance) that were more sensitive to the individual voter. Wicksell, in turn, imported the ideas of Hare and Mill into his defense of the near-unanimity rule—and in so doing, produced a near-perfect replica of Calhoun's thought, without once referencing Calhoun himself.[141] The fact is that the Calhounian philosophy of minority veto could deliver very different political results, depending on the context in which it was applied and the given distribution of wealth and power.

The question of Buchanan's political affiliation to Calhoun is both more controversial and more complex. One would be hard-pressed to find any political affinity between Wicksell and Calhoun, despite the former's intellectual debt to the latter. And Buchanan was not the only public finance economist of his time to draw on the Swedish thinker's work. In fact, Wicksell was undergoing something of a revival in American public finance circles at the time he was allegedly "rediscovered" by Buchanan, and his work was of interest to progressive economists such as Richard Musgrave also.[142] What nevertheless points to a clear affinity between Buchanan and Calhoun is the political lineage that leads from the Bourbon and Redeemer Democrats of the late nineteenth century to the conservative southern Democrats of one-party rule, and the role of Calhounian "states' rights" doctrine in rationalizing their restorationist agenda. As we will see in the next chapter, Buchanan was closely aligned with the political tradition of the conservative southern Democrats.

The southern historian Lacy K. Ford argues counterintuitively that the cult of Calhoun only really came into its own after the Confederate defeat in the Civil War. Calhoun's strategies for defending the South never gained wide acceptance during his lifetime, and despite their apparent vindication in the lead-up to the Civil War, they were not fully embraced as a guide to Southern unity before the 1870s. It was in the half century after the defeat of the Confederacy, writes Ford, that "Lost Cause" mythologists "invented a Calhounian Confederacy, a South united behind a noble if doomed cause."[143] The mythology sanitized the reality of Southern division during the Civil War, but in so doing it enabled the Southern states to unite as never before and to wrest a kind of posthumous victory from the jaws of defeat. The self-declared Redeemers, who returned to power at the end of Reconstruction, thus "came closer to achieving Calhoun's goal of a unified South than their Confederate predecessors."[144] The Southern Democrats, who formed the Solid South of one-party rule after the defeat of the Populists in the 1890s, "also approximated the Calhounian ideal of a South united to maximize its political influence" and retain its racial privileges.[145]

Ironically, then, it was only when Calhoun's purist dream of Southern nullification and secession had become a lost cause that the South Carolina senator achieved his greatest influence. Calhoun was a radical conservative, intent on preserving the racial order of slavery from political contestation; those who followed him were counterrevolutionaries, who invoked the cause of "states' rights" to restore white supremacy, even after its formal defeat.[146] Calhoun had proposed the constitutional instruments of nullification and the supermajority vote to preempt the possibility of slave emancipation; the conservative southern Democrats who glorified his memory were seeking to claw back power they had lost and contain freedoms that had been won. As intellectual heir to the southern Democrats, Buchanan gave new expression to this long counterrevolutionary tradition.

Buchanan's entry into political philosophy occurred at a time when the long civil rights movement was making significant headway in the realm of voting rights and African Americans were for the first time enjoying some of the benefits of postwar public spending, after years of obstruction by the southern Democratic bloc in the Senate. For many conservative southern Democrats, it seemed that this was the time to revive Calhoun's dream in its purest form: in 1956, the General Assembly of the state of Virginia responded to the *Brown v. Board of Education* decision by adopting a nullification resolution announcing its intent to disobey federal antisegregation edicts.[147] Buchanan, by contrast, accepted that nullification and secession were no longer an option. Democratic Party pragmatists had "not been impressed by latter day Calhounians," he noted curtly, in what was for him an unusually explicit reference to the political stakes at hand.[148] Instead, he turned to a more adaptive and defensive solution, which he would later describe as "internal exit without secession": this involved the adoption of constitutional limits allowing white property owners to excuse themselves from the tax burdens of the racially redistributive state without seceding from its territory.[149] If taxpayers could no longer escape from the territorial space of the union or nullify federal edicts, they could nevertheless avail themselves of tax and spending limits to secede from the obligations of the fiscal state.

The strategy was not entirely novel. It had been successfully deployed by the southern Democrat Redeemers of the late nineteenth century, who formally accepted their territorial defeat in the Civil War while doing all in their power to block the new fiscal and redistributive powers of Southern states.[150] The Redeemers came into being as a resistance movement against the fiscal project of Reconstruction, which had invested Southern states with new tax and spending powers and compelled them to provide newly freed slaves and impoverished whites with a minimal level of social welfare. White landowners, who saw state appropriations as a threat to the one form of property that remained securely theirs, bitterly resented these new powers. As historical beneficiaries of landed wealth, they could expect to be disproportionately subject to taxation while having little interest in the public services funded by them. The threat was made real when public education became compulsory for all students, Black and white, across the South, and a new *ad valorem* property tax was established to cover the greatly increased need for public monies. As the representatives and champions of white landowners, the Redeemers fought hard to block the public spending mandates of Reconstruction and turned to constitutional constraints as a way to stave off any future government claims.[151] Redeemer governments, writes historian C. Vann Woodward, "frankly constituted themselves champions of the property owner against the propertyless and allegedly untaxed masses...often describing themselves as the 'rule of the taxpayer.'"[152] The Alabama state constitution of 1875 was the first to enact limits on the collection of state and local property taxes, the first to establish a debt ceiling, and the first to implement a supermajority voting requirement for appropriations—a suite of techniques that would all be revived in the tax revolt of the 1970s. It was followed soon after by Texas, Arkansas, Georgia, and Kentucky, where constitutional tax limits were introduced in 1876, 1883, 1890, and 1908, respectively.[153] Calhoun's defense of states' rights and minority interests no doubt served as an important source of inspiration for these constitutional reforms, but in the postbellum context, the threatening majority had expanded to include former slaves as well as northern elites. Southern wealth holders now imagined themselves as a tax-producing minority under siege from an alliance of nonproductive tax enforcers (pro-Reconstruction Republicans) on the one hand and nonproductive tax consumers (African Americans and poor whites) on the other. This double-sided critique, which depicts the property owner as assailed from above and below by unproductive parasites, has remained a feature of white taxpayer populism until this day.

In this tax revolt, as in subsequent ones, the conflict around fiscal transfers was sharpened by the historically racialized nature of property ownership in the American polity. Why would long-standing property owners be willing to see their wealth confiscated, in the form of taxes, and transferred to a class of people who, as slaves, had once served as their principal form of taxable property? Not all taxes were equal in the eyes of southern Democrats. The property tax was especially resented because it targeted those who were the historical beneficiaries of private wealth accumulation; sales and other consumption taxes were far less controversial because they were borne by all citizens alike, Black and white, property-owning and propertyless.[154] For this reason the constitutional tax limits implemented by southern states focused obsessively on the taxation of wealth but gave legislators free rein to cover their spending needs with exorbitant—and regressive—consumption and excise taxes.[155]

In many cases, the tax and spending limits implemented by the Redeemers remained inscribed in southern state constitutions well into the twentieth century and, over time, were supplemented by constitutional changes to the procedural rules governing the approval of taxes. In 1934, Arkansas became the first state to introduce a supermajority vote for tax increases; it remained the sole state to enforce such a provision for three decades.[156] But with the rise of the civil rights movement and the extension of Great Society welfare programs to the poorest citizens of the South, many other states adopted similar constraints. After 1965, southern states one by one adopted supermajority requirements in an effort to block future tax increases and the further transfers of wealth from the white propertied classes to the Black and white poor. In 1966, Louisiana was the first in a new wave of states to amend its constitution, now requiring a two-thirds supermajority to increase any tax in the state. Mississippi and Florida followed suit in 1970 and 1971.[157] These supermajority amendments were the immediate political precursors to the California tax revolt and very likely the proximate inspiration for Buchanan's near-unanimity rule, despite his overt references to Knut Wicksell.

In some respects, then, it might be argued that California merely imported a tax revolt that had been initiated in the South nearly a century earlier. Yet the California tax revolt was a watershed precisely because of the very different fiscal history of California as a big-spending, big-tax state. When southern states introduced tax limits and supermajority rules in the 1960s and 1970s, they were reverting to form and entrenching what was already a highly regressive tax regime with limited room for fiscal transfers. They simply did not have much of a public sector to pare down. The situation in California could not have been more different. In the 1950s and 60s, public services in the Golden State were ranked among the most generous in the country, and state and local expenditures remained well above the national average right into the 1970s.[158] Both Republican and Democratic governors invested heavily in public infrastructure and poured money into schools, community colleges, universities, hospitals, and parks to keep up with the expanding population.[159] Even Governor Reagan was not able to arrest the momentum.

The passage of Prop 13 was a turning point, triggering a huge but short-lived drop in total state and local tax revenues and a permanent decline in the share of revenues derived from property.[160] When compared with other states, the overall (visible) tax burden on Californian citizens went from well above average in the 1970s to average in the first decade of the twenty-first century.[161] And yet the public demand for government spending did not diminish along with tax receipts. Searching around for new sources of revenue, state and local governments generally resorted to new sales taxes that, despite their inherently regressive nature, rarely generated the same public outrage as the more immediate, lump-sum taxes on property. But they also steadily increased their reliance on less visible sources of income such as user fees and charges—consumption taxes in anything but name.[162]

Comparing the tax composition of American states from the 1950s to 2000s, Newman and O'Brien found that northeastern and midwestern states had much higher property tax rates than southern states in the 1950s, with western states lying somewhere between the two. By the 2000s, however, western states such as California had moved much closer to the tax composition of southern states, where regressive sales and consumption taxes—and, we might add, invisible forms of taxation such as user fees and fines—had long outweighed the contribution of property taxes.[163] Its public services wore the consequences. Californian public schools and infrastructure now rank well below the national average, bringing the state much closer to the South in terms of its commitment to social redistribution.[164]

The California tax revolt was a phenomenal victory for the right precisely because it managed to import a southern tax structure into a high-spending state and to permanently reorient its tax composition in a regressive direction. The experiment would soon be replicated nationwide.

THE REGRESSIVE TAX STATE

By the early 2000s, twenty-seven states had some kind of tax and expenditure limitation in place, while fourteen states required a legislative supermajority and two an electoral supermajority to approve any tax increase.[165] Tax and spending constraints have also been widely adopted at the local level, with one in eight municipalities now subject to some kind of constitutional or statutory limit on its ability to spend.[166] But even in the absence of such constitutional limits, the mere threat of a voter referendum on public spending appears to have permanently altered the landscape of local and state politics, turning electoral debates into contests around fiscal restraint and persuading candidates that new spending initiatives are too hot to touch.

By all accounts, constitutional tax and expenditure limits have failed to substantially reduce overall volumes of public spending. What they have succeeded in doing is significantly transforming how public spending is financed and what public money is allocated to.[167] Hard tax and spending limits have invariably forced governments to take on more, not less, debt, although the type and purpose of bond issuance has shifted dramatically. The public choice gospel that government debt is sinful (at least when used to finance social redistribution) finds an unexpected solution in the supply-side insight that the same debt can be issued ad infinitum so long as the benefits are channeled upward and the risks downward. In practice, then, it turns out that constitutional limits to tax and spending are easily circumvented by nonguaranteed or off-budget debt issuance: the real impact of such interventions is to reserve debt-financed spending for private development and to shift the burden of revenue collection from progressive to regressive taxes.

Since the late 1970s, both state and municipal governments have opted for increased reliance on unguaranteed revenue bonds as one way of dealing with budget shortfalls.[168] Although limits to state and municipal bonded indebtedness have been in place since the late nineteenth century, they do not generally extend to revenue bonds, making the latter a useful device for eluding more recent tax and expenditure constraints.[169] As a rule, revenue bonds incur higher borrowing costs than general obligation securities since they are not backed by the "full faith and credit" of the government and its general taxing power. Instead, they are paid for with the revenue generated by the project in question—for the most part, regressive consumption taxes such as user fees, tolls, and utility bills.[170] The nonguaranteed debt that surged after the tax revolt reflected the growing tendency of municipal government to issue public debt on behalf of private projects: as governments turned to "self-financing" developments capable of generating high consumption taxes (shopping malls, fast food franchises, and sports stadiums), their spending on freely available public space and infrastructure declined accordingly.[171]

One particular funding structure that has flourished in the wake of tax and expenditure limits is the combination of revenue bond and tax increment finance (TIF). In this arrangement, a municipal government issues debt to pay the local infrastructure costs necessary for the success of a private real estate or infrastructure development. The bond is issued on the assumption that the completed project will enhance the real estate value of the area in question, allowing the municipality to collect higher-than-expected revenues even in the face of hard constitutional tax limits.[172] The hypothetical increment in tax revenue, it is argued, will eventually return to the city's residents in the form of better public services. But the promised trickle-down is put on hold for a period of two to three decades, during which time the increment is embargoed for general use and diverted to the exclusive purpose of paying down the debt. If the deal works out, the private developer will have received a risk-free loan for the duration of the project and any resulting increment in its property tax payments will be sequestered from the general tax fund to pay off its own initial costs. If it fails, the municipality is on the hook (even though it has not given its "full faith and credit" to the original bond issue) and will have to raise taxes or cut spending to repay bondholders.[173] In either case, TIF is always a bad deal for renters or low-income home buyers because it makes public service provision dependent on permanently rising real estate values.[174] Tax increment finance is supply-side economics translated into urban development policy. The same dynamic of real estate inflation that keeps property tax revenues rising even when tax ratios are subject to constitutional limits is also calculated to make the city less and less affordable to those who live and work there.

As far as revenue collection is concerned, the tax composition of states—always less progressive than that of local and federal government—has become even more regressive, as state governments vie with each other to offer the most attractive tax incentives to business.[175] In a self-defeating attempt to ensure their future growth prospects through business tax cuts, states have overseen a steady decline in revenues from corporate income and a corresponding rise in sales and consumption taxes. Most states have also expanded the portion of their revenue they derive from user fees, in some cases dramatically.[176]

The regressive drift has been even more marked at the local level, where counties, cities, municipalities, and special districts have performed fiscal acrobatics to make up for diminishing property tax revenues. When forced to choose among invidious alternatives, local governments have shown a marked preference for increasing consumption or sales taxes or introducing new ones. Despite their regressive nature, these are the easiest political option since sales taxes are absorbed into the price of consumer goods and are less perceptible to taxpayers than annual tax returns on income.[177] Much more so than states, local governments have also resorted to the subterfuge of increasing user fees and other miscellaneous consumption charges.[178] Such fees rose from 27 to 37 percent of own-source revenues for all American cities between 1970 and 2008, up from 10 percent at midcentury.[179] The figures are much higher in traditionally regressive tax states such as Alabama, South Carolina, Idaho, Mississippi, and Wyoming.[180] User fees can apply to anything from "recreational" facilities such as parks, pools, and libraries to services that are generally considered indispensable, such as garbage collection, sewer systems, ambulance transport, or parking. Increasingly, municipal courts also collect user charges to finance local criminal justice systems; these include both court-ordered fees imposed as part of the punishment process and fees-for-service to cover the cost of public defenders, private probation, rehabilitation services, or simply time spent in jail. Recourse to penal fees has escalated since the 1980s, precisely when many local governments came under pressure from falling tax revenues.[181]

In some local government areas, typically the most disadvantaged and those that have least opportunity to collect property and sales tax, fines have come to serve as another form of invisible taxation. Following the shooting of Michael Brown in 2014, the city of Ferguson, Missouri, gained notoriety for its practice of generating revenue from a panoply of absurd monetary sanctions. But Missouri has far from the worst record on this count. According to a survey of 2013 census data, Louisiana, Arkansas, Georgia, Mississippi, and Illinois topped the list of states whose local governments relied most heavily on fines and forfeitures as a source of revenue.[182] It turns out that many cities and counties increased their reliance on such miscellaneous revenue sources following the Great Recession of 2007. Indeed, one study of local government finances found that, on average, per capita revenues from user fees grew by 7 percent between 2007 and 2012, while revenue from formal tax sources and state aid declined by an equal amount.[183]

Buchanan had long advocated the pathway toward greater tax regressivity. As early as 1960, in the first edition of his textbook introduction to public finance, Buchanan was calling for the expansion of consumption taxes relative to graduated taxes on income and wealth.[184] Dismissing the distinction between progressive and regressive taxation as "spurious," he predicted that both federal and state levels of government would need to introduce or increase the share of their revenues coming from sales taxes if they were to continue their present path toward increased public spending.[185] Buchanan also assigned an important role to user fees as a future revenue source, especially in light of the fact that they could be included "off the fiscal account" and thereby sold as substitutes for taxation rather than an alternative form of taxation.[186]

As federal and state governments launched themselves into new public infrastructure projects such as the federal highway system and intensified public investments in higher education and health care in the 1950s and 1960s, Buchanan produced a number of influential policy papers in favor of the "user pays" principle.[187] User pricing, he argued, was more efficient than the free provision of public services, not only in light of its self-financing qualities but also because it curbed the otherwise limitless appetite for public services.[188] The user fee encapsulated Buchanan's ideal form of taxation: it targeted consumption rather than production or investment, and it tailored individual benefit to individual burden following the rule of "proportional" (as opposed to progressive) taxation. With per-unit levies on consumption, there was no risk of paying more tax into a general fund than one extracted in the form of individual benefits. The more one consumed in the form of "public services," the more one had to pay in taxes and vice versa, such that every tax-payer could "choose" how much he would be taxed. The user fee, in short, was Buchanan's market quid pro quo transferred into the realm of fiscal politics.

In the 1960 version of his textbook, Buchanan anticipated that a retreat from redistributive objectives was likely in the near future and predicted increases in public investment primarily in the area of defense.[189] But he was soon compelled to revise his predictions, avowing his personal astonishment that "since 1965, we have witnessed an almost wholly unpredicted explosion in federal [non-defense] spending along with incessant demands for still further expansion."[190] As the federal government assumed a greater role in the provision of public services, Buchanan became ever more adamant that such services should be financed by the consumer. The 1960 version of his textbook calls for a greater use of motor vehicle license and registration fees to fund road infrastructure and curb congestion; the 1965 version commends the recent introduction of automated parking meters in city streets.[191] Each successive update recommends more extensive reliance on user fees at the local level for general and recreational facilities as well as the reintroduction of tuition fees to fund state universities.[192]

At the time Buchanan was reflecting on pricing public services through user fees, his Chicago school colleague Gary Becker was following a similar line of reasoning with respect to the criminal justice system. Becker opened his classic 1968 article "Crime and Punishment" by lamenting what he saw as the excessive paternalism of the late twentieth-century social state, whose punitive powers had grown beyond the traditional space of criminal law to regulate the farthest reaches of social life. "Since the turn of the century," he wrote, "legislation in Western countries has expanded rapidly to reverse the brief dominance of laissez faire during the nineteenth century. The state no longer merely protects against violations of person and property through murder, rape or burglary but also restricts 'discrimination' against certain minorities, collusive business arrangements, 'jaywalking,' travel, the materials used in construction and thousands of other activities."[193] Becker was a priori opposed to the expansion of the carceral state and could even be described as a "prison abolitionist" of sorts, albeit one who would scarcely be recognizable to contemporary abolitionists on the left. In his characterization of punitive excess, for instance, he included the growing field of administrative law—incorporating everything from antidiscrimination statutes to government regulation of pollution, consumer products, and corporate monopoly. Indeed, it was the expansion of *administrative* rather than *criminal* law that he found most concerning.

In Becker's view, administrative overreach was regrettable not only because it threatened the fundamental economic freedoms of the market actor but also because it represented a growing fiscal burden on the state, one that in the future was likely to be transferred to the ordinary citizen in the form of taxes. Already in the late 1960s, Becker was concerned with the enormous social costs of an expanding prison system. "Currently about $1 billion is being spent each year in the United States on probation, parole, and institutionalization alone," he lamented, "with the daily cost per case varying tremendously from a low of $0.38 for adults on probation to a high of $11.00 for juveniles in detention institutions."[194]

From the outset, Becker dispensed with psychotherapeutic or sociological theories of crime—the "special theories of anomie, psychological inadequacies, or inheritance of special traits" that Michel Foucault described as the hallmarks of normative or disciplinary modes of power—and instead sought to imagine a system of punishment informed by microeconomic reason alone.[195] Becker, in fact, was much closer to the mature Jeremy Bentham, who in his later work was fascinated by the penological uses of the so-called pecuniary sanction, than he was to the Bentham of the panopticon, which Foucault saw as the very prototype of disciplinary power.[196] As such, Becker posed the question of punishment in terms of a Benthamite calculus of pleasure and pain. If we begin by assuming that the crime represents a social loss to victims and a private benefit to offenders, he asked, what is the threshold of punishment required to deter a maximum number of crimes at a price that is palatable to the taxpayer? At what point does the would-be offender determine that the price of committing a crime outweighs the pleasure she derives from it? And when does the taxpayer decide that the price of preventing and punishing crime exceeds the costs of the crime itself? Put differently and, Becker conceded, somewhat strangely, "How many offenses *should* be permitted and how many offenders *should* go unpunished?"[197]

Becker's neo-utilitarian imaginary saw all human behavior as deriving from an economic calculus of pleasure and pain, where incentives and disincentives to action can be imagined in the form of price signals. In this view, every act has a price, although one that is not necessarily expressed in economic terms (a price signal may just as easily manifest in the nonmonetary form of perceived risk or expected pain, for instance). Consequently, Becker was less interested in the outright prohibition of criminal acts—an impossible task, he observed, and one whose costs would be exponential—than in finding the best way of calibrating the trade-off between expected costs and benefits.

The form of punishment most likely to achieve this aim, he thought, was the administrative fine—a pecuniary sanction that could be issued out of court and liquidated with a simple exchange of money and minimal transaction costs. We could in fact reap all the benefits of harsher forms of punishment much more efficiently, he urged, if we extended the scope of the fine into the realm of criminal law and calibrated its price as a function of the perceived gravity of the wrongdoing. "Is it merely an accident," he asked, "or have optimality conditions determined that today, in most countries, fines are the predominant form of punishment, with institutionalization reserved for the more serious offenses?"[198] Pushing this logic just a little bit further would allow us to absorb almost all criminal offenses within the civil law of torts and thereby translate all wrongdoing into a question of economic harm and compensation. The monetary sanction, in this way, could be established as a universal form of punishment, serving as both a fine for economic trespass and a user fee for the costs of legal services rendered. Becker thus pushed Buchanan's fiscal argument in favor of the user fee into the realm of criminal law and sought to deconstruct the administrative/carceral state with the tools of neo-utilitarian reason.

Buchanan's argument in favor of user fees had an immediate impact on the recomposition of public finances after Prop 13 and has subsequently become a pillar of Virginia school thinking on public-sector reform.[199] As the tax revolt gained momentum, Lewis Uhler translated Buchanan's rather arcane academic writings on public finance into more digestible form and reflected on the likely effects of tax limitations:

> If there were strict limitations on funds available to government, the politicians would probably begin to make some basic changes. To prevent the development of demands for services which cannot be met, the politicians would try to shift the political "heat" by juxtaposing tax costs with benefits.

The politician would say, "we're willing to give you this service, but here is what it will cost *you*, the recipient of the service, not someone else. And here is the user fee or the specific tax that *you* will have to bear." Furthermore, the fee or tax would be more likely to represent the full cost, not the subsidized cost, of the service. This combination of actions would produce a true pricing system and would have the immediate effect of reducing demand.[200]

As Uhler predicted, local governments did indeed find that they had few alternatives other than user fees when faced with immediate and dramatic cuts to their formal tax revenue. In the wake of the tax revolt, even liberal public finance experts were won over, sometimes mustering arguments that were indistinguishable from those of public choice economists to justify both the inevitability and greater efficiency of consumption-sensitive charges.[201] Becker's plea in favor of monetary sanctions has also left its mark, since fines have become a favorite source of revenue-generation for cash-strapped municipalities. And although Becker recommended the monetary sanction as an alternative to the fiscal burdens of the criminal justice system, a distorted version of his program for reform has been realized in the guise of expanded user fees *within* courts, jails, and prisons.[202] The criminal justice system is one of the few public services that has expanded dramatically over the last few decades; to cover these expenditures, state and local government have shifted their priorities from higher education to prison funding, and wherever possible they have transferred costs to defendants in the form of proliferating fees-for-service.[203] Few municipalities offer a better illustration of the long-term impact of Virginia school fiscalism than that of Ferguson, Missouri.

FERGUSON, MISSOURI

The 2014 shooting of Michael Brown in Ferguson, Missouri, was the catalyst for the Black Lives Matter movement, a long wave of struggles protesting the collusion between police violence, the local court system, and the fiscal politics of the neoliberal state. Ferguson, like many other cities across the United States, had seen its ability to spend on essential public services dramatically curtailed in the wake of popular tax revolts. In 1980, the state of Missouri passed the Hancock Amendment—its own version of California's Proposition 13—

which required local government authorities to call an election and win a majority of votes for almost every new tax or tax increase.[204] Small municipal governments were particularly hard hit by the consequent decline in property taxes and were left scrambling for alternative sources of income. In 1991, the Missouri Supreme Court provided some relief by exempting certain user fees from the category of taxes, while in 1995, the passage of a law designed to place an upper limit on traffic fines inadvertently opened the door to the massive use of municipal ordinance violations as an alternative source of revenue.[205] Following these changes, cities, towns, and boroughs became heavily dependent on the revenues extracted from user fees and fines, including the court fines that are imposed when a fine defaulter fails to appear at a court hearing or the multiple legal fees that accrue to the low-waged offender. Missouri state senator Eric Schmitt has aptly referred to this as a system of "taxation by citation," whereby the police are authorized to issue on-the-spot stealth taxes in response to a panoply of often absurd municipal ordinance violations.[206]

Thrust into the public gaze by the murder of Michael Brown, the story of Ferguson, Missouri, is not so different from those of many other local government areas that were left struggling to reconcile mounting public service responsibilities and dwindling tax resources in the long aftermath of the tax revolt. What sets Ferguson apart is the extreme fragmentation of the St. Louis County region in which it is located, a jurisdictional maze forged by decades of white flight and facilitated by the state of Missouri's lax rules on municipal incorporation. Under the home rule provisions that were enshrined in the state's 1875 constitution and effective until the late 1970s, local communities of any size were free to incorporate and to dictate their own zoning laws with almost no oversight from the state.[207] White middle-class residents who moved out of the central city into the suburbs beginning in the early twentieth century at first used restrictive deeds and covenants to exclude African Americans from their communities. But when these were struck down by the Supreme Court in the *Shelley v. Kraemer* case of 1948, they turned instead to municipal incorporation and zoning laws as a way of keeping out low-income whites and Blacks. While suburban tax resisters in Los Angeles could only dream of secession, municipal secession was such an easily accessible option in St. Louis County, Missouri, that it served almost as a substitute for urban planning.[208] Within a matter of weeks, a group of white homeowners could incorporate as a new municipality replete with zoning rules such as a requirement for large allotments or a ban on multifamily housing projects that were calculated to keep out impoverished whites and African Americans. The process was repeated many times over, as low-income whites followed their middle-class peers into the suburbs and African Americans followed in greater numbers after the 1960s. Wealthier white residents responded to successive waves of outmigration by steadily abandoning their old suburbs and moving further and further westward, leaving in their wake an archipelago of independent local jurisdictions. By the early twenty-first century, St. Louis County alone included ninety separate municipal governments ranging in population size from tens of thousands to a few hundred people, each with the legal authority to zone, to tax, and to provide its own public services.[209] The result was an extreme segregation of tax revenues that enabled wealthier communities to finance generous public services at minimal per capita cost while compelling poorer communities to fund dilapidated schools and urban infrastructure at proportionately greater cost to their residents.

When the state of Missouri passed the Hancock Amendment to limit property taxes in 1980, its impact was somewhat belated and redundant. The deindustrialization of St. Louis had been in full swing for over a decade, the city was hemorrhaging taxpaying workers and industries, and property taxes had long been in decline. Meanwhile, many municipalities in the wealthier outer suburbs of St. Louis County had already lowered property taxes of their own accord and replaced them with a new local sales tax.[210] As elsewhere, the introduction of tax and spending limits led to a paring away of progressive taxes on real wealth and a simultaneous burgeoning of regressive consumption taxes, whose costs were always much greater for the income- and asset-poor.[211] After the passage of the Hancock Amendment, municipalities in St. Louis County entered into open competition for mobile consumers and their attendant sales tax revenues. Local government areas vied to poach shoppers and their tax revenues from each other by constructing ever larger, more spectacular shopping malls—a zero-sum game that has unsurprisingly worked in favor of wealthier suburbs and left behind a cemetery of abandoned, almost new shopping malls across the county.[212] The fact that sales taxes are paid by all consumers, resident and nonresident alike, means that wealthier municipalities can offload a good part of their revenue needs onto outsiders while hoarding the benefits for themselves. Many wealthier communities have managed to entirely discard the tax on wealth, which weighs on them in particular, while relying primarily on regressive sales taxes. The poorer towns struggle to maintain a stable tax base and so double down on their own residents to extract the most regressive kinds of taxes.

To make matters worse, the menu of regressive tax options available to local governments in Missouri is even narrower than elsewhere, thanks to a clause in the Hancock Amendment that specifies that even the introduction of "user fees" should be subject to voter approval.[213] This apparently unintentional detail has resulted in years of litigation seeking to determine the metaphysical difference between a tax and a user fee and has made it that much harder for local governments to introduce new user fees at will. For this reason, it seems, cash-strapped municipalities have for the most part followed the path of least resistance and resorted to increasing traffic fines, municipal code violation fines, and court fees whenever they need to make up for revenue shortfalls. According to a 2015 Department of Justice report, the City of Ferguson's finance director simply turned to the police force and exhorted them to write more tickets when faced with the "not insignificant issue" of "a substantial sales tax shortfall."[214] As neighboring communities face off in a relentless, cutthroat struggle to plunder one another's sales tax base, the fiscal fortunes of any one town can change dramatically from year to year. The village of St. Ann, for instance, had been living reasonably well off the sales revenue from its Northwest Plaza shopping mall. But when the mall lost its customers to a competing development and was forced to close down in 2010, local authorities set up radar traps on the highway and ratcheted up court fines and fees to almost 40 percent of general revenues in an effort to make up for lost sales taxes.[215]

For all its notoriety, Ferguson is not the worst offender in St. Louis County. A report released by the public interest law firm ArchCity Defenders found that the small, predominantly African American town of Bel-Ridge collected some $450 per household in municipal court fines in 2014, making such sanctions its largest source of revenue.[216] In Ferguson, fines were the second-largest source of revenue, and in Florissant, the largest town in St. Louis County, fines came third. As a source of revenue, fines have the virtue of being endlessly elastic. The poorest municipalities already issue a large number of citations for unpaid user fees—overdue utilities bills, failure to register or insure a car, expired driver's licenses, or unpaid garbage collection fees. But local police can generate a further mass of fines virtually at will by citing arcane municipal code violations, ranging from uncut grass to loitering or wearing baggy pants. These, in turn, can be supplemented by the many penal fines that await the fine defaulter once she arrives in a local court or jail.

To the extent that fines are generated for the exclusive purpose of plugging holes in revenue, their relationship to public service provision becomes ever more tenuous. Taxation, in this context, loses any redistributive pretensions and becomes a pure act of confiscation, indistinguishable from punishment. If we can speak of a public service here, it has become so threadbare as to consist almost entirely of the act of extracting tax itself. In Ferguson, schools, sidewalks, and streetlights are left in disrepair, while the police and municipal courts—listed as "public safety"—absorb 40 percent of the budget.[217] When Buchanan's recipe for tax regression is pursued to its logical conclusion, the poorest residents—those who cannot buy their way out of public service provision by resorting to private alternatives—are plunged into states of cumulative indebtedness by the mere act of existing in and traversing public space.

Much has been written about the connection between declining public investment in human services and ballooning household debt in recent years. The economists Aldo Barba and Massimo Pivetti have shown how even middle-income, asset-holding households have been forced to take on debt in order to maintain access to formerly public or government-subsidized services such as education, health, and housing, and how this expanding debt burden has come to replace government deficit spending as a stimulus to demand.[218] But while mortgage, credit card, medical, and student loan debt are the usual suspects here, far less attention has been paid to the peculiar forms of debt that afflict the income- and asset-poor as a result of public service attrition. Like the high-cost payday loans that cater to the poor, these burdens remain invisible to the secure wage earner, for whom the flat-rate pricing of user fees such as motor vehicle registration, public transport, and utilities might appear unremarkable.[219] But in areas such as northern St. Louis County, where roughly a quarter of residents live below the poverty line, the mere act of moving through "public space" or consuming a "public service" has become a minefield by virtue of the fact that it incurs so many fees, each one liable to blossom into cumulative debt burden via late penalties, interest charges, and court sanctions.[220]

The woman who works in a distant mall but can't afford to register her car or renew her license runs the risk of incurring an arrest warrant if she is pulled over on her way to work. If she avoids court because she can't afford the fine she is liable to spend time in jail, where she will incur further fees. The man who is behind on his sewer bills may find himself arraigned before court by the Metropolitan St. Louis Sewer District.[221] The household debt burdens of North County's African American residents have skyrocketed in recent decades, in large part due to the increasingly regressive nature of municipal tax regimes. These communities continued to bear the brunt of the subprime meltdown long after the crisis was deemed over: almost ten years out from the initial shock, municipalities such as Ferguson, Black Jack, Spanish Lake, and parts of Florissant were still reporting unusually high rates of mortgage distress and foreclosure.[222] The African American residents of the North County area of St. Louis also report astonishing levels of vehicle-related and utilities debt—very specific liabilities that reflect the rising costs of nominally public infrastructure for those who are most dependent on it.[223]

The disproportionate impact of debt on African Americans, even when compared to their low-income white neighbors, can in large part be explained by their historical exclusion from housing wealth. Following the subprime crisis of 2007, the homeownership rate among African American households in St. Louis fell to 40 percent, a drop of almost 10 percentage points; among white residents, it fell to 76 percent, a drop of only 3 percent. Nationwide, the chasm between white and Black homeownership is at its widest point since the 1940s.[224] However astronomical their debt and however precarious their income flows, homeowners can at least rest assured that their debt is collateralized by property, which in the best-case scenario can be leveraged to access more credit and in the worst case can be liquidated as a way of paying off outstanding debt. By contrast, the debt burdens of the asset-poor are collateralized by little more than themselves and whatever portion of their debt burden they can share with friends and family.

How is any of this debt ever redeemed? The jailing of fine defaulters is one very obvious and dramatic way of seizing collateral, and it is no surprise that debtor incarceration has flourished in recent years.[225] But jail time doesn't actually liquidate liabilities—indeed, it very often plunges the fine defaulter into a further spiral of debt through the accumulation of fees-for-service.

Alongside the rise of debt-induced incarceration, then, we have also seen the return of peonage systems that convert debt burdens into forced labor. With collection agencies now increasingly turning to the courts to pursue even the smallest of household debts, court-ordered wage garnishing has risen sharply and often targets those who are already on low and precarious incomes.[226] Most cities have also extended their so-called "community service" programs—a euphemism for workfare—to criminal justice debtors, so that someone who has accumulated a debt and been jailed simply for accessing so-called public services can now be mobilized to perform municipal service work for free.[227] Permanent indebtedness to the public purse becomes redeemable as a fount of unpaid public service labor.

James M. Buchanan was one of the few American neoliberals who acknowledged the necessary relationship between contractual freedom and non-contractual coercion in free market economics. His theory of constitutional order presumes that political freedom belongs legitimately to those who have already accumulated wealth—the property owners and producers—and that it must be strenuously protected from all threats of confiscation on the part of the rentiers—the nonproductive poor and their bureaucratic allies. This implies that the freedom of wealth holders can only be upheld if we agree to curtail the power of the state to commandeer the resources of property owners through taxation. Any public service provided by the state must be funded proportionately—that is, regressively—since to do otherwise would be to infringe upon the freedom of wealth-holders. If tax regression means that the asset-poor cannot afford to move in public space or earn a living without incurring a debt to the public purse, then the threat of forced work or jail time must be actively enforced. In Buchanan's words: "vague thoughts or promises to cut off...charity in the absence of work on the part of the recipient parasite will remain empty unless there is demonstrated willingness to carry out such threats."[228] The tax producers must be protected from the tax consumers, if necessary by denying both their freedom of movement and labor. This, it seems, represents the logical outcome of the tax revolt.

Constitutional Austerity: Virginia School Neoliberalism and the Balanced Budget Amendment

A few years out from the subprime meltdown of 2007, the U.S. political process was brought to a standstill when Tea Party Republicans forced a showdown on the issue of government debt. Incensed by the deficits which they saw as the predictable outcome of Obama's fiscal stimulus spending, a cadre of newly elected Republicans refused to approve a rise in the debt ceiling unless a balanced budget amendment were submitted to the states.[1] By any standard, this was an act of extraordinary brinkmanship. If the debt limit were not raised in time, the United States would have to default on its sovereign obligations to domestic and foreign lenders, a scenario that could have permanently tarnished the creditworthiness of the American dollar. As it happened, Standard and Poor's ended up downgrading the credit rating of the United States for the first time in its history.[2] The standoff was resolved only two days before the Treasury exhausted its borrowing power, with the passage of a Budget Control Act requiring Congress to vote on a balanced budget amendment in the near future.[3]

Yet less than a decade later, Republicans were overcome with amnesia as Trump, with the blessing of his supply-side advisors, voted in the largest corporate tax cut in U.S. history and approved a $1.3 trillion omnibus spending bill that was astonishingly generous to the military.[4] The Congressional Budget Office, a nonpartisan body that estimates the fiscal impact of legislation, reported that Trump's tax cuts would raise the primary deficit by $1.3 trillion and debt-service costs by roughly $600 billion.[5] But Republicans were less concerned with their tax cut expenditures than the burden of health-care entitlements such as Medicare and Medicaid, and as soon as the tax bill was passed, they began to worry about their impact on the national debt. Almost no one was surprised when the same congressional Republicans who had approved a historically unprecedented tax cut almost immediately rediscovered their fear of deficits and promptly moved to pass a constitutional amendment in favor of balanced budgets.[6] And as anyone who had followed the long balanced budget crusade might have predicted, as soon as Republicans lost control of the House in the midterm elections, the momentum was taken up from the outside by the American Legislative Exchange Council (ALEC), which for many years had been trying to call a state convention under Article V of the Constitution, an alternative route to constitutional change that would allow the states to circumvent Congress entirely.[7]

This theater of the absurd has played out many times over throughout the last few decades, with more than a dozen such bills brought before the Senate and House since 1980.[8] When Republicans win power in Congress they propose a balanced budget amendment, which invariably fails to win the necessary supermajority in either the House or Senate. When the congressional route to an amendment is blocked or when power swings to the Democrats, Republicans seek to bypass Congress by petitioning for a state convention. But although Republicans themselves have never been constrained by the deficit and have each time failed in their efforts to pass a balanced budget amendment—perhaps by design—they have been remarkably adroit at forcing Democrats into a corner. Since the 1970s, Democrats have largely resisted the amendment campaign, fearful that it would mean the complete evisceration of programs such as Medicaid and Medicare, yet only the Democrats have taken the cause of budget balance seriously, and only President Clinton has managed to generate a surplus, at the expense of his own more progressive policy ambitions. In practice, Republicans, with the exception of George H. W. Bush, have been indifferent to the deficit when it comes to their own spending preferences (tax cuts and the military) but adept at maneuvering the specter of catastrophic debt burdens when it comes to the Democrats' meager efforts to fund public welfare.

How have Republicans managed to wield the cause of the balanced budget amendment so skillfully, even when their supply-side tax cuts and military escapades account for the lion's share of the national debt? And why have Democrats consented to a fiscal *danse macabre* in which Republicans reap all the moral dividends of balanced budgets while at the same time enacting extravagant tax cuts, with Democrats typecast as the sober enforcers of spending restraint? After all, before the Goldwater campaign and the presidential victory of Reagan, Republicans were solidly committed to the cause of balanced budgets, even when this meant raising taxes, while Democrats were increasingly won over to the idea that deficit spending (and indeed tax cuts) could be strategically used as instruments of ongoing macroeconomic stimulus. The GOP of the postwar years was dominated by so-called Eisenhower Republicans, who accepted the necessity of New Deal social spending without endorsing the more "functional" uses of deficit spending advocated by American Keynesians such as Abba Lerner and Alvin Hansen.[9] Today, the tables are turned, and Democrats appear to have accepted their position as ersatz "Eisenhower Republicans" (or worse), perpetually whipped into line by spendthrift Republicans brandishing the threat of constitutional debt limits.

Today's campaign for a balanced budget amendment can be traced back to the 1970s, when a new generation of right-wing lobbyists successfully transformed a once fringe issue into a national cause célèbre. But the issue itself is enmeshed in the much longer history of state-level battles around budget deficits, taxation, and racial redistribution that raged across the American South from the post-Reconstruction period onward. The state of Virginia, along with its leading statesman, Harry Flood Byrd Sr., played a critical role in the story of the balanced budget amendment owing to the exorbitant influence of southern Democrats in the Senate throughout much of the twentieth century. The work of James M. Buchanan, intellectual figurehead of the Virginia school of political economy, also proved vital in translating the southern Democratic politics of low public spending and taxation into a general constitutional agenda for fiscal austerity.

The historian Nancy MacLean is the first to have drawn attention to the elective affinity between Buchanan and Senator Harry F. Byrd. Although there is no evidence that Buchanan and Byrd ever met, she notes, "the two men were soul mates when it came to fiscal policy and social reform."[10] MacLean's pathbreaking work on the history of Virginia school public choice has made it impossible to ignore the deep resonance between Buchanan's enduring philosophical concerns and the political context of midcentury Virginia. Yet MacLean has little to say about the multidecade movement to pass a federal balanced budget amendment—a campaign that Byrd initiated in the 1950s and Buchanan helped revive in the tumultuous 1970s. Having translated Senator Byrd's early efforts to mandate balanced budgets into an elaborate philosophy of constitutional austerity, Buchanan was personally involved in efforts to draft and relaunch the balanced budget amendment in the 1970s, and thereafter lent his incomparable intellectual authority to a succession of movement organizers, who have kept the cause alive to this day.

This chapter traces the political and intellectual history of the balanced budget amendment in an effort to illuminate how a regionally specific formula for austerity was progressively abstracted from its deep roots in the racial politics of the South and elevated to the status of fiscal common sense, applicable outside the American South and legible beyond the partisan circles of southern Democrats. It follows the migration of the balanced budget cause from the conservative southern wing of the Democratic Party to the emergent Republican Sunbelt, represented by such antiestablishment figures as Barry Goldwater, Ronald Reagan, and Newt Gingrich. Buchanan's personal and intellectual trajectory was deeply shaped by these party tectonics. He was born and raised in Tennessee, a stronghold of the "Solid South" in which Democrats reigned supreme.[11] Steeped in the "family populist tradition," he recalls, "I grew up in a solidly Democratic setting, with Roosevelt emerging as the popular leader in the 1930s."[12] By 1965, however, in a letter addressed to the editor of the *Times* of London, Buchanan confessed to being one of the many white, Anglo-Saxon, middle-class (traditionally Democrat-voting) southerners who had backed Goldwater in 1964.[13] In the following years, as a whole generation of southern Democratic senators retired from the political scene and passed the baton of the balanced budget amendment to Sunbelt Republicans, Buchanan's alliances shifted enduringly to the Republican right. Having collaborated with small-budget antitax organizations in the 1970s, he served on the academic advisory board to the Koch brothers' Citizens for a Sound Economy in the 1980s, and thus lent his imprint to the long constitutional counterrevolution leading from Newt Gingrich in the 1990s to the Tea Party movement of the 2010s and beyond.

Buchanan's was a willfully unorthodox voice in the context of postwar American economics. As Keynesian ideas about deficit spending gained a foothold

in respected economics departments across the country, Buchanan continued to hammer home the lessons of classical public finance. By this reckoning, public borrowing was sometimes necessary but always unproductive: in
sucking up the savings of private investors, it crowded out productive investments in the private sector; and in demanding future interest payments from
the state, it placed an undemocratic tax burden on future generations. When
Keynesian economists attained real access to power through their positions in
the Kennedy/Johnson Council of Economic Advisers and started teaching that
deficit spending could be modified at will to adjust to the ups and downs of
the business cycle, Buchanan stood undeterred. But his tone became increasingly hysterical. Keynes, he claimed, was a decadent elitist who had brushed
aside the ascetic principles of Victorian public finance without considering
how his private immorality might contaminate the public. Placed in the hands
of the democratic masses, Keynesianism had destroyed America's "old fiscal
religion" and unleashed a deluge of private and public extravagance.[14] "We
do not need to become full-blown Hegelians to entertain the general notion
of zeitgeist, a 'spirit of the times,'" wrote Buchanan and his student Richard
Wagner in the 1970s. "Such a spirit seems at work in the 1960s and 1970s,
and is evidenced by what appears as a generalized erosion in public and private manners, increasingly liberalized attitudes toward sexual activities, a
declining vitality of the Puritan work ethic, deterioration in product quality,
explosion of the welfare rolls, widespread corruption in both the private and
the governmental sector, and, finally, observed increases in the alienation of
voters from the political process."[15] Rising public debt and a growing resort to
deficit spending were the most egregious symptoms of this widespread breakdown in moral convention.

The moralizing tenor of Buchanan's tirades against public debt must have
struck an odd note among mainstream economists of the time, who were
more likely to subscribe to the "functionalist" idea that debt and deficit spending were neither good nor bad in themselves, only more or less stimulative
as a function of overall macroeconomic trends. But it would have been all
too familiar to the people of Virginia, who had grown up under the one-party
rule of conservative Democrat Harry Byrd, with his endless tirades against
the sin of public debt. As state governor in the 1920s, Byrd was one of the
most intransigent foes of state deficit spending across the American South. As

U.S. senator, he spent three decades doing all in his power to thwart, veto, or reverse attempts by the federal government to fund public welfare and impose civil rights legislation on the states.[16] Appointed chair of the all-important Senate Finance Committee in 1955, Byrd wielded extraordinary power to obstruct federal decisions on taxation and spending at a crucial moment in its history and left an indelible negative imprint on the shape of the American welfare state.[17] Byrd expressed his visceral aversion to public debt and deficit spending in terms strikingly similar to Buchanan. Debt-financed public spending, he warned, would crowd out private investment, inflate prices, and transfer an intolerable tax burden onto the shoulders of future generations.[18] The activist use of deficit spending advocated by American Keynesians was a symptom of moral as well as fiscal irresponsibility: "I believe that improvident political promises and programs are sinful; that they are evils perpetrated on innocent citizens by demagogues."[19]

As enforcer-in-chief of public austerity in Virginia, Byrd boasted that he "would vastly prefer to take the Virginia philosophy of government to Washington than to bring the current Washington theories to Virginia."[20] This driving ambition could just as easily characterize Buchanan, who through his work on constitutional budget limits sought to place the same fiscal constraints on the federal government as those self-imposed by the state of Virginia. The affinity was one that Buchanan readily acknowledged. Throughout the 1970s, as Buchanan was composing his mature work on public debt, he each year wrote a deferential letter to Byrd's son and political heir, Senator Harry Flood Byrd Jr., asking him to send a copy of the annual budget report. The "concerns that you have been expressing for many years," he wrote in one letter, are "concerns that I have, also, been trying to express at a different level."[21] The letter came enclosed with an outline of the book, *Democracy in Deficit*, which Buchanan was preparing to write with Richard Wagner.

Harry Flood Byrd Sr. liked to characterize himself as a small government Jeffersonian.[22] But a more proximate source of inspiration could be found in the bitter struggles over the management of public debt that pitted Virginians against each other for several decades after Reconstruction. Like many other former Confederate states, Virginia had emerged from the Civil War in economic ruin but still liable for the heavy debts it had accumulated in more prosperous times.[23] In the years leading up to the Civil War, Southern states had invested heavily in railways, toll roads, and canals, secure in the knowledge that debt burdens could be paid off by taxes on slaves and arable lands. Much of this infrastructure was destroyed by the Civil War, along with the South's primary tax base. Yet interest on the debt continued to accumulate, and this was especially problematic for Virginia, which owed more per capita than any other state in the country. Well aware of the fact that they could not honor their obligations to creditors without condemning themselves to years of penury, most former Confederate states defaulted on or repudiated part of their debt. Virginia was unique in choosing to honor its antebellum liabilities, a decision that, ironically, forced the state to run continual deficits and bleed public institutions dry, including the very popular public schools that had been set up as part of Reconstruction.[24]

As tensions over the fate of public schools intensified, two competing parties emerged to contest Virginia's elections: on the one hand, the Readjusters, who favored renegotiation of the debt and argued that the welfare of the state's citizens, both Black and white, was more important than the interests of creditors, and on the other the Funders, who insisted that debts must be honored at their original value and the state budget definitively balanced in order to retain its long-term creditworthiness.[25] As the state legislature shut down dozens of schools to fund its interest payments, the Readjusters were propelled into power, supported by an altogether unique coalition of small landowning whites and African Americans.[26] They retained power from 1880 until 1885, when the Funder-dominated Democratic Party recaptured control of the state and proceeded to rewrite the history of this extraordinary episode, intent that it should never happen again.[27] Over the following decades, the Democrats took full advantage of their victory to spell out what they saw as the catastrophic political consequences of public deficit spending and debt finance. As an imperative that had been foisted on them by the victorious Northeast, Democrats associated public spending on behalf of the poor with the bitter memories of congressional Reconstruction and the destruction of an older, more honorable way of life.[28] Pointing to the unnatural racial alliances fostered by the Readjuster movement, they rammed home the lesson that generous public spending was tantamount to fomenting communism and the political ambitions of Blacks; budget austerity, by implication, was the most reliable means of maintaining the traditional race and class hierarchies of the South.[29]

The Democrats' efforts to marginalize African Americans and poorer whites from political life culminated with the Constitutional Convention of 1901 and 1902, which reintroduced the poll tax and literacy tests as a prerequisite to voting and excluded those convicted of petty crime.[30] With half of the white male electorate and 90 percent of African American men thereby disenfranchised, the Democratic Party seized control of almost every federal, state, and local office in Virginia and utterly dominated the state's politics until the late 1960s.[31] This was the political lineage that Harry Byrd was born into: following in the footsteps of his uncle and father, both Democratic Funders, Byrd was so personally imbued with the budget-balancing zeal of his Funder forbears that his name soon became synonymous with state Democratic politics. As a young senator and chair of the Virginia Democratic Party's central committee in the 1920s, Byrd shot to fame by blocking a proposal for a bond issue to fund a state highway system, insisting instead that any large government outlay should be financed on a pay-as-you-go basis by earmarked user fees.[32] The so-called Byrd organization—or Byrd machine, according to its detractors—henceforth became the dominant force in Virginia politics as Byrd went from party chairman in 1922, to state governor in 1925 to U.S. senator for the state of Virginia between 1933 and his death in 1965.[33] Byrd's opening salvo on the issue of state bond issues proved to be the signature stance of his entire career: at the state level, he assiduously blocked every attempt to open government purse strings in favor of public services such as schools, welfare, or employment relief, and when the federal government attempted to override state decision-making on these matters, he became even more ferocious in his opposition to public spending.

The Virginia Democrats' deference to their Funder forbears ensured that the state remained as if locked in time until the mid-1960s, its citizens compelled to pay literal and figurative tribute to an antebellum past its leaders would not let go of. As a consequence of the state's singular refusal to renegotiate the terms of its antebellum debt, Virginians continued to pay taxes on this debt into the middle of the twentieth century, long after the roads, canals, and railways it had been created for had fallen into disrepair or been replaced.[34] In the meantime, their welfare, health, and education services were pared to the bone (the state of Virginia spent less on public schools than any other southern state).[35] Since the dearth of state funds transferred the burden of spending onto local municipalities or private citizens, the Byrd machine's parsimony ensured exactly the outcome that the Funders had always wanted: a radically divided and segregated school system, with wealthier white municipalities able to afford better public schools or private alternatives and poorer whites and African Americans condemned to a second-class education.

Byrd's sphere of influence, like that of conservative southern Democrats in general, extended well beyond state lines.[36] Beginning in the Great Depression, southern Democrats skillfully leveraged their minority position within the majority Democratic Party to make sure that the New Deal did not infringe on their jealously guarded traditions of racial and class paternalism. The procedural convention that assigned congressional committee positions to long-standing incumbents conferred a fatal advantage on southern Democrats, who were often elected in one-party states and therefore tended to remain in office for many years on end. Thanks to these seniority rights, southern Democrats chaired key committees in both chambers of Congress and so wielded an effective veto power over New Deal legislation.[37] In the Senate, their power was so entrenched that one outside observer described it as a "*Southern* Institution, engrafted upon or growing in at the heart of, this ostensibly national institution of the sages."[38]

Southern Democrats were masters of the filibuster, a procedural quirk unique to the Senate that allowed them to delay legislation or block it entirely by triggering a supermajority vote. Conservatives liked to romanticize the filibuster as a venerable Senate tradition designed to protect minority rights against the tyranny of the majority: in fact, the institution was unknown to the framers of the Constitution and emerged in its modern form only after 1917, when southern Democrats took hold of a new supermajority voting rule to block any move toward civil rights.[39] With this instrument at their disposal, southern Democrats mercilessly blackmailed the more progressive elements within the Democratic Party. If Roosevelt ignored their demands, they could scuttle the entire New Deal project by voting with Republicans. If he wanted them on side, he would have to sacrifice some of the New Deal's universalism to the special interests of the South. When it came to civil rights legislation in particular, southern Democrats weaponized the filibuster to block progress altogether: between the early 1920s and mid-1940s, three anti-lynching bills and three bills to end the poll tax succumbed to the southern Democratic filibuster.[40] The overall effect of their obstruction was to cast a dead weight on historical change, in much the same way that Virginia's antebellum debt continued to exact its toll into the twentieth century.

During congressional hearings for the Social Security Act of 1935, southern Democrats made full use of their political whip hand to protect the interests of large southern landowners. Fearing that the social insurance provisions of the New Deal would liberate sharecroppers and tenant farmers from the paternalist grip of large landowners, they intervened to exclude agricultural workers, domestic servants, and casual laborers from the core elements of the Social Security Act of 1935—old age and unemployment insurance.[41] The mostly Black workers who were ousted by these provisions were relegated to less generous and secure public assistance programs, which southern Democrats fought to keep under the watchful oversight of state and local authorities.

Southern Democrats were just as conscientious in their efforts to attenuate Aid to Dependent Children, the New Deal's public assistance program for widowed mothers and their children. ADC (later renamed Aid to Families with Dependent Children, or AFDC) fell under the terms of the Social Security Act of 1935 but left the states to implement the program, with the federal government offering matching grants to compliment state funding. As the New Deal's ADC provisions wended their way through congress, southern Democrats in both House and Senate Committees worked hard to curtail the more generous elements of the draft legislation.[42] As was the case with old age assistance, they made sure that any reference to reasonable subsistence levels was stripped from the final legislation. And in the House Ways and Means Committee, they removed a work exemption for the primary carer, thus leaving open the possibility that states, in the future, could force welfare mothers to work. In the years ahead, southern states one by one introduced "employable mother" rules that redirected African American women from welfare offices to the fields or homes of white landowners.[43] A panoply of other provisions made sure that unmarried, divorced, insufficiently pious, or morally dubious women were almost always deemed ineligible for public assistance.[44] During this period, southern states made abundant use of "man-in-the-house," "substitute father," and "suitable home" rules to exclude African American women from the rolls, on the grounds that their nonmarital relationships with men made them both morally suspect and better served by the private provision of a de facto husband.

Even among conservative southern Democrats, Byrd stood out for his relentless obstructionism.[45] Where other southern Democrats played a double game, welcoming federal relief funds that would subsidize their flailing economies while at the same time thwarting any measure that would empower tenant farmers, laborers, or domestic workers, Byrd wielded an indefatigable veto power. He was one among only a handful of senators to vote against the Social Security Act en bloc.[46]

Byrd was particularly fearful that the activist use of public deficit spending, authorized by the growing influence of Keynes upon American economists, would afford the federal government untold powers of intervention into state affairs, allowing them to overcome the hierarchical social structures carefully held in place by state-level frugality. Roosevelt himself only ever made reluctant and pragmatic use of deficit spending. But when the president was forced to resume federal stimulus efforts in the late 1930s, as the nation plunged back into recession, Byrd very publicly expressed his distaste for the new Keynesian economics, via a debate with the then chairman of the Federal Reserve, Marriner Eccles.[47] In an open letter published in 1939 by major newspapers throughout the country, Byrd denounced "the dogma and doctrine of that erratic English economist, Dr. J.M. Keynes" and reasserted the fundamental distinction between private and public indebtedness.[48] The distinction was particularly important to southern conservatives because the South's entire system of racial paternalism rested on the fact that African Americans were very often personally indebted to local landowners, who thereby assumed the multiple functions of welfare provider, protector, and employer in lieu of the state.[49] Throughout the South, sharecropping and tenant farming had replaced the brutal exploitation of slavery with a more personal but no less vicious system of racial paternalism which locked African Americans into intimate relations of obligation and dependence on landlords and subsumed them within the extended household economy of the white master. These private obligations were so important to the southern agricultural economy that state law granted planters first lien on any outstanding debt.[50] As Byrd recognized, however, they would be gravely threatened if the federal government were to assume the responsibility for deficit spending on behalf of the poor. After all, if public debt-financing were used to provide an alternative source of welfare, it would usurp the first-claim status of private creditors and allow African Americans to escape the personal bonds of indebtedness that tied them to their landlords. "A public debt is a universal mortgage," Byrd warned. "It is a first lien on every acre of land, on every house and home, on every piece of property, on every service that is rendered, on every transaction that is made."[51]

In the wake of World War II, Byrd doubled down on his commitment to fiscal conservatism, even as most Democrats and mainstream Republicans embraced the new normal of sustained public spending and a permanently expanded tax base. Like other southern Democrats, he was outraged by Truman's attempts to extend Roosevelt's experiment into the domain of civil rights via poll tax repeal and desegregation.[52] Byrd was instrumental in forging the southern Democratic/Old Guard Republican alliance that would thwart the progressive ambitions of successive federal administrations for years to come.[53] With this alliance in place, conservative Democrats and Republicans united to defeat Truman's national health-insurance program and consistently blocked attempts to extend federal aid to public schools, fearful that federal funding flows would come replete with antisegregation clauses.[54] When the Supreme Court achieved the same objective in the *Brown v. Board of Education* decision of 1954, the state of Virginia, at Byrd's behest, embarked on a campaign of "massive resistance" which saw dozens of integrated public schools close their doors and thousands of African American and poor white children excluded from education for several years.[55] This was an almost perfect replay of the public school funding crisis of 1870, although this time the conflict was as much external as internal to the state of Virginia. Inspired by the teachings of John C. Calhoun, in 1956 the Virginia General Assembly adopted a nullification resolution expressing its intention to disobey federal laws it deemed unconstitutional.[56] The nullification option proved unworkable in the long run, but Byrd would soon turn to constitutional budget constraints as an alternative means of blocking federal intrusions on state's rights.

Byrd had been one of the few Democrats to welcome the Republican president Eisenhower with open arms, fully expecting him to restore some semblance of fiscal common sense. He was disappointed when Eisenhower proved more flexible on the issue of public finance than he had anticipated and outright alarmed when the president embarked on a series of ambitious federal initiatives, ranging from a boost to Social Security benefits and a national highway construction program to the creation of a new federal agency, the Department of Health, Education and Welfare (HEW). Recalling the state-level battles of his early career, Byrd was enraged when one of Eisenhower's advisors suggested that a new national highway scheme should be funded via the issuing of public bonds and fought tooth and nail to block the proposal, convinced that any departure from budget balance, even for so-called capital investment, would set a dangerous a precedent for the expansion of federal powers.[57]

Eisenhower himself was for the most part committed to balanced budgets, but he had no intention of giving up on the federal government's new role in shaping the fiscal affairs of the nation. Indeed, it was Eisenhower who established the new Republican common sense that balanced budgets were to be achieved through sustained and progressive taxation rather than public spending cutbacks.[58] As a consequence, Byrd found himself in the unexpected position of opposing many of the president's initiatives from the fiscal conservative right. Again, southern Democrats found common ground with Old Guard Republicans such as Barry Goldwater, who refused to accept the centrist compromise politics of the new Republican Party and insisted that balanced budgets should be combined with low taxes—a formula that was designed to cripple public spending and reverse the gains of the New Deal.[59]

In the years following World War II, as southern Democrats and Old Guard Republicans came to the gradual realization that they could no longer rely on the Republican mainstream to reverse the Keynesian fiscal revolution, they turned to the constitutional instruments deployed by the Progressive movement in the early twentieth century. The constitutional scholar Clement E. Vose coined the term "conservatism by amendment" to describe fiscal conservatives' new passion for constitutional activism during this period.[60] As noted by Vose, this amounted to an attempted counterrevolution. The "constitutional revolution" of 1936 (when the Supreme Court swung decisively behind Roosevelt's New Deal legislation) was the high point of progressive attempts to interpret the constitution in such a way that the federal government would exercise greater control over taxing and spending decisions. With this shift, the Supreme Court gave its blessing to Franklin Roosevelt's New Deal and opened the floodgates to federal intervention in every area of economic life, from minimum wages to welfare.[61] By the 1950s, however, states' rights defenders were attempting to reverse these gains, often exploiting the very same instruments of constitutional reform that were pioneered by New

Deal progressives.[62] Among the many amendments they put forward were proposals to permanently reduce the federal income tax, to mandate balanced budgets, and to facilitate the Article V (or state convention) route to constitutional amendment. Harry Byrd was at the forefront of this would-be counterrevolution.

In the summer of 1953, Byrd used his powerful new position on the Senate Finance Committee to block Eisenhower's request to lift the debt ceiling. This was the first debt ceiling showdown in American history and the first instance in which a threatened default on the national debt was used to force through spending cuts.[63] The following year, Byrd joined Republican senator Styles Bridges of New Hampshire to propose another first—this time a constitutional amendment to enforce balanced budgets.[64] The idea of placing constitutional shackles on federal deficit spending had originated with Thomas Jefferson, who in 1798 wrote: "I wish it were possible to obtain a single amendment to our constitution...I mean an additional article, taking from the federal government the power of borrowing."[65] But this was the first time in U.S. history that someone had seriously attempted to put the idea into practice. In 1956, Byrd and Bridges would submit a second such resolution; soon after, Republican senator Carl Curtis of Nebraska would follow up with a third.[66] All three of these balanced budget resolutions died on the Senate floor. But the idea lived on in the work of James M. Buchanan, who over the next few decades focused his considerable intellectual energies on the question of how to impose hard constitutional limits on deficit-financed public spending.

JAMES M. BUCHANAN AND THE BALANCED BUDGET AMENDMENT

James M. Buchanan's first monograph, *Public Principles of Public Debt: A Defense and Restatement*, published in 1958, emerged directly out of Senator Byrd's battles with the Eisenhower administration around the use of public borrowing. In the lead-up to the congressional debate around Eisenhower's proposed highway construction project, Buchanan was engaged by the business-led public policy organization, the Committee for Economic Development, to consult on the best means of financing such a project: public borrowing or pay-as-you-go.[67] The committee preferred the solution of raising taxes to ensure increased public spending would not be financed by government borrowing, but specified that such taxes should be "earmarked" for highway construction and thus drawn out of user fees such as gasoline taxes, vehicle registration, and toll roads rather than general funds.[68] Byrd would present the same case in Congress a month later.[69] Buchanan claims that prior to this consulting experience, he, like many other postwar economists, had more or less accepted the "new orthodoxy" of American Keynesians such as Abba Lerner and Alvin Hansen, that active public investment policies, if necessary involving the use of deficit spending, were needed to cope with the realities of modern economic management—although he concedes that there are few indications of this in his written work.[70] Buchanan's engagement with the federal highway project, however, convinced him that the old-fashioned views of ordinary citizens (and Senator Byrd) made sense in the nondeflationary environment of the postwar economy. The old orthodoxy of classical public finance had been right all along: public borrowing was a moral and fiscal evil to be avoided at all costs. In one of his many moments of populist epiphany, Buchanan found himself "somewhat to [his] surprise...in the camp of the much-maligned man on the street, the holder of the allegedly vulgar and unsophisticated ideas about the public finances." "This heresy," obliged him "to spell out the ideas involved in [his] proposed overthrow of the ruling orthodoxy carefully and precisely."[71]

As the title of the book suggests, *Public Principles of Public Debt: A Defense and Restatement* was less a refutation of the new Keynesian macroeconomics than a serene reaffirmation of classical public finance principles. Buchanan hardly bothered to engage with the conceptual innovations of Keynesian economics—the notion that deficit spending might have a "multiplier" effect on national income, for example—much less the "new economics" of the American Keynesians, with their far more radical suggestion that deficit spending might be used as a permanent stimulus to economic growth.[72] The debate, as Buchanan understood it, remained firmly ensconced in the zero-sum world of classical physics, where capital could be moved around to more or less productive effect, but never created anew. Hence, the book amounted to a calm reiteration of the nostrums of classical sound finance. Public borrowing, in this view, was incapable of increasing national income; it merely diverted income from the productive private sector to the unproductive public sector, crowding out commercial investment as it did so. And since public debt added no surplus to the national income, it could never be outpaced by economic growth and so would inevitably fall on the shoulders of future generations in the form of taxes.

As we have seen, the immediate prompt to Buchanan's meditation on public debt was a proposal to fund Eisenhower's federal highway system through a public bond issue. For the time being, however, Buchanan was less concerned by Eisenhower's public spending record than he was with the long-term threat of the new Keynesian economics. After all, although Truman and Eisenhower had failed to roll back the elevated spending of the 1930s and 1940s, they had never questioned the basic wisdom of balanced budgets, and so had almost always funded their public spending ventures with higher taxes rather than reckless borrowing.[73] Their ambitions were for the most part confined to the relatively uncontroversial matter of investment in capital assets such as infrastructure and defense and did not challenge the racial limits of New Deal social welfare. But Buchanan was conscious of the fact that the American Keynesianism of Alvin Hansen and Abba Lerner considered social welfare to be a legitimate object of government investment and sanctioned the use of active deficit spending to fund it. Although this version of Keynesianism had made little headway in Washington, it was conventional wisdom in the economics departments of Harvard and MIT and could conceivably be put into practice by future Democratic presidents, who might also question the class, race, and gender exclusions built into the postwar consensus. With this in mind, Buchanan concluded his book with a warning: if in the future the "current majority" happens to "be controlled by the poorer classes who are determined to utilize the fiscal system in all possible ways to benefit their own group at the expense of the richer classes," then the "whole fiscal process [could take] on the appearance of a purely partisan struggle."[74]

As the 1960s unfolded, Buchanan's fears were confirmed as first the Supreme Court and then Congress took steps to challenge voter disenfranchisement in the South. Beginning with the landmark *Baker v. Carr* decision of 1962, a quick succession of Supreme Court cases established "one person, one vote" as the new constitutional standard for evaluating voting and districting practices. With the passage of the Voting Rights Act of 1965, minority voters no longer had to rely on case-by-case litigation to protest unfair practices: federal observers were appointed to monitor states with a history of voter suppression and gerrymandering, while poll taxes and literacy tests were banned outright.[75] As poor white and Black voters assumed greater weight in state and federal elections, Buchanan was increasingly convinced that constitutional action was needed to protect the soon-to-be-minoritarian "richer classes" from exploitation at the hands of the state. In *The Calculus of Consent*, a founding text of Virginia school neoliberalism, Buchanan and Tullock developed a searching critique of majority rule against the background of the *Baker v. Carr* case.[76] The book pivoted around a central question: what limits can be placed on the expropriation of private wealth in a context where the non-property-owning poor acquire new powers to influence the allocation of tax monies? *The Calculus of Consent* was the first of Buchanan's monographs to comprehensively address the issue of preconstitutional rule-setting and its impact on tax and spending decisions. It was also the first work in which he explicitly identified the importance of constitutional limits as a necessary antidote to the changing composition of the voting majority.[77] For the time being, however, Buchanan's interest in constitutional limits was confined to the issue of taxation and did not extend to deficit spending as such. His solution, the supermajority vote, offered the perfect means for blocking the newly enfranchised majority of poor white and Black voters who might be tempted to claim too much from the property-owning minority in the way of shared public services.[78] As we have seen, this was far from the blunt instrument of Calhounian "nullification" that southern Democrats had brandished against the Supreme Court's edict on school desegregation. After all, Buchanan and Tullock weren't seeking to annul the Supreme Court's decisions in cases such as *Baker v. Carr*. They were merely hoping to contain its unwelcome consequences by transferring a veto power to the voting minority. And although the supermajority rule was formally identical to Calhoun's "concurrent majority," Buchanan and Tullock could point to the precedent of the liberal progressive Knut Wicksell as a sign of their impeccable political credentials.

Very soon, however, Buchanan concluded that constitutional limits on tax voting procedures were insufficient to stem the rising tide of illegitimate claims on private wealth. The idea of implementing a constitutional supermajority to veto tax decisions made sense in a context where both major political parties abided by a tacit balanced budget rule, since this implied that any restraint on taxation would be reflected in diminished spending. But the issue became much more complicated in the mid-1960s, when Supreme Court decisions on the democratic franchise were solidified and enforced by Congress and the balanced budget norm itself appeared to be losing its legitimacy. In quick succession, the Civil Rights Act of 1964, the Voting Rights Act of 1965, and the Fair Housing Act of 1968 all passed Congress, despite the herculean efforts of southern Democrats to filibuster progress in the Senate.[79] By outlawing racial discrimination in both the public and private sectors and authorizing the federal government to enforce the "one person, one vote" rule across the South, this troika of civil rights statutes profoundly transformed the landscape of electoral power, opening up the prospect of a massive redistribution of taxpayer dollars to the African American poor.

But even more alarming, for Buchanan, was the fact that this extension of the democratic franchise occurred at a time when politicians were losing their instinctive fear of deficit spending, thanks to the suasions of Keynesian economists at the Council of Economic Advisers. Under the influence of the "new economics," politicians were now being told that the deficit was neither good nor bad per se, merely "functional" to different ends. Indeed, with proper care, the deficit could be permanently wielded as an instrument of macroeconomic stimulus.[80] If the "new economics" of the American Keynesians was merely an intellectual threat when Buchanan wrote his first major book, *Public Principles of Public Debt*, by the mid-1960s it was being deployed as an active political weapon in the service of greater redistribution. The year 1965 was a "historical watershed," Buchanan wrote. "Before this date, the fiscal politics of America was at least partially 'pre-Keynesian' in both rhetoric and reality. After 1965, the fiscal politics became definitely 'post-Keynesian' in reality." [81] Buchanan was not wrong in identifying 1965 as a historical turning point in American public finance. When President Johnson arrived in the White House, he initiated an upward trend in social spending that would accelerate into the 1970s: social expenditures doubled between 1963 and 1969, for the first time increasing faster than defense.[82] And as Johnson sought to juggle the spending priorities of the Great Society and the Vietnam War without raising taxes, he resorted to deficits to fund them. Johnson's successors, Nixon and Ford, would go on to break multiple budget deficit records in the 1970s.[83]

As a consequence, Buchanan was compelled to rethink his prescriptions for constitutional restraint. Although still necessary, the minority veto power on tax decisions, outlined in *The Calculus of Consent*, was no longer sufficient to rein in the spending power of the state, since politicians now felt emboldened to spend above and beyond the limits of their incoming revenues, either by issuing public debt or relying on the Federal Reserve to monetize government debt or a bit of both. As politicians lost their once instinctive respect for budget balance—what Buchanan referred to as an implicit fiscal and moral constitution—their spending decisions were no longer constrained by hard revenue limits or the threat of voter backlash against rising tax burdens.[84] If revenue fell short, the tax burden could simply be transferred into the future, where it would fall upon the shoulders of hard-earning producers for decades to come. Or else it would be converted, via inflation, into a form of stealth taxation on bond holders and savers.[85] "Governments increasingly enact public expenditure programs that confer benefits on special segments of the population, with the cost borne by taxpayers generally," Buchanan lamented. "Many such programs might not be financed in the face of strenuous taxpayer resistance but might well secure acceptance under debt finance. The hostility to the expenditure programs is reduced in this way, and budgets rise; intergroup income transfers multiply"—yet the intergroup conflict we might otherwise expect is averted by transferring some of the costs to future generations.[86] By delegitimizing the balanced budget rule, Buchanan contended, Keynesian economists had transformed what was once a zero-sum game among competing social interests into a free-for-all where each unproductive "special interest" could accumulate unearned public service "rents," seemingly without end.

In his earlier work, Buchanan had established that even under the normal circumstances of majority rule, the most honest of politicians would be inclined to increase the size of the public sector and distribute an inefficient volume of public service "rents" to potential voters.[87] But when the biases of majority rule were combined with reckless deficit spending, Buchanan warned, the results would be catastrophic.[88] Legislative limits alone could not be relied upon to contain political self-interest: Who could trust a politician to police himself? What was needed was a limit on the power to spend in deficit, and this limit would need to be embedded in the constitution so as to neutralize the predictable attempts of politicians and bureaucrats to get around it. Published at the height of the deficit debates of the 1970s, James M. Buchanan and Richard Wagner's *Democracy in Deficit: The Political Legacy of Lord Keynes* concluded with an impassioned defense of the balanced budget amendment as the final bulwark against Keynesian follies. "Precisely because we have allowed the Keynesian teachings to destroy the constraining influence...of our previously informal fiscal constitution," they wrote, "restoration must now involve something more formal, more specific, more explicitly confining than that which fell victim to the Keynesian onslaught. Restoration will require a constitutional rule that will become legally as well as morally binding, a rule that is explicitly written into the constitutional document of the United States."[89] In short, Buchanan now threw his whole intellectual weight behind the solution that Senator Byrd had come up with in the 1950s—an amendment to the U.S. Constitution obliging the federal government to balance its annual budget.

Buchanan and Wagner's *Democracy in Deficit* became something of a manifesto for the balanced budget campaign of the 1970s.[90] In correspondence with Milton Friedman, Buchanan shared his quiet conviction that this, among all his published works, was the most likely to have some lasting impact on American political life.[91] In 1975, Buchanan was invited to read out a draft chapter for a Senate Judiciary Committee hearing on a proposed balanced budget amendment. And by the time the book was published two years later, movement organizers had recruited both Buchanan and his arguments into a new and invigorated national campaign for constitutional counterrevolution.

THE BALANCED BUDGET RESOLUTION OF 1975

When a group of conservative Democrat and Republican senators banded together to relaunch Senator Byrd's balanced budget idea in the 1970s, the context was much more propitious than it had been in the postwar era. For several decades, the Keynesian formula for macroeconomic management had proved so successful that mainstream politicians from both sides of the political spectrum were adopting its methods. Even Nixon, at the outset of the 1970s, would concede that he was "a Keynesian in economics."[92] By the middle of the decade, however, the leading economic indicators seemed to be signaling that something was seriously amiss with the Keynesian rulebook. The creeping inflation that had begun in the late 1960s was now accompanied by high rates of unemployment, in seeming contradiction with the expectations built into the Phillips curve formula. And after chalking up surpluses for decades on end, governments were now routinely running deficits. The high unemployment of the 1970s revealed latent tensions in the Great Society social compact, pitting unionized white workers against nonunionized Blacks, workers against students, and almost all constituencies against Black welfare mothers. As conservative pundits (and a handful of scholars) pressed home the spurious connections between deficit spending, inflation, and high interest rates, the deficit became a convenient symbol of growing popular discontent with the Great Society experiment.

By the 1970s, moreover, the American political landscape had shifted in such a way that white voters as a whole were becoming much more receptive to the balanced budget and low-tax arguments of southern Democrats. The turning point, as suggested by Buchanan, seems to have been around 1965, when Johnson extended the purview of civil rights legislation to include expanded public spending programs for low-income minorities. White voters outside the South had for the most part tolerated the Civil and Voting Rights Acts of 1964 and 1965, which targeted segregation and voter suppression in the South. But when civil rights legislation on housing threatened their own interests as homeowners and taxpayers, they abruptly withdrew their support.[93] With the passage of state and federal fair housing laws, conflicts around public debt, taxation, and racial redistribution that were once largely confined to the rural South were now being played out in suburbs across the nation, spreading from the new city fringes of the South across the country. In 1960s Atlanta, white residents twice voted against public bond initiatives to upgrade schools, streets, and sewers, fearing that any improvement to recently desegregated public space would benefit Blacks more than whites.[94] In 1964, Californians voted against a state fair housing law that sought to end racial discrimination by private landlords.[95] And in 1979, a predominantly white working-class suburb of Detroit chose to forfeit millions in federal urban renewal funds that mandated rezoning for low-income housing.[96]

All of a sudden, the white suburban homeowners who had been the chief beneficiaries and supporters of the postwar New Deal consensus were beginning to appreciate the states' rights, low-tax, and balanced budget arguments of southern Democrats and Old Guard Republicans. Eisenhower's signature fiscal politics of balanced budgets and progressive taxation was acceptable as long as it ensured a high level of public spending on the private asset holdings of white

CONSTITUTIONAL AUSTERITY

suburban home dwellers, but when public spending extended to racial others, white homeowners outside the South began to understand why southerners had always preferred balanced budgets *and* low taxes—quite simply, the latter combination was a recipe for fiscal austerity. An early observer of this profound political realignment, John Egerton, commented that the "South and the nation are not exchanging strengths as much as they are exchanging sins." The "South [was] just about over as a separate and distinct place" not because civil rights legislation had put an end to racial injustice but because the rest of the country was now reliving old southern battles on suburban territory.[97] Now, at last, southern Democrats and their Old Right Republican allies seemed to have found the perfect conditions for reviving Senator Byrd's balanced budget amendment.

In 1975, Senator Carl Curtis, a Republican from Nebraska and a veteran of Byrd's 1950s antideficit campaign, approached Senator William L. Scott, a Republican from Virginia, to cosponsor a new resolution in favor of a balanced budget amendment.[98] The hearings were a who's who of Sunbelt conservatives and southern states' rights defenders.[99] They included Harry Flood Byrd Jr., who continued to fight his father's battles in the Senate long after the latter's death in 1966, and Strom Thurmond, the segregationist southern Democrat turned Republican, along with representatives from both the Tax Foundation and the National Taxpayers Union, the oldest and youngest antitax organizations in the country, respectively. Written statements were provided by Barry Goldwater, the Old Guard Republican and Sunbelt conservative, and George Wallace, the populist segregationist from Alabama. The 1975 resolution was self-consciously palimpsestic. Throughout the hearing, speakers acknowledged the precedent set by Harry Flood Byrd Sr. two decades earlier.[100] This time, however, their efforts were greatly enhanced by the expert testimony of James M. Buchanan, whose case for constitutional limits lent a new aura of intellectual rigor to Byrd's commonsense grievances against government irresponsibility.[101] If anyone could bring the politics of Virginia to Washington, it was Buchanan.

FROM BALANCED BUDGET RESOLUTION TO CONSTITUTIONAL CONVENTION

As it turned out, the 1975 balanced budget proposal failed to pass muster on the Senate floor. But key sponsors of the resolution soon discovered an alternative strategy that they thought could force the hand of Congress. Throughout the postwar era, disgruntled states' rights defenders and small government conservatives became increasingly interested in the so-called Article V convention as a way of short-circuiting the centralization of power in Washington.[102] Article V of the United States Constitution outlines two ways in which the nation's founding document can be amended. The first pathway, and the only one to be successfully applied thus far, depends on Congressional initiative and requires two-thirds of votes in Congress to be ratified by three-quarters of the states. The other, somewhat obscure method, unused since 1789, allows state legislatures to petition Congress for a convention of states to amend the Constitution. The so-called Article V convention must be called by two-thirds of state legislatures and ratified by three-quarters for an amendment to be valid. As many constitutional lawyers have pointed out, the Article V convention presents significant risks, not least of which is the lack of historical precedent and consequent uncertainty around its scope of application (what, for example, would stop a state convention, once called, from amending the entire Constitution?)[103] And while for the most part political activists have used the Article V convention as a provocation and a way of spurring Congress into action, others seem to be deadly serious in their intention to push it as far as it can go.[104]

The state of Virginia, in 1973, was the first to pass a resolution petitioning Congress to summon a convention of states, followed soon after by Maryland and Mississippi.[105] A Democratic state senator from Maryland then enlisted the support of James Dale Davidson, chairman of the National Taxpayers Union (NTU), to muster support for the campaign across the nation.[106] This was a defining moment for Davidson and his fledgling, student-run libertarian group. The anarcho-capitalist Murray Rothbard identified Davidson as the most successful libertarian strategist of his time, attributing much of his success to his political stealth.[107] Davidson, he pointed out, had managed to drum up support for ten libertarian legislative goals in one year (winning some of them outright) by quietly prevailing on key decision-makers in the Senate. This he had achieved by muting his more extravagant libertarian ambitions and working with strange bedfellows from the antiwar left and states' rights South to stunt the federal government's tax and spending powers on single-issue votes. "How does the young and handsome Davidson, operating with virtually no help and on a shoestring budget, do it?" Rothbard asked.

"One way is by getting to know and influence key aides to key Senators, who in turn influence the rest of the Senate: and another of his crucial tactics is to do what the Marxists call 'exploiting the contradictions within the ruling class.' In other words, to push a piece of libertarian legislation or to block a piece of particularly egregious statism, Davidson finds out which interests within the Establishment, not ordinarily libertarian, can be developed as allies on this particular issue."[108] For the most part, these "interests" turned out to be southern Democrats such as Harry Byrd Jr. and Russell Long, whose opposition to federal power stemmed from different sources but very often dovetailed with the pro-market, antistate ideas of libertarians. And although the NTU, in its public manifestations, made concerted efforts to reach out to the antiwar left and Eisenhower Republicans, its board of directors was a solid mix of right-wing libertarian, Old Guard Republican, and conservative southern Democrat.[109] In the early 1970s, the organization counted the Austrian neoliberals Ludwig von Mises and Henry Hazlitt on its board of advisors and Murray Rothbard on its executive committee. By the 1980s, it had accumulated a respectable list of business supporters, including Koch Industries, and James M. Buchanan was serving on its board of directors.[110]

Having settled for the state convention route to constitutional change after their failure in the Senate, balanced budget campaigners turned this defensive gambit into a badge of honor. They were, they claimed, safeguarding the rights of states against an overbearing federal machinery, and more implausibly, giving voice to the will of the people, free of the distortions of representative democracy. For his part, James Buchanan, who was well known for embracing Kenneth Arrow's thesis that no such thing as a general social welfare function could be derived from individual self-interest, saw no contradiction in invoking a general *will of the people* in defense of the state convention process.[111] In a workshop on the convention process organized by the American Enterprise Institute, Buchanan castigated his fellow presenters for displaying an exaggerated trust in the integrity of politicians and a barely concealed contempt for the people.[112] James Dale Davidson and Harry F. Byrd Jr. followed suit, denouncing critics of the balanced budget convention as enemies of the popular will.[113]

The argument was disingenuous in the extreme. In most states that had petitioned Congress to call a convention, there had been very little in the way of legislative, much less public, debate. State resolutions in favor of a balanced budget amendment were passed effortlessly precisely because there was so little awareness of their real intent. No state-level resolution made any mention of the future spending cuts that would result from an amendment, although campaign organizers were determined that balanced budgets should not be achieved at the price of tax increases.[114] And while campaign organizers were comforted by opinion polls revealing overwhelming public support for the *idea* of a balanced budget amendment, the endorsement was less straightforward than it seemed given that substantial majorities also opposed spending restraint in every significant area of federal spending.[115] NTU campaigners were well aware that secrecy was vital to their success. By 1979, they had managed to persuade thirty states to pass a convention resolution, just short of the thirty-four that were needed for the convention to be called. But the campaign was scuttled at the last minute when Governor Edmund Gerald (Jerry) Brown of California unthinkingly boasted of his intention to support it.[116] Having proceeded thus far by stealth, the state convention campaign was now exposed to the unflattering glare of public scrutiny.[117] The California state legislature was the first to submit the proposal to serious debate, with a full cast of constitutional lawyers, state representatives, and economists convened to discuss its merits.[118] As a consequence, the resolution failed to pass in California, while other states moved to rescind resolutions they had passed in previous years.

In the meantime, however, the NTU was joined by Lewis K. Uhler's National Tax Limitation Committee, which lent its support to the state convention campaign but also set to work on a new draft amendment that it hoped would prove more congenial to Congress.[119] Buoyed by the success of California's Proposition 13, neither organization felt compelled to mollify Eisenhower Republicans anymore, and both dropped any pretense that they might be favorable to tax increases to achieve balanced budgets.[120] As tax revolt fervor gripped the country, campaign organizers now declared out loud that the only acceptable way to balance the budget was through the deliberate ratcheting down of spending *and* taxes. During the final six months of 1978, Uhler called on the veterans of the Californian tax and spending limit referendum, including James M. Buchanan and his student William Craig Stubblebine, to work on a federal amendment that would achieve both these tasks.[121] After six months of intensive draft sessions, the NTLC came up with a balanced budget amendment that was more flexible with regard to annual receipts and outlays than its predecessor while actually introducing greater stringency with regard to methods. The amendment limited annual growth in federal spending to a percentage increase in the previous year's gross national product, with even tighter limits to apply when inflation was expanding government revenues by pushing people into higher tax brackets.[122] It was envisaged that with such constraints in place, Congress would be forced to use its surplus revenue to either retire existing debt or enact tax reductions.[123] In this way, the NTLC sought to preclude the expansionary "Eisenhower" solution to balanced budgets and instead place a permanent break on federal spending and taxes alike. A slightly revised version of this proposal was presented before Congress, with Reagan's support, in 1982.

Beginning in the 1970s, James Dale Davidson and Lewis K. Uhler adopted Buchanan's political philosophy as their campaign vernacular and assiduously popularized his theory of democratic excess. The balanced budget amendment, Davidson wrote in 1979, signaled an end to the "good-will theory of government," which assumed that politicians acted in the service of an illusory public interest. Congressmen "continue to spend money," he wrote, "not because they believe expenditures are in the public interest, but because they know such expenditures are in their own interests." The politician satisfies his own self-interest by catering to "special interests" and multiplies his opportunities for doing so by resorting to deficit spending.[124]

Lewis K. Uhler, too, never tired of repeating the argument that "our political system permits special interests to gain private benefits at the expense of the taxpayers." "There is no law," he lamented, "against the majority voting to strip the producers of 100 percent of their income!" And since "the legislative approach doesn't promise much" (it is "illogical to suppose that legislators who, as a group, vote *for* new spending every time they have a chance, will vote *against* new spending" on principle), this "leaves only the *Constitutional approach*" as a way of permanently restraining the deficit-fueled excesses of majoritarian democracy.[125] Targeting the full range of media outlets from respectable newspapers to the libertarian press and the think-tank policy pipeline, Davidson and Uhler performed the invaluable task of transcribing Buchanan's intricate academic arguments back into the commonsense language of the "man on the street," from whom he had allegedly drawn inspiration in the first place.

By 1980, it seemed as though the southern Democratic politics of Harry

Byrd Sr. had triumphed on the national stage. Although no amendment had been passed, the campaign had acquired a seemingly unstoppable momentum and the cause itself had migrated from the extremist fringes into everyday political parlance. At the very moment that Byrd's ideas were acquiring national resonance, however, the southern Democratic faction he had represented for so many years was fading from the scene, along with its aging senators. During the 1960s, the national Democrats had thrown their support behind civil and voting rights legislation and thus destroyed the power base of southern Democrats within their own party. As the Democratic party moved to the left, however, Republicans were strategically moving to the right, first by courting the votes of former white Democrats in the South, then, as "southern" politics moved nationwide, by riding the wave of white suburban resentment across the country.

The balanced budget resolution of 1975 was charged with the memory of Senator Byrd and the racial history of Virginia. Yet by the time it was proposed, the influence of southern Democrats in the Senate was on the wane, while Sunbelt Republicans were just beginning to emerge as a recognizable bloc.[126] Byrd had once been the uncontested leader of the postwar coalition between southern Democrats and Old Guard Republicans. By the 1970s, a new generation of southern and southwestern Republicans were making inroads in the solid Democratic South and agitating for a more ruthless conservative politics within the GOP. These included Senator Trent Lott of Mississippi, a Republican who had replaced and was endorsed by a conservative southern Democrat in 1972; Newt Gingrich, who had won over the Sixth District of Georgia when it was vacated by a southern Democrat in 1978; Dick Armey of Dallas, Texas, and Tom DeLay of Houston, Texas, both of whom had dislodged Democratic incumbents in 1984; and on the campaign front, Lee Atwater of South Carolina, a protégé of Dixiecrat cum Republican senator Strom Thurmond, who had served as southern coordinator of Reagan's 1980 campaign, deputy manager of his 1984 reelection campaign, and manager of the George H. W. Bush campaign of 1988.[127] All but Lee Atwater, who died prematurely, would return as architects of the Republican revolution of 1994, when Gingrich emerged as uncontested champion of the balanced budget and orchestrated a scorched-earth campaign against Clinton's fiscal agenda.

While this new cohort of Sunbelt Republicans wielded the cause of the balanced budget with all the zeal of old southern Democrats before them, they

CONSTITUTIONAL AUSTERITY

271

modulated the tone and focus of their fiscal jeremiads to suit the sensibilities of their new suburban constituents. It was no longer the southern planter class but middle-class homeowners congregated in the newly affluent and de facto segregated suburbs of Georgia, Arizona, Texas, and California who dictated the script of balanced budget politics. The question of racial redistribution continued to fire the debate. Yet nowhere could one find the overt calls for segregation embraced by Byrd and the advocates of "massive resistance." In the aftermath of the civil rights era, Sunbelt Republicans spoke to the racial anxieties of white homeowners through the filtered lens of inflation-driven bracket creep, property taxes, and crime rates, all of which they traced back to the original sin of unbalanced budgets.

By the end of the decade, the once quintessentially southern Democratic cause of balanced budgets and low taxes was now practically owned by Sunbelt Republicans, whose rising star, Ronald Reagan, played it for all it was worth.

SUNBELT REPUBLICANS AND THE BALANCED BUDGET AMENDMENT

That Reagan should sell himself as the champion of a balanced budget amendment was ironic. No American president before Reagan had invested so much rhetorical value in the cause of a balanced budget. And no other president had done so much to ensure it wouldn't happen. Having entered office vowing to curb the wasteful government spending that had "piled deficit upon deficit" and "mortgag[ed] our future and our children's future for the temporary convenience of the present," Reagan presided over record budget deficits—which rose from $40 billion in fiscal year 1979 to $221 billion in 1986—and tripled the dollar size of the debt.[128] This could in part be attributed to the automatic rise in unemployment insurance costs and diminished tax base of the early 1980s, as Federal Reserve chairman Paul Volcker plunged the economy into its worst downturn since the Great Depression.[129] But the situation was exacerbated by Reagan's resolve to slash taxes and pump up military spending. Even as he paid lip service to balanced budgets, then, Reagan's perseverance in pursuing both tax cuts and the largest buildup in military spending since the Korean War was destined to produce a permanent shortfall in revenues.[130] In the face of this contradiction, Reagan's budget director, David Stockman, quietly persuaded him to drop his campaign pledge to enact a balanced budget amendment.[131]

It is not clear how many people actually believed the radical supply-side proposition that tax cuts would pay for themselves in increased revenues, but by the early months of the Reagan administration, many, including Reagan himself, were convinced by the more pragmatic argument that tax cuts were the best way of cornering the Democrats.[132] The "starve the beast" strategy implied that Reagan need not search for an immediate spending offset to his tax cuts since Democrats would in the long run be forced to enact these anyhow, under the goad of out-of-control deficits. In a speech marketing his proposed tax cuts, Reagan remarked that "there were always those who told us that taxes couldn't be cut until spending was reduced. Well, you know we can lecture our children about extravagance until we run out of voice and breath. Or we can cure their extravagance by simply reducing their allowance."[133] By itself, Reagan's cavalier approach to tax cuts might not have succeeded in reversing the established roles between Democrats and Republicans. But the Democrats fell straight into the trap and made the politically fatal decision to make Reagan's deficit record rather than his spending cuts their primary focus of attack.[134] Thus they became the unwitting defenders of standalone austerity in the face of a Republican administration that was artfully playing in both registers, combining direct spending cuts to stigmatized public spending programs with an extravaganza of tax cuts for more deserving others.

In the first year of his presidency alone, Reagan managed to push through a stunning $787 billion in tax reductions and $130.5 billion in spending cuts—a victory he achieved with the help of conservative Democrats.[135] But as deficits mounted and the promised revenue windfall failed to materialize, Reagan was unable to muster the same coalition for the much more drastic cuts to Medicare, Medicaid, and welfare he proposed in 1982 and suffered a resounding defeat in his efforts to privatize Social Security.[136] As time went on, the manifest contradictions in Reagan's position made it harder for him to convince Congress that the budget would sort itself out of its own accord, and this threatened his chances in the midterm elections. At this point, Reagan's senior advisors prevailed on him to end his silence on the balanced budget amendment and issue an official statement of support. A White House memorandum sent to senior presidential aides in April 1982 outlined the strategic value of such an endorsement. "Caught as we are, proposing a deficit which demoralizes our strongest supporters, we have one good way out," the memo advised. The "President, who is a notorious foe of deficits, could almost totally reclaim the initiative by committing all the political resources of the Administration in support of the balanced-budget, tax-limitation constitutional amendment." "At one stroke, we would restore the fighting vigor of our core supporters and steal from our opponents the major issue on which they are making headway against us. Liberal Democrats who have been decrying the deficits would face an insoluble problem. Most of the pain of the 1983 deficit would ease. The market would surely rally. The effect on long-term interest rates would probably be dramatic." At the same time, the memo continued, ratification of a balanced budget amendment by three-fourths of the states "would likely be some time down the road, thus buying us time to cope with the bulge in social spending that we inherited from previous administrations." Presidential endorsement of the balanced budget amendment "would restore intact in 1982 the 1980 Reagan winning coalition."[137]

This, in a nutshell, was the game Republicans would play over the following decades. From Reagan onward, with the notable exception of George H. W. Bush, Republicans learned to leverage the cause of the balanced budget to maximum effect while at the same time behaving like fervent supply-siders in practice. Deficits didn't matter, as long as they were financing tax cuts or the military. They mattered a lot, however, when they served to finance domestic spending other than prisons and police. Indeed, whenever Republicans were caught in the act of creating deficits, they would point to the dead weight of entitlements that previous administrations had bequeathed them, forever underscoring the point that wasteful social spending was the true culprit. In sum, Republicans opposed the kinds of deficits that Democrats were liable to create and when faced with these became pious defenders of balanced budgets. As few Democrats supported the cause of the balanced budget amendment after 1980, and as their opposition made it unlikely that Congress, much less a full three-quarters of states, would ever approve one, Republicans were able to make full rhetorical use of the amendment cause without facing the consequences with regard to their own spending preferences. As the internal Reagan administration memo of 1982 foresaw, Republicans could use the mere threat of a balanced budget amendment to enforce a very selective kind of fiscal austerity, even when they recognized in private that its passage was unlikely and perhaps even undesirable.

If the strategy hadn't quite worked under Reagan, who ended up raising taxes again in 1982, Newt Gingrich perfected it in the 1990s, when he proved how completely an incumbent Democratic president could be shackled by the mere threat of a balanced budget amendment. In the 1970s, Gingrich was one of several up-and-coming Republicans to have been groomed by the New Right impresario Paul Weyrich, with the long-term goal of radicalizing the GOP from within.[138] Like his mentor, Gingrich felt that the Republican Party of the postwar years had become so comfortable in its minority status that it had forgotten how to wield power. In the absence of any real opposition party, American politics had devolved into a polite dialogue, in which Democrats had the winning hand and Republicans moved inexorably toward the center. Gingrich saw polarization as an end in itself. Republicans had no chance of ever winning a House majority unless they learned to pull away from the center and sharpen the contradictions. When questioned in one interview how much damage he was prepared to inflict in pursuit of this goal, he replied that the House had to be brought down before it could be built up again.[139]

As a junior House member during the Reagan administration, Gingrich tested out the hardball tactics he would perfect in the years ahead. In 1983, he marshalled allies into the Conservative Opportunity Society, a caucus of insurgent Republicans that tried to steer Reagan away from intraparty compromise.[140] Gingrich and his COS allies spent the Reagan years railing against the president's tergiversations on fiscal issues, urging him to adopt a hard budget limit and despairing when he wound back some of his first-year tax cuts. Reviving the methods of Senator Harry Byrd Sr., Gingrich in 1982 announced his intention to vote against a rise in the debt ceiling unless Congress considered "dramatic spending cuts" and threatened to shut down the government for weeks on end to extract this concession.[141] Later, he distributed a letter cosigned by fifty-three other Republican conservatives urging the House to preserve Reagan's first-year tax cuts, to enact spending cuts in the billions, and to pass a constitutional amendment balancing the federal budget.[142] While Gingrich and his allies were too weak to do anything but rant from the sidelines during the 1980s, they would come into their own during the Clinton years, when Gingrich emerged as a formidable House minority whip, capable of making and breaking Republican moderates.

When George H. W. Bush, in 1990, reneged on his infamous "read my lips" pledge to introduce no new taxes, Newt Gingrich incited an internal revolt from which Republican moderates would never recover. In retrospect, it is clear that the showdown served as a watershed in Republican Party fiscal politics: from this point on, radical tax cutters gained the moral high ground, and moderates such as Robert Dole could no longer entertain tax increases even in the face of deficits.[143] Where Reagan was continually brokering between the supply-siders and fiscal conservatives in his administration, Gingrich, a longtime admirer of Jack Kemp, taught Republicans that deficits don't matter—unless of course they were the consequence of liberal social welfare spending. A consummate practitioner of the "starve the beast" strategy diagnosed by former Kemp advisor Bruce Bartlett, Gingrich saw no contradiction between his support for sweeping tax cuts and his commitment to a balanced budget amendment.[144] This was a logical contradiction that was not meant to be resolved: instead, it served as a useful weapon against Democrats, who in the absence of any more courageous fiscal vision, would be forced to perform the Sisyphean task of paring back social spending as fast as Republicans could slash taxes.

President Clinton was already on the defensive within his first few months of entering office. Although he had campaigned on a promise to invest in infrastructure, research, and education, he was quickly persuaded by his economic advisor Robert Rubin and Federal Reserve chairman Alan Greenspan that he would need to balance the budget first. Hence, Clinton's first budget bill, the Omnibus Budget Reconciliation Act of 1993, included a suite of spending cuts and moderate tax increases on high-income earners and corporations, with very little left over for public investment.[145] This, along with the early defeat of Clinton's national health insurance bill, signaled a fatal readiness to surrender. As Clinton wryly remarked, "Where are the Democrats? We are all Eisenhower Republicans."[146] Yet as Democrats would soon learn, even Eisenhower Republicanism would not appease the Gingrich Republicans.

JAMES M. BUCHANAN AND THE REPUBLICAN REVOLUTION

Gingrich's moment of glory arrived with the midterm elections of 1994, when Republicans seized both the House and Senate for the first time in four decades. More than half of the losses inflicted on the Democrats came from the South, a final confirmation that the once solid Democratic South now leaned Republican. While it was true that the GOP's majorities were smaller and less immovable than those once enjoyed by southern Democrats, the significance of the event went beyond mere numbers. The volatile young southern Republicans who had goaded Reagan from the sidelines during the 1980s now held the reins of power in Congress, where they set the new tone of GOP politics: with the inauguration of the 104th Congress, Newt Gingrich assumed the position of Speaker of the House, Dick Armey and former COS member Tom Delay were nominated for House majority leader and House majority whip, respectively, and another COS alumnus, Trent Lott of Mississippi, was the new Senate majority whip.[147]

While most Republicans were not expecting such a resounding victory in the midterm elections, Newt Gingrich had been preparing for this very conjuncture since the 1980s and was determined to use it as aggressively as possible. Fearing that a Republican majority might be short-lived and easily squandered, Gingrich had prevailed on Republicans to sign on to a preelection manifesto setting out the party's legislative agenda. The Contract with America, coauthored by Newt Gingrich and Dick Armey, called for a set of sweeping operational and fiscal reforms to be enacted within the first one hundred days of the 104th Congress. These ranged from anticorruption measures such as term limits and a crusade against government waste; tort law reforms designed to limit product liability protections for consumers; a reduction in the capital gains tax; tax expenditures on child and elderly care; strengthened truth-in-sentencing laws and a diversion of social spending to fund prison construction; a root-and-branch overhaul of the much-maligned welfare program, Aid to Families with Dependent Children (AFDC); and last but not least, a balanced budget amendment to the Constitution.[148] The contract's tax expenditures alone, designed to increase in value at higher income levels, looked certain to violate the proposed balanced budget rule within a few years, at which point Republicans would be sure to call for more extensive spending cuts.[149]

In reality, incoming Republicans had much more radical ambitions than those outlined in the Contract with America. Gingrich returned to office as Speaker of the House, vowing to abolish the Department of Education, eviscerate the Earned Income Tax Credit for the working poor, and cut spending on Medicare, not just the stigmatized public assistance program of Medicaid.

And although Social Security was explicitly exempted from the contract's assault on public spending, Gingrich, in private, made clear his intention to go after it when the time was right.[150]

The Contract with America, Gingrich explained, would "transfer power back to the states and to local governments and back to families."[151] If this sounded like extreme austerity, it was also designed to flatter the self-image of suburban homeowners, who were constantly told that their household wealth had been privately generated—in contrast to the public wealth squandered on inner-city scroungers. Gingrich held up his own district of Cobb County in suburban Atlanta as an exemplar of private-property-owning autarchy. Middle-class suburbanites, he charged, were sick of "sending more money to inner-city mayors": they wanted to segregate their tax dollars within the family and local community, to have a "neighborhood where their children are safe…a chance to save what they earn, the right to spend it themselves."[152] Gingrich's romanticization of the postwar suburb as a bastion of economic independence conveniently neglected the role of federal money in making homeownership accessible to white male workers across the country. It egregiously misrepresented the history of suburban landscapes in the Sunbelt South and West, many of which had been brought into existence under the combined auspices of federal highway money, government mortgage insurance, and billions of dollars in defense outlays. At the time Gingrich took up his position as House Speaker, his own Cobb County was receiving more federal dollars per capita than any other suburban area in the nation, with the exception of Arlington County in Virginia (which houses the CIA and Pentagon) and Brevard County in Florida (home to the NASA Space Center).[153] Small wonder that Gingrich's program of extreme austerity was also highly selective, exempting military spending from the cutbacks that were reserved for public assistance and other domestic discretionary programs for the poor.

Gingrich understood all too well that the balanced budget amendment, or the credible threat thereof, was critical to his agenda. "The budget is the transformational document for the system," he explained to the House Republican Conference on the eve of victory. "When you've changed the budget, you've really changed government, and until you change the budget, you've just talked about changing government."[154] And in conversation with a biographer, he hailed the "balanced budget" as the "only thing that gives you the moral imperative to change the whole structure of the welfare state."[155] Whatever its moral value, the strategic utility of the balanced budget lever was beyond question. Having exempted Social Security and defense from budget negotiations, the Republicans could wield the threat of a hard budget limit to force Clinton's hand, giving him no choice but to look for savings in social welfare programs.

It was during the Clinton years that a new think tank—Citizens for a Sound Economy—emerged as a powerful driving force behind the movement to enact a balanced budget amendment. Established in 1984 by Charles and David Koch, Citizens for a Sound Economy (CSE) had maintained a low public profile until the early years of the Clinton administration, when it won a first battle against Clinton's proposed energy tax, and went on to prove its mettle as the chief federating force behind the campaign to defeat a national health-care bill (about which we will hear more in the following chapter).[156] The organization began life as a discreet mediator between legislators and business interests. Although a nonprofit and thus, in principle, committed to "social welfare" rather than specific political interests, CSE cultivated friendly relations with Republican legislators who might be willing to block or expedite the legislative process in the service of CSE's business clients. In the era prior to the 2010 *Citizens United v. Federal Election Commission* ruling, corporations could contribute only a limited amount of money to political candidates. There were no such restrictions on the charitable donations they could make to non-profits such as CSE, however. By keeping its funding sources secret, CSE could defend the interests of corporations in the halls of power, while allowing them to present a scrupulously impartial face to the outside world.[157]

When Clinton was elected in 1992, CSE lost its direct line to Republican legislators and so made a tactical decision to cultivate a "grassroots" presence beyond the Washington beltway.[158] To this end, it established an ongoing working relationship with the National Federation of Independent Business (NFIB) and other small business associations, whose members soon proved their worth as main street foot soldiers in the campaign against Clinton's health-care reform.[159]

The once obscure NFIB had much to gain from this alliance. As the poor cousin to the Chamber of Commerce, the organization had a large member base and extensive networks at the local and state level, but weak links to federal legislators. With CSE on its side, the NFIB could make use of unimaginable resources and untrammeled access to Republicans in Congress. As a result, the organization assumed a newly prominent position in the world of politically active trade associations.[160] What CSE gained in return was priceless—a locally embedded, politically energized base, whose hundreds of thousands of members could be relied upon to mob state legislators and turn out en masse at the ballot box.[161] The forging of this alliance, notes Nancy MacLean, resolved a problem that had long haunted organized libertarianism: how to recruit soldiers into a movement that had only an officer class.[162] Small business owners had been energetic defenders of market freedom since the tax revolt of the late 1970s and so provided the perfect Main Street cover for the legislative agenda of Koch's big business donor base.

In the course of its feuds with the Clinton administration, CSE forged a tight working relationship with Gingrich Republicans, virtually requisitioning Gingrich's office as its de facto headquarters during the campaign against health-care reform.[163] By the time of the Republican landslide of 1994, the relationship was so symbiotic that a handful of CSE staff members went to work for Gingrich allies on Capitol Hill, while CSE threw its full weight into the battle to implement the Contract with America.[164] As exultant Republican freshmen pressed forward under Gingrich's marching orders, the CSE presented itself as a disinterested business stakeholder commenting from the sidelines. Yet it was far from impartial when it came to those it considered to be Republican moderates. When neoconservative William Kristol, at the time a top Republican strategist, called for compromise on the issue of a balanced budget, the CSE went on the attack. "We want Republicans to draw a line in the sand and not blink," CSE spokesman Brent N. Bahler announced.[165] As Gingrich well understood, the blackmail of the balanced budget was nonnegotiable.

The presence of the well-financed CSE at the very heart of the Republican Revolution gave new momentum to a campaign that until this point had been entirely sustained by the small-budget National Taxpayers Union and the National Tax Limitation Committee. When old-timers such as James Dale Davidson and Lewis K. Uhler turned up to defend the balanced budget amendment in Congress, they now stood shoulder to shoulder with high-powered CSE spokesmen, with their subterranean links to Republican congressmen and their incomparable financial resources.[166]

The CSE's oratory struck a familiar note. In a speech in favor of the balanced budget amendment, CSE president Wayne Gable evoked the specter of unnamed "special interests," hell-bent on using the deficit to line their own pockets at the expense of average taxpayers.[167] The reason why a Balanced Budget Amendment was necessary, Gable continued, was that "in a representative democracy like the United States, a fundamental imbalance biases the political process in favor of those who seek more federal spending on specific programs and against the average citizen who has to pay the bill."[168] For "about 150 years, policymakers had taken it for granted that deficit spending was irresponsible—indeed, even immoral." But these attitudes had begun to erode in the 1930s, along with the import of Keynesian ideas.[169]

If CSE representatives sounded like they were speaking fluent public choice, there was good reason for this. Buchanan had long-standing connections with the Charles G. Koch Foundation and in 1975 had attended the organization's inaugural seminar in Virginia.[170] In 1977, Charles G. Koch was one of several right-wing luminaries to whom Buchanan sent a personal copy of the recently published *Democracy in Deficit*, with its resounding endorsement of the balanced budget amendment; in response, Koch wrote back to say how "excited" he was "about developments in the economics profession" and how much he appreciated Buchanan's "important role...in bringing them about."[171] When Charles and David Koch founded CSE in 1984, they looked to Buchanan's colleagues and former students to join their staff. It was Buchanan who advised Charles Koch to appoint fellow George Mason University scholar Richard Fink as the organization's president.[172] Over the following years, several generations of graduates from the University of Virginia, Virginia Polytechnic Institute, and George Mason University joined its ranks. James C. Miller III, a public choice protégé and graduate of the University of Virginia, had spent several years pushing a radical privatization agenda as head of Reagan's Federal Trade Commission and budget director. In 1988, he resigned from the Office of Management and Budget to serve as chairman of CSE.[173] Robert D. Tollison, who had written his PhD under Buchanan's supervision at the University of Virginia, was appointed to the CSE board of directors in 1986 and remained there until 2000. Tollison's academic work reflected his long-standing ties with the tobacco industry, which paid him and several other Virginia school scholars to oppose excise taxes and other mooted public health regulations using the ostensibly neutral language of public choice economics. Buchanan himself was a member of CSE's academic advisory board.[174]

At the same time that the Koch-funded CSE was making its mark in federal politics, another organization was flexing its muscles at the state level. The American Legislative Exchange Council (ALEC) was cofounded in 1973 by New Right impresario Paul Weyrich—later a mentor to Newt Gingrich.[175] One of many organizations that Weyrich set up and promptly delegated to others over the years, ALEC was designed to counter the formidable influence of left-wing public-sector unions in state politics. At the time it was established in the early 1970s, activist unions such as the National Education Association had established a beachhead in state legislatures and were leveraging this position to push through model legislation across the country.[176] Like many of the New Right's institutions, ALEC was created as a mirror image of and competitor to an existing power bloc on the left. Although its focus and methods would change over the years, its animus against public-sector unions burned on, later erupting into the dramatic legislative assaults orchestrated by Tea Party governors in the 2010s.

In its first decade of existence, ALEC tried unsuccessfully to bridge the divide between business interests and religious conservatives—the two poles of the New Right agenda—but ended up alienating the trade associations it wanted to work with.[177] In the course of the 1980s, the organization settled on a more comfortable division of labor, largely ceding the religious conservative terrain to other New Right institutions such as the Council for National Policy while it attended more closely to the pressing policy concerns of business.[178]

ALEC's breakthrough moment as a middleman between trade associations and state legislators was a campaign to weaken tort law protections for consumers—later taken up at the federal level by Gingrich's Contract with America. By the late 1980s, the organization had become involved in the state convention process to petition for a balanced budget amendment and was working in close collaboration with the NTLC's Lew Uhler.[179] During the 1990s, Koch Industries was one of ALEC's most active dues-paying members, working closely with another member Enron to push for energy deregulation across the country.[180] At the same time, ALEC and the Koch-funded CSE were working side by side on the campaign to enact a balanced budget amendment at the state and federal level, respectively. This was one early instance of coordinated activism between the New Right–founded ALEC and another entirely Koch-directed and financed endeavor, CSE—a coalition of New Right and Koch interests that would become ubiquitous with the Tea Party movement of the early 2010s.

The Contract with America's balanced budget amendment came within a hair's breadth of success. It passed the House of Representatives in January of 1995 (the first such amendment to do so) but fell one vote short of the requisite two-thirds supermajority in the Senate.[181] Following a script that had been established in the 1970s, the impetus for the campaign then shifted to the states, where the increasingly powerful ALEC (of which the NTU and NTLC were now members) took the initiative in pushing for a constitutional convention.[182]

BILL CLINTON, NEW SOUTHERN DEMOCRAT

In the meantime, Clinton was convinced by centrist advisors that he would need to enact a plan to balance the budget anyhow. What followed was a test of wills in which Republicans set out a draconian wish list of spending hits to Medicare, Medicaid, and education, and Clinton responded with a qualified counteroffer that made him look reasonable by comparison.[183] Gingrich then upped the ante by refusing to raise the debt ceiling—a form of blackmail that had been test-run by Senator Byrd in the 1950s, brandished by a young Gingrich in the 1980s, and subsequently incorporated into the Republican arsenal as a regular weapon in its budget battles with Democrats.[184]

Republicans forced two government shutdowns between the end of 1995 and the beginning of 1996.[185] In the short term, the standoff worked against Gingrich, who was eventually forced to back down and accept an earlier offer from Clinton. But the episode ultimately solidified Republican strategy—as set out in the previously cited internal Reagan administration memo of 1982—and confirmed their intuition that the battle was half won when Democrats were speaking the language of balanced budgets. If Clinton once thought that balancing the budget of his own accord would give him the green light to spend later, he now understood that Republicans saw spending moderation as an end in itself. Clinton's most progressive proposal, a complete reform of health-care insurance to cover America's millions of uninsured, died in Congress after a vicious attack by CSE and Gingrich Republicans.[186] His most regressive proposal, the promise "to end welfare as we know it," ended up conceding far more ground to Republicans than he would have liked (including a five-year exclusion for legal migrants) and was emptied of all of the mitigating expenditures on increased childcare and job training he had originally envisaged.[187]

If Clinton, the "New Democrat" from Arkansas, had been turned into an Eisenhower Republican during his first years in office, after the midterm elections of 1994 he was governing like an old-time southern Democrat. No late twentieth-century Republican president ever made a comparable effort to downsize the government. Under Clinton's watch, total federal expenditures fell from 21.9 to 18.1 percent of GDP, amounting to a total decline of 17.1 percent between 1992 and 2000. And although New Democrats celebrated this as a fiscal "peace dividend" afforded by the now obsolete Cold War, it is remarkable that Clinton made no effort to divert the resulting savings toward other ends, instead opting to introduce further cuts in education (minus 23.9 percent), science (minus 19.1 percent), income security (minus 17.6 percent), and transportation (minus 10 percent).[188] The New Democrat president who had entered office calling for a cornucopia of new investments in science, infrastructure, and R&D, ended up authorizing a $25.6 billion reduction in these same areas of federal spending.[189] And despite significant cuts in Cold War military infrastructure, defense spending remained over five times higher than federal outlays on education.[190]

Clinton's fiscal politics were exceptional by any standard. Democrats, after all, had traditionally outperformed Republicans when it came to domestic (nondefense) discretionary spending—the annual budget appropriations, not covered by statutory mandates or entitlements, that fund such essential services as infrastructure, national parks, public health, consumer protection, education, and myriad assistance programs for the urban poor. Clinton, by contrast, made parsimonious use of this option. His total domestic discretionary spending was not only lower than that of his Democratic predecessors, but it also underperformed with respect to the Republican administrations of Bush, Reagan, and Nixon.

Placed on the defensive by a ruthlessly aggressive Gingrich coalition, Clinton made much of his resolve to protect Medicare from Republican attacks and reaped the rewards in terms of popularity. But as a consequence of this concession to the deserving middle class, a disproportionate share of Clinton's cuts fell on programs for the poor, including AFDC, SSI, food stamps, public housing, and other less visible antipoverty programs covered by discretionary spending.[191]

Under the shadow of a de facto balanced budget rule, Clinton's policy choices bore an uncanny resemblance to those of conservative southern Democrats at midcentury. This was particularly true of Clinton's welfare reform legislation of 1996—the Personal Responsibility and Work Opportunity Reconciliation Act—that eliminated the old AFDC (Aid to Families with Dependent Children) as a federal entitlement and replaced it with the much more restrictive TANF (Temporary Assistance for Needy Families).[192] In deference to the principle of fiscal federalism, the Personal Responsibility Act eliminated welfare's original open-ended funding structure and replaced it with state block grants that allowed for no leeway in response to economic recessions or rising poverty levels. States had to make do with a fixed welfare budget, whether caseloads rose or fell, and therefore had no choice but to tighten the screws and shrink individual benefits.[193]

The principle of fiscal federalism had been celebrated by Republicans from Nixon to Reagan as a cure-all for the excesses of the liberal welfare state. But as noted by journalist Elizabeth Drew, it also "had more than a whiff of the old states' rights approach" that had long sanctioned the right of southern Democrats to discriminate against the poor and nonwhite.[194] Under its auspices, states were authorized to enact their own experiments in welfare discipline—they might, for example, introduce faith-based instruction in abstinence and monogamy or divert welfare money to middle-class marriage counseling—as long as they hewed to a federal baseline. In the meantime, the new standard set by the federal government had itself become so punitive that it compelled all states to implement poor-law rules that were once overwhelmingly associated with the South.[195]

During House and Senate negotiations over the Social Security Act of 1935, Harry Byrd and other conservative Democrats in Congress had carved out a southern exception to the universal social insurance principles of the New Deal, segregating the region's mostly African American agricultural and domestic workers into a poor-law regime of unfree labor enacted under the blunt compulsion of hunger. This space of exception allowed Byrd and other large southern landowners to push down wages at will, safe in the knowledge that sharecroppers, tenant farmers, farm laborers, and domestic servants had no option but to accept what work was available.

The welfare-to-work provisions in Clinton's Personal Responsibility Act of 1996 played a similar wage-depressing role in the service, retail, and logistics sector of late industrial America. By placing a two-year time limit on welfare benefits, beyond which beneficiaries would need to accept the first job offer made to them, the legislation delivered hundreds of thousands of welfare recipients into the low-wage economy, without the education funding Clinton had originally hoped to provide. Aware that employers would not want to train these workers on their own account, Clinton's Welfare to Work Partnership program of 1998 instead provided tax credits to companies that were willing to employ workers straight off the welfare rolls.

The Chamber of Commerce, the most vocal trade champion of welfare to work, had called for further concessions to businesses that pledged to employ people coming off welfare: it had recommended a probationary period in which minimum wages, maximum working hours, and overtime pay would be frozen and employers exempted from antidiscrimination laws, "prevailing wage" policies for government contracts, and medical and family leave policies.[196] But even when Clinton blocked these requests, there was no lack of interest on the part of employers. As the first round of welfare beneficiaries to come under the new two-year time limit were pushed off the rolls, the Welfare to Work Partnership shunted them into low-wage work in pharmacies, fast-food franchises, temp agencies, nursing homes, distribution warehouses, and meat processing plants across the country.[197] There was good reason why unemployment reached record lows during the late 1990s without generating any wage growth at the bottom of the workforce.[198] When their two-year time limit was up, welfare recipients had to accept the first job that was offered them or disappear from the welfare rolls altogether. The poor-law tradition of the large southern farm was reborn in the sprawling retail, health care, and logistics sweatshops of the late twentieth century.

This is not to say that unfree labor was the only weapon available to the poor-law tradition. The nineteenth-century workhouse or post–Civil War sharecropping system had always operated in concert with a less recognized instrument of capitalist discipline: the state-imposed assertion of kinship relations as an alternative to public welfare.[199] During the 1930s, southern states had made abundant use of "family" or "spousal responsibility" rules to police the intimate relationships of female welfare claimants and force them wherever possible into private dependence on a man. Welfare agencies across the South routinely cited man-in-the-house, substitute father, and suitable home rules to exclude impoverished women from the welfare rolls, on the grounds that their intimate relationships with men made them undeserving claimants or de facto dependants on a man's care.[200] Although southern welfare programs were the most brutal and threadbare by a long shot, northern states began to follow their lead in the 1950s and 1960s, as the number of divorced or never-married women rose and northern welfare agencies saw a growing influx of African American migrants from the South.[201]

The Supreme Court eventually outlawed these poor-law rules in the late 1960s and 1970s, forcing southern states to align their welfare programs with a more generous federal minimum.[202] Republican legislators would do all in their power to erode these gains over the following decades. But their success was minimal when compared to Clinton's landmark legislation, which reinstated the poor-law rule of paternal responsibility at the very heart of the new welfare system. Clinton not only revived the old "absent father" rule once cherished by southern states but also enshrined it in federal legislation, where it had never been recognized before, turning the new welfare program TANF into a much more punitive system than its New Deal forerunner. Welfare agencies were now instructed to pursue every avenue in search of the biological fathers of children on benefits (now deemed legally responsible for child support whatever their past or actual relationship to the mother), and they would disburse funds only once all options of private paternal provision had been exhausted.[203] Thus, a self-professed New Democrat infused new life into the poor-law regime of the old South and turned a once shameful exception into a federal baseline. Gingrich Republicans may have pushed him there, but even Clinton's closest advisors were shocked by the scale of his surrender.[204] By contrast, Clinton resolutely defended tax expenditures on "working families" from a growing chorus of critique by Gingrich Republicans. The Earned Income Tax Credit (EITC) was the Democratic Leadership Council's preferred alternative to direct spending on welfare.[205] Chicago school economist Milton Friedman had first come up with the idea in the early 1970s, and southern

Democrat Russell Long had championed it as a novel way of pushing African American welfare mothers off the rolls and into the low-wage workforce.[206] Its value, in the eyes of each of these stakeholders, was its ability to deliver government expenditures in the retroactive form of the tax credit, which could be claimed only as a result of working. The EITC program had grown dramatically after Reagan's 1986 Tax Reform Act, thanks to the enthusiasm of the Christian right for a measure that ticked both the antitax and profamily boxes, and was scaled up under both George H. W. Bush and Clinton. During the 1990s, the total cost of the program, expressed in constant 2000 dollars, grew from just under $10 billion to over $32 billion. As a result, tax expenditures on the working poor now surpassed direct spending on the stigmatized welfare and food stamp programs—a reflection of the bipartisan consensus that government support, if tolerated at all, was best disbursed in the indirect, work-incentivizing form of the tax credit.[207] For the poorest of the poor, there was to be no escape from the low-wage labor market.

PERMANENT FISCAL COUNTERREVOLUTION

The spirit of the Gingrich-led Republican Revolution returned in force with the election of Barack Obama, when Republicans were once again caught off guard by a charismatic Democratic centrist and insurgents emerged from the right flank to put the party on a war footing. Dick Armey, a key actor in both episodes, described the Tea Party wave of 2010 as the culmination of a long series of intraparty revolts, each leading the GOP closer to a state of ideological rigor. The opening salvo was the presidential bid of Barry Goldwater, who had inspired a young Armey to enter politics. Then came the Reagan revolution, where antiestablishment Republicans got their first taste of executive power, and finally the 1994 Gingrich takeover of Congress, resulting "in the impossible—a balanced budget amendment."[208] For Armey, the Tea Party movement promised to achieve what these earlier movements had not: an enduring constitutional counterrevolution restoring America to its founding state of limited government and individual freedom.[209]

It is hard to contest this lineage. Like Gingrich, the Tea Party freshmen who surged to power in the 2010 elections were not afraid to "burn down the house" to achieve their ends. Determined to disarm their opponents if they could not hold power themselves, Tea Party legislators were possessed of the same single-minded resolve to block, delay, or repeal any attempt by the Democratic administration to pursue an expansive fiscal politics—or simply to maintain the status quo. But if Gingrich was no stranger to fiscal sabotage, making deliberate and shameless use of the debt ceiling and a threatened balanced budget amendment to extract concessions, the Tea Party took the art of obstruction to another level. In each year between January 2011, when a wave of Tea Party–affiliated freshmen swept into the House of Representatives, and January 2017, when Obama left office, congressional Republicans managed to turn at least one major budgetary deadline into a show of force. The standout moments in this war of attrition included the August 2011 showdown over the debt limit and forced vote on the passage of a balanced budget amendment, the fiscal cliff of 2012, the government shutdown of 2013, and the near shutdown of 2014.[210] But no list of punctual events can convey the sheer relentlessness of Tea Party obstructionism—the months of gridlock, the endless delay tactics deployed to defer the implementation of legislation that had already passed, and the time wasted in grueling negotiations, almost always prolonged until the eleventh hour.

In the Senate also, Republicans turned gridlock into a procedural art form. The Republican minority under Mitch McConnell made more use of threatened filibusters than any other minority party in American history, blocking or delaying everything from contested legislation, judicial nominations, and executive branch appointments to the most routine government decisions.[211] Having aligned himself with the Tea Party as a matter of political survival, McConnell turned the filibuster from a weapon of last resort into a permanent modus operandi. Even when Democrats had the numbers to invoke a cloture and defeat a filibuster, they now spent so much time overcoming the hurdles placed in their way by Republican senators that the entire business of governing slowed to a glacial pace. The political scientist Sean Theriault refers to this new generation of hyperadversarial Republican senators as "Gingrich senators": many of them, he notes, first served in the House of Representatives alongside Newt Gingrich in the 1980s and later took Gingrich's peculiar style of partisan warfare into the upper chamber.[212]

At once a populist movement and a business-led legislative crusade, the Tea Party upsurge was driven at the elite level by some of the same para-party machines that had risen to prominence during the Gingrich Revolution. In 2004, internal rivalries within the Koch-funded CSE led to the organization's dissolution, with core members taking up positions in two new outfits, Americans for Prosperity and FreedomWorks.[213] While former CSE president Richard Fink took up the leadership of Americans for Prosperity, it was Dick Armey, former House majority leader and chairman of CSE, who took the helm at FreedomWorks. Along with FreedomWorks' other staff members, George Mason University alumni Matt Kibbe and Wayne Brough, Dick Armey was a conscientious practitioner of public choice economics.[214] In an interview conducted in the midst of the Tea Party uprising of 2009, Armey confessed that he "was largely influenced by a unique American contribution called Public Choice Theory that was pioneered by Dr. James Buchanan in the state of Virginia."[215] A trained economist who had chaired the Department of Economics at North Texas State University before entering politics, Armey clarified that while his "intellectual" grounding was in the Austrian school economics of Ludwig von Mises and Friedrich Hayek, his "methodological" inclinations were shaped by public choice.[216] This twin heritage does much to illuminate Armey's punitive and fatalistic posture toward austerity-induced deflation (a feature of Austrian neoliberalism) and his methodological expertise in the arts of countermajoritarian rule (with its obvious debt to the teachings of Buchanan).

It should be stressed that Americans for Prosperity and FreedomWorks did not create but rather harnessed the power of the emerging Tea Party movement, in much the same way that Citizens for a Sound Economy annexed the energy of small business associations and the religious right in the 1990s. When a smattering of citizen groups got together to protest Obama's federal stimulus bill in 2009, Americans for Prosperity and FreedomWorks immediately identified a political opportunity and reached out with financing, training, and a direct conduit to media personalities such as Glenn Beck and Rush Limbaugh.[217] This combination of movement energy and organizational acumen delivered Republicans a historic landslide in the midterm elections of 2010.[218] Two years into Obama's first term, Republicans picked up sixty-three seats in the House of Representatives—the largest midterm gain of any party since 1938—while six new seats in the Senate gave Republicans sufficient numbers to filibuster all Democratic initiatives. Many of the incoming members of the House were Tea Party–endorsed freshmen, intent on undoing or blocking Obama's legislative achievements by whatever means possible.[219]

These Tea Party freshmen lost no time in making their presence felt. The debt ceiling crisis of 2011 (outlined in the introduction to this chapter) was the first in a series of standoffs that pitted Tea Party house members against mainstream Republicans and Democrats alike. Despite numerous attempts by House Speaker John Boehner (himself a veteran of the Gingrich insurgency) to break the deadlock with draconian spending cuts, Republican negotiators were ultimately held hostage by radicals within the new Tea Party Caucus, who were determined to extract much more radical concessions.[220] A hard core of no more than thirty Tea Party–affiliated legislators were responsible for holding the line on the debt ceiling, yet their sway over Republican Party dynamics was magnified by the outside influence of groups such as Freedom-Works, Americans for Prosperity, and the Club for Growth. These groups kept a vigilant eye on Republican roll calls, threatening to unleash primary challenges against any incumbent officeholder who defected from the Tea Party line.[221]

In the meantime, Tea Party legislators refused to authorize a debt ceiling increase unless both chambers approved a balanced budget amendment—a near-impossible feat given the two-thirds supermajority requirement in both the House and Senate.[222] In the weeks of back-and-forth that followed, thirty Tea Party hardliners refused to cede ground, instead demonstrating an apocalyptic readiness to take the United States to the edge of default. Ultimately, the fiasco provoked the ratings agency Standard and Poor's to downgrade U.S. debt from AAA to AA+. If few bond investors really expected the United States to stop paying interest on treasuries (and could rest assured that their own claims would be prioritized in the event of default), the willingness of Tea Party Republicans to hold the entire political process to ransom introduced a new level of uncertainty into economic forecasts. In the press release announcing its decision to downgrade, Standard and Poor's explained that the "political brinkmanship of recent months highlights what we see as America's governance and policymaking becoming less stable, less effective and less predictable than what we previously believed. The statutory debt ceiling and the threat of default have become political bargaining chips in the debate over fiscal policy."[223]

Debt default was averted in the nick of time, when an agreement was reached that gave Republicans almost everything they wanted. The Budget Control Act of July 31, 2011, exchanged a debt ceiling hike of $900 billion for spending cuts of approximately equal value. Furthermore, it created a super-committee of legislators charged with identifying additional spending cuts of at least $1.3 trillion (to be spread over a decade) or passing a balanced budget amendment by the end of the year. If the committee failed in either of these endeavors, the $1.3 trillion in cuts would automatically go into effect at the start of 2013.[224] The Obama administration tried its best to paint the bill as a compromise. But in reality, it was a win-win for Republicans.[225] If the House, as was inevitable under the circumstances, were unable to muster the two-thirds supermajority to pass a balanced budget resolution, Republicans would get what they wanted anyway—a brutal halt to every economic stimulus effort for a decade to come. In 2011, the United States was still struggling to emerge from the economic doldrums, home foreclosures were still common in many regional markets, and unemployment rates remained stubbornly high.[226] Yet Tea Party Republicans turned Keynesian countercyclical policy on its head, insisting that this was the time to cut government spending still further. The economist Josh Bivens calculates that the 2011 Budget Control Act generated an antistimulus effect that was almost twice as large as the stimulus effect of Obama's 2009 Recovery Act.[227] The result, in the words of Lawrence Summers, was a lingering or "secular" state of stagnation characterized by historically low rates of new capital investment, sluggish consumer spending, and unemployment figures that looked presentable only because so many of the working-age population were no longer actively seeking work.[228]

Ultimately, it was at the state and city level that the impact of Tea Party austerity was felt most acutely.[229] The majority of states had already implemented their own draconian cuts to core public services in the first years of the recession, as plummeting house prices dried up property and sales tax revenue.[230] Until this point, some relief had come in the form of federal emergency funds to states, which had been legislated as part of the Obama Recovery Act of 2009. But the budget concessions extracted by congressional Republicans shrank the normal flow of federal transfers to states at precisely the moment when emergency aid was tapering off, leaving state legislatures vulnerable to the austere designs of newly elected Tea Party governors. The

2010 midterms had delivered historic gains to Republicans at the state as well as federal level: the GOP picked up six new governors and 675 new legislators as part of the Tea Party electoral sweep. As a result, they now held 53 percent of total state legislative seats, the highest number since 1928.[231] This gave Republican-controlled state legislatures an unusual degree of power to implement Tea Party directives from above. Once the Tea Party faction had completed its work in Congress, then, Republican governors were on their marks, ready to launch a coordinated legislative strike on the state public sector. The speed with which right-to-work laws, antiunion measures, and various restrictions on welfare and other aid programs were rolled out, in textually identical form, across different states left no doubt as to their provenance. Groups such as ALEC and its close collaborator, the State Policy Network, had been crafting and testing out model legislation for years and were determined to exploit the Tea Party landslide of 2010 to the full.[232] In state after state, Republican legislators turned against their public employees, took a hatchet to unemployment benefits, and used the state legislative process to block the ACA-mandated expansion of Medicaid from below.

In some states, these attacks on the public sector were conspicuously paired with efforts to criminalize migrants or to empower armed citizens to enforce vigilante justice. When the Arizona state legislature passed SB1070, a law allowing police to stop and search anyone suspected of being an undocumented migrant, local Tea Party groups rallied to the cause.[233] Many states sought to pass ALEC-designed "stand-your-ground" laws in the same flurry of legislation that went after public-sector unions and social welfare programs.[234] But even when such overt measures were absent, there could be no doubt as to the racially charged nature of Tea Party austerity. The public sector was not only the last redoubt of American unionism but also a leading employer of African Americans and a relative haven from the stark racial disparities of the private-sector workplace.[235] The drive to shrink and disarm the public-sector workforce was always going to impact the employment and wages of African Americans to a disproportionate degree.[236] This was one among several factors that contributed to the much higher levels of unemployment among nonwhites in the wake of the financial crisis.[237]

If the state-level Tea Party assault on public provision for the low-income and out of work in many ways recalled the Gingrich-led (and Clinton-enabled) dismantling of welfare in the mid-1990s, the Tea Party took this campaign to another level. The targeted vitriol that had once been reserved for stigmatized public assistance programs such as AFDC now extended to core programs of the Social Security Act such as unemployment insurance, which middle-class whites had long considered to be an earned right of the contributing tax-payer. In the lingering aftermath of the Global Financial Crisis, sixteen states responded to the swelling ranks of the long-term unemployed by moving to restrict benefits, either by slashing payments or shortening the length of time a person could stay on the rolls.[238] Others introduced "work experience" options similar to the welfare-to-work provisions inflicted on welfare mothers in the 1990s.[239] The fickleness of Tea Party value judgments when it comes to public aid is easier to grasp when we consider changing program demograph-ics. In the wake of the financial crisis of 2008, long-term unemployment was largely an African American problem—and it remained so as the financial cri-sis was transmuted into a manufactured fiscal crisis of the state. Under these circumstances, it made sense for a movement of white retirees, many of them out of the workforce but now in receipt of Social Security and Medicare, to resignify unemployment insurance as a program for the undeserving poor.

A simmering racial resentment was also at work in the Tea Party's relent-less opposition to the Affordable Care Act. The expansion of Medicaid to previ-ously uninsured categories was without a doubt the most radical of the ACA's initiatives and the one that provoked the most outrage among Tea Partiers. Prior to the passage of the ACA in 2010, states were obliged to pay benefits to pregnant women, poor children and their parents, the disabled, and the elderly who were not covered by Medicare. Only eight states offered full Medicaid cov-erage to impoverished adults without children, however, leaving millions with no health insurance at all.[240] Under the terms of the ACA, states were sud-denly obliged to extend public insurance to millions of working-age adults without children, thus granting many younger, poorer, and disproportionately minority citizens and long-term residents the same or similar protections that older white people had long enjoyed under Medicare.[241] And it was this that affronted the sensibilities of Tea Party sympathizers, more than a straight-forward calculus of costs and benefits: the ACA in their eyes represented an immoral transfer of wealth from productive white citizens to the unproduc-tive, perhaps nonwhite or migrant poor.[242] Their suspicions hardened in the lead-up to the midterm elections of 2010, when Republican candidates will-fully misrepresented facts to claim that the ACA's expansion of Medicaid would be paid for with $716 billion in cuts to Medicare, the health-care program that Tea Party supporters passionately defended as the just rewards for their many years of work.[243] Nothing could have better dramatized the fear that President Obama, whose own citizenship status was endlessly challenged by Tea Party "birthers," was providing for undeserving others at the expense of the productive taxpayer.

Congressional Republicans did everything in their power to repeal or hobble the Affordable Care Act. But it was at the state level that they found the most leverage, thanks to a 2012 Supreme Court ruling defending the right of states to opt out of the ACA's expanded Medicaid provisions on the grounds that they constituted a coercive use of the federal spending power.[244] The mandate imposed virtually no new fiscal burdens on states (the federal government promised to cover the full costs of new enrollees for the first three years, and 90 percent thereafter).[245] Yet in apparent defiance of their own self-interest, an astonishing number of Republican-controlled states went out of their way to refuse the new Medicaid funds, so determined were they to secure the borders of the fiscal state against undeserving claimants. In 2017, the number of refuseniks stood at nineteen. As of 2022, a dozen states were still holding out.[246]

The Tea Party grassroots and national umbrella organizations did not always walk in lockstep. Dick Armey, who advocated amnesty for long-term residents, castigated the Tea Party base for its crude xenophobia and advised against the rollout of punitive anti-immigration laws: nativism, he thought, was a strategic mistake for a party that needed desperately to cultivate the Latino vote.[247] By the same token, FreedomWorks, Americans for Prosperity, and their allied legislators were often much more extreme in their visions of fiscal austerity than the Tea Party base. As several movement ethnographers found, Tea Party supporters revealed a great deal of cognitive dissonance when it came to the issue of government spending: while they demonized programs such as TANF and food stamps as symptomatic of government excess, they were fiercely protective of the much more expensive entitlement programs of Social Security and Medicare, which many of them were personally dependent on.[248] "Hands off our Medicare," the slogan that so baffled outside observers of the Tea Party grassroots, makes more sense when we understand this as a movement to defend the limited New Deal welfare state rather than a straight-forward rejection of public spending as such.[249] By contrast, Tea Party legislators such as Paul Ryan were determined to go after everything, including Medicare and Social Security.

The new Republican brinkmanship reflected profound changes in the GOP itself, which in many respects was no longer acting like a traditional party machine. The combined effect of the Bipartisan Campaign Reform Act or McCain-Feingold Act of 2004, which limited the ability of parties to raise money, and the Supreme Court *Citizens United* ruling of 2010, which allowed corporations and wealthy individuals to make unlimited, unregulated donations to election campaigns, was to wrest power from national party leaders and transfer it to "shadow parties" who had no particular allegiance to established partisan structures.[250] Without consulting local party organizations, billionaire donors could use super PACs to funnel money to dark horse candidates who would challenge party incumbents from the far right. Even when these outside candidates had little chance of winning, they had sufficient funding to saturate the media and stay in the race to the last minute, thereby setting the parameters of debate for the Republican incumbent.[251]

The torrent of outside money scrambled bonds of allegiance, creating candidates that were as much (if not more) obligated to donors as they were to their own party. In the House and Senate, the ever-present threat of a primary challenge exerted a profound disciplinary effect on congressional voting and fatally undermined the authority once wielded by leaders and Speakers. Congressional Tea Partiers stubbornly refused to cooperate with Speaker of the House John Boehner and more than once threatened to eject him at the next primaries. He eventually resigned under duress in 2015, just as the House Freedom Caucus was preparing to oust him.[252] Even those who shamelessly curried favor with the Tea Party were not immune from its wrath. The self-proclaimed "Young Guns," Eric Cantor, Paul Ryan, and Kevin McCarthy, who had toured the country whipping up support for Tea Party candidates in the 2010 elections, were all at some point disciplined by the movement they helped to create.[253] Under Tea Party influence, the Republican Party was no longer marching to its own orders or following its own chain of command. Instead, it was acting as if possessed by an outside force, purging one former ally after another in a convulsive search for ideological purity.

It is only when we appreciate how thoroughly the Tea Party transformed the internal dynamics of the GOP that we can understand how someone like Trump could come out of nowhere and still command such blind loyalty from Republican Party ranks. Long before they sold their souls to Trump, Republicans had been pummeled into submission by the Tea Party waves of 2010 and 2014. No longer beholden to its own agenda, the party was in a state of constant upheaval as its congressional representatives suffered wave after wave of contestation from the revolutionary far right. Political commentators who recoiled in disbelief when a majority of Republicans condoned the Capitol Hill insurrection of 2021 were forgetting that Republicans had been waging a campaign of fiscal insurrection for many years now. Almost a decade to the day before far-right insurgents stormed the Capitol, Tea Party legislators had entered Congress with the full intention of playing Russian roulette with the national debt.[254] And this in many ways represented a much more serious threat to American democracy.

For those who had observed or participated in more than one debt ceiling showdown in the past, it was abundantly clear that Tea Party Republicans were playing a much more serious game. In previous such episodes, a clear element of political pantomime was at play: failure to raise the debt ceiling served as a useful stalling mechanism in negotiations, but it was always assumed that neither party had anything to gain from precipitating a default.[255] With the Tea Party in the ascendant, however, there could be no guarantee that negotiators would pull back from the edge. Indeed, several prominent Tea Party congressmen seemed to be deadly serious about the need for debt default. Others were shockingly sanguine about the consequences, should it occur.[256]

Few better illustrated this kamikaze spirit than John Tamny, vice president of FreedomWorks, who in the midst of the budget negotiations of 2011 declared that "it's time we learn to love the idea of a U.S. default."[257] For Tamny, who believed that the buildup of government debt was a crisis in waiting, default was in any case inevitable and might well be the best cure for government excess. "Government spending is our economy's unspoken ill," he lamented, "and the day a default leads to the starvation of this economy-retarding beast is the day the U.S. economy really starts to boom."

James M. Buchanan was less inclined to romantic millenarianism. But he too thought that default on the national debt could be justified under certain circumstances. This was the case, for instance, with debt-financed "current" expenditures, as opposed to capital expenditures on national infrastructure or civic works. It was especially the case when it came to debt-financed spending on social welfare, which he saw as subsidizing the unproductive poor at the ultimate expense of the productive taxpayer.[258] If no attempt was made to rein in this kind of debt, and new generations were expected to pay off a debt they had never consented to, then taxpayers (in Buchanan's view) might have good reason to favor default. Writing in the late 1980s, Buchanan adduced the growing size of the national debt as damning evidence of profligate spending on social welfare. In the coming decades, he predicted, the question of default on the national debt—"a major issue of public policy"—would "move directly into the domain of moral philosophy," where the proponents of debt default would have sound arguments on their side.[259] While others might see default as a catastrophic injury to the monetary sovereignty of the United States, Buchanan never subscribed to the national—or what he called organismic—frame. Instead, he theorized political federations as composites of individual "votes" that could at any time disaggregate and fracture into constituent blocs, without doing damage to democracy as he understood it.[260] Just as the confederate states had seceded from the union in 1861, one group of taxpayers and their congressional representatives might refuse to honor the nation's debt if they felt it was being exploited to finance undeserving others.[261] Debt default was the fiscal equivalent to territorial secession and, in Buchanan's eyes, perfectly justified on moral grounds.

JUDICIAL COUNTERREVOLUTION

For many years, Ronald Reagan had denounced the Voting Rights Act of 1965 as "humiliating to the South."[262] Yet in 1982, he extended the law for twenty-five years and thus sealed the fate of the modern Republican Party for the next few decades: the battle to defend racial, class, and economic privilege would now be fought on the fiscal terrain of public spending decisions rather than the judicial and legislative terrain of voting rights. At the time, the ever-cynical Reagan strategist Lee Atwater offered the following analysis of the Republican party's strategic evolution on this matter: "As to the whole Southern strategy that Harry S. Dent, Sr. and others put together in 1968, opposition to the Voting Rights Act would have been a central part of keeping the South. Now you don't have to do that. All that you need to do to keep the South is for Reagan to run in place on the issues that he's campaigned on since 1964, and that's fiscal conservatism, balancing the budget, cut taxes, you know, the whole cluster."[263]

The interviewer pressed Atwater on the relationship between balanced budgets, social spending cuts, and race, suggesting that "Reagan does get to the Wallace voter and to the racist side of the Wallace voter by doing away with legal services, by cutting down on food stamps."[264] Atwater responded that the strategy was one of abstraction: "Y'all don't quote me on this. You start out in 1954 by saying, 'Nigger, nigger, nigger.' By 1968 you can't say 'nigger'—that hurts you. Backfires. So you say stuff like forced busing, states' rights and all that stuff. You're getting so abstract now [that] you're talking about cutting taxes, and all these things you're talking about are totally economic things and a byproduct of them is [that] blacks get hurt worse than whites."[265]

The constitutional economics of James M. Buchanan did much to accomplish this work of abstraction. In the wake of the Voting Rights Act of 1965, Buchanan shifted his attention to the fiscal terrain, intent on discovering budget rules that would permanently strangle the power of formal voting rights to redistribute economic wealth. He was thus able to give new life to the counter-majoritarian politics of southern Democrats while plausibly denying any intent to disenfranchise African Americans and the poor. As Atwater suggests, the balanced budget amendment was a rear-guard struggle to snuff out the democratic voice of African Americans by other means. Although the amendment has repeatedly failed to pass (and would likely be immediately circumvented if it did come to pass), the campaign itself has more than achieved its goal of permanently tying the hands of legislators. The mere threat of a balanced budget amendment casts a pall over federal budget decisions in much the same way that the state of Virginia's lingering antebellum debt continued to punish its' poorest constituents well into the twentieth century. Buchanan's fiscal counter-revolution has been enshrined in practice, if not in constitutional law.

Today, it must be recognized that Republicans have gone much further. The GOP now possesses many of the instruments of minority veto that once belonged to conservative southern Democrats, and as a party, it has moved far to the right. Where southern Democrats once ruled the Senate with gentlemanly malice, thanks to the privileges of one-party rule and the selective use of the filibuster, recent demographic shifts have endowed Republicans from the smallest, most conservative states with an outsized influence over an institution that has the power to block any legislation that comes its way. In recent decades, a clear partisan split has emerged in the distribution of Senate seats, making it far more likely for Democrats to represent high-population states, while Republicans monopolize the vote in smaller-population states. The equal representation rule for each state has reliably skewed the Senate in favor of the GOP: in 2021, for instance, Republican senators represented nearly forty million fewer voters than Democratic senators in a Senate that was split 50–50.[266] The overrepresentation of rural states in the chamber gives a disproportionate voice to white voters, in a near-replica of the status quo before the landmark voting rights legislation of the 1960s.

Like southern Democrats before them, Republicans have become virtuosi of the filibuster. Under the leadership of Mitch McConnell, however, Republicans turned the Jim Crow filibuster, selectively deployed by southern Democrats to kill off civil rights legislation, into an indiscriminate tool of obstruction designed to block almost any legislative initiatives proposed by the Democrats apart from the annual budget reconciliation process. As the historian Adam Jentleson points out, the full-spectrum filibuster developed by McConnell comes close to realizing the ideal instrument of minority veto called for by Senator John Calhoun a century earlier.[267]

And it is this that has enabled Republicans to pursue the project of constitutional counterrevolution much further than Buchanan had envisaged. With McConnell as Senate Majority leader between January 2015 and January 2021, Republicans ruthlessly exploited Senate procedure to stack the federal courts at every level and install three Federalist Society–approved justices in the Supreme Court. After blocking a centrist Supreme Court nominee put forward by President Obama, McConnell cynically voided the filibuster for Supreme Court confirmations once Trump arrived in power, allowing Republicans to install an ultraconservative supermajority on the basis of a simple Senate majority.

In a trio of cases, an increasingly reactionary Supreme Court has gutted the Voting Rights Act of 1965, stopping just short of unwinding it altogether. In *Abbott v. Perez* (2018), the court upheld nearly all of Texas's gerrymandered maps and ruled that the state legislature had not intentionally discriminated against Latino and African American voters in drawing them.[268] In *Rucho v. Common Cause* (2019), it ruled that partisan gerrymandering claims, even when "incompatible with democratic principles," were beyond the purview of the federal courts.[269] And in *Brnovich v. DNC* (2021), it upheld two voter restriction laws in Arizona and recommended that in future rulings the court should look kindly on state laws purporting to prevent voter fraud.[270]

Their rulings confirmed the outcome of two earlier cases, *Shelby County v. Holder* (2013), which voided a key part of the Voting Rights Act of 1965 by exempting states with a history of racist election practices from having to "preclear" any new voting laws with the Justice Department, and *Vieth v. Jubelirer* (2004), which ruled that partisan gerrymandering was a political question that could only be dealt with by the elected branches of government, not the Supreme Court.[271]

Taken together, these decisions have sanctioned a long wave of state-level voter restrictions.[272] The Tea Party electoral surge of 2010 appears to have been the key turning point. What we have witnessed since then, write political theorists Paul Pierson and Jacob Hacker, is "the most sustained and coordinated assault on voting rights since Reconstruction, over a century ago, and it's being led by one party."[273] Following the 2010 Tea Party wave, approximately half of state legislatures introduced voter restrictions of some kind, ranging from voter ID laws, voter registration rules, and limits on postal votes. Many of these new laws were inspired by ALEC-drafted model legislation and were explicitly designed to prevent African American, Latinos, the poor, and younger people from voting.[274]

Even more valuable to Republicans has been the practice of partisan gerrymandering, which has delivered a clear electoral advantage at both the state and federal levels. In the eighteen states where they gained control of both legislative chambers in 2010, Republicans seized the opportunity to aggressively redraw electoral lines at both the U.S. House and state legislature levels so as to dilute the votes of African Americans and Latinos.[275] Their efforts have placed Democrats at a permanent disadvantage in U.S. House elections: with newly drawn districts in place, for instance, Democratic candidates received almost one million more votes than Republicans in the 2012 elections, yet Republicans ended up with a comfortable majority of seats.[276] Until these biases are neutralized, Democratic candidates will have to pass a much higher hurdle than Republicans to win control of the House.

Today's Republicans have taken minority rule several steps further than southern Democrats a century earlier. They now wield a minority veto not only in the Senate, where they have transformed the filibuster into a formidable tool of systemic obstruction, but also in the House and the Supreme Court, where an unelected minority seems intent on sanctioning every Republican transgression. This has enabled them to renew and radicalize the agenda of outright democratic disenfranchisement that southern Democrats were forced to give up on in the 1960s. As the twentieth century's foremost philosopher of minority rule, Buchanan saw the southern Democrats' last-ditch defense of Calhounian nullification as a lost cause. Accepting the landmark civil and voting rights legislation of this era as a fait accompli, he turned his attention to fiscal solutions, such as the balanced budget amendment, that could permanently puncture the dream of racial wealth redistribution, even when formal democracy was respected to the letter. Republicans today no longer see nullification as a lost cause: in fact, they have federalized it, turning what Calhoun imagined as a dissenting state's right to nullify federal laws deemed unconstitutional into a project of counterrevolution imposed on all states from above. With the help of an unelected supermajority in the Supreme Court, Republicans have come close to nullifying the Voting Rights Act of 1965 and have thus infused new life into Jim Crow, this time at the federal rather than the state level. The de facto "new Jim Crow" that many diagnosed in the emerging welfare and carceral practices of the 1980s now increasingly extends to the realm of formal rights, too.[277]

CHAPTER FIVE

Aborting America: The Reproductive Politics of the National Debt

With the midterm elections of 2010, a small army of politically inexperienced Tea Party Republicans entered the White House and proceeded to unleash a hitherto unimagined program of fiscal chaos upon the United States. As newly elected Tea Partiers scrambled to legislate a wave of state-level restrictions around women's access to abortion and birth control, House Republicans brought the government to the verge of shutdown in April 2011 over the alleged federal funding of abortion. At issue was a $300 million grant in Title X funding that would have provided states with matching funds for family planning and other health services. Federal funding of abortion had been banned since the Hyde Amendment of 1976. Yet Republicans were undaunted by this detail. Title X funding, they insisted, could easily be laundered to allow abortion providers to ply their trade.[1] When questioned why Republicans were so obsessively focused on women's bodies at a time of record unemployment, Congressman Mike Pence warned that there could be "no lasting prosperity without a moral foundation in law" and no lasting solution to America's mountain of debt without careful attention to the equivalent problem of moral bankruptcy.[2] "America's darkest moments have come when economic arguments trumped moral principles," he told a gathering of right-to-life activists. Yes, the focus should be on the budget, but: "Let's start by denying all federal funding for abortion at home and abroad. The largest abortion provider in America should not also be the largest recipient of federal funding under Title X. The time has come to deny any and all federal funding to Planned Parenthood of America."

In October 2013, the same House Republicans refused to approve an increase in the debt ceiling unless Obama agreed to defund the Affordable

Care Act or removed birth control from its preventative health-care provisions. Instigated by Senator Ted Cruz, the standoff brought the United States to the brink of default, risking its creditworthiness in the eyes of international investors for the second time in two years, and forced the government to shut down for two weeks.[3] The argument that the Affordable Care Act—Obamacare to its detractors—was a Trojan horse for socialized medicine, rampant deficit spending, and state eugenics had been steadily gaining momentum on the Tea Party right for several years now. Shortly after Obama's presidential win, a journalist writing for the *American Spectator* warned that the president-elect was planning to implement a "radical abortion agenda"—consisting of generous Title X spending and sex education budgets—within the first hundred days of his administration. This agenda would surely take a heavy toll on the nation's finances and raise an already overburdened national debt to catastrophic levels.[4]

As the government went into shutdown in April 2011, Concerned Women for America issued a "Declaration on America's Fiscal Crisis" calling for a repeal of Obamacare—as the first step in a program to abolish all entitlement spending, including Medicare and Social Security. The more debt the government took on to pay for such entitlements, the argument went, the more tax burdens fell on the American family and the less money it had to provide for its members. The escalating federal debt measured the declining fortunes of the family—literally so, when it came to Obamacare, which, it was alleged, funneled money to sexually active "unmarried women" and served as cover for the taxpayer funding of abortion.[5] In the meantime the former president of the Family Research Council, Gary Bauer, argued against all evidence that the Affordable Care Act was the most pro-abortion legislation to have passed Congress in decades while Sarah Palin warned of the "death panels" that would soon decide who was productive enough to live.[6]

The single-minded zeal with which this new cohort of Republicans, once in office, sought to track down and stamp out every possible source of federal funding for abortion and birth control came as a surprise to the many commentators who had assumed that the Tea Party was nothing but a front for the economic libertarianism of the Koch brothers. Nancy Cohen, one of the earliest and most astute observers of the movement, suggests that this misperception was carefully cultivated: anyone who had followed the Tea Party on the ground would have been aware that the religious conservative element was at least as strong as the economic libertarian, yet the movement's political operatives knew better than to advertise this. The point was to capture Congress—and the GOP—by stealth, by planting as many Tea Party activists as possible in Republican primaries and sidelining their establishment rivals.[7]

In support of this thesis, the political scientists Robert Putnam and David Campbell found that the best predictor of Tea Party affiliation, after being a Republican, was a "desire to see religion play a prominent role in...politics."[8] Others have pointed out that the movement was internally divided: business-funded groups such FreedomWorks and Charles and David Koch's Americans for Prosperity that latched onto the Tea Party in 2009 downplayed its religious right elements before the general public, although only FreedomWorks' Dick Armey actively sought to dampen the influence of Christian conservatives within the movement.[9] When the Council for National Policy, or CNP, came on board in 2010, however, it deliberately amplified the role of religious fundamentalists and was joined by the ostensibly agnostic Americans for Prosperity in sponsoring pro-life Tea Party events.[10]

It would be tempting to disentangle the religious conservative and economic libertarian sensibilities of the Tea Party grassroots—to posit one as cover for the other—as observers of American populism have so often done in the past. But to do this one would have to disregard the self-presentation of Tea Party activists themselves, who very loudly affirm the inseparability of moral and fiscal politics and refuse to see the one subordinated to the other. As noted by Phyllis Schlafly, the pioneering voice of the religious right turned Tea Party cheerleader under Obama, the "media are forever trying to create a division in the Republican Party between those who care most about so-called social issues and those who want priority for fiscal issues.... The truth is that social and fiscal issues cannot be pried apart. Those who emphasize runaway government spending and out-of-control debt and deficits must face the fact that those trillions of dollars are being spent by government on social problems.... It's the breakdown in our culture that has caused millions of Americans to depend on government for their living expenses and for solutions to their personal problems.... Fiscal and social conservatives need each other. Remedying the culture and restoring a marriage society is the only way to reduce the size and costs of the welfare state."[11]

Nowhere is this fusion of moral and fiscal concerns more apparent than around the issue of abortion, which Christian conservatives routinely diagnose as both the source of family breakdown and the driver of the nation's crippling national debt. In an appeal to outraged taxpayers, Tea Party senator Jim DeMint calculated that "total spending on abortion since *Roe v. Wade* in America" was "equal to $22 billion," and this without counting the "significant medical costs of post-abortion psychological problems, infertility, and increased cancer risk." But the "direct costs of abortion" paled in comparison to "the economic cost of the loss of 44 million American workers, consumers, and taxpayers" who were no longer able to fill the government's coffers with their productive tax dollars.[12] Beyond their more familiar moral objections, DeMint and others like him are outraged that hardworking taxpayers are expected to subsidize the abortions of future American citizens. Isn't this equivalent to aborting the American nation?[13]

Such arguments have been ubiquitous in religious right discourse since the 1970s, when Catholics first joined forces with evangelicals and fundamentalists to oppose the government funding of abortion. Despite their often conflicting positions on economic politics, Catholics and born-again Christians were able to forge a durable alliance around the idea that America's moral and fiscal pathologies were deeply entangled.[14] However perplexing it might look to outside observers, then, the chain of associations between the national debt, family breakdown, and abortion is not in itself new. What is astoundingly new is the ability of the religious right, in the guise of the Tea Party, to activate such ideas within the ambit of the Republican Party.

Christian conservatives have been reliable, if unsatisfied, allies of the GOP since the late 1970s, when the New Right first brought them into the Republican fold. But the trade-off has more often worked in favor of the Republican mainstream, which has repeatedly leveraged the religious right to implement its economic agenda while holding back on the full realization of its moral politics. With the rise of the Tea Party, the balance of power has shifted, freeing up religious conservatives to impose their will on the Republican Party coalition. Although Tea Party Republicans are just as intent on balancing the budget and cutting taxes as their libertarian peers, they have logically pursued this program by targeting what they perceive to be the underlying cause of America's fiscal problems—the alleged federal funding of abortion.

In the wake of the 2022 Supreme Court ruling that overturned *Roe v. Wade*, it is easy to forget how central the fiscal issues of government health-care spending and taxation have been to the religious right's crusade against abortion. Long before the *Dobbs v. Jackson* decision, however, Christian conservatives had already succeeded in making abortion, birth control, and other sexual-health services as hard to access as possible. The moral counterrevolution arrived in fiscal form, before an ultraconservative Supreme Court imposed it by judicial fiat. In the wake of *Dobbs*, these economic constraints have become more decisive than ever, as women in anti-abortion states are faced with prohibitive travel costs and missed wages, not to mention criminal prosecution, when they need to terminate a pregnancy. The women most affected are lower-income and disproportionately African American or Latina. It is ironic, then, to say the least, that the religious right has consistently framed its quest to outlaw abortion as a crusade against eugenics.

HOWARD PHILLIPS

One of the few political operatives to have traveled the road from the religious right of the 1970s to the Tea Party movement of the 2010s was Howard Phillips, identified by some as the "founding father" of the movement.[15] An often forgotten member of the New Right coalition of the 1970s, Phillips was one of the key instigators of the new religious right and a personal convert to fundamentalist Protestantism of the Christian Reconstructionist variety. For many years he attempted to transform the Republican Party from within before breaking off to form the U.S. Taxpayers (later Constitution) Party in the early 1990s. With its amalgam of libertarian economics, antiimmigrant nativism, and Christian Reconstructionism, the U.S. Constitution Party spawned many of the political figures who later returned to the GOP as Tea Party Republicans in the 2010 midterm elections.[16] Although unremarked at the time, their triumphant return to the ranks of the Republican Party represented a vindication of sorts for Phillips, who had himself spent many years attempting to reform government from within and who decided, in the 1990s, that the option of outsider extremism would yield more dividends than reformist compromise. When Tea Party activists returned to the fold in 2010, they set about implementing the strategy of institutional implosion that Phillips had tested out in the 1970s—with a particular focus on the defunding of birth control and sex-ual health services for low-income women.

Howard Phillips was the consummate political strategist. In 1960, he cofounded Young Americans for Freedom, a group of young Republicans who had been energized by Goldwater's hard-right challenge to the Eisen-hower mainstream and who sought to fashion an enduring alliance of eco-nomic libertarians and social conservatives from within the younger, more activist ranks of the GOP.[17] Phillips went on to work for Nixon at a time when the Republican president was seeking to court the votes of southern racists and blue-collar conservatives. In 1973, after winning his second election on a promise of hard-right reform, Nixon appointed Phillips to the position of act-ing director of the Office of Economic Opportunity (OEO) with the express purpose of dismantling the agency from within. This he set about doing with extreme care.

Phillips's special targets were legal service programs that combined a focus on antipoverty activism, welfare rights, and sexual freedom for low-income women and teenagers. Although funded by the OEO, these services often walked a tightrope between the pursuit of government directives and activist reform. In the 1960s and 1970s, left-wing public interest firms (in part subsidized by the OEO) were challenging the moral conditionalities imposed on welfare clients and the punitive practices associated with government-funded family planning services. Phillips was particularly incensed by the work of the UCLA-based National Legal Program on Health Problems of the Poor, which in the years before *Roe v. Wade* had contributed legal advice and amicus briefs in test cases challenging everything from involuntary steril-ization laws, parental consent requirements for access to birth control, and state anti-abortion laws. Public interest lawyers for the National Legal Pro-gram underscored the extreme dangers faced by poor women when seeking to terminate a pregnancy: at a time when abortion could be requested if the mother's life was deemed to be in danger, white middle-class women were able to access legal abortions with relative ease in private hospitals, while abor-tion in public-indigent hospitals was much more tightly policed.[18] As a result, nonwhite women were five times more likely to die of abortions performed in illegal clinics and simultaneously more liable to be "offered" unwanted sterilizations in public hospitals. Even as they helped contest eugenic state sterilization laws, then, National Legal Program lawyers challenged the nonimplementation of federal directives that were supposed to guarantee Medicaid and AFDC coverage of birth control, fought for the abolition of parental consent laws for sexual-health services, and advocated the legalization of abortion.[19] The fact that these public interest lawyers were seeking to use public money to enable the sexual freedom of the poor and the young was particularly outrageous to Phillips.[20] Tax-funded welfare was egregious enough. But taxes paid in the service of women's sexual freedom, especially when those women were low-income and nonwhite, was the special target of Phillips's ire.

In a series of articles published in the conservative *Human Events* after his departure from the OEO, Phillips provided a detailed report on what he called the "abortionist activities" of the "legal services program."[21] Here he elaborated a chronicle of decline that made abortion the symptom and cause of all that was wrong with American culture: not simply its moral fall from grace but also its fiscal and monetary woes. The idea that an increasingly liberal welfare state was responsible for the breakdown of the family, the burgeoning of the national debt, and inflation was already a familiar refrain among secular neoconservatives.[22] But religious conservatives such as Phillips went one step further and identified abortion as the literal manifestation of national and familial decline. Indeed, the questions of the national debt and abortion were never far removed from each other in his reflections: the loss of economic foundation signaled by Nixon's abandonment of the dollar-gold standard, the routine deficits now factored into government budget projections, and the record-breaking national debt were all signs of moral as well as fiscal bankruptcy in his eyes. With the expansion of the welfare state, he lamented, hardworking taxpayers were now expected to subsidize the nonproductive shirker and parasite. More than this, with the extension of federal funds to cover birth control and (for a brief moment after *Roe v. Wade*) abortion, the productive were being asked to finance the active destruction of the nation's future. "If there's no shame attached to living off someone else's labor, a lot of people…will gleefully dive for the dole," Phillips reflected, adding that "the same kind of moral irresponsibility…results annually in the abortion of millions of healthy babies, killed with little stigma (and a lot of federal money) because they were inconvenient to those who decreed their death."[23] Why should the productive be forced to subsidize the unproductive and the willfully sterile? Wasn't this equivalent to asking ordinary taxpayers to pay for the abortion of their own future?

When Republican president Gerald Ford proposed a national health insurance bill in his inaugural address to Congress, Phillips joined forces with old friends from his Young Americans for Freedom days in shouting down the threat of "socialized medicine." Just as "the federal government now finances and encourages abortion with funds from HEW and OEO," he warned, "in a few years your taxes may be used to underwrite the 'termination' of your grandparents, your parents, or perhaps even you.... Life would become hard for doctors who decline to follow the guidelines of HEW or of their local 'termination' commission."[24] Following up on this warning, Congressman Robert Bauman (R-MD), a former chairman of Young Americans for Freedom, sent out a petition on behalf of Americans against Socialized Medicine alerting his constituents that "welfare chiselers who refuse to work" were about to get "free abortions...which you will pay for" and "free VD clinics...which you will pay for."[25]

By this time, Phillips was no longer working at OEO. His appointment had been terminated after only six months, when the Supreme Court found it to be unconstitutional. Yet his half year of institutional destruction would remain a model for a small group of strategists (including Phillips himself) who came together after Nixon's resignation under the banner of the New Right. In the years ahead, New Right activists would seek to scale up Phillip's short-lived trial run at the OEO by making the defunding of "abortionist activities" the centerpiece of a national grassroots campaign with close links to key congressional actors. Well before many on the Republican right, the New Right four recognized that economically progressive Catholics could be lured away from the Democrats on the single issue of abortion, while politically apathetic evangelicals and fundamentalists could be transformed into energized Republican militants if the party pandered to their moral concerns. For all their differences around the issues of economic welfare, Catholics and born-again Christians could be persuaded to work together to oppose the use of tax dollars in the funding of abortion. By the election of Ronald Reagan in 1980, the defunding of Planned Parenthood and Title X programs had become a familiar refrain on the Republican right and Howard Phillips himself had become the champion of a larger crusade to "defund the left."

We commonly locate the emergence of the religious right in the years immediately prior to the Reagan revolution of 1980. Yet Republican strategists had been calling for a mobilization of cross-denominational religious forces for well over a decade before Reagan entered office and briefly persuaded Nixon to reach out to blue-collar religious conservatives in the lead-up to his second term. These strategists were convinced by George Wallace's showings in the presidential elections of 1968 that the New Deal Democratic coalition was unravelling: a former southern Democrat who appealed to the blue-collar workers with a mix of anti-plutocratic economic populism, white supremacism, and a solid dose of fundamentalist moralism, Wallace had attracted a sizeable portion of votes from white southerners when he ran as an independent in the 1968 elections. For Republican thinkers such as Kevin Phillips, M. Stanton Evans, Pat Buchanan, and William Rusher, this suggested that the white workers who had once been solidly attached to the Democratic Party might be lured away with a few select inducements.[26] As is well known, this reasoning gave birth to the so-called Southern Strategy, by which the Republicans sought to lure southern and lower middle-class suburban voters away from the Democratic Party via an attack on racial redistribution. Less well known but just as consequential in the long run were Nixon's early efforts to sign up religious conservatives to the Republican side.[27]

As Nixon prepared to contend with the progressive Democratic candidate George McGovern in the 1972 elections, Republican strategist Kevin Phillips (no relation to Howard) predicted an overwhelming victory for Nixon, as long as he fought hard to attract the religious conservative vote.[28] At a time when most pundits were focused on the impact of the countercultural "youth bloc," Phillips presaged a longer-term and more important shift in voting patterns in line with changing economic conditions. The Democratic Party had for many years represented the white agricultural South, industrial Northeast, and northern Midwest as against the northeastern Republican establishment. But the McGovernite Democrats were now more reliant on an emergent class of knowledge workers and professional bureaucrats who were both economically privileged and socially liberal. These voters assumed an alliance of interests with the traditionally Democratic working class, Phillips observed, but the attraction was not necessarily mutual, and the old white working class was more likely to feel alienated from the McGovernite campaign than included in it. This was particularly true of white "ethnic" Catholic voters in the Northeast, who as passionate opponents of abortion had every reason to fear McGovern's association with the student and progressive left.[29] By Kevin Phillips's reckoning, the Democratic Party was "going to pay heavily for having become the party of affluent professionals, knowledgeable industry executives, social cause activists and minorities of various sexual, racial, chronological and other hues."[30]

This literature is best understood as performative rather than descriptive. Drawing on the all-too-familiar equation between the non-working welfare poor, the professional-managerial class, and the parasitic rentier, the inclusion of "sexual, racial [and] chronological" minorities within the ranks of the economic elite confuses populist resentment with actual class formation and so endorses what it purports to diagnose. But whatever the deficiencies of the analysis, the prospect of an overwhelming swing to the Republican Party was alluring enough to convince Nixon to test the waters. After a trial run in California in 1970, where the State Republican Committee organized for Catholic voters to register en masse with the GOP in protest against the State Democratic Party's support for decriminalizing abortion, Nixon took the strategy to the national stage in the run-up to the 1972 election.[31] In April 1971 he ostentatiously rescinded a directive allowing military bases to perform therapeutic abortions, even though his own administration had introduced the directive two years before. He then rejected the findings of a report on population and family planning that he himself had commissioned, on the grounds that unrestricted abortion would demean human life.[32] When Nixon began his second term in 1973, his appointment of Howard Phillips to the position of acting director of the Office of Economic Opportunity signaled the seriousness of his words: Phillips, after all, was intent on dismantling community action programs in general, but his personal obsession was with the "abortionist activities" of the OEO and the fact that taxpayers' money was being used to fund them.[33] Nixon could not have found a better way to express his newfound commitment to fiscal and social conservatism.

But Nixon proved to be an unreliable partner and was backtracking on this strategy even before the eruption of the Watergate scandal, much to the disappointment of Howard Phillips and other party conservatives. When Gerald Ford beat their favorite, Ronald Reagan, as successor in the White House, and when President Ford nominated the quintessential moderate Nelson Rockefeller as vice president, a group of young right-wing activists embarked on a new strategy of coalition building from the party margins. Immediately after the appointment of Rockefeller, the former executive secretary of Young Americans for Freedom Richard Viguerie invited a group of like-minded conservatives to form the so-called New Right—a militant caucus that refused to make its peace with the party's centrists. Its core members were Viguerie himself, Paul Weyrich, John Terrence "Terry" Dolan, and Howard Phillips.[34]

THE NEW RIGHT

As veterans of the 1964 Goldwater campaign, the New Right four shared their candidate's investment in fiscal conservatism and hardline anti-communism. What separated them from Goldwater, however, was their unerring focus on the "family issues" so dear to religious conservatives, hence their willingness to pursue Catholics, southern fundamentalists, and born-again Christians as political allies. As explained in an editorial for the New Right's *Conservative Digest*, for the past half century, "conservatives have stressed almost exclusively economic and foreign policy. The New Right shares the same basic beliefs of other conservatives in economic and foreign policy matters, but we feel that conservatives cannot become the dominant political force in America until we stress the issues of concern to ethnic and blue-collar Americans, born-again Christians, pro-life Catholics, and Jews. Some of these issues are busing, abortion, pornography, education, traditional Biblical moral values, and quotas."[35]

As conscientious students of Nixon-era realignment strategists, the leaders of the New Right were determined to take things up where Nixon had left off. They would revive Nixon's strategy of courting Christians while discarding his conservative welfarism in favor of Goldwater-style small government libertarianism. But having learned the lesson that well-meaning presidents could promise the world and still end up buckling under pressure, they needed to find some more enduring way of holding legislators to account. Grassroots coalition building was essential to their vision, as was the cultivation of young, suitably hardline congressional candidates to the right of the Republican mainstream. The point was less to attract new religious voters to an existing party apparatus than to harness Christian conservatives as agents of wholesale party transformation. If this meant sacrificing incumbent Republican congressmen deemed too moderate, then so be it. As Paul Weyrich explained, we "are radicals who want to change the existing power structure. We are not conservatives in the sense that conservative means accepting the status quo."[36] More important than partisan loyalties was the higher cause of conservative counterrevolution.

Before coming together as a collective, the New Right four had for many years practiced the coalition politics they now sought to scale up into a national movement. Although all except Howard Phillips had been raised in blue-collar Catholic families, they did not share the almost automatic allegiance to the New Deal Democratic Party that was so common among low-income Catholic migrants. As young men, they had earned their political stripes in the militant youth wings of the Republican Party but were also more than happy to reach across political and theological lines to work with conservative Democrats and southern fundamentalists.

Born in Texas in 1933, Richard Viguerie had been raised by a family of devout Catholics of Louisiana French origins. Viguerie had spent his early career working for the radio evangelist Billy James Hargis, an old-time fundamentalist who preached against the evils of desegregation and communism.[37] It was in this role that Viguerie discovered the wonders of direct mail as a way of amassing donor funds and circumventing the mainstream media. He would later put these skills to work in the service of the Old Guard Republican Barry Goldwater and the segregationist Dixiecrat George Wallace. Paul Weyrich was the child of blue-collar German Catholic immigrants who had settled in the Midwest. Active in the local Young Republicans of Racine, Milwaukee, he had spent his early career as a TV and radio news reporter before launching himself into Barry Goldwater's 1964 presidential campaign. Weyrich's Catholicism was so orthodox that he later joined the Eastern Rite Church in protest against the liberalized liturgy of the post–Vatican II church. Terry Dolan, too, was a devout Catholic Midwesterner who at age thirteen had been one of the youngest volunteers to sign up for the Goldwater campaign. Dolan spent much of his short life vociferating against gays, lesbians, and feminists. He died of complications from AIDS in 1986. The sole non-Catholic among the New Right four, Howard Phillips was a lower-middle-class Jew who shared his friends' horror of abortion. Sometime in the mid-1970s he converted to an extreme form of Calvinism known as Christian Reconstructionism under the guidance of its founder and leading theologian, Rousas John Rushdoony. For the rest of his life, he would refer to Rushdoony as his "wise counselor."[38]

In their public accounts of themselves, the New Right four unfailingly zoomed in on their blue-collar Catholic origins. Although, ironically enough, they all earned their living in the "unproductive" media and culture industries they purported to disdain, they felt perpetually scorned by the "country club" Republicanism of the Anglo-Protestant Northeast and conjured up a simulacrum of class warfare to make sense of this.[39] The figure of the plain-talking, clean-living blue-collar worker loomed large in their collective imagination. More than a personal reference point, all three Catholic members of the New Right and its one fundamentalist convert understood their own sense of exclusion as indicative of wider fault lines in American culture. With a bit of forcing, they thought, these fault lines might be leveraged to crack up the entire New Deal coalition. Thus, they paid close attention when Irish Catholics organized against school busing in Boston or when the hard-hat workers turned on Vietnam War protestors in New York.[40] Beyond the usual suspects—the white ethnic Catholics that Nixon-era strategists had identified—New Right operatives at various points thought that they could herd middle-class Blacks, urban Jews, and active union members into their nets.[41]

Their aspirations were sometimes grandiose. Even without the intercession of the AFL-CIO, which launched a publicity blitz against the New Right in the late 1970s, the movement was never going to make massive inroads among trade unionists, given its simultaneous activism in favor of right-to-work laws and against workplace picketing.[42] Nor did they have much hope of attracting middle-class Blacks, given their history of chasing former George Wallace voters and their animus against school busing. Where they did meet with success was among religious conservatives, who were looking to scale up and professionalize their efforts at precisely the moment when New Right activists were scouting for militants on the ground.

With half a century of activism against "artificial birth control" behind them, the Catholic right-to-life movement had something the New Right could only dream of—a ground army of Christian soldiers dedicated to waging war against murderous women and their political enablers.[43] It was among Catholic activists in the National Right to Life Committee that the New Right found its first religious conservative allies. And it was they who helped triangulate the alliance by bringing conservative protestants on board. The National Right to Life Committee had been reaching out to evangelicals and fundamentalists since the *Roe v. Wade* decision of 1973. The New Right followed their lead and managed to establish a lasting pact with Jerry Falwell in the late 1970s.[44] Born-again Christians looked like natural allies of the Republican right: their numbers were exploding at a time when the mainline Protestant churches were stagnant, and their leaders had been cultivating ties to the Republican Party since Eisenhower.[45] The fact that almost half of them were not registered to vote only increased their attractiveness in the eyes of New Right strategists.[46] With southern fundamentalists and evangelicals on side, the New Right was gifted a grassroots infrastructure of megachurches and media outlets powerful enough to compete with the New Deal labor unions. What religious conservatives received, in exchange, was a conduit into political circles and a means of exerting direct pressure on the electoral process. "Common consensus had it that somehow we planned and plotted to mobilize these millions of people," Weyrich reflected in hindsight, but "the fact is, they already had all of the structural resources necessary for an organization." All they lacked was a sense of "how to maneuver in politics."[47]

INCONGRUOUS ALLIANCES

Of all the political reshufflings that took place in the turbulent 1970s, the emergence of an interdenominational alliance of conservative Christians was surely the most incongruous. Before this time, few could have foreseen a truce between fundamentalists and evangelicals, much less Catholics and Protestants. The idea that these different denominations might actively work together was unthinkable. Southern fundamentalists had spent decades doing battle with their modernizing brethren, the evangelicals, whose optimistic embrace of political change in general and civil rights in particular they saw as a fatal capitulation to the secular world.[48] But fundamentalists and evangelicals were united in their distrust of American Catholics, who for much of the twentieth century were suspected of secret loyalty to the Vatican. The Catholic philosophy of life, and the radical opposition to abortion it inspired, was deeply alien to American Protestant sensibilities. Born-again Christians were fervent defenders of moral purity, to be sure, but the notion that abortion constituted an assault on unborn life was too closely embedded in natural-law doctrine to warrant their blessing.[49] Indeed, up until the mid-1970s, even the most conservative Baptist and fundamentalist churches in the South expressed support for the legalization of therapeutic abortions within certain time limits.[50]

As the decade progressed, however, religious conservatives began to feel they were more threatened by the growing liberalization of American culture than they were by each other and learned to set aside doctrinal differences in the interests of united action.[51] The abortion issue served as an improbable source of consensus as evangelical and fundamentalist Protestants began to see the traditionally Catholic pro-life position as a bulwark against a general state of moral decline. Abortion in this view was more than a perversion of natural law; it was also a symbol of the multiple threats to the family that abounded in American culture. As Jerry Falwell explained, "in another context we would be shedding blood" but "our commitment to the family has brought those of us of differing views and backgrounds together to fight a just cause . . . to fight for the family."[52]

Yet if Catholics and conservative Protestants found common cause in the defense of the family, their many other differences proved challenging. The most obvious source of tension resided in their strikingly different attitudes toward the welfare state and the role of progressive taxation in funding it. As impoverished migrants hailing from the economic margins of Europe, American Catholics had been natural allies of the New Deal Democrats and were themselves actively involved in the campaign to institute a family wage in the early twentieth century. Indeed, in the American context, Catholic social doctrine played a crucial but often unacknowledged role in popularizing the idea that each male worker should earn enough to provide for himself, his wife, and children.[53]

A symptom of this entanglement, the term "right to life," which we now automatically associate with the anti-abortion movement of the 1970s, was first coined by the Catholic social philosopher John Ryan as a defense of the male breadwinner family wage.[54] Drawing on the Thomist natural-law tradition and the social doctrine of Pope Leo XIII, Ryan preached that every male worker had a right to a "living wage" by virtue of the universal sacredness of human life. By insisting on the value of all life—irrespective of class, race, or nationhood—Catholic natural law sanctioned a radical vision of social welfare. Yet the same argument undergirded Ryan's defense of the large family and his strident opposition to any form of "unnatural" birth control, which he understood as both a deviation from natural law and a form of race suicide.[55]

Catholics were the most vocal opponents of Margaret Sanger's movement to liberalize birth control in the 1920s and began campaigning against the eugenics movement in the 1930s, at a time when coercive population control measures very often targeted fellow Catholics from the fringes of Europe.[56] So inseparable were the issues of social welfare and the protection of the fetus in their minds that when the American Medical Association endorsed the legalization of birth control in 1937, one Catholic cleric warned that the degradation of unborn life would lead to a general backlash against the rights of workers.[57]

The flourishing eugenics movement of the 1920s and 1930s was enduringly discredited, in the wake of World War II, by the full revelation of Nazi atrocities (which is not to say that eugenic *practices* did not survive).[58] At this point, American Catholics sought to have the rights of the unborn enshrined in the founding documents of human-rights law.[59] Although their campaign was only partially successful—the unborn were recognized in the United Nations General Assembly's Declaration of the Rights of the Child in 1959, but not in the 1948 Universal Declaration of Human Rights—Catholics never abandoned the idea that a comprehensive vision of human rights should be imbued with the spirit of natural law. In the years ahead, they continued to weave together the themes of social welfare, the Holocaust, and the human rights of the unborn, making the equation between genocide and abortion a staple of right-to-life discourse by the end of the century.[60]

The universalist, non-race-specific pronatalism espoused by Catholics made their critique of eugenics remarkably adaptable to different times and circumstances. In the 1960s, when Black nationalist leaders organized their own campaigns against federal family planning clinics in poor neighborhoods, they were often joined by Catholic progressives who saw the defense of unborn Black life as a natural extension of their civil rights work.[61] A new generation of Black activists, from Malcolm X to the Black Panthers to a number of more reformist civil rights leaders, were convinced that federal funding of birth control, which became available in 1965 under the auspices of the OEO, was a plot to exterminate the Black race.[62] Whether inspired by the religious conservatism of the Nation of Islam or the revolutionary Marxism of the Black Panthers, Black nationalists understood the reproduction of race as foundational to their project and saw women as an instrument to this end ("man's field to produce his nation," in the words of Elijah Muhammad).[63]

They had good reason to be suspicious of government-funded family planning: the resurgence of Malthusian overpopulation theories in the 1960s, often couched in the language of environmental limits to growth, occurred just at the moment when Black liberation and anti-imperialist movements were gaining ground across the world. The population lobby was beset by conflict during this period, as Planned Parenthood and other foundations sought to distance themselves from the increasingly authoritarian and racist positions of latter-day Malthusians in the nascent environmental movement.[64] Critics who suspected the motives behind federal family planning programs were vindicated when it was revealed in the early 1970s that a number of Black women and girls had been sterilized without their consent in HEW-funded clinics across the South.[65] Nevertheless, African American women, including prominent members of the Black Panthers, had their own reasons for welcoming the state-funded provision of birth control and abortion. Faced with the combined threats of coerced sterilization, inadequate access to birth control, and life-threatening abortions, Black feminists forged an expanded notion of reproductive justice, which demanded freedom from both state and communal coercion—hence, the right to end a pregnancy on their own terms.[66] Yet for this reason their male peers often accused them of collaborating with the eugenic state. As designated bearers of racial continuity, women in charge of their own reproductive decisions could be just as threatening to the future Black nation as neo-Malthusian advocates of population control.[67]

During this period, Black nationalists borrowed heavily from the Catholic anti-eugenic repertoire to couch their arguments against government-funded family planning and women's liberation alike.[68] For their part, the many Catholic clergymen who fought alongside Black nationalists to shut down birth control clinics expanded their vocabulary to include the themes of Black geno-cide and slavery. Catholics who had cast the defense of the unborn as an exten-sion of the fight for workers' rights and universal welfare in the 1930s, and who had compared birth control to the Holocaust in the postwar era, now con-figured the pro-life cause as a resurgence of the abolitionist movement and the defining civil rights issue of the time.[69]

In his illuminating prehistory of the right-to-life cause, the historian Daniel K. Williams notes that we routinely forget the movement's origins in Catholic social welfare and civil rights activism, thanks in large part to its sub-sequent domination by free-market-oriented evangelicals. The anti-abortion movement, he goes so far as to claim, began as a "liberal" cause.[70] More accu-rately, we could say that it emerged from the combination of social conser-vatism and redistributive economics espoused by Catholics (and many other New Deal Democrats) at midcentury. For those who had grown up in a polit-ical culture in which abortion was illegal, birth control was barely accessi-ble, and women were relegated to the role of mother and wife, the connection between social welfare and defense of the unborn was perfectly logical. The same mix of sexual conservatism and economic progressivism was at play in the civil rights and Black liberation movements of the 1960s and 1970s. For the many Catholic clergy who were sympathetic to these movements, it would have made perfect sense to fight for the welfare and civil rights of African Americans even while they vehemently opposed the expansion of women's sexual freedom. As universal bearers of reproductive life, women could not assert their right to bodily autonomy without being accused of eugenic intent.

The politico-economic leanings of conservative Protestants at midcen-tury could not have been further removed from those of Catholics. As self-identified native-born whites concentrated in the South and Southwest, most evangelicals, Southern Baptists, and fundamentalists were naturally inclined to small government conservatism.[71] While Catholics looked to natural law and the idiom of universal human rights to construct their social theology, conservative Protestants declared their allegiance to the American Constitu-tion, which they infused with the literal word of God.[72] Evangelicals and fun-damentalists were just as fervently engaged in the defense of sexual morality as Catholics, but whereas Catholics sought to conform state welfare institu-tions to their own moral doctrine, born-again Christians believed that the family was the most perfect form of welfare, which therefore needed defending *against* the state. Their signature political campaigns (much more frequent than their professed quietism would seem to suggest) involved the defense of private Christian enclaves against the corrupting influence and tax impositions of federal government. Beginning in the 1950s and extending into the 1960s, fundamentalists fought against Supreme Court orders forcing all-white Christian schools to desegregate and federal edicts prohibiting mandatory prayer in public schools.[73] They were some of the most impassioned opponents of Truman's plans to introduce "socialized medicine"—that is, government-funded health care—after World War II, convinced that it was a Trojan horse for socialist "totalitarianism."[74]

As attention turned increasingly to the federal threat to the family in the 1970s, evangelicals and fundamentalists launched an unremitting assault on Nixon's early efforts to introduce free public childcare, surprising all with the ferocity of their attack.[75] This was the first in a series of campaigns that would pit them against the tax-funded transgressions of public school teachers and the social welfare system. Throughout the decade, born-again Christians translated the concerns of free market economists into the language of family decline, charging that inflation-induced bracket creep was eroding the foundations of the male breadwinner wage and forcing housewives into paid work.[76] The family's private wealth, they claimed, was being suctioned away in the form of property and income taxes to pay for the wages of public schoolteachers and other agents of the social state—hell-bent, it was feared, on undermining parental authority over children.[77] In 1978, fundamentalists and evangelicals turned their anger against the IRS when it threatened to withdraw the tax-exempt status of private Christian schools that had failed to enforce affirmative action mandates.[78] This and other less spectacular battles with the IRS only served to confirm their belief that the federal government was using taxation as a weapon against the white Christian family. There was considerable cognitive dissonance in these tirades against the welfare state. After all, tax exemption was itself a form of government expenditure, and this was only one of several forms of support that conservative evangelicals and fundamentalists received from government during this period. With the proliferation of federal funding contracts in the mid-1960s, along with the Great Society preference for the devolution of service provision, conservative

Protestants were financing an ever-greater proportion of their colleges, nursing homes, and other social services with the help of direct or indirect federal expenditures. In practice, what mattered most to them was not the source of funding but the ability to use it without following federal antidiscrimination directives.[79] Thus, even while their own institutions were increasingly dependent on government money, born-again Christians continued to rail against the evils of tax-funded secularism. With their sensibilities so finely attuned to the links between fiscal and moral decadence, it was only natural that they would frame the abortion issue in these terms also, as a tax-funded crime against the family.

By contrast, most of the Catholics who launched themselves into antiabortion activism in the wake of *Roe v. Wade* were direct heirs to the New Deal right-to-life movement and its embrace of social welfare. Their favored response to the *Roe v. Wade* decision—constitutional recognition of the right to life from the moment of conception—was so intimately shaped by this history that many saw it as a prelude to the expansion of welfare rights for the unborn.[80] Yet Catholics also had a long tradition of selectively campaigning against the use of tax dollars to pay for the distribution of birth control in public hospitals.[81] In what proved to be an enduring obsession, Catholics successfully blocked the disbursement of local welfare funds to Planned Parenthood clinics as early as the 1950s. In 1959, Catholic bishops issued a statement warning that Catholic voters, representing a quarter of the American voting public, would never tolerate the use of their tax dollars to promote birth control, abortion, or sterilization for poor women, either at home or abroad.[82] In 1965 the New York State Catholic Welfare Committee, followed by many others around the country, accused the state government of using "tax funds to condone promiscuous conduct" when it ventured to provide birth control information to single mothers on welfare.[83] Without renouncing their more ambitious agenda to achieve constitutional recognition of the unborn, Catholics continued to make use of such targeted antitax arguments in the wake of *Roe v. Wade.*

It was this minor tradition in Catholic activism that ultimately facilitated the dialogue with evangelicals and fundamentalists. For all their historical allegiance to the welfare state, Catholics were virulently opposed to the use of taxpayer money when it subsidized the destruction of unborn life. Born-again Christians, for their part, continued to denounce the welfare state as a totalitarian attack on the family while conveniently disavowing their own growing dependence on tax dollars. Thus, the fight against tax-funded abortion emerged as an obvious point of convergence between unlikely allies.

UNITED AGAINST EUGENICS AND SOCIALIZED MEDICINE

The leaders of the New Right made first contact with the right-to-life movement in early 1975, when they invited Mildred Jefferson to attend the Conservative Political Action Conference.[84] The daughter of a Methodist minister, a staunch Texas Republican, and the first African American woman to graduate from Harvard Medical School, Jefferson had recently been elected president of the National Right to Life Committee and charged with the mission of building bridges between Catholics and Protestants, white and Black activists. Her strategic objectives dovetailed perfectly with those of the New Right. Both Jefferson and her New Right allies were convinced that evangelicals and fundamentalists would need to be brought into the fold to create a credible national movement, and both felt that Catholic Democrats would need to dampen their social welfare instincts to properly collaborate with evangelicals and fundamentalists.[85]

In September 1975, Mildred Jefferson invited Weyrich's Committee for the Survival of a Free Congress to help train her and thirty other anti-abortion activists in the art of coordinating national campaigns.[86] The perfect opportunity for testing out these new skills presented itself in early 1976, when Congressman Henry Hyde, a Catholic Republican from Illinois, proposed amending the House appropriations bill to disallow Medicaid funding of abortions. As soon as the amendment was approved by the House of Representatives, the National Right to Life Committee swung into action to ensure it wouldn't be quashed in the Senate.[87] In the lead-up to the November elections, Jefferson and her collaborators kept the issue permanently in the spotlight, pressing candidates Jimmy Carter and Gerald Ford for statements, extracting an interview from a contrite Ronald Reagan (who regretted his decision to legalize abortion in California), and threatening to out any congressional hopeful who wavered from the anti-abortion line.[88] Keen to exploit the growing fractures within the New Deal Democratic coalition, Jefferson invoked a feminine version of Nixon's "silent majority" to warn candidates that pro-life women were ready to defect from the Democratic to the Republican side over this one issue.[89]

Although she was no doubt driven by her own deep religious convictions, Jefferson was the perfect decoy for the New Right. With an African American woman at its helm, the National Right to Life Committee was able to present itself as a disinterested defender of the vulnerable, even as it was campaigning to defund abortion services for low-income women. At the same time that the Hyde Amendment was being debated in Congress, National Right to Life Committee events made ample use of Catholic and Black nationalist arguments that abortion was a form of genocide practiced against the poor and the nonwhite.[90] In the meantime, the organization's monthly magazine regularly reported on the welfare rights campaign against the forced sterilization of low-income women, assiduously ignoring the fact that Black and feminist welfare-rights militants also supported women's right to abortion and birth control.[91] As an outsider on all counts, Jefferson was a formidable foil against would-be progressive critics of the right-to-life movement. Jefferson was neither a Catholic nor a civil rights activist—alongside her anti-abortion work, she also dabbled in anti–school busing protests organized by Howard Phillips[92]—but her status as a Black woman helped deflect charges that the movement was unfairly targeting the rights of low-income minority women.[93]

The congressional debate leading up to the Senate vote demonstrated just how useful the tax issue had become in building a bridge between Catholic and Protestant opponents of abortion. The bill's sponsor, Henry Hyde, appeared to be channeling both Catholic right-to-life and traditional small government arguments when he asked why taxpayers should be forced to pay for the "slaughter of innocent, inconvenient, unborn children."[94] When pressed to account for the seeming injustice of a law that impacted poor, minority women in particular, Hyde foregrounded the even greater injustice suffered by the unborn child from the ghetto. "I regret that I certainly would like to prevent, if I could legally, anybody having an abortion, a rich woman, a middle-class woman, or a poor woman," he told his audience. "Unfortunately, the only vehicle available is the HEW Medicaid bill. A life is a life. The life of a little ghetto kid is just as important as the life of a rich person. And so we proceed in this bill."[95] Brandishing a recent statement by Planned Parenthood, in which abortions were credited with future savings to the welfare state, Hyde lamented the false economy that lavished federal money on abortions to save federal money on welfare. "We spend about $50 million a year to pay for about 300,000 abortions under Medicaid," he observed, often on the grounds that it "costs too much to bring these welfare kids into the world." In protest, Hyde was "prepared to pay the price to see that they get an education, decent housing, and adequate clothing."[96]

By contrast, non-Catholic conservatives were more inclined to believe that government-funded abortion really did place a significant fiscal burden on the state. Utah Republican senator Orrin Hatch, one of a batch of congressional freshmen cultivated by the New Right, saw the federal funding of abortion as continuous with the welfare state itself, that is, as a dangerous diversion of tax dollars to finance the destruction of the family. Like Howard Phillips, Hatch discerned a somewhat tortuous connection between the federal funding of abortion and the vertiginous growth in the national debt. There is a "remarkable similarity," he observed, "between many of those who believe in abortion and...[those] who are bankrupting this country monetarily." The same people "who vote for abortion," Hatch averred, are those who foster the idle poor.[97] Hatch's views on the relationship between the welfare state and abortion were completely at odds with those of fellow Catholic congressmen. Only a shared horror before the taxpayer funding of "genocide" could bridge their differences.

On June 29, 1977, after a year of federal court challenges and congressional debates, the Senate voted in favor of the Hyde Amendment, with the proviso that exemptions could be granted when the mother's life was in danger, or in cases of rape or incest. Earlier that same day, the Supreme Court had given the amendment its constitutional imprimatur.[98] This was not only the first and most enduring legislative victory of the right-to-life movement but also the moment in which the formative alliances of the new religious right were sealed, thanks in large part to the ambidextrous appeal of the fiscal argument against abortion. As the New Right had understood from the very beginning, the defunding of abortion services for low-income women was the fastest route to success and the best way of ensuring unity among the diverse factions of the religious right.

In hindsight, the congressional debate surrounding the Hyde Amendment appears as an inflection point. At the time of the debate, Catholic and non-Catholic supporters of the bill were still expounding markedly different perspectives on the welfare state, even while they found a point of consensus in their opposition to tax-funded abortion. In the years that followed, the difference between Catholic and evangelical voices in the right-to-life movement became increasingly muted, thanks to the movement's shifting partisan politics and growing alignment with the Republican Party. Astonishingly, Democratic and Republican positions on the issue of abortion completely reversed in the course of the 1970s. At the beginning of the decade, more Republicans than Democrats—68 percent to 58 percent—were pro-choice. By 1979, a growing number of Senate Republicans were professing pro-life positions, no doubt alert to the growing contingent of conservative evangelicals preparing to vote for them. House Democrats, by contrast, were becoming more pro-choice, as onetime abortion foes such as Ted Kennedy, Al Gore, and Jesse Jackson revised their former positions.[99] The presidency of the southern evangelical Jimmy Carter, who briefly reunited Christian voters from the South around the Democratic Party, proved to be decisive. Southern evangelicals and fundamentalists who had put their faith in Carter, only to be disappointed by his relative cultural liberalism in office, concluded that the Republican Party was their only real option.

Not all Catholics were happy with the growing alliance between the religious right and the Republican Party. And some pro-life Catholics, including the National Conference of Catholic Bishops, would continue to oppose social welfare cuts in the name of a broader right to life, making them enduring if fractious allies of the Democrats.[100] But many more Catholics were content to mute the full force of their New Deal right-to-life politics in exchange for a president who would vouch for the welfare of the unborn in utero. By the end of the decade, then, the distinct Catholic and conservative Protestant positions that were still discernible in the Hyde Amendment debate were beginning to blur, as Catholics toned down their earlier pro-welfare positions and evangelicals erased any memory of their earlier indifference to abortion. What remained of Catholics' older, more comprehensive right-to-life politics was a concern with the genocidal violence of the eugenic state and a rhetorical focus on the Black fetus as its most vulnerable target.[101] This topos was close enough to long-standing fundamentalist fears of "socialized medicine" that it was embraced by conservative Protestants also, who no doubt saw it as a welcome opportunity for disavowing their own compromised history on the matter of civil rights. Henceforth, the combined threats of taxpayer-funded abortion and state-enabled eugenics would become the mainstays of right-to-life rhetoric.

THE GHOST OF MARGARET SANGER

It was during this period that religious conservatives resurrected the figure of Margaret Sanger as the villain of the right-to-life movement. Catholics had been harsh critics of Sanger in the 1920s and 1930s, but she barely appears in Catholic denunciations of the abortion "holocaust" for much of the postwar period, only returning from the grave in the late 1970s and early 1980s.

Sanger was indeed an ambivalent figure who remained a lifelong campaigner for women's rights while gradually abandoning her earlier anarchist and socialist convictions in favor of a distinctly feminist version of eugenics.[102] Frustrated with the general lack of interest in women's reproductive autonomy among feminists and labor activists, Margaret Sanger turned to the science of eugenics at the same time as she launched herself into the campaign to liberalize birth control laws and provide free clinics to working-class women.[103] Sanger was outraged that middle and upper-class women had ready access to birth control, while working-class women, who bore the brunt of the Comstock anti-obscenity laws, were condemned to continuous unwanted pregnancies and early death.

In her writings on birth control, Sanger fulsomely adopted the eugenic language of racial purification to advance arguments that most eugenicists strenuously rejected. The pervasiveness of a male-inspired sexual morality, she argued, had condemned women to a state of sexual ignorance, which ultimately led to the degeneration of the race. While embracing the eugenicists' language of racial uplift as her own, Sanger argued against the eugenicist mainstream that this goal could only be achieved if women were granted full legal and sexual equality.

During the 1920s, she made overtures to recognized eugenicists, hoping to conscript them in the birth control cause, and published several anti-immigrant and racist texts in her journal the *Birth Control Review*. The official eugenic movement, however, clung to the idea that unconstrained female sexuality was itself a form of racial degeneracy and in a general meeting held in 1925 cast a resounding vote against the liberalization of birth control laws.

By 1930, Margaret Sanger and the eugenics movement had parted ways. The early twentieth-century science of eugenics itself would soon be divested of its mainstream professional legitimacy.

For religious conservatives, Margaret Sanger's embrace of eugenics was more than a historical footnote: as the founder of Planned Parenthood, she was the through line that led from the eugenic laws of the 1910s and 1920s to the involuntary sterilizations of Black women in the 1960s and 1970s and the *Roe v. Wade* decision of 1973. This history proved to them that legalized abortion (and the feminism that demanded it) was an irredeemably racist project. The story is complicated by the fact that Sanger was resolutely opposed to both abortion and state sterilization laws. But if religious conservatives fudge the details when it comes to Sanger's stance on abortion, they willfully misrepresent the history of the modern, interdenominational right-to-life movement, which was much more directly prompted by the feminist threat to *reproduction as such* than by the eugenic politics of selective reproduction.

Evangelicals and fundamentalists had never been overly troubled by pregnancy termination as a family planning measure and only embraced the Catholic "right-to-life" position when abortion came to be associated with the feminist demand for sexual freedom. Catholics, by contrast, have always fought against the eugenic and feminist threat to the natural family with equal ferocity, discerning no clear difference between the coercive control of women's childbearing by the state and women's own power to terminate their pregnancies. In the period after *Roe v. Wade*, religious conservatives of all stripes turned most of their attention to curbing women's right to voluntary abortion. Yet in public representations of their politics, they have consistently muted their desire to curtail women's bodily freedoms, instead presenting themselves wherever possible as crusaders against racist eugenics and the genocidal totalitarian state. To this end, they have brandished the figure of Margaret Sanger as evidence that feminism and eugenics are in any case one and the same thing.[104]

If references to Margaret Sanger were few and far between in the right-to-life literature of the 1970s, she becomes a ubiquitous figure in the following decades.[105] Beginning in the 1980s, religious conservatives developed a counterhistory of Planned Parenthood, which ironically enough drew heavily on the critical feminist historiography of the early birth control movement.[106] A defining moment here was the 1988 publication of *Grand Illusions:*

The Legacy of Planned Parenthood, a revisionist text written by George Grant, a Christian Reconstructionist and close ally of Howard Phillips.[107] Widely disseminated in the broader right-to-life movement and reissued multiple times, *Grand Illusions* evoked the case of one "Roxanne Robertson...young, Black, uninformed, frightened, unmarried, pregnant, and best of all, government subsidy eligible," whose vulnerability made her "just the kind of customer that Planned Parenthood [was] looking for."[108] The family planning establishment, Grant contended, had amassed millions of taxpayer dollars to fund its eugenic designs against the welfare poor. Like its founder, the "frivolous" and "wastrel" Margaret Sanger, Planned Parenthood worshipped at the shrine of mammon, laundering tax dollars to make "filthy lucre" and finance "concupiscence."[109] While Grant was no doubt aware that Margaret Sanger was not Jewish, her early socialism was reason enough to tar her with the brush of financial avarice, thanks to the enduring mythology of Judeo-Bolshevism. The American far right has long seen socialism and Nazism as two faces of the same coin: it was only one step from here to the idea that Margaret Sanger, the former socialist and phantasmatic Jew, was also a Nazi and a white supremacist.[110] The bottom line, according to Grant, was that "Planned Parenthood was self-consciously organized, in part, to promote and enforce White Supremacy. Like the Ku Klux Klan, the Nazi Party, and the Mensheviks, it has been from its inception implicitly and explicitly racist."[111]

And so the Black fetus on the one hand and the eugenic totalitarian state on the other became stock figures of right-to-life discourse as it solidified in the 1980s, allowing Catholics and evangelicals to exculpate themselves on every front. In the meantime, with no apparent sense of irony, the right-to-life movement continued to wage an unrelenting war on family planning services for low-income and minority women.

DEFUNDING THE LEFT: THE NEW RIGHT, CHRISTIAN CONSERVATIVES, AND REAGAN

The new Christian right was exhilarated by the election of Ronald Reagan in 1980, secure in the knowledge that the president owed his stunning victory to their historical mobilization. No president had ever promised so much to religious conservatives and never before had evangelicals and fundamentalists so wholeheartedly thrown their lot in with one party. At the Republican Convention of July 1980, the party reiterated its opposition to *Roe v. Wade*, called for the protection of private Christian academies against the IRS, and promised the "appointment of judges at all levels of the judiciary who respect traditional family values and the sanctity of innocent human life."[112] A month later, Reagan was the only presidential candidate to accept an invitation to speak before a mass rally of Southern Baptists in Dallas, Texas. The event had been stage-managed by Ed McAteer, former national field director of Howard Phillips's Conservative Caucus; it thus represented the first public meeting of New Right activists and southern fundamentalists with Reagan.[113]

Although not without risks, the dividends were clear for all to see in the election results of 1980. A sign of the decisive swing of evangelicals and fundamentalists behind the GOP, Reagan resoundingly defeated the born-again Democrat Jimmy Carter as every southern state except Georgia moved into the Republican camp. Of the forty-three House and Senate candidates endorsed by state Moral Majority chapters, forty were elected.[114] Mindful that Reagan would inevitably be subject to the pressures of factional influence once inside the White House, an umbrella organization, the Council for National Policy, or CNP, was created to maintain communication between Reagan's inner circle and the conservative movement that had brought it to power. Founded in 1981 by the evangelical Tim LaHaye and codirected by Howard Phillips and LaHaye during its first years of existence, the CNP was conceived as a conservative equivalent to the liberal Council on Foreign Relations. Ultimately, its aim was to hold Reagan to account by facilitating traffic between the Republican mainstream and the activist margins, where Christian Reconstructionists mingled with gun rights activists and cheerleaders of central American death squads. In its triannual meetings, Reagan administrators and right-wing funders congregated under the same roof as far-right militants, ensuring that White House insiders were never too far removed from the radical grassroots.[115]

But for those who thought the war was almost over with the election of Reagan, the pace of change proved frustratingly slow. The fragmentation of Reagan's constituencies placed him in a difficult position. Although the rallying of an interdenominational religious right behind his cause had no doubt secured Reagan his winning edge, figures such as Jerry Falwell were anathema to more secular Republican voters, and any real progress on the religious right's major demands was likely to alienate the bulk of his supporters.[116] With this in mind, Reagan opted for a strategy of prevarication: although he never missed an occasion to vocalize his personal sympathy with religious conservatives, he mysteriously absented himself when it came to key legislative decisions.

Religious conservatives were baffled by the mixture of intimacy and distance that characterized their relationship to the Reagan administration. Their support was apparently so precious to Reagan that he created a position of permanent liaison between himself and the movement. This position was filled by none other than Morton Blackwell, a close associate of the New Right from Young Americans for Freedom days who had worked for Richard Viguerie's direct mail operation and served as contributing editor for their movement paper *Conservative Digest*. At the same time, however, the handful of evangelicals appointed to senior positions within the administration fell far short of the 30 to 40 percent (proportional to their overall percentage of the population) promised by Reagan. Although religious conservatives were seeded throughout the lower levels of government and saw one of their own, C. Everett Koop, selected as surgeon general, only one evangelical—the secretary of the interior, James Watt—was appointed to the cabinet during Reagan's first term.[117] At the same time, Reagan's powerful triumvirate of cabinet advisors—Chief of Staff James Baker, Deputy Chief of Staff Michael Deaver, and Counselor to the President Edwin Meese—called for patience. The moral issues could wait; first Reagan had to attend to the more urgent fiscal issues of the deficit and tax cuts.[118] These advisors formed a kind of cordon sanitaire around Reagan, carefully filtering the lines of communications between the president and his contingent of zealous religious supporters.[119] Recounting the words of an anonymous White House insider, the journalist Sidney Blumenthal reported that cabinet members had been advised to keep the religious right in a state of "perpetual mobilization."[120] The plan was to create an expectation of imminent action by soliciting endless consultations while pulling back from decisive action at the last minute. Whether he knew it or not, public liaison Morton Blackwell had been appointed as distractor in chief.

In the meantime, Reagan did much to disappoint his conservative Christian supporters. During his first year in office, he appointed Sandra Day O'Connor, an Arizona judge who supported abortion rights, to a newly vacant position on the Supreme Court, directly flouting the Republican Convention's promises of the previous year.[121] The president also proved less than helpful when it came to the right-to-life movement's long-term goal of undermining *Roe v. Wade* through constitutional or legislative means. Christian conservatives descended into infighting over which one of two proposals to support: a constitutional amendment that would allow states to pass their own abortion laws, proposed by Utah Republican senator Orrin Hatch, or a bill declaring that human life began at conception, proposed by Republican senator Jesse Helms of North Carolina. After he refused to enter the fray, Reagan's lack of initiative ultimately doomed both ventures to failure.[122]

In January 1982, a group of conservative activists and businessmen, many of them members of the CNP, met at the Mayflower Hotel in Washington, DC, to take stock of Reagan's first year in office. After a day of invitation-only discussions, the attendees issued a collective statement pointing to serious deficiencies in the administration's performance.[123] While reiterating their enthusiasm for Reagan the man, the signatories expressed alarm that senior advisors seemed to be thwarting his attempts to fulfill his mission as defined by the New Right. By far the most vexing issue in their eyes was the inertia of key administration appointees, many of whom had been selected on the basis of prior bureaucratic experience and continued to reflect the general liberal bias of the managerial elite. It was evident to all that "in agency after agency," dedicated supporters of Reagan were "a distinct minority, if not entirely isolated." Whatever their merits on other grounds, career bureaucrats were "ill-equipped to carry through the Reagan program," which required people who were "audacious, resolute and willing to brave the liberal furies without flinching."[124] These appointments had worked against Reagan even with regard to his priority economic reforms. But the problem was most visible when it came to the cultural and moral issues that were most important to the religious right: in the Justice Department, for instance, most personnel were "drawn from sectors of our culture opposing the social themes on which the President was elected."[125] As a corrective to this institutional stalemate, the signatories urged a complete overhaul of administration appointments: the Reagan revolution required passionate zealots, not pragmatists or professional paper-pushers.

A few months later, the New Right's flagship journal, *Conservative Digest*, dedicated an entire issue to the problem of "how Washington funds the left."[126]

The special issue, which published a list of 175 government-funded organizations allegedly serving as left-wing fronts, was designed to alert the public to the immensity of the institutional challenge. The editors declared themselves to be enthusiastic supporters of Reagan's tax and spending cuts (indeed, they wanted to see such efforts pushed further) but fiscal austerity alone would not fulfill Reagan's mandate. What was also needed was an unflinching focus on the root of the problem—"entrenched career leftists at the lower levels of the bureaucracy, where most grant decisions are made."[127] It was conceded that Reagan had won some significant victories: one-quarter of funds allocated to the Legal Services Corporation, Howard Phillips's bête noire, had been cut; the federal Comprehensive Employment and Training Act program, CETA, was slated for closure in 1982; VISTA, or Volunteers in Service to America, a program that paid a lowly wage to volunteers on antipoverty projects, was soon to be overhauled.[128] Reagan was also congratulated for pushing ahead with the agenda of state-oriented "federalism," which aimed to eviscerate what remained of Johnson's community action programs: by consolidating existing categorical grants into a smaller number of block grants and slashing overall funding by one-quarter, Reagan had forced states and cities to shut down many of the programs inherited from the War on Poverty.[129] But the scale of financial abuse allegedly uncovered by *Conservative Digest*—from tax-funded naked lesbian theater to the promotion of sodomy and teenage sex—suggested that the project of defunding the left had far to go.

The special issue credited Howard Phillips with pioneering the "defund the left" strategy. Having bench tested the idea during his short tenure at the Office of Economic Opportunity, Phillips went on to develop a full-time research unit out of his Conservative Caucus and charged it with the task of tracking down left-leaning recipients of government aid.[130] Because federal departments were not legally required to provide such information, this research work was precious for would-be right-wing demolition teams. Indeed, much of the information publicized in same issue of *Conservative Digest* had been compiled as part of this venture by Howard Phillips's sister, Susan, whom he had employed as full-time research assistant.

Despite religious conservatives' frustration with the pace of change, Reagan had in fact appointed a small army of highly motivated reformers to sub-cabinet positions in the department that mattered most, Health and Human

Services. As reported by the *Washington Post*, "anti-abortionists have won without fanfare key positions in the Reagan administration and launched an effort to alter federal policy not just on abortion, but sex education, family planning and world population control."[131] The same article leaked the news that two anti-abortion militants had secured a meeting with Office of Management and Budget Director David Stockman and Reagan within the first few months of his inauguration, where they presented a white paper urging the president to merge his fiscal and social conservative objectives into one coordinated attack on federal family planning programs. These militants, it was later revealed, were Judie and Paul Brown of the hardline American Life Lobby.[132] The white paper provided a list of the dozen or so statutes, from the well-known Title X to more obscure sources, under which family planning services could be funded and included the usual salacious details on sex education programs for teenagers. By thwarting these funding sources, it was explained, Reagan could rein in the deficit and "at the same time do a great deal to advance the family and take the U.S. government out of the abortion and anti-family business."[133] Later that year, the Browns commissioned Howard Phillips to train their followers in movement strategies for attacking the institutional power of the left. "There's no secret to de-funding the programs of the left," Phillips explained to American Life Lobby delegates: "First you must learn how they get their money in the first place, then you monitor legislative and executive 'decision points' when the funding or program is renewed, and finally you build popular opinion and grassroots pressure to get the program eliminated." But, he concluded, "in order to make this whole process effective, we need all the organizations…working at every level of Government monitoring these programs and coordinating our unified action."[134] The Browns stood to the far right of the right-to-life movement (they had established the American Life Lobby as an alternative to the National Right to Life Committee in 1979, when the latter made allowances for abortion in the event of rape or incest). As such they were natural allies of the extremist Howard Phillips, with whom they often acted in concert.

But even more moderate, public relations–conscious allies of the pro-life movement were diligent in pursuing the New Right agenda of defunding federal family planning services. To the critical post of secretary of Department of Health and Human Services, Reagan appointed the abortion opponent

Richard Schweiker, who in turn appointed Marjory Mecklenburg, founder of Minnesota Citizens Concerned for Life, to a subcabinet position with jurisdiction over Title X family planning programs.[135] According to the testimony of one former HHS employee, Mecklenburg kept a copy of *Conservative Digest*'s 1982 special issue on "how to defund the left" on her desk and instructed staff to refuse grants to any of the 175 organizations listed there.[136] Schweiker and Mecklenburg spent their first year at HHS pursuing Planned Parenthood for suspected misuse of Title X funds: reserved for birth control and sex education services, the religious right had long accused Planned Parenthood of secretly diverting these funds to finance abortions.[137] But as these investigations were unlikely to find any hard evidence of wrongdoing and were designed to harass more than anything else, HHS officials soon turned their attention to Title X funds themselves, apparently convinced that guidelines to provide birth control to teenagers were undermining parental authority in the family and that many forms of birth control were abortifacients anyhow.[138] Title X sustained a 23 percent drop in funding between 1981 and 1982.

Religious conservatives would continue this institutional war of attrition throughout Reagan's second term. Yet while their campaign of bureaucratic harassment succeeded in putting family planning services on the defensive, no new major breakthroughs on a par with the Hyde Amendment were forthcoming.[139] New Right leaders were disappointed that Reagan had been so thoroughly fenced in by his advisors. "As a conservative, I reject the notion that our role in American politics is to 'lose as slowly as possible,'" Howard Phillips told the *New York Times* on the eve of Reagan's second term.[140] Looking back on the 1980s, Richard Viguerie reflected that although Reagan had been elected as a true movement conservative, party insiders had prevented him from governing as a conservative once in office. "Our next challenge," he concluded, "will be to nominate and elect a conservative as president, and provide him or her with a conservative majority in Congress and the states so that he or she can actually *govern* as a conservative."[141]

For a while, the New Right four thought they had found this messianic figure in the person of Pat Robertson, the Christian charismatic and televangelist who had served as president of the CNP between 1985 and 1986. Robertson ran against George H. W. Bush for the Republican presidential nomination of 1988, with the full backing of Weyrich's Free Congress Foundation.[142] When this campaign failed, however, the once unified New Right core was left in disarray as individual members found different ways of responding to failure.

Paul Weyrich put his energies behind the Christian Coalition, a national, interdenominational federation of Christian activists that Pat Robertson had pieced together out of the ruins of his election campaign.[143] Weyrich envisaged the Christian Coalition as a more sophisticated version of Falwell's Moral Majority, which was winding down just as the Christian Coalition was getting started. It was Weyrich who convinced the young Republican Ralph Reed to take up the position of executive director.[144] Reed was the ideal figure to lead a New Right–endorsed political coalition and the perfect instrument for Weyrich's own strategic designs. A founding member of Christians for America, a religious counterpart to Young Americans for Freedom, he too had begun his political career on the radical fringes of the Republican Party. Like Weyrich, however, he also had the personal and political discipline to play the long institutional game.[145]

The Christian Coalition evinced a new realism with regard to the relationship between religious conservatives and the Republican Party. Where Falwell had rashly proclaimed the majority status of moral Americans, fully expecting to parachute into the Republican Party from without, conservative Christians who had spent the decade struggling to assert themselves within a ruling Republican bloc were now forced to reckon with their current (and perhaps) enduring minority status. Robertson, Weyrich, and Reed responded to this impasse by adopting a new posture of moderation. The Christian Coalition would be a bridge builder, cultivating connections with other faiths, races, and ethnicities and with nonreligious conservatives on the Republican right. Its leaders set their sights on the long game. Instead of attempting a coup d'état on the Republican Party, they would seek to build influence from the ground up, inserting themselves in local, state, and primary campaigns, where gains were easier won. "We think the Lord is going to give us this nation back one precinct at a time, one neighborhood at a time, and one state at a time," Ralph told a journalist at *Christianity Today*. "We're not going to win it all at once with some kind of millennial rush at the White House."[146]

While this may have looked like a confession of weakness, it also concealed a long-term strategy to capture the Republican Party agenda by less than transparent means. Reporting on a leadership meeting of the Christian Coalition incognito in 1992, one political journalist attended a session in which local activists were instructed on how to infiltrate the Republican National Convention.[147] The coalition's field director explained that only 15 percent of eligible voters were required to swing a presidential election; in low-turnout city council and state legislature elections, the swing vote could be as low as 6 or 7 percent. If the Christian Coalition could successfully place congenial candidates in the running and deliver its legions of energized members to the polls on election day, it would have a good chance of replacing incumbent Republicans one precinct at a time. Ralph Reed spoke of the group's voter mobilization plans as if he were describing a covert military operation: "I want to be invisible. I do guerrilla warfare. I paint my face and travel at night. You don't know it's over until you're in a body bag. You don't know until election night."[148]

Among the original New Right four, Howard Phillips was the most pessimistic about the possibility of continuing to work within Republican Party structures. At the end of Reagan's second term, his assessment of the president's record had barely shifted from 1983, when he accused Reagan of a "conscious policy of detente with the left" and lambasted him for failing to take down "the big banks, the Great Society infrastructure, the imperial judiciary, the Pharisaic lawyers, the cultural priesthood of humanism in the media, the corporate socialists and the twisters of truth who continue to dominate our education institutions."[149] Phillips's gloomy outlook was confirmed when Pat Robertson dropped out of the primaries and the GOP's new presidential candidate turned out to be George H. W. Bush, an "establishment" Republican who until recently had been an outspoken supporter of Planned Parenthood. A sign of the now entrenched influence of religious conservatives over the Republican Party, Bush was forced to renege on his pro-choice past in the lead-up to the election. But when the newly elected Bush appointed a moderate to the Supreme Court, the ever-intransigent Phillips turned his back on the Republican Party for good and revived the New Right's old dream of creating a third party to the extreme right of the GOP.[150]

Howard Phillips was far from alone in his appraisal of the situation. While many Christian conservatives followed Robertson, Reed, Weyrich, and Viguerie in their long march through Republican institutions, many others now opted for extralegal forms of direct action or terrorism.[151] For movement radicals, the uncompromising fundamentalism of Christian Reconstructionism was the obvious ideological refuge from the Christian Coalition's moderation.

From this point onward, it appeared that Howard Phillips and his old New Right associates were traveling on two nonintersecting orbits, the one patient and pragmatic, the other so extreme and uncompromising it must surely have been doomed to failure. Yet the estrangement was not as total as it looked. As Phillips spun off to the far right, Viguerie and Weyrich doubled down on the inside/outside strategy they had adopted since the 1970s, with one foot in the conventional electoral politics of the Republican Party and the other in the miasma of far-right groupuscules that existed on its fringe. Ever mindful, however, that they needed a reliable conveyer belt between populist movement conservatives, congressional representatives, and Washington lobbyists, the remaining New Right stalwarts strengthened their investment in the CNP during these years.[152]

Even as the president of a far-right third party, Phillips, like other militants of the radical right, was a regular invitee to the triennial meetings of the CNP, which he had after all directed in its early years. Here, he was free to mingle with Republican congressmen, Beltway lobbyists, and professional compromisers such as Ralph Reed and Pat Robertson, as if the moment of rupture had never happened at all.[153] The mere existence of this intermediary space helps explain why movement activists who parted ways during the Clinton years could reunite so effortlessly under different circumstances. In 2010, when the CNP threw its weight behind the Tea Party movement, in which Howard Phillips and his far-right associates were fully embedded, the founding members of the New Right once again found themselves traveling on the same arc.

"HILLARYCARE" AND THE SPECTER OF EUGENICS

Just when everyone was pronouncing the death of the Christian right, however, religious conservatives surprised everyone when they managed to secure the defeat of President Clinton's national health-care plan.[154] The coup was unexpected because conservative Catholics and born-again Christians had expressed markedly different positions on the value of universal health care at the outset of the Clinton administration. Their shared focus on the issue of abortion coverage, however, ultimately ended up scuttling the plan altogether. For operatives of the New Right such as Ralph Reed, this not altogether concerted collaboration proved that religious conservatives could be formidable foot soldiers in the defeat of wider social initiatives and indispensable partners in Gingrich's gathering Republican Revolution—if only these same Republicans would recognize it.

The battle was a watershed in the politics of the religious right: not only had it turned economically progressive Catholics into saboteurs of a project they otherwise supported on social and economic grounds, but it also enduringly shifted the politics of many evangelicals much further to the right. Evangelicals who had once held centrist views on the value of universal health care (in line with the Republican Party itself), now became hardened foes of a project they saw as irredeemably "humanistic" and "socialist."[155] From this point on, the issues of universal health care and abortion became inextricably linked in the American political imagination, and would-be reformers could hardly contemplate the prospect of universal health care without triggering a storm of protest around the issue of tax-funded abortion. The campaign against "Hillarycare," as the Health Security Act came to be known on the right, represented the first major collaboration between religious conservatives connected to the New Right's Council for National Policy and the free market militants organized around the Koch-funded Citizens for a Sound Economy. As such, it must be seen as a trial run for the Tea Party campaign against the Affordable Care Act, or "Obamacare," which brought together a similar coalition between the Council for National Policy and the Koch-funded Americans for Prosperity more than a decade later.

When Democrats set to work on health-care reform in the first few months of 1993, there was a sense of urgency on all sides. Hillary Clinton, who took up a position as leader of the health reform task force five days after Bill Clinton's inauguration, warned that the Democrats needed to move as quickly as possible if they wanted to avoid defeat at the next presidential elections.[156] The New Right protégé Newt Gingrich, then second in command of House Republicans, understood just how significant this project was to the fortunes of the Democrats: universal health care was the missing piece of the unfinished New Deal project; if successful, it would represent the first major act of social legislation to be passed since the 1960s. As such, Gingrich feared that the passage of universal health care would enduringly seal the allegiance of American citizens to the social state, both as patients and workers in an expanded health-care sector, and in so doing, create a permanent natural constituency for the Democratic Party. By the same token, if Republicans were able to defeat Clinton's cherished reform in the first year of his administration, they would destroy all confidence in his abilities and give Republicans a much greater chance of winning control of Congress at the next elections.[157]

For Wanda Franz, president of the National Right to Life Committee, passage of the Clinton health-care bill would be a "calamity" for the pro-life movement because it risked extending health-care coverage to all abortion procedures, whether the woman in question was poor or middle-class.[158] If Clinton's health-care plan, as she feared, was set to define abortion as a routine medical practice, then even the partial victory of the Hyde Amendment would be lost as women on Medicaid were absorbed into a national system of coverage. The Christian Coalition's Ralph Reed, for his part, summoned up a long tradition of fundamentalist attacks on "socialized medicine" to denounce the plan as a "bureaucratic, Byzantine, European-style syndicalist nightmare."[159]

By the time Clinton presented his plan to a joint session of Congress in September 1993, he had lined up an impressive contingent of supporters, including groups as diverse as the AFL-CIO unions, the Business Roundtable, the National Association of Manufacturers, and even the once intractable Chamber of Commerce.[160] From the outset, Catholics were among the most important assets in this coalition. Both the Catholic Health Association, or CHA, which represented hundreds of hospitals and nursing homes across the country, and the United States Conference of Catholic Bishops (USCCB) were long-standing advocates of universal health care. Given their significant presence in the nation's health-care system (with over 10 percent of hospitals and 15 percent of hospital beds under the auspices of the CHA), Catholic allegiance to the Clinton plan was an all-important trump card.[161] Prominent Catholic allies were duly invited to every official announcement of the plan's progress.[162]

Yet as details of the plan emerged, the question of abortion coverage became an intractable sticking point. At first muted in their dissent, the USCCB and CHA became increasingly vocal in their opposition as it emerged that abortion coverage was indeed to be included under the wide-ranging category of "pregnancy-related services." Although Catholics were assured that they could opt out by invoking the plan's "conscience clause," the fact that abortion was covered at all proved too much for these once staunch allies. Leveraging their power as some of the nation's major health-care stakeholders, the USCCB and CHA refused to put their final stamp of approval on a plan that would permit the taxpayer funding of abortion.[163] And as the Clinton administration attempted to push the plan toward closure, the conspicuous reserve of these once vocal allies became a dangerous liability.

If the Catholic leadership was conflicted in its stance on universal health care, there was no such ambivalence among pro-life activist groups such as the Catholic-dominated National Right to Life Committee. The NRLC had been on high alert since Clinton's first few days in office, when he signed a volley of executive orders overturning Republican restrictions on everything from fetal tissue research to USAID funding of family planning services.[164] At the time, the federal legislative director of the NRLC, Douglas Johnson, had warned that these "were just the opening shots in a much bigger battle that the pro-life movement must win—the battle to block Clinton's plan to federally mandate abortion coverage for the entire nation, through his forthcoming proposal for a nationalized health system."[165]

It would not take long for the NRLC to announce its blanket opposition to health-care reform. Wanda Franz predicted that a Clinton-led program of universal health care would "institutionalize" abortion by turning it into routine medical care, subsidized at the taxpayer's expense.[166] Franz cited the bill's cost efficiency measures—which the Clinton administration had included as a preemptive concession to free market critics—as evidence of eugenic intent. Beyond its obvious risks to the unborn, Franz reasoned, the bill "might also be a massive threat to the born who are physically imperfect, disabled, or frail and old. Infanticide, denial of medical care, and euthanasia may well be the fruits of a misguided approach to health care."[167] Mothers, Franz predicted, "would find themselves under pressure to abort their children because the bureaucrats administering the government's health plan will be under pressure to save money by avoiding more costly services for birth. The disabled, the seriously ill, and the old and frail might be in danger of having treatment denied if their quality of life is judged too low to justify medical treatment. Physicians, nurses, pharmacists, hospitals…would find themselves enmeshed in a government-imposed system that mandates killing as medical 'service.'"[168]

By this point, right-to-life Catholics were just as well versed in the language of taxpayer rights as evangelicals and fundamentalists. Richard Doerflinger, associate director of pro-life activities for the United States Conference of Catholic Bishops, complained that Clinton's health-care reform was "not 'pro-choice' for taxpayers," who would "be forced, under threat of fines and imprisonment, to pay for hundreds of thousands of procedures that many of us recognize as the killing of young children."[169] Notwithstanding their concern for taxpayers, however, most Catholic anti-abortion activists maintained their long-standing support for maternalist welfare measures and state support to the family. Thus, they were often outraged by the fact that federal coverage for abortion was being contemplated at the same time that certain states were restricting welfare benefits for mothers and children through the use of antinatalist welfare caps. For Doerflinger, Clinton's proposed health-care reform was "not even 'pro-choice' for poor women." "Low-income women don't have abortions because they favor them," he continued; "they generally have them in situations of social and economic pressure...pressure that can only increase when the government provides unlimited funding for abortion, even as it cuts off payment for additional children under various forms of so-called 'welfare reform.' Under Clinton's policy, the poor will have the abortions that the rich want them to have."[170]

Evangelical groups such as Concerned Women for America, Focus on the Family, and the Family Research Council were allergic to the very idea of social welfare but brandished the same specters of eugenics, latter-day slavery, and state-run death panels to express their opposition. The press secretary of Concerned Women for America quipped that while the Clinton administration had included a "conscience clause" for nurses and doctors, no such provision had been made for taxpayers, who would be forced against their will to subsidize assaults on the family.[171] The Christian taxpayer, she worried, would be compelled to finance rehabilitation programs for drug addicts, the care of AIDS patients, and proposed school-based clinics "dispens[ing] condoms and other birth control methods to junior and senior high school students without permission from parents."[172] Much of this was pure speculation; some of it (including an alleged "promiscuity benefit" for sexually active women) was outright fantasy.

The Eagle Forum's Phyllis Schlafly was unusual among Catholics (but in sync with New Right Catholics such as Viguerie and Weyrich) in adopting a hard line against social insurance of any kind. "Is America ready for the totalitarian state?" she asked readers of her monthly report; "Hillary Clinton's health care proposal is genuine socialism—an attempt to control every aspect of U.S. health care under a National Health Board functioning like a Communist Central Committee."[173] Turning the logic of social insurance on its head, Schlafly predicted that universal coverage would lead to less, not more, care. Under the proposed National Health Board, a "network of bureaucrats wielding unprecedented power would limit costs by "denying treatment to those whom the Gatekeepers determine have a very poor 'quality of life.'"[174] And while taxpayers succumbed to the sovereign power of the bureaucrat, their tax dollars would be siphoned off to pay for the Clintons' "special interest kinds of health care" such as "all abortions, all mental disorders, all substance abusers, and condom clinics in all public schools."[175]

As a self-declared feminist and child of the 1960s, it was the first lady and not the president who came to embody all the dangers of overbearing statism in the eyes of religious conservatives. Variously assumed to be a voracious man-eater and a castrating lesbian, a child-hating feminist and an indulgent champion of children's rights, Hillary Clinton represented fantasized contradictions that could not be resolved into the reassuring dialectic of mother or whore.[176] Her proximity to state power turned her into a latter-day Margaret Sanger, a representative of state eugenics in feminist garb. She was, in Rush Limbaugh's words, a "feminazi"—a portmanteau of pro-choice feminist and national socialist.[177]

In contrast to the white feminazi, African American women figured in right-to-life discourse as would-be mothers and unwitting victims of a feminist white supremacist medical complex. Any public figure who deviated from this picture of the maternal ingenue was subject to an onslaught of vitriol. The young African American lawyer Anita Hill was one such target: when Hill brought sexual harassment allegations against George H.W. Bush's Supreme Court nominee, the Catholic conservative Clarence Thomas, she earned the enduring hatred of religious conservatives.[178] Another prominent African American woman and Clinton's choice for surgeon general, Dr. Joycelyn Elders, was also subject to relentless attack. Elders's unapologetic embrace of a risk-reduction approach to sexual health and recreational drug use made her unusable as a pietà figure.[179] If religious conservatives could not depict her as a victim of eugenic feminism, they concluded that she must be a collaborator and race traitor. In the words of Texe Marrs, head of the fundamentalist Living Truth Ministry in Texas: "Although Joycelyn Elders is, herself, a black American, she, Hillary, and their liberal friends seem to be especially fascinated about providing the $500 per unit Norplant implant to black teenagers from ghetto and slum neighborhoods in decaying urban centers where pregnancy rates are now soaring. Naturally taxpayers will be required to foot the bill."[180]

As the health-care debate intensified, the NRLC and other prominent groups on the religious right were swept up in the juggernaut of the Christian Coalition's heavily funded, multipronged campaign. When Ralph Reed announced the organization's opposition to Clinton's health-care plan in September 1993, it was in language that gave equal weight to fiscal and moral concerns. The coalition, reported the *Wall Street Journal*, intended "to weigh in on health-care reform, fighting funding of elective abortions in any national plan, opposing mandatory membership in health cooperatives that might limit families' choice of doctors and resisting requiring small businesses to pay for employees' health coverage."[181] The framing reflected Reed's determination to augment the power of the religious right by broadening its focus beyond the question of sexuality.

In a position piece published in the Heritage Foundation's *Policy Review* in the summer of 1993, Reed presented his case that the religious right could not win on single-issue campaigns alone.[182] Recent polls suggested that relatively few voters were prepared to choose between candidates on the sole basis of their religious convictions, and even committed Christian conservatives were often more motivated by the larger fiscal issues of taxation, public spending, and the deficit than they were by abortion. If this might have discouraged someone more purist in approach, Reed sensed an opportunity for "widening the net." Economic and religious conservatives might differ on the question of legislating sexual morality, he argued, but their convergence around fiscal issues reflected a basic concern that excessive government spending was a threat to the interests of the private family. If the Christian Coalition could convincingly frame moral issues in fiscal terms and vice versa, then it would make itself legible to a much wider spectrum of right-wing voters. The tension between religious and economic conservatives was overstated, Reed claimed: "What most conservative religious folk want is not to use government to impose their values on others, but to shrink and delimit government so the left can no longer impose its secular values on churches and families.... By using fiscal policy as social policy—shifting control of education to the local level, ending tax subsidies for abortion, and transferring certain welfare functions to the civil society—social conservatives could reduce the size of government in such a way as to measurably advance traditional values."[183] This need not mean abandoning the religious conservative's favorite issues, Reed reassured his fellow Christians.[184] Indeed, conservative Christians could achieve previously unattainable goals on the anti-abortion front by embedding the issue of taxpayer-funded abortion within a larger struggle against the very idea of social welfare. If "religious and economic conservatives [could] cooperate where possible and remain civil in disagreement," Reed predicted, they would "accomplish far more together than separately."[185]

In opting for this strategy, the Christian Coalition was seeking not only to reach a greater section of the voting public, but also to wedge itself more permanently in Republican Party structures. To have any hope of doing this, Reed calculated, the Christian Coalition needed to hitch a ride with the then more powerful small government conservatives on the Republican right. Reed envisaged the Christian Coalition as a "pro-family equivalent" to the insurgent Sunbelt Republicans that had gathered around Newt Gingrich and the Koch-funded Citizens for a Sound Economy.[186] The Christian Coalition could only aspire to enter this alliance as a junior partner. But if it could prove itself indispensable to the long-term success of Gingrich's Republican right, Reed calculated, it might eventually secure a role as equal partner in the ruling coalition.[187]

The Clinton Health Security bill was the perfect opportunity for putting this plan to the test. The free market campaign against health-care reform was driven by the Koch-funded Citizens for a Sound Economy, which represented the many smaller, noncorporate business interests that were most opposed to employer-mandated health care. These included a handful of small business associations such as the National American Wholesale Grocers Association, the National Retailers Federation, the National Restaurant Association, and, most significant of all, the National Federation of Independent Business, whose many small business members feared (for the most part erroneously, given planned exemptions) that they would be forced to contribute to the health care of workers.[188] Throughout the campaign, Citizens for a Sound Economy worked in close collaboration with Newt Gingrich's office on Capitol Hill.[189]

There was much that predisposed the Christian Coalition and Citizens for a Sound Economy to work together. Both organizations had emerged from the Reagan and Bush years convinced that they needed to establish a grassroots presence beyond the Washington Beltway if they wanted to push their agenda any further.[190] By the early Clinton years, both presided over a network of smaller associations that were able to mobilize angry constituents at a moment's notice. Their respective membership bases were well suited to joint action. As noted by Ralph Reed, there was considerable overlap between CSE's legions of small business owners and the foot soldiers of the Christian Coalition: a full 43 percent of small business owners represented by the National Federation of Independent Business were evangelical Christians.[191]

During the summer of 1993, as Hillary Clinton set out on a nationwide bus tour to promote the proposed health-care bill, the Christian Coalition and Citizens for a Sound Economy marshaled their combined forces in ambush.[192] At every small town the Clinton caravan stopped off at, it was shouted down by a crowd of small business owners and religious right activists carrying placards inscribed with messages such as "Abortion is Not Health Care for Babies" or "Stop Hillary's Rationing Plan."[193] Protesters came prepared with scripted soundbites to read to the mainstream media, while Rush Limbaugh, in close collaboration with Gingrich's office, used his nationally syndicated program to broadcast the protesters' message through local radio stations.[194] In an inspired piece of campaign propaganda, anti-health-care activists responded to the televised image of Hillary Clinton holding up a red, white, and blue Health Security Card by handing out a replica "ration card" emblazoned with the message "Stop Socialized Medicine." The card could be mailed back to the president with the following message boxes ticked: "DO NOT want the government to choose my doctor!... DO NOT want by tax dollars used to pay exorbitant medical bills created by immoral lifestyles! REFUSE to pay for the murder of innocent little babies! DO NOT WANT TO PAY HIGHER TAXES to finance SOCIALIZED MEDICINE IN AMERICA!"[195]

At the same time as it was curating this spectacle of popular outrage, Citizens for a Sound Economy kept up steady pressure on the business and political allies of the Clinton plan. Having conscripted the National Federation of Independent Business (NFIB) into its own ranks, the CSE campaign threatened to undercut the power of other more established trade associations. As the once renegade Chamber of Commerce lined up with the Business Round-table in support of Clinton's health-care plan, the newly visible NFIB—for many years the chamber's poor cousin—was now threatening to poach the latter's members.[196] The crisis forced Richard Lesher to abruptly reverse the organization's position on health care. The Business Roundtable followed suit.[197] As key allies such as these drifted away, Democrats themselves were beginning to waver, thanks in large part to the intervention of the United States Conference of Catholic Bishops.[198]

The Clinton Health Security Act was officially shelved in September 1994. It had taken less than a year for a seemingly unbeatable bill to be banished from the political agenda. And the Christian Coalition could claim a good part of the credit for this spectacular turnaround. High on this victory, religious conservatives threw themselves behind Newt Gingrich in the midterm elections of 1994, convinced that they now held the bargaining power to implement their own agenda.[199]

When the full scale of the Republican sweep of Congress became apparent, the Christian Coalition had every reason to feel emboldened. Evangelicals had turned out in droves to support the Republican right. A *Washington Post* exit poll found that one in four voters identified as "evangelical" or "born again" Christians, while a postelection survey sponsored by the Christian Coalition reported that "religious conservatives" accounted for 33 percent of all voters—double the 15 percent threshold its strategists had identified as necessary to swing an election in their favor.[200] As pointed out by the conservative weekly *Human Events*, thirty-eight of the fifty-two Republican House freshmen were either religious conservatives themselves or closely aligned with them.[201] Even critics of the religious right thought that Gingrich Republicans owed an enormous debt to their Christian foot soldiers. Arthur J. Kropp, president of the liberal think tank People for the American Way, remarked that the "biggest story in Washington, D.C., isn't the Republican Party takeover of Congress. It's the ascendancy of a political movement that was once considered to be 'political exotica' and which now, amazingly, commands the loyalty of both houses of Congress."[202] The election, Ralph Reed claimed, "ended once and for all the myth that we are a liability rather than an asset in the Republican Party."[203]

His elation was short-lived, however, as the Christian Coalition soon found itself sidelined by Republican allies once again. The coalition's consolation prize for backing the Contract with America—a ten-point Contract with the Family calling for a ban on late-term abortion and the abolition of the Department of Education—received Gingrich's official blessing, but in the absence of real support among House Republicans, languished in congressional committee.[204] By the time of Clinton's decisive reelection in 1996, the Christian Coalition had little to show for its efforts.[205] For Howard Phillips, the saga confirmed what he had suspected all along—for the moment at least, the path to Christian victory lay outside the bounds of electoral politics.

DEBT MILLENNIALISM

By the final year of the George H. W. Bush administration, Howard Phillips was so frustrated with the Republican mainstream that he created a breakaway venture, the U.S. Taxpayers Party (renamed the Constitution Party in 1999). Announcing his decision at the New Right's annual Conservative Political Action Conference, or CPAC, in April 1991, he told his audience that the pragmatism of alliance formation "doesn't work—at least not in the long run."[206] And Phillips's sights were set on the long run. The Republican Party was a "house divided," he claimed. "The workers oppose Planned Parenthood, safe sodomy, high taxes and the New World Order but the leaders favor all of the above. In the Republican Party, the conservatives get the platform but the liberals get the government."[207] The GOP would split in two, perhaps within the next decade, he reassured his audience. In the meantime, only a third party would have the necessary freedom to implement the kind of "radical reform" agenda he had in mind: nothing less than the "radical reconstruction of America as it ought to be."[208]

Phillips's use of the term "reconstruction" was far from casual. For those who were familiar with the terminology, it would have been clear that the U.S. Taxpayers Party platform was steeped in the principles of Christian Reconstructionism, the fringe current in Reformed (Calvinist) theology to which Phillips had converted in the mid-1970s. Christian Reconstructionism had taught Phillips that the framers of the American Constitution were inspired by Old Testament law. This idiosyncratic reading of American history saw the Declaration of Independence as the preamble to the Constitution and refused to recognize any amendment passed after the Civil War. Christian

Reconstructionists such as Phillips denied that America had no religion of state: if the First Amendment prohibited Congress from making any law "respecting an establishment of religion," it placed no such stricture on the states, each of which had their own official religion at the time of independence.[209] America, moreover, was not a democracy: rather, it was a republic of theocratic states founded on biblical law.[210]

Most important, for Phillips, was the claim that the government had no right to exercise functions that were not explicitly enumerated in the original text of the Constitution.[211] Like all fiscal conservatives, Phillips rejected the New Deal constitutional revolution that purported to uncover an expanded federal power to tax and spend in the general welfare clause (Article 1, Section 8, Clause 1) of the Constitution. All redistribution was theft, whether performed at the point of a gun or voted in at the ballot box.[212] The family, in this view, was the only legitimate source of welfare. Public spending on secular welfare services, education, and health was not only unconstitutional but also contrary to biblical law. The government had no mandate to create debt or collect income taxes. Nor did the Federal Reserve have the authority to print money or inflate away the debt: it would have to be abolished.

From Reconstructionism also, Phillips inherited a sense of prophetic urgency in the face of an always imminent day of reckoning. "Both political parties have given us a debt of historic proportions," he warned in a 1992 campaign interview.[213] Not only had they squandered America's credit by spending beyond their means, they had funneled this excess of spending into the subsidization of "moral decline."[214] By directing money to organizations such as Planned Parenthood and Gay Men's Health Crisis, both Republicans and Democrats had spent "millions of dollars...in promoting a way of life which is counterproductive and destructive." A final accounting would come soon enough, Phillips warned. "Debt," like sin, "is not without consequences." [215] Unless it changed course within a few years, America would be engulfed in an "inflationary depression" the likes of which had never been experienced before. The Taxpayers Party could soften the blow by immediately withdrawing funds from social welfare—with proposed cuts of $500 billion to public spending—and commencing the long-overdue work of moral reconstruction.

A fundamentalist offshoot of the Reformed (or Calvinist) church, Christian Reconstructionism was founded by the Presbyterian theologian Rousas

John Rushdoony in the mid-1960s. Arising out of the ferment of John Birch Society tax resistance and Protestant reaction that raged across the Sunbelt at the height of the Cold War, it represents one of the most sustained attempts yet to unite the precepts of free market economics and sexual austerity. Like the early New England Puritans, Christian Reconstructionists recognize no rupture between the Old and New Testament: the vengeful God of the old covenant was not superseded by the forgiving God of the new when Jesus died on the cross, Rushdoony told his followers.[216] But Reconstructionists go further than most Calvinists in holding that the civil and criminal (not just moral) laws of the Old Testament still hold sway, unless explicitly overturned by New Testament revelation.[217] In this spirit, Rushdoony's infamous masterwork *The Institutes of Biblical Law* seeks to retrieve a complete casuistry of moral, civil, and criminal laws from the books of the Old Testament with the ultimate goal of implementing them in present-day America.[218]

As adherents to a postmillennial eschatology, Christian Reconstructionists place great faith in institutional and legal activism as a means of precipitating the millennium. Unlike the vast majority of modern evangelicals, who as premillennials believe that Christians must passively await the return of God before they can rule, at best saving as many souls as possible along the way, Reconstructionists are convinced they must establish the Kingdom of God on earth before he will deign to return. As such, they see proselytism as necessary but insufficient. Beyond evangelism, their biblical mandate is to start immediate construction work on the coming Kingdom, if necessary occupying the interstices of the secular state to seed them with alternative institutions under Old Testament law.

This is by no means a pacifist solution, although it might present itself as such at first. Christian Reconstructionists see no neutral ground between the religious and the secular; one or the other will triumph in the long run.[219] Yet they condone the tactical occupation of "neutral" space in the interests of establishing a long-term advantage. For example, they teach that the quintessentially liberal right to "religious freedom" can be exploited to create a standing army of true believers outside and beyond the state, who at some millenarian turning point will rise up and swallow the same liberal state that has so kindly tolerated them.[220] It is easy to see how this message might have appealed to someone like Howard Phillips, who was a long-term strategist as much as he was a purist. As futile as third parties often were within the bipolar landscape of American electoral politics, Christian Reconstruction offered some hope that victory might be achieved by other means, through theism patient cultivation of Christian enclaves—the home school, the Christian militia, and the biblical law court. This was not a frontal assault on the state so much as an exhortation to institutional counterinsurgency. If party politics within the Republican Party offered the prospect of "losing slowly," Christian Reconstructionism reassured Howard Phillips that by occupying the margins he could in fact "win slowly."[221]

Rushdoony's attempt to amalgamate Christian theocracy and economic libertarianism was not without precedent. In the first decades of the twentieth century, fundamentalist Protestants armed themselves against the social gospel of the progressive era and the even greater threat of the New Deal by forging a unique hybrid of Christian conservatism and libertarian economics. This fusionist tendency was so dominant within the libertarian movement at midcentury that its signature publication, *Faith and Freedom*, was responsible for introducing the major figures in Austrian economics (Ludwig von Mises and Friedrich von Hayek) onto the American scene and regularly featured texts by both fundamentalist Christians and the major American exponents of Austrian-inspired libertarianism (Henry Hazlitt and Murray Rothbard).[222] When the libertarian movement started sidelining its Christian exponents in the 1960s, Rushdoony was so well established he felt able to continue the project on his own. Hoping to place Christian economics on sounder theological grounds, he commissioned the services of a young disciple, Gary North, to forge an overarching synthesis between Austrian economics and Reconstructionist theology. With Rushdoony as mentor, North secured a series of key positions working for major libertarian organizations such as the Volker Fund and the Foundation for Economic Education in the early 1960s.[223] The result of his apprenticeship was the *Introduction to Christian Economics*, a Christian libertarian primer published in 1974 as a companion volume to Rushdoony's *Institutes of Biblical Law.*[224]

From the Austrian neoliberals and their American libertarian followers, North derived the idea that a truly free market could be established only on the basis of honest money, that is, money backed by an immutable referent such as gold or silver. The libertarians contrasted the honesty of commodity money with the fraudulence of modern state money, with its trio of subterfuge: legal tender laws, authorizing the state to monopolize the creation of money; fractional reserve banking, allowing state-licensed banks to create money out of thin air without equivalent collateral; and most treacherous of all, central banking, an institution by which the state performs the same sleight of hand at the expense of its hardworking citizens.[225] For economic libertarians, the state-based creation of money and debt represents the most dangerous of modern economic institutions and an affront to market freedom. To be sure, the state can always steal from its citizens through the blunt instrument of taxation and distribution. But the Treasury can also avoid the inevitable conflicts associated with taxation by issuing its own debt and allowing the state to spend beyond its means. When the central bank then exchanges this debt for newly created money, it both debases the currency and inflates prices and imposes a form of stealth taxation on its most productive citizens. Inflation is the worst of economic crimes because it redistributes wealth from creditors to debtors, and from savers to consumers.

North was a dutiful student of the Austrian school economists. Yet he was convinced that Christian Reconstructionism offered something they lacked. After all, although Ludwig von Mises and Murray Rothbard saw clearly enough that market freedom stood or fell on the premise of scarce metal, they ultimately could not explain why there should be austerity rather than abundance. North's theological reductionism dug deeper and found God. "God has cursed the earth (Gen 3:12–19). This is the starting point for all economic analysis," North wrote. "The earth no longer gives up her fruits automatically. Man must sweat to eat."[226] Where the Austrian economists saw debt, North saw guilt, and where they saw bankruptcy, North saw sin.

North scoured the Old Testament in search of biblical foundations for free market principles. Thus, he contended, the libertarian doctrine of honest money was justified by the Old Testament's insistence on reliable weights and measures. Inflation he denounced as running counter to the biblical law of scarcity. The collection of interest from debt was sinful among fellow believers, but allowable when applied to heretics. Debt denoted sin but could be rationalized if it was fully collateralized. Personal debt was forbidden unless secured by its equivalent in hard money, commodities, or labor, while failure to pay a personal debt could legitimate the enslavement of the debtor. Public debt, by contrast, was sinful under all circumstances because it was never meant to be repaid and violated the biblical injunction against the pledging of collateral to multiple creditors. "The public debt of the federal government...is steadily eroding the monetary unit," North wrote; "from a biblical standpoint, this is utterly corrupt. 'The wicked borroweth and payeth not again' (Ps 37:21). The civil authorities do not intend to reduce this debt and repay the principal. They favor perpetual indebtedness. Laws that are transgressed in God's universe will be found to contain their own built-in punishment."[227] Not only were inflation and public debt acts of fraud committed against the taxpaying citizen; they were transgressions of biblical law and as such destined to be punished.

For Christian Reconstructionists, the fiscal sins of the state are intimately entangled with the moral corruption of the family. For much of the debt issued by the modern state, North explains, stems from its efforts to replace the biblically mandated functions of the family with a panoply of corrupt welfare-state institutions, from the public school to socialized medicine and social welfare itself. By creating alternatives to family welfare, the profligate, big-spending state nullifies intergenerational bonds and undermines the incentive to bequeath wealth. As the state takes over the natural bonds of kinship, the young lose all sense of their genealogical connection to parents, while the old abandon all investment in their children's future.

The inevitable result is warfare between the young and the old: generations that no longer depend on each other for family-based welfare learn to see each other as unproductive burdens and so become inured to the eugenic evils of the modern state. "By abandoning the principle of family responsibility," North writes, "the modern messianic state wastes a culture's capital and makes more acceptable both euthanasia (which reduces the expense of caring for the unproductive elderly) and abortion (which reduces the expense of training and caring for the unproductive young)."[228] But the more the state usurps the role of the family, the more precarious are its own economic foundations. By offering too much economic security, the welfare state disincentivizes productive work and erodes the tax base, thereby forcing itself to take on ever greater levels of debt.[229] Once initiated, the dynamic becomes self-reinforcing. If abortion is the literal manifestation of the family's self-implosion, North predicts the same fate for the American nation, which at some point will collapse under its cumulated burden of economic debt and moral guilt. "The pseudo-family state is an agent of social, political and economic bankruptcy.... *The pseudo-family is suicidal.*"[230] Thus North elucidates the secret relationship between public debt and abortion that is so often simply assumed in conservative Christian rhetoric.

With an audience reaching beyond the small circle of Christian Reconstructionists to include survivalists, militia members, and economic libertarians, Gary North has played a seminal role in stoking a pervasive fear of imminent economic collapse on the American far right. In North's hands, Austrian economic theory—already more attentive than most economic traditions to the grand cycles of boom and bust—is infused with a millenarian sensibility, predicting inevitable punishment for the hubris of wanton fiat money creation on the part of the state. The precise contours of the coming collapse have shifted with remarkable frequency (from the third world debt crisis of the 1980s to the millennium bug and the subprime crisis of the early twenty-first century), but North has never wavered from the idea that the day of reckoning is nigh. The "world faces a crisis," he wrote in the mid-1980s, "either more debt to insolvent debtors, or a default. Either more inflation to make the loans, or a giant international bank run. And all of it has come about because the masters of finance and the politicians they buy refuse to honor basic Biblical principles of debt."[231] Only a complete reconstruction of society, extending from the prohibition of abortion to a "Bible-based monetary reform," could avert the coming crisis.[232] But whether this could be accomplished peacefully is uncertain. The necessary reform "may have to come through economic collapse, which will involve the destruction of the present world monetary system. Then, out of the rubble...something else will arise." In the meantime, North advises his followers to start hoarding gold, silver, and nonperishable foods in preparation for the cataclysm to come.[233]

There is in North's work a kind of reckless fatalism in the face of economic collapse. If default is the prelude to moral reconstruction, he seems to be saying, then bring it on. This reflects the growing radicalism of American libertarians in general, who in recent years have become much more willing than their Austrian forefathers to recommend catastrophic depression and debt deflation as a useful catalyst to systemic reform.[234] Convinced as they are that the United States is headed toward default, libertarians have come to believe that it might be better to hasten the event rather than see it deferred through another round of inflation. "Default will be painful," observed Ron Paul at the height of the government debt ceiling showdown of July 2011, "but it is all but inevitable for a country as heavily indebted as the US."[235] Better to push the United States over the fiscal cliff now than condemn the country to the much more painful fate of hyperinflation somewhere down the road. "Continuously raising the debt ceiling" will "only forestall the day of reckoning and ensure that when it comes, it will be cataclysmic," he intoned. Ron Paul's language was almost millenarian. Gary North's was explicitly so. "Economic judgment is coming," North warned.[236] To force the United States to default on its obligations—and to do so on the specific issue of funding abortion—would perhaps bring terrible suffering to bear on the American people, but it would also act as a moral purgative and prelude to reconstruction.

That such ideas should circulate among Tea Party activists is less surprising when we consider that Christian Reconstructionism is one of several varieties of fusionism that have flourished in the orbit of Ron Paul's Libertarian Party. For several decades now, Ron Paul has played to multiple audiences, presenting himself on the main stage as a purist economic libertarian of the Cato Institute variety while also cultivating close links with the paleoconservative alt-right and Christian Reconstructionists in the wings. Ron Paul's connection to Gary North is long-standing. North served as Paul's first staff economist in the mid-1970s and was more recently commissioned to create Ron Paul's home-schooling curriculum, based, in North's words, on the "biblical principle of self-government and personal responsibility."[237] Ron Paul was just as warmly disposed toward Howard Phillips and frequently keynoted Constitution Party gatherings, while Christian Reconstructionists were among Ron and Rand Paul's most devoted constituencies.[238] The porousness of the boundaries between Christian Reconstructionism and the ostensibly secular circles of Ron and Rand Paul goes some way toward explaining why Tea Party Republicans who presented as radical economic libertarians in the electoral process ended up pursuing an unrelenting assault on birth control once in office. Purist economic libertarians might have been just as intransigent on the issue of the debt ceiling, but only theocratic libertarians would be prepared to sacrifice the creditworthiness of the U.S. dollar to abolish the sin of abortion. Theirs was a millenarian long game, which Democrats and mainstream Republicans mistook for a bluff.

With its position at the margins of the new religious right of the 1970s, Christian Reconstruction has long maintained an idiosyncratic attachment to the nativist and segregationist politics of the old Protestant right.[239] The repression of this past was one of the founding acts of the new religious right. Catholics who held conservative positions on the family and the role of women were more likely than not to skew progressive on the question of migration and civil rights. The postwar evangelical movement had distinguished itself from its fundamentalist brethren by embracing the civil rights movement and the moderate Republicanism of Eisenhower. Die-hard fundamentalists, by contrast, had taken active part in the "massive resistance" campaign against the *Brown v. Board of Education* decision to end segregation in public schools and preached that racial integration was against God's will well into the 1960s.[240] More than its oft-cited (but dubious) quietism, it was this exceptionalism on the question of race that prevented any broader alliance with other religious conservatives and any durable relationship between Protestant fundamentalists and the mainstream Republican Party. When Catholics and evangelicals joined forces with the fundamentalist Jerry Falwell in the late 1970s, it was on condition that he disavow his segregationist past.[241] This act of treason earned him the enduring contempt of old-time fundamentalists such as Bob Jones Jr. and Carl McIntire, who in turn faded into insignificance.[242]

The Christian right of the 1980s fought hard to forget the historical alliance between fundamentalists and white supremacists, even while its churches and congregations remained overwhelmingly white. In the 1990s, denialism was replaced by active remembering and remorse, as Ralph Reed's Christian Coalition made real overtures toward historically Black conservative churches.[243] Christian Reconstructionism remained immune to these pressures, however, and indeed moved even further to the right during the 1990s when its leading theologian, Rushdoony—along with his disciple Howard Phillips—forged closer institutional and theological ties with the neo-Confederate and nativist movements. For a long time, this ensured that the Constitution Party was relegated beyond the pale of mainstream right-wing politics. But as the nativist movement acquired momentum in the early twenty-first century and as more and more Republicans lent their voices to the campaign against birthright citizenship, the GOP itself moved closer to the Constitution Party—until, with the rise of the Tea Party and its success in the midterm elections of 2010, the religious and nativist far right began to overwhelm the party's mainstream.

At its founding in 1992, these issues were not at the forefront of the U.S. Taxpayers Party's agenda. This period saw a phenomenal upsurge in attacks on abortion clinics as the most radical member of the religious right refused the consensus politics of the Christian Coalition and turned instead to civil disobedience and terrorism.[244] By all accounts, the U.S. Taxpayers Party was one of the prime catalysts behind the resurgent patriot militia movement of the 1990s, which in its early years was overwhelmingly focused on the moral and fiscal impositions of the federal government (in the guise of legal abortion and taxes) and the right to defend oneself against them. Early associates of the party included the militant pro-life activists Randall Terry, founder of Operation Rescue, and Matthew Trewhella, founder of Missionaries for the Preborn, who pushed tactics of civil disobedience, clinic obstruction, and personal harassment as far as they could go without falling afoul of the law while also nurturing many of the militants who would go on to commit arson or murder.[245] The Christian Reconstructionist Gary North was an important source of inspiration for this activism: North had edited a collection on the theology of Christian resistance in the early 1980s, and this book had served as an instruction manual for the whole gamut of patriot militias.[246] Indeed, at least one scholar of the American far right has suggested that Christian Reconstruction was the real nerve center of militia activity during this period.[247]

By the late 1990s, however, the Constitution Party was casting its net wider to reach out to anti-immigrant nativists and neo-Confederate defenders of a white southern culture.[248] A sign of this shift, the lineup of speakers at the U.S. Taxpayers Convention of 1996 included Larry Pratt, an anti-abortion activist who was also the founder of English First, a nativist anti-immigrant group, and the executive director of Gun Owners of America.[249] The change of tone was also reflected in the party's executive circles. Between 1996 and 1999, the position of party chairman was held by William K. Shearer, a former member of David Duke's Populist Party and cofounder of the American Independent Party, which in 1968 had nominated the segregationist George Wallace as its first presidential candidate.[250]

The Constitution Party's lurch to the white supremacist right was confirmed with the election of George W. Bush, a president whose foreign interventionism and color-blind conservatism made him almost as intolerable as a Democrat. The nativist far right was outraged when Bush supported amnesty for undocumented migrants and appointed Black American moderates or neoconservatives such as Colin Powell and Condoleezza Rice to key defense positions. The Constitution Party's presidential candidate for 2004 was Michael Peroutka, who was both an uncompromising opponent of abortion and a member of the neo-Confederate League of the South, a group that celebrated the pre–Civil War South and the strategy of secession.[251]

This did not come entirely out of the blue. Christian Reconstructionism has a much longer intellectual connection with the neo-Confederate movement than is often recognized. Indeed, as early as the 1960s, Rushdoony's work helped to revive the idea that the Civil War was less a struggle over slavery than a battle between a white Christian South and a heretical North.[252] It was only in the late 1990s, however, that Christian Reconstructionism as a movement made common cause with the neo-Confederate right. Shortly after the League of the South was founded in 1994, Rushdoony's journal the *Chalcedon Report* published a symposium of responses to the Civil War that included both for and against positions on the neo-Confederate cause. Five years later, the *Chalcedon Report* was only publishing papers in support of neo-Confederacy, while the League of the South was itself adopting a much more explicit Christian Reconstructionist reading of the Civil War.[253] The Christian and neo-Confederate far right had merged into one, and this synthesis was reflected in the Constitution Party's choice of candidates.

When Barack Obama was elected the first Black president of the United States in 2008, he became a lightning rod for nativist and neo-Confederate anxieties about the boundaries of citizenship. As Fox News anchors and conservative radio hosts obsessed over the question of whether Obama qualified for birthright citizenship, the natalism of the Christian far right entered into a new and sometimes fractious alliance with the nativism of the white supremacist far right. The so-called birther movement collapsed the disparate nightmares of the far right and projected them onto the figure of Obama, a man who was himself a fusion of terrifying opposites: the son of a single white mother and a Black father, not quite African American but politically identified with the African American community, Black but well educated and "articulate" (in the memorable words of Joe Biden), American-born but raised in the Muslim-majority country of Indonesia, a Black man who was also a feminist and supporter of women's reproductive choice.[254] Faced with these contradictions, the birther movement gave voice to the pervasive suspicion that Obama was not in fact a real American. This suspicion fueled an insatiable litigiousness over the question of Obama's birthright.

Howard Phillips's Constitution Party was ground zero for the birther movement. Jerome Corsi, a close associate of Phillips's and at one point a candidate for party leadership, was the chief purveyor of the theory that Obama was not born on American soil at all and was therefore not eligible for American citizenship, a theory that failed to die even when Obama released his long-form birth certificate.[255] Corsi's bestselling investigation into the details of Obama's birth unfolded a spectacular kaleidoscope of fears. In addressing the question of *ius soli*, Corsi referred to Obama as our "undocumented worker" in the White House and evoked in passing what he saw as the related issue of "anchor babies," the children that noncitizen women allegedly give birth to on American soil so as to secure the right to citizenship.[256] He went on to draw a distinction between "natural born" citizens under the terms of the original Constitution and the birthright citizens recognized after the Civil War with the passage of the Fourteenth Amendment—only the former, he argued, have the constitutional right to serve as presidents, an argument that stealthily undermines the full citizenship rights of African Americans and dog whistles to the constitutional revisionism of the far right.[257] These and similar suspicions about a Black man's "natural" right to citizenship were pervasive in the wider Tea Party movement.

Interestingly, however, the embrace of nativism on the part of Christian Reconstructionists has not lessened their commitment to the universalist pronatalism that was so formative of the alliance between Catholics and born-again Christians in the 1970s. Thus, in the midst of an argument seeking to prove the illegitimacy of a Black president's birthright, Jerome Corsi turned abruptly to the issue of the rights of the unborn. Obama, he charged, "chooses conveniently to ignore the great harm done to African American communities" by abortion. "The staggering number of African American abortions since *Roe v. Wade* in 1973 would suggest the 'abortion on demand insistence of the political left is permitting genocide to be waged against blacks in America.'"[258]

Christian Reconstructionists, in fact, have been some of the most prolific and influential traffickers in the idea that Planned Parenthood is an agent of genocide against Black Americans. Their convictions have only become louder in recent years, at the very moment they have turned sharply toward white supremacism.[259] This has served to create a very real schism within the wider far right. For while the nonreligious wing of the nativist far right subscribes to classic eugenic ideas about the need for targeted population control, the conservative Christians associated with the Tea Party are much more selective in their distribution of nativist and natalist sympathies. Their nationalism, in other words, attributes unconditional citizenship to the unborn, but immediately qualifies this at the moment of birth, when the child all of a sudden acquires a whole host of particular qualities that bar him or her from full citizenship.

As a fetus, Obama would surely have merited their ostentatious love; once born, he is an anchor baby sucking the welfare state dry; as a man, he becomes a superpredator and a terrorist. This confusion of nativist and natalist arguments explains why Tea Party activists could obsess over Obama's birthright (accusing him of being Muslim, socialist, a Black nationalist, a chimp) and simultaneously argue that the Affordable Care Act, through its eugenic funding of family planning, had to be opposed because it served the racist goal of aborting Black children. As a singular example of the generic unborn, the Black fetus serves as an object of universal love and a convenient token of color-blind nationalism. The postnatal Obama, by contrast, represents all that is most feared by the Tea Party right: an "Indonesian Muslim turned welfare thug and a racist in chief," in the words of one Tea Party activist.[260] As perfect a disavowal as one could find, the charge of eugenic "totalitarianism" brandished against Obama allowed Tea Party militants to whitewash their own history while presenting a Black president as both a singular threat to the minority fetus and a general threat to the American nation.

"THE LONG NEW RIGHT": FROM THE TEA PARTY TO TRUMP

By the conventional standards of electoral politics, Howard Phillips's Constitution Party was a crushing failure. The party never polled more than 0.2 percent of the vote and saw no candidates elected to the House of Representatives or the Senate, though a few members have held public office at the state level. Every effort to recruit a powerful front-runner candidate—most notably Pat Buchanan, who in 1996 threatened to defect to the U.S. Taxpayers Party if the Republicans nominated a pro-choice vice president—came to nothing. For most of its existence, the mainstream news media treated the Constitution Party as a comic sideshow of John Bircher diehards and martyrs to the unborn.[261] With a few notable exceptions, academic historiography has not looked kindly on Howard Phillips either, by and large dismissing him as the lost son of the New Right.[262] With the rise of the Tea Party, however, Phillips seemed to be everywhere. Representatives who had been active in state chapters of the Constitution Party or its affiliates were now running as Tea Party candidates on Republican tickets. Tea Party activists were being schooled in the Constitution by Phillips's associates. The Tea Party as a whole seemed to be speaking the language of Christian law espoused by Phillips and his "wise counselor," Rushdoony. Howard Phillips's sudden ubiquity seemed to suggest that existing histories of American politics had missed some important channel of communication between the Republican Party, economic libertarianism, and the religious far right.

The missing link was the New Right's Council for National Policy, or CNP, and its ever-tighter funding links with the libertarian Koch brothers. In the lead-up to the 2010 midterm elections, the Tea Party and its various groups were receiving a "merry-go-round" of funding from the Koch brothers and the CNP.[263] This was less a case of rivalry than symbiosis. Despite their indifference to the "social" issues of abortion and religious freedom, the Koch brothers have never been able to connect with a popular base and so have become ever more dependent on CNP connections to animate the libertarian cause. The CNP, in turn, has always lacked the formidable financial means of the Koch brothers.[264] Alone, the Koch brothers and the CNP could only get so far. Together, they had organizational prowess, money to burn, and a seemingly inexhaustible fount of anger.

But the role of the religious far right within the Tea Party was truly solidified when the CNP decided to follow the Koch brothers in backing it. Howard Phillips rode both of these funding streams. Many of the political figures who became active as Tea Party agitators or congressional candidates were longstanding members of the CNP. Others had connections with both the CNP and the Constitution Party: apart from Howard Phillips himself, this was the case for birther in chief, Jerome Corsi, and the League of the South's Michael Peroutka.[265] As one of the most significant figures on the religious far right and a founding member of the CNP, it would have been surprising had Howard Phillips not been right in the thick of things.

In January 2010, Richard Viguerie, now an elder statesman of the CNP, addressed a meeting of more than one hundred Tea Party leaders with the words: "Hi. Where have you been? [pause] I've been waiting for you. [pause] I've been waiting for fifty years for you people."[266] With its fusion of economic libertarianism, racial backlash, and religious fanaticism, the Tea Party ticked every New Right box and seemed to possess the same boisterous momentum as the religious right of the 1970s. The movement did not yet have a presidential candidate of the caliber of Reagan, but it had a much tighter grip on the electoral process than the earlier religious right and enjoyed incomparable media resonance.[267]

The midterm elections of November 2010 "turned out to be almost everything [Viguerie] had hoped," securing the Republicans more seats in the House than in any other midterm since the 1930s.[268] Viguerie, who had once complained that Reagan was thwarted by his lack of congressional enablers, could now rest assured that any future president elected under the auspices of the CNP would be able to truly govern as a conservative, surrounded as he would be by hard-right yes-men. That these were no ordinary Republicans was made clear within the first few months of 2011, when newly elected Tea Party representatives brought the government to the brink of shutdown over the approval of Title X funds. With numbers on their side, religious conservatives were now in a position to refuse the subordinate posture imposed on them since the time of Reagan. No longer would they let themselves be sidelined by the Republicans' economic agenda. Instead, they would seize upon the budget process itself—appropriation bills and annual debt ceiling approvals—as a means of forcing through their moral commandments. As subsequent showdowns would soon make clear, Tea Party Republicans were prepared to jeopardize the creditworthiness of the U.S. dollar to achieve their long-standing dream of defunding Planned Parenthood. The new-look Republican Party was acting as if possessed by the debt millenarianism of a Gary North or a Howard Phillips.

In retrospect, it is becoming clear just how cataclysmic the midterm elections of 2010 really were. Political scientists Bryan Gervais and Irwin Morris convincingly argue that conventional wisdom has underestimated both the scale and durability of the hard-right takeover of the IIIth Congress.[269] Most analyses take formal affiliation with the short-lived House Tea Party Caucus as a proxy for membership of the faction, but this would exclude many of the most prominent Tea Party representatives. If we appreciate that there was more than one mode of affiliation to the Tea Party faction (financial, personal, and ideological) and that the faction's influence extended well beyond the brief lifetime of the Tea Party Caucus, then we get a very different perspective on the recent history of the GOP. Republican congressmen who were not affiliated with the Tea Party after 2010 were an embattled minority. It was not Trump who demolished the Republican mainstream, then. It was the Tea Party—or, if we adopt the cross-generational perspective of Daniel Schlozman and Sam Rosenfeld, the "long New Right."[270]

With his bad press among evangelicals, Trump was not the CNP's first choice. This was Ted Cruz, a disciple of Christian dominionism—a form of postmillennial evangelicalism with close ties to Christian Reconstructionism.[271] But when it became clear that Trump was soaring above his rivals in the primaries, the then president of the CNP, Tony Perkins, proposed a deal. The CNP could offer Trump the decisive edge on other candidates by gifting him both their evangelical voter bloc and their incomparable hold over regional media and politics. Invited to make his case before an audience of a thousand or so evangelical and CNP leaders at the Times Square Marriott in June 2016, Trump emerged with their full blessing. In return, Trump nominated the "evangelical" Catholic Michael Pence (Paul Weyrich's favorite) as his running mate and set up an evangelical advisory board consisting of Tea Party agitators and CNP members to help rewrite the Republican platform.[272] Crucially, he promised to consult them before making any federal judicial nominations, a promise he more than kept with his legacy of three Supreme Court justices.[273]

In power, Trump surrounded himself with CNP members. His former chief strategist, Stephen K. Bannon, was a member; his campaign manager, Kellyanne Conway, once served on the CNP's executive committee; Jay Sekulow, the lead attorney on Trump's personal legal team, was on the board of governors; Richard DeVos Sr., the father-in-law of Education Secretary Betsy DeVos, twice served as president and is one of the organization's major donors; Betsy DeVos's mother, Elsa Prince Broekhuizen, was also among its executive members and donor circle; Trump's vice president, Mike Pence, was trained by the Leadership Institute, run by CNP founding member Morton Blackwell; Pence was also a regular guest at the weekly strategy lunch organized by CNP veteran Paul Weyrich.[274]

Although Trump's personal politics appears to lie closer to the nativist and neo-Confederate wing of libertarianism, if indeed he is libertarian at all, his biggest political debt is owed to the Christian right via his connection to the CNP. Trump may never have been the perfect vessel, but his "deep state" was Christian fundamentalist and just as hostile to business as usual as he was. Trump proved his willingness to appease them when in 2019 he introduced a gag rule that forced Planned Parenthood to abandon the entirety of its Title X funding.[275] A victory that the religious right had been pursuing for many years, the decision was bound to hurt the low-income, underaged, and minority women who had always benefited most from Title X services. And so a president who was only casually pro-life went further than any other in fulfilling the religious right's dream of defunding Planned Parenthood.

DOBBS, ANTI-EUGENICS, AND THE RETURN OF FETAL PERSONHOOD

There can be no question, however, that Trump's most important gift to the religious right was his appointment of three conservative Supreme Court justices. Trump had promised to stack the court with pro-life justices in his June 2016 meeting with evangelicals and CNP members.[276] Once in office, he followed through on this pledge with uncharacteristic discipline. In the space of one presidential term, he appointed Justices Neil Gorsuch, Brett Kavanaugh, and—at the eleventh hour, days before he lost the presidency—Amy Coney Barrett, thus handing conservatives a 6–3 supermajority. The new Supreme Court did not disappoint. Within its first term it gave religious conservatives the victory they had been awaiting for decades. In a 6–3 decision, the *Dobbs v. Jackson Women's Health Organization* of 2022 overturned *Roe v. Wade* and ended five decades of constitutional protections for the right to abortion.[277]

Soberingly, the decision is unlikely to be the Supreme Court's last word on the matter. For decades, religious conservatives have wanted to overturn *Roe v. Wade* and return abortion laws to state legislatures. But they have never seen this as the be-all and end-all of their struggle. For the right-to-life movement that emerged in the 1970s, the reversion of authority to states was only a stepping stone on the road to a higher goal: a federal prohibition on abortion that would overrule the ability of *any* state to authorize the practice.[278] The recognition of fetal personhood was a key plank in this agenda.

Because of the long-standing Catholic topos of abortion as eugenics, some of the earliest legal challenges to state abortion rights were framed in terms of racial justice. In the years leading up to the 1973 *Roe v. Wade* decision, anti-abortion activists called on state and federal courts to recognize the civil rights of the unborn.[279] They appealed to the Declaration of Independence, with its affirmation of an unalienable right to life, and to the Fourteenth Amendment to argue that the unborn deserved equal protection and due process like any other racial minority. In several instances, they cited as precedent the 1954 *Brown v. Board of Education* decision outlawing segregation, hoping to convince the courts that fetuses, like African Americans under Jim Crow, were natural persons unjustly deprived of their full rights to life.

Their efforts were unceremoniously rebuffed by Justice Harry A. Blackmun, author of the majority opinion in *Roe v. Wade*, who argued that fetal personhood was nowhere to be found in the text of the Constitution, and that in any case the court had no authority to rule on a matter that was unresolved among religious scholars and biologists.[280] Crucially, however, Blackmun acknowledged that if the concept of "person" could somehow be construed to apply to the unborn, then no one could legitimately deny due process and equal protection rights to fetuses—and the case for abortion rights would "collapse."[281]

In the wake of *Roe*, religious conservatives remained hopeful they could work through Congress and the states to secure a constitutional amendment that would establish the personhood of the fetus once and for all.[282] Their hopes faded in 1983, when the most promising of several such proposals died on the floor of Congress.

At this point, they resorted to less direct ways of inserting the concept of fetal personhood into law. Beginning in the mid-1980s and accelerating after the *Planned Parenthood v. Casey* decision of 1992, anti-abortion activists fought for fetal homicide laws, late-term abortion bans, fetal pain legislation, and state edicts compelling women to view ultrasound images of fetuses before abortion.[283] In adopting these more incremental measures, religious conservatives were conceding tactical defeat. Yet they never lost sight of the strategic endgame. The legal changes they fought for were designed to turn the idea of fetal personhood into common sense, such that an accumulation of minor laws could be invoked as precedent when the time was right. With a 6–3 conservative supermajority and a Republican Party that has moved far to the right, that time has clearly arrived. Anti-abortion activists are now returning to their original goal—"the recognition of fetal personhood and the criminalization of abortion" in all states.[284]

In preparing the ground for this challenge, anti-abortion activists have revived the race-based arguments that they first tried out in the 1970s. Feminist legal scholars Melissa Murray and Jeannie Suk Gersen have pointed to a recent spate of "anti-eugenic" state laws as a likely prompt to future Supreme Court assaults on abortion and a springboard for the recognition of fetal personhood.[285] In recent years, a number of states have passed laws banning abortions that are motivated by a presumed intent to discriminate against the fetus on the grounds of race, sex, or disability.[286] In 2016, the Indiana state legislature passed a particularly draconian version of these "trait selection anti-discrimination laws." HEA 1337 was framed as a belated response to Indiana's early twentieth-century history of state-enforced eugenics. Just ten years previously, the same state legislature had issued an official apology for its "role in the eugenics movement in this country and the injustices done under eugenic laws." Recognizing that the state's eugenic laws had "targeted the most vulnerable among us, including the poor and racial minorities . . . for the claimed purpose of public health and the good of the people," the General Assembly "urge[d] the citizens of Indiana to become familiar with the history of the eugenics movement" and "repudiate the many laws passed in the name of eugenics and reject any such laws in the future."[287] In signing bill HEA 1337 into law, Pence self-consciously reprised this language, affirming that "a society can be judged by how it deals with its most vulnerable—the aged, the infirm, the disabled and the unborn."[288]

The law was subsequently invalidated as unconstitutional by the Federal Appeals Court, on the grounds that it imposed an "undue burden" on a woman's right to abortion. The Supreme Court declined to take up the case, with the *Box v. Planned Parenthood* decision in 2019 postponing any further consideration of the issue until other courts of appeals had weighed in on similar laws from other states. Significantly, however, Supreme Court justice Clarence Thomas took this occasion to pen a lengthy reflection on the subject of abortion, race, and eugenics. While agreeing with the court that the case law was not yet ready for review, Thomas thought the issue significant enough to warrant a detailed solo opinion, in which he laid out the reasons why he thought such laws should ultimately be legitimated.

At stake in "this law and other laws," he wrote, is nothing less than a "State's compelling interest in preventing abortion from becoming a tool of modern-day eugenics."[289] In what follows, Thomas rehearsed a refrain that has been perfected by the right-to-life movement since the 1970s. Making indiscriminate use of the historical scholarship, he drew a logical chain of equivalence from Margaret Sanger's eugenicist arguments in favor of voluntary birth control to early twentieth-century state sterilization laws, and from there to *Roe v. Wade*, without once acknowledging the existence of feminist (much less Black feminist) defenses of abortion as a right to bodily autonomy.[290] Thomas closed his opinion by endorsing the views of 1960s Black nationalists who saw "'family planning' as a euphemism for race genocide."[291]

Thomas's position was anticipated by future Supreme Court justice Amy Coney Barrett, who in her then capacity as judge of the U.S. Federal Court of Appeals for the Seventh Circuit contested the court's refusal to consider the "validity of an anti-eugenics law."[292] The idea that abortion constitutes a form of eugenics has since been reaffirmed by Mike Pence. In a speech before the 2022 National Pro-Life Summit, the former vice president proclaimed that abortion today "is being used as a tool of eugenics for the elimination of children of the wrong sex or race or those suffering with disability." He continued with the now requisite reference to "Margaret Sanger, the founder of Planned Parenthood," who "once wrote that eugenics, in her words, was, quote 'the most adequate and thorough avenue in the solution of racial, political and social problems.'" Today, Pence concluded, "Planned Parenthood shamelessly builds on Margaret Sanger's legacy."[293]

The consensus between Justice Clarence Thomas (a former Black nationalist and errant Catholic) on the one hand, and Mike Pence (a self-described evangelical Catholic) and Amy Coney Barrett (a Catholic charismatic) on the other makes perfect sense when we reflect back on the early alliance making between these communities in the 1970s. Never before, however, have exponents of this view been so well represented in the Supreme Court, and never before has the Supreme Court been so closely aligned with the ultraconservative religious faction of the Republican right.

In recent public lectures, Thomas has invoked his personal trajectory as a former student radical and lapsed Catholic to make a biographical case for the alliance between Catholic conservatism and Black nationalism. Raised out of maternal poverty by a Catholic grandfather and placed in a local Catholic school, a young Thomas embraced the teachings of the church as a theological answer to the oppression of Blacks in the Jim Crow South. Thomas credits the nuns at school for teaching him that as a "child of God there [was] no force on this earth that [could] make [him] any less than a man of equal dignity and equal worth." This truth was "repeatedly restated and echoed throughout the segregated world of our youth," Thomas recalls, and "reinforced our proper roles as equal citizens, not the perversely distorted and reduced role offered us by Jim Crow."[294]

It was the conviction that God "transcends all law"—including the white supremacist laws of the U.S. government—that led Thomas to choose the priesthood as his original vocation.[295] His brief stint as the only Black student in a southern seminary was cut short, however, when he was forced to reckon with the assassination of Martin Luther King Jr. in 1968 and the contemptuous attitudes he encountered among his fellow students.

At this point, Thomas moved north to enroll in the College of the Holy Cross, an integrating liberal arts institution in Massachusetts. Throwing himself into the student Black Power movement, Thomas became a voracious reader of Malcolm X and stood out even among other Black radicals for his uncompromising views on racial separatism and the immorality of interracial relationships.[296] In retrospect, he recalls his younger self as clear-sighted in his assessment of American racism but hopelessly destructive in the solutions he found.[297]

Over the next decade, Thomas experienced a series of abrupt political and personal epiphanies. By 1980, he had ceased to be a Democrat and was openly supportive of Ronald Reagan, who appointed him chair of the Equal Employment Opportunity Commission. In 1991, he was nominated to the Supreme Court by President George H. W. Bush, a position he took up after the sexual harassment charges laid against him by former employee Anita Hill were dismissed. At some point in the 1990s, Thomas returned to Catholicism, after "twenty-five years in the wilderness away from the Church."[298]

None of this involved a simple break with the Black nationalism of his student years, however. The political theorist Corey Robin convincingly argues that Thomas remains a Black nationalist to this day, even as he has moved from the radical left to the radical right.[299] As a Republican, Thomas has clung to the most conservative elements of the Black Power movement—its fealty to racial purity and male domination—while gradually replacing the revolutionary left principles of economic self-determination and mutual aid (variously espoused by Malcolm X and the Black Panthers) with the neoliberal ones of personal, familial, and communal responsibility (associated most notably with Louis Farrakhan).[300]

In the process, I would suggest, Thomas also found a new way of reconciling the warring parties in his personal philosophy—Catholicism and Black nationalism. With his return to the Catholic faith, Thomas retrieved his early intuition that racial equality was ordained by Catholic natural law. Instead of elevating God's law above human law, however, he now believed that natural law was compatible with, and indeed mandated by, the founding texts of the American Constitution. This reconciliation, as we have seen, had already been attempted by Catholic legal scholars in the 1970s, who sought to gain recognition of fetal personhood by appealing to a constitutional "right to life" embedded in the Declaration of Independence and the Fourteenth Amendment. Thomas, however, claims to have received the same revealed wisdom on the basis of his personal journey back to the church. Studying the Declaration of Independence in the mid-1980s, he recalls, felt "like a return to familiar ground.... The Declaration captured what I had been taught to venerate as a child but had cynically rejected as a young man. All men are created equal, endowed by their creator with certain unalienable rights."[301] As "I rediscovered the God-given principles of the declaration and our founding," he continues, "I eventually returned to the Church, which had been teaching the same truths for millennia."[302]

Thomas's concurring opinion in *Box v. Planned Parenthood* simply extended this Catholic reading of the rights of man from the Declaration of Independence to the Fourteenth Amendment and from the Black man raised in the Jim Crow South to the fetus. The progression is compelling—even unavoidable—

for someone who has accepted the Catholic teaching that universal person-hood is located in the figure of the unborn child. If the American Constitution is to fulfill its promise of "equal protection" for all life, stripped of racial predicates, the ultimate test of this promise must lie in its willingness to protect Black life from the moment of conception.

The whole point of recent trait-selection anti-abortion laws is to put the Supreme Court to the test on this issue. In passing these laws, state legislators such as Pence are asking a leading question, fully expecting it to be tested in the courts, and no doubt hoping that the matter will make it all the way to an ultraconservative Supreme Court. In providing state legislators with the answer they want—that prenatal genetic testing does indeed have eugenic potential—Thomas is not only impugning this specific practice but also making a much more momentous argument about the legal rights of the unborn. Thomas's whole framing of the question in terms of equal protection assumes that the status of the fetus has already been resolved and is beyond debate. "What is really at stake" here, writes legal scholar Jeannie Suk Gersen, "is an idea of fetal person-hood." In effect, "if the right to be free of discrimination on the basis of race, sex, or disability can be made relevant to a fetus, then fetuses are figured as entities with anti-discrimination rights—like people. This move imbues the fetus with rights that the pregnant person—and, by extension, the abortion provider—might violate."[303] While claiming to weigh in on the discrete practice of genetic diagnosis, Thomas is laying the groundwork for the federal prohibition of abortion and the criminalization of aborting women as murderers.

It is not hard to find evidence for that ambition in the *Dobbs* decision. Written by Justice Samuel Alito, the text of the decision brims with comparisons between *Roe v. Wade*, fetal nonpersonhood, and the status of African Americans under slavery or segregation. Throughout the opinion, Alito goes out of his way to represent the fetus as a natural person who has been subject to a long and egregious history of persecution comparable to that of African Americans. At stake here is an interpretation of the Fourteenth Amendment that contests its use to defend the liberty (and sexual privacy) of women in *Roe v. Wade* while endorsing its redeployment as grounds to protect the right to life of the fetus. At several points, Alito compares the "misuse" of the Fourteenth Amendment's substantive due process clause in *Roe* to the "disastrous" use of the same clause in *Dred Scott*—the infamous 1857 decision to exclude African Americans from citizenship on federal territories.[304] Elsewhere he counters the argument that *Roe v. Wade* should be left in place on the basis of stare decisis, the doctrine that advises judges to err on the side of precedent when urged to reconsider established law. Here he invokes *Plessy v. Ferguson*—the decision that justified segregation on the principle that African Americans were "separate but equal"—to argue that at key moments in its history the Supreme Court has had no other ethical option but to depart from precedent. *Roe v. Wade* was "egregiously wrong and on a collision course with the Constitution from the day it was decided," he writes, just like the "infamous decision in *Plessy v. Ferguson*."[305] The court was justified in overturning *Roe v. Wade* for the same reason it was right to overrule segregation in the 1954 *Brown v. Board of Education* ruling.[306] By implication, Alito is suggesting that anyone who recognizes the civil rights of African Americans should be prepared to extend those rights to fetuses too.

The equation is spelled out explicitly in a footnote, in which Alito directly considers Clarence Thomas's concurrent opinion on anti-Black eugenics in *Box v. Planned Parenthood*. While claiming, disingenuously, to have no interest in questioning the "motives of those who have . . . opposed laws restricting abortion," Alito nevertheless declares it "beyond dispute that *Roe* has had [the] demographic effect" of suppressing the size of the African American population.[307] In another passage, he outlines the legitimate grounds on which a state might restrict abortion and refers to both the protection of "life at all stages of development" and the "prevention of discrimination on the basis of race, sex or disability."[308] Clearly, Alito is laying the foundations for a case in which the validation of state "anti-eugenic" laws is taken to its logical conclusion—as a pretext for recognizing full fetal personhood.

The different treatment that Alito reserves for sexual and racial oppression is instructive here. At the same time that he proposes *race* discrimination as a reason for banning abortion, Alito dismisses out of hand any suggestion that banning abortion might constitute a form of *sex* discrimination. In response to long-standing feminist arguments that the right to abortion might be grounded in the Fourteenth Amendment's Equal Protection Clause as it relates to women, he bluntly retorts that the "State's regulation of abortion is not a sex-based classification and is thus not subject to the heightened scrutiny that applies to such classifications."[309]

In his defense, he cites the 1974 *Geduldig v. Aiello* case, infamous in the feminist legal scholarship for deploying a concept of abstract (sex-neutral) personhood as a reason to deny the charge of sex discrimination against women.[310] In this case, the Supreme Court ruled that pregnant women were not owed coverage under the state of California's disability insurance program because pregnancy was not an experience particular to women: the relevant distinction, the court argued, was not between women and men but between "pregnant women and non-pregnant persons."[311] In other words, while the raced (or sexed or ability-based) particularity of the fetus is sufficient to render it vulnerable to discrimination and hence worthy of equal protection, the sexed specificity of the female body during pregnancy does not distinguish it from the abstract, universal (presumptively male) person, thereby invalidating any claim to equal protection on the grounds of sexed embodiment. (However well intentioned, the widespread adoption of the movement term "pregnant person" by feminist legal scholars risks obscuring and thereby repeating this sleight of hand.[312] Despite the claims of legal conservatives, anti-abortion laws do not target the abstract person or universal subject of rights; they marshal sexed bodies into the unfree labor of reproduction and therefore actively assign femaleness, independently of and sometimes in spite of gender identification. The work of patriarchy is to render bodily specificities deterministic and inescapable such that the ability to bear a child becomes the imperative to do so. In this instance at least, trans men and nonbinary people fall under the hammer of laws designed to discipline and define women.)

Alito's message could not be clearer. When rights come into conflict, the personhood of the fetus must take precedence over that of women. The modern religious right's obsession with abortion reflects the enduring assumption that female bodies are duty bound to bear the father's name and biological essence across generations. For those committed to the defense of lineage, the sexual freedom of women will always be problematic since it endows them with the unique ability to undermine the proper ends of reproduction—or to refuse it altogether.[313] Within the imaginary of the modern religious right, the unborn child is valued as a promissory note for the future of the race—where race is posited in its most indeterminate, not yet specified form; as life itself. This future can only be perfectly secured if women's bodies are conscripted into the labor of reproduction, their legal personhood made subservient to the interests of the unborn child.

The patriarchal logic of racial reproduction is clear enough when it comes to hegemonic formations of race such as white nationalism. But leftists often shy away from the fact that the subordination of women is intrinsic to the project of racial reproduction, hegemonic or not. Any politics that sets out to defend the integrity of the race—conceived of as an order of reproduction or genealogical lineage—will inevitably regard women with suspicion, since any freedom they have to withdraw their reproductive labor places the future of the race in their hands. Antiracism need not take this reproductivist form, but when it does it is just as implacable in its enforcement of patriarchal imperatives as majoritarian nationalism.

As noted by Corey Robin, Thomas's nationalism was always biological rather than territorial.[314] In his travels from the radical left to radical right, Thomas has never stopped seeing the reproduction of (the Black) race as the horizon and endgame of his politics. As secretary of the Black Students Union at the College of the Holy Cross, he subscribed to the manifesto that "the Black Man wants...the right to perpetuate his race."[315] For all his political conversions, he never abandoned the belief that "the salvation of our race" depends upon "the strength and the will of black men."[316]

This enduring commitment to the ends of racial reproduction explains why Thomas was vehemently opposed to interracial marriage well into the 1980s (before he met his second wife, Virginia Lamp Thomas, in 1986) and why he has always advocated for the merits of institutional segregation.[317] Notwithstanding the charge that he has abandoned community in favor of individualism, Thomas has always taken equality to mean an equality of and between (not necessarily within) races. This is a position that can be comfortably accommodated within Catholic universalism.

Catholicism has proven historically useful in bringing together conservatives of different denominational, ethnic, and racial provenance because it offers a universalist philosophy of life, under which singular claims to reproductive lineage can be housed and momentarily reconciled.[318] With its elevation of *life as such* over particular forms of life, Catholicism distills the abstract kernel of genealogical law common to all nationalisms—territorial, racial, or cultural—and proclaims their equality in the eyes of God. But for the same reason it recognizes the equality of all forms of reproductive life, Catholicism must deny equal personhood to women. As bodily instrument of reproduction, after all, a woman's right to life must always be conditional upon her willingness to obey this higher imperative. The figure of the unborn child is that imperative in iconic form.

While this iconography was once unique to Catholics, it has now become the lingua franca of the religious right. Catholic natural law is inclusive and abstract enough that it can unite sworn enemies around a shared defense of the unborn before releasing them back into a postnatal world of implacable racial enmities and enduring Black oppression. In the 1970s, it created an improbable coalition of Catholics and Protestants, modernizing evangelicals and nostalgic fundamentalists, as well as white Christians and Black nationalists. Today, oddly enough, it is a language embraced by an African American Supreme Court justice and fellow travelers of Howard Phillips, who share little else but the compulsion to reproduce their lineage.

On Fiscal and Monetary Revolution

This was always "a counterrevolution without revolution," to paraphrase Bernard Harcourt, a preemptive strike against an incipient social revolution that was not to be.[1] For years, that counteroffensive has undermined the power of unions, eviscerated public services, and reinstated the private family as the welfare provider of last resort while for the most part leaving formal rights intact. In the last decade or so, the counterrevolution has gone into overdrive. Feeding off its own paranoia more than any real threat from the left, it is now seeking to extinguish even the legacy of civil, labor, and sexual rights won in a previous era. The escalation is visible everywhere. We have only to look to the Republican Party and its hijacking by the far-right fringe. The constant congressional obstructionism that seeks to torpedo even the most routine acts of government spending. A Federal Reserve that has done all in its power to sustain the wealth of asset holders while resorting to maximum firepower when faced with the mere whiff of rising wages in the lower echelons of the labor market. A Supreme Court that has eviscerated the major voting rights legislation of the 1960s, curtailed the power of unions, and overturned the constitutional right to abortion.

Talk of revolution appears as untimely as ever, except for the fact that the left is alive in a way it has not been in a very long time. From wildcat teacher strikes in right-to-work states to union breakthroughs at Amazon and Starbucks and a new wave of militancy driven by the university's academic precariat, the labor movement has emerged from its multidecade torpor. The Black liberation movement too has acquired a new momentum, even in the face of far-right backlash. Black Lives Matter has forced the issue of systemic police racism onto the public agenda as never before, and it has done so by making explicit the links between mass incarceration, everyday criminal indebtedness, and local government austerity. The feminist movement was dealt a devastating juridical blow with the *Dobbs* decision of 2022. Yet the decision was met on the ground by a resurgence of mutual aid initiatives not seen since the feminist health movement of the 1970s. While the revival of the left has hardly dented the self-fueled delirium of the far right, we have at least retrieved the sense that things could be otherwise.

This is no small thing. By far the most insidious legacy of the neoliberal counterrevolution was its foreclosure of the political imagination. In the wake of Reagan and Thatcher, more than a few disillusioned leftists embraced the realpolitik of neoliberal compromise. Indeed, "third-way" neoliberals such as the New Democrats in the United States or New Labor in the United Kingdom often ended up implementing austerity measures with more zeal and efficacy than their right-wing counterparts. This was more than simple reformism. By ceding to the triad of central bank independence, balanced budgets, and regressive tax cuts, third-way neoliberals came to believe that Keynesianism itself was utopian. Political ambition, even of the most moderate kind, was sacrificed on the altar of economic realism. The left could fantasize as much as it liked—we simply could not afford social democracy anymore, much less revolutionary change.

Yet this dogma is becoming harder to maintain, if only because neoliberal monetary and fiscal authorities have so blatantly transgressed their own rules of self-restraint during the last decade or so of financial crisis. When the Federal Reserve is prepared to stimulate asset price inflation without apparent technical limit, on what grounds could it oppose the same intervention on behalf of wages or social welfare? When the only limit it is willing to recognize is that of wage inflation—phantasmatic or otherwise—it becomes that much harder to hide the real political stakes. It is not "inflation" as such that is the real bogeyman, but the prospect of wage rises outrunning corporate profits or eroding asset values.

One reason why modern monetary theory (MMT) has become widely legible in recent years is the fact that the Federal Reserve has so perfectly enacted its economic agenda—*in reverse.*[2] A politically simplified translation of leftist post-Keynesian theory, MMT teaches that we can afford anything we have the current labor power to do: in a fiat money regime, the central bank has only to activate its money-printing powers to pay for any spending the Treasury might want to initiate. While this knowledge is no secret to central bankers, neoliberal monetary orthodoxy has shrouded it in mystery—lest it be misused in the service of (social) wage inflation. Yet in the last decade or so, the Federal Reserve has selectively broken its own taboo to implement an upside-down version of MMT, in which the state's powers of fiat money creation are deployed in the almost exclusive service of asset holders. If we have learned anything at all from this experience, it is that pseudoscientific laws of price stability can be transgressed at will, so long as the resulting wealth is redistributed upward. The limits to wealth creation are political, not technical.

But is the left prepared to act on this knowledge? Contemporary Marxist critiques of modern monetary theory—of which there are many—sometimes read as a counsel of despair.[3] When they dismiss the theory as a Keynesian half-measure, they are stating the obvious. There is undeniable value in the quasi-Spinozist claim that fiscal and monetary actions should be judged by their real-world effects, not their distance from transcendent economic laws. But in other respects, MMT remains committed to the Keynesian/Hegelian project of dialectical mediation, with all its built-in buffers—the distinction between productive and unproductive labor, the confinement of social democracy within national borders, and the fear of overexuberant wage growth. Tellingly, both MMT and neoliberal monetary orthodoxy are in agreement that the one "technical" limit to central bank extravagance is excessive wage inflation.

That this is a limited project goes without saying. The whole point of Keynesianism is to moderate the relationship between labor and capital so that central bank money creation and the state's power to tax and spend never tip over into a full-blown socialization of finance. Yet in their zeal to demonstrate the obvious—that technocratic Keynesianism can never eliminate capitalist austerity—Marxist critics sometimes seem to suggest there is no response to austerity at all. At their most despairing, they replace the praxis of social change with the consolations of eschatology. If we just wait long enough, capitalism's long slowdown will release us from capture.

For those who think that Marxism is supposed to be more—not less—ambitious than Keynesianism, this cannot be enough. Given the ever more blatant role of nominally public fiscal and monetary authorities in sustaining the summits of private wealth, it is hard to avoid a confrontation with the politics of money. There can be no truly radical challenge to capitalism today without some larger vision of collectivized money creation and spending. The question of how to organize money creation while releasing it from the constraints of private property is key to a postcapitalist praxis.[4] Without this horizon, anarchist mutual aid becomes a leftist adaptation to austerity and Marxist antireformism an admission of defeat. What then would it take to radicalize the project of socialized finance? If Keynesian monetary theory is hamstrung by its need to mediate between labor and capital, how might we collectivize and redistribute wealth beyond these class limits—as well as beyond the gendered, racial, and national limits within which the welfare state has historically been confined? How would we implement a social wage divested of all the sexual and racial conditionalities of the Fordist family wage? What would monetary and fiscal extravagance look like from the left?

The knowledge that extravagance is technically possible is small consolation, of course, when the chasm between technical possibility and political reality is as vast as ever. While blueprints for a wider distribution of wealth have flourished in the wake of the Global Financial Crisis, we cannot expect progressive reform (much less revolutionary change) to be delivered by technocratic fiat.[5] The emergency response to the coronavirus pandemic was greeted by many on the left as a demonstration project in fiscal and monetary abundance. Yet central banks are now doing all in their power to punish wage earners for this brief moment of transgression, as if terrified by the possibilities it might have unleashed. It must be conceded that the balance of power is considerably less favorable than it was in the early 1970s, when labor unions briefly eroded the profit share of national income and wage-push inflation instilled terror in financial markets. Today, we are faced with profit-push and not wage-push inflation, and financial asset holders have fared remarkably well in the face of interest rate hikes that are crippling the rest of the economy.[6]

Most important perhaps, the evolution of the capitalist state has profoundly altered the terrain on which anticapitalist struggles take place. Keynesianism describes the strategy by which the state transfers a growing share of social risks and responsibilities onto its ledger. Its operating logic is centripetal: it is always seeking to incorporate and neutralize class struggle. As such, the anarcho-communists of the 1970s saw themselves as working "in and against the state" to radicalize the Keynesian project of wealth distribution while eluding absorption within its institutional and normative constraints.[7] The neo-liberal state, by contrast, is animated by the centrifugal spirit of secession: without renouncing any of its punitive powers, it is desperate to disown its his-torically assumed social obligations and actively aids and abets private efforts to elude its sphere of regulatory oversight. How then might we return to the spirit of 1970s anarcho-communism, while acknowledging the very different challenges thrown up by the neoliberal antisocial state? Is anarchism des-tined to play the game of unwitting collaborator when capitalism itself is cast-ing off its former social functions? And is a resurgent socialism always going to be the midwife to Keynesianism, a statist dampener on more revolution-ary desires? (The latter danger has become very real with the rollout of Presi-dent Biden's industrial policy and the possible emergence of a green military Keynesianism.)

In recent times, some of the most helpful reflections on strategy vis-à-vis the neoliberal state have come from the Debt Collective, a group that emerged out of the Occupy Wall Street movement of 2011.[8] Originally conceived as a union of student debtors, the collective and its offshoots have since coordi-nated a series of strategic defaults involving a much broader array of personal debt, with a view to consolidating them into an effective counterforce against the combined powers of private finance and the state. Via its Rolling Jubilee, the collective has purchased portfolios of medical, student, payday, probation, and judgment debt on secondary markets with the express purpose of can-celing the associated liabilities.[9] By the time unpaid debt has been sold on to the secondary market, it has lost much of its market value in the eyes of creditors. The burden on the individual debtor, however, remains as daunt-ing as ever owing to the accumulation of interest rates, penalty fees, and tar-nished credit scores. Thus, while the Debt Collective claims to have annulled an impressive $832 million of personal debts, its interventions are worth far more than this. By rescuing the debtor from the devastating personal ordeal of being hounded by debt collectors for years on end, mass debt cancelation deac-tivates the entire disciplinary mechanism that sustains the economy of private credit. Collectivized debt default, in this instance, plays much the same role as full employment in Michał Kalecki's reflections on Keynesianism: it is one method by which the neoliberal antisocial state can be forced to reckon with its own limits.

The Debt Collective begins from the premise that the sheer ubiquity of unmanageable household indebtedness can be tapped as a source of solidarity and leveraged as a way of releasing people from the experience of individual fault and punishment. The largest financial institutions rely on the size of their liabilities and their interconnectedness to other actors to demand Treasury bailouts and central bank monetary accommodation. How then might consumer and wage-earner debtors consolidate their liabilities such that they too become a systemic risk—hence, too big to fail? While simultaneously agitating for the reform of interest rate regulations and bankruptcy laws, the collective's actions are driven by the more ambitious agenda of socializing finance.[10] If pursued at scale, after all, the effect of collective default is to transfer private and familial debt back onto the state balance sheet, where it assumes the status of a free public service. This is one very direct way of pushing the fiscal levers from below such that government is forced to assume costs it would rather outsource to the household. While rarely articulated as such, this same strategy of collective debt transfer is at stake in any call for free health care, education, or a living wage.

This strategic lens can be usefully extended to labor activism also, which at its most forceful can profoundly shift the tectonic plates of fiscal and monetary distribution. The possibilities are most obvious in the public sector, of course, where every dispute around formal wages has immediate repercussions for state budgets and the social wage. With their visible dependence on government support, public-sector movements have no choice but to confront fiscal and monetary issues that are usually sidelined in the wage-bargaining process: the relationship between labor income, asset prices, and government spending; the distributional stakes of taxation and credit creation; the challenges of administering a public service or managing welfare under conditions of austerity. That such challenges can become sources of strength is demonstrated by recent initiatives to build coalitions between striking public-sector workers and their so-called clients in a united front against permanent austerity. To get a sense of how far-reaching such campaigns can be, the United Teachers Los Angeles (UTLA) has fought to lift the commercial property-tax limit on school funding, to turn school-owned vacant land into affordable housing, and to contain the power of the private equity funds that exploit renters (through their real-estate portfolios) as well as teachers (through state tax policies that privilege capital gains at the expense of funding for schools).[11]

Public-sector unionism is sometimes dismissed as peripheral to the real work of anticapitalist struggle on the anachronistic grounds that the fulcrum of capitalist power relations lies in the profit-making private sector. This assumption misreads the last century of capitalist organization, which saw "private-sector" surplus-value production massively underwritten by the state, whether through direct subventions, tax expenditures, or government contracts, and thereby misses the hidden affinities between public- and private-sector unionism. Today the dividing line between private- and public-sector labor is more tenuous than ever. Private health-care clinics are dependent on government-insured Medicare and Medicaid patients and nominally public universities have transferred a growing share of their costs to students, while corporations rely on a cornucopia of tax expenditures and bailouts to fund their private initiatives.

The interests of private- and public-sector workers are therefore more closely aligned than one might think. Take the General Motors strike of 2019, which saw 48,000 United Auto Workers members walk off the job in protest against stagnant wages and insecure conditions, a decade after the company was bailed out to the tune of $50 billion by the U.S. Treasury and one year after the Trump tax cuts delivered trillions of dollars in stock buybacks to GM shareholders.[12] The action was successful in the short term: striking workers managed to secure wage gains and a guarantee of job security in exchange for the closure of the Lordstown, Baltimore, and Warren transmission plants. But how much more powerful could industrial action be if it intervened at the scene of the crime: that is, if it sought to block the diversion of bailout and tax-cut funds into stock buybacks in the first place? Today there can be little doubt that the union movement's embrace of pension-fund capitalism was a fatal error: by trading rising share prices for rising wages, union pension funds helped inflate the wealth of the largest individual portfolio owners while delivering very little to wage earners, with their very small stock holdings and ever more precarious work trajectories.[13] At GM as in so many other nominally private sectors of the economy, what we have seen in recent decades is a direct infusion of public money into the hands of the wealthiest asset holders (the chief beneficiaries of bailouts and tax cuts) while mere wage earners are left to pay the price. Thus, the wider issues of fiscal and monetary policy loom large in private- as well as public-sector disputes.

For all the efforts by the right to reinvigorate, in symbolic form, the race, ethnic, and gender fault lines that divided workers in the 1970s, we are no longer dealing with the same set of class relations. Blue-collar workers in construction and transportation are no longer overwhelmingly white. Independent contractors may operate as genuine small business owners or the most exploited of dependants. White-collar workers are not automatically middle-class. The real wages of workers in the same institution can differ wildly as a function of student debt burdens and inherited wealth. Public universities are increasingly funded by their students and thus de facto privatized, while whole cohorts of graduate students are positioned as low-rung workers in the same institutions. The last few decades of asset price inflation have expanded the focus of class conflict (including such issues as unaffordable housing and soaring rents) while introducing new fault lines within the one wage-earner class (homeowner versus renter, inheritor versus non-inheritor). We can be sure that something profound has shifted in the class composition of the American workforce when the United Auto Workers is winning its most decisive victories in the higher education sector through the organizing efforts of postdoctoral fellows, nontenured instructors, graduate students, and other precarious academic workers.[14] But we can also observe that the scope of class conflict is itself in flux when the most militant unions regularly address the issue of housing alongside wages. The recent demands by wildcat strikers at UC Santa Cruz for wage rises equal to soaring house prices in coastal California are a case in point: by articulating what is at present impossible—that wages be indexed to asset price inflation—such actions threaten the basic hierarchy between capital and wage income and strike at the heart of our contemporary capitalist regime.[15]

The experience of (social) wage austerity, alongside asset-holder abundance, is one that is shared by public- and private-sector workers alike, administrators of public services and their so-called clients. It extends beyond the formal wage relation to include those who routinely encounter the violence of racially targeted policing when moving through urban space and anyone who traverses a minefield of user fees in exchange for the use of nominally public services. While the class positions of graduate students, auto workers, public school teachers, the chronically overpoliced, the long-term unemployed, and the welfare-dependent cannot be conflated, public spending austerity is the common thread running through their diverse experiences. The challenge of addressing the seemingly distant spheres of monetary and fiscal policy is less technocratic than it seems. As the strike-driven wage-push inflation of the early 1970s demonstrated, "old-fashioned" forms of action can be the most effective means of corroding the value of financial assets and redistributing wealth from below. Labor strikes, rent strikes, strategic defaults, urban riots, occupations of public space, and squatting can all have an acute effect on the value of private wealth and the calculation of public spending priorities. The real challenge is coordinating and consolidating such actions at scale such that they enduringly shift the levers of fiscal and monetary action in an egalitarian direction. The left will never be able to afford the revolutionary change it longs for unless some effort is made to collectivize the process of money creation and public spending. How to make such change affordable is the process of revolution itself.

Acknowledgments

I have many people to thank for helping to make this book possible.

I owe a huge debt to all those who gave me the opportunity to test out first drafts en route to finding my thesis. I am especially grateful to Michael Szalay and Annie McClanahan at UC Irvine, Leslie Salzinger at UC Berkeley, Dorit Geva from the Central European University, and Paul North at Yale.

Much of this book was written during a time of immense institutional and epidemiological upheaval. I would like to thank my colleagues and students at the Australian National University for creating such a kind and enabling working environment. I was lucky to receive a Discovery Grant from the Australian Research Council (DPI80101197) to carry out my early archival research at the James M. Buchanan papers at George Mason University. I owe a special debt to the many archivists who scanned documents, sent microfiche reels by snail mail, or otherwise went out of their way to make material available during lockdown.

Some of this material first saw the light of day in *Capitalism: A Journal of History and Economics*, *Dissent Magazine*, and *The Baffler*. Editors Julia Ott, Zach Webb, Nick Serpe, and Natasha Lewis went above and beyond in their efforts to sharpen my prose and refine my arguments. Online interlocutors Bruce Bartlett, Nancy McLean, and Bethany Moreton were especially generous with comments, critiques, and suggestions. Several people intervened to provide crucial missing ingredients, sometimes unbeknownst to them. These are Katrina Forrester, Will Bateman, Veena Dubal, Mark Gawne, Jeremy Walker, Jason Stanley, Daniel Judt, Amy Kapczynski, Corinne Blalock, and Brendon O'Connor. Michel Feher, Wendy Brown, Meighan Gale, Julie Fry, and Greg McNamee were inordinately professional, reassuring, and patient throughout the editorial process.

Finally, I would be nowhere without Ari Heinrich, Joe Butters, Catherine Waldby, Paul K. Jones, Meredith Williams, Louise Boon-Kuo, Regrette Etcetera, Peter Banki, Hilary Caldwell, Elena Jeffreys, Janelle Fawkes, Melissa McAdam, Diablotine Cysique, and Lucette Cysique.

This book is dedicated to Marina.

Notes

INTRODUCTION: FISCAL AND MONETARY COUNTERREVOLUTION

1. In his own careful analysis of the crisis of Keynesian "crisis management," the German political sociologist Claus Offe underscored the diagnostic similarities between left and right perspectives on the 1970s. Claus Offe, "'Ungovernability': The Renaissance of Conservative Theories of Crisis," in *Contradictions of the Welfare State* (London: Routledge, 1984), p. 65.

2. James M. Buchanan, *The Limits of Liberty: Between Anarchy and Leviathan* (Carmel, IN: Liberty Fund, 1975), p. 218.

3. James M. Buchanan and Richard E. Wagner, *Democracy in Deficit: The Political Legacy of Lord Keynes* (Indianapolis: Liberty Fund, 1977), pp. 66–67.

4. James M. Buchanan, *Better Than Plowing and Other Personal Essays* (Chicago: University of Chicago Press, 1992), p. 115.

5. Ibid., p. 123.

6. Arthur B. Laffer, Memorandum for the Secretary, "Doomsday and the Stock Market," September 17, 1974, William E. Simon Papers, 1972–1977, Series II: Internal Memoranda, Drawer 10 Internal Memoranda: J-R, Folder 11—Arthur B. Laffer (Consultant to the Secretary): 1973–1975, Special Collections and College Archives, David Bishop Skillman Library, Lafayette College. Laffer presented this paper to the Institute of Chartered Financial Analysts in New York on September 18, 1974.

7. James O'Connor, *The Fiscal Crisis of the State* (New York: St. Martin's Press, 1973).

8. Ibid., pp. 221–26.

9. "It is our contention that the only lasting solution to the crisis is socialism." Ibid., p. 221. O'Connor's vision of social revolution can be usefully compared with that of the London–Edinburgh Weekend Return Group of the Conference of Socialist Economists, who saw themselves as pursuing a practice of revolutionary change "in and against the state." London Edinburgh Weekend Return Group, *In and against the State: Discussion Notes for Socialists* (London: Pluto Press, 2021). Both visions of leftist strategy vis-à-vis the state have obvious affinities with the later work of Marxist philosopher Nicos Poulantzas. See "The State, Social Movements, Party: Interview with Nicos Poulantzas," *Viewpoint Magazine*, December 18, 2017.

10. Joseph A. Schumpeter, "Crisis of the Tax State," in *The Economics and Sociology of Capitalism* (Princeton, NJ: Princeton University Press, [1917] 1991), pp. 99–140. For contemporary reflections on the changing nature of political conflict in the twentieth-century social state, see W. Elliot Brownlee, *Federal Taxation in America: A History* (Cambridge: Cambridge University Press, 2018), pp. 69–117; Martin Slater, *The National Debt: A Short History* (London: Hurst and Company, 2018), pp. 104–108. For an elucidation of the context in which Schumpeter was writing, see Clara E. Mattei, *The Capital Order: How Economists Invented Austerity and Paved the Way to Fascism* (Chicago: University of Chicago Press, 2022), on the revolutionary upsurge that followed the Great War and the deep fear it provoked among leading liberal economists. As Mattei explains, it was the activist government spending of World War I, with its demonstration of the possibilities of generous public spending, that emboldened workers across Europe to imagine an enduring exit from economic scarcity (pp. 7–10). Mattei traces the invention of modern state austerity politics to this moment.

11. Schumpeter, "Crisis of the Tax State," p. 117.

12. Ibid., pp. 116, 130.

13. Communist revolution, it is presumed, is punctual and explosive, emerging at the point of maximal antagonism between workers and the capitalist state. By contrast, Schumpeter's feared revolution looks incremental and subversive, an immanent force that takes hold of the state's social concessions and hijacks them from within. The difference is often summarized as a conflict between reform and revolution. The dichotomy is overdrawn, however, and misrepresents the complexity of Marx (and Marxian) understandings of revolution. Already in the *Communist Manifesto*, Marx and Engels were calling for the "centralization of credit in the banks of the state by means of a national bank with state capital and an exclusive monopoly." Karl Marx and Friedrich Engels, *The Communist Manifesto* (London: Pluto, [1848] 2017), p. 83. The question of how to reorganize public money and debt creation under communism was of critical concern also to the Russian revolutionaries, despite the frequent marginalization of such issues from the historiography. Among the first actions taken by the Bolsheviks after the 1917 coup was the nationalization of banks and the repudiation of all debts contracted by the Tsarist and Provisional governments—to this day the largest default in history. Hassan Malik, *Bankers and Bolsheviks: International Finance and the Russian Revolution* (Princeton, NJ: Princeton University Press, 2018), pp. 1–5, 186–97.

The same nuance can be found in early twentieth-century Marxist attitudes toward social welfare. In meetings of the Second International, which lasted from 1889 to 1914, deep cleavages between revolutionary Marxists and Social Democrats emerged, especially around the issue of whether to collaborate with mainstream parties in the building of welfare state institutions. Yet in many respects, the dichotomy between social welfare and revolution was overdetermined by the peculiar experience of Germany, where Otto von Bismarck had implemented the first modern welfare state as a means of staving off the socialist threat. The equation was seemingly confirmed by the subsequent evolution of social democratic parties, many of which abandoned their revolutionary ambitions after World War I and took active part in the development of Keynesian welfare states. In revolutionary Russia, however, the dichotomy was far from apparent. In the years leading up to the Russian Revolution of 1917, both Mensheviks and Bolsheviks sought very deliberately to take control of nascent social insurance structures with the aim of radicalizing them from below. Sally Ewing, "The Russian Social Insurance Movement, 1912–1914: An Ideological Analysis," *Slavic Review* 50, no. 4 (1991): pp. 914–26. For a history of modern welfare that emphasizes the catalytic role of class struggle, see Alexander Hicks, *Social Democracy and Welfare Capitalism: A Century of Income Security Politics* (Princeton, NJ: Princeton University Press, 1999).

14. Schumpeter, "Crisis of the Tax State," p. 131.

15. On Keynesianism as a form of Hegelianism, see Geoff Mann, *In the Long Run We Are All Dead: Keynesianism, Political Economy, and Revolution* (New York: Verso, 2017). In a much earlier essay, Antonio Negri makes the cognate argument that Keynesianism can be understood as a form of social insurance against the catastrophic risk of communism. Antonio Negri, "Keynes and the Capitalist Theory of the State," in *Labor of Dionysus: A Critique of the State-Form*, ed. Michael Hardt (Minneapolis: University of Minnesota Press, [1967] 1994), pp. 22–51.

16. Michał Kalecki, "Political Aspects of Full Employment," *Political Quarterly* 14, no. 4 (1943): pp. 322–30.

17. Ibid., p. 330.

18. Ron Paul, *End the Fed* (New York: Hachette, 2009).

19. I propose this concept of the unofficial dual mandate in contrast to the official dual mandate that is commonly understood to have governed monetary policy since the Federal Reserve Act of 1977. This act identifies full employment and stable inflation as the twin goals of monetary policy. Board of Governors of the Federal Reserve System, "Monetary Policy Principles and Practice" (2023).

20. On floating exchange rates as a technical release from domestic budget and balance-of-payment constraints, see Michael Hudson, *Super Imperialism: The Origins and Fundamentals of U.S. World Dominance* (London: Pluto Books, [1972] 2003), pp. x–xv, 18. Despite the sharpness of his account, Hudson is unable to explain why U.S. social policy became so deliberately austere at the very moment it was technically released from spending limits.

21. Jefferson Cowie, *Stayin' Alive: The 1970s and the Last Days of the Working Class* (New York: New Press, 2010), pp. 221–23; Kim Phillips-Fein, *Invisible Hands: The Businessmen's Crusade against the New Deal* (New York: Norton, 2010), pp. 153–56.

22. Milton Friedman, *Money Mischief: Episodes in Monetary History* (New York: Harcourt Brace Jovanovich, 1992), pp. 15–16. Friedman is referencing Irving Fisher, *The Purchasing Power of Money* (New York: Macmillan, [1911] 1929), p. 131.

23. Friedman, *Money Mischief*, p. 254.

24. Ibid.

25. On the institutional separation between the central bank and the Treasury and the origins of the taboo against debt monetization, see Josh Ryan-Collins and Frank van Lerven, *Bringing the Helicopter to Ground: A Historical Review of Fiscal-Monetary Coordination to Support Economic Growth in the 20th Century* (UCL Institute for Innovation and Public Purpose Working Paper Series, 2018); Daniela Gabor, *Revolution without Revolutionaries: Interrogating the Return of Monetary Financing* (Berlin: Heinrich Böll Stiftung, 2021); and Will Bateman and Jens van 't Klooster, "The Dysfunctional Taboo: Monetary Financing at the Bank of England, the Federal Reserve, and the European Central Bank," *Review of International Political Economy* (2023). For a discussion of the wider political ramifications of "central bank independence," see Jocelyn Pixley, *Central Banks, Democratic States and Financial Power* (Cambridge: Cambridge University Press, 2018), pp. 305–56. In Pixley's words, the "(silenced) rules" of central bank independence were "to increase unemployment at a hint of wage rises, to refuse state debt being monetized, and harp against deficits while busily monetizing bank debt" (p. 321). Pixley describes central bank independence as a deliberate insulation of monetary policy from democracy (p. 306). Stefan Eich, too, argues that the alleged "depoliticization" of central banking would be better described as "dedemocratization." Stefan Eich, *The Currency of Politics: The Political Theory of Money from Aristotle to Keynes* (Princeton, NJ: Princeton University Press, 2022), pp. 196–203. See also Joseph Vogl, *The Ascendancy of Finance* (Cambridge: Polity Press, 2017), pp. 19–131, for an excellent *longue durée* history of central bank independence, with a particular focus on the Deutsche Bundesbank.

26. Gabor, *Revolution without Revolutionaries*, p. 11. As Gabor notes, this transition occurred a lot earlier in the United States because of the Treasury-Fed Accord of 1951, which freed the Federal Reserve from its obligation to keep long-term interest rates down and minimized (but did not eliminate) the option of monetizing government debt. Thus, much of the 1970s hysteria around money printing as a source of wage-push inflation in the U.S. economy was completely misplaced (pp. 14, 24). The Federal Reserve departed from the recommendations of the accord only twice during this period, both times in response to military emergencies, not trade union activism or social demands. The final major round of debt monetization occurred in 1970, when it was feared that a billion-dollar issue of Treasury notes would fail following Nixon's decision to invade Cambodia. Bateman and van 't Klooster, "The Dysfunctional Taboo," p. 12.

27. William L. Silber, *Volcker: The Triumph of Persistence* (New York: Bloomsbury, 2012), p. 298.

28. Ibid., p. 164.

29. In 1966, Greenspan proffered the following lucid analysis of the role of the pure gold standard: "In the absence of the gold standard, there is no way to protect savings from confiscation through inflation.... The financial policy of the welfare state requires that there be no way for the owners of wealth to protect themselves. This is the shabby secret of the welfare statists' tirades against gold. Deficit spending is simply a scheme for the 'hidden' confiscation of wealth. Gold stands in the way of this insidious process. It stands as

a protector of property rights. If one grasps this, one has no difficulty in understanding the statists' antagonism toward the gold standard." The essay was published in Ayn Rand's journal *The Objectivist*. Alan Greenspan, "Gold and Economic Freedom," *The Objectivist* 7 (July 1966): pp. 12–13. For a reflection on the paradox of a former gold bug heading the Federal Reserve, see E. Ray Canterbery, *Alan Greenspan: The Oracle behind the Curtain* (London: World Scientific, 2006), p. 12.

30. Sebastian Mallaby, *The Man Who Knew: The Life and Times of Alan Greenspan* (London: Bloomsbury, 2016), pp. 49–52, 208–14.

31. Paul Pierson popularized the term "permanent austerity" in his classic essay "Coping with Permanent Austerity: Welfare State Restructuring in Affluent Democracies," in *The New Politics of the Welfare State*, ed. Paul Pierson (Oxford: Oxford University Press, 2001), pp. 410–56. It has given rise to a rich literature on the theme of welfare state austerity. See, for example, Armin Schäfer and Wolfgang Streeck, *Politics in the Age of Austerity* (London: Polity, 2013). Despite his perceptive analysis of the shift toward austerity, Pierson tends to see this trend as driven by demographic and economic forces beyond the reach of political contestation. Moreover, as others have pointed out, Pierson overestimates the inertia of the New Deal welfare state in the face of neoliberal attacks and underestimates the actual attrition of major entitlement programs. A number of scholars have focused on per capita benefits rather than overall program spending to argue that the austerity effect was more significant than Pierson acknowledges. James P. Allan and Lyle Scruggs, "Political Partisanship and Welfare State Reform in Advanced Industrial Societies," *American Journal of Political Science* 48, no. 3 (2004): pp. 496–512; and Walter Korpi and Joakim Palme, "New Politics and Class Politics in the Context of Austerity and Globalization: Welfare State Regress in 18 Countries, 1975–95," *American Political Science Review* 97, no. 3 (2003): pp. 425–46.

32. Richard A. Viguerie, "Defund the Left," *New York Times*, August 11, 1982.

33. Ruth Wilson Gilmore, *Golden Gulag: Prisons, Surplus, Crisis, and Opposition in Globalizing California* (Berkeley: University of California Press, 2007), pp. 54–127. On the paradox of increased criminal justice spending by the neoliberal "anti-state state," see Ruth Wilson Gilmore (with Craig Gilmore), "Beyond Bratton," in *Abolition Geography: Essays towards Liberation*, ed. Alberto Toscano and Brenna Bhander (New York: Verso, 2022), pp. 288–317. On the state preference for corrections spending over higher education, see Suzanne Mettler, *Degrees of Inequality: How the Politics of Higher Education Sabotaged the American Dream* (New York: Basic Books, 2014), pp. 120–27.

34. Natalia Mehlman Petrzela, *Classroom Wars: Language, Sex, and the Making of Modern Political Culture* (Oxford: Oxford University Press, 2015). On the recent history of these attacks, with their combination of economic and social grievances, see Jack Schneider and Jennifer Berkshire, *A Wolf at the Schoolhouse Door: The Dismantling of Public Education and the Future of School* (New York: New Press, 2020).

35. Frank Sammartino and Eric Toder, *Tax Expenditure Basics* (Washington, DC: Urban Institute, 2020). The concept of the "tax expenditure" was first proposed in 1967 by Assistant Secretary of the Treasury Stanley Surrey, who was concerned that legislators were

using the tax code to offer hidden subsidies to their favorite constituencies. The first tax expenditure report was published by the Treasury Department in 1968. Since then, both the Office of Tax Analysis in the U.S. Department of the Treasury and the congressional Joint Committee on Taxation have published annual lists of tax expenditures.

36. Christopher G. Faricy, *Welfare for the Wealthy: Parties, Social Spending, and Inequality in the United States* (Cambridge: Cambridge University Press, 2015), p. 99.

37. Joshua T. McCabe, *The Fiscalization of Social Policy: How Taxpayers Trumped Children in the Fight against Child Poverty* (Oxford: Oxford University Press, 2018), p. 61.

38. On the Republican Party bias toward tax expenditures, see Faricy, *Welfare for the Wealthy*, pp. 140–44, 169–200. The concept of the "hidden welfare state" is explored by Christopher Howard in *The Hidden Welfare State: Tax Expenditures and Social Policy in the United States* (Princeton, NJ: Princeton University Press, 1999) and *The Welfare State Nobody Knows: Debunking Myths about U.S. Social Policy* (Princeton, NJ: Princeton University Press, 2006).

39. "Policy Basics: Federal Tax Expenditures," Center on Budget and Policy Priorities, December 8, 2020; Tom Neubig and Agustin Redonda, "Tax Expenditures—the $1.5 Trillion Elephant in the (Budget) Room," *Bloomberg Tax*, September 7, 2021. As noted by Neubig and Redonda, annual reports released by the Treasury Department and Joint Committee on Taxation cover only income-related tax expenditures. The revenue foregone from other expenditures—relating to payroll taxes, excise taxes, or estate and gift taxes—is not included. Therefore, U.S. figures are likely to underestimate the total cost of tax expenditures.

40. Faricy, *Welfare for the Wealthy*, pp. 86, 100, 181. With the exception of social tax expenditures such as the EITC and the Child Tax Credit, most income-based tax expenditures are designed to subsidize the kinds of employment-based social insurance or asset-based wealth generation available to the already well-off. Neubig and Agustin Redonda, "Tax Expenditures" and "Addressing Tax Expenditures Could Raise Substantial Revenue," Committee for a Responsible Federal Budget, January 6, 2022.

41. Peter K. Eisinger, *The Rise of the Entrepreneurial State: State and Local Economic Development Policy in the United* States (Madison: University of Wisconsin Press, 1988); David Brunori, "Principles of Tax Policy and Targeted Tax Incentives," *State and Local Government Review* 29, no. 1 (1997): pp. 50–61; and Nathan M. Jensen and Edmund J. Malesky, *Incentives to Pander: How Politicians Use Corporate Welfare for Political Gain* (Cambridge: Cambridge University Press, 2018).

42. On the municipal bond market, see Jason Hackworth, *The Neoliberal City: Governance, Ideology, and Development in American Urbanism* (Ithaca, NY: Cornell University Press, 2007), pp. 17–30; Destin Jenkins, *The Bonds of Inequality: Debt and the Making of the American City* (Chicago: University of Chicago Press, 2021).

43. On the scale of these purchases, see Adam Tooze, *Crashed: How a Decade of Financial Crises Changed the World* (New York: Penguin Press, 2019), pp. 367–68, 471–79; Adam Tooze, *Shutdown: How Covid Shook the World's Economy* (New York: Viking, 2021),

pp. 129–45; and Lev Menand, *The Fed Unbound: Central Banking in a Time of Crisis* (New York: Columbia Global Reports, 2022), p. 59. On the turn to debt monetization as the breaking of a taboo, see Tooze, *Shutdown*, p. 145; Gabor, *Revolution without Revolutionaries*; and Eich, *The Currency of Politics*, pp. 207–209.

44. For a critical overview of the "neo-feudal" thesis, see Evgeny Morozov, "Critique of Techno-Feudal Reason," *New Left Review* 133/134 (2022): pp. 1–38.

45. Andrew Bowman, Ismail Erturk, Julie Froud, Sukhdev Johal, Adam Leaver, Michael Moran, and Karel Williams, "Central Bank–Led Capitalism?," *Seattle University Law Review* 36, no. 2 (2013): pp. 455–87; Tooze, *Shutdown*, pp. 119–28; Menand, *The Fed Unbound*, pp. 13, 119–23.

46. The term "neoliberal thought collective" is proposed by Philip Mirowski and Dieter Plehwe as a way of defining the social and ideological networks associated with thinkers in the Mont Pelerin Society, founded in 1947 at a first meeting in Mont Pèlerin, Switzerland. Philip Mirowski and Dieter Plehwe, eds., *The Road from Mont Pèlerin: The Making of the Neoliberal Thought Collective* (Cambridge, MA: Harvard University Press, 2009).

47. Robert A. Mundell and Members of the Conference, "Options in Therapy: The Role of Fiscal and Monetary Policy," in *Inflation as a Global Problem*, ed. Randall Hinshaw (Baltimore: Johns Hopkins University Press, 1972), p. 122.

48. Wanniski is here referring to presidential candidate Bob Dole's vow to pass a balanced budget amendment at any cost. Quoted in Jacob Weisberg, "The National Interest: Tax Cutups," *New York Magazine*, June 10, 1996, p. 21. Virginia school public choice theorists retorted with charges of supply-side "inflationism." See, for instance, Leland B. Yeager, "Supply-Side Inflationism," *Cato Policy Report* 7, no. 6 (July/August 1984): pp. 1, 3–4, 6.

49. This proposition was outlined in Wanniski's "Santa Claus theory" of Republican renewal. Jude Wanniski, "Taxes and a Two-Santa Theory," *National Observer*, March 6, 1976, pp. 6–8. The clearest expression of the supply-side anti-austerity message comes from Congressman Jack Kemp, who told the Republican Convention in 1980 that "austerity is not the answer. Austerity is the problem.... We can have growth, expansion, hope, and opportunity…or we can have contraction, suffering and austerity—with the bitter social divisiveness that these conditions bring." Jack Kemp, "A Republican Tidal Wave, July 15, 1980," in *The American Idea: Ending Limits to Growth* (Washington, DC: American Studies Center, 1984), p. 3.

50. Mark S. Mizruchi, *The Fracturing of the American Corporate Elite* (Cambridge, MA: Harvard University Press, 2013); Gerald F. Davis, *The Vanishing American Corporation: Navigating the Hazards of a New Economy* (New York: Penguin Random House, 2016); Doug Henwood, "Take Me to Your Leader: The Rot of the American Ruling Class," *Jacobin*, April 27, 2021.

51. Steve Fraser, "Playing God: The Rebirth of Family Capitalism," in *Mongrel Firebugs and Men of Property* (New York: Verso 2019), p. 232.

52. Davis, *The Vanishing American Corporation*, pp. 85–92; Jonathan Levy, *Ages of American Capitalism* (New York: Random House, 2021), p. xxvii.

53. In a speech at the Brookings Institution, Powell cited rising wages in service sectors ranging from hospitality to hairdressing as the "most important category for understanding the future evolution" of prices. Federal Reserve Chair Jerome Powell, *The Economic Outlook, Inflation and the Labor Market*, November 30 (Washington, DC: Brookings Institution, 2022), p. 5. Powell has continued to worry about wage inflation, even as evidence of profit-push inflation on the part of large corporations mounts up. See Servaas Storm, "Profit Inflation Is Real," INET Institute for New Economic Thinking, June 15, 2023; Isabella M. Weber and Evan Wasner, "Sellers' Inflation, Profits and Conflict: Why Can Large Firms Hike Prices in an Emergency?," Economics Department University of Massachusetts Amherst Working Paper Series 343 (2023).

54. London Edinburgh Weekend Return Group, *In and against the State*. For an excellent engagement with this group and its practice, see Katrina Forrester, "Quentin Skinner Lecture: 'In and against the State': Revolutionary Feminism during Deindustrialisation," Cambridge University, June 9, 2023.

55. L. Randall Wray, *Modern Money Theory: A Primer on Macroeconomics for Sovereign Monetary Systems* (London: Palgrave, 2012); Stephanie Kelton, *Modern Monetary Theory and the Birth of the People's Economy* (London: John Murray, 2020).

CHAPTER ONE: CAPITAL GAINS

1. Ben Schreckinger, "Reagan's Supply-Side Warriors Blaze a Comeback under Trump," *Politico Magazine*, April 22, 2019. Laffer played a leading role in shaping President Reagan's personal income tax cuts of 1981. The other four figures all held positions in the Reagan administration. Stephen Moore served as research director of Reagan's Commission on Privatization; Steve Forbes was Reagan's appointee to direct the Board of International Broadcasting, which managed the operation of Radio Free Europe/Radio Liberty; Lawrence Kudlow served as Reagan administration budget official; and David Malpas was Reagan's deputy assistant treasury secretary. Trump nominated each of these figures to key positions within his administration. In September 2017, he appointed Malpass as undersecretary of the treasury for international affairs, and two years later nominated him to the position of president of the World Bank. In late 2018, Trump appointed Kudlow as director of the National Economic Council. He later tried but failed to nominate the non-economist Stephen Moore to the board of the Federal Reserve. In June 2019, Trump awarded Arthur Laffer the Presidential Medal of Freedom for his contributions to economics. For an overview of the supply-siders' recommendations to Trump, see Arthur B. Laffer and Stephen Moore, *Trumponomics: Inside the America First Plan to Revive Our Economy* (New York: St. Martin's Press, 2018).

2. On the supply-siders' advice to Trump during the coronavirus pandemic, see Jonathan Chait, "The Fatal Calculations of the Economists Steering Our Public Health," *Intelligencer*, April 25, 2020.

3. Schreckinger, "Reagan's Supply-Side Warriors."

4. Peter Cary, "Republicans Passed Tax Cuts—Then Profited," Center for Public Integrity, January 24, 2020.

5. Patricia Cohen and Jesse Drucker, "Tax Plan Crowns a Big Winner: Trump's Industry," *New York Times*, December 5, 2017.

6. The growing critical literature on neoliberalism as a "thought collective" identifies at least four distinct schools: the Virginia school, the Chicago school, the Austrian school, and ordoliberalism. There now exists a growing critical literature on the Chicago and Virginia schools of economics, both of which played an important role in the development of American neoliberalism. See, for example, Philip Mirowski and Dieter Plehwe, eds., *The Road from Mont Pèlerin: The Making of the Neoliberal Thought Collective* (Cambridge, MA: Harvard University Press, 2009). On Chicago school neoliberalism, see Rob Van Horn and Philip Mirowski, "The Rise of the Chicago School of Economics and the Birth of Neoliberalism," in ibid., pp. 139–80; Robert Van Horn, Philip Mirowski, and Thomas A. Stapleford, eds., *Building Chicago Economics: New Perspectives on the History of America's Most Powerful Economics Program* (Cambridge: Cambridge University Press, 2011); and Jamie Peck, *Constructions of Neoliberal Reason* (Oxford: Oxford University Press, 2010). On Virginia school neoliberalism, see S. M. Amadae, *Prisoners of Reason: Game Theory and Neoliberal Political Economy* (Cambridge: Cambridge University Press, 2015); Nancy MacLean, *Democracy in Chains: The Deep History of the Radical Right's Stealth Plan for America* (New York: Viking, 2017); and Thomas Biebricher, *The Political Theory of Neoliberalism* (Stanford, CA: Stanford University Press, 2018). Supply-side economics has received far less scholarly attention and has only rarely been considered part of the "neoliberal thought collective" posited by Dieter Plehwe and Philip Mirowski. Important exceptions are Robert M. Collins, *More: The Politics of Economic Growth in Postwar America* (Oxford: Oxford University Press, 2000); Molly Michelmore, *Tax and Spend: The Welfare State, Tax Politics, and the Limits of American Liberalism* (Philadelphia: University of Pennsylvania Press, 2012); and Monica Prasad, *Starving the Beast: Ronald Reagan and the Tax Cut Revolution* (New York: Russell Sage Foundation, 2018).

7. It was the economist Herbert Stein who in 1976 coined the term "supply-side fiscalism" to describe the ideas of Robert Mundell, Jude Wanniski, and Arthur Laffer. Although the term was meant to be disparaging, Wanniski embraced it in the simplified form of "supply-side economics." Brian Domitrovic, *Econoclasts: The Rebels Who Sparked the Supply-Side Revolution and Restored American Prosperity* (Wilmington, DE: Intercollegiate Studies Institute, 2009), pp. 14–15. On the considerable importance accorded to supply-side Keynesian initiatives in postwar US liberalism, see Brent Cebul, *Illusions of Progress: Business, Poverty, and Liberalism in the American Century* (Philadelphia: University of Pennsylvania Press, 2023).

8. Robert A. Mundell and Members of the Conference, "Options in Therapy: The Role of Fiscal and Monetary Policy," in *Inflation as a Global Problem*, ed. Randall Hinshaw (Baltimore: Johns Hopkins University Press, 1972), p. 122.

9. On the supply-siders' nostalgia for the pure gold standard and turn to institutional price stability as a workable alternative, see Domitrovic, *Econoclasts*, pp. 39–50, 244–68. As noted by his biographer William L. Silber, Paul Volcker's anti-inflationary policy of 1979

functioned as a kind of "gold standard without gold." See William L. Silber, *The Triumph of Persistence* (New York: Bloomsbury, 2012), p. 164.

10. On this lineage, see Collins, *More*, pp. 176–77. A more logical line of descent would lead to Treasury Secretary Andrew Mellon, who between 1921 and 1932 presided over an austere mix of balanced budgets and tax cuts. Mellon also apparently believed that tax reductions could lead to higher revenues. Supply-siders only sometimes cite Mellon as a forebear, presumably because his associations with regressive giveaways to "special interests" make him something of a public relations liability. On the affinities between Mellon and the supply-siders, see Julia Ott, "Tax Preference as White Privilege in the United States, 1921–1965," *Capitalism: A Journal of History and Economics* 1, no. 1 (2019): pp. 92–165.

11. The period from 1973 to 1995 witnessed a long slowdown in productivity and GDP rates. This trend was briefly reversed under Clinton, who achieved an average GDP of 3.7 percent and a productivity growth rate of 1.9 percent between 1993 and 2000. At the time, both the Clinton White House and Greenspan's Federal Reserve hailed these figures as the sign of a "New Economy" fueled by the commercialization of new information technologies and an ebullient stock market. As noted by Robert Pollin, Clinton's macroeconomic record does indeed compare favorably with that of Nixon, Ford, Carter, Reagan, and Bush Sr., but it falls far short of the economic record of the Kennedy/Johnson years, when GDP was at 4.8 percent and productivity growth at 3.4 percent. Robert Pollin, *Contours of Descent: US Economic Fractures and the Landscape of Global Austerity* (New York: Verso, 2003), pp. 33–47. Private-sector fixed investment also bounced back during the Clinton era, as businesses adapted to the arrival of new information and communication technologies, but this development too was short-lived. See David M. Kotz, *The Rise and Fall of Neoliberal Capitalism* (Cambridge, MA: Harvard University Press, 2015), pp. 92–95, 112.

12. Robert Brenner, *The Economics of Global Turbulence: The Advanced Capitalist Economies from Long Boom to Long Downturn, 1945–2005* (New York: Verso, 2006), pp. 1–11. In Brenner's words, the "sharp deterioration in the economic performance of the advanced capitalist economies over the last quarter-century... is self-evident. Throughout these economies, average rates of growth of output, capital stock (investment), labour productivity, and real wages for the years 1973 to the present have been one-third to one-half of those for the years 1950–73, while the average unemployment rate has been more than double" (p. 4). Brenner accords a special significance to manufacturing profits as a marker of capitalism's general state of health (pp. 4, 6). But by focusing exclusively on the economic indicators appropriate to mid-twentieth-century Fordism, Brenner misses the vigorous capital gains made by asset holders during the so-called long stagnation of the last four decades. What at first appears as an eschatological theory of capitalism's inexorable decline turns out to be wildly optimistic.

My analysis of the U.S. economy, as it developed after 1980, is closely aligned with that of the historian Jonathan Levy, who speaks of "the capitalism of asset appreciation, which directs the bulk of fresh income gains not to labor earnings, or pay, but to the owners of capital." Jonathan Levy, *Ages of American Capitalism* (New York: Random House, 2021), p. xxvii.

13. Jacob A. Robbins, "Capital Gains and the Distribution of Income in the United States," *NBER* (December 2018). One response to this finding would be to discard measures of "savings" altogether. Another, adopted by Robbins, is to expand the concept of savings so as to include the automatic increases in wealth deriving from capital gains. This leads Robbins to question the standard story of a post-1980 decline in savings.

14. Ibid. Robbins's attempt to develop a comprehensive account of asset price appreciation and its impact on income inequality places him within the lineage of earlier economists such as Robert Murray Haig and Henry C. Simons, who first proposed the so-called Haig-Simons concept of capital gains.

There is a long-standing debate among economists about how to measure asset price appreciation or, in accounting terms, capital gains. Throughout the first decades of the twentieth century, tax scholars and economists turned to the issue of whether capital gains should be counted (hence taxed) as ordinary income at a time when the general income tax was itself a recent innovation. Among economists, Irving Fisher was the most hostile to the idea that asset price appreciation should be accorded any special significance as a contributor to income. In his view, the concept of income could be defined as "returns to saving," which in turn could be measured by the sum of one's enjoyment. If income was equivalent to what one consumed, the best and fairest option would be to subject all forms of income to a flat-rate consumption tax. Irving Fisher, *The Works of Irving Fisher: The Nature of Capital and Income* (London: Routledge, [1906] 1997), pp. 108–109.

This definition of income has obvious distributional drawbacks. After all, it is well known that wage earners consume a much larger proportion of their income than investors and asset holders, who may well hold vast amounts of wealth that they never consume. Fisher glossed over the issue of inequality by insisting that consumption could take any form—psychic as well as material—with the implication that the poorest of wage workers might compare with the wealthiest of investors if we only looked at the sum of their enjoyments, monetary or otherwise.

Others offered a more sophisticated account of capital gains. Robert Murray Haig replaced the consumption theory of income with a theory of power as leverage and extended the concept of satisfaction to include anything money could value, whether or not it was consumed or realized as a transaction. Under this conception, "income becomes the increase or accretion of one's power to satisfy his wants in a given period in so far as that power consists of (a) money itself, or (b) anything susceptible of valuation in terms of money." In other words, income is *the money-value of the net accretion to one's economic power between two points in time.* Robert Murray Haig, "The Concept of Income—Economic and Legal Aspects," in *The Federal Income Tax*, ed. Robert Murray Haig (New York: Columbia University Press, 1921), p. 7. Henry C. Simons, father of the Chicago school of economics, endorsed this definition of capital gains but called for a more radical rejection of neoclassical premises, which assume that any increment to income flows from savings and investment and is measurable as consumption. After all, he observed, the income in capital gains "is not saved or spent." Henry C. Simons, *Personal Income Taxation: The*

Definition of Income as a Problem of Fiscal Policy (Chicago: University of Chicago Press, 1938), p. 98. Rather, it appreciates and depreciates as a function of market valuations. Like Haig, Simons stressed that asset price appreciation functioned as a tremendous lever to economic power, whether or not the resultant capital gain was sold or consumed, that is, "realized." "One may gain without realizing and realize without gaining," Simons wrote, but "gain is the true *sine qua non*" (p. 84).

In public finance theory, the so-called Haig-Simons definition of income refers to the idea that capital gains should be measured at the market value of asset price appreciation. That is, even *unrealized* capital gains need to be counted if we want to generate an accurate picture of the national distribution of income and wealth.

It should be noted here that although "capital gains" are commonly (and intuitively) conceptualized as an increment in capital, they are often treated as if they were convertible into income (that is, as so-called putative income) in these secondary accounts, presumably because capital gains are almost always taxed as income rather than wealth.

15. Greta Krippner, *Capitalizing on Crisis: The Political Origins of the Rise of Finance* (Cambridge, MA: Harvard University Press, 2011), pp. 27–57. See also Brett Christophers, *Rentier Capitalism: Who Owns the Economy and Who Pays for It?* (New York: Verso, 2020), for an excellent account of this shift with respect to the United Kingdom. Christophers replaces Krippner's category of "financial profits" with that of "rents" and extends his purview from financial services to real estate and other sectors not normally associated with financialization. While carefully distancing his use of the concept "rent" from the well-worn moral taxonomies of earned and unearned income, Christophers retains the core distinction between a rentier capitalism defined by "having" and a non-rentier capitalism defined by "doing" (p. xviii). In this view, only non-rentier capitalism can "create" wealth; rentierism simply extracts. My own typology dispenses with this distinction altogether and focuses instead on different logics of investment and wealth creation, as shaped by the larger fiscal and monetary environment.

16. Simon Kuznets, *National Income and Its Composition: 1919–1938* (Washington, DC: National Bureau of Economic Research, 1947), p. 12.

17. Brenner, *The Economics of Global Turbulence*, pp. 1–11.

18. Michael Hudson and Steven Pressman both point to Piketty's relative neglect of capital gains as a serious shortcoming of his wealth and income statistics. Michael Hudson, "Piketty versus the Classical Economic Reformers," *Real-World Economics Review* 69, no. 7 (2014): pp. 122–30; Steven Pressman, *Understanding Piketty's Capital in the Twenty-First Century* (London: Routledge, 2015), p. 24.

In fact, Piketty does consider capital gains data at certain points in his analysis, but his reservations speak volumes about the conceptual and methodological challenges he encounters here. Thus, he dismisses capital gains windfalls as too volatile to account for the "structural increase" in top income shares during the past few decades (by contrast, Robbins's examination of the data shows that despite volatility in particular markets, average long-term increases in capital gains have been very high). See Thomas Piketty, *Capital in the Twenty-First Century*, trans. Arthur Goldhammer (Cambridge, MA: Harvard University Press, 2014), p. 295.

This is more than an interpretative detail. Not only does Piketty rely on Kuznets's mid-twentieth-century wealth and income metrics to measure inequality, but his causal account of rising inequality also rests on the neoclassical assumption that wealth is generated through a cumulative process of savings from production and investment from savings, in which collective expectations play little role. Piketty's entire conceptual apparatus is blind to the dynamics of asset price appreciation. The epistemological difficulty is nicely brought out by Suresh Naidu, who writes that Piketty "ends up trapped by the Marshallian apparatus he has built," where "capital—wealth—is treated more as a stock of accumulated savings rather than a claim on future output." Suresh Naidu, "A Political Economy Take on W/Y," in *After Piketty: The Agenda for Economics and Inequality*, ed. Heather Boushey, J. Bradford DeLong, and Marshall Steinbaum (Cambridge, MA: Harvard University Press, 2017), p. 100. For an illuminating discussion of the conceptual issues at stake here, see Levy, *Ages of American Capitalism*, pp. xiii–xvii.

19. Thomas Piketty and Emmanuel Saez, "Income Inequality in the United States, 1913–1998," *Quarterly Journal of Economics* 118, no. 1 (2003): pp. 1–41.

20. Robbins, "Capital Gains and the Distribution of Income in the United States," pp. 4–5, 22–25.

21. This is not to minimize the role of noneconomic factors in the reproduction of class. However, financial assets and their income-generating capacities are bequeathed in a much more direct way than taste, skills, education, and wages. I do not literally inherit the income-earning capacity of my parents by virtue of my genetic endowment, *pace* the claims of human capital theorists such as Gary Becker and Milton Friedman.

22. On George H. W. Bush's reference to "voodoo economics," see "The End Game for Reagan," *Time*, May 19, 1980, p. 25. George H. W. Bush is often remembered as the last Republican to have resisted the charms of the supply-side movement. In fact, he was only critical of the populist, Lafferite wing of the supply-side movement. Elite supply-side figures such as Martin Feldstein played an important role during his presidency.

23. For accounts of the *Wall Street Journal* supply-side movement, written by those involved, see Bruce R. Bartlett, *Reaganomics: Supply-Side Economics in Action* (Westport, CT: Arlington House, 1981); Robert L. Bartley, *The Seven Fat Years: And How to Do It Again* (New York: Free Press, 1992); and Jude Wanniski, *The Way the World Works, 20th Anniversary Edition* (Lanham, MD: Gateway Editions, [1978] 1998).

24. On the "theology of capital formation," see Robert Kuttner, *Revolt of the Haves: Tax Rebellions and Hard Times* (New York: Simon & Schuster, 1980), pp. 250–71.

25. My contention that the wider supply-side movement must be understood as incorporating an elitist and populist wing is built on the observation that (1) several of the leading figures in each wing had close connections with the other (Arthur Laffer had worked as economic advisor to William E. Simon between 1973 and 1975; the "capital formation" theorist Norman B. Ture worked with Jack Kemp and Paul Craig Roberts on the Kemp-Roth tax

bill); (2) the key figures of the populist wing, such as Jude Wanniski, were early proponents of the ideas of Martin Feldstein and other capital formation theorists in the pages of the *Wall Street Journal*; and (3) Reagan understood these two wings as contributing to a comprehensive supply-side agenda that he incorporated into his 1981 tax legislation.

The existence of two supply-side wings is implicitly acknowledged by scholars when they nominate Norman B. Ture (a crossover figure who straddles the two factions) as a supply-side economist. As for Martin Feldstein, his importance as a legitimating figure and broker of institutional access for the larger supply-side movement is confirmed by one of its more populist exponents, Bruce Bartlett. See Bartlett, *Reaganomics*, p. 7. For the most part, however, scholars have tended to privilege one wing over the other. Robert Kuttner, for instance, identifies the elite "capital formation" stalwarts as the real supply-side economists. He writes: "William Simon, President Gerald Ford's Treasury Secretary, sounded the alarm that government borrowing was 'crowding out' more productive uses of capital by private capital markets. Subsequently, capital formation was appropriated as a rallying cry by business groups resisting demands by tax reformers for higher taxes on capital gains. The so-called supply-side school associated with Arthur Laffer never represented more than a tiny fraction of economists and was essentially just a more outlandish version of the mainstream business claims. But the supply-siders popularized the capital-supply worries of Wall Street and imbued them with a democratic flavor since they offered a rationale that rewards to the rich would unlock new prosperity and growth for all." See Robert Kuttner, *Economic Illusion: False Choices between Prosperity and Social Justice* (Philadelphia: University of Pennsylvania Press, 1984), p. 52. For her part, Monica Prasad pushes back against the entire literature on the elite business offensive of the 1970s to reframe the supply-side movement as a whole as populist. But in doing, she too is obliged to privilege one wing of the supply-side movement over the other. Prasad, *Starving the Beast*.

26. Martin Feldstein, "Supply-Side Economics: Old Truths and New Claims," *American Economic Review* 76, no. 2 (1986): p. 27.

27. G. William Domhoff, *The Corporate Rich and the Power Elite in the Twentieth Century: How They Won, Why Liberals and Labor Lost* (London: Routledge, 2019); Kim McQuaid, *Uneasy Partners: Big Business in American Politics, 1945–1990* (Baltimore: Johns Hopkins University Press, 1994); David Vogel, *Fluctuating Fortunes: The Political Power of Business in America* (Washington, DC: Beard Books, 1989); Kim Phillips-Fein, *Invisible Hands: The Businessmen's Crusade against the New Deal* (New York: Norton, 2010), pp. 154–212; Benjamin C. Waterhouse, *Lobbying America: The Politics of Business from Nixon to NAFTA* (Princeton, NJ: Princeton University Press, 2014).

28. Vogel, *Fluctuating Fortunes*, p. 197.

29. Kotz, *The Rise and Fall of Neoliberal Capitalism*, p. 64.

30. On wage-push inflation and its presentation in the mainstream business press, see Jefferson Cowie, *Stayin' Alive: The 1970s and the Last Days of the Working Class* (New York: The New Press, 2010), pp. 221–23; Phillips-Fein, *Invisible Hands*, pp. 153–56.

31. On the relationship between rising wages and consumer prices, on the one hand,

and asset price depreciation, on the other, see Joseph J. Minarik, "The Distributional Effects of Inflation and Their Implications," in *Stagflation: The Causes, Effects and Solutions* (Washington DC: Joint Economic Committee, U.S. Congress, 1980), pp. 225–77; Edward N. Wolff, "The Distributional Effects of the 1969–75 Inflation on the Holdings of Household Wealth in the United States," *Review of Income and Wealth* 25, no. 2 (1979): pp. 195–207; and Douglas A. Hibbs, *The American Political Economy: Macroeconomics and Electoral Politics* (Cambridge, MA: Harvard University Press, 1987), pp. 63–124. On falling returns to financial assets during the 1970s, see Gerald A. Epstein and Arjun Jayadev, "The Rise of Rentier Incomes in OECD Countries: Financialization, Central Bank Policy and Labor Solidarity," in *Financialization and the World Economy*, ed. Gerald A. Epstein (Cheltenham, UK: Edward Elgar, 2005), p. 54; and Òscar Jordà, Katharina Knoll, Dmitry Kuvshinov, Moritz Schularick, and Alan M. Taylor, "The Rate of Return on Everything, 1870–2015," *Quarterly Journal of Economics* 134, no. 3 (2019): pp. 1280–81.

32. Kenneth L. Hirsch, "Inflation and the Law of Trusts," *Real Property, Probate and Trust Journal* 18, no. 4 (1983): p. 601. The threat posed by inflation to inheritable wealth was a frequent topic of concern in the business and legal press during this period. See Jules Blackman, "Price Inflation Threatens Estate Planning," *Trusts and Estates*, March 1979, pp. 22, 30; and "Conserving Your Estate: Wise Planning Is Now Essential for Any Estate above $60,000," *BusinessWeek*, July 26, 1976, pp. 121–28.

33. "The Death of Equities," *BusinessWeek*, August 13, 1979, pp. 54–59.

34. Henry C. Wallich, "Investment Income during Inflation," *Financial Analysts Journal* 34, no. 2 (1978): pp. 34–37.

35. Robert Metz, "Market Place; Making a Case for Buying Bonds," *New York Times*, May 1, 1981.

36. McQuaid, *Uneasy Partners*, p. 155.

37. Vogel, *Fluctuating Fortunes*, p. 200.

38. Gerald Epstein, *The Political Economy of Central Banking: Contested Control and the Power of Finance, Selected Essays* (Cheltenham, UK: Edward Elgar, 2019), p. 6.

39. On these organizations and their historically divergent relationship to the New Deal consensus, see Domhoff, *The Corporate Rich*, pp. 191–225; McQuaid, *Uneasy Partners*, p. 150.

40. Leonard Silk, "McGovern Tax Proposals Examined," *New York Times*, July 5, 1972.

41. Michael J. Graetz, "The Democrats' Tax Program," *Wall Street Journal*, August 11, 1976.

42. Jimmy Carter, "Tax Reduction and Reform, Message to the Congress, January 20, 1978," in *Public Papers of the Presidents of the United States: Jimmy Carter, 1978, Book 1—January 1 to June 30, 1978* (Washington, DC: U.S. Government Printing Office, 1979), p. 167.

43. The following biographical details on Norman B. Ture are drawn from Ronald Brownstein and Nina Easton, *Reagan's Ruling Class: Portraits of the President's Top 100 Officials* (Washington, DC: Presidential Accountability Group, 1982), pp. 6–10. Ture occupies an important place in supply-side mythology because he is the one figure to have actively

participated in both the Kennedy and Reagan administration tax cuts. According to the latter-day supply-sider Brian Domitrovic, by the time Ture arrived in Washington in 1976, he "had been pushing Capitol Hill in a supply-side direction for two decades." Domitrovic, *Econoclasts*, p. 128.

44. Norman B. Ture, *Accelerated Depreciation in the United States: 1954–60* (New York: National Bureau of Economic Research, 1967).

45. Norman B. Ture, *Tax Policy, Capital Formation, and Productivity* (Washington, DC: National Association of Manufacturers, 1973); and Norman B. Ture and B. Kenneth Sanden, *The Effects of Tax Policy on Capital Formation* (New York: Financial Executives Research Foundation, 1977).

46. Norman B. Ture served as advisor to chairman Wilbur D. Mills of the House Ways and Means Committee during the Eisenhower years. Stanley S. Surrey had worked for the treasury during the Roosevelt administration, advised members of the House Ways and Means Committee on tax matters in the late 1950s, and served as assistant secretary of the treasury for tax policy between 1961 and 1969. When Kennedy arrived in the White House in 1961, he set up a taxation task force that included both Norman B. Ture and Stanley Surrey. Julian E. Zelizer, *Taxing America: Wilbur D. Mills, Congress, and the State 1945–1975* (Cambridge: Cambridge University Press, 2000), p. 180.

47. On the Haig-Simons concept of income, see note 13. On Surrey's pragmatic interpretation of the Haig-Simons concept, see Reuven S. Avi-Yonah and Nir Fishbien, "Stanley Surrey, the Code, and the Regime," *Florida Tax Review* 25 no. 1 (2021): pp. 119–39.

48. Stanley S. Surrey, *Pathways to Tax Reform: The Concept of Tax Expenditures* (Cambridge, MA: Harvard University Press, 1973), p. 60.

49. Norman B. Ture, "Tax Aids in the Federal Budget," in *General Tax Reform: Objectives and Approaches to Tax Reform and Simplification, Committee on Ways and Means, Part I of II, February 5, 1973* (Washington, DC: U.S. Government Printing Office, 1973), pp. 169–78; Norman B. Ture, "Ture's Unreleased Testimony on Tax Expenditures," *Tax Notes* 13, no. 25 (1981): pp. 1535–39. As undersecretary of the treasury during the Reagan administration, Ture would seek (unsuccessfully) to abolish the tax expenditure budget altogether. Paul F. Harstad, "Treasury and OMB Clash on Tax Expenditure Concept," *Tax Notes* 13, no. 23 (1981): pp. 1407–8. For an extended discussion of the intellectual traditions underlying the "tax expenditure" concept, and efforts by Norman B. Ture and others to abolish or revise the tax expenditure budget, see Bruce Bartlett, "The End of Tax Expenditures as We Know Them?," *IRET Policy Bulletin*, June 13, 2001.

50. Ture, "Tax Aids in the Federal Budget" and "Ture's Unreleased Testimony on Tax Expenditures."

51. Soma Golden, "Superstar of the New Economists," *New York Times Magazine*, March 23, 1980. For further details on Feldstein's career, especially his role at the NBER, see the journalistic accounts of Anna Bernasek, "The Next Greenspan?," *Fortune*, June 14, 2004, p. 124; and David Leonhardt, "Scholarly Mentor to Bush's Team," *New York Times*, December 1, 2002. For academic accounts of Martin Feldstein's influence, see Mark Blyth, *Great*

Transformations: Economic Ideas and Institutional Change in the Twentieth Century (Cambridge: Cambridge University Press, 2002), pp. 158–60; and Michael Perelman, *The Confiscation of American Prosperity* (New York: Palgrave Macmillan, 2007), pp. 189–96.

52. Collins, *More*, p. 189.

53. Martin Feldstein and Joel Slemrod, "Inflation and the Excess Taxation of Capital Gains on Corporate Stock," *National Tax Journal* 31, no. 2 (1978): pp. 107–18; and Martin Feldstein, "Inflation and the Stock Market," *American Economic Review* 70, no. 5 (1980): pp. 839–47.

54. Martin S. Feldstein, "The New Economics and Government Policy," *Business Horizons* 22, no. 4 (1979): pp. 11–13.

55. Martin Feldstein, "Inflation and Capital Formation," *Wall Street Journal*, July 27, 1978.

56. Martin S. Feldstein, "The United States Saves Too Little!," *Society* 14 (1977): pp. 76–78.

57. Michael J. Boskin, "An Economist's Perspective on Estate Taxation," in *Death, Taxes and Family Property*, ed. Edward C. Halbach Jr. (St. Paul, MN: West, 1977), p. 61.

58. Ibid.

59. Ibid., 64.

60. William E. Simon was nominated as deputy secretary of the Treasury Department on January 22, 1973. He became secretary of the treasury in June 1974, just three months before Nixon resigned, and continued in this role throughout the Ford administration. For the argument that William E. Simon should be considered a supply-sider, see the archival work of Paul Macavoy, "'Don't Just Stand There…': Treasury Secretary William E. Simon and Fiscal Policy During Stagflation, 1975–76," *Atlantic Economic Journal* 31, no. 3 (2003): pp. 213–18; Susan L. Averett, Edward N. Gamber, and Sheila Handy, "William E. Simon's Contribution to Tax Policy," *American Economic Journal* 31, no. 3 (2003): pp. 233–41.

61. John F. Witte, *The Politics and Development of the Federal Income Tax* (Madison: University of Wisconsin Press, 1985), pp. 187 and 216; Macavoy, "Don't Just Stand There."

62. Averett, Gamber, and Handy, "William E. Simon's Contribution to Tax Policy," pp. 235–36.

63. Interestingly, Simon's chief economic advisor during his first years in office was none other than Arthur Laffer, who later emerged as the media face of populist supply-side economics. Arthur B. Laffer (Consultant to the Secretary): 1973–1975, William E. Simon Papers, 1972–1977, Series II: Internal Memoranda, Drawer 10 Internal Memoranda: J-R, Folder 11, Special Collections and College Archives, David Bishop Skillman Library, Lafayette College.

64. An in-depth account of Charls ("Charlie") E. Walker and his many lobbying hats can be found in Elizabeth Drew, "Charlie: Portrait of a Lobbyist," in *Interest Group Politics*, ed. Allan J. Cigler and Burdett A. Loomis (Washington, DC: CQ Press, 1983), pp. 217–50. Walker was a trained economist who had served as economic advisor to the secretary of the treasury under Eisenhower and deputy secretary of the treasury under Nixon. On his role in establishing the Business Roundtable, see Drew, "Charlie," pp. 221–23.

65. McQuaid, *Uneasy Partners*, p. 157. The American Council for Capital Formation

was briefly known under the all-too-transparent name of the American Council on Capital Gains and Estate Taxation. McQuaid notes that the organization "was run by high-ranking tax officials from the Nixon and Ford administrations." Apart from Walker, the original board of the ACCF also included Robert B. Anderson and David Kennedy, who served as Treasury secretaries under Eisenhower and Nixon, respectively.

66. Ture was nominated to the board of directors of the American Council for Capital Formation in 1977. See Norman B. Ture, "Biographical Sketch of Norman B. Ture," in *Nominations of Norman B. Ture and Beryl Wayne Sprinkel: Hearing before the Committee on Finance, United States Senate, Ninety-Seventh Congress, First Session* (Washington, DC: U.S. Government Printing Office, 1981), p. 2. For Ture's perspective on the estate tax as a disincentive to capital formation, see Ture, *Tax Policy, Capital Formation, and Productivity*, p. 32; and Ture and Sanden, *The Effects of Tax Policy on Capital Formation*, p. 66.

67. Kuttner, *Revolt of the Haves*, p. 244; Vogel, *Fluctuating Fortunes*, pp. 175–76; Drew, "Charlie," pp. 239–40.

68. Ibid., p. 242.

69. To convince Democratic members of the House Ways and Means Committee to vote for the amendment, Walker told them that "although they were going to exempt the sale of homes, the perception was out there that homes would be included, or people would say 'Well they're leaving out homes this time, but they'll get them the next time.' If they'd kept on with that, I was going to do a TV treatment of an Archie Bunker type trying to sell his home." Drew, "Charlie," p. 239. As noted by Kim McQuaid, "Democrats not only got beaten, they got scared. Fears of middle-class disenchantment had rocked Congress in 1978, when a majority of Democrats staged their own tax cut revolt against Carter." McQuaid, *Uneasy Partners*, p. 167.

70. In the words of Molly Michelmore, the bill "provided a dress rehearsal for the tax politics of the Reagan era" and beyond. Michelmore, *Tax and Spend*, p. 128.

71. Kim Moody, *From Welfare State to Real Estate: Regime Change in New York City, 1974 to the Present* (New York: New Press, 2007), pp. 40–41.

72. John H. Mollenkopf, "The Crisis of the Public Sector in America's Cities," in *The Fiscal Crisis of American Cities: Essays on the Political Economy of Urban America with Special Reference to New York*, ed. Roger E. Alcaly and David Mermelstein (New York: Vintage Books, 1976), pp. 125–26.

73. Kim Phillips-Fein, *Fear City: New York's Fiscal Crisis and the Rise of Austerity Politics* (New York: Henry Holt, 2017), pp. 79–88. For a comparative study of bondholder exit in San Francisco, which makes a compelling case for the manufactured nature of the crisis, see Destin Jenkins, *The Bonds of Inequality: Debt and the Making of the American City* (Chicago: University of Chicago Press, 2021).

74. Moody, *From Welfare State to Real Estate*, p. 16.

75. Joshua B. Freeman, *Working-Class New York: Life and Labor since World War II* (New York: New Press, 2000); Phillips-Fein, *Fear City*, pp. 4–5; and Moody, *From Welfare State to Real Estate*, pp. 16–18.

76. William E. Simon, *A Time for Truth* (New York: Reader's Digest Press, 1978), p. 154.

77. Mollenkopf, "The Crisis of the Public Sector in America's Cities," pp. 118, 122, 126–27.

78. Moody, *From Welfare State to Real Estate*, pp. 12, 14, 57.

79. Alexis N. Walker, *Divided Unions: The Wagner Act, Federalism, and Organized Labor* (Philadelphia: University of Pennsylvania Press, 2020), p. 54.

80. Moody, *From Welfare State to Real Estate*, p. 57.

81. Rona B. Stein, "The New York City Budget: Anatomy of a Fiscal Crisis," *Federal Reserve Board of New York Quarterly Review* (Winter 1976): pp. 5–8, 11.

82. H. J. Maidenberg, "Inflation Is Ravaging the Bond Market," *New York Times*, July 7, 1974.

83. "New York City's Financial Situation," Statement of the Honorable William E. Simon, Secretary of the Treasury, Before the Senate Committee on Banking, Housing and Urban Affairs, Thursday, October 9 at 9:30AM, The Department of the Treasury News, William E. Simon Papers, 1972–1977 (microfiche), Series IIIB: Subject Files (Secretary), Drawer 24 Minimum Tax—The Penny, Folder 24: 33 New York City: 1975 (Oct), Special Collections and College Archives, David Bishop Skillman Library, Lafayette College. Simon noted that "municipal governments are facing the same pressures as all other borrowers: a diminishing supply of capital at higher and higher rates caused primarily by inflation and the growing Federal usurpation of the supply of credit in this country" (p. 12). Simon's crowding-out thesis originally applied to private borrowers only, but here he extended it to municipal governments competing with a voracious federal government.

84. Anthony Sampson, *The Money Lenders: Bankers and a World in Turmoil* (New York: Viking, 1981), pp. 118–28.

85. Moody, *From Welfare State to Real Estate*, pp. 10–11, 34–35; Lynne A. Weikart, *Follow the Money: Who Controls New York City Mayors?* (Albany: State University of New York Press, 2009), pp. 30–31; and Phillips-Fein, *Fear City*, pp. 75–77.

86. Moody, *From Welfare State to Real Estate*, p. 29.

87. Fred Ferretti, "City's Realty Tax Will Rise by 11.3%," *New York Times*, June 28, 1975. This, however, was not enough to compensate for the systemic underassessment of property values under Mayor Lindsay's commercial construction boom, and as a consequence the property tax actually declined as a percentage of local tax revenue during these years. See Moody, *From Welfare State to Real Estate*, p. 58.

88. Moody, *From Welfare State to Real Estate*, pp. 35–41; Weikart, *Follow the Money*, p. 46.

89. James Ring Adams, *Secrets of the Tax Revolt* (New York: Harcourt Brace Jovanovich, 1984), p. 118.

90. Moody, *From Welfare State to Real Estate*, pp. 39–40, 72, 133.

91. Jonathan Soffer, *Ed Koch and the Rebuilding of New York City* (New York: Columbia University Press, 2010), pp. 143–44; Weikart, *Follow the Money*, p. 49.

92. Temporary Commission on City Finances, *The City in Transition: Prospects and Policies for New York* (New York: Arno Press, 1978). On the importance of this report, from a

supply-side friendly and supply-side critical perspective, respectively, see Moody, *From Welfare State to Real Estate*, p. 66; Ring Adams, *Secrets of the Tax Revolt*, p. 118.

93. Temporary Commission on City Finances, *The City in Transition*, pp. 11, 149, 160.

94. Ibid., pp. 11, 142, 144.

95. Ibid., p. 144.

96. Eric Lichten, *Class, Power, and Austerity: The New York City Fiscal Crisis* (South Hadley, MA: Bergin & Garvey, 1986), p. 64.

97. U.S. General Accounting Office, *The Long-Term Fiscal Outlook for New York City: Report to the Congress* (Washington DC: U.S. General Accounting Office, 1977).

98. Adrian deWind, *Report of the Special Task Force on Taxation to the Council on the Economy of New York* (New York: Municipal Assistance Corporation, 1976).

99. Temporary Commission on City Finances, *The City in Transition*, pp. 1, 12–14.

100. Ring Adams, *Secrets of the Tax Revolt*, pp. 120–21.

101. Samuel Stein, *Capital City: Gentrification and the Real Estate State* (New York: Verso, 2019), pp. 36–40, 43–48.

102. Moody, *From Welfare State to Real Estate*, p. 66.

103. John H. Mollenkopf, *A Phoenix in the Ashes: The Rise and Fall of the Koch Coalition in New York City Politics* (Princeton, NJ: Princeton University Press, 1994), p. 146, and Moody, *From Welfare State to Real Estate*, p. 71.

104. Alex S. Vitale, *City of Disorder: How the Quality of Life Campaign Transformed New York Politics* (New York: New York University Press, 2008), pp. 109–10.

105. Mollenkopf, *A Phoenix in the Ashes*, pp. 146–49.

106. Wayne Barrett, *Trump: The Deals and the Downfall* (New York: HarperCollins, 1992), pp. 117–53; Phillips-Fein, *Fear City*, pp. 256–60; and Andrea Bernstein, *American Oligarchs: The Kushners, the Trumps, and the Marriage of Money and Power* (New York: Norton, 2020), pp. 71–82.

107. On the lifetime of gifts, intergenerational transfers, and inherited wealth that Trump has received, beginning at the age of three, see the New York Times special investigation by David Barstow, Susanne Craig, and Russ Buettner, "Trump Engaged in Suspect Tax Schemes as He Reaped Riches from His Father," *New York Times*, October 2, 2018. On Trump's inheritance of his father's political networks, see Andrea Bernstein, "Turning Politics into Money," *Trump, Inc.* (podcast), January 23, 2020.

108. Charles V. Bagli, "A Trump Empire Built on Inside Connections and $885 Million in Tax Breaks," *New York Times*, September 17, 2016.

109. Trump successfully sued Koch for refusing a ten-year tax exemption for Trump Tower. Bernstein, *American Oligarchs*, pp. 84–88.

110. Bagli, "A Trump Empire Built on Inside Connections and $885 Million in Tax Breaks."

111. "The Supply-Side Saves New York," *Wall Street Journal*, February 23, 1981.

112. "On to the Next Challenge: A Crumbling Foundation," *BusinessWeek*, July 23, 1984, pp. 109–12.

113. Soffer, *Ed Koch and the Rebuilding of New York City*, pp. 146–47.

114. Adams, *Secrets of the Tax Revolt*, p. 119.

115. Molly Ivins, "Carey's Budget Urges Major Welfare Cuts, Some Tax Reductions," *New York Times*, January 19, 1977.

116. Richard J. Meislin, "Carey Plans to Put Income Tax Cuts in Effect on July 1," *New York Times*, January 6, 1978.

117. Weikart, *Follow the Money*, pp. 51 and 55.

118. "The Supply-Side Saves New York."

119. See also Adams, *Secrets of the Tax Revolt*, pp. 120–21.

120. If this was the case, however, then real estate had little to do with it: the relative contribution of property taxes to New York City's revenue base actually fell from 55.6 percent in 1975 to 34 percent in 1983; consumption taxes on utilities, by contrast, were rising, and these are more readily distributed downward. Moody, *From Welfare State to Real Estate*, pp. 70–71.

121. Simon, *A Time for Truth*, p. 193.

122. Ibid., p. 226.

123. Ibid.

124. Hobart Rowen, "The Dollar's Slide: What It Means," *Washington Post*, August 20, 1978. On the history of the dollar depreciation crisis and the Carter administration's disputes with its trading partners, see W. Carl Biven, *Jimmy Carter's Economy: Policy in an Age of Limits* (Chapel Hill: University of North Carolina Press, 2014), pp. 95–121.

125. On the "locomotive theory" of joint reflation that Carter had hoped to lead, see Biven, *Jimmy Carter's Economy*, pp. 96–97; Eric Helleiner, *States and the Reemergence of Global Finance: From Bretton Woods to the 1990s* (Ithaca, NY: Cornell University Press, 1994), pp. 131–32.

126. Rowen, "The Dollar's Slide."

127. William Greider comments that the "Federal Reserve officials tried to downplay the importance of international finance in forcing their hand" for "obvious political reasons." William Greider, *Secrets of the Temple: How the Federal Reserve Runs the Country* (New York: Simon & Schuster, 1989), p. 118.

128. Quoted in Biven, *Jimmy Carter's Economy*, p. 239.

129. On Volcker's pragmatic use of monetarism, see Silber, *Volcker*, pp. 163–64. Volcker's apparent monetarist turn was motivated by political optics above all. By focusing on monetary targets and letting banks do the dirty work of raising interest rates in its stead, the Fed could blame others for the pain it inflicted. Biven, *Jimmy Carter's Economy*, p. 242; Krippner, *Capitalizing on Crisis*, p. 108.

130. Paul A. Volcker, "Testimony before the Committee on Banking, Finance, and Urban Affairs, U.S. House of Representatives, July 21, 1981," *Federal Reserve Bulletin* 67, no. 8 (1981): p. 614.

131. Paul Volcker, "Statement before the Joint Economic Committee of the U.S. Congress, January 26, 1982," *Federal Reserve Bulletin* 68, no. 2 (1982): p. 89. For a discussion

of Volcker's views on wage-push inflation, see Michael Perelman, *The Pathology of the U.S Economy: The Costs of a Low-Wage System* (New York: Palgrave Macmillan, 1996), pp. 42–43; Michael A. McCarthy, *Dismantling Solidarity: Capitalist Politics and American Pensions since the New Deal* (Ithaca, NY: Cornell University Press, 2017), pp. 138–39. On the Federal Reserve's continuing preoccupation with wage-push inflation, see Daniel J. B. Mitchell and Christopher L. Erickson, "Not Yet Dead at the Fed: Unions, Worker Bargaining, and Economy-Wide Wage Determination," *Industrial Relations* 44, no 4. (2005): pp. 565–606.

132. McCarthy, *Dismantling Solidarity*, p. 141.

133. On the multiple reasons for the record debt under Reagan, see Robert Heilbroner and Peter Bernstein, *The Debt and the Deficit: False Alarms/Real Possibilities* (New York: Norton, 1989), pp. 21–27.

134. For an insider's account of these rifts, see David A. Stockman, *The Triumph of Politics: Why the Reagan Revolution Failed* (New York: HarperCollins, 1987).

135. On the long history of the "crowding-out" thesis, see Richard M. Salsman, *The Political Economy of Public Debt* (Cheltenham, UK: Edward Elgar, 2017), pp. 76–77 and 113. On Simon's mobilization of the "crowding-out" thesis, see Kuttner, *Economic Illusion*, p. 52. On the pervasiveness of this argument in the early Reagan administration, see Krippner, *Capitalizing on Crisis*, p. 94.

136. David Stockman, who had once identified as a supply-sider, referred to these people as the "central committee" of supply-side economics. See Stockman, *The Triumph of Politics*, p. 344. Other members of the "central committee" who were not in the early Reagan administration were Jude Wanniski and the neoconservative supporter of supply-side economics Irving Kristol.

137. Jude Wanniski, "Taxes and a Two-Santa Theory," *National Observer*, March 6, 1976, pp. 6–8.

138. As Mundell explained to conference colleagues in 1971, in an open economy with floating exchange rates, "there may be a possibility of getting more resources than you are currently producing." This was because, in an "open economy" with relatively free capital movements, "you could get the resources by following a less expansionary monetary policy which, through a high interest rate, would attract capital from abroad. This would allow the economy to have a deficit on current account which would increase the national supply of goods and services." Robert A. Mundell and Members of the Conference, "Options in Therapy: The Role of Fiscal and Monetary Policy," in *Inflation as a Global Problem*, ed. Randall Hinshaw (Baltimore: Johns Hopkins University Press, 1972), p. 122.

139. Paul Craig Roberts, "Idealism in Public Choice Theory," *Journal of Monetary Economics* 4, no. 3 (1978): pp. 603–15.

140. See Krippner, *Capitalizing on Crisis*, pp. 94–95, for an illuminating analysis of this moment in the early Reagan administration.

141. Krippner, *Capitalizing on Crisis*, pp. 100–101.

142. Beryl W. Sprinkel, "Statement of the Honorable Beryl W. Sprinkel, under Secretary for Monetary Affairs, United States Treasury Department, October 27, 1983," in *Foreign*

Exchange Value of the Dollar: Joint Hearings before the Subcommittee on International Trade, Investment, and Monetary Policy and the Subcommittee on Domestic Monetary Policy of the Committee on Banking, Finance, and Urban Affairs, House of Representatives, Ninety-Eighth Congress, First Session, October 5, 25, 27; November 1 and 2, 1983 (Washington, DC: U.S. Government Printing Office, 1984), p. 83.

143. Sprinkel, "Statement of the Honorable Beryl W. Sprinkel," p. 84.

144. Ibid., pp. 84–85.

145. "H.R. 4242—97th Congress: Economic Recovery Tax Act of 1981," July 23, 1981. Confusingly, the Tax Act of 1981 is also referred to as the Kemp-Roth Tax Act. I have avoided using this formulation here, since it is easy to mistake it for earlier bills bearing the name "Kemp-Roth."

146. Indeed, in their haste to put their signature on a bill they saw as unstoppable, Democrats engaged in a bidding war to add concessions of their own and ended up pushing things much further than Reagan had dared to hope. Ronald Reagan, *An American Life* (New York: Simon & Schuster, 1990), p. 286.

147. "During the 1980 campaign," Reagan wrote, "a new term, *supply-side economics,* came into vogue. People said I embraced this theory, and several economists claimed credit for inventing its principles, which they said I had then adopted as the basis for my economic recovery program." Reagan countered that his embrace of the tax-cut credo in fact stemmed from his personal experience. "At Eureka College, my major was economics, but I think my own experience with our tax laws in Hollywood probably taught me more about practical economic theory than I ever learned in a classroom or from an economist, and my views on tax reform did not spring from what people called supply-side economics." Reagan, *An American Life*, p. 231. He continued: "A few economists call this…supply-side economics. I just call it common sense" (p. 232).

148. Reagan, *An American Life*, p. 288. On Reagan's personal devotion to the supply-side credo and the tensions this later caused with administration pragmatists, see Brownstein and Easton, *Reagan's Ruling Class*, pp. 12–19; Thomas S. Langston, *Ideologues and Presidents* (London: Routledge, 2017), pp. 199–200. On Reagan's California encounter with Arthur Laffer in the late 1970s and Jack Kemp's decision to endorse Reagan's presidential bid (instead of running on a supply-side platform himself), see William Kleinknecht, *The Man Who Sold the World: Ronald Reagan and the Betrayal of Main Street America* (Philadelphia: Nation Books, 2009), pp. 65–66, 96.

149. Members of the American Council for Capital Formation, the Business Roundtable, the U.S. Chamber of Commerce, and other business associations had been meeting informally for a year before the election and had already come up with a set of new accelerated depreciation rules before Reagan came into office. McQuaid, *Uneasy Partners*, pp. 167–68l; Witte, *Politics and Development of the Federal Income Tax*, pp. 218–21; and Vogel, *Fluctuating Fortunes*, pp. 242–43. According to Witte, Charls E. Walker had been meeting with other business insiders at the Carlton hotel in Washington in the lead-up to Reagan's inauguration (Vogel traces the origins of this group back to 1975). Besides Walker,

other members of the so-called Carlton Group included Ernest Christian, another former officeholder in the Nixon/Ford Treasury Department, Richard Rahn, chief economist for the U.S. Chamber of Commerce and former executive director of the American Council for Capital Formation, and Mark Bloomfield, who had succeeded Rahn at the ACCF.

150. According to another member of the team, Walker "tried to put together a program which expressed what the President wanted, a marriage of the capital formation and the populist people" within the wider supply-side movement. The anonymous source is quoted in Aaron Wildavsky and Joseph White, *The Deficit and the Public Interest: The Search for Responsible Budgeting in the 1980s* (Berkeley: University of California Press, 1989), p. 79.

151. The position of Treasury tax advisor had been conjured up by Ture himself. In his contribution to the Heritage Foundation's *Mandate for Leadership*, a digest intended to guide Reagan's transition into the presidency, Ture had called for a new position of under-secretary for tax and economic affairs to be created within the Treasury Department. Norman B. Ture, "Treasury," in *Mandate for Leadership: Policy Management in a Conservative Administration*, ed. Charles Heatherly (Washington, DC: Heritage Foundation, 1981), pp. 647–94. The position was duly established by Treasury Secretary Donald Regan, who appointed Ture as its first incumbent. Although not a supply-sider himself, Regan was a conscientious translator of the president's will. In Donald Regan's words, "I read what President Reagan said during the campaign, and he made clear he was in favor of what is called supply-side tax cuts. I tried to find the best men with those views." Quoted in Rowland Evans and Robert Novak, *The Reagan Revolution: An Inside Look at the Transformation of the U.S. Government* (New York: Dutton, 1981), p. 97.

152. Langston, *Ideologues and Presidents*, pp. 191–92.

153. According to the economist Douglas Hibbs, the reductions in tax liability resulting from the ERTA increased monotonically with adjusted gross income. This he attributes primarily to the impact of tax expenditures such as the reduction in the capital gains tax and accelerated depreciation schedules, which are naturally of greatest benefit to those who derive most of their income from investment rather than labor. Hibbs calculates that for the top 2 percent of taxpayers by income, disposable incomes were 21 to 26 percent higher in 1984 than they would have been otherwise. For the 38 percent of taxpayers with annual incomes less than $10,000, by contrast, disposable incomes were 0.3 to 1.8 percent higher. Hibbs, *The American Political Economy*, p. 311.

154. The Carlton Group came up with the so-called 10-5-3 accelerated depreciation schedule (ten years for buildings, three years for vehicles, and five years for all other capital equipment) in the lead-up to the Reagan election. Vogel, *Fluctuating Fortunes*, p. 243. As undersecretary for tax and economic affairs, Ture put forward a slightly revised version of this model. Peter Grier, "Reagan's Man for Tax Policy a Backer of Cuts-for-Stimulus," *Christian Science Monitor*, January 19, 1981.

155. David Warsh, "Bull Run," *New York Times*, January 21, 2001.

156. David A. Vise, "The Stock Market from the Roaring '80s to the Sober '90s," *Washington Post*, December 31, 1989.

157. Matthew Winkler, "How to Take a Bull Market in Bonds by the Horns," *Wall Street Journal*, October 19, 1988; Walter L. Updegrave, "Capital Gains: The Twisting Path to Appreciation," *Money*, December 1988, p. 83.

158. R. S. Salomon Jr. and Mallory J. Lennox, "Returns on Various Types of Investments," in *The 1987 Dow Jones-Irwin Business and Investment Almanac*, ed. Sumner N. Levine and Caroline Levine (Homewood, IL: Dow Jones-Irwin, 1987), p. 267. The 1980s witnessed a wave of asset price surges across the world. In the United States, the commercial real estate and stock price surge of the 1980s would be followed by the dot-com boom of the late 1990s, the housing boom of the early 2000s, and a new stock price boom after the financial crisis of 2007 to 2009. Although the fortunes of specific asset classes would wax and wane, asset price appreciation as a general tendency had become the new normal of the post-1980s economic world. See Garry J. Schinasi and Monica Hargraves, "'Boom and Bust' in Asset Markets in the 1980s: Causes and Consequences," in *Staff Studies for the World Economic Outlook* (Washington, DC: International Monetary Fund, 1993), pp. 1–27.

159. On the impact of capital gains tax cuts on triggering a wave of venture capital investments and leveraged buyouts, see Kenneth W. Rind, "Overview of Venture Capital," in *Investing in Venture Capital and Buyouts*, ed. Sumner N. Levine (Homewood, IL: Dow Jones-Irwin, 1985), p. 1.

160. George P. Baker and George David Smith, *The New Financial Capitalists: Kohlberg Kravis Roberts and the Creation of Corporate Value* (Cambridge: Cambridge University Press, 1998).

161. Baker and Smith, *The New Financial Capitalists*, pp. 64–68.

162. Bruce Nussbaum, "Deal Mania," *BusinessWeek*, November 24, 1986, pp. 74–76; Ellyn E. Spragins, "The Corporate Shopping Spree Roars on and On," *BusinessWeek*, July 21, 1986, pp. 110–11.

163. Michael C. Jensen and William H. Meckling, "Theory of the Firm: Managerial Behavior, Agency Costs and Ownership Structure," *Journal of Financial Economics* 3, no. 4 (1976): pp. 305–60.

164. Jack Hirshleifer, Michael C. Jensen, Robert E. Hall, Andrei Shleifer, and William H. Meckling, "Economics and Organizational Innovation," *Contemporary Economic Policy* 12, no. 2 (1994): pp. 1–20.

165. Louis Lowenstein, "No More Cozy Management Buyouts," *Harvard Business Review* 64, no. 1 (1986): pp. 147–56.

166. George Anders, *Merchants of Debt: KKR and the Mortgaging of American Business* (New York: Basic Books, 1992), p. 21. Tax deductions on corporate and other forms of debt had been in place since 1909, but it was only in the newly abundant credit conditions of the 1980s that this fact encouraged a widespread substitution of debt for equity finance.

167. Lowenstein, "No More Cozy Management Buyouts," p. 153.

168. Chris Katterjohn, "Gaining on Capital Gains," *Indianapolis Business Journal* 7, no. 29 (1986): p. 9A. On "mirror subsidiaries," see Anders, *Merchants of Debt*, p. 220.

169. Ford S. Worthy, "Wes Threatens to Pull out of Wesray," *Fortune*, July 21, 1986, p. 50; Robert McKay, "Dollar Bill Simon," *Cincinnati Magazine*, November 1986, pp. 132–36.

170. McKay, "Dollar Bill Simon," p. 133.

171. On the decline in business investment relative to GDP, see Kotz, *The Rise and Fall of Neoliberal Capitalism*, pp. 92–93.

172. Peter T. Kilborn, "Americans Saving Less Now than before the '81 Tax Act," *New York Times*, September 6, 1983. The article quotes Norman B. Ture, who found the results "disturbing" and "very surprising." On the long-term decline in the U.S. savings rate, see Kotz, *The Rise and Fall of Neoliberal Capitalism*, pp. 93–94.

173. Greider, *Secrets of the Temple*, p. 552.

174. As noted by Jonathan Levy, "future 'return on equity,' or the trajectory of the stock, replaces 'return on investment,' or the return on the company's past outlay of resources, in order to produce something and sell it above its cost of production." Levy, *Ages of American Capitalism*, p. 621. By incorporating unrealized capital gains into a revised concept of savings, Jacob A. Robbins contests the view that the United States experienced a precipitous decline in savings and "investment" after 1980. Robbins, "Capital Gains and the Distribution of Income in the United States," pp. 1–4.

175. *Utilization of Pension Plan Assets in Leveraged Buyouts and Related Transactions: Hearing before the Subcommittee on Oversight of the Committee on Ways and Means, House of Representatives, One Hundred First Congress, First Session*, April 27, 1989, vol. 4 (Washington, DC: U.S. Government Printing Office, 1989).

176. McCarthy, *Dismantling Solidarity*, p. 77.

177. For an illuminating analysis of shareholder activism on the part of employee pension funds, both in the public and private sector, see Sanford M. Jacoby, *Labor in the Age of Finance: Pensions, Politics, and Corporations from Deindustrialization to Dodd-Frank* (Princeton, NJ: Princeton University Press, 2021).

178. Kenneth B. Noble, "Revival for Stock Options?," *New York Times*, June 28, 1981. For a history of the stock option as a form of executive compensation, see William Lazonick, *Sustainable Prosperity in the New Economy? Business Organization and High-Tech Employment in the United States* (Kalamazoo, MI: W. E. Upjohn Institute for Employment Research, 2009), pp. 48–50.

179. Lazonick, *Sustainable Prosperity in the New Economy?*, p. 50.

180. Ibid., pp. 51–66.

181. Jensen and Meckling, "Theory of the Firm."

182. Lawrence Mishel and Jared Bernstein, *The State of Working America 1994–95* (Armonk, NY: M. E. Sharpe, 1994), p. 52.

183. Ibid., pp. 52–53.

184. Ibid., p. 248.

185. As noted by Mishel and Bernstein, "most wealth growth arose from the appreciation (or capital gains) of preexisting wealth and not from savings out of income." Ibid., p. 246.

186. On the extraordinary tax shelter opportunities opened up by the ERTA's accelerated depreciation rules, see C. Eugene Steuerle, *The Tax Decade: How Taxes Came to Dominate the Public Agenda* (Washington, DC: Urban Institute Press, 1991), pp. 48–50.

187. Kuttner, *Economic Illusion*, pp. 197–99.

188. Real estate industry insiders were keenly attuned to these special benefits from the moment the ERTA was passed. See Howard L. Braitman, James J. Klink, and Bernard M. Shapiro, "Real Estate Industry Benefits from ERTA 1981," *CPA Journal* 52, no. 3 (1982): pp. 32–38.

189. On Carter's tentative reindustrialization policies, see Collins, *More*, pp. 172–74.

190. Cathie J. Martin notes that the chief advocates of the ERTA's accelerated depreciation schedules were primary industry, particular timber and steel, and capital-intensive manufacturing. Cathie J. Martin, *Shifting the Burden: The Struggle over Growth and Corporate Taxation* (Chicago: University of Chicago Press, 1991), pp. 115, 117.

191. Norman B. Ture, "Ture on Supply-side Policies and Reindustrialization," *Tax Notes* 19, no. 14 (1982): p. 236.

192. Barry Bluestone and Bennett Harrison, *The Deindustrialization of America* (New York: Basic Books, 1982), pp. 6–10. Even the small increase in capital spending that occurred after Reagan's 1981 tax cuts revealed a worrying preference for short-term capital equipment (trucks and cars) over new plants. Much of this new capital equipment was imported. Steven Greenhouse, "Pitfalls in the Capital Spending Boom," *New York Times*, June 3, 1984. On the growing portfolio of real estate investments held by Fortune 500 corporations in the 1980s, see John R. Logan and Harvey L. Molotch, *Urban Fortunes: The Political Economy of Place* (Berkeley: University of California Press, 1987), p. 230.

193. Stein, *Capital City*, p. 45. For earlier discussions of the autonomization of real estate, see Susan S. Fainstein, *The City Builders: Property, Politics, and Planning in London and New York* (Oxford, UK: Blackwell, 1994), pp. 220–23; Jason Hackworth, *The Neoliberal City: Governance, Ideology, and Development in American Urbanism* (Ithaca, NY: Cornell University Press, 2007), pp. 77–78; and Rachel Weber, *From Boom to Bubble: How Finance Built the New Chicago* (Chicago: University of Chicago Press, 2015), pp. 50–54. Much of this literature builds on Harvey's early theses on real estate. Harvey was among the first to recognize the newly central role of real estate to the urban and global economy of the 1980s. However, his argument rested on a dubious distinction between the primary and secondary circuits of capitalism that saw real estate as merely responding to booms and busts in the sphere of "real production." Thus, according to Harvey's early "capital switching" thesis, capital switched into the "secondary" circuit of real estate investment only when there was overaccumulation in the "primary circuit" of industrial production. David Harvey, "The Urban Process under Capitalism: A Framework for Analysis," in *Urbanization and Urban Planning in Capitalist Society*, ed. Michael Dear and Allen J. Scott (London: Methuen, 1981), pp. 91–121. Although indebted to Harvey, much of the subsequent literature has challenged his heuristics of primary and secondary, real and fictitious sources of production.

194. Stein, *Capital City*, p. 37.

195. Marx's "general formula for capital" is a precise definition of capital gains. "Value is here the subject of a process in which, while constantly assuming the form in turn of money and commodities, it changes its own magnitude, throws off surplus-value from itself considered as original value, and thus valorizes itself independently. For the movement in the course of which it adds surplus-value is its own movement, its valorization is therefore self-valorization [*Selbstverwertung*]. By virtue of being value, it has acquired the occult ability to add value to itself. It brings forth living offspring, or at least lays golden eggs." Karl Marx, *Capital: A Critique of Political Economy*, trans. Ben Fowkes (London: Penguin Books, 1990), p. 1:255.

196. Moody, *From Welfare State to Real Estate*, pp. 12, 57.

197. Stein, *Capital City*, p. 66.

198. Ibid., pp. 57–58, 65–66; Rachel Weber, "Selling City Futures: The Financialization of Urban Redevelopment Policy," *Economic Geography* 86, no. 3 (2010): pp. 251–74.

199. Lynn E. Browne and Karl E. Case, "How the Commercial Real Estate Boom Undid the Banks," *Federal Reserve Bank of Boston* 36 (1992): p. 63.

200. Ibid., p. 66.

201. Min Hwang, "Financing Real Estate Development: A Case Study of the US Real Estate Market in the 2000s," in *The Global Financial Crisis and Housing: A New Policy Paradigm*, ed. Susan Wachter, Man Cho, and Moo Joong Tcha (Cheltenham, UK: Edward Elgar, 2014), p. 154.

202. Browne and Case, "How the Commercial Real Estate Boom Undid the Banks," pp. 64–66; Martin Lowy, *High Rollers: Inside the Savings and Loan Debacle* (New York: Praeger, 1992), p. 87.

203. Jason Barr, Fred H. Smith, and Sayali J. Kulkarni, "What's Manhattan Worth? A Land Values Index from 1950 to 2014," *Regional Science and Urban Economics* 70 (2019): p. 10.

204. As pointed out by Sheldon Pollack, the combined effect of these deductions was to create a negative tax rate. "With a negative tax rate, an investor could be economically better off making an entirely worthless investment solely on account of the tax benefits. In effect, a positive subsidy was paid out of the federal Treasury to support the taxpayer's investment." Sheldon D. Pollack, *The Failure of U.S. Tax Policy: Revenue and Politics* (University Park: Pennsylvania State University Press, 2010), p. 91.

205. David Cay Johnston, *The Making of Donald Trump*, 2nd ed. (London: Hardie Grant, 2018), pp. 104–105. Johnston offers a lengthy reflection on Trump's use of accelerated depreciation rules. On the use of the pass-through partnership form in real estate, see Joe Light, "Trump Companies Were in the Red: He's Reaped the Rewards Since," *National Real Estate Investor*, May 15, 2019.

206. Donald J. Trump and Tony Schwartz, *Trump: The Art of the Deal* (London: Penguin Books, 1987), p. 219.

207. Hyman P. Minsky, "The Bubble in the Price of Baseball Cards, Paper 94," Hyman

Minsky Archive (1990), p. 6. For an extended exegesis of this text with close reference to Trump's business dealings of the time, see Kevin W. Capehart, "Hyman Minsky's Interpretation of Donald Trump," *Journal of Post-Keynesian Economics* 38, no. 3 (2015): pp. 477–92.

208. Minsky, "The Bubble in the Price of Baseball Cards," p. 7.

209. For Minsky, hedge finance refers to a situation where cash flows from an investment are large enough to meet the entire payment commitments on a debt. Speculative finance takes place when the cash flows from an investment are large enough to meet current interest payments but not sufficient to pay down principal. Speculative investors must continually refinance their positions and are vulnerable to interest rate hikes, which may exceed their current returns on investment. Ponzi finance occurs when current payments on a debt must be financed by further borrowing. Hyman P. Minsky, *Can "It" Happen Again? Essays on Instability and Finance* (Armonk, NY: M. E. Sharpe, 1982), pp. 66–67; Hyman P. Minsky, "On the Non-Neutrality of Money," *Federal Reserve Bank of New York Quarterly Review* 18, no. 1 (1992–1993): pp. 77–82. In the latter work, Minsky noted that "construction financing is almost always a prearranged Ponzi financing scheme that is to be validated by the payment on completion, usually by funds derived from a takeout mortgage" (p. 80).

210. Minsky, "The Bubble in the Price of Baseball Cards," p. 7.

211. On the poverty of Minsky's thought when it comes to taxation, see Tim Edgar, "Financial Instability, Tax Policy, and the Tax Expenditure Concept," *SMU Law Review* 63, no. 2 (2010): pp. 969–1032. Minsky supported a progressive income tax on income from labor but was opposed to the corporate income tax.

212. Edgar, "Financial Instability, Tax Policy, and the Tax Expenditure Concept," p. 1000. See also pp. 1014–17 on the capital gains tax preference in particular. This accords with Pistor's claim that financial assets are legally created and enforced. Katharina Pistor, *The Code of Capital: How the Law Creates Wealth and Inequality* (Princeton, NJ: Princeton University Press, 2019).

213. William Niskanen, *Reaganomics: An Insider's Account of the Policies and the People* (Oxford: Oxford University Press, 1988), p. 86; Michael Wine, "Industries Give Surprising Support to Senate Tax Plan," *Los Angeles Times*, May 10, 1986.

214. Tax Reform Act of 1986, Public Law 99–514 (H.R. 3838). For an account of the political machinations behind the Tax Reform Act of 1986 and the defeat of the original ERTA coalition, see Jeffrey H. Birnbaum and Alan S. Murray, *Showdown at Gucci Gulch: Lawmakers, Lobbyists, and the Unlikely Triumph of Tax Reform* (New York: Random House, 1987); Timothy J. Conlan, Margaret T. Wrightson, and David R. Beam, *Taxing Choices: The Politics of Tax Reform* (Washington, DC: Congressional Quarterly, 1990).

215. Niskanen, *Reaganomics*, p. 104.

216. Tax Reform Act of 1986, Public Law 99–514 (H.R. 3838), Secs. 301 and 302. 26 U.S. Code § 1 (j) and 6 U.S. Code § 1202.

217. 26 U.S. Code § 469. In fact, the Reagan administration had already signaled its willingness to backtrack on accelerated depreciation rules as early as 1982, when soaring

deficits and interest rates convinced Reagan that some of the more radical provisions contained in the ERTA needed to be scaled back. Martin, *Shifting the Burden*, pp. 135–58. The Tax Equity and Fiscal Responsibility Act (TEFRA) of 1982, introduced barely a year after the passage of the ERTA, repealed an additional liberalization of accelerated depreciation provisions that was scheduled to begin in 1985. Tax Equity and Fiscal Responsibility Act (TEFRA) of 1982, Pub. L. No. 97–248, 51 U.S.L.W. 5 (1982).

218. Roy E. Cordato, "Destroying Real Estate through the Tax Code," *CPA Journal* 61, no. 6 (1991): pp. 8, 79.

219. Hwang, "Financing Real Estate Development," pp. 153–54.

220. Lowy, *High Rollers*; Kitty Calavita, Henry N. Pontell, and Robert Tillman, *Big Money Crime: Fraud and Politics in the Savings and Loan Crisis* (Berkeley: University of California Press, 1997).

221. Russ Buettner and Susanne Craig, "Decade in the Red: Trump Tax Figures Show over $1 Billion in Business Losses," *New York Times*, May 8, 2019.

222. John Cassidy, "Donald Trump's Business Failures Were Very Real," *New Yorker*, May 10, 2019; Henry Grabar, "Donald Trump Lost a Billion Dollars—Just Not His Own," *Slate*, May 8, 2019.

223. Bernstein, *American Oligarchs*, p. 101.

224. Quoted in ibid., 102.

225. Gwenda Blair, *Donald Trump: Master Apprentice* (New York: Simon & Schuster, 2005), p. 175.

226. On the evolution of corporate and business bankruptcy from the New Deal to 1978, see David Steel, *Debt's Dominion: A History of Bankruptcy Law in America* (Princeton, NJ: Princeton University Press, 2014), pp. 160–84. On the rise of strategic bankruptcy in the 1990s, see Kevin J. Delaney, *Strategic Bankruptcy: How Corporations and Creditors Use Chapter 11 to Their Advantage* (Berkeley: University of California Press, 1998).

227. On the history of this campaign by the major real estate trade associations and Trump's role within it, see Justin Miller, "How the Real Estate Lobby—and Trump—Got a Huge Tax Break," *American Prospect*, October 7, 2016.

228. Donald J. Trump, *The Credit Shortage: Is It Stifling Economic Recovery? Hearing before the Task Force on Urgent Fiscal Issues of the Committee on the Budget House of Representatives, One Hundred and Second Congress, First Session, November 21, 1991* (Washington, DC: U.S. Government Printing Office, 1992), p. 24.

229. Ibid., p. 25.

230. Ibid., p. 27.

231. Ibid.

232. Daniel N. Shaviro, "Narrowing the Passive Loss Rules: The New Rental Exception for Real Estate Operators," *Tax Management Real Estate Journal* 9, no. 11 (1993): p. 209.

233. Nicholas Confessore and Binyamin Appelbaum, "How a Simple Tax Rule Helped Trump Turn a Huge Loss into a Plus," *New York Times*, October 3, 2016. The Revenue Act of 1918 was the first to allow businesses to use their annual net operating losses to offset

their tax liabilities in previous or future years, on the grounds that they should not be punished for the volatilities of the business cycle. The act limited the carryforward and carryback period to one year. It now stands at twenty years. Many states offer similar provisions on state tax liabilities. "The Tax Treatment of Net Operating Losses: In Brief," *Congressional Research Service*, October 4, 2017.

234. Russ Buettner and Susanne Craig, "Decade in the Red: Trump Tax Figures Show over $1 Billion in Business Losses," *New York Times*, May 8, 2019.

235. Buettner and Craig, "Decade in the Red"; Gabriel J.X. Dance and Aaron Byrd, "How Donald Trump Avoided Taxes Using Other People's Money," *New York Times*, October 31, 2016. Trump claims to have received over $200 million for *The Apprentice* and *The Celebrity Apprentice* but paid no federal income tax on this.

236. On Trump's use of other people's money to concoct his own bailout, see Dance and Byrd, "How Donald Trump Avoided Taxes"; Light, "Trump Companies Were in the Red: He's Reaped the Rewards Since."

237. On self-appreciation as a psychic economy, see Michel Feher, "Self-Appreciation; or, The Aspirations of Human Capital," *Public Culture* 21 no. 1 (2009): pp. 21–41. According to Feher, "an investor in his or her human capital is concerned less with maximizing the returns on his or her investments—whether monetary or psychic—than with appreciating, that is, increasing the stock value of the capital to which he or she is identified. In other words, insofar as our condition is that of human capital in a neoliberal environment, our main purpose is not so much to profit from our accumulated potential as to constantly value or appreciate ourselves—or at least prevent our own depreciation" (p. 27). The pertinence of this analysis to an understanding of Trump's political persona is striking.

238. Quoted in Confessore and Appelbaum, "Simple Tax Rule."

239. On the supply-side influence in the George W. Bush administration, see Jacob S. Hacker and Paul Pierson, "Tax Politics and the Struggle over Activist Government," in *The Transformation of American Politics: Activist Government and the Rise of Conservatism*, ed. Theda Skocpol and Paul Pierson (Princeton, NJ: Princeton University Press, 2007), pp. 256–80; James T. Patterson, "Transformative Economic Policies: Tax Cutting, Stimuli, and Bailouts," in *The Presidency of George W. Bush: A First Historical Assessment*, ed. Julian E. Zelizer (Princeton, NJ: Princeton University Press, 2010), pp. 114–38. On the elite supply-side views of Marin Feldstein, Lawrence Lindsey, and R. Glenn Hubbard and their influence on the Bush administration, see Daniel Altman, *Neoeconomy: George Bush's Revolutionary Gamble with America's Future* (New York: Public Affairs, 2004); Ron Suskind, *The Price of Loyalty* (New York: Simon & Schuster, 2013), pp. 33–34; Leonhardt, "Scholarly Mentor to Bush's Team."

240. Bernasek, "The Next Greenspan?"

241. Lawrence B. Lindsey, *The Growth Experiment: How the New Tax Policy Is Transforming the U.S. Economy* (New York: Basic Books, 1990), pp. 180–95.

242. Leonhardt, "Scholarly Mentor to Bush's Team"; Altman, *Neoeconomy*, pp. 39 and 42.

243. Only a few political journalists recognized Feldstein's supply-side credentials. The

New York Times quoted former Clinton advisor Jonathan Gruber, according to whom Feldstein was "basically the father of supply-side economics—not the Laffer curve, the stupid side of supply-side economics." Leonhardt, "Scholarly Mentor to Bush's Team," p. 12. *Fortune* magazine quoted Feldstein, who declared himself "a true supply-sider" while admitting that "some of the extreme statements people were making were giving it a bad name." Bernasek, "The Next Greenspan?," On the Democrats' side, Ed Kilgore of the Democratic Leadership Council recognized that Bush was running a supply-side operation by stealth. Ed Kilgore, "Starving the Beast: If President Bush Keeps Listening to Grover Norquist, Republicans Won't Have a Government to Kick Around Anymore," *Democratic Blueprint* 22 (2003): pp. 9–11.

244. On this shift in Republican Party tax politics, see Hacker and Pierson, "Tax Politics and the Struggle over Activist Government," pp. 256–80; James T. Patterson, "Transformative Economic Policies: Tax Cutting, Stimuli, and Bailouts," in Zelizer, *The Presidency of George W. Bush*, pp. 114–38.

245. "O'Neill Says Cheney Told Him, 'Deficits Don't Matter,'" *Chicago Tribune*, January 12, 2004. The full version of Cheney's observation, as recounted by Paul O'Neill, was this: "Reagan proved deficits don't matter." O'Neill, who was concerned about the impact of Bush's tax cuts on the deficit, was dismissed in December 2002, a few months after this exchange with Cheney.

246. Bernasek, "The Next Greenspan?"

247. W. Elliot Brownlee, *Federal Taxation in America: A History* (Cambridge: Cambridge University Press, 2018), pp. 247–48.

248. Brownlee, *Federal Taxation in America*, p. 250.

249. Patterson, "Transformative Economic Policies," p. 122.

250. Martin Feldstein, "Kill the Death Tax Now," *Wall Street Journal*, July 14, 2000. According to Feldstein, the estate tax had the perverse effect of encouraging high income earners "to retire early or simply to work less, save less and take less investment risk. The result is not only to waste their talents but also to hurt those who would otherwise benefit from their efforts, their entrepreneurship, their management skills and their saving and investment."

251. Brownlee, *Federal Taxation in America*, pp. 262–63; Patterson, "Transformative Economic Policies," pp. 125–26.

252. Brownlee, *Federal Taxation in America*, p. 265.

253. On the responsiveness of the private equity market to changes in the tax rate on capital gains, see Alex Holcomb, Paul Mason, and Harold H. Zhang, "Investment Income Taxes and Private Equity Acquisition Activity," *Journal of Empirical Finance* 59, no. C (2020): pp. 25–51. The authors calculate that private equity acquisitions increased more than 75 percent following the 2003 tax cut. On the Bush-era private equity boom, see Emily Thornton, "Gluttons at the Gate," *BusinessWeek*, October 30, 2006, pp. 58–66.

254. Eileen Appelbaum and Rosemary Batt, *Private Equity at Work: When Wall Street Manages Main Street* (New York: Russell Sage Foundation, 2014), pp. 3, 32–33, 55. It is the

general partner, as distinct from the limited partners, who stands to gain most from this arrangement: besides receiving 20 percent of the fund's value in management fees for the duration of the fund, the standard agreement reserves a full 20 percent of the gains from investment for the general partner, once a hurdle profit of 8 percent has been achieved.

255. Further to these incentives, debt-funded investment is protected by special tax preferences on interest, and in a private equity deal, the legal liability for debt in in any case borne by the target company. See ibid., pp. 32–33.

256. Ibid., p. 16, and "Buyout Industry: Thank You Sarbanes-Oxley," *Corporate Financing Week* 32, no. 39 (2006): p. 5.

257. Lazonick, *Sustainable Prosperity in the New Economy?*, pp. 244–45.

258. On the relationship between stock price appreciation, capital gains, and buybacks, see Joe Hughes, "Democrats Seek to Eliminate the Stock Buyback Advantage," *Just Taxes Blog*, ITEP Institute on Taxation and Tax Policy, November 4, 2021.

259. In 1997, for the first time, share repurchases outpaced dividends as the dominant form of shareholder cash distribution in the United States—a historic shift that even some shareholder value exponents saw as a dereliction of managerial duties. Liyu Zeng and Priscilla Luk, "Examining Share Repurchasing and the S&P Buyback Indices in the U.S. Market," *S&P Dow Jones Indices*, March 2020, pp. 1–20.

260. *Jobs and Growth Tax Relief Reconciliation Act of 2003: Explanation and Analysis as Signed by the President on May 28, 2003* (Chicago: CCH Incorporated, 2003), p. 31.

261. Jennifer Blouin and Linda Krull, "Bringing It Home: A Study of the Incentives Surrounding the Repatriation of Foreign Earnings under the American Jobs Creation Act of 2004," *Journal of Accounting Research* 47, no. 4 (2009): pp. 1027–59.

262. John R. Boatright, "Compensation: Unjust or Just Right," in *The Oxford Handbook of Business Ethics*, ed. George G. Brenkert and Tom L. Beauchamp (Oxford: Oxford University Press, 2012), p. 165.

263. Boatright, "Compensation: Unjust or Just Right," p. 164.

264. Several scholars have commented on Greenspan's apparent conversion from monetary hawk to monetary enabler in the late 1990s. See, for example, Frederick Sheehan and William A. Fleckenstein, *Greenspan's Bubbles: The Age of Ignorance at the Federal Reserve* (New York: McGraw-Hill, 2008), pp. 22–26; Peter Hartcher, *Bubble Man* (New York: Norton, 2006), pp. 132–38.

265. Sebastian Mallaby is illuminating when it comes to the evolution of Greenspan's thinking on asset price appreciation and capital gains. Mallaby's account provides an important corrective to those who see Greenspan's actions in the late 1990s as either an incomprehensible about-face or an example of his blind commitment to the efficient markets hypothesis. See Sebastian Mallaby, *The Man Who Knew: The Life and Times of Alan Greenspan* (London: Bloomsbury, 2016), pp. 49–52, 208–14.

266. Ibid., pp. 209–14.

267. In a 1999 speech before Congress, Greenspan observed that "when we can be preemptive, we should be" before emphasizing that preemptive action was not possible in the

case of asset price inflation. The central bank, he insisted, "cannot effectively directly target stock or other asset prices. Should an asset bubble arise, or even if one is already in train, monetary policy properly calibrated can doubtless mitigate at least part of the impact on the economy. And obviously, if we could find a way to prevent or deflate emerging bubbles, we would be better off. But identifying a bubble in the process of inflating may be among the most formidable challenges confronting a central bank, pitting its own assessment of fundamentals against the combined judgement of millions of investors." With this admission of defeat, he concluded that it was "the job of economic policy makers to *mitigate the fallout when it occurs and, hopefully, ease the transition to the next expansion*" (my italics). Alan Greenspan, "Testimony of Chairman Alan Greenspan, the Federal Reserve's Semiannual Report on Monetary Policy before the Committee on Banking and Financial Services," U.S. House of Representatives, July 22, 1999. Greenspan reiterated the point in 2002 before the Economic Club of New York. Alan Greenspan, "Issues for Monetary Policy: Remarks by Mr. Alan Greenspan, Chairman of the Board of Governors of the US Federal Reserve System," December 19, 2002.

268. Sandeep Dahiya, Bardia Kamrad, Valerio Poti, and Akhtar Siddique, "Fed Put in the Equity Options Markets," *Social Science Research Network*, August 24, 2022.

269. Jennifer Dauble, "CNBC Exclusive: CNBC Transcript Alan Greenspan, Former Federal Reserve Chairman, on CNBC's 'Squawk Box' Today," CNBC, July 1, 2010.

270. Lev Menand, *The Fed Unbound: Central Banking in a Time of Crisis* (New York: Columbia Global Reports, 2022), pp. 47–48.

271. For accounts of the Federal Reserve's actions since 2008, see Adam Tooze, *Crashed: How a Decade of Financial Crises Changed the World* (New York: Penguin Press, 2019), pp. 367–68, 471–79; Adam Tooze, *Shutdown: How Covid Shook the World's Economy* (New York: Viking, 2021), pp. 119–45; and Menand, *The Fed Unbound*. On the Federal Reserve as de facto central bank to the world, see Stefan Eich, *The Currency of Politics: The Political Theory of Money from Aristotle to Keynes* (Princeton, NJ: Princeton University Press, 2022), p. 211. On the Federal Reserve as dealer or market maker of last resort, see Perry Mehrling, *The New Lombard Street* (Princeton, NJ: Princeton University Press, 2010), p. 137.

272. On quantitative easing (QE) as "trickle-down" policy, see Karen Petrou, *Engine of Inequality: The Fed and the Future of Wealth in America* (New York: Wiley, 2021), pp. 38–39. Four years into the experiment, Ben Bernanke was still predicting that "declining yields and rising asset prices" would at some point "ease overall financial conditions and stimulate economic activity" across the economy. Ben Bernanke, "Monetary Policy since the Onset of the Crisis," Federal Reserve Bank of Kansas City Economic Symposium, Jackson Hole, Wyoming, August 31, 2012.

273. Jesse Colombo, "The U.S. Is Experiencing a Dangerous Corporate Debt Bubble," *Forbes*, August 29, 2018. On the use of leverage to finance cash distributions, see William Lazonick and Jang-Sup Shin, *Predatory Value Extraction: How the Looting of the Business Corporation Became the US Norm and How Sustainable Prosperity Can Be Restored* (Oxford: Oxford University Press, 2019), p. 80.

274. Editorial Board, "Private Equity's Risky Cheap Debt Move," *Financial Times*, September 23, 2020; Davide Scigliuzzo, Kelsey Butler, and Sally Bakewell, "Everything Is Private Equity Now," *BusinessWeek*, October 9, 2019.

275. The last three chairs of the U.S. Federal Reserve have been loath to acknowledge any link between unconventional monetary policy and soaring inequality. Other central bank officials have been surprisingly forthcoming. In 2012, an anonymous report in the Bank of England's quarterly bulletin admitted that rising asset prices had overwhelmingly benefited the top 5 percent of households, due to the disproportionate share of financial assets such as stocks and bonds in their wealth portfolios. Anonymous, "The Distributional Effects of Asset Purchases," *Bank of England Quarterly Bulletin* 52, no. 3 (2012): 254–66. Although more evasive on the question of their own responsibility, both the bank's former governor Mark Carney and former chief economist Andrew Haldane have recognized the role played by QE in exacerbating extreme wealth concentration. Emily Cadman, "Mark Carney Warns of Dangers of Growing Inequality," *Financial Times*, May 28, 2014; Andrew G. Haldane, "Unfair Shares," Bristol Festival of Ideas, May 21, 2014. Others, including in-house economists at the Federal Reserve and Bank for International Settlements, have added their voice to the chorus, while in the meantime a handful of academic economists have undertaken the slow work of demonstrating the causal connections between ultra-low interest rates, central bank asset purchases, and the swollen asset portfolios of the wealthiest households. See, for instance, Stephen D. Williamson, "Quantitative Easing: How Well Does This Tool Work?," Federal Reserve Bank of St. Louis, August 18, 2017; Dietrich Domanski, Michela Scatigna, and Anna Zabai, "Wealth Inequality and Monetary Policy," *BIS Quarterly Review* (March 2016): pp. 45–64. On the different distributive effects of real estate and stock price surges, see Moritz Kuhn, Moritz Schularick, and Ulrike Steins, "Income and Wealth Inequality in America, 1949–2016," *Journal of Political Economy* 128, no. 9 (2020): pp. 3469–519. For an extensive analysis of the links between Federal Reserve monetary policy and rising inequality, see Petrou, *Engine of Inequality*.

276. Kuhn, Schularick, and Steins, "Income and Wealth Inequality in America, 1949–2016," p. 3473.

277. Chase Peterson-Withorn, "How Much Money America's Billionaires Have Made during the Covid-19 Pandemic," *Forbes*, April 30, 2021.

278. Chuck Collins, Joe Fitzgerald, Helen Flannery, Omar Ocampo, Sophia Paslaski, and Kalena Thomhave, *Silver Spoon Oligarchs: How America's 50 Largest Inherited Wealth Dynasties Accelerate Inequality* (Washington, DC: Institute for Policy Studies, 2021), p. 11.

279. Peter W. Bernstein and Annalyn Swan, *All the Money in the World: How the Forbes 400 Make—and Spend—Their Fortunes* (New York: Knopf, 2008), pp. 176–81; Kate Vinton, "Meet the 14 Unicorn Start-ups That Have Created 25 Billionaires," *Forbes*, March 6, 2016; Stephen Todd Walker, *Understanding Alternative Investments* (New York: Palgrave Macmillan, 2017), pp. 81–82.

280. Bernstein and Swan, *All the Money in the World*, pp. 13–15.

281. Alfred D. Chandler Jr., *The Visible Hand: The Managerial Revolution in American*

Business (Cambridge, MA: Belknap Press of Harvard University Press, 1977), pp. 9–10. For a critical commentary on the history of family capitalism and its place in the mainstream of organizational theory, see Harold James, *Family Capitalism: Wendels, Haniels, Falcks, and the Continental European Model* (Cambridge, MA: Belknap Press of Harvard University Press, 2006), pp. 6–20. As noted by James, the continued existence of closely held family businesses in continental Europe throughout the twentieth century was seen as evidence of these countries' industrial backwardness.

282. Richard Lachmann, "Coda: American Patrimonialism: The Return of the Repressed," *Annals of the American Academy of Political and Social Science* 636, no. 1 (2011): p. 220.

283. The "Berle and Means" corporation refers to the work of the legal scholar Adolf Berle and the economist Gardiner Means, who postulated that the modern publicly traded corporation involved a separation between ownership (now distributed among public shareholders) and control (now consigned to a meritocratic class of professional managers). Adolf Berle and Gardiner Means, *The Modern Corporation and Private Property* (New York: Harcourt, Brace, and World, 1932).

284. For a general discussion of the decline of the public corporation, see Gerald F. Davis, *The Vanishing American Corporation: Navigating the Hazards of a New Economy* (New York: Penguin Random House, 2016). And for an insightful reflection on the differences between "managerial" and "dynastic capitalism," see Steve Fraser, "Playing God: The Rebirth of Family Capitalism," in *Mongrel Firebugs and Men of Property* (New York: Verso, 2019), pp. 223–40. On the rise of private capitalism as a reactionary development, see Doug Henwood, "Take Me to Your Leader: The Rot of the American Ruling Class," *Jacobin*, April 27, 2021.

285. The argument is made most forcefully by sociologist Mark Mizruchi, who contends that the early successes of the business revolt during the Reagan administration—including the deregulation of commercial banking and tax cuts to capital gains—ultimately dissolved the class foundations of the corporate managerial elite that had driven the revolt in the first place. The hostile takeover wave of the 1980s produced a new generation of corporate stockholders whose skill set brought them closer to the financial trader than the long-sighted corporate manager of the postwar era. Thus, although the "corporate elite...had...seemingly won the war," its victory had the "unintended consequence" of "undoing the elite itself." Mark S. Mizruchi, *The Fracturing of the American Corporate Elite* (Cambridge, MA: Harvard University Press, 2013), p. 197. Incidentally, the success of the business revolt also led to the marginalization of the Business Roundtable and the rise of a new generation of business lobbies. Jacob S. Hacker and Paul Pierson. *American Amnesia: How the War on Government Led Us to Forget What Made America Prosper* (New York: Simon & Schuster, 2017), p. 237. Hacker and Pierson note that by the late 1990s "the Business Roundtable had lost its once preeminent position" (p. 206) and explain its fading relevance by noting that "the Roundtable's founders had built their entire political strategy around a corporate model that was fast disappearing" (p. 205).

286. Michael C. Jensen, "Eclipse of the Public Corporation," *Harvard Business Review* 67, no. 5 (1989): pp. 61–74.

287. On the rise of private capital markets, see Dawn Lim and David Brooke, "The Boom in Private Markets Has Transformed Finance," *Washington Post*, July 18, 2022. On the regulatory conditions that facilitated their growth, see Allison Herren Lee, "Going Dark: The Growth of Private Markets and the Impact on Investors and the Economy," U.S. Securities and Exchange Commission, October 12, 2021. On the rise of private companies financed outside the public markets, see Jakob Wilhelmus and William Lee, *Companies Rush to Go Private*, August (Santa Monica, CA: Milken Institute, 2018).

288. Elisabeth de Fontenay, "The Deregulation of Private Capital and the Decline of the Public Company," *Hastings Law Journal* 68 (2017): p. 448.

289. Ibid., pp. 447, 456–59, 463.

290. Ibid., pp. 455, 461.

291. Ironically, dual-class share structures became popular in the 1980s as a defense against leveraged buyouts. In the long run, however, both leveraged buyouts and dual-class share structures have had the same effect of elevating the power of small groups of owners (private equity partners, hedge fund managers, or in this case, shareholders with disproportionate voting rights). As noted by Daniel Wells, "in 2005, only 1% of IPOs on U.S. exchanges comprised dual (or more) classes of stock, but by 2017 this figure was 19%. In 2004, Google was one of the first major technology companies to employ the structure, and now it is almost de rigueur among technology start-up and other, 'unicorn' (start-ups worth $1 billion) IPOs. In the last ten years alone, Facebook, GoPro, Groupon, LinkedIn, Square, TripAdvisor, Yelp, Zillow, and Zynga have all gone public with dual-class share structures. Snapchat's parent company, Snap Inc., appears to have presented something of a high-water mark in 2017 by issuing only non-voting shares to its ordinary shareholders at IPO." Daniel Wells, "Shareholder Inequity in the Age of Big Tech: Public Policy Dangers of Dual-Class Share Structures and the Case for Congressional Action," *Northeastern University Law Review* 13 no. 1 (2021): p. 46.

292. According to Robert J. Jackson Jr., nearly half of the companies that went public with dual-class shares since 2003 have given corporate insiders outsized voting rights in perpetuity. Commissioner Robert J. Jackson Jr., "Perpetual Dual-Class Stock: The Case Against Corporate Royalty," U.S. Securities and Exchange Commission, February 15, 2018.

293. In 2019, the research firm Campden Wealth estimated the global value of single-family offices at almost $6 trillion—larger than the entire hedge fund industry. James Beech "Global Family Office Growth Soars," CampdenFB, July 18, 2019.

294. Family offices can take the form of single-family private investment firms or multifamily offices catering to a client base of several or more families. While family offices in general have been on the rise since the 1980s, the more recent trend has been toward the establishment of single-family offices. I therefore focus my analysis on the single-family office here. For an ethnographic account of the family office, see Luna Glucksberg and Roger Burrows, "Family Offices and the Contemporary Infrastructures of Dynastic Wealth," *Sociologica* 2 (2016): pp. 1–23.

295. Peter Collier and David Horowitz, *The Rockefellers: An American Dynasty* (New York: Holt, Rinehart, and Winston, 1975), pp. 52–54.

296. Chuck Collins, *The Wealth Hoarders* (London: Polity, 2021), p. 97.

297. Anupreeta Das and Juliet Chung, "New Force on Wall Street: The 'Family Office,'" *Wall Street Journal*, March 10, 2017.

298. Mark S. Greenfield and Garry J. Padrta Jr., "The Family Office as Private Equity Investor," *Bloomberg Law*, September 4, 2020. The most recent surveys of family offices report that 96 percent of U.S.-based family offices invest in private equity, either directly or by partnering with funds. Campden Wealth, *The North America Family Office Report* (London: Campden Wealth, 2021), p. 32; UBS, *Global Family Office Report* (Zurich: UBS, 2022), pp. 11, 25–26. As a rule, even *passive* private equity investments generate higher returns than the average portfolio of stocks and bonds or shares in an exchange-traded fund; *active* private equity investments, however, can generate even higher returns. *The North America Family Office Report*, p. 32.

299. On the growing competition between family offices, private equity firms, and hedge funds, see Das and Chung, "New Force on Wall Street."

300. On the limitation of partners and assets to kin, see "Family Office: A Small Entity Compliance Guide," U.S. Securities and Exchange Commission, November 21, 2011. On the organizational affinities between family offices, private equity, and hedge funds, see Tom Burroughes, "How Private Equity Moulds Shape of Single-Family Offices," Wealth-BriefingAsia, July 19, 2019. The organizational similarities go further than this, however. Megan Tobias Neely argues that the world of hedge fund investment already operates in a "patrimonial" manner, where the manager's personal or familial wealth typically represents a significant portion of seed funding and employment relations are organized in a patrilineal fashion that privileges white upper-class men. She observes that hedge fund managers are frequently referred to as "kings" and "chiefs." The most successful of them—Julian Robertson's Tiger Fund, for instance—spawn whole lineages of investment firms sharing the founder's signature trading style. While there are numerous examples of hedge fund managers preparing their sons for succession, Neely notes that she has only seen one instance of intergenerational handover involving a daughter. Megan Tobias Neely, *Hedged Out: Inequality and Insecurity on Wall Street* (Berkeley: University of California Press, 2022), pp. 13–14, 159–64, 191–94.

301. Simone Foxman, "Wealthy Families Are Winning Deals Away from Private Equity," Bloomberg.com, October 20, 2017; "The Rise of Permanent Capital: Single Family Offices and Direct Investing," The Stephens Group, May 31, 2019.

302. Squire Patton Boggs, "The Family Office Rule under the Investment Advisers Act," Family Office Insights, 2017; Noam Scheiber and Patricia Cohen, "For the Wealthiest, a Private Tax System That Saves them Billions," *New York Times*, December 29, 2015; Collins, *The Wealth Hoarders*, pp. 105–106. The "private advisor" exemption was first introduced under the Investment Advisors Act of 1940.

303. This is referred to as the "step-up" basis for the calculation of capital gains tax. See

James Poterba and Scott Weisbenner, "The Distributional Burden of Taxing Estates and Unrealized Capital Gains at Death," in *Rethinking Estate and Gift Taxation*, ed. William G. Gale, James R. Hines, and Joel Slemrod (Washington, DC: Brookings Institution Press, 2001), p. 422.

304. Only the nonprofit, which is exempt from the capital gains tax altogether, can claim to be more advantaged. The closest equivalent to the family capital gains tax exemption is the so-called 1031 exchange, which allows a taxpayer to postpone capital gains tax on an investment property—perhaps indefinitely—so long as they exchange it for an investment of equal market value. But while the 1031 exchange is limited to one asset class—real estate—the family tax exemption applies to *all assets* passed from one generation to another and is therefore much more comprehensive in scope.

305. Poterba and Weisbenner, "The Distributional Burden of Taxing Estates," p. 439.

306. Chye-Ching Huang and Chloe Cho, "Ten Facts You Should Know about the Federal Estate Tax," Center on Budget and Policy Priorities, October 30, 2017. I am unable to find more recent figures for unrealized capital gains, but given the enormous increase in asset prices during the pandemic, we can assume that the ratio of unrealized capital gains to overall wealth among the top one percent has increased still further.

307. These include the grantor-retained annuity trust and the dynastic trust fund. On these trust forms, see respectively Huang and Cho, "Ten Facts You Should Know about the Federal Estate Tax," and Eric Kades, "Of Piketty and Perpetuities: Dynastic Wealth in the Twenty-First Century (and Beyond)," *Boston College Law Review* 60, no. 1 (2019): pp. 145–215.

308. Fraser, "Playing God: The Rebirth of Family Capitalism," p. 224.

309. Anna Palmer and Abby Phillip, "Corporations Not Funding Super PACs," *Politico*, March 8, 2012.

310. Karl Evers-Hillstrom, "In Hyperpartisan Political Environment, Major Corporations Stay Away from Super PACs," *Open Secrets*, April 12, 2019.

311. Nicholas Confessore, Sarah Cohen, and Karen Yourish, "The Families Funding the 2016 Presidential Election," *New York Times*, October 10, 2015.

312. Marlène Benquet and Théo Bourgeron, *Alt-Finance: How the City of London Bought Democracy* (London: Pluto Press, 2022), pp. 42, 58–60. Others have posited the rise of institutional asset managers such as BlackRock, State Street, and Vanguard as the defining characteristic of early twenty-first-century capitalism. See, for example, Benjamin Braun, "Asset Management Capitalism as a Corporate Governance Regime," in *American Political Economy: Politics, Markets, Power*, ed. Jacob S. Hacker, Alexander Hertel-Fernandez, Paul Pierson, and Kathleen Thelen (New York: Cambridge University Press, 2021), pp. 270–94; Brett Christophers, *Our Lives in Their Portfolios: Why Asset Managers Own the World* (New York: Verso, 2023). Without denying the importance of this development, I follow Benquet and Bourgeron in identifying *style* of asset management—"active" versus "passive"—as a key point of distinction, the former describing the aggressive buy-and-sell strategies of genuine private equity funds and the latter characterizing the market-averaging strategies of

index and exchange-traded funds and other safe forms of institutional investment. To be sure, some firms deploy both styles of asset management and may thus have conflicting interests with regard to financial regulation. Thus, while BlackRock was spun off from the private equity firm Blackstone in 1994, it now functions primarily as an "institutional investor for institutional investors," deploying passive investment strategies on behalf of pension funds, mutual funds, and other clients. Active private equity investment now represents only one of its many services.

313. Confessore, Cohen, and Yourish, "The Families Funding the 2016 Presidential Election."

314. Michelle Celarier, "Meet the Wall Street Titans Who Back Trump," *Intelligencer,* June 22, 2016; Lucinda Shen and Stephen Gandel, "Nope, Clinton Is Not Completely Annihilating Trump among Hedge Fund Donors," *Fortune,* August 2, 2016; Gillian Tett, "Distressed-Debt Players Rule the Roost in Trump's White House," *Financial Times,* April 28, 2012.

315. A widely reported but misleading *Wall Street Journal* article published in July 2016 claimed that hedge fund donors favored Hillary Clinton over Trump. John Carney and Anupreeta Das, "Hedge Fund Money Has Vastly Favored Clinton over Trump," *Wall Street Journal,* July 29, 2016. However, the nonprofit group Open Secrets, whose data was incorrectly used in the original *Wall Street Journal* article, contested these findings. According to their data, Republicans attracted the vast majority of money from hedge funds during the 2016 cycle, though little of it went to Trump. See Alec Goodwin, "Setting It Straight: Hedge Funds to Clinton Plus Super PACs, $25.6 Million; to Trump, $2,000," *Open Secrets,* August 3, 2016.

316. Confessore, Cohen, and Yourish, "The Families Funding the 2016 Presidential Election."

317. Michela Tindera, "Here Are the Billionaires Who Donated to Joe Biden's 2020 Presidential Campaign," *Forbes,* February 17, 2021.

318. Confessore, Cohen, and Yourish, "The Families Funding the 2016 Presidential Election." On this point, I see the political composition of second-wave finance somewhat differently from Benquet and Bourgeron. Taking the Brexit campaign as their case study, Benquet and Bourgeron conclude that second-wave financial elites skew toward the right or far right and are disproportionately allied with fossil fuel and construction companies. Benquet and Bourgeron, *Alt-Finance,* p. 114. While it is true that the most publicly visible second-wave finance players in the United States seem to confirm this analysis, it is also notable that one and the same private equity firm or hedge fund (Renaissance Technologies, for instance) can include prominent donors to both Republicans and Democrats. Moreover, while second-wave finance donors to the Republican right are certainly closely allied with the fossil fuel and construction industries, another segment has close connections to the high-tech sector and appears to favor the Democrats.

319. Misyrlena Egkolfopoulou, "Private Equity Donors Favor Biden over Trump on Bet to End Chaos," *Bloomberg,* June 19, 2020.

320. Benjamin I. Page, Jason Seawright, and Matthew J. Lacombe, *Billionaires and Stealth Politics* (Chicago: University of Chicago Press, 2018), pp. 2–3, 48–49, 128, 132–33.

321. Jaime Lowe, "With 'Stealth Politics,' Billionaires Make Sure Their Money Talks," *New York Times Magazine*, April 7, 2022.

322. Henwood, "Take Me to Your Leader."

323. Derrick Wetherell, "The Bush 100," Center for Public Integrity, January 14, 2002.

324. Michela Tindera, "The Definitive Net Worth of Donald Trump's Cabinet," *Forbes*, July 25, 2019.

325. Wetherell, "The Bush 100." The Center for Public Integrity noted that the "corporate character of the Bush administration is both substantive and stylistic."

326. Daniel Scott Souleles, *Songs of Profit, Songs of Loss: Private Equity, Wealth, and Inequality* (Lincoln: University of Nebraska Press, 2019), pp. 5–6; Kevin Dowd, "Nine Politicians Who Went from Public Servant to Private Equity," *PitchBook*, May 12, 2016.

327. Leslie Wayne, "Elder Bush in Big G.O.P. Cast Toiling for Top Equity Firm," *New York Times*, March 5, 2001.

328. In March 2020, Powell's Federal Reserve bailed out floundering corporate debt markets, thus delivering record capital gains to private equity firms like the Carlyle Group. Christopher Leonard, *The Lords of Easy Money: How the Federal Reserve Broke the American Economy* (New York: Simon & Schuster, 2022), pp. 161–63, 165–69, 221–27, 236, 269, 279.

329. The Democrats, too, have their ties to the world of private investment, although far less extensive than those of the Republicans. Timothy Geithner, who served as secretary of the treasury under Obama, went on to become president of Warburg Pincus, while former president Clinton served as an advisor to Yucaipa Companies after leaving office. Robert Rubin, longtime executive at Goldman Sachs and former secretary of the treasury under Clinton, ended his career at the private equity firm Centerview Partners. Dowd, "Nine Politicians Who Went from Public Servant to Private Equity." With several advisors from the world of private capital, the Biden cabinet was nevertheless worth less than either the Obama or Trump teams. Chad Day, Luis Melgar, and John McCormick, "Biden's Wealthiest Cabinet Officials: Zients, Lander, Rice Top the List," *Wall Street Journal*, March 23, 2021; Dan Alexander and Michela Tindera, "The Net Worth of Joe Biden's Cabinet: President Biden's Cabinet Is Worth a Fraction of Donald Trump's—and Barack Obama's," *Forbes*, June 29, 2021.

330. Tett, "Distressed-Debt Players Rule the Roost in Trump's White House." For an excellent discussion of Trump's privileged relationship to bankruptcy and the world of distressed debt, see Quinn Slobodian, "Donald Trump Is Once More Walking Away from Failure at a Profit," *New Statesman*, December 1, 2020.

331. Adam Lewis, "Untangling the Trump Administration's Private Equity Ties," *PitchBook*, March 28, 2017; Tett, "Distressed-Debt Players Rule the Roost in Trump's White House."

332. Adele M. Stan, "What We Do Is Secret: Trumpism as Private Capital Scam," *Baffler*, June 2017.

333. Mary L. Trump, *Too Much and Never Enough: How My Family Created the World's Most Dangerous Man* (London: Simon & Schuster, 2020), p. 10.

334. Ibid., pp. 39–59.

335. Ibid., p. 98.

336. Ibid., pp. 76–79.

337. Ibid., p. 10.

338. Ibid., p. 16.

339. Ibid., pp. 90–91, 102–103, 107, 114. Mary Trump's narrative is here based in part on Barstow, Craig, and Buettner, "Trump Engaged in Suspect Tax Schemes as He Reaped Riches from His Father."

340. Ibid., pp. 133–34.

341. Ibid., pp. 134–35.

342. Among the most prominent examples of this genre are Bandy X. Lee, ed., *The Dangerous Case of Donald Trump: 37 Psychiatrists and Mental Health Experts Assess a President—Updated and Expanded with New Essays* (New York: St. Martin's Press, 2019); Dan P. McAdams, *The Strange Case of Donald J. Trump: A Psychological Reckoning* (Oxford: Oxford University Press, 2020).

343. The intern was a grandson of Robert F. Kennedy, who worked as volunteer in Jared Kushner's coronavirus task force. With this quote, he was referring specifically to the Trump administration's pandemic response. Jane Mayer, "A Young Kennedy, in Kushnerland, Turned Whistle-Blower," *New Yorker*, September 28, 2020, p. 14. The Trump Organization LLC functions as both a holding company for the family's hundreds of business ventures and a single-family office, responsible for administering the family's legal, financial, and tax concerns.

344. James Beech and Nicholas Moody, "The Oval Office as the Trump Family Office," CampdenFB, May 3, 2017; Lachlan Markay, "Make Nepotism Great Again: 20 Families Got Jobs in Trump Administration," *Daily Beast*, November 20, 2017.

345. Matt Ford, "An Administration Run by Temp Workers," *New Republic*, June 20, 2019.

346. I am here drawing on Jeffrey D. Broxmeyer's illuminating analysis in "A Political Machine for the 21st Century: The Trump Organization as Platform Capitalism," *Public Seminar*, August 22, 2019.

347. Ibid.

348. Paul Kiel and Jesse Eisinger, "How the IRS Was Gutted," *ProPublica*, December 11, 2018; Chairman John Yarmuth, "Funding the IRS Pays Off: Preventing Tax Dodging by Wealthy Filers Is the First Step to Fixing Our Tax Code," House Committee on the Budget, October 1, 2020.

349. Jeffrey D. Broxmeyer, "The Patrimonial Turn in the American State," *Clio* 28, no. 2 (2019): p. 21.

350. While much has been made of the losses he incurred on his golf courses, clubs, and hotels, thanks to the polarizing effect of his presidential persona, this should not

overshadow the much more substantial gains he made on his commercial properties during his term in office. Shahien Nasirpour and Caleb Melby, "Trump's Net Worth Rises to $3 Billion Despite Business Setbacks," *Bloomberg*, June 12, 2019; Eric Lipton and Steve Eder, "For Trump Organization, Office Skyscrapers Make up for Lagging Hotels," *New York Times*, January 13, 2021.

351. Cohen and Drucker, "Tax Plan Crowns a Big Winner."

352. Cary, "Republicans Passed Tax Cuts—Then Profited."

353. Kevin Breuninger, "Trump Rails against Powell a Day after the Fed Cuts Rates for a Third Time This Year," CNBC, October 31, 2019.

354. Cary, "Republicans Passed Tax Cuts—Then Profited."

355. Max Weber's account of "patrimonial power" can be found in *Economy and Society*, ed. Guenther Roth and Claus Wittich (Berkeley: University of California Press, [1922] 1968), pp. 957–1029. The most sustained and convincing use of "patrimonial power" as a lens for understanding the Trump presidency is Jeffrey Broxmeyer's "The Patrimonial Turn in the American State."

356. Weber, *Economy and Society*, pp. 1028–29.

357. Ibid. By contrast, writes Weber, the modern "Kontor (office) is separated from the household, business from private correspondence, and business assets from private wealth" (p. 957).

358. Weber, *Economy and Society*, p. 1006.

359. "Patrimonialism is compatible with capitalism," writes Weber (*Economy and Society*, p. 1091). However, Weber also thought that the arbitrary and discretionary character of patrimonial rule rendered it unsuitable as a long-term foundation for capitalist development (p. 1095). On the indeterminacy of Weber's pronouncements on the relationship between patrimonialism and capitalism, see Ivan Ermakoff, "Patrimonial Rise and Decline: The Strange Case of the Familial State," in *Political Power and Social Theory*, ed. Diane E. Davis and Christina Proenza-Coles (Bingley, UK: Emerald Group, 2008), p. 268. For an extensive case study of the alliance between patrimonialism and capitalism, see Julia Adams's *The Familial State: Ruling Families and Merchant Capitalism in Early Modern Europe* (Ithaca, NY: Cornell University Press, 2007). The Dutch Golden Age offers one very clear instance of an early modern capitalist state in which powerful families played an all-important role both as merchants and political actors. Unless we are to assume a straightforwardly progressive view of history, there is no reason why we should not consider the Dutch familial state as a specific style (as opposed to stage) of capitalism—distinct from the modern bureaucratic style of corporate capitalism but no less capable of commercial or financial innovation. If we focus attention on the fiscal and monetary conditions that enabled such regimes, it is easier to see them as recurrent possibilities within the longer history of capitalism rather than transitional moments in a march toward the modern.

360. For Weber's historical examples of patrimonialism, see, for example, *Economy and Society*, p. 1013. On Weber's own family as inspiration for his study of "patrimonialism,"

see Lutz Kaelber, "How Well Do We Know Max Weber after All? A New Look at Max Weber and His Anglo-German Family Connections," *International Journal of Politics, Culture, and Society* 17, no. 2 (2003): pp. 307–27.

361. For a critical overview of the "neo-feudal" thesis, see Evgeny Morozov, "Critique of Techno-Feudal Reason," *New Left Review* 133/134 (2022): p. 1–38.

362. I borrow the term "long Gilded Age" from historian Leon Fink in *The Long Gilded Age: American Capitalism and the Lessons of a New World Order* (Philadelphia: University of Pennsylvania Press, 2015). Fink extends the period from 1880 to 1920. According to the latest figures, wealth inequality today now actually exceeds the Gilded Age. Thomas Piketty, Emmanuel Saez, and Gabriel Zucman, "Twenty Years and Counting: Thoughts about Measuring the Upper Tail," *Journal of Economic Inequality* 20, no. 1 (2022): p. 262.

363. On the family-based "horizontal consolidations" of the Gilded Age and their gradual replacement by the "vertically integrated" managerial corporation, see Chandler, *The Visible Hand*, pp. 438–39, 452, 457, 491.

364. Alan Dawley, "The Abortive Rule of Big Money," in *Ruling America: A History of Wealth and Power in a Democracy*, ed. Steve Fraser and Gary Gerstle (Cambridge, MA: Harvard University Press, 2005), pp. 156–57.

365. Gabriel Zucman, "Global Wealth Inequality," *Annual Review of Economics* 11 (2019): p. 120.

366. W. Elliot Brownlee, *Federal Taxation in America: A History* (Cambridge: Cambridge University Press, 2018), pp. 124–28.

367. After pursuing a disastrously contractionary policy during the Great Depression, the Federal Reserve was granted new powers to abandon gold and to purchase (or "monetize") Treasury debt, thus allowing for a much more expansive use of monetary policy in the service of New Deal spending objectives and a greater cooperation between the Federal Reserve and Treasury. Although gold convertibility was restored in January 1934, the Federal Reserve remained free from its constraints due to the war in Europe and the consequent international influx of gold into the United States. The Treasury-Federal Reserve Accord of 1951 officially terminated this almost two-decade period of cooperation between the Treasury and the Federal Reserve. Charles W. Calomiris and David C. Wheelock, "Was the Great Depression a Watershed for American Monetary Policy?," in *The Defining Moment: The Great Depression and the American Economy in the Twentieth Century*, ed. Michael D. Bordo, Claudia Goldin, and Eugene N. White (Chicago: University of Chicago Press, 1998), pp. 23–65.

368. Christopher W. Shaw, *Money, Power, and the People: The American Struggle to Make Banking Democratic* (Chicago: University of Chicago Press, 2019), and Jakob Feinig, *Moral Economies of Money: Politics and the Monetary Constitution of Society* (Stanford, CA: Stanford University Press, 2022).

369. Emmanuel Saez and Gabriel Zucman, *The Triumph of Injustice: How the Rich Dodge Taxes and How to Make Them Pay* (New York: Norton, 2019), pp. xvi, 21–23, 32–44.

1. Quoted in Michele Lamont, Bo Yun Park, and Elena Ayala-Hurtado, "Trump's Electoral Speeches and His Appeal to the American White Working Class," *British Journal of Sociology* 68, no. S1 (2017): p. S164.

2. Candace Smith and John Santucci, "Trump Calls on Working Class to 'Strike Back' in Final Day of Campaigning," ABC News, November 8, 2016.

3. Thomas Frank, "Millions of Ordinary Americans Support Donald Trump: Here's Why," *Guardian*, March 8, 2016.

4. Nate Cohn, "Why Trump Won: Working-Class Whites," *New York Times*, November 9, 2016.

5. Philip Bump, "Donald Trump Got Reagan-Like Support from Union Households," *Washington Post*, November 10, 2016. For a repudiation of this comparison, see Kim Moody, *On New Terrain: How Capital Is Reshaping the Battleground of Class War* (Chicago: Haymarket Books, 2017), p. 178.

6. Thomas Frank, *Listen, Liberal: Or, What Ever Happened to the Party of the People?* (New York: Henry Holt, 2016), p. 35.

7. Michael Lind, *The New Class War: Saving Democracy from the Metropolitan Elite* (New York: Penguin Random House, 2020), pp. 18–19. Another prominent contributor to this genre is Joan C. Williams, who explicitly equates working-class status with low educational achievement and follows the convention of referring to the working class as "blue-collar." Although Williams concedes that the equation between working-class and "blue-collar" is questionable, her entire analysis rests on the assumption that liberals have condemned themselves to political obsolescence by ignoring the blue-collar white man. Joan C. Williams, *White Working Class: Overcoming Class Cluelessness in America* (Cambridge, MA: Harvard Business Review Press, 2017), pp. 9–12, 137.

8. Reece Peck, *Fox Populism: Branding Conservatism as Working Class* (Cambridge: Cambridge University Press, 2019), pp. 155–84.

9. Most of the poll data that is adduced to confirm Trump's success among the white working class includes information on the educational status of the voter and only sometimes correlates this to income. Only rarely is this data correlated to wealth or homeownership, almost never to employment or occupational status (employee, independent contractor, manager, or small business owner), and never to household/student debt—although each of these categories is critical to building a nuanced picture of class position today.

10. Arthur C. Wolfe, "Trends in Labor Union Voting Behavior, 1948–1968," *Industrial Relations: A Journal of Economy and Society* 9, no. 1 (1969): p. 5.

11. Ibid.

12. David Halle, *America's Working Man: Work, Home, and Politics among Blue Collar Property Owners* (Chicago: University of Chicago Press, 1984), p. 228.

13. Ibid., pp. 165–70.

14. Tamara Draut, *Understanding the Working Class* (New York: Demos, 2018), p. 6. For

a book-length reflection on this data, see Tamara Draut, *Sleeping Giant: The Untapped Economic and Political Power of America's New Working Class* (New York: Knopf Doubleday, 2016). Gabriel Winant notes that the bulk of job creation now takes place in the low-wage care economy. This category "encompasses the provision of direct and indirect services to develop and sustain human capacities, including tending to the young, old, disabled, and sick and supporting daily life through housekeeping, food service and domestic work." Health care accounts for the largest part of this economy. The care economy "accounted for 56 percent of all job growth in the 1980s, 63 percent in the 1990s, and 74 percent in the 2000s." Gabriel Winant, *The Next Shift: The Fall of Industry and the Rise of Health Care in Rust Belt America* (Cambridge, MA: Harvard University Press, 2021), p. 3.

15. Current Employment Statistics (Establishment Data): Table B-1, Employees on Non-farm Payrolls by Industry Sector and Selected Industry Detail, Federal Reserve Bank of St. Louis, April 1, 2021.

16. Moody, *On New Terrain*, pp. 37–39.

17. See "Warehouse and Storage" under "Household Data Annual Averages 18, Employed Persons by Detailed Industry, Sex, Race, and Hispanic or Latino Ethnicity," U.S. Bureau of Labor Statistics, January 22, 2021. For a detailed analysis, see "General Warehouse Worker: Demographics in the US," Zippia Career Research, January 29, 2021.

18. Ruth Milkman, *Immigrant Labor and the New Precariat* (Cambridge, UK: Polity Press, 2020), p. 78. On 2020 statistics, see "Construction" in U.S. Bureau of Labor Statistics, "Household Data, Annual Averages, 2020."

19. Barbara and John Ehrenreich first coined the term "professional-managerial class" in 1977 as an attempt to understand the class position of educated New Left activists vis-à-vis blue-collar workers. Barbara and John Ehrenreich, "The Professional-Managerial Class," *Radical America* 11, no. 2 (1977): pp. 7–32. Here they argue that "technical workers, managerial workers, 'culture' producers, etc.—must be understood as comprising a distinct class in monopoly capitalist society. The Professional-Managerial Class ('PMC') cannot be considered a stratum of a broader 'class' of 'workers' because it exists in an objectively antagonistic relationship to another class of wage earners (whom we shall simply call the 'working class')" (p. 11). The category coexisted with and sometimes overlapped with neoconservative critiques of the "New Class" of educated, politically liberal professionals and an older analysis of the "managerial class" proposed by the conservative political thinker James Burnham in *The Managerial Revolution: What Is Happening in the World* (New York: John Day, 1941). A cofounder, with William Buckley, of the *National Review*, Burnham influenced both neoconservative and paleoconservative (far-right) views on class. The term "PMC" has now become commonplace on the American alt-right and far right, as well as the "Dirt Bag Left," thanks to a hybridization between Burnham's thought and the concept as proposed by Barbara and John Ehrenreich. In a recent interview, however, Barbara Ehrenreich asserts that the "PMC lies in ruins": "what happened to the blue-collar working class with deindustrialization is now happening with the PMC." See Alex Press, "On the Origins of the Professional-Managerial Class: An Interview with Barbara Ehrenreich," *Dissent*, October 22, 2019.

20. While the average schoolteacher's salary stands at roughly $60,000, as Jack Schneider and Jennifer Berkshire note, most teachers earn less than that, thanks to the influx of younger teachers, with starting salaries of less than $40,000 in a majority of states. Jack Schneider and Jennifer Berkshire, *A Wolf at the Schoolhouse Door: The Dismantling of Public Education and the Future of School* (New York: New Press, 2020), pp. 31–32. Overall, they note, "the wages of teachers have fallen sharply, even as the wages of other college-educated professionals have risen.… [While] teacher salaries had been commensurate with other comparable workers in 1994, roughly a quarter of a century later, it was 18.7 percent lower" (p. 32).

21. By 2011, around 10 percent of low-wage workers had a four-year college degree or more, almost double the number recorded in 1979. John Smith and Janelle Jones, "Low-Wage Workers Are Older and Better Educated than Ever," *CEPR Center for Economic and Policy Research* (April 2012): pp. 1–6.

22. Gary Roth, *The Educated Underclass: Students and the Promise of Social Mobility* (London: Pluto Press, 2019), pp. 107–108.

23. Nicholas Carnes and Noam Lupu, "It's Time to Bust the Myth: Most Trump Voters Were Not Working Class," *Washington Post*, June 5, 2017. The final results of this research can be found in Nicholas Carnes and Noam Lupu, "The White Working Class and the 2016 Election," *Perspectives on Politics* 19, no. 1 (2021): pp. 55–72.

24. On the numerical and analytical limits of this assumption, see Moody, *On New Terrain*, pp. 176–77. See also Mike Juang, "A Secret Many Small-Business Owners Share with Mark Zuckerberg," CNBC, July 9, 2017.

25. Helaine Olen, "Small-Business Owners Have a Thing for Donald Trump," *Slate*, May 9, 2016; Gene Marks, "If It Were Up to Small Business, Trump Would Get His Second Term," *Guardian*, February 27, 2020. See Michael McCarthy, "The Revenge of Joe the Plumber," *Jacobin*, October 26, 2016, for an excellent review of the literature indicating heavy support for Trump among small business owners and the self-employed.

26. Mike Davis, "Election 2016," *New Left Review*, January–February 2017.

27. Ibid.

28. Jacob S. Hacker and Paul Pierson, *Let Them Eat Tweets: How the Right Rules in an Age of Extreme Inequality* (New York: Liveright, 2020), pp. 171–95.

29. Peck, *Fox Populism*, pp. 121–84.

30. Ibid., p. 172.

31. For an incisive analysis of the productivity debates of the 1970s and their gendered underpinnings, see Natasha Zaretsky, *No Direction Home: The American Family and the Fear of National Decline, 1968–1980* (Chapel Hill: University of North Carolina Press, 2007), pp. 105–42. For a contemporary revival of these debates, see Aaron Benanav, "Service Work in the Pandemic Economy," *International Labor and Working-Class History* 99 (2021): pp. 66–74.

32. Samuel J. Wurzelbacher and Thomas N. Tabback, *Joe the Plumber: Fighting for the American Dream* (Austin, TX: Pearlgate Publishing, 2008). It turns out that Joe Wurzel-

bacher was just as confused about his occupational status as the right-wing media. Although he had apparently worked for a licensed plumber, he did not hold a license himself and had never completed an apprenticeship. His dreams of buying the plumbing business he worked for were therefore somewhat fanciful. Larry Vellequette and Tom Troy, "'Joe the Plumber' Isn't Licensed," *Blade*, October 16, 2008.

33. On the electoral minority status of the Republican Party prior to Reagan, see Robert Mason, *The Republican Party and American Politics from Hoover to Reagan* (Cambridge: Cambridge University Press, 2011). Between 1933 and 1989, Republicans held the White House, the House, and the Senate for only two years, at the outset of the Eisenhower administration. While Republicans controlled the White House for a total of twenty-four years, public opinion polls throughout this period showed that Democrats enjoyed a decisive edge over Republicans when it came to popular support (pp. 1–2, 7–8). The minority status of the GOP also extended to the realm of policy ideas, where Democrats generally set the agenda.

34. Mabel Berezin is illuminating on the prominent place of the building trades in Trump's political pageantry. Mabel Berezin, "On the Construction Sites of History: Where Did Donald Trump Come From?," *American Journal of Cultural Sociology* 5, no. 3 (2017): p. 329.

35. Quoted in Lamont, Yun Park, and Ayala-Hurtado, "Trump's Electoral Speeches and His Appeal to the American White Working Class," pp. S165–66.

36. Paul Prescod, "We Can't Abandon the Building Trades Unions to the Right," *Jacobin*, March 5, 2020.

37. President Donald J. Trump, "Remarks at the North America's Building Trades Unions 2017 Legislative Conference," April 4, 2017.

38. Prescod, "We Can't Abandon the Building Trades Unions to the Right"; Dylan Matthews, "Donald Trump's Real Political Inspiration: Richard Nixon," *Vox*, July 18, 2016.

39. Jefferson Cowie, *Stayin' Alive: The 1970s and the Last Days of the Working Class* (New York: New Press, 2010), p. 149.

40. Grace Palladino, *Skilled Hands, Strong Spirits: A Century of Building Trades History* (Ithaca, NY: Cornell University Press, 2012), p. 157.

41. Thomas O'Hanlon, "The Unchecked Power of the Building Trades," *Fortune*, December 1968, p. 209.

42. G. William Domhoff, *The Corporate Rich and the Power Elite in the Twentieth Century: How They Won, Why Liberals and Labor Lost* (London: Routledge, 2019), p. 191.

43. Gilbert Burck, "The Building Trades versus the People," *Fortune*, October 1970, p. 95.

44. O'Hanlon, "The Unchecked Power of the Building Trades," p. 104.

45. On the lower rates of unionization in the South and Southwest, see Palladino, *Skilled Hands, Strong Spirits*, pp. 147–48. On fear of contagion among nonunion construction workers, see O'Hanlon, "The Unchecked Power of the Building Trades," pp. 103–104.

46. O'Hanlon, "The Unchecked Power of the Building Trades," p. 104; Marc Linder,

Wars of Attrition: Vietnam, the Business Roundtable, and the Decline of Construction Unions, 2nd ed. (Iowa City, IA: Fanpihua Press, 2000), pp. 50, 58.

47. O'Hanlon, "The Unchecked Power of the Building Trades," p. 107.

48. Ibid., p. 106.

49. Ibid., p. 107.

50. Palladino, *Skilled Hands, Strong Spirits*, pp. 142–43.

51. Joshua B. Freeman, "Hardhats: Construction Workers, Manliness, and the 1970 Pro-War Demonstrations," *Journal of Social History* 26, no. 4 (1993): p. 732.

52. Ibid., pp. 726–27, 730–31.

53. Trevor Griffey, "From Jobs to Power: The United Construction Workers Association and Title VII Community Organizing in the 1970s," in *Black Power at Work: Community Control, Affirmative Action, and the Construction Industry*, ed. David Goldberg and Trevor Griffey (Ithaca, NY: Cornell University Press, 2010), pp. 170–73.

54. Freeman, "Hardhats," p. 732.

55. On the history of the CUAIR, see David Vogel, *Fluctuating Fortunes: The Political Power of Business in America* (Washington, DC: Beard Books, 1989), p. 198; Linder, *Wars of Attrition*, pp. 182–97; Palladino, *Skilled Hands, Strong Spirits*, pp. 173–74; Benjamin C. Waterhouse, *Lobbying America: The Politics of Business from Nixon to NAFTA* (Princeton, NJ: Princeton University Press, 2014), pp. 83–87; and Domhoff, *The Corporate Rich and the Power Elite*, pp. 191–96. According to Vogel, the Business Roundtable was formed in 1972 from a merger between three groups—the CUAIR, the March Group (an informal lobbying group for CEOs), and the Labor Law Study Committee (a counterweight to organized labor). Vogel, *Fluctuating Fortunes*, p. 198. However, Domhoff argues that the CUAIR and these other study groups, along with the Business Roundtable, were all offshoots of the Business Council, which had served as the main broker between the state and the corporate elite beginning in the New Deal. According to Domhoff, some scholars "make the Business Roundtable sound like a new organization, but it was in fact the Business Council adding a new [lobbying] function." G William Domhoff, *The Power Elite and the State: How Policy Is Made in America* (New York: Routledge, 2017), p. 267.

56. Palladino, *Skilled Hands, Strong Spirits*, p. 145.

57. Ibid. The Labor Management Relations Act of 1947, otherwise known as Taft-Hartley, watered down the provisions of the 1935 National Labor Relations Act so as to prevent unions from engaging in "unfair labor practices" such as closed shops (which allowed employers to hire unionized workers only), jurisdictional strikes, wildcat actions, or donations to political parties.

58. Linder, *Wars of Attrition*, pp. 191, 198–99, 220, 236; Palladino, *Skilled Hands, Strong Spirits*, p. 173.

59. "Editorial: Breaking Up a Labor Monopoly," *Fortune*, September 1969, pp. 85–86.

60. On the federal government's alleged indulgence of the building trades unions, see O'Hanlon, "The Unchecked Power of the Building Trades," p. 209.

61. Palladino, *Skilled Hands, Strong Spirits*, p. 170.

62. Richard Nixon, Proclamation 4031—Proclaiming the Suspension of the Davis-Bacon Act of March 3, 1931, 36 Fed. Reg. 2855, 3457, February 23, 1971.

63. Palladino, *Skilled Hands, Strong Spirits*, p. 157.

64. David Goldberg and Trevor Griffey argue that the Black Power movement was deeply involved in the struggle to integrate building sites in the late 1960s and in this respect was responsible for radicalizing the long-standing tradition of civil rights activism against the sector. See the essays collected in David Goldberg and Trevor Griffey, eds., *Black Power at Work: Community Control, Affirmative Action, and the Construction Industry* (Ithaca, NY: Cornell University Press, 2010), for more detail on this period of crossover between Black Power and labor activism.

65. Thomas O'Hanlon, "The Case against the Unions," *Fortune*, January 1968, p. 190

66. This was a revised version of President Johnson's aborted "Philadelphia Plan" for construction. Nixon's Philadelphia Plan was watered down soon after implementation, first by the AFL-CIO's attempts to establish alternative systems of voluntary compliance and subsequently by Nixon's own neglect. The program did achieve moderate success, however, lifting the nonwhite membership of the skilled trades from about 1 percent or less to 15 percent by the end of the 1970s. Linder, *Wars of Attrition*, pp. 253–54, and David Hamilton Golland, *Constructing Affirmative Action: The Struggle for Equal Employment Opportunity* (Lexington: University Press of Kentucky, 2011), pp. 151–69.

67. Linder, *Wars of Attrition*, pp. 276–84. Full-length accounts of the hard-hat riots can be found in Penny Lewis, *Hardhats, Hippies, and Hawks: The Vietnam Antiwar Movement as Myth and Memory* (Ithaca, NY: Cornell University Press, 2013), pp. 159–85, and David Paul Kuhn, *The Hardhat Riot: Nixon, New York City and the Dawn of the White Working-Class Revolution* (Oxford: Oxford University Press, 2020).

68. Freeman, "Hardhats," pp. 735–36.

69. Philip S. Foner, *US Labor and the Vietnam War* (New York: International Publishers, 1989), pp. 95–96.

70. That organized labor would support Nixon's foreign policy was hardly surprising, given the long-standing collusion between the most powerful unions and the Cold War defense state. In the wake of World War II, first the AFL and then the CIO embraced Truman's Cold War policy, and both were ruthless in their attempts to cleanse the ranks of dissidents. Ibid., pp. 4–7. The AFL-CIO pact with the Cold War state was motivated by more than a pragmatic interest in the employment opportunities offered by defense contracts. Under Meany's reign, the AFL-CIO's Department of Foreign Affairs collaborated closely with the CIA in seeking to purge communists from its partner unions around the world and offered material support in seeking to overthrow left-wing governments in Central America (pp. 7–8). At the outset of the Vietnam War, George Meany declared that the AFL-CIO would support U.S. intervention—"no matter what the academic do-gooders may say, no matter what the apostles of appeasement may say"—and accused those who criticized the war as being "victims of Communist propaganda" (pp. 20–21). Member unions for the most part kept their doubts behind closed doors until in 1969 the comparatively

progressive leader of the United Auto Workers, Walter Reuther, removed his union from the AFL-CIO and formed an improbable alliance with the Teamsters. Joined together as the Alliance for Labor Action, the UAW and Teamsters promptly called for an immediate end to the war and encouraged many other unions to break with the AFL-CIO line over the following years (pp. 69–71).

71. Freeman, "Hardhats," p. 734.

72. Quoted in Foner, *US Labor and the Vietnam War*, pp. 108.

73. Golland, *Constructing Affirmative Action*, pp. 153–55.

74. Robert Mason, *Richard Nixon and the Quest for a New Majority* (Chapel Hill: University of North Carolina Press, 2004), pp. 72–74; Cowie, *Stayin' Alive*, pp. 133–34.

75. Jerome M. Rosow, *The Problem of the Blue-Collar Worker* (Washington, DC: U.S. Department of Labor, 1970), p. 2.

76. Ibid., p. 4.

77. Ibid., p. 8.

78. Ibid.

79. Ibid., p. 14. Most of these suggestions were an extension of Nixon's (later aborted) Family Assistance Plan—itself originally conceived as a kind of male breadwinner wage for the African American man. On the history of Nixon's Family Assistance Plan and its conceptualization as a family wage supplement for African American men, see Marisa Chappell, *The War on Welfare: Family, Poverty, and Politics in Modern America* (Philadelphia: University of Pennsylvania Press, 2009).

80. Kevin P. Phillips, *The Emerging Republican Majority* (New York: Doubleday, 1969). On Kevin Phillips and the Republican realignment strategy, see Mason, *Richard Nixon and the Quest for a New Majority*, pp. 47–50, and Cowie, *Stayin' Alive*, pp. 130–32.

81. Freeman, "Hardhats," p. 737; Linder, *Wars of Attrition*, p. 286; Cowie, *Stayin' Alive*, p. 138.

82. Cowie, *Stayin' Alive*, p. 161.

83. Freeman, "Hardhats," p. 737.

84. Mason, *Richard Nixon and the Quest for a New Majority*, p. 194.

85. Nixon was certainly capable of cashing in on promises while deferring the moment of action indefinitely—a habit that earned him the sobriquet "Tricky Dick." For discussions of Nixon's intentions vis-à-vis organized labor, see Mason, *Richard Nixon and the Quest for a New Majority*, p. 203, and Cowie, *Stayin' Alive*, p. 134.

86. "The Year of Confrontation," *Time*, April 13, 1970, p. 87, and Judson Gooding, "Blue-Collar Blues on the Assembly Line," *Fortune*, July 1970, p. 69.

87. "The Blue Collar Worker's Lowdown Blues," *Time*, November 9, 1970, p. 69.

88. "The Year of Confrontation," pp. 87–88.

89. J. D. Hodgson, *Analysis of Work Stoppages, 1970*, Bureau of Labor Statistics Bulletin 1727 (Washington, DC: U.S. Department of Labor, 1970), p. 1.

90. "The Blue Collar Worker's Lowdown Blues," p. 68. Real wage increases were considerably lower, averaging 1.7 percent per year between 1966 and 1973. However, the profit rate

saw a real decline during the same period, losing 29.5 percent of its 1966 value by 1973. This disparity was reflected in a rising labor share of national income. David M. Kotz, *The Rise and Fall of Neoliberal Capitalism* (Cambridge, MA: Harvard University Press, 2015), p. 64.

91. "The Blue Collar Worker's Lowdown Blues," p. 69.

92. Ibid., pp. 71, 74.

93. "The U.S. Can't Afford What Labor Wants," *BusinessWeek*, April 11, 1970, p. 104.

94. "The Blue Collar Worker's Lowdown Blues," p. 71.

95. "The U.S. Can't Afford What Labor Wants," pp. 104–105.

96. "Revolt of the Robots," *New York Times*, March 7, 1972.

97. "Sabotage at Lordstown?," *Time*, February 7, 1972, p. 76.

98. Agis Salpukas, "U.A.W. Seeks End of Job Boredom," *New York Times*, September 3, 1972.

99. Gooding, "Blue-Collar Blues on the Assembly Line," p. 69.

100. Cal Winslow, "Overview: The Rebellion from Below, 1965–81," in *Rebel Rank and File: Labor Militancy and Revolt from Below in the Long 1970s*, ed. Aaron Brenner, Robert Brenner, and Cal Winslow (London: Verso, 2010), pp. 1–36.

101. Aaron Brenner, "Preface," in ibid., pp. viii–ix.

102. "Wage-Wage Inflation," *Wall Street Journal*, June 27, 1973.

103. Labor increased its share of national income at the expense of capital in the period between 1966 and the first oil price shock of 1973. After 1973, however, real (inflation-adjusted) wages declined in absolute terms, but to a far lesser extent than real profits. The real wage fell by 4.4 percent between 1973 and 1979, while real profits fell by 17.8 percent over the same period. Kotz, *The Rise and Fall of Neoliberal Capitalism*, pp. 63–65.

104. Laird Hart, "Fickle Formulas: 'Stagflation' Reminds Economics Professors How Little They Know," *Wall Street Journal*, September 6, 1974.

105. A.W. Phillips, "The Relation between Unemployment and the Rate of Change of Money Wage Rates in the United Kingdom 1861–1957," *Economica* 25, no. 100 (1958): pp. 283–99.

106. Milton Friedman, "The Role of Monetary Policy," *American Economic Review* 58, no. 1 (1968): pp. 1–17. Edmund S. Phelps published a similar rebuttal of the Phillips curve in the same year. Edmund S. Phelps "Money-Wage Dynamics and Labor Market Equilibrium," *Journal of Political Economy* 76, no. S4 (1968): pp. 678–711.

107. Martin S. Feldstein, *Lowering the Permanent Rate of Unemployment: A Study Prepared for the Use of the Joint Economic Committee Congress of the United States, September 18* (Washington, DC: U.S. Government Printing Office, 1973). Feldstein republished the results of this report in several follow-up articles, including Martin S. Feldstein, "Unemployment Insurance: Time for Reform," *Harvard Business Review*, March 1975, pp. 51–61.

108. Feldstein, *Lowering the Permanent Rate of Unemployment*, pp. 11, 15, 17, 20.

109. Ibid., pp. 11, 16.

110. Ibid., pp. 41–42, 47.

111. Ibid., p. 34.

112. "Bankrolling the Strikers," *BusinessWeek*, August 26, 1972, p. 84; "Will Congress Approve Food Stamps for Strikers?," *Human Events* 32, no. 27 (1972): p. 4. These media reports draw on a Wharton School monograph published that same year: Armand Thiebault and Ronald M. Cowin, *Welfare and Strikes: The Use of Public Funds to Support Strikers* (Philadelphia: Industrial Research Unit, Wharton School of Finance and Commerce, University of Pennsylvania, 1972).

113. Feldstein, *Lowering the Permanent Rate of Unemployment*, p. 41. On lower taxation rates during the Great Depression, see Martin S. Feldstein, "The Social Security Explosion," Donald Gilbert Memorial Lecture Series, Department of Economics, University of Rochester, April 19, 1974.

114. Feldstein, *Lowering the Permanent Rate of Unemployment*, pp. 11, 41–42.

115. Ibid., p. 41.

116. Ibid., pp. 41–42.

117. Ibid., p. 20.

118. Ibid., p. 51.

119. Michał Kalecki, "Political Aspects of Full Employment," *Political Quarterly* 14, no. 4 (1943): pp. 322–30.

120. Ibid.

121. "Breaking the Tax Barrier," *Wall Street Journal*, January 8, 1975. The article is republished in Jude Wanniski, *The Way the World Works: 20th Anniversary Edition* (Lanham, MD: Gateway Editions, [1978] 1998), p. 244. We can therefore assume that Wanniski is the author.

122. James O'Toole et al., *Work in America: Report of a Special Task Force to the Secretary of Health, Education, and Welfare* (Washington, DC: Department of Health, Education, and Welfare, 1972).

123. Ibid., p. 13.

124. Ibid., p. 20.

125. Ibid., p. 13.

126. "The Great Male Cop-out from the Work Ethic," *BusinessWeek*, November 14, 1977, pp. 156, 161–66. See Zaretsky, *No Direction Home*, pp. 110–21, for a reading of this and other texts in light of contemporary debates around productivity and the male breadwinner wage.

127. George F. Gilder, *Sexual Suicide* (New York: Bantam Books, 1973), pp. 90–95.

128. Ibid., pp. 96–97.

129. Ibid.; George Gilder, *Visible Man: A True Story of Post-Racist America* (New York: Basic Books, 1978).

130. George F. Gilder, *Wealth and Poverty* (New York: Basic Books, 1981), pp. 68–69.

131. Ibid., pp. 16, 87.

132. "What has been happening is a drive, conscious or not, on the part of the government, to flush the wife out of the untaxed household economy and into the arms of the IRS. Accompanying her in her emergence from the home are a host of previously private and

untaxed expenses, for everything from food preparation to childcare, increasingly including, so it would seem from the proliferation of massage parlors around most American cities, the ministrations of sex." Ibid., pp. 16–17.

133. Ibid., p. 16.

134. On these three stages of public-sector militancy, see Deborah Bell, "Unionized Women in State and Local Government," in *Women, Work and Protest: A Century of U.S. Women's Labor History,* ed. Ruth Milkman (Boston: Routledge, 1985), p. 283.

135. Alexis N. Walker, *Divided Unions: The Wagner Act, Federalism, and Organized Labor* (Philadelphia: University of Pennsylvania Press, 2020), p. 20.

136. Ibid., pp. 5, 17–18.

137. Joseph E. Slater, *Public Workers: Government Employee Unions, the Law, and the State, 1900–1962* (Ithaca, NY: Cornell University Press, 2004), p. 109.

138. B. Guy Peters, "The United States: Absolute Change and Relative Stability," in *Public Employment in Western Nations,* ed. Richard Rose (Cambridge: Cambridge University Press, 1985), pp. 234–35.

139. Slater, *Public Workers,* p. 6.

140. Marjorie Murphy, "Militancy in Many Forms: Teacher Strikes and Urban Insurrection, 1967–1974," in Brenner, Brenner, and Winslow, *Rebel Rank and File,* pp. 229–50.

141. In 1960, the United States saw only thirty-six strikes by public-sector workers. That number increased to 412 in 1970 and 536 in 1980. Joseph A. McCartin, "Solvents of Solidarity: Political Economy, Collective Action, and the Crisis of Organized Labor, 1968–2005," in *Rethinking US Labor History: Essays on the Working-Class Experience, 1756–2009,* ed. Donna T. Haverty-Stacke and Daniel J. Walkowitz (New York: Continuum, 2010), p. 222.

142. On federal employment and the "black collar" worker, see Frederick W. Gooding, *American Dream Deferred: Black Federal Workers in Washington, D.C., 1941–1981* (Pittsburgh, PA: University of Pittsburgh Press, 2018). On women's employment as public schoolteachers, see John Shelton, *Teacher Strike! Public Education and the Making of a New American Political Order* (Urbana: University of Illinois Press, 2017), pp. 8–13.

143. Linda M. Blum, *Between Feminism and Labor: The Significance of the Comparable Worth Movement* (Berkeley: University of California Press, 1991), p. 25.

144. Ibid., p. 25.

145. Walker, *Divided Unions,* pp. 70–72. Much of the early organizing in the public sector grew out of and beyond Johnson's Great Society initiatives, which frequently served as de facto job creation programs for members of the same communities they were designed to serve. This contingent of new public-sector workers soon became the target of organizing campaigns on the part of large multisectoral unions such as the American Federation of State, County, and Municipal Employees, or AFSCME, which helped them secure better working conditions and wages. Bell, "Unionized Women in State and Local Government," p. 285. The effect was to force the hand of federal government to enact a more ambitious job creation program than it had originally intended.

146. On the postal workers strike of 1970, see Philip F. Rubio, *There's Always Work at the Post Office: African American Postal Workers and the Fight for Jobs, Justice, and Equality* (Chapel Hill: University of North Carolina Press, 2010), pp. 233–61.

147. Walker, *Divided Unions*, pp. 72–73.

148. Palladino, *Skilled Hands, Strong Spirits*, p. 176.

149. Cowie, *Stayin' Alive*, p. 12; Walker, *Divided Unions*, p. 83.

150. James O'Connor, *The Fiscal Crisis of the State* (New York: St. Martin's Press, 1973), pp. 236–48.

151. "The Need for a Little Backbone," *Wall Street Journal*, July 25, 1975.

152. "Power to the Public Sector," *Wall Street Journal*, August 2, 1976.

153. Paul W. McCracken, "The New Mood on Public Spending," *Wall Street Journal*, October 29, 1976.

154. "People with middle-class incomes…earned the hard way, as they see it, do find themselves in neighborhoods where others live just as well and do not work because they find it more congenial to work all the angles of federal programs." McCracken, "The New Mood on Public Spending." On the tensions that sometimes emerged between public-sector workers and their clients, see Jonna Perrillo, *Uncivil Rights: Teachers, Unions, and Race in the Struggle for School Equity* (Chicago: University of Chicago Press, 2012).

155. Slater, *Public Workers*, p. 5.

156. As the decade progressed, the *Wall Street Journal* watched with alarm as teachers' unions extended their outreach to nurses and other health-care professionals. "Teachers Union Opens Drive to Sign Nurses, Other Health Workers," *Wall Street Journal*, November 30, 1978.

157. Shelton, *Teacher Strike*, pp. 8–16, 178–85.

158. Lee Smith, "The EEOC's Bold Foray into Job Evaluation," *Fortune*, September 11, 1978, p. 58.

159. *Wall Street Journal* op-eds publicized Feldstein's work on the privatization of Social Security and the alleged disincentivizing effects of unemployment insurance. See "Breaking the Tax Barrier." On Wanniski's claim that he "discovered" Feldstein by publicizing his work on the privatization of Social Security, see Anna Bernasek, "The Next Greenspan?," *Fortune*, June 14, 2004, p. 124. Wanniski makes the same boastful claim in his personal correspondence, which offers an interesting insight into the fraught relationship between the populist and elite supply-siders. In a letter dated June 1980, Wanniski describes Feldstein as "an occasional ally of the Lafferians, although he does take pot shots at Art [Laffer] as a professional competitor." He continues: "He [Feldstein] does have incentives in his model, but seems to think they only work on capital, not labor. In other words, cut business taxes, because business will use the extra cash productively, forming 'capital.' Don't cut personal tax rates, because people will only squander their money on personal goods. Right?" See Letter to Ms. Soma Goldman, *New York Times*, from Jude Wanniski, 23 March 1980, Jude Wanniski Papers, 1965–2006, Box 1, Correspondence 1965–2001, Hoover Institution Library and Archives.

160. The Full Employment and Balanced Growth Act of 1976, otherwise known as the Humphrey-Hawkins bill, promised to revive and consolidate the Full Employment Act of 1946. It is widely thought to have won the Democrats the Senate, House, and presidency in 1976. By the time the act was passed in 1978, however, it had been rendered largely toothless. Steven Attewell, *People Must Live by Work: Direct Job Creation in America from FDR to Reagan* (Philadelphia: University of Pennsylvania Press, 2018), pp. 210–11.

161. Yanek Mieczkowski, *Gerald Ford and the Challenges of the 1970s* (Lexington: University Press of Kentucky, 2005), pp. 189–93.

162. James P. Gannon, "Unemployment as a Political Issue," *Wall Street Journal*, February 12, 1976.

163. Jude Wanniski, "Looking for the Right Broom," *Wall Street Journal*, August 17, 1976.

164. Jude Wanniski, "It's Time to Cut Taxes," *Wall Street Journal*, December 11, 1974. Paraphrasing Mundell, Wanniski wrote that with "announcement of a major tax cut, the capital market would instantly perceive that it is more profitable to do business in the United States than the rest of the world. Capital that is now flowing out would remain; foreign capital going elsewhere would come in. The increased real economic growth would mean the U.S. would run a sizable trade deficit as the U.S. would keep more of what it produces and buy more goods from abroad."

165. Infamously, Eisenhower had refused to spend an end-of-term budget surplus, instead using it to retire a portion of government debt. For Eisenhower's incoming statement on the importance of budget balance, see Dwight D. Eisenhower, *Public Papers of the Presidents of the United States: Dwight D. Eisenhower, 1953* (Washington, DC: U.S. Government Printing Office, 1960), p. 48. For a wider analysis of Eisenhower's horror of unbalanced budgets, see Iwan Morgan, "Taxation as a Republican Issue in the Era of Stagflation," in *Seeking a New Majority: The Republican Party and American Politics, 1960–1980*, ed. Robert Mason and Iwan Morgan (Nashville, TN: Vanderbilt University Press, 2013), pp. 180–81.

166. Jude Wanniski, "Taxes and a Two-Santa Theory," *National Observer*, March 6, 1976, pp. 6–8.

167. For accounts of the meeting between Jude Wanniski and Jack Kemp, see Bruce R. Bartlett, *Reaganomics: Supply-Side Economics in Action* (Westport, CT: Arlington House, 1981), p. 127; Morton Kondracke and Fred Barnes, *Jack Kemp: The Bleeding-Heart Conservative Who Changed America* (New York: Sentinel, 2015), p. 30.

168. Jack Kemp, *American Renaissance: Strategy for the 1980s* (New York: Harper & Row, 1979), p. 37.

169. Ibid., p. 38. Kemp's most significant offering to date had been the Job Creation Act of 1975, a bill that proposed to accelerate depreciation schedules while reducing taxation on capital gains, dividends, and other capital income. Codesigned by Kemp's staff economist Paul Craig Roberts and the ubiquitous Norman B. Ture, the act was advertised as a trickle-down alternative to the Humphrey-Hawkins bill. Bartlett, *Reaganomics*, p. 126.

170. Kondracke and Barnes, *Jack Kemp*, p. 39.

171. Monica Prasad speaks of a process of "alchemy" between Wanniski and Kemp which "transformed" both of their perspectives. Monica Prasad, *Starving the Beast: Ronald Reagan and the Tax Cut Revolution* (New York: Russell Sage Foundation, 2018), p. 33. For an insightful analysis of Kemp's trajectory, see Robert M. Collins, *More: The Politics of Economic Growth in Postwar America* (Oxford: Oxford University Press, 2000), pp. 175–77.

172. Kemp's hold on his blue-collar district was so secure by the late 1970s that Democrats had ceased to contest it. Adam Clymer, "Washington: Quarterbacking for the GOP," *Atlantic Monthly*, December 1978, p. 17.

173. Bartlett, *Reaganomics*, p. 120. The so-called Kennedy-Johnson tax cut of 1964 was crafted by the Council for Economic Advisors, the Treasury, and the House Ways and Means Committee during the Kennedy administration, but was only implemented in 1964, after President Kennedy's death. The legislation reduced the marginal corporate tax rate from 52 to 48 percent and cut federal income taxes by 20 percent across the board.

174. Kondracke and Barnes, *Jack Kemp*, p. 45.

175. Ibid., pp. 46–52.

176. Ibid., p. 52.

177. Norman B. Ture, "Statement on the Roth-Kemp Tax Reduction Proposal, July 14, 1978," in *Individual and Business Tax Reduction Proposals, Hearing before the Subcommittee on Taxation and Debt Management, Committee on Finance, U.S. Senate* (Washington, DC: U.S. Government Printing Office, 1978), pp. 213–18. Wanniski made reference to Ture's calculations as early as 1976. See Jude Wanniski, "Taxes and the Kennedy Gamble," *Wall Street Journal*, September 23, 1976.

178. Roberts, *The Supply-Side Revolution*, p. 31. Roberts resented Laffer and Wanniski's influence on Kemp and accused them of rewriting history to exaggerate their own role in the birth of supply-side economics. According to Roberts, Wanniski "created the impression that supply-side economics began in 1976 when he and Laffer met an untutored Kemp and introduced him to the Laffer curve." Paul Craig Roberts and Norman B. Ture were excluded from the picture. It is likely that Wanniski's narrative is the reason why supply-side populism is often taken to represent the supply-side movement as a whole.

179. Bartlett, *Reaganomics*, p. 132.

180. Ibid.; Milton Friedman, "The Kemp-Roth Free Lunch," *Newsweek*, August 7, 1978, p. 59. Bruce Bartlett himself, the designer of Kemp-Roth, later argued that the spending austerity was the primary strategic rationale behind across-the-board tax cuts. Bruce Bartlett, "'Starve the Beast': Origins and Development of a Budgetary Metaphor," *Independent Review* 12, no. 1 (2007): pp. 5–26.

181. Bartlett, *Reaganomics*, p. 135.

182. Robert R. Keller, "Supply-Side Economic Policies during the Coolidge-Mellon Era," *Journal of Economic Issues* 16, no. 3 (1982): pp. 773–90. Wanniski invokes the Coolidge-Mellon tax cuts in Jude Wanniski, "Taxes, Revenues, and the 'Laffer Curve,'" *Public Interest* 50 (Winter 1978): p. 14.

183. Jude Wanniski, "Taxes and the Kennedy Gamble," *Wall Street Journal*, September

23, 1976; "Editorial: JFK Strikes Again," *Wall Street Journal*, February 23, 1977. For a more recent exposition of this argument, see Lawrence Kudlow and Brian Domitrovic, *JFK and the Reagan Revolution* (New York: Penguin Books, 2016). The fact that the tax specialist Norman B. Ture had a hand in designing both the Kennedy and Kemp-Roth tax cuts lent historical weight to the comparison.

184. Between January 1961 and November 1964, the Council of Economic Advisors (CEA) operated under the leadership of the American Keynesian and Harvard economics professor Alvin Hansen. During this period, the CEA counted Keynesian economists such as Walter Heller, Kermit Gordon, and James Tobin among its members. On the role and influence of "Kennedy's CEA," see Alice O'Connor, *Poverty Knowledge: Social Science, Social Policy, and the Poor in Twentieth-Century U.S. History* (Princeton, NJ: Princeton University Press, 2001), pp. 140–58; Christopher Frenze, *The Mellon and Kennedy Tax Cuts: A Review and Analysis, A Staff Study Prepared for the Use of the Subcommittee on Monetary and Fiscal Policy of the Joint Economic Committee Congress of the United States, June 18* (Washington, DC: U.S. Government Printing Office, 1982), p. 2.

185. Frenze, *The Mellon and Kennedy Tax Cuts*, p. 16. Seiichiro Mozumi, however, argues that the Kennedy-Johnson tax cuts of 1964 were much closer in spirit to the Reagan-era supply-side tax cuts than is often acknowledged. Mozumi points out that Kennedy's original tax reform was meant to include a significant base-broadening component—proposed by the Treasury and House Ways and Means Committee, not the CEA—that would have significantly increased the tax burden on capital gains. These progressive tax reforms were abandoned under pressure from business elites. Seiichiro Mozumi, "The Kennedy–Johnson Tax Cut of 1964, the Defeat of Keynes, and Comprehensive Tax Reform in the United States," *Journal of Policy History* 30, no. 1 (2018): pp. 25–61.

186. In Galbraith's words, "when the conservatives found out that Keynes could be had by tax cuts, they would embrace the faith with too much fervor. If that happened, it would become permanently more difficult to implement Keynes through the expenditure route." John Kenneth Galbraith, "The Public Sector Is Still Starved (1967)," in *Interviews with John Kenneth Galbraith*, ed. James Ronald Stanfield and Jacqueline Bloom Stanfield (Jackson: University Press of Mississippi, 2004), p. 18.

187. Edward Walsh, "President Links Budget Austerity and Social Goals," *Washington Post*, December 9, 1978.

188. Jack Kemp, "Coalition Needed between Labor and the GOP," *Human Events*, September 22, 1979, p. 14.

189. Ibid.

190. Jack Kemp, "The New Populist Consensus in America," in *The American Idea: Ending Limits to Growth* (Washington, DC: American Studies Center, 1984), p. 252.

191. Wanniski, "It's Time to Cut Taxes."

192. "Breaking the Tax Barrier."

193. Paul Craig Roberts, "Idealism in Public Choice Theory," *Journal of Monetary Economics* 4, no. 3 (1978): p. 612.

194. Ibid., p. 613.

195. For an illuminating insight into views on house values, the property tax, and public-school funding among blue-collar workers during the late 1970s, see the interviews in Halle, *America's Working Man*, pp. 220–30.

196. "What's Wrong with Labor?," *Wall Street Journal*, June 27, 1978. For an illuminating discussion of the *Wall Street Journal*'s attempts to exploit the tensions between private- and public-sector unions, see Joseph Anthony McCartin, *Collision Course: Ronald Reagan, the Air Traffic Controllers, and the Strike That Changed America* (Oxford: Oxford University Press, 2011), pp. 215–17.

197. Molly Michelmore, *Tax and Spend: The Welfare State, Tax Politics, and the Limits of American Liberalism* (Philadelphia: University of Pennsylvania Press, 2012), pp. 107, 118, 127–28.

198. Douglas A. Hibbs, *The American Political Economy: Macroeconomics and Electoral Politics* (Cambridge, MA: Harvard University Press, 1987), pp. 308–309.

199. "What's Wrong with Labor?"

200. Natalia Mehlman Petrzela, *Classroom Wars: Language, Sex, and the Making of Modern Political Culture* (Oxford: Oxford University Press, 2015), pp. 203–18.

201. Ibid., pp. 205–209.

202. According to Romain Huret, "middle-class tax resisters expounded in newsletters and pamphlets their belief that the leviathan state [had] increased both permissiveness among citizens and the waste of tax-payers' money.... Taxpayers feared that liberal policymakers were usurping their authority as parents.... In San Francisco, the organization Parents and Taxpayers established a place for itself by attacking welfare policy as an agent of moral decay.... The association's bulletin devoted many articles to the multiple causes of evil, including busing, the Black Panthers, and welfare programs.... The *Roe v. Wade* (1973) decision was compared to the *Dred Scott* (1857) decision, prophesying a civil war to come." Romain Huret, *American Tax Resisters* (Cambridge, MA: Harvard University Press, 2014), p. 211.

203. Halle, *America's Working Man*, pp. 61, 66–68, 74, 294.

204. Clarence Y. H. Lo, *Small Property versus Big Government: Social Origins of the Property Tax Revolt* (Berkeley: University of California Press, 1990), pp. 31–32, 93–101, and 137–41. For an in-depth discussion of the heterogeneous political sentiments animating the early tax revolt movement, see Isaac William Martin, *The Permanent Tax Revolt: How the Property Tax Transformed American Politics* (Stanford, CA: Stanford University Press, 2008).

205. Quoted in Lo, *Small Property Versus Big Government*, p. 105.

206. Quoted in Walker, *Divided Unions*, p. 90.

207. Wanniski hailed the vote as a "dramatic test" of Laffer curve economics and its capacity to mobilize the popular vote. "The array of elite opposition to 13 was almost total," he remarked. "Democratic Governor Jerry Brown, Democrats and Republicans of the state legislature, mayors, county executives, labor unions, the Business Roundtable, and the

news media, 'liberal' and 'conservative,' all opposed Proposition 13, many with doomsday predictions of fiscal collapse." Jude Wanniski, "Introduction to the Revised and Updated Edition," in *The Way the World Works: 20th Anniversary Edition*, p. 347. See also Jack Kemp, "Prop 13 Fever," *New York Daily News*, July 23, 1979.

208. In fact, any business of whatever size that was organized as a "pass through" was obliged to pay individual, not corporate, taxes, and to this extent stood to gain from across-the-board income tax cuts. Kim McQuaid, *Uneasy Partners: Big Business in American Politics, 1945–1990* (Baltimore: Johns Hopkins University Press, 1994), p. 130; Waterhouse, *Lobbying America*, p. 213; Prasad, *Starving the Beast*, p. 130. This detail was of little relevance in the 1970s, when most pass-through businesses were effectively small, but it would become significant in the decades ahead, when wealthy hedge funds, private equity firms, and other limited liability companies (LLCs) could avail themselves of personal income tax cuts in the same way as genuine small businesses.

209. Independent truckers had occupied a parallel world to regulated company drivers since the New Deal, when farming interests prevailed upon federal regulators to exclude the drivers of nonmanufactured agricultural products from the oversight of the Motor Carrier Act of 1935. Shane Hamilton, *Trucking Country: The Road to America's Wal-Mart Economy* (Princeton, NJ: Princeton University Press, 2014), p. 51. In the winter of 1973–1974 and again in the summer of 1979, they orchestrated a series of road blockages across the country in protest against rising fuel prices, government regulation, and union protectionism. Independent owner operators had joined the Teamsters in the 1960s as a way of accessing work in protected freight markets. The Teamsters' efforts to drive up the wages of long-haul company drivers had a flow-on effect for independent truckers, who in the 1960s were earning higher piecework wages (minus benefits) than their regulated peers. Hamilton, *Trucking Country*, p. 208; D. Daryl Wyckoff and David H. Maister, *The Owner-Operator: Independent Trucker* (Lexington, MA: Lexington Books, 1975), pp. 8, 16, 17, 18. However, when independent drivers saw their earnings drop below that of regular company drivers following the oil price hikes of the 1970s, they turned their rage against the combined powers of the Teamsters and federal regulators. Hamilton, *Trucking Country*, pp. 217–18. Ultimately, their actions strengthened the hand of would-be reformers who had for many years been looking for an opportunity to deregulate the sector. In 1980, President Carter abolished the federal government's power to control freight prices and widened the independent trucking exemption to include manufactured as well as nonmanufactured agricultural commodities. Jimmy Carter, "Motor Carrier Act of 1980: Remarks on Signing S. 2245 into Law (July 1)," American Presidency Project. On the small business identification and aspirations of independent truckers, see Hamilton, *Trucking Country*, p. 187; Wyckoff and Maister, *The Owner-Operator*, p. 66.

210. Graham Russell Gao Hodges, *Taxi! A Social History of the New York City Cabdriver* (Baltimore: Johns Hopkins University Press, 2007), p. 4.

211. Paul Bullock, Cara Anderson, Jack Blackburn, Edna Bonacich, and Richard Steele, *Building California: The Story of the Carpenters' Union* (Los Angeles: Center for Labor

Research and Education, Institute for Industrial Relations, University of California, 1982), p. iii. Mark Erlich and David Goldberg make a similar observation: the "vast majority of building trades workers collect a paycheck" and work as fixed-term employees, but trades-men and women "who will never open their own businesses have temporary escapes from the status of a hired hand…. Whether it be working 'side jobs' or buying a pick-up truck for tools and materials, from time to time most construction workers will grapple with a fuzzy self-definition that straddles strict class boundaries. Autoworkers, checkout cashiers, and nurse's aides are unlikely to open a factory, supermarket, or hospital, but carpenters and other building trades workers can harbor small-scale designs of independence, within their occupation. The chances of truly 'making it' are remote, but the nine hundred thou-sand self-employed builders counted in the census do underpin a construction culture in which distinctions between employer and employed are sometimes blurred and the com-mon concerns of everyone who builds for a living can be exaggerated." Mark Erlich and David Goldberg, *With Our Hands: The Story of Carpenters in Massachusetts* (Philadelphia: Temple University Press, 1986), p. 17.

212. Erlich and Goldberg, *With Our Hands*, p. 18.

213. Waterhouse, *Lobbying America*, pp. 202–203.

214. Kim Phillips-Fein, *Invisible Hands: The Businessmen's Crusade against the New Deal* (New York: Norton, 2010), pp. 199–207.

215. Lesher was nominated president of the Chamber of Commerce in 1975 and remained in this position until 1997. Ann Crittenden, "A Stubborn Chamber of Commerce Roils the Waters," *New York Times*, June 27, 1982.

216. On this tradition, see Lawrence B. Glickman, *Free Enterprise: An American History* (New Haven, CT: Yale University Press, 2019), pp. 79–110. On the long arc of this tradition, which traces its evolution from the anti–New Deal "old right" of the prewar period to the formation of the John Birch Society in 1954 and the Goldwater presidential campaign of 1964, see Robert B. Horwitz, *America's Right: Anti-Establishment Conservatism from Gold-water to the Tea Party* (Cambridge, UK: Polity Press, 2013), pp. 23–51. On Goldwater's role in positing and denouncing a secret symbiosis between big business, big government, and the Republican Party establishment, see McQuaid, *Uneasy Partners*, pp. 128–30.

217. On the Business Roundtable's position, see Lo, *Small Property versus Big Govern-ment*, p. 24. For the *Nation's Business* response to the California tax revolt, see "Taxpayers in Revolt," *Nation's Business*, July 1978, p. 19; Robert T. Gray, "The Taxpayer Fights Back," *Nation's Business*, April 1978, pp. 25–28.

218. Richard L. Lesher, "Full Employment without Inflation: A Tax Cut Now," *Vital Speeches of the Day* 44, no. 10 (1978): p. 320. On the alignment between the U.S. Cham-ber of Commerce and supply-side populism, see Gregory A. Elinson, "Shifting Coalitions: Business Power, Partisan Politics, and the Rise of the Regulatory State," PhD diss., Univer-sity of California, Berkeley, 2015, pp. 137–38.

219. Richard L. Lesher, "Right-Wing Extremism," *Economic Progress: It's Everybody's Business* (Washington, DC: Chamber of Commerce, 1980), pp. 26–27. This book brings

together a collection of the weekly syndicated columns, called "The Voice of Business," that Richard Lesher began writing in 1975. The article "Right-Wing Extremism" was originally published in 1979.

220. The chamber also had a weekly television program, compèred by Lesher himself, and in the early 1980s set up its own satellite news network. Crittenden, "A Stubborn Chamber of Commerce"; Edward Cowan, "News with a Business Point of View," *New York Times,* June 3, 1983.

221. See, for instance, the following account of readers' responses to Reagan's supply-side tax cuts, "Sound off Response: Siding with the Supply-Siders," *Nation's Business,* July 1981, p. 87.

222. James J. Kilpatrick, "The Case against ERA," *Nation's Business,* January 1975, p. 9; "How Illegal Aliens Rob Jobs from Unemployed Americans," *Nation's Business,* May 1975, pp. 18–22; James J. Kilpatrick, "Fireworks Ahead among the Majority Sex," *Nation's Business,* September 1977, pp. 13–14; Carole Feldman, "Uncle Sam's Unwelcomed Boarders: Immigration Reform Is an Idea Whose Time Seems to Have Come," *Nation's Business,* April 1982, pp. 26–29.

223. James J. Kilpatrick, "New Hope for Employers Harassed by OSHA," *Nation's Business,* March 1977, pp. 15–16; "What to Do When the OSHA Inspector Knocks," *Nation's Business,* February 1978, pp. 48–49; "Moving a Mobile America, a Conversation with James D. Edgett, Who Rose from Baggage Boy to North American Van Lines President in American Horatio Alger Tradition," *Nation's Business,* February 1969, pp. 74–79; "From One Secondhand Truck to a Giant Truckline," *Nation's Business,* July 1978, pp. 41–46; Martin Wilbur, "Amway Founder: A Salesman for Free Enterprise," *Nation's Business,* May 1979, pp. 68–73.

224. "How the Customer Is Wronged by Washington: Guess Who Pays through the Nose when the Benefits of Regulations Are Not Weighed against the Costs?," *Nation's Business,* March 1975, pp. 28–32; "The Need to Reform Obsolete and Unnecessary Regulations," *Nation's Business,* June 1975, pp. 34–35; "Employee Benefits: Now a Third of Payroll Costs," *Nation's Business,* October 1976, pp. 36–37; "How Job-Injury Benefits Are Rising," *Nation's Business,* June 1977, pp. 38–40; Barbara Hackman Franklin, "Viewpoint: Easing the Regulatory Load for Small Business," *Nation's Business,* September 1978, pp. 54–55.

225. Phillips-Fein, *Invisible Hands,* pp. 201–202.

226. "Lessons of Leadership: Jay Van Andel of Amway Corporation," *Nation's Business,* October 1973, p. 66. Van Andel served as the chamber's chairman from 1979 to 1980 and as member of the Senior Council from 1980 to 1985. See also Wilbur, "Amway Founder: A Salesman for Free Enterprise."

227. "'Invisible Rich' Located," *New York Times,* January 26, 1979.

228. Davor Mondom, "Compassionate Capitalism: Amway and the Role of Small-Business Conservatives in the New Right," *Modern American History* 1 (2018): p. 346; Nicole Woolsey Biggart, *Charismatic Capitalism: Direct Selling Organizations in America* (Chicago: University of Chicago Press, 1988), pp. 33–42.

229. Mondom, "Compassionate Capitalism," p. 344.

230. Ibid., pp. 343–61.

231. Stephen Butterfield, *Amway: The Cult of Free Enterprise* (Boston: South End Press, 1985), pp. 111–28. See also Woolsey Biggart, *Charismatic Capitalism*, pp. 70–96.

232. Butterfield, *Amway: The Cult of Free Enterprise*, p. 112.

233. According to Butterfield, Amway actually used the vocabulary of "generations" and "family trees" to map out the different branches of a contractual chain. Ibid., p. 126.

234. Richard DeVos and Charles Paul Conn, *Believe!* (New York: Pocket Books, 1983), p. 166. The historical divergence of the corporate and family business form should not be overstated, however. In her history of Walmart, the initially privately owned and later closely held but incorporated retail behemoth, Bethany Moreton shows how the Waltons deliberately attempted to style their employment relations around the gendered model of small household production. Bethany Moreton, *To Serve God and Walmart: The Making of Christian Free Enterprise* (Cambridge: Cambridge University Press, 2010), pp. 50–53.

235. Under the terms of New Deal legislation, comprising the Social Security Act of 1935, the National Labor Relations Act of 1935, and the Fair Labor Standards Act of 1938, the employee was granted a panoply of rights unheard of under the old common law of employment. These ranged from minimum wage laws, the right to collectively bargain, to form a union, and to take strike action, and the right to social insurance protections, including old age benefits, workers' compensation, and unemployment benefits. Yet New Deal labor legislation was notoriously vague when it came to deciding who was an "employee" and who was not; and it ultimately fell to the courts to provide this definition. In *National Labor Relations Board v. Hearst* (1944), the Supreme Court offered an expansive interpretation of the spectrum of employment arrangements to be covered under the collective bargaining provisions of the National Labor Relations Act. On the significance of this case, see Veena B. Dubal, "Wage Slave or Entrepreneur: Contesting the Dualism of Legal Worker Identities," *California Law Review* 105, no. 1 (2017): pp. 83–88; Marc Linder, *The Employment Relationship in Anglo-American Law: A Historical Perspective* (New York: Greenwood Press, 1989), pp. 186–89. Acknowledging the existence of hybrid cases among the "myriad forms of service relationship," the court advised against the adoption of a narrow common-law definition of employment, in which direct control over the means and manner of production was taken as the sole deciding criterion. In its interpretation of the congressional intent informing NLRA provisions, the Supreme Court ruled that the worker's employment status should be considered "a matter of economic fact" as opposed to common-law orthodoxy. In subsequent rulings, the Supreme Court reaffirmed this position as it applied to the Fair Labor Standards and Social Security Acts, determining that "in the application of social legislation, employees are those who, as a matter of economic reality, are dependent upon the business to which they render service," *United States v. Silk*, 331 U.S. 704 (1947), p. 130. Thus, newspaper sellers, truckers, and taxi drivers could be (and often were) considered employees under the terms of New Deal legislation. Linder, *The Employment Relationship in Anglo-American Law*, pp. 193–95.

This accommodative reading of New Deal labor legislation was brutally upended, however, when Republicans took control of both houses of Congress in 1947. Determined to placate their business constituents and rein in the power of organized labor, the 80th Congress extolled the virtues of the old common-law employment test and wielded it as a weapon against New Deal reforms. Passed over Truman's veto, the Labor Management Relations Act of 1947, otherwise known as the Taft-Hartley Act, curtailed the power of unions as outlined in the National Labor Relations Act and revised its definition of "employee" to exclude "any individual having the status of independent contractor." Quoted in ibid., p. 196. See also Dubal, "Wage Slave or Entrepreneur," p. 86. One year later, Congress again overruled Truman's veto and passed a resolution excluding independent contractors from the reach of the Social Security Act. Linder, *The Employment Relationship in Anglo-American Law*, pp. 204–8. Any worker who could be construed as independent under the narrow common-law definition of employment would now be barred from receiving a pension, unemployment benefits, or workers' compensation. In Senate hearings, the Treasury Department objected that the resolution would be especially harmful to salesmen, taxi drivers, domestic workers, contract loggers, and contract construction workers. Ibid., p. 206. Until the 1970s, however, the full implications of this shift remained obscure, thanks to the growing hegemony of the standard contract of employment. Dubal, "Wage Slave or Entrepreneur," p. 88.

236. On company truckers as employees, see Michael H. Belzer, *Sweatshops on Wheels: Winners and Losers in Trucking Deregulation* (Oxford: Oxford University Press, 2000), pp. 21–22; Steve Viscelli, *The Big Rig: Trucking and the Decline of the American Dream* (Berkeley: University of California Press, 2016), pp. 12–14; Hamilton, *Trucking Country*, p. 8. On the taxi driver as employee, see Hodges, *Taxi!*, pp. 127, 140–41; Veena B. Dubal, "The Drive to Precarity: A Political History of Work, Regulation, and Labor Advocacy in San Francisco's Taxi and Uber Economies," *Berkeley Journal of Employment and Labor Law* 38, no. 1 (2017): pp. 101–102.

237. In the taxi industry, for instance, fleet owners who had hitherto treated their drivers as employees and paid them on commission reorganized themselves as leasing companies and transferred the entire risk of fluctuating revenue to their workers—now reclassified as independent contractors. On the shift from a commission-based to a leasing model in the taxi industry, see Biju Mathew, *Taxi!: Cabs and Capitalism in New York City* (Ithaca, NY: ILR Press, 2005), pp. 53, 68–79. When asked to rule on these specific cases of misclassification, the DC Circuit decided in favor of the taxi fleet owners. Dubal, "Wage Slave or Entrepreneur," p. 90.

238. Marc Linder, "The Involuntary Conversion of Employees into Self-Employed: The Internal Revenue Service and Section 530," *Clearinghouse Review* 22 (1988): pp. 14–22.

239. Mark Erlich, "Misclassification in Construction: The Original Gig Economy," *Industrial & Labor Relations Review* 74, no. 5 (2021): pp. 1208–1209.

240. Ronald Reagan, "Independents vs. IRS," Program 78–02, 27 January 1978, Ronald Reagan Radio Commentary Sound Recordings, Box/Folder 2:3, Hoover Institution Library and Archives.

241. Ibid.

242. McQuaid, *Uneasy Partners*, pp. 164–65. John Connally had served as treasury secretary under Nixon and was a mentor to Charls E. Walker.

243. Reagan hosted the General Electric Theater television program and traveled the country as the company's public relations envoy between 1954 and 1962. For an account of Ronald Reagan's time at General Electric, his close relationship with its vice president of labor, Lemuel Boulware, and Boulware's influence on his political views, see Thomas W. Evans, *The Education of Ronald Reagan: The General Electric Years and the Untold Story of His Conversion to Conservatism* (New York: Columbia University Press, 2008).

244. In an early memoir, Reagan lamented that professional actors "have been and are discriminated against tax-wise. In all the half million words that make up the senseless hodgepodge of the income tax law, there are only two references to actors. One says we are not entitled to the deductions granted businessmen because we are professionals and the other says we aren't professionals because we receive a salary instead of a fee." Ronald Reagan and Richard G. Hubler, *Where's the Rest of Me? The Autobiography of Ronald Reagan* (New York: Duell, Sloan and Pearce, 1965), p. 264. Reagan was elected to the board of directors of the Screen Actors Guild in 1941. He became vice president in 1946 and was elected president in 1947. He was reelected to this role six times, completing his last term in 1959.

245. Ronald Reagan, *An American Life: The Autobiography* (London: Hutchinson, 1990), pp. 117 and 231.

246. Lou Cannon, *Reagan* (New York: G. P. Putnam's Sons, 1982), pp. 91, 324.

247. As noted by Kim Phillips-Fein, Reagan "celebrated the individual risk-taker, the small proprietor, not the life-long executive or bureaucrat." *Invisible Hands*, p. 247.

248. Wanniski, "Introduction," p. 351.

249. Ibid. The meeting was attended by Kemp, Laffer, and Wanniski. Wanniski and Laffer had originally hoped that Kemp would run in the Republican primaries. However, Kemp pledged allegiance to Reagan in the summer of 1979, claiming that "he is eighty-five percent with us on the issues" (p. 349). For a discussion of this meeting, see Kondracke and Barnes, *Jack Kemp*, pp. 65–67. Kemp reiterated Wanniski's assessment of Reagan in an interview with political journalist Frank van der Linden. In Kemp's words, "Reagan is different. His strength comes from the blue-collar worker, the small shopkeeper, those men and women who really want to aspire to more." Frank Van der Linden, *The Real Reagan: What He Believes, What He Has Accomplished, What We Can Expect from Him* (New York: Morrow, 1981), p. 198.

250. Having slipped up once in the early months of 1980, when he carelessly told a reporter that he wanted to apply antitrust laws to organized labor, Reagan became much more curated in the final months of the campaign. Rowland Evans and Robert Novak, "Reagan's Blue Collar," *Washington Post*, April 25, 1980; Rachelle Patterson, "The Stretch Drive: Reagan Goes after the Blue-Collar Voter," *Boston Globe*, September 2, 1980; David S. Broder, "Reagan Makes Pitch to Labor, but First He Changes the Key," *Washington Post*, October 9, 1980; and Art Pine, "Ronald Reagan: Rewrapping a Massive Package of Tax Cuts for 1981," *Washington Post*, October 26, 1980.

251. Lou Cannon, "Reagan, Echoing 'New Deal,' Woos Hard-Hats," *Washington Post*, October 2, 1980.

252. Quoted in Van der Linden, *The Real Reagan*, p. 239. The quote is taken from Reagan's speech before a group of Teamsters in Columbus, Ohio.

253. Cannon, "Reagan, Echoing 'New Deal,' Woos Hard-Hats."

254. Phillips-Fein, *Invisible Hands*, pp. 242–47.

255. "H.R. 4242—97th Congress: Economic Recovery Tax Act of 1981," July 23, 1981. Confusingly, the Tax Act of 1981 is also referred to as the Kemp-Roth Tax Act. I have avoided using this formulation here, since it is easy to confuse with earlier bills bearing the name "Kemp-Roth."

256. On this schism, see Waterhouse, *Lobbying America*, pp. 202–14. Monica Prasad argues that Reagan's 1981 income tax cuts disprove the thesis of an overwhelming business influence on the early neoliberal agenda. Monica Prasad, "The Popular Origins of Neoliberalism in the Reagan Tax Cut of 1981," *Journal of Policy History* 24, no. 3 (2012): pp. 351–83. Yet she ignores the considerable support coming from the small business sector, represented at the time by the Chamber of Commerce.

257. Prasad, "The Popular Origins of Neoliberalism," p. 373.

258. Paul R. Abramson, John H. Aldrich, and David W. Rohde, *Change and Continuity in the 1980 Elections* (Washington, DC: CQ Press, 1983), pp. 98–99.

259. For a nuanced discussion of the "Reagan Democrats" and the considerable fluctuation in union and white working-class party allegiance from one election cycle to the next, see Marie Gottschalk, *The Shadow Welfare State: Labor, Business, and the Politics of Health Care in the United States* (Ithaca, NY: Cornell University Press, 2018), pp. 31–36.

260. Hibbs, *The American Political Economy*, p. 323; Kevin Phillips, *The Politics of Rich and Poor: Wealth and the American Electorate in the Reagan Aftermath* (New York: Random House, 1990), p. 80.

261. Hibbs, *The American Political Economy*, pp. 308–10; Phillips, *The Politics of Rich and Poor*, pp. 81–82, 87.

262. Steve Babson, *The Unfinished Struggle: Turning Points in American Labor, 1877–Present* (Lanham, MD: Rowman & Littlefield, 1999), p. 156.

263. "Text of Reagan Talk on Strike," *New York Times*, August 4, 1981. In the draft of his 1980 State of the Union speech, Reagan confided his view that excessive taxation and an over-powerful public sector had diminished U.S. economic competitiveness: "We have lost our international economic competition, not only because we have become overgoverned, overregulated and overtaxed but because…our method of taxation has discouraged investment risk and enterprise, and the results of overtaxation have siphoned people and their work from the private sector which accounts for our production, to the public sector which is not only the least productive segment of our economy, but devotes much of its activity to impeding production and stimulating consumption." Ronald Reagan, "'State of the Union' Speech, March 13, 1980," in *Reagan in His Own Hand*, ed. Annelise Anderson, Martin Anderson, and Kiron K. Skinner (Waterville, ME: Thorndike Press, 2001), p. 769.

264. Babson, *The Unfinished Struggle*, pp. 156–58.

265. Ibid., p. 158. The ruling in question is *NLRB v. Mackay Radio & Telegraph Co.*, 304 U.S. 333 (1938). For an extensive discussion of this ruling, see James Gray Pope, "How American Workers Lost the Right to Strike, and Other Tales," *Michigan Law Review* 103, no. 3 (2004): pp. 527–34.

266. Richard B. Freeman, "Contraction and Expansion: The Divergence of Private Sector and Public Sector Unionism in the United States," *Journal of Economic Perspectives* 2, no. 2 (1988): pp. 63–88.

267. Mike Davis, *Prisoners of the American Dream: Politics and Economy in the History of the US Working Class* (New York: Verso, 1999), pp. 102–56.

268. Linder, *Wars of Attrition*, p. 356.

269. Ibid., p. 393.

270. Ibid., p. 356.

271. *The Construction Chart Book*, 4th ed. (Silver Spring, MD: CPWR Center for Construction Research and Training, 2008), section 22.

272. Peter Philips, Garth Mangum, Norm Waitzman, and Anne Yeagle, "Losing Ground: Lessons from the Repeal of Nine 'Little Davis-Bacon' Acts," Working Paper, Economics Department, University of Utah, 1995.

273. Erlich, "Misclassification in Construction," pp. 1203, 1212.

274. Marc Linder, "Dependent and Independent Contractors in Recent U.S. Labor Law: An Ambiguous Dichotomy Rooted in Simulated Statutory Purposelessness," *Comparative Labor Law and Policy Journal* 21, no. 1 (1999): p. 221.

275. Erlich, "Misclassification in Construction," p. 1203. See also Russell Ormiston, Dale Belman, and Mark Erlich, *An Empirical Methodology to Estimate the Incidence and Costs of Payroll Fraud in the Construction Industry* (Washington, DC: National Alliance for Fair Contracting, 2020). Ormiston, Belman, and Erlich calculate that in an average month of 2017, between 12.4 percent and 20.5 percent of the construction industry workforce was either misclassified as independent contractors or working "off-the-books" (p. 3).

276. In much of the recent labor scholarship, subcontracting has become a byword for labor precarity. However, this equation cannot be assumed for the building trades, which have never followed the standard organizational structure of the vertically integrated corporation. In an industry dominated by small-to medium-size companies, the largest builders have always operated "like a federation of small independent companies" rather than an integrated corporation. The place of workers within this network of contractual relations was once mediated by the union hiring hall and collective bargaining powers, ensuring them a voice at least equal to that of the industrial wage worker in a standard employment arrangement. Frederick Abernathy, Kermit Baker, Kent Colton, and David Weil, *Bigger Isn't Necessarily Better: Lessons from the Harvard Home Builder Study* (Lanham, MD: Lexington Books, 2012), p. 106.

277. Ibid.

278. Erlich, "Misclassification in Construction," p. 1207.

279. On the transition from the unionized general contractor to the union-hostile contract manager, see David Weil, "The Contemporary Industrial Relations System in Construction," *Labor History* 46, no. 4 (2005): p. 451; Erlich, "Misclassification in Construction," pp. 1206–207.

280. On the "master-servant"-style labor relationship that reigns between day laborers and labor brokers, see Rebecca Berke Galemba, *Laboring for Justice: The Fight against Wage Theft in an American City* (Stanford, CA: Stanford University Press, 2023), pp. 49–71. On the phenomenon of migrant workers being exploited by labor brokers in their own social or kin networks, see Ruth Milkman, *L.A. Story: Immigrant Workers and the Future of the U.S. Labor Movement* (New York: Russell Sage Foundation, 2006), pp. 95–97. On the continuing importance of family ownership in construction, see Belén Villalonga and Raphael Amit, "Family Control of Firms and Industries," *Financial Management* 39, no. 3 (2010): pp. 863–904. It is notable today that the most prominent business lobby in the sector is the antiunion contractor group ABC (Associated Builders and Contractors), which claims to represent "small, family owned and closely held" nonunion construction companies. "ABC Celebrates Passage of Historic Tax Reform Bill," ABC (Associated Builders and Contractors), December 20, 2017. To be clear, although most construction firms are small to medium in size, it is doubtful that ABC represents any but the largest and wealthiest among these. In a 2012 investigation, the labor studies scholar Thomas J. Kriger found that no more than 1 percent of licensed construction contractors nationwide were ABC members. David Moberg, "Union Busting Is as Easy as ABC (the Associated Builders and Contractors)," *In These Times*, June 5, 2012. It is true, however, that most construction businesses are privately held and a disproportionate number of them are family owned. On the continuing dominance of small-to medium-sized firms in the construction industry, despite the recent rise of large publicly traded home builder companies, see Abernathy et al., *Bigger Isn't Necessarily Better*, pp. 40–48.

281. For an extensive discussion of these developments and the pivotal role of the small business contractor, see David Weil, *The Fissured Workplace: Why Work Became So Bad for So Many and What Can Be Done to Improve It* (Cambridge, MA: Harvard University Press, 2014), pp. 8–9 and 17; Gerald F. Davis, *The Vanishing American Corporation: Navigating the Hazards of a New Economy* (New York: Penguin Random House, 2016), pp. 81–94. For a fascinating account of the role of the small business third-party seller in Amazon's platform-mediated retail model, see Moira Weigel, *Amazon's Trickle-Down Monopoly: Third-Party Sellers and the Transformation of Small Business* (New York: Data & Society Research Institute, 2023). Weigel's concept of the "trickle-down monopoly," which grants the third-party seller all the risks and responsibilities but little of the freedom of true entrepreneurship, is clearly relevant to many other sectors of the economy today.

282. Abernathy et al., *Bigger Isn't Necessarily Better*, p. 106.

283. Weil, *The Fissured Workplace*, pp. 7–8, 142–43.

284. The Fair Labor Standards Act of 1938 established the right of employees to minimum wages and overtime. It also outlawed the use of child labor. Under a little-known

provision, the FLSA was amended in 1989 to exempt small business owners. Small business referred to any business making less than $500,000 per year but employing up to ten workers. A similar exemption had been included in the original FLSA owing to concerns that federal limits on local business activity would be considered unconstitutional. However, the exemption was almost immediately subject to strict oversight and was removed by the 1960s as the Supreme Court came to recognize a vastly expanded commerce power. The 1989 amendments reinstated the exemption at precisely the moment when more and more employees were falling under the authority of small business owners. The labor historian Marc Linder notes that the impact of the exemption was especially harsh in the construction industry, where small business contractors are pervasive. Marc Linder, "The Small Business Exemption under the Fair Labor Standards Act: The 'Original' Accumulation of Capital and the Inversion of Industrial Policy," *Journal of Law and Policy* 6 (1998): pp. 403–535.

285. Martin S. Feldstein, "The United States Saves Too Little!," *Society* 14 (1977): pp. 76–78.

286. According to Michael Sherraden, Kemp became interested in the idea of "asset-based welfare" during his time as secretary of housing and urban development (HUD) under President George H.W. Bush. In 1991 and 1992, Kemp initiated several meetings between Sherraden and high-level officials in the Bush administration and set about proposing a number of bills modeled directly on Sherraden's ideas. These included a proposed change to the welfare asset limit from $1000 to $10,000 and legislation to enact individual development accounts, or IDAs, for public housing residents. Michael Sherraden, "Asset-Building Policy and Programs for the Poor," in *Assets for the Poor: The Benefits of Spreading Asset Ownership*, ed. Thomas M. Shapiro and Edward N. Wolff (New York: Russell Sage Foundation, 2001), pp. 306–307.

287. Michael B. Katz, *The Price of Citizenship: Redefining the American Welfare State* (Philadelphia: University of Pennsylvania Press, 2008), p. 122; Alan F. Zundel, *Declarations of Dependency: The Civic Republican Tradition in U.S. Poverty Policy* (Albany: State University of New York Press, 2000), p. 55. For details on Reagan's attack on urban poverty programs, see Helene Slessarev, *The Betrayal of the Urban Poor* (Philadelphia: Temple University Press, 1997).

288. Katz, *The Price of Citizenship*, p. 126; Timothy P. R. Weaver, *Blazing the Neoliberal Trail: Urban Political Development in the United States and United Kingdom* (Philadelphia: University of Pennsylvania Press, 2016), pp. 31–33, 40, 84. In June 1980, Kemp joined Democratic Representative Robert Garcia in cosponsoring an "enterprise zone" bill. The Kemp-Garcia bill would have allowed tax abatements and other incentives to encourage small business creation in inner-city areas with high rates of unemployment. Unlike the British version, the Kemp-Garcia enterprise zone would not have exempted businesses from minimum wage laws and federal health and safety regulations.

289. Stuart M. Butler, "The Conceptual Evolution of Enterprise Zones," in *Enterprise Zones: New Directions in Economic Development*, ed. Roy Green (Newbury Park, CA: Sage,

1991), pp. 30–31. On the role of supply-side advocates in promoting the "enterprise zone" framework, see Stuart M. Butler, "'Supply-Side' in the Inner-City Enterprise Zones in America," *Built Environment* 7, no. 1 (1981): pp. 42–49. For a meticulous account of the transplant of neoliberal ideas around property-owning democracy from Britain to the United States, see Daniel Stedman-Jones, *Masters of the Universe: Hayek, Friedman, and the Birth of Neoliberal Politics* (Princeton, NJ: Princeton University Press, 2012), pp. 273–328. On Reagan's "enterprise zone" initiatives as a uniquely austere form of supply-side state intervention, see Brent Cebul, *Illusions of Progress: Business, Poverty, and Liberalism in the American Century* (Philadelphia: University of Pennsylvania Press, 2023), pp. 310–14.

290. David L. Birch, *The Job Generation Process* (Cambridge, MA: MIT Program on Neighborhood and Regional Change, 1979); David L. Birch, *Job Creation in America: How the Smallest Companies Put the Most People to Work* (New York: Free Press, 1987). For an analysis of the importance of David Birch's work to the "enterprise zone" project, see Mark Bendick Jr. and David W. Rasmussen, "Enterprise Zones and Inner-City Economic Revitalization," in *Reagan and the Cities*, ed. George E. Peterson and Carol W. Lewis (Washington, DC: Urban Institute Press, 1986), pp. 101–109. For an insight into Kemp's reliance on the work of David Birch, see Jack Kemp, *HUD Programs and Policies with Secretary Jack Kemp, Hearing before the Committee on Banking, Finance, and Urban Affairs, House of Representatives, One Hundred First Congress, First Session, March 7, 1989* (Washington, DC: U.S. Government Printing Office, 1989), p. 29. In a systematic review of Birch's methods published later in the decade, Hamilton, Medoff, and Brown found that Birch had misleadingly included the chain store and franchise outlet under the small business category, so that the figure of eight out of ten jobs created by small businesses was closer to six out of ten. The most important finding to come out of their research, however, was that small businesses are also responsible for most job losses, because 60 to 80 percent fail within the first five years. Charles Brown, James Hamilton, and James Medoff, *Employers Large and Small* (Cambridge, MA: Harvard University Press, 1990), pp. 2, 23–24.

291. On the role of the American Legislative Exchange Council in the state-level dissemination of the enterprise zone model, see Karen Mossberger, *The Politics of Ideas and the Spread of Enterprise Zones* (Washington, DC: Georgetown University Press, 2000).

292. Margaret G. Wilder and Barry M. Rubin, "Rhetoric versus Reality: A Review of Studies on State Enterprise Zone Programs," *Journal of the American Planning Association* 62, no. 4 (1996): pp. 473–91.

293. On the neglect of urban poverty, see Joe R. Feagin and Robert Parker, *Building American Cities: The Urban Real Estate Game* (Englewood Cliffs, NJ: Prentice-Hall, 2002), p. 58. On the prioritization of manufacturing companies, see Alan H. Peters and Peter S. Fisher, *State Enterprise Zone Programs: Have They Worked?* (Kalamazoo, MI: W. E. Upjohn Institute, 2002), p. 1.

294. For a long-term perspective on the use of tax incentives, which traces the shift from supply-side to demand-side policies of economic development, beginning in the early twentieth century, see Peter K. Eisinger, *The Rise of the Entrepreneurial State: State and*

Local Economic Development Policy in the United States (Madison: University of Wisconsin Press, 1988). On the explosion of business tax incentives in the 1990s, see David Brunori, "Principles of Tax Policy and Targeted Tax Incentives," *State and Local Government Review* 29, no. 1 (1997): pp. 50–61. On tax incentives as a form of political as well as economic tribute, see Nathan M. Jensen and Edmund J. Malesky, *Incentives to Pander: How Politicians Use Corporate Welfare for Political Gain* (Cambridge: Cambridge University Press, 2018).

295. Jack Kemp, *Secretary Jack Kemp Speaks to the National Association of Home Builders Remarks at the Annual Convention, Atlanta, Georgia, January 21, 1991* (Washington, DC: Department of Housing and Urban Development, 1991), p. 4.

296. Katz, *The Price of Citizenship*, p. 122; Zundel, *Declarations of Dependency*, p. 55.

297. Zundel, *Declarations of Dependency*, p. 55.

298. As secretary of housing and urban development under President George H. W. Bush, Kemp included the same plan for public housing privatization in the 1990 Housing Act. However, during his four years of tenure, HUD managed to sell only 135 public housing units to tenants. Katz, *The Price of Citizenship*, p. 123.

299. In his State of the Union address of January 1984, Reagan asked the Treasury Department to propose a plan for action to simplify the entire tax code so that all taxpayers, big and small, were treated more fairly. Determined to avoid the fallout of his 1981 tax cuts, Reagan advised that the final bill would need to be "revenue neutral": his stated intention was to remain faithful to the spirit of tax reduction while at the same time broadening the base through the careful elimination of tax shelters. This call eventually led to the Tax Reform Act of 1986. See W. Elliot Brownlee, *Federal Taxation in America: A History* (Cambridge: Cambridge University Press, 2018), pp. 197–209. The Kemp-Kasten proposal was one of several early responses to Reagan's call, all of which bore the mark of supply-side thinking.

300. Jack Kemp, "A Fair, Simple, and Pro-Growth Tax Reform," *Cato Journal* 5, no. 2 (1985): p. 484. Kemp saw Reagan's second round of tax reforms as a valuable chance to consolidate the Republicans' strategy of blue-collar realignment. David E. Rosenbaum, "A Decidedly Different Tax Debate: Everything's Up for Grabs This Year—and Business Is Split as Never Before," *New York Times*, March 24, 1985.

301. Kemp, "A Fair, Simple, and Pro-Growth Tax Reform," p. 484.

302. Ibid., pp. 487–89. Along with the so-called marriage penalty in tax law, the issue of the personal tax exemption was taken up by religious conservatives in the 1980s as part of a wider interest in the interactions between taxation and the family. On the emergence of taxation as a central issue for the religious right, see Molly Michelmore, "Creating the Marriage Penalty: Tax Politics, Gender, and Political Realignment in 1970s America," *Journal of Women's History* 30, no. 2 (2018): pp. 136–60. While the problem of an alleged "marriage penalty" within the tax code was the theme of choice for several years, by the end of Reagan's first term religious conservatives had redirected their attention to the question of "personal exemptions" and their impact on the traditional family. By his own admission, the tax specialist Eugene Steuerle inadvertently inspired this new obsession when

he published a study pointing to the diminishing value of personal tax exemptions in the decades after World War II. C. Eugene Steuerle, *Contemporary U.S. Tax Policy* (Lanham, MD: Rowman & Littlefield, 2008), pp. 114, 125. The study, presented at an American Enterprise Institute conference on tax and the family, showed that the growing income tax burden paid by the working poor and households with dependants could be attributed in part to the steady erosion in the relative and real value of personal exemptions. Eugene Steuerle, "The Tax Treatment of Households of Different Size," in *Taxing the Family: A Conference Sponsored by the American Enterprise Institute for Public Policy Research*, ed. Rudolph G. Penner (Washington, DC: American Enterprise Institute, 1983), pp. 73–91.

303. Kemp, "A Fair, Simple, and Pro-Growth Tax Reform," p. 491.

304. Ibid., pp. 491–92.

305. Ibid., p. 495. At the time the bill was proposed, the long-term capital gains rate stood at 20 percent, as set by Reagan's ERTA in 1981.

306. Ronald Reagan, "Remarks on Signing the Tax Reform Act of 1986," Reagan Library Archives, October 22, 1986.

307. For a summary of all provisions in the Tax Reform Act of 1986, see Brownlee, *Federal Taxation in America*, pp. 204–205.

308. Kemp, *Secretary Jack Kemp Speaks to the National Association of Home Builders*, p. 2.

309. Ibid., p. 4.

310. Ibid. In their attempts to sell the proposed capital gains tax cut to the public, Republicans argued that average homeowners would be major beneficiaries. H. Jane Lehman, "Tax Cut Issue Focuses on Homeowners," *Washington Post*, February 10, 1990; H. Jane Lehman, "GOP Advocates an End to Tax on House Sales," *Washington Post*, August 22, 1992.

311. "Greenspan Defends Tight Money Policy: Says Taming Inflation Can Extend Economic Growth Beyond 1990," *Los Angeles Times*, March 22, 1989.

312. Quoted in Rowland Evans and Robert Novak, "Pressure on the Fed," *Washington Post*, May 26, 1989. Kemp kept up a lively correspondence with Greenspan over the following decade, repeatedly pleading with him to ease up on interest rates and unleash consumer credit. Even in the late 1990s, Greenspan was too much of a monetary hawk for Kemp. For insight into Kemp's continuing efforts to persuade Greenspan, see "Greenspan, Alan, 1997–1999," Box 239, Jack Kemp Papers, Manuscript Division, Library of Congress, Washington, DC.

313. Alan Greenspan, "Stock Prices and Capital Evaluation," *Proceedings of the Business and Economic Statistics Section of the American Statistical Association* 6, no. 1 (1959): pp. 2–26. For an analysis of Greenspan's views on asset price dynamics, see Sebastian Mallaby, *The Man Who Knew: The Life and Times of Alan Greenspan* (London: Bloomsbury, 2016), pp. 49–52 and 208–14.

314. Mallaby, *The Man Who Knew*, p. 208.

315. Alan Greenspan, "Speculative Excesses Hit Housing Rather than Stock Market," *Notes from the Joint Economic Committee* 4, no. 1 (1978): p. 2.

316. Greenspan's speeches and commentaries of the late 1990s and early 2000s faithfully reproduce the terms of his earlier analysis. For Greenspan's most extensive discussion of the relationship between capital gains, both realized and unrealized, and consumer demand, see Alan Greenspan, "Capital Gains Trends in the United States: Opening Remarks by Alan Greenspan, Chairman of the Board of Governors of the US Federal Reserve System," Symposium Sponsored by the Federal Reserve Bank of Kansas City, Jackson Hole, Wyoming, August 31, 2001. In a later interview, Greenspan outlined his commonsense but academically heterodox views on savings and wealth accumulation as follows: "As far as your average American household is concerned, they would argue that they are saving more than enough [despite low official savings rates]. The reason for that mindset is they've looked at their 401(k)s, and they've looked at the value of their homes, and they've looked at their assets generally—and while we economists may say that capital gains do not finance real capital investment and standards of living, the average household couldn't care less." Addison Wiggin and Kate Incontrera, "Interview with Dr. Alan Greenspan," in *I.O.U.S.A: One Nation, Under Stress, In Debt* (Hoboken, NJ: John Wiley & Sons, 2008), p. 169.

317. Mallaby, *The Man Who Knew*, pp. 209–14. Greenspan was still lobbying for a change in the national income accounts three decades later. Alan Greenspan, "Capital Gains Trends in the United States."

318. Alan Greenspan, "The Escalation of Wages in Construction," *District Court Jurisdiction over Unfair Labor Practice Cases Hearings before the Subcommittee on Separation of Powers of the Committee on the Judiciary, United States Senate, Ninety-First Congress, Second Session on S. 3671, July 21, 22, 23* (Washington, DC: United States Congress, 1970), pp. 247–77. This testimonial reproduced a report that Greenspan's private consulting firm, Townsend-Greenspan & Co., had produced on commission to the Association of General Contractors.

319. Sherraden's ideas were picked up simultaneously by both Jack Kemp and the New Democrat caucus of the Democratic Leadership Council, or DLC. Mark Schmitt, "Michael Sherraden's Compounding Interest," *Washington Monthly*, July 2012. On the role of the DLC's Progressive Policy Institute in promoting asset-based welfare, see Lily Geismer, *Left Behind: The Democrats' Failed Attempt to Solve Inequality* (New York: Public Affairs, 2022), pp. 112–15.

320. A final insult, President George H. W. Bush was forced to veto Kemp's federal enterprise zone legislation of 1992 after the Democrats laced it with tax hikes. Weaver, *Blazing the Neoliberal Trail*, pp. 64–65.

321. HOPE legislation was passed in 1990. Roger Biles, *The Fate of Cities: Urban America and the Federal Government, 1945–2000* (Lawrence: University Press of Kansas, 2011), pp. 297–98.

322. On Clinton's federal empowerment zone legislation and its continuity with Kemp's earlier proposals, see Weaver, *Blazing the Neoliberal Trail*, pp. 66, 71, 135–45. As noted by Michael Katz, "the Clinton administration's more vigorous urban policy did not reject

the strategic direction of the Reagan/Bush era. Rather, with renewed optimism about the future of American cities, it tried to implement them more effectively." Katz, *The Price of Citizenship*, p. 123. During this period, the third-way Democratic Leadership Council actively fostered collaboration between the Clinton White House and "empowerment conservatives" such as Jack Kemp. See Joe Klein, "In the Leadership Vacuum after L.A., Will Ross Perot Become America's Fantasy?," *New York Magazine*, May 18, 1992, pp. 22–27. Accordingly, Clinton's hom ownership policy also borrowed heavily from Kemp's ideas and vocabulary. For a broader perspective on the continuities and differences between Reagan's supply-side urban policy and that of the New Democrats under Clinton, see Cebul, *Illusions of Progress*, pp. 267–96.

323. Congress passed the Housing and Community Development Act of 1992 in the final days of the Bush administration. Replete with a $300 million federal grant program to incentivize market alternatives to public housing, the project was referred to as HOPE VI in homage to Jack Kemp's HOPE (Homeownership for People Everywhere) idea. Geismer, *Left Behind*, pp. 209–10.

324. Quoted in ibid., p. 213.

325. Ibid., pp. 215, 225.

326. Katz, *The Price of Citizenship*, p. 125.

327. Kenneth Harney, "Tax Breaks for the Well-Off," *Washington Post*, October 2, 1996.

328. Lehman, "GOP Advocates an End to Tax on House Sales."

329. Cushing N. Dolbeare, "Housing Policy: A General Consideration," in *Homelessness in America*, ed. Jim Baumohl (Westport, CT: Oryx Press, 1996), p. 41.

330. Vikas Bajaj and David Leonhardt, "Tax Break May Have Helped Cause Housing Bubble," *New York Times*, December 18, 2008.

331. For accounts of Clinton's surrender to hawks in the Treasury and Federal Reserve, accomplished within the first few months of his presidency, see Bob Woodward, *The Agenda: Inside the Clinton White House* (New York: Simon & Schuster, 1994), pp. 68–71; Robert E. Rubin and Jacob Weisberg, *In an Uncertain World: Tough Choices from Wall Street to Washington* (New York: Random House, 2003), pp. 118–20. For a full account of Clinton's downsizing of the state, see Flavio Romano, *Clinton and Blair: The Political Economy of the Third Way* (London: Routledge, 2013), pp. 54–58.

332. Sheldon Pollack, *Refinancing America: The Republican Anti-Tax Agenda* (Albany: State University of New York Press, 2002), p. 90.

333. Robin Blackburn, *Banking on Death or Investing in Life: The History and Future of Pensions* (New York: Verso, 2002), pp. 387–88.

334. Richard Minns, *The Cold War in Welfare: Stock Markets versus Pensions* (New York: Verso, 2001), pp. 102–10. In Feldstein's words, "although President Clinton's Social Security proposal is awful in itself and based on a remarkable accounting sham, it also contains and endorses the key building blocks of a very desirable reform—creating individual accounts, using projected surpluses, and investing in equities." Martin Feldstein, "Clinton's Social Security Sham," *Wall Street Journal*, February 1, 1999.

335. J. Bradford DeLong and Barry Eichengreen, "Between Meltdown and Moral Hazard: International and Financial Policies of the Clinton Administration," in *American Economic Policy in the 1990s*, ed. Jeffrey A. Frankel and Peter Orszag (Cambridge, MA: MIT Press, 2002), pp. 197–204.

336. Robert Pollin, *Contours of Descent: US Economic Fractures and the Landscape of Global Austerity* (New York: Verso, 2003), p. 52.

337. According to Bob Woodward, "Greenspan hypothesized at one point to colleagues within the Fed about the 'traumatized worker'—someone who felt job insecurity in the changing economy and so was accepting smaller wage increases. He had talked with business leaders who said their workers were not agitating and were fearful that their skills might not be marketable if they were forced to change jobs." Bob Woodward, *Maestro: Greenspan's Fed and the American Boom* (New York: Simon & Schuster, 2000), p. 168. On the degradation of work under Clinton and the role of the "traumatized worker" in Greenspan's conversion from monetary hawk to dove, see Pollin, *Contours of Descent*, pp. 53–56; Michael Perelman, *The Invisible Handcuffs of Capitalism: How Market Tyranny Stifles the Economy by Stunting Workers* (New York: New York University Press, 2011), pp. 47–54. Daniel J. B. Mitchell and Christopher L. Erickson point out that there has always been a strong interest in union wage settlements and their impact on wage-price inflation in Federal Open Market Committee meetings. This preoccupation with wage-push pressures, they note, remained as strong as ever even after the massive drop in unionization that occurred in the Reagan years. Greenspan began to have doubts about the continuing power of workers to push up wages in the late 1980s but did not act on these doubts for several more years. Daniel J. B. Mitchell and Christopher L. Erickson, "Not Yet Dead at the Fed: Unions, Worker Bargaining, and Economy-Wide Wage Determination," *Industrial Relations* 44, no. 4 (2005): pp. 565–606.

338. Peter Hartcher, *Bubble Man: Alan Greenspan and the Missing Seven Trillion Dollars* (New York: Norton, 2005), pp. 19, 132.

339. Edward M. Gramlich, "Consumption and the Wealth Effect: The United States and the United Kingdom," Speech by Mr. Edward M. Gramlich, Member of the Board of Governors of the US Federal Reserve System, before the International Bond Congress, London, 20 February 2002.

340. At the turn of the millennium, Greenspan and other economists at the Federal Reserve were busily investigating the differential consumption effects of stock and home-ownership. For an insight into some of their early hypotheses, see Greenspan, "Capital Gains Trends in the United States." Testifying before Congress in late 2002, Greenspan noted that "a dollar of equity extracted from housing has a more powerful effect on consumer spending than does a dollar change in the value of common stocks." Alan Greenspan, "The Economic Outlook: Testimony before the Joint Economic Committee," U.S. Congress, November 13, 2002. Fleckenstein and Sheehan calculate that home equity withdrawal accounted for a very significant part of GDP growth in the post-2001 period. They note that without it, "the economic growth from 2001 to 2007 would barely have registered

as an economic expansion by historic standards." William A. Fleckenstein and Frederick Sheehan, *Greenspan's Bubbles: The Age of Ignorance at the Federal Reserve* (New York: McGraw Hill, 2008), pp. 170–71.

341. Although most of the president's senior economic advisers could be described as elite supply-siders, as detailed in the preceding chapter, George W. Bush also advanced a supply-side populist agenda under the influence of Karl Rove. On Karl Rove's role in helping to shape Bush's "ownership society" agenda, see Jerome M. Mileur, "Incumbency, Politics, and Policy: Detour or New Direction?," in *A Defining Moment: The Presidential Election of 2004*, ed. William J. Crotty (London: Routledge, 2005), pp. 151–54; Larry Kudlow, "The Supply Side of Karl Rove," *National Review*, July 29, 2005. From outside the White House, Stephen Moore's Club for Growth played an important role in pushing for Bush's "ownership society." Stephen Moore, *Bullish on Bush: How George Bush's Ownership Society Will Make America Stronger* (Lanham, MD: Madison Books, 2004). On the housing boom as vindication of the "ownership society," see Larry Kudlow, "The Housing Bears Are Wrong Again," *National Review*, June 20, 2005.

342. Asha Bangalore, "Housing Market—Another Information Tidbit," *Northern Trust Company Economic Research Department Daily Economic Comment*, May 23, 2005. Follow-up studies using retrospective census data corroborated these results. Kathryn J. Byun, "The US Housing Bubble and Bust: Impacts on Employment," *Monthly Labor Review* December (2010): pp. 3–17; Christopher J. Goodman and Steven M. Mance, "Employment Loss and the 2007–09 Recession: An Overview," *Monthly Labor Review* (April 2011): pp. 3–12.

343. Abernathy et al., *Bigger Isn't Necessarily Better*, pp. 40–48.

344. On revenue growth in residential construction during this period, see Andrew Haughwout, Richard W. Peach, John Sporn, and Joseph Tracy, *The Supply Side of the Housing Boom and Bust of the 2000s: Federal Reserve Bank of New York Staff Reports No. 556* (New York: Federal Reserve Bank of New York, 2012), pp. 19–20. A survey conducted by the National Association of Home Builders recorded rising profits for both large and small home builders as early as 2001, when the rest of the economy was still mired in recession. David F. Seiders, "Profits Outpace Average: Despite Recession, Home Builders Perform Well," *Builder*, March 2002, pp. 66, 68. On the importance of small business expansion during this business cycle, see Manuel Adelino, Antoinette Schoar, and Felipe Severino, "House Prices, Collateral and Self-Employment," *Journal of Financial Economics* 117, no. 2 (2015): pp. 288–306. Small firms were in high demand from both large home-building companies and homeowners looking to remodel. Marc Doussard, *Degraded Work: The Struggle at the Bottom of the Labor Market* (Minneapolis: University of Minnesota Press, 2013), p. 160.

345. Adelino, Schoar, and Severino, "House Prices, Collateral and Self-Employment."

346. Daniel Gross, "As the McMansions Go, So Goes Job Growth," *New York Times*, November 20, 2005; Phillip Reese and Mehul Srivastava, "Meet the Bosses the Real Estate Boom Inspired," *Sacramento Bee*, August 20, 2006; and Byun, "The US Housing Bubble and Bust: Impacts on Employment," p. 10.

347. Doussard, *Degraded Work*, p. 144.

348. Milkman, *Immigrant Labor and the New Precariat*, pp. 77–78. As noted by Milkman, it was not undocumented migrants who lowered wages or undercut union power in residential construction and other sectors of the blue-collar workforce. Rather, the line of causation ran in the other direction: following decades of deunionization and informalization, employers increasingly sought out undocumented workers to fill positions that had long been abandoned by citizen workers (pp. 12–13). A recent study of the California construction industry shows that the wage differential between white U.S-born and foreign workers has little to do with specialization or training: Latinos make approximately $0.70 on the dollar compared to white workers across all skill levels. Surprisingly also, union membership, not education or citizenship status, is the deciding factor in wage gains among foreign-born workers. Alex Lantsberg and Scott Littlehale, "The 1,000,000 Homes Challenge: Will Workers Who Build New Housing Be Left Housing Cost-Burdened?," CAFWD, November 10, 2016.

349. Doussard, *Degraded Work*, pp. 149–50, 163.

350. Theda Skocpol, Vanessa Williamson, and John Coggin, "The Tea Party and the Remaking of Republican Conservatism," *Perspectives on Politics* 9, no. 1 (2011): p. 33; Theda Skocpol and Vanessa Williamson, *The Tea Party and the Remaking of Republican Conservatism* (Oxford: Oxford University Press, 2016), pp. 23–24 and 57.

351. A summary of the Cato Institute survey conducted at the Virginia Tea Party Convention in 2010 by David Kirby and Emily Ekins can be found in Emily Ekins, "The Character and Economic Morality of the Tea Party Movement," *APSA Annual Meeting Paper*, January 2011. The *Politico* survey can be found at Edison Research, Politico/TargetPoint Poll Topline Results, conducted April 15, 2010, at the Washington DC Tax Day Tea Party.

352. Nils C. Kumkar, *The Tea Party, Occupy Wall Street, and the Great Recession* (New York: Palgrave Macmillan, 2018), p. 71.

353. Ibid.

354. Ekins, "The Character and Economic Morality of the Tea Party Movement," p. 9.

355. Labor sociologists report that the category of managerial independent contractor accounts for a growing proportion of employment among older white people. This is precisely the demographic that the Tea Party appeals to. Eileen Appelbaum, Arne Kalleberg, and Hye Jin Rho, *Nonstandard Work Arrangements and Older Americans, 2005–2017* (Washington, DC: Economic Policy Institute, 2019).

356. Kumkar, *The Tea Party*, p. 69.

357. Both Arlie Hochschild and Jonathan Metzl suggest as much in their studies of the Tea Party movement. Arlie R. Hochschild, *Strangers in Their Own Land: Anger and Mourning on the American Right* (New York: The New Press, 2016); Jonathan M. Metzl, *Dying of Whiteness: How the Politics of Racial Resentment Is Killing America's Heartland* (New York: Basic Books, 2019).

358. Quoted in Yuri Maltsev and Roman Skaskiw, *The Tea Party Explained: From Crisis to Crusade* (Chicago: Open Court, 2013), p. 48. This text contains a full transcript of Santelli's rant (pp. 48–50).

359. For an insight into the scale of small business failure in this period, see Ayşegül Şahin, Sagiri Kitao, Anna Cororaton, and Sergiu Laiu, "Why Small Businesses Were Hit Harder by the Recent Recession," *Federal Reserve Bank of New York Current Issues in Economics and Finance* 17, no. 4 (2011): pp. 1–7. On the scale of the recession in the residential housing sector, see Goodman and Mance, "Employment Loss and the 2007–09 Recession," p. 5. Goodman and Mance note that "even considering the volatile history of the construction industry, the 2007–09 downturn stands out. Declines from the prerecession peak in construction employment easily exceeded those of the earlier housing busts in the 1980s and 1990s, and are the steepest since the labor dislocations during WWII" (p. 5). On the impact on residential construction businesses in particular, see Katie Hafner, "Builders and Homeowners under Strain," *New York Times*, March 7, 2008; David Phelps, "Bailout Bidding," *Star Tribune* (Minneapolis), March 30, 2008; Dev Strischek and Marla McIntyre, "Red Flags and Warning Signs of Contractor Failure," *RMA Journal* 90, no. 6 (2008): pp. 72–77.

360. Skocpol and Williamson, *The Tea Party and the Remaking of Republican Conservatism*, p. 29.

361. "Tea Party participants simply did not come from the groups that have borne the brunt of the recent US economic crisis." Ibid., p. 30.

362. Christopher Ellis and Christopher Faricy, *The Other Side of the Coin: Public Opinion toward Social Tax Expenditures* (New York: Russell Sage Foundation, 2021).

363. Tess Wise, "Personal Bankruptcy and Race: When the Public-Private Welfare State Is Predatory," Working Paper, June 18, 2020. Wise is here building on Christopher Howard's concept of the "hidden welfare state." Christopher Howard, *The Hidden Welfare State: Tax Expenditures and Social Policy in the United States* (Princeton, NJ: Princeton University Press, 1999). Small businesses can file under several different chapters in bankruptcy law. Chapter 7 allows a business owner to wipe out both personal and business debts in a single case; Chapter 11, the form of bankruptcy repeatedly used by Donald Trump, allows a company to restructure and survive after bankruptcy and was originally designed for larger companies; Chapter 13 covers only personal debts and so applies only to businesses that are organized as sole proprietorships. Chapter 11 was until recently quite onerous for small business but was made more accessible in 2020 in the midst of the coronavirus crisis.

364. Debbie Gruenstein-Bocian, Wei Li, and Keith S. Ernst, *Foreclosures by Race and Ethnicity: The Demographics of a Crisis* (Durham, NC: Center for Responsible Lending, 2010). Gruenstein-Boclan, Li, and Ernst report that between 2007 and 2009, Black and Hispanic borrowers experienced foreclosure rates of 7.9 percent and 7.7 percent, respectively, as compared to a 4.5 percent rate among white borrowers. They attribute this disparity to the fact that nonwhite borrowers were more likely to be offered nonconventional, high-interest-rate loans, even when comparing for income and wealth levels. However, it can also be explained by their differential access to bankruptcy protections. On racial differences in access to and outcomes of bankruptcy protection, see Paul Kiel and Hannah Fresques, "How the Bankruptcy System Is Failing Black Americans," ProPublica,

September 27, 2017. On the growing financial barriers to filing bankruptcy since passage of the 2005 Bankruptcy Abuse Prevention and Consumer Protection Act, see Stefania Albanesi and Jaromir Nosal, *Insolvency after the 2005 Bankruptcy Reform: Staff Report No. 725* (New York: Federal Reserve Bank of New York, 2015). Albanesi and Nosal find that declining bankruptcy filings are associated with a rise in the foreclosure rate and that a growing number of low-income, non-asset-owning debtors have no access to legal protections at all. Finally, the crucial question of whose property was foreclosed upon (mortgaged homeowner or investor) was strangely absent from most analyses of the housing crisis. However, we do know that 80 percent of foreclosures in the first two years of the housing crisis involved owner–occupiers, leaving a remaining 20 percent of investors who foreclosed on investment properties. For a rare examination of the investor foreclosure and its racial dimensions, see John I. Gilderbloom, Joshua D. Ambrosius, Gregory D. Squires, Matthew J. Hanka, and Zachary E. Kenitzer, "Investors: The Missing Piece in the Foreclosure Racial Gap Debate," *Journal of Urban Affairs* 34, no. 5 (2012): pp. 559–82. These two types of foreclosure represent very different experiences of default, especially because there is ample evidence that many investors were resorting to strategic default to offload devalued properties. See "When Borrowers Default on Second Homes," *New York Times*, December 2, 2010.

365. *New York Times*/CBS Polls, "National Survey of Tea Party Supporters," April 5–12, 2010.

366. For an excellent analysis of these tensions, see Kim Phillips-Fein, "The Business Lobby and the Tea Party," *New Labor Forum* 23, no. 2 (2014): pp. 14–20.

367. Quoted in Lisa Lerer and John McCormick, "The Devil You Don't Know," *BusinessWeek*, October 2010, p. 71.

368. For a detailed analysis of the Tea Party's "small business" perspective on each of these policy points, see Scott Shane, "Why Small Business Owners Trust the Tea Party," American Enterprise Institute, 2010, and "Big Business Risks Alienating Small Business by Shunning the Tea Party," *Entrepreneur*, November 1, 2013.

369. Marlene Satter, "How Did the ACA Affect the Small-Business Insurance Market," ALM Benefits Pro, April 27, 2020.

370 The legal scholar Lisa Phillips has carried out an extensive literature review of this practice in the United States and Canada. Phillips combines insights from observational and analytic studies of small business to conclude that rising self-employment has been accompanied by a hidden growth in "unpaid market labor," for the most part performed by household members and relatives. These hidden forms of labor follow highly gendered patterns of distribution: where young men are more likely to perform unpaid market labor in young adulthood as a prelude to taking over a family business, women continue to perform the same kind of labor as spouses, even when they also work outside the household. Lisa Phillips, "Helping Out in the Family Firm: The Legal Treatment of Unpaid Market Labor," *Wisconsin Journal of Law, Gender and Society* 23, no. 1 (2008): pp. 65–112. For a nuanced analysis of unpaid family labor among migrant small business owners, see

Floya Anthias and Nishi Mehta, "The Intersection between Gender, the Family and Self-Employment: The Family as Resource," *International Journal of Sociology* 13, no. 1 (2003): pp. 105–16.

371. Palmer Schoening and Patrick Fagan, "Repealing Death Tax Will Create Jobs and Boost Economy," *Insight* (Family Research Council), September 2009, p. 4.

372. Josh Kraushaar, "Club for Growth Fueling, and Fueled by, GOP's Rightward Shift," *National Journal*, September 15, 2011. The organization had a former life as the smaller, more informal Political Club for Growth, founded in the 1980s by the investment banker Richard Gilder. It was turned into a formal organization in 1999 by Heritage economist Stephen Moore and president of *National Review* Thomas (Dusty) Rhodes.

373. Marc Ambinder, "The Club: Making GOP Establishment Vehicles Insecure since 1999," *Atlantic*, June 3, 2010.

374. Jane Mayer, *Dark Money: How a Secretive Group of Billionaires Is Trying to Buy Political Control in the US* (Melbourne: Scribe, 2016), pp. 297–98.

375. Robert G. Boatright, *Getting Primaried: The Changing Politics of Congressional Primary Challenges* (Ann Arbor: University of Michigan Press, 2013), p. 197.

376. Brendan Fischer, "Club for Growth Flexing Muscle in Races across the Country, with Help from Big Donors," *PR Watch*, August 31, 2012.

377. For an overview of the metrics and philosophy behind the index, see Arthur B. Laffer, Stephen Moore, Rex A. Sinquefield, and Travis H. Brown, *An Inquiry into the Nature and Causes of the Wealth of States: How Taxes, Energy, and Worker Freedom Change Everything* (Somerset, NJ: John Wiley & Sons, 2014), pp. 23–52.

378. Erica Williams and Nicholas Johnson, "ALEC Tax and Budget Proposals Would Slash Public Services and Jeopardize Economic Growth," Center on Budget and Policy Priorities, February 13, 2013.

379. "Supply-Side Economist Laffer Enjoys Renewed Popularity," Gannett News Service, May 25, 2012, and Rachael Bade, "Arthur Laffer Is Back as GOP Tax Man," *Politico Magazine*, October 14, 2013.

380. On Walker's active role in ALEC during his time as state legislator, see Alexander Hertel-Fernandez, *State Capture: How Conservative Activists, Big Businesses, and Wealthy Donors Reshaped the American States—and the Nation* (Oxford: Oxford University Press, 2019), p. 35. Walker's longtime political associate and campaign strategist R. J. Johnson was also an advisor to the Wisconsin Club for Growth. Scott Walker, *Unintimidated: A Governor's Story and a Nation's Challenge* (New York: Sentinel, 2014), pp. 83, 91, 187, 256. The group spent lavishly on media campaigns in support of Walker's legislation and dedicated nine million to the recall election of 2012. "Wisconsin Club for Growth," Sourcewatch, 2019.

381. Andrew E. Kersten, *The Battle for Wisconsin: Scott Walker and the Attack on the Progressive Tradition* (New York: Farrar, Straus and Giroux, 2011), pp. 1–10.

382. Lee Sustar, "Who Were the Leaders of the Wisconsin Uprising," in *Wisconsin Uprising: Labor Fights Back*, ed. Michael D. Yates (New York: Monthly Review Press, 2010), p. 71.

383. Richard W. Hurd and Tamara L. Lee, "Can U.S. Public Labor Relations Survive the

Tea Party," *Dispute Resolution in the Workplace: The Proceedings of the National Academy of Arbitrators* 66 (2014): pp. 327–28.

384. "Transcript of Koch-Walker Prank Call," Madison.com, March 5, 2011.

385. Joseph A. McCartin, "The Strike That Busted Unions," *New York Times*, August 2, 2011.

386. "Scott Walker's Tax-Cut-Driven Economic Plan," Citizens for Tax Justice, July 28, 2015.

387. Lawrence Tabak, *Foxconned: Imaginary Jobs, Bulldozed Homes, and the Sacking of Local Government* (Chicago: University of Chicago Press, 2021), p. 12.

388. These incentives were to be reproduced at progressively greater cost each year. Jason Stein, Patrick Marley, and Lee Bergquist, "Walker's Budget Cuts Would Touch Most Wisconsinites," *Milwaukee Journal Sentinel*, March 1, 2011.

389. "Scott Walker's Tax-Cut-Driven Economic Plan," Teodor Teofilov, "Which Taxpayers Saved the Most from Tax Cuts under Gov. Scott Walker?," *The Observatory*, March 20, 2018.

390. Walker confessed as much in a telephone conversation with one of his donors, Diane Hendricks. Unbeknownst to Walker, a documentary filmmaker captured the conversation. When "Hendricks...asked if Wisconsin would ever become a right-to-work state, Walker responded enthusiastically. 'The first step is, we're going to deal with collective bargaining for all public-employee unions,' he said, 'because you use divide-and-conquer.'" Dan Kaufman, *The Fall of Wisconsin: The Conservative Conquest of a Progressive Bastion and the Future of American Politics* (New York: Norton, 2019), p. 48.

391. Abby Scher, "The Attack on Unions: Right-Wing Politics and Democratic Possibilities," *Public Eye* 26, no. 2 (2011): pp. 1, 19–25.

392. Quoted in Sustar, "Who Were the Leaders of the Wisconsin Uprising," p. 72. On the concessions made by private-sector unions in the lead-up to Walker's assault on public-sector unions, see ibid., pp. 64–67.

393. Quoted in Scher, "The Attack on Unions: Right-Wing Politics and Democratic Possibilities," p. 22.

394. Ibid.

395. Meg Jones, "Walker Supporters Rally at Serb Hall," *Milwaukee Journal Sentinel*, March 3, 2011.

396. Daniel Martinez HoSang and Joseph E. Lowndes, *Producers, Parasites, Patriots: Race and the New Right-Wing Politics of Precarity* (Minneapolis: University of Minnesota Press, 2019), pp. 19–46. For a longer history of the assault on teachers' unions, see Schneider and Berkshire, *A Wolf at the Schoolhouse Door*. Without downplaying the peculiar viciousness of Republican attacks, Schneider and Berkshire point out that the demonization of teachers' unions was always a bipartisan affair (pp. 54–58).

397. Kaufman, *The Fall of Wisconsin*, p. 167.

398. Ibid., p. 32. Highway construction was one of the few public infrastructure items that Walker was prepared to spend on lavishly, even dipping into the state's general fund to

finance highway improvements. By contrast, he flatly refused the Obama administration's offer of $810 million in federal stimulus money to fund a high-speed rail line between Milwaukee and Madison. As Republican state legislatures veered to the right under the influence of the Tea Party movement, infrastructure spending became heavily partisan. For Republican legislators such as Walker, private transport on toll-collecting superhighways represented economic freedom in contrast to the suspiciously collectivist solution of mass transport. Thus, Walker refused Obama's high-speed rail project on principle, even if it would have delivered construction jobs at no cost to the state. Steve Hiniker, "Walker Road Plan Driving Him Crazy," *Milwaukee Journal Sentinel*, April 16, 2011. On the polarization of infrastructure funding, see Clayton Nall, *The Road to Inequality: How the Federal Highway Program Polarized America and Undermined Cities* (Cambridge: Cambridge University Press, 2018), pp. 70–106.

399. Kaufman, *Fall of Wisconsin*, pp. 84–85. The bill passed in 2013.

400. Tabak, *Foxconned*.

401. Jon Shelton, "The Factory That Ate Wisconsin," *Dissent*, Fall 2018, pp. 99–103.

402. Danielle Paquette, "Foxconn Scraps Plan to Build Factory in Wisconsin, Will Hire White-Collar Workers Instead," *Washington Post*, January 30, 2019.

403. Glenn Schmidt, "Wisconsin, Round Two: Walker Attacks Private Sector Workers," *Labor Notes*, March 5, 2015.

404. Sharon O'Malley, "Wisconsin Repeals Prevailing Wage Law," *Construction Dive*, July 15, 2015.

405. Frank Manzo IV, Kevin Duncan, Jill Gigstad, and Nathaniel Goodell, *The Effects of Repealing Prevailing Wage in Wisconsin* (Saint Paul, MN: Midwest Economic Policy Institute MEPI, 2020).

406. Lee Sustar notes that, despite the early show of support for Governor Walker by the most conservative construction unions, many rank-and-file private-sector workers, including factory workers and some in the building trades, demonstrated alongside teachers outside the Wisconsin State Capitol. Sustar, "Who Were the Leaders of the Wisconsin Uprising," pp. 60–62.

407. Daniel R. Alvord, "Reversal of the Kansas Tax 'Experiment': The Social Limits of Supply-Side," PhD diss., University of Kansas, 2019, p. 67.

408. Scott Rothschild, "Brownback Tax Cut Law Produces Winners and Losers, KU Tax Law Professor Says," *Lawrence Journal World*, June 16, 2012.

409. On the contribution of these organizations to the Brownback campaign, see Irin Carmon, "Kansas Gets Even Crazier," *Salon*, August 16, 2012. David Kensinger, chief of staff to Sam Brownback during his term as U.S. senator and continuing into his first year as state governor, also headed the Kansas chapter of the Club for Growth during this period. David M. Drucker, "Brownback Aides Mentioned for Congressional Seats," *Roll Call*, December 3, 2007. George Pearson, chairman of Kansas Policy Institute's board of trustees during Governor Brownback's tenure, was a longtime associate and aide to the Koch brothers. "Kansas Policy Institute," Sourcewatch, November 3, 2020.

410. Sam Zeff, "Elections Question: How Are the Kochs Influencing Campaigns in Kansas This Year," KCUR, October 20, 2016; Bill Wilson, "Alan Cobb to Head Kansas Chamber," *Wichita Business Journal*, March 24, 2017.

411. Scott Rothschild, "Task Force Working in Secret on Tax Proposal," *Lawrence Journal World*, October 8, 2011.

412. Alvord, "Reversal of the Kansas Tax 'Experiment,'" pp. 70–73.

413. Patrick Caldwell, "What's the Matter with Sam Brownback?," *Mother Jones*, September 25, 2014.

414. Chye-Ching Huang, *Tax Cuts for the Wealthy Would Do Little to Help Small Businesses and the Economy* (Washington, DC: Center on Budget and Policy Priorities, 2017), pp. 8–9. On the abuse of the pass-through income exemption by wealthy individuals, see "Editorial: KU Coach Bill Self and the Myth of Trickle-Down Economics," *St. Louis Post Dispatch*, June 15, 2016.

415. Michael Mazerov, *Kansas Provides Compelling Evidence of Failure of "Supply-Side" Tax Cuts* (Washington, DC: Center on Budget and Policy Priorities, 2018), pp. 7–8.

416. Patricia Murphy, "Sam Brownback's Kansas Catastrophe," *Daily Beast*, July 20, 2014.

417. Zachary A. Goldfarb, "In Kansas, Brownback Tried a Red-State 'Experiment'; Now He May Be Paying a Political Price," *Washington Post*, July 30, 2014; Alvord, "Reversal of the Kansas Tax 'Experiment,'" pp. 66–124.

418. In a recent statement on its tax position, ABC states that the "overwhelming majority of construction businesses are organized as pass-through entities, meaning that their income is taxed at the individual level. These job-creating small and medium-sized businesses would bear the brunt of higher marginal tax rates, wealth surcharges, and corporate-only attempts to reform or alter the code." "Tax and Fiscal Policy," ABC, 2022.

419. Pamela Prah, "GOP Targets State Construction Labor Projects," Pew Trust, September 14, 2012. The state and federal lobbying effort to repeal PLAs was spearheaded by ABC. However, AGC has also been opposed to PLAs for many years. See "AGC Testifies in Opposition to President Clinton's Proposed Executive Order on Project Labor Agreements," *PR Newswire*, April 30, 1997.

420. Daniel McCoy, "New KDOT Director Is Mike King of McPherson," *Wichita Business Journal*, March 23, 2012.

421. "Kansas Contractors Out to Curb State Raids of Highway Funds," *Real Estate Monitor Worldwide*, October 14, 2016.

422. "Dollars and Sense: Brownback Wants the Real Story on Taxes Out, So Here It Is," *Hutchinson News*, December 18, 2015.

423. Benjy Sarlin, "The GOP Tried Trump-Style Tax Cuts in Kansas; What a Mess," NBC News, October 23, 2017; Dan Kaufman, "Scott Walker's Wisconsin Paved the Way for Donald Trump's America," *New York Times*, July 6, 2021.

424. On this lineage, see Ray Kiely, "Locating Trump: Paleoconservatism, Neoliberalism, and Anti-Globalization," *Socialist Register* 55 (2019): pp. 126–49; Peter Kolozi,

Conservatives against Capitalism: From the Industrial Revolution to Globalization (New York: Columbia University Press, 2017), pp. 167–89.

425. Davis, "Election 2016."

426. Pew Research Center, *Trump's Staunch GOP Supporters Have Roots in the Tea Party* (Washington, DC: Pew Research Center, 2019). On Trump's enduring support base among small business owners, see Olen, "Small-Business Owners Have a Thing for Donald Trump"; Marks, "If It Were Up to Small Business Owners, Trump Would Get His Second Term"; Michael McCarthy, "The Revenge of Joe the Plumber."

427. Regularly updated data on the demographics of the Capitol Hill rioters can be found on the following website created by Robert Pape and colleagues at the University of Chicago, "The Face of American Insurrection," Chicago Project on Security and Threats at the University of Chicago. See also the data summary in Robert A. Pape, "The Jan. 6 Insurrectionists Aren't Who You Think They Are," *Foreign Policy*, January 6, 2022. As of June 8, 2022, a total of 213 out of 599 arrested protestors (that is, over one-third) were either business owners or self-employed. Among those charged were real estate brokers, CEOs, shop owners, accountants, and lawyers. The Capitol Hill crowd differed from the Tea Party base in its more even spread across age cohorts and the large numbers of active militia members, primarily Oath Keepers and Proud Boys, it its ranks. The Chicago Project reports that 18 percent overall of those arrested were serving or former members of the military or law enforcement; 10 percent were active members of far-right militias. For media commentary on these findings, see Eugene Scott, "Data about the Capitol Rioters Serves Another Blow to the White, Working-Class Trump-Supporter Narrative," *Washington Post*, April 12, 2021.

428. With a membership base of acting and former soldiers and police officers, the Oath Keepers have historically taken action to defend white landowners and businesses against federal law enforcement, petty criminals, and left-wing rioters. According to a recent CSIS report, approximately two-thirds of the Oath Keepers are former military or law enforcement officers. A further 10 percent are on active duty in the military or currently employed in law enforcement. Eric McQueen, "Examining Extremism: The Oath Keepers," CSIS (Center for Strategic & International Studies), June 17, 2021. On the Oath Keepers' history of interventions to defend property owners, including their actions to protect small businesses in Ferguson, Missouri, after the police killing of Michael Brown in 2014, see Sam Jackson, *Oath Keepers: Patriotism and the Edge of Violence in a Right-Wing Antigovernment Group* (New York: Columbia University Press, 2020), pp. 47–52.

429. "My family came from a communist country," Tarrio recounts. "The only way to true freedom is entrepreneurship." Brendan O'Connor, *Blood Red Lines: How Nativism Fuels the Right* (Chicago: Haymarket Books, 2021), p. 105.

430. "WSJ BLOG/Washington Wire: Ted Cruz Interview: On Obama, GOP and Big Business," *Dow Jones Institutional News*, May 29, 2012.

431. Donald J. Trump, *Crippled America: How to Make America Great Again* (New York: Threshold Editions, 2015), p. 74.

432. Ibid., p. 82.

433. "President Trump Meeting with Small Business Leaders," C-Span, August 1, 2017. Sidney Plotkin makes the astute point that in its organizational style, if not its asset holdings, "Trump's private business organization has always been more akin to a small loosely run family enterprise than a corporate hierarchy." Sidney Plotkin, *Veblen's America: The Conspicuous Case of Donald J. Trump* (London: Anthem Press, 2018), p. 236. The Associated General Contractors of America (AGC) apparently shares the same assessment. A leaked PowerPoint presentation from one of the association's executives accused Trump of running his administration like a "bad family-owned small business." The executive later specified that this was not meant to be pejorative. Justin Elliott, "An Industry Group Says the Trump Administration is Run 'Like a Bad Family-Owned Small Business'—And They Love It," ProPublica, March 1, 2018.

434. Arthur B. Laffer and Stephen Moore, *Trumponomics: Inside the America First Plan to Revive Our Economy* (New York: St. Martin's Press, 2018), p. 114.

435. Ibid., pp. 114–15.

436. Ibid., p. 114.

437. Aaron Krupkin and Adam Looney, "Nine Facts about Pass-Through Businesses," Brookings, May 15, 2017.

438. Wyoming was the first state to do this in 1977. The validity of the LLC was confirmed by the IRS in 1988 and facilitated by the introduction of "check-the-box" rules in the mid-1990s. Ibid.

439. Ibid.

440. Ryan Erickson and Brendan V. Duke, "The Art of the Pass-Through," Center for American Progress Action Fund, August 10, 2016.

441. I borrow the expression from Ryan Erickson and Brendan V. Duke in "The Art of the Pass-Through."

442. Claire Sasko, "Trump Comes to PA., Talks Almost Exclusively about Truckers," *Philadelphia*, October 12, 2017.

443. Brian Straight, "Text of Trump's Speech to Truckers," *Freightwaves*, October 12, 2017.

444. Josh Barro, "Trump Has Been Lying a Lot about His 'Small Business' Tax Cut," *Business Insider*, October 13, 2017. Barro calculates that only about 1.8 percent of genuine small businesses would have benefited from this tax break.

445. Greg Sargent, "This May Be Trump's Most Insulting Scam Yet: We Need to Repeal the Estate Tax to Help American Truckers, Trump Will Say Today," *Washington Post Blogs*, October 11, 2017.

446. See especially Michael Lind, "Why Big Business Fears the Tea Party," *Politico*, June 15, 2014.

447. On the enduring importance of the family business in these sectors, see Villalonga and Amit, "Family Control of Firms and Industries."

448. It is well known that the Trump Organization has left behind a trail of destruction among its actual small business contractors. Michelle Mark, "Hundreds of Small

Businesses and Employees Have Accused Donald Trump of not Paying Them," *Business Insider,* June 10, 2016.

449. Olen, "Small-Business Owners Have a Thing for Donald Trump." Moira Weigel notes this same ambivalent relationship of loyalty and capture among Amazon's third-party sellers. Weigel, "Amazon's Trickle-Down Monopoly."

450. See Adele Stan on the prevalence of private companies in Trump's inner circle. Adele Stan, "What We Do Is Secret: Trumpism as a Private-Capital Scam," *Baffler,* June 2017. On the specifically dynastic form of these private companies, see Steve Fraser, "Playing God: The Rebirth of Family Capitalism," in *Mongrel Firebugs and Men of Property* (New York: Verso 2019), pp. 223–40.

451. Stan, "What We Do Is Secret."

452. Josh Israel, "Trump's Tax Cuts for Betsy DeVos and the Very Rich are Being Paid for by Education Cuts," ThinkProgress, April 10, 2019.

453. Doug Henwood, "Take Me to Your Leader: The Rot of the American Ruling Class," *Jacobin,* April 27, 2021. Henwood is here drawing on the work of Patrick Wyman, "American Gentry," *Atlantic,* September 23, 2021.

454. "Top Contributors, Federal Election Data for Donald Trump, 2016 cycle," Open-Secrets, 2016; "Top Contributors, Federal Election Data for Donald Trump, 2020 Cycle," OpenSecrets, 2020.

455. On the history of the Koch-founded Citizens for a Sound Economy and the latter's spinoffs FreedomWorks and Americans for Prosperity, see Mayer, *Dark Money,* pp. 27–156. On the history of the Council for National Policy and its connections to the DeVos family, see Anne Nelson, *Shadow Network: Media, Money, and the Secret Hub of the Radical Right* (New York: Bloomsbury, 2019), pp. 20–34. On the connections between the CNP and the DeVos and Prince dynasties, see ibid., p. 71. On the ties between the Family Research Council and the DeVos and Prince dynasties, see Zack Stanton, "How Betsy DeVos Used God and Amway to Take Over Michigan Politics," *Politico,* January 15, 2017; "Rich DeVos: The Salesman Who Helped Launched the Modern Right," *Politico,* December 30, 2018.

456. On the Koch's growing influence on the Republican Party and the concurrent marginalization of the Business Roundtable, see Jacob S. Hacker and Paul Pierson, *American Amnesia: How the War on Government Led Us to Forget What Made America Prosper* (New York: Simon & Schuster, 2017), pp. 201–37.

CHAPTER THREE: INFINITE REGRESS

1. Buchanan makes this claim throughout his work. In a representative passage, he contends that "the position...I advance is neutral with respect to ideological or normative content. I am simply proposing, in various ways, that economists concentrate attention on the institutions, the relationships, among individuals as they participate in voluntarily organized activity, in trade or exchange, broadly considered. People may, as in my swamp-clearing example, decide to do things collectively. Or they may not. The analysis, as such, is neutral in respect to the proper private-sector–public-sector mix." James M. Buchanan,

What Should Economists Do? (Indianapolis: Liberty Fund, 1979), p. 36. Buchanan distinguished his "constitutional" approach to economics from the "allocational" view by insisting that he was demonstrating the distributional outcomes to be expected from any given set of constitutional rules, not prescribing some optimal distribution of goods. He was, in other words, simply presenting the informed citizen with a menu of possible constitutional choices or game rules (pp. 136–38).

2. Richard E. Wagner, *James M. Buchanan and Liberal Political Economy* (Lanham, MD: Lexington Books, 2017), p. 2.

3. In his excellent study of the origins of social choice economics, for instance, Jacob Jensen argues that "Buchanan's work was mostly a political failure." Jacob Jensen, *The Marketizers: Public Choice and the Origins of the Neoliberal Order* (London: Goldsmiths Press, 2022), p. 109. While acknowledging that Buchanan's prescriptions for tax and spending limits were effective at the local and state level, he contends that "Buchanan's concern was with introducing limits at the federal level, an ambition that never materialized" (pp. 110–11). Nancy MacLean, who presents a maximalist view of Buchanan's political influence, largely confines this influence to institution-building and the transmission of ideas. She offers relatively little insight into his involvement in specific campaigns. Nancy MacLean, *Democracy in Chains: The Deep History of the Radical Right's Stealth Plan for America* (New York: Viking, 2017).

4. James M. Buchanan, *Better Than Plowing and Other Personal Essays* (Chicago: University of Chicago Press, 1992), pp. 1–2.

5. Ibid., pp. 4–5. For a detailed account of Buchanan's intellectual encounters at the University of Chicago, see Marianne Johnson, "James M. Buchanan, Chicago, and Post-War Public Finance," *Journal of the History of Economic Thought* 36, no. 4 (2014): pp. 479–97.

6. Buchanan, *Better Than Plowing*, p. 71.

7. Ibid., p. 72.

8. MacLean, *Democracy in Chains*, pp. 45–60, 94–95. I borrow the term "neoliberal thought collective" from Philip Mirowski and Dieter Plehwe, who use it to encompass the multiplicity of international scholars associated with the Mont Pelerin Society. Philip Mirowski and Dieter Plehwe, eds., *The Road from Mont Pèlerin: The Making of the Neoliberal Thought Collective Cambridge* (Cambridge, MA: Harvard University Press, 2009). I follow common usage in identifying at least four distinct schools of neoliberalism: the Virginia school, the Chicago school, the Austrian school, and ordoliberalism. At the time that neoliberal public choice theory being established at the University of Virginia, the University of Chicago and UCLA economics departments (heavily influenced by the Chicago school) were the two major institutional outposts of neoliberal thinking in the United States.

9. "I have not, and I do not reject this label." Buchanan, *Better Than Plowing*, p. 93.

10. Wagner, *James M. Buchanan*, pp. 2, 16; Buchanan, *Better Than Plowing*, p. 100. The committee was renamed as the Public Choice Society in 1968.

11. MacLean, *Democracy in Chains*, p. 85.

12. Buchanan notes that "Tullock and I formed a splinter subgroup [in the *Public Choice*

Society], one that was not fully appreciated by our peers in the more comprehensive program." Buchanan, *Better Than Plowing*, p. 100.

13. Unless otherwise stated, the following detail on the investigation into the Jefferson Center and Buchanan's departure from the University of Virginia is taken from MacLean, *Democracy in Chains*, pp. 95–101. Buchanan's curt account can be found in Buchanan, *Better Than Plowing*, pp. 15–16. For Ronald Coase's account of the institutional hostility endured by himself and his colleagues, see Thomas W. Hazlett, "Looking for Results: An Interview with Ronald Coase," *Reason*, January 1, 1997.

14. MacLean, *Democracy in Chains*, p. 96.

15. Ibid., p. 99.

16. Buchanan, *Better Than Plowing*, p. 16.

17. The experience is recounted in the uncharacteristically polemical James M. Buchanan and Nicos E. Devletoglou, *Academia in Anarchy: An Economic Diagnosis* (New York: Basic Books, 1970).

18. Buchanan, *Better Than Plowing*, p. 101.

19. Ibid., p. 100.

20. The first of Buchanan's books to give full expression to this change in outlook is James M. Buchanan, *The Limits of Liberty: Between Anarchy and Leviathan* (Carmel, IN: Liberty Fund, 1975).

21. Wagner, *James M. Buchanan*, p. 16; MacLean, *Democracy in Chains*, pp. 108–109.

22. Buchanan, *Better Than Plowing*, p. 114.

23. Ibid., pp. 123–24.

24. Ibid., p. 126.

25. The so-called Nobel Prize in economics is the Sveriges Riksbank Prize in Economic Sciences in Memory of Alfred Nobel and is not connected to the actual Nobel Prize. Philip Mirowski, "The Neoliberal Ersatz Nobel Prize," in *Nine Lives of Neoliberalism*, ed. Dieter Plehwe, Quinn Slobodian, and Philip Mirowski (New York: Verso, 2020), pp. 219–54.

26. On Buchanan's move to George Mason University and his relationship with Charles Koch, see MacLean, *Democracy in Chains*, pp. 195–97.

27. James M. Buchanan, "America's Third Century in Perspective," *Atlantic Economic Journal* 1 (November 1973): pp. 9–12.

28. James M. Buchanan and Richard E. Wagner, *Democracy in Deficit: The Political Legacy of Lord Keynes* (Indianapolis: Liberty Fund, 1977), pp. 3–4.

29. Buchanan, "America's Third Century," p. 6; James M. Buchanan, "The Economic Constitution and the New Deal: Lessons for Late Learners," in *Regulatory Change in an Atmosphere of Crisis: Current Implications of the Roosevelt Years, April 1978*, ed. Gary M. Walton (New York: Academic Press, 1979), p. 13.

30. Buchanan, "The Economic Constitution and the New Deal," p. 13.

31. Ibid., pp. 22, 19.

32. W. Elliot Brownlee, *Federal Taxation in America: A Short History* (Cambridge: Cambridge University Press, 1996), pp. 89–129; Theodore Sky, *To Provide for the General*

Welfare: A History of the Federal Spending Power (Newark: University of Delaware Press, 2003), pp. 327–41.

33. Buchanan, "America's Third Century," p. 7.

34. Buchanan's aversion to majoritarian democracy is shared by other neoliberal thinkers such as Milton Friedman and Friedrich von Hayek. For a subtle overview of their differences and commonalities, see Thomas Biebricher, *The Political Theory of Neoliberalism* (Stanford, CA: Stanford University Press, 2018), pp. 79–108.

35. James M. Buchanan and Gordon Tullock, *The Calculus of Consent: Logical Foundations of Constitutional Democracy* (Ann Arbor: University of Michigan Press, 1962), pp. 74, 82.

36. Robert F. Crea, "Racial Discrimination and Baker v. Carr," *Journal of Legislation* 30, no. 2 (2004): pp. 289–304.

37. I agree with Nancy MacLean that the *Baker v. Carr* case can be discerned in the background of Buchanan and Tullock's *Calculus of Consent*. MacLean, *Democracy in Chains*, pp. 74–87. The connection is suggested by Gordon Tullock's 1965 speech to the American Conservative Union, which refers to the arguments in *The Calculus of Consent* to illuminate the issue of electoral apportionment. Gordon Tullock, carbon copy of speech before American Conservative Union, June 10, 1965, Box 95, Gordon Tullock Papers, Hoover Institution Archives, Hoover Institution, Stanford University (hereafter Gordon Tullock Papers). For a comprehensive discussion of Buchanan and Tullock's views on the "one person, one vote" rule, see Daniel Kuehn, "James Buchanan, Gordon Tullock, and the 'Radically Irresponsible' One Person, One Vote Decisions," *Journal of the History of Economic Thought* 44, no. 3 (2022): pp. 413–36. As Kuehn observes, *The Calculus of Consent* offers a hesitant case for state malapportionment, although the argument is somewhat obscured by the use of the opaque term "numbers diversity" to describe it. Ibid., pp. 419–20. The relevant pages can be found in Buchanan and Tullock, *The Calculus of Consent*, pp. 244–46. In other texts, Buchanan referred to the Supreme Court voting rights decisions as "radically irresponsible." "Financing a Viable Federalism," in *State and Local Tax Problems*, ed. H. L. Johnson (Knoxville: University of Tennessee Press, 1969), p. 4. He also called them "extremely naïve": "Student Revolts, Academic Liberalism, and Constitutional Attitudes," *Social Research* 35, no. 4 (1968): p. 677. Remarkably, Kuehn has unearthed private correspondence from 1966 in which Buchanan urged congressional Republicans to support a constitutional amendment overturning "one person, one vote" (p. 422).

38. Buchanan and Tullock, *The Calculus of Consent*, p. 194.

39. Ibid., p. 311.

40. Ibid.

41. On this point they defer to the economist Kenneth J. Arrow, whose 1951 study *Social Choice and Individual Values* had demonstrated the impossibility of deriving public interest, social welfare, or a collective will from a simple aggregation of individual preferences or votes. Arrow, *Social Choice and Individual Values* (New Haven, CT: Yale University Press, 1951). In the years since its publication, Arrow's "impossibility theorem" has lent itself to

diverse, sometimes contradictory interpretations. Some read it as an indictment of methodological individualism itself. Others, including Amartya Sen and Anthony Downs, saw it as a challenge for identifying the conditions under which collective interests could be better apprehended and translated into practice. For an overview of these diverse interpretations, see Jeja-Pekka Roos, *Welfare Theory and Social Policy: A Study in Policy Science* (Helsinki: Societas Scientiarum Fennica, 1973), pp. 131–64. Buchanan, by contrast, seized on it as proof that *any* attempt to define or implement collective social welfare was doomed: the relevant unit of analysis could only be the individual. Buchanan's early response to Arrow's "impossibility theorem" was one of the building blocks of his intellectual development and a stepping stone toward the analysis carried out with Tullock in *The Calculus of Consent.* See James M. Buchanan, "Social Choice, Democracy, and Free Markets," *Journal of Political Economy* 62, no. 2 (1954): pp. 114–23. On the importance of Arrow's impossibility theorem for Buchanan's work, see S. M. Amadae, *Rationalizing Capitalist Democracy: The Cold War Origins of Rational Choice Liberalism* (Chicago: University of Chicago Press, 2003), pp. 135–36; Jensen, *The Marketizers*, p. 123.

42. The basic premises of the theory of voluntary exchange informing *The Calculus of Consent* are laid out in James M. Buchanan, "The Pure Theory of Government Finance: A Suggested Approach," *Journal of Political Economy* 57, no. 6 (1949): pp. 496–505; James M. Buchanan, "Individual Choice in Voting and the Market," *Journal of Political Economy* 62, no. 4 (1954): pp. 334–43. See Buchanan and Tullock, *The Calculus of Consent*, p. 250, for a restatement. For an extensive discussion of these earlier texts of Buchanan, see Amadae, *Rationalizing Capitalist Democracy*, p. 139, and Jensen, *The Marketizers*, pp. 114–16, 124–28.

43. Buchanan and Tullock, *The Calculus of Consent*, pp. 89, 148.

44. Ibid., p. 166.

45. Ibid., p. 168.

46. Ibid., p. 166.

47. Ibid., p. 72.

48. For a historically informed reading of Wicksell's contribution, see Marianne Johnson, "Wicksell's Social Philosophy and His Unanimity Rule," *Review of Social Economy* 68, no. 2 (2010): pp. 187–204. For an analysis of Buchanan's reading of Wicksell, see S. M. Amadae, *Prisoners of Reason: Game Theory and Neoliberal Political Economy* (Cambridge: Cambridge University Press, 2015), pp. 197–204, and a consideration of the diverse (pro and antigovernment) readings of Wicksell that circulated in postwar public finance, see Marianne Johnson, "Wicksell's Unanimity Rule: Buchanan's Dominance Considered," *American Journal of Economics and Sociology* 64, no. 4 (2005): pp. 1049–71. In his memoirs, Buchanan claims that he first discovered Wicksell after finishing his PhD thesis when he happened to pull the German version of Wicksell's 1896 study on taxation—"untranslated and unknown"—from the library shelves. Buchanan, *Better Than Plowing*, p. 5. The study in question was Knut Wicksell, *Finanztheoretische Untersuchungen: Nebst Darstellung und Kritik des Steuerwesens Schwedens* (Jena: Verlag von Gustav Fisher, 1896). Buchanan was responsible for translating the second chapter of this study into English. Knut Wicksell,

"A New Principle of Just Taxation," in *Classics in the Theory of Public Finance* (1896), trans. James M. Buchanan, ed. Richard Musgrave and Alan Peacock (New York: St. Martin's Press, 1958), pp. 72–118. Marianne Johnson offers a skeptical account of Buchanan's serendipitous discovery of Wicksell in "James M. Buchanan, Chicago, and Post-War Public Finance," pp. 488–91. In fact, she argues, Buchanan was already familiar with Wicksell's work at the time he wrote his doctoral thesis but later "rediscovered" him in the context of a wider renaissance of interest in the Swedish philosopher's thinking. Buchanan, she argues, offered a highly partial account of Wicksell's oeuvre, focusing almost exclusively on the second chapter of the *Untersuchungen* to buttress his account of a free market model of taxation. Johnson, "Wicksell's Unanimity Rule."

49. Buchanan and Tullock, *The Calculus of Consent*, pp. 60, 73, 94–96.

50. Ibid., pp. 254–58.

51. Buchanan, *Better Than Plowing*, pp. 113–14. See also pp. 11–12.

52. Ibid., p. 113.

53. James J. Gosling, *Budgetary Politics in American Governments*, 6th ed. (London: Routledge, 2016), pp. 13–14.

54. On this shift in welfare jurisprudence, see Martha F. Davis, *Brutal Need: Lawyers and the Welfare Rights Movement, 1960–1973* (New Haven, CT: Yale University Press, 1993); Shep Melnick, *Between the Lines: Interpreting Welfare Rights* (Washington, DC: Brookings Institution Press, 1994).

55. Buchanan, *The Limits of Liberty*, p. 207.

56. Leo Panitch and Sam Gindin, *The Making of Global Capitalism: The Political Economy of American Empire* (New York: Verso, 2013), p. 112.

57. Buchanan, "America's Third Century," p. 7.

58. Buchanan, *Limits of Liberty*, p. 21.

59. Buchanan and Wagner, *Democracy in Deficit*; James M. Buchanan, "The Moral Dimension of Debt Financing," in *Liberty, Market and State: Political Economy in the 1980s* (Brighton, UK: Wheatsheaf Books, 1986), p. 190.

60. On the welfare recipient and student militant as net consumers of public services or "parasites," see James M. Buchanan, "The Samaritan's Dilemma," in *Altruism, Morality, and Economic Theory*, ed. Edmund S. Phelps (New York: Russell Sage Foundation, 1975), pp. 74, 78–79, 82, 83. On the connections among loss of authority in the household, the decline of patriotism, and the funding of public services, in particular higher education, see Buchanan and Devletoglou, *Academia in Anarchy*. In a subsection of that book entitled "The American Tragedy of Race," Buchanan and Devetoglou identify Black students in particular as professional abusers of taxpayer largesse and useful alibis for the antics of white student militants (pp. 128–30). That Buchanan saw the white working poor as the most marginalized of social groups is confirmed by his candid quip, in correspondence with Gordon Tullock, that "the poor whites" are "the ones getting the screw as always. C9est [*sic*] la vie." James M. Buchanan to Gordon Tullock, July 12, 1965, Box 95, Gordon Tullock Papers.

61. For a wider perspective on the backlash against Great Society tax and spending

programs, see Molly C. Michelmore, *Tax and Spend: The Welfare State, Tax Politics, and the Limits of American Liberalism* (Philadelphia: University of Pennsylvania Press, 2012).

62. Jensen, *The Marketizers*, p. 128.

63. Buchanan, "Individual Choice in Voting and the Market," p. 340.

64. The reason why freedom was best fulfilled in the market was the "absence of negative results of individual [market] choices and, therefore, of the direct coercion which requires that the individual accept unchosen alternatives." Ibid., p. 341.

65. Buchanan, *Limits of Liberty*, pp. 5–9. The "libertarian" thinkers mentioned by name in the book include the philosopher Robert Nozick, the Mises-inspired libertarian and anarcho-capitalist Murray Rothbard, and the Austrian neoliberal Friedrich von Hayek. For Buchanan's critique of *The Calculus of Consent*, see pp. 9–12.

66. Ibid., p. 8.

67. Ibid., p. 9. On this shift in Buchanan's thought, see Jensen, *The Marketizers*, pp. 124, 136–47. Buchanan clarifies the difference between Chicago school and Virginia school perspectives on contractual freedom and coercion in the following quote: "Markets fail, governments fail. Demonstration of these propositions is straightforward once *homo economicus* is plugged into the model of interaction. Even in those aspects of economic intercourse that involve no externalities or spillover effects in the Pigovian sense, some limits must be imposed on the working of pure self-interest. Individuals must abide by behavioral standards which dictate adherence to law, respect for personal rights, and fulfillment of contractual agreements—standards which may not, in specific instances, be consistent with objectively measurable economic self-interest. Absent such standards as these, markets will fail even where there are no imperfections of the sort that have attracted the attention of the welfare theorist." James M. Buchanan, "Methods and Morals in Economics: The Ayres-Knight Discussion," in *Science and Ceremony: The Institutional Economics of C. E. Ayres*, ed. William Breit and William Patton Culbertson Jr. (Austin: University of Texas Press, 1976), p. 169. With regard to Hayek's depiction of the market as the product of spontaneous evolutionary process, Buchanan writes that "my basic criticism of F. A. Hayek's profound interpretation of modern history and his diagnoses for improvement is directed at his apparent belief or faith that social evolution will, in fact, ensure the survival of efficient institutional forms. Hayek is so distrustful of man's explicit attempts at reforming institutions that he accepts uncritically the evolutionary alternative. We may share much of Hayek's skepticism about social and institutional reform, however, without elevating the evolutionary process to an ideal role. Reform may, indeed, be difficult, but this is no argument that its alternative is ideal." Buchanan, *The Limits of Liberty*, p. 211n1. It has been noted by others that Buchanan's mature recognition of the noncontractual foundations of market order brought him closer to the ordoliberal school of neoliberalism. On this point, see Gabriele Ciampini, "Democracy, Liberalism, and Moral Order in Wilhelm Röpke: A Comparison with James M. Buchanan," in *Wilhelm Röpke (1899–1966): A Liberal Political Economist and Conservative Social Philosopher*, ed. Patricia Commun and Stefan Kolev (Cham, Switzerland: Springer, 2018), pp. 237–58.

68. Buchanan, "The Moral Dimension of Debt Financing," p. 190.

69. Buchanan, *Limits of Liberty*, p. 10.

70. Ibid., pp. 210, 212.

71. Ibid., p. 212.

72. Ibid., p. 210.

73. Ibid., p. 223.

74. Buchanan and Tullock, *The Calculus of Consent*, p. 194.

75. James M. Buchanan and Marilyn Flowers, "An Analytical Setting for a 'Taxpayers' Revolution,'" *Western Economic Journal* 7, no. 4 (1969): p. 355.

76. Ibid.

77. Ibid.

78. Ibid.

79. Buchanan, *Limits of Liberty*, pp. 20, 116.

80. Ibid., p. 205; Geoffrey Brennan and James M. Buchanan, *The Power to Tax: Analytical Foundations of a Fiscal Constitution* (Cambridge: Cambridge University Press, 1980), p. 6.

81. Buchanan, *Limits of Liberty*, pp. 191–94; Brennan and Buchanan, *Power to Tax*, p. 154.

82. Buchanan, "The Samaritan's Dilemma." On the "producerist" rhetoric of the American populists, see Michael Kazin, *The Populist Persuasion: An American History* (New York: Basic Books, 1995), pp. 35–36, 52–54, 143–44. Despite their very real commitment to economic redistribution, and significant instances of cross-racial organizing, the American Populists also had their nativist tendencies. Thus, as noted by Kazin, African Americans and recent migrants were frequently included in the class of "unproductive elites" by virtue of their apparent readiness to collude with the monopolists in performing low-paid work (p. 35).

83. On the welfare and student rent-seeker, see "The Samaritan's Dilemma." On the public-sector worker as bureaucratic rent-seeker, see Buchanan, *Limits of Liberty*, pp. 197–204. For a wider perspective on the public choice theory of the rent-seeker, see James M. Buchanan, Robert D. Tollison, and Gordon Tullock, eds., *Toward a Theory of the Rent-Seeking Society* (College Station: Texas A&M University Press, 1980). On the historical evolution of the term "special interest" from Progressive critique of big business to neo-populist tax resistance, see Joel Anderson, "'Special Interests' and the Common Good: The Construction of an Opposition," in *A Cultural Lexicon: Words in the Social*, ed. D. Moore, K. Olson, and J. Stoeckler (Evanston, IL: Center for Interdisciplinary Research in the Arts, 1991), pp. 91–102.

84. Buchanan, *Better Than Plowing*, p. 5.

85. James M. Buchanan, "Direct Democracy, Classical Liberalism, and Constitutional Strategy," *Kyklos* 54, nos. 2–3 (2001): p. 236.

86. Buchanan's critique of majoritarian rule, for instance, comes very close to that of anti–New Deal libertarians such as H. L. Mencken, Albert Jay Nock, and Frank Chodorov,

who combined an elitist suspicion of majoritarian democracy with a right-wing popu-list concern for the average taxpayer. Significantly, the anti–New Deal right (sometimes referred to as the "Old Right") also repurposed the American Progressive language of "spe-cial interests" to denounce the alliance between the New Deal state, unions, and public-sector workers. On the limits of majoritarian democracy, see H. L. Mencken, *Notes on Democracy* (New York: Knopf, 1926). On teachers and veterans as "special interests," chas-ing after government money and soaking the taxpayer, see H. L. Mencken, "What Is Going On in the World," *American Mercury* 28, no 4 (April 1933): pp. 385–90; Albert Jay Nock, *Our Enemy, the State* (Caldwell, ID: Caxton Printers, 1935); on the progressive income tax, special privileges, and unproductive state dependants, see Frank Chodorov, *The Income Tax: Root of All Evil* (New York: Devin-Adair Co., 1954). An even more obvious precursor was the public philosopher Walter Lippmann, a former Progressive who from the 1920s onward developed a comprehensive theory of the limits of majoritarian democracy. Walter Lippmann, *Public Opinion* (New York: Harcourt, Brace, and Company, 1922); *The Phantom Public* (New York: Harcourt, Brace, and Company, 1925); *American Inquisitors: A Commen-tary on Dayton and Chicago* (New York: Macmillan, 1927). It was Lippmann's *Inquiry into the Principles of the Good Society* (1937) that inspired the Colloque Walter Lippmann of 1938, a meeting that brought together the leading figures of what would soon be called the Mont Pelerin Society. Walter Lippmann, *Inquiry into the Principles of the Good Society* (Boston: Little Brown and Company, 1937).

87. Buchanan, *Limits of Liberty*, pp. 188–89.

88. For details on Wicksell's progressive politics, see Johnson, "Wicksell's Social Phi-losophy and His Unanimity Rule." Johnson lays out the considerable political differences between Wicksell and Buchanan in "Wicksell's Unanimity Rule: Buchanan's Dominance Considered."

89. Buchanan, "Direct Democracy," p. 237.

90. Sidney Plotkin and William E. Scheuerman, *Private Interest, Public Spending: Bal-anced Budget Conservatism and the Fiscal Crisis* (Boston: South End Press, 1994), p. 139; George E. Peterson, "Intergovernmental Financial Relations," in *Reality and Research: Social Science and US Urban Policy since 1960*, ed. George C. Galster (Washington, DC: Urban Institute Press, 1996), p. 218.

91. Colin H. McCubbins and Mathew D. McCubbins, "Proposition 13 and the California Fiscal Shell Game," *California Journal of Politics and Policy* 2, no. 2 (2010): p. 3.

92. Joe Mathews and Mark Paul, *California Crackup: How Reform Broke the Golden State and How We Can Fix It* (Berkeley: University of California Press, 2010), p. 85. Mathews and Paul's claims about the minority position of the Republican Party in the Californian legis-lature remains true to this day. In fact, California Democrats have held a trifecta—majori-ties in both chambers of the state legislature and the governor's office—since 2011.

93. David O. Sears and Jack Citrin, *Tax Revolt: Something for Nothing in California* (Cam-bridge, MA: Harvard University Press, 1985), p. 22.

94. Peterson, "Intergovernmental Financial Relations," p. 208.

95. Ibid., p. 209.

96. Ibid., p. 208.

97. Kenneth T. Jackson, *The Crabgrass Frontier: The Suburbanization of the United States* (Oxford: Oxford University Press, 1985), pp. 190–245; Louis Hyman, *Debtor Nation: The History of America in Red Ink* (Princeton, NJ: Princeton University Press, 2012), pp. 45–72.

98. Clarence Y. H. Lo, *Small Property versus Big Government: Social Origins of the Tax Revolt* (Berkeley: University of California Press, 1990), pp. 152, 163.

99. Sears and Citrin, *Tax Revolt*, pp. 47–49.

100. Ibid., p. 49.

101. Molly Michelmore is particularly illuminating on the symbolic role of AFDC in the larger tax revolt movement. Michelmore, *Tax and Spend*, pp. 3–4.

102. Romain D. Huret, *The American Tax Resisters* (Cambridge, MA: Harvard University Press, 2014), p. 211; Natalia Mehlman Petrzela, *Classroom Wars: Language, Sex, and the Making of Modern Political Culture* (Oxford: Oxford University Press, 2015), pp. 203–18.

103. Buchanan and Flowers, "An Analytical Setting," p. 355.

104. Brennan and Buchanan, *Power to Tax*, p. 25.

105. Ibid.

106. California was one of the few states to require a supermajority legislative vote to approve state budgets, a provision that had been introduced as far back as 1933. However, the supermajority vote did not apply to taxes before Prop 13.

107. Uhler wrote to Buchanan in July 1972, insisting that he was "indispensable to our effort." See Letter from Lewis K. Uhler to James M. Buchanan, July 18, 1972, C0246, Correspondence Box 32, Folder "Reagan, Ronald 1972–1974," James M. Buchanan Papers, Special Collections Research Center, George Mason University Libraries, George Mason University, Fairfax, Virginia. It appears that Uhler and Buchanan met in Blacksburg, Virginia, later that year, where Buchanan had assembled a team of colleagues to work further on the draft amendment before the whole committee was reconvened in Los Angeles in December. See Letter from Lewis K. Uhler to James M. Buchanan, November 9, 1972, C0246, Correspondence Box 32, Folder "Reagan, Ronald 1972–1974," James M. Buchanan Papers. See also William Craig Stubblebine, Interview by Enid H. Douglass, "The Development of Proposition #1," Governmental History Documentation Project: Ronald Reagan Era (Claremont, CA, Oral History Program Claremont Graduate School, 1982), p. 5; Lewis K. Uhler, Interview by Enid H. Douglass, "Chairman of Task Force on Tax Reduction," ibid., pp. 15–16. For a detailed overview of Lewis K. Uhler's role in state and federal campaigns to limit tax and spending, see Isaac William Martin, *Rich People's Movements: Grassroots Campaigns to Untax the One Percent* (Oxford: Oxford University Press, 2013), pp. 168–71.

108. James M. Buchanan to Lewis K. Uhler, July 24, 1972, C0246, Correspondence Box 32, Folder "Reagan, Ronald 1972–1974," James M. Buchanan Papers. It was Buchanan who suggested the names of Tullock, Friedman, Niskanen, and Ture as potential members of the committee.

109. Without mentioning Buchanan by name, Uhler's publications during this period faithfully translate Buchanan's theory of constitutional revolution into policy-friendly language. See Lewis K. Uhler, "A Constitutional Limitation on Taxes," *Proceedings of the Annual Conference on Taxation Held under the Auspices of the National Tax Association—Tax Institute of America* 66 (1973): pp. 379–88; "The Case for Constitutional Tax Limitation," *Ripon Quarterly* 1 (1974): pp. 13–22; "Tax Limitation: An Idea Whose Time Has Come," *Human Events* 34, no. 17 (1974): p. 43. Uhler was apparently responsible for pushing the idea that Reagan's tax reduction strategy should take a specifically *constitutional* form. See Uhler, Interview by Enid H. Douglass, p. 13. Buchanan's student, Stubblebine, notes that he was skeptical of the project until it had been formulated in constitutional terms, as "some kind of amendment—something that had some kind of relationship to theory and some aspect of enforceability, predictability, or control aspect of it." In language strongly redolent of Buchanan, he explains that Prop 1 was an attempt to "place the elected officials in a different institutional environment, a different environment within which to make decisions. The whole exercise is predicated on the basis that elected officials respond to the kinds of pressures that they find come to bear on them.... That is, there's a bias in the democratic process and that these constitutional limitations on the power of legislatures to tax and to spend are ways of dealing with an inherent bias in the situation." See Stubblebine, "The Development of Proposition #1," pp. 21, 45–46.

110. Robert Kuttner, *Revolt of the Haves* (New York: Simon & Schuster, 1980), pp. 277–78.

111. Buchanan, "America's Third Century," p. 9. The speech was published in November 1973 (the same month as the ballot) but delivered at the first conference of the Atlantic Economic Society held in Richmond, Virginia, on September 28–29, 1973.

112. Buchanan, "America's Third Century," p. 12.

113. Lewis Uhler to Ronald Reagan, April 26, 1973, Box 344, Folder 1–3 "Task Force 1972–1973," Edwin Meese Papers, 1941–1991, Hoover Institution Library and Archives. I am grateful to the historian Alexander Gourse for uncovering this correspondence. Alexander Gourse, "Restraining the Reagan Revolution: The Lawyers' War on Poverty and the Durable Liberal State, 1964–1989," PhD diss., Northwestern University, 2015, pp. 260–64. Gourse also provides an excellent account of Reagan's Prop 1 campaign.

114. Governor Ronald Reagan, "Reflections on the Failure of Proposition #1," *National Review* 25, no. 49 (1973): p. 1358.

115. Garin Burbank, "Governor Reagan's Only Defeat: The Proposition 1 Campaign in 1973," *California History* 72 (1993/1994): p. 365.

116. Ibid., pp. 365, 372.

117. Ibid., p. 365.

118. Kuttner, *Revolt of the Haves*, pp. 277–79.

119. James Ring Adams, *Secrets of the Tax Revolt* (New York: Harcourt Brace Jovanovich, 1984), pp. 168, 282; Sears and Citrin, *Tax Revolt*, p. 21.

120. On the importance of "direct democracy" to the 1970s tax revolt and the

increasingly cynical use of ballot initiatives by political entrepreneurs, see Daniel A. Smith, *Tax Crusaders and the Politics of Direct Democracy* (London: Routledge, 1998).

121. On the role of the Populist and Progressive movements in the introduction of direct democracy in California, see John M. Allswang, *The Initiative and Referendum in California, 1898–1998* (Stanford, CA: Stanford University Press, 2000), pp. 1–31.

122. On the "producerism" of the American Populists, see Kazin, *The Populist Persuasion*, pp. 34–36, 52–54, 143–44. Through the creation of a "producerist coalition," Kazin writes, "activists tended to inflate their definition of producer and labor into a grand abstraction that ignored most differences of income and occupation.... Insurgents denounced the misery caused by unemployment, low wages, and tight money. But...few criticize[d] employers or property-owners as a class" (p. 34). There is a vast literature exploring the ambivalence of the Populist and Progressive movements on questions of race and gender. See, for example, Thomas Goebel, *A Government by the People: Direct Democracy in America, 1890–1940* (Chapel Hill: University of North Carolina Press, 2003); Noralee Frankel and Nancy S. Dye, eds., *Gender, Class, Race and Reform in the Progressive Era* (Lexington: University Press of Kentucky, 1991).

123. Ajay K. Mehrotra, "Envisioning the Modern American Fiscal State: Progressive-Era Economists and the Intellectual Foundations of the U.S. Income Tax," *UCLA Law Review* 52 (2005): pp. 1793–866.

124. In his encounters with the Democratic governor Pat Brown and the League of Women Voters, Stubblebine presented the referendum as an instrument of radical democracy and a defense against the elitist tendencies of the Democratic Party. Stubblebine, "The Development of Proposition #1," pp. 37, 46–47.

125. Uhler, "A Constitutional Limitation on Taxes," pp. 380–81.

126. Buchanan, "Direct Democracy," p. 240.

127. Ibid.

128. Gordon Tullock to James M. Buchanan, July 13, 1965, Box 95, Gordon Tullock Papers.

129. This seems to be a shortcoming of Nancy MacLean's otherwise compelling account of Buchanan's work in *Democracy in Chains*. When MacLean looks for empirical examples of Buchanan's influence, she cites Chile's 1980 constitutional reform under Pinochet (pp. 154–68) but does not consider the more proximate example of the California tax revolt. Where Pinochet's Chile seems to corroborate her representation of Virginia school neoliberalism as an elite and shadowy force imposing antidemocratic reform from above, this analysis is harder to maintain when it comes to Prop 13. For a sustained inquiry into the populist origins of the neoliberal turn, which moves from the 1970s tax revolt to Reagan's 1981 income tax cuts, see Monica Prasad, "The Popular Origins of Neoliberalism in the Reagan Tax Cut of 1981," *Journal of Policy History* 24, no. 3 (2012): pp. 351–83.

130. Jonathan Metzl develops this argument at length in his study of the Tea Party, *Dying of Whiteness: How the Politics of Racial Resentment Is Killing America's Heartland* (New York: Basic Books, 2019).

131. In Kazin's words, "the romance of producerism had a cultural blindspot: it left unchallenged strong prejudices toward not just African-Americans but also toward recent immigrants…. Many insurgents who lauded the producer also stated or hinted that certain groups of people lacked the capacity to take on the monopolists in a sustained, ideologically stalwart way." Kazin, *The Populist Persuasion*, p. 35. For further analysis of the role of producerism in American right-wing populism, see Chip Berlet and Matthew Lyons, *Right-Wing Populism in America: Too Close for Comfort* (New York: Guilford, 2000), pp. 6–7, and for a perspective on Tea Party producerism during the Obama administration, see Daniel Martinez HoSang and Joseph E. Lowndes, *Producers, Parasites, Patriots: Race and the New Right-Wing Politics of Precarity* (Minneapolis: University of Minnesota Press, 2019), pp. 19–46.

132. Charles Pinnegar, *Virginia and State Rights, 1750–1861: The Genesis and Promotion of a Doctrine* (Jefferson, NC: McFarland, 2009), pp. 35–38.

133. Adam Jentleson, *Kill Switch: The Rise of the Modern Senate and the Crippling of American Democracy* (New York: Norton, 2021), p. 27.

134. Ibid., pp. 22–23.

135. Lacy K. Ford Jr., "Inventing the Concurrent Majority: Madison, Calhoun, and the Problem of Majoritarianism in American Political Thought," *Journal of Southern History* 60, no. 1 (1994): pp. 19–58.

136. Ibid., p. 48. The argument that Calhoun invented the Senate filibuster in its modern form is made by Adam Jentleson in *Kill Switch*, pp. 35, 48–58.

137. John Caldwell Calhoun, *A Disquisition on Government* (New York: Peter Smith, 1853), pp. 38–39.

138. Ibid.

139. MacLean dedicates the opening chapter of her book to exploring Buchanan's debt to Calhoun. See MacLean, *Democracy in Chains*, pp. 1–12. The argument is by no means new but only became controversial when it was publicized by MacLean's highly critical and best-selling book. For earlier instances of the argument, see Douglas W. Rae, "The Limits of Consensual Decision," *American Political Science Review* 69, no. 4 (1975): pp. 1270–94, which provoked a fierce rebuttal from Gordon Tullock in "Comment on Rae's 'The Limits of Consensual Decision,'" *American Political Science Review* 69, no. 4 (1975): pp. 1295–97. For a more recent argument from within the public choice movement, see Alexander Tabarrok and Tyler Cohen, "The Public Choice Theory of John C. Calhoun," *Journal of Institutional and Theoretical Economics* 148, no. 4 (1992): pp. 655–74. And for a comparison that is more critical of Virginia school public choice, see Daniel Rodgers, *Age of Fracture* (Cambridge, MA: Belknap Press, 2011), pp. 86–87. Michael Lind sees the entire Republican right of the Gingrich years as being driven by a Calhounian or confederate theory of the constitution. Michael Lind, *Up from Conservatism: Why the Right Is Wrong for America* (New York: Free Press, 1996), pp. 208–34.

140. The point is forcefully made in Clement H. Kreider, "Is the 'Rational Actor a Calhounian?," PhD diss., Rutgers University, 2012, pp. 98–138. As Kreider notes, John Stuart

Mill seems to have admired Calhoun without favoring either outright minority veto or slavery. Mill was significantly less pessimistic about the political wisdom of the voting majority than Calhoun and supported the extension of the vote to both working men and upper-class women. Yet he was also concerned that the voice of educated, freethinking men like him would be drowned out by the ignorant masses should universal suffrage and party politics become a reality. A solution to the problem was provided by the lawyer Thomas Hare, who drew on Calhoun's work as a justification for replacing majority voting by districts with proportional representation. The two most relevant texts here are John Stuart Mill, *Considerations on Representative Government* (London: Parker, Son, and Bourn, 1861), and Thomas Hare, *The Election of Representatives, Parliamentary and Municipal* (London: Longman Green, 1865).

141. Kreider, "Rational Actor" (pp. 139–59) makes a point-by-point textual comparison between Wicksell's arguments in "A New Principle of Just Taxation" and Calhoun's *A Disquisition on Government* to demonstrate that Wicksell faithfully reproduced the latter's logic. Given the absence of any reference to Calhoun, he surmises that the translation occurred indirectly, via Wicksell's reading of Thomas Hare, who had reproduced whole chunks of the *Disquisition* in his own work.

142. Marianne Johnson, "The Wicksellian Unanimity Rule: The Competing Interpretations of Buchanan and Musgrave," *Journal of the History of Economic Thought* 28, no. 1 (2006): pp. 57–79.

143. Lacy K. Ford Jr., "Prophet with Posthumous Honor: John C. Calhoun and the Southern Political Tradition," in *Is There a Southern Political Tradition?*, ed. Charles W. Eagles (Jackson: University Press of Mississippi, 1996), p. 23.

144. Ibid.

145. Ibid., pp. 23–24. On Calhoun as a source of inspiration for the countermajoritarian tactics of the conservative southern Democratic bloc, see David Morris Potter, *The South and the Concurrent Majority* (Baton Rouge: Louisiana State University Press, 1972).

146. On the post-Reconstruction era as counterrevolution, see W. E. B. Du Bois, *Black Reconstruction in America, 1860–1880* (New York: Free Press, 1998), pp. 580–636.

147. As noted by historian Susan Dunn, it was James Kilpatrick, editor of the *Richmond News Leader*, who had suggested the tactic of reviving Calhoun's doctrine of nullification. Susan Dunn, *Dominion of Memories: Jefferson, Madison, and the Decline of Virginia* (New York: Basic Books, 2007), p. 221.

148. Buchanan, "Financing a Viable Federalism," p. 4. Buchanan is here referring to the failure of efforts to challenge Supreme Court decisions outlawing racial malapportionment.

149. That Buchanan rejected the Calhounian solution of nullification and secession was understood by his most astute critics. The libertarian economist Murray Rothbard took Buchanan to task for precisely this reason. Murray N. Rothbard, "The Anatomy of the State," in *Egalitarianism as a Revolt Against Nature and Other Essays*, ed. R. A. Childs Jr. (Auburn, AL: Ludwig von Mises Institute, 2000), p. 79. Interestingly, MacLean's reading

of Buchanan sometimes seems to apply better to Rothbard, who did advocate a Calhounian strategy of secession. But while both Rothbard and Buchanan describe themselves as "libertarians," Buchanan, unlike Rothbard, does not belong to the American libertarian tradition inspired by the Austrian neoliberal Ludwig von Mises. On Buchanan's theory of "internal exit without secession," see James M. Buchanan and Roger L. Faith, "Secession and the Limits of Taxation: Toward a Theory of Internal Exit," *American Economic Review* 77, no. 5 (1987): pp. 1023–31. Buchanan and Faith note that "internal exit" is not only an alternative to secession but also an alternative *form of secession*. The authors are candid in describing internal secession as an option more readily available to the rich, who can easily leverage the threat of tax evasion to extract tax concessions from the state (p. 1031).

150. Du Bois, *Black Reconstruction in America*, pp. 604–605; Eric Foner, *Reconstruction: America's Unfinished Revolution, 1863-1877* (New York: Harper & Row, 1988), pp. 587–89; John Hope Franklin, *Reconstruction after the Civil War*, 3rd ed. (Chicago: University of Chicago Press, 2013), pp. 189–220.

151. Katherine S. Newman, and Rourke L. O'Brien, *Taxing the Poor: Doing Damage to the Truly Disadvantaged* (Berkeley: University of California Press, 2011), pp. 35–36.

152. C. Vann Woodward, *Origins of the New South, 1877–1913* (Baton Rouge: Louisiana State University Press, 1961), p. 59.

153. Newman and O'Brien, *Taxing the Poor*, pp. 33–34. See also Kasey Henricks and David G. Embrick, *State Looteries: Historical Continuity, Rearticulations of Racism, and American Taxation* (London: Routledge, 2016), pp. 10–27, for a rich analysis of this period and its resonances in present-day America.

154. Newman and O'Brien, *Taxing the Poor*, pp. 1–30.

155. Anne Permaloff and Carl Grafton, "Political Geography and Power Elites: Big Mules and the Alabama Constitution," in *The Constitutionalism of American States*, ed. George E. Connor and Christopher W. Hammons (Columbia: University of Missouri Press, 2008), pp. 248–50.

156. Newman and O'Brien, *Taxing the Poor*, p. 32.

157. Ibid., pp. 40–41. For an in-depth discussion of the southern tax revolt of the 1960s and 1970s, see Kevin Kruse, "The Politics of Race and Public Space: Desegregation, Privatization, and the Tax Revolt in Atlanta," *Journal of Urban History* 31, no. 5 (2005): pp. 610–33.

158. Sears and Citrin, *Tax Revolt*, pp. 23–24.

159. Jonathan Bell, *California Crucible: The Forging of Modern American Liberalism* (Philadelphia: University of Pennsylvania Press, 2012).

160. Terry Schwadron and Paul Richter, *California and the American Tax Revolt: Proposition 13 Five Years Later* (Berkeley: University of California Press, 1984), pp. 8–9.

161. Mathews and Paul, *California Crackup*, p. 84.

162. Schwadron and Richter, *California and the American Tax Revolt*, p. 11; McCubbins and McCubbins, "Proposition 13," pp. 19–20.

163. Newman and O'Brien, *Taxing the Poor*, pp. 40–42.

164. Mathews and Paul, *California Crackup*, p. 87.

165. David Brunori, "The Limits of Justice: The Struggle for Tax Justice in the United States," in *Tax Justice: The Ongoing Debate*, ed. Joseph J. Thorndike and Dennis J. Ventry Jr. (Washington, DC: Urban Institute Press, 2002), pp. 203–204.

166. Leah Brooks, Yosh Halberstam, and Justin Phillips, "Spending within Limits: Evidence from Municipal Fiscal Restraints," *National Tax Journal* 69, no. 2 (2016): pp. 315–52.

167. McCubbins and McCubbins, "Proposition 13," p. 2.

168. Jon A. Baer, "Municipal Debt and Tax Limits: Constraints on Home Rule," *National Civic Review* 70, no. 4 (1981): pp. 204–10; D. Roderick Kiewiet and Kristin Szakaly, "Constitutional Limitations on Borrowing: An Analysis of State Bonded Indebtedness," *Journal of Law, Economics, and Organization* 12, no. 1 (1996): pp. 62–97; Ruth Wilson Gilmore, *Golden Gulag: Prisons, Surplus, Crisis, and Opposition in Globalizing California* (Berkeley: University of California Press, 2007), pp. 97–102; and Destin Jenkins, *The Bonds of Inequality: Debt and the Making of the American City* (Chicago: University of Chicago Press, 2021), p. 29.

169. Kiewiet and Szakaly, "Constitutional Limitations on Borrowing," pp. 63, 68.

170. Ibid., p. 69.

171. Ibid., pp. 72 and 73.

172. Rachel Weber, "Selling City Futures: The Financialization of Urban Redevelopment Policy," *Economic Geography* 86, no. 3 (2010): pp. 251–54, 258–60.

173. Ibid., p. 260.

174. Rachel Weber and Sara O'Neill-Kohl, "The Historical Roots of Tax Increment Financing, or How Real Estate Consultants Kept Urban Renewal Alive," *Economic Development Quarterly* 27, no. 3 (2013): pp. 193–207; Rachel Weber, "Embedding Futurity in Urban Governance: Redevelopment Schemes and the Time Value of Money," *Environment and Planning A: Economy and Place* 53, no. 3 (2021): pp. 503–24; and Samuel Stein, *Capital City: Gentrification and the Real Estate State* (New York: Verso, 2019), pp. 57–58, 65–66.

175. Brunori, "The Limits of Justice," pp. 193–201, 207–208.

176. South Carolina, Alabama, and Utah all derive around a quarter of their state revenue from such sources, a trend that accentuates their historically regressive tax profile. David J. Sjoquist and Rayna Stoycheva, "Local Revenue Diversification: User Charges, Sales Taxes, and Income Taxes," in *The Oxford Handbook of State and Local Government Finance*, ed. Robert D. Ebel and John E. Petersen (Oxford: Oxford University Press, 2012), pp. 438–39.

177. Sjoquist and Stoycheva, "Local Revenue Diversification," p. 439.

178. Terry Nichols Clark, "Small Is Innovative: Local Government Innovation Strategies in the United States and Other Countries," in *Strategic Changes and Organizational Reorientations in Local Government: A Cross-National Perspective*, ed. Nahum Ben-Elia (London: Macmillan, 1996), p. 30.

179. Clark, "Small Is Innovative," p. 31; Sjoquist and Stoycheva, "Local Revenue Diversification," p. 430.

180. Sjoquist and Stoycheva, "Local Revenue Diversification," p. 439.

181. Alexes Harris, Beth Huebner, Karin Martin, Mary Pattillo, Becky Pettit, Sarah Shannon, Bryan Sykes, Chris Uggen, and April Fernandes, *Monetary Sanctions in the Criminal Justice System: A Review of Law and Policy in California, Georgia, Illinois, Minnesota, Missouri, New York, North Carolina, Texas and Washington, April* (Houston, TX: Laura and John Arnold Foundation, 2017), pp. 51, 156, 173, 186, 201.

182. Emily Shaw, *Where Local Governments Are Paying the Bills with Police Fines* (Washington, DC: Sunlight Foundation, 2016).

183. Lincoln House Blog, "Cities' Increasing Reliance on Fees as Other Revenues Fall," Lincoln Institute of Land Policy, May 7, 2015.

184. James M. Buchanan, *The Public Finances: An Introductory Textbook*, 1st ed. (Homewood, IL: Richard D. Irwin, 1960), p. 434.

185. Ibid., p. 433.

186. Ibid., pp. 503–16. For a general discussion of the importance of user fees for Buchanan's theory of public finance, see David Reisman, *The Political Economy of James M. Buchanan* (London: Macmillan, 1990), pp. 170–71.

187. James M. Buchanan, "The Pricing of Highway Services," *National Tax Journal* 5, no. 2 (1952): pp. 97–106; "The Inconsistencies of the National Health Service: A Study in the Conflict between Individual Demand and Collective Supply," in *Constitutional Economics* (London: Basil Blackwell, 1991), pp. 112–32.

188. Buchanan, *The Public Finances*, pp. 402, 507–508.

189. Ibid., p. 539.

190. James M. Buchanan, *The Public Finances: An Introductory Textbook*, 3rd ed. (Homewood, IL: Richard D. Irwin, 1970), p. 482.

191. Buchanan, *The Public Finances*, 1st ed., pp. 522–23; *The Public Finances: An Introductory Textbook*, 2nd ed. (Homewood, IL: Richard D. Irwin, 1965), p. 469.

192. For general user fees, see Buchanan, *The Public Finances*, 1st ed., p. 508; 2nd ed., p. 434; 3rd ed., p. 356. For public university tuition, see Buchanan, *The Public Finances*, 1st ed., p. 509; 2nd ed., pp. 428–29; 3rd ed., p. 351.

193. Gary Becker, "Crime and Punishment: An Economic Approach," *Journal of Political Economy* 76, no. 2 (1968): p. 169. Becker's work belongs to a wider conversation among Chicago school "law and economics" scholars concerning the most efficient management of crime and punishment. See George J. Stigler, "The Optimum Enforcement of Laws," *Journal of Political Economy* 78, no. 3 (1970): pp. 526–36; Richard A. Posner, "An Economic Theory of the Criminal Law," *Columbia Law Review* 85, no. 6 (1985): pp. 1193–231. For an alternative reading of this tradition, focusing on the work of Richard Posner, see Bernard Harcourt, *The Illusion of Free Markets: Punishment and the Myth of Natural Order* (Cambridge, MA: Harvard University Press, 2011).

194. Becker, "Crime and Punishment," p. 180.

195. Ibid., p. 170.

196. Foucault's classic reading of Bentham's panopticon can be found in Michel Foucault, *Discipline and Punishment: The Birth of the Prison*, trans. Alan Sheridan (New York:

Vintage Books, 1977). Here, Foucault advanced the idea that the expansion of the prison in the nineteenth century dislodged an earlier regime of spectacular sovereign punishment. However, as political theorist Pat O'Malley points out, the most common form of sanction prior to the late eighteenth century was in fact the fine, whose logics Foucault almost completely neglected. Pat O'Malley, "Politicizing the Case for Fines," *Criminology & Public Policy* 10, no. 3 (2011): p. 548. For Bentham's reflections on the "pecuniary sanction," see Jeremy Bentham, "Principles of Penal Law," *The Works of Jeremy Bentham*, vol. 1 *(Principles of Morals and Legislation, Fragment on Government, Civil Code, Penal Law)*, ed. John Bowring (Edinburgh: William Tait, 1843), pp. 390–580.

197. Becker, "Crime and Punishment," p. 170.

198. Ibid., p. 193.

199. For a collection of Virginia school perspectives on user fees, see Richard E. Wagner, ed., *Charging for Government: User Charges and Earmarked Taxes in Principle and Practice* (London: Routledge, 1991).

200. Uhler, "A Constitutional Limitation on Taxes," p. 383.

201. Selma J. Mushkin, "The Case for User Fees," in *Taxing and Spending* (San Francisco: Institute for Contemporary Studies, 1979), pp. 16–19.

202. As pointed out by Pat O'Malley, the United States remains an outlier in the sense that it maintains a tight relationship between the administration of everyday fines and the court system. Other countries, such as Australia and the United Kingdom, have come much closer to Becker's prescriptions in expanding the use of on-the-spot administrative fines as an outright alternative to the court system. Pat O'Malley, *The Currency of Justice: Fines and Damages in Consumer Society* (Oxford: Routledge-Cavendish, 2009), pp. 46–47.

203. Alexes Harris, *A Pound of Flesh: Monetary Sanctions as Punishment for the Poor* (New York: Russell Sage Foundation, 2016), pp. 9–11.

204. The Hancock Amendment was passed by popular initiative in November 1980 and is now enshrined in Article X, Taxation, sections 16–24 of the Missouri Constitution. The amendment used a complex formula to limit the amount of taxes that could be raised by state and local governments; capped the rate of increase in assessed property values to the consumer price index or below; and prohibited local government from levying any new or increased "tax, license or fee" without the approval of voters. See Laura A. Harrison, "The Missouri Hancock Amendment: A Case Study of a Tax Limitation Law," MPA thesis, University of Montana, 1984; Walter Johnson, *The Broken Heart of America: St. Louis and the Violent History of the United States* (New York: Basic Books, 2020), pp. 399–400.

205. The relevant Missouri Supreme Court decision on user fees and taxes is *Keller v. Marion County Ambulance Dist. 820 S.W.2d 301* (1991). Macks Creek Law was passed with the intention of limiting the exorbitant generation of fine revenue from traffic tickets in some local government areas. However, it also effectively validated such practices by setting a generous upper bound of 30 percent on traffic fine revenue and implicitly authorized cash-strapped municipal governments to generate further revenue from non-traffic fines such as municipal ordinance violations.

206. Marshall Griffin, "Debate Begins on Traffic Revenue Limits in Missouri Legislature," St. Louis Public Radio, January 22, 2015. For helpful analyses of the economy of fines in St. Louis, see Johnson, *The Broken Heart of America*, pp. 418–21; Colin Gordon, *Citizen Brown: Race, Democracy, and Inequality in the St. Louis Suburbs* (Chicago: University of Chicago Press, 2019), pp. 135–42; and Jackie Wang, *Carceral Capitalism* (New York: Semiotext(e), 2018), pp. 151–92. On the links between fiscal austerity and racialized violence, see Ruth Wilson Gilmore (with Craig Gilmore), "Beyond Bratton," in *Abolition Geography: Essays towards Liberation*, ed. Alberto Toscano and Brenna Bhander (New York: Verso, 2022), pp. 288–317. Gilmore positions the post-Ferguson movement as a revolt against "profound austerity and the iron fist necessary to impose it" (p. 316).

207. Colin Gordon, *Mapping Decline: St. Louis and the Fate of the American City* (Philadelphia: University of Pennsylvania Press, 2014), pp. 43–45.

208. Since the 1970s, Los Angeles has seen multiple attempts at secession, most of them originating from southern counties. Raphael J. Sonenshein, *The City at Stake: Secession, Reform, and the Battle for Los Angeles* (Princeton, NJ: Princeton University Press, 2013). For a broader reflection on the secessionist impulse in neoliberal economics, see Quinn Slobodian, *Crack-Up Capitalism: Market Radicals and the Dream of a World without Democracy* (New York: Metropolitan Books, 2023).

209. Clarissa Hayward, "After Ferguson," *Washington Post*, November 24, 2014.

210. Better Together St. Louis, *General Administration, Report #2: Municipal Structure, Powers, Funding, Operations* (St. Louis: Better Together St. Louis, 2015), 13.

211. According to the association Better Together St. Louis, "the St. Louis region has gone from having *no* municipal sales tax [prior to 1969] to gathering 36.7% of its regional revenue from sales taxes. Sixty-nine of the ninety-two local governments in the St. Louis region count sales taxes as their number-one source of revenue." See Better Together St. Louis, *General Administration*, p. 13. Moreover, three of the wealthiest municipalities in the St. Louis region no longer levy a property tax at all (p. 20).

212. Gordon, *Mapping Decline*, p. 219; Sarah Kendzior, "In Ferguson, There Are No Malls Left to Boycott," *Quartz*, November 30, 2014.

213. Harrison, "The Missouri Hancock Amendment," pp. 16–19.

214. U.S. Department of Justice Civil Rights Division, *Investigation of the Ferguson Police Department*, March 4 (Washington, DC: Department of Justice, 2015), p. 2.

215. Better Together St. Louis, *General Administration*, p. 25.

216. ArchCity Defenders, *Municipal Courts White Paper* (St. Louis, MO: ArchCity Defenders, 2014), pp. 30–34.

217. Aubrey Bryon, "In Much of Ferguson, Walking in the Street Remains the Only Option," Strong Towns, February 20, 2018; Tracy Gordon and Sarah Gault, "Ferguson City Finances: Not the New Normal," *Urban Institute*, April 8, 2015.

218. Aldo Barba and Massimo Pivetti, "Rising Household Debt: Its Causes and Macroeconomic Implications—a Long-Period Analysis," *Cambridge Journal of Economics* 33, no. 1 (2009): pp. 113–37. The transfer of deficit-spending from the state to the household is

sometimes referred to as "privatized Keynesianism"; see Colin Crouch, *The Strange Non-death of Neoliberalism* (London: Polity Press, 2011), pp. 97–124.

219. On the exorbitant risks of payday loans as a form of consumer credit, see Mehrsa Baradaran, *How the Other Half Banks: Exclusion, Exploitation, and the Threat to Democracy* (Cambridge, MA: Harvard University Press, 2015), pp. 102–37.

220. For detail on poverty rates in the North County area of St. Louis County, see Arch-City Defenders, *Municipal Courts White Paper*, 35.

221. It seems that sewer bills are those that most often end up bringing people before the courts. Because sewer services cannot easily be cut off, residents who face several over-due bills will typically leave this one till last. Paul Kiel and Annie Waldman, "The Color of Debt: How Collection Suits Squeeze Black Neighborhoods," ProPublica, October 8, 2015.

222. Kouichi Shirayanagi, "Mortgage Crisis Still Persists in North St. Louis City, County," *St. Louis Post-Dispatch*, July 4, 2015.

223. Kiel and Waldman, "The Color of Debt."

224. Uliana Pavlova, "Gap in White and Black Homeownership Grew in St. Louis in Past Decade," *St. Louis Post-Dispatch*, July 9, 2017. According to census data, Black home-ownership rates have been falling across the United States since 2004. See Laura Kusisto, "Black Homeownership Drops to All-Time Low," *Wall Street Journal*, July 15, 2019.

225. ACLU, *In for a Penny: The Rise of America's New Debtors' Prisons* (New York: ACLU, 2010).

226. Kiel and Waldman, "The Color of Debt." According to this report, the most common plaintiffs seeking to use the courts to recoup debt from consumers are utilities, hospi-tals, debt buyers, banks, and auto and payday lenders—in other words, a mix of public and private organizations.

227. Lucero Herrera, Tia Koonse, Melanie Sonsteng-Person, and Noah Zatz, *Work, Pay or Go to Jail: Court-Ordered Community Service in Los Angeles* (Los Angeles: UCLA Labor Center, 2019). Although focused on Los Angeles, this report also includes a survey of com-parable practices across the United States. The authors find that "all 50 states authorize court-ordered community service in at least some criminal cases, and at least thirty-six states use community service as an alternative to court debt in some circumstances, with many states actively considering bills to expand their use" (p. 6).

228. Buchanan, "The Samaritan's Dilemma," pp. 81, 76.

CHAPTER FOUR: CONSTITUTIONAL AUSTERITY

1. Ewen MacAskill, "US Debt Crisis: Tea Party Intransigence Takes America to the Brink," *Guardian*, July 31, 2011.

2. Zachary Goldfarb, "S&P Downgrades U.S. Credit Rating for First Time," *Washington Post*, August 6, 2011.

3. The Budget Control Act of 2011, Pub. L .112–25, S. 365, 125 Stat. 240 was signed into law by President Barack Obama on August 2, 2011.

4. Peter Cary and Allan Holmes, "Workers Barely Benefited from Trump's Sweeping

Tax Cut, Investigation Shows," *Guardian*, April 30, 2019. On the influence of supply-side economists on Trump's fiscal politics, see Ben Schreckinger, "Reagan's Supply-Side Warriors Blaze a Comeback under Trump," *Politico Magazine*, April 22, 2019.

5. Congressional Budget Office, "How the 2017 Tax Act Affects CBO's Projections," Congressional Budget Office, April 20, 2018.

6. Tara Golshan, "House Republicans Are Voting to Make Deficits Unconstitutional after Their $1.5 Trillion Tax Cut," *Vox*, April 12, 2018.

7. Matt Sedensky, "Conservatives Want to Bypass Usual Way to Amend Constitution," AP News, November 4, 2018.

8. For a list of all Senate and House Judiciary Committee meetings, as well as House and Senate floor debates proposing a balanced budget bill, see James V. Saturno and Megan Suzanne Lynch, *A Balanced Budget Constitutional Amendment: Background and Congressional Options* (Washington, DC: Congressional Research Service, 2018), pp. 12–23. This list does not include two further House votes on a balanced budget amendment in November 2011 and April 2018.

9. On this shift in Republican budgetary politics, see Monica Prasad, *Starving the Beast: Ronald Reagan and the Tax Cut Revolution* (New York: Russell Sage Foundation, 2018), pp. 5–7. The American Keynesian Abba Lerner argued that public spending decisions should be judged by their stimulus effects rather than their adherence to a priori accounting rules such as the balanced budget. Abba P. Lerner, "Functional Finance and the Federal Debt," *Social Research* 10, no. 1 (1943): pp. 38–51. Another American Keynesian, Alvin Hansen, advanced a less radical critique of balanced budget orthodoxy but nevertheless called for permanent (rather than merely compensatory or countercyclical) use of government deficit spending as a way of stimulating the economy. Alvin H. Hansen, *Fiscal Policy and Business Cycles* (New York: Norton, 1941).

10. Nancy MacLean, *Democracy in Chains: The Deep History of the Radical Right's Stealth Plan for America* (New York: Viking, 2017), p. 49.

11. James M. Buchanan, *Better Than Plowing and Other Personal Essays* (Chicago: University of Chicago Press, 1992), pp. 30–31.

12. Ibid., p. 4.

13. James M. Buchanan, Letter to the Editor, *Times* (London), 25 June 1965, Box 95 Correspondence 1958–1966, Folder 1—Buchanan, James 1965, Gordon Tullock Papers, Hoover Institution Archives, Hoover Institution, Stanford University.

14. James M. Buchanan and Richard E. Wagner, *Democracy in Deficit: The Political Legacy of Lord Keynes* (Indianapolis: Liberty Fund, 1977), pp. 3–24; James M. Buchanan, John Burton, and Richard Wagner, *The Consequences of Mr. Keynes* (London: Institute of Economic Affairs, 1978), pp. 16–18, 47–51.

15. Buchanan and Wagner, *Democracy in Deficit*, pp. 66–67.

16. James R. Sweeney, "Harry Byrd: Vanishing Policies and Enduring Principles," *Virginia Quarterly Review* 52, no. 4 (1976): pp. 596–612.

17. J. Harvie Wilkinson III, *Harry Byrd and the Changing Face of Virginia Politics,*

1945–1966 (Charlottesville: University Press of Virginia, 1968), pp. 65, 68–69. Conservative Southern Democrats in general had a disproportionate impact on U.S. politics in the wake of World War II because of their ability to leverage the seniority privileges of one-party rule to occupy key decision-making positions in Senate committees.

18. Harry Flood Byrd, "The Importance of Balancing the Budget: Our Number One Problem," *Vital Speeches of the Day* 21, no. 18 (1955): pp. 1318–22.

19. Quoted in Sweeney, "Harry Byrd," p. 603.

20. Quoted in Wilkinson III, *Harry Byrd and the Changing Face of Virginia Politics*, p. 67.

21. Letter from James M. Buchanan to Senator Harry F. Byrd, Jr., 16 January 1976, Correspondence Box "B" 1975–1978 (Folder 1), James M. Buchanan Papers, C0246, Special Collections Research Center, George Mason University Libraries (hereafter James M. Buchanan Papers).

22. Susan Dunn, *Dominion of Memories: Jefferson, Madison, and the Decline of Virginia* (New York: Basic Books, 2007), pp. 215–16.

23. Brent Tarter, *A Saga of the New South: Race, Law, and Public Debt in Virginia* (Charlottesville: University of Virginia Press, 2016), p. 2.

24. Jane Dailey, *Before Jim Crow: The Politics of Race in Postemancipation Virginia* (Chapel Hill: University of North Carolina Press, 2000), pp. 28–29.

25. Tarter, *A Saga of the New South*, pp. 35–52.

26. James Tice Moore, *Two Paths to the New South: The Virginia Debt Controversy, 1870–1883* (Lexington: University Press of Kentucky, 1974), pp. 45–53; Tarter, *A Saga of the New South*, pp. 53–68; Dailey, *Before Jim Crow*, pp. 33, 44–45.

27. Moore, *Two Paths to the New South*, pp. 27–44, 109–18; Tarter, *A Saga of the New South*, pp. 79–81.

28. Tarter, *A Saga of the New South*, p. 180.

29. Ibid., pp. 79–81; Moore, *Two Paths to the New South*, p. 27.

30. Tarter, *A Saga of the New South*, pp. 176, 180–81; Moore, *Two Paths to the New South*, p. 36.

31. Tarter, *A Saga of the New South*, pp. 5, 176–77.

32. Ibid., p. 178.

33. Ronald L. Heinemann, *Depression and New Deal in Virginia: The Enduring Dominion* (Charlottesville: University Press of Virginia, 1983), pp. 133–35.

34. Tarter, *A Saga of the New South*, p. 174,

35. Wilkinson III, *Harry Byrd and the Changing Face of Virginia Politics*, pp. 38–48.

36. Ibid., p. 62.

37. Nicol C. Rae, *Southern Democrats* (Oxford: Oxford University Press, 1994), pp. 36–38. As Rae makes clear, the convention of assigning committee positions based on age was a relatively recent one, dating back to 1910. There is some debate as to whether southern Democrats really voted as a "solid bloc" during the New Deal and subsequent decades. The assumption was famously contested by political scientist V.O. Key in his landmark *Southern Politics in State and Nation* (New York: Knopf, 1949). The more recent

literature has tended to confirm that southern Democrats in Congress did indeed unite to defend the class and race prerogatives of the southern plantation elite. For a thorough analysis of southern Democratic roll calls in the period between 1933 and 1955, see Ira Katznelson and Quinn Mulroy, "Was the South Pivotal? Situated Partisanship and Policy Coalitions During the New Deal and Fair Deal," *Journal of Politics* 74, no. 2 (2012): pp. 604–20. On southern Democratic positions against progressive labor legislation in particular, see Sean Farhang and Ira Katznelson, "The Southern Imposition: Congress and Labor in the New Deal and Fair Deal," *Studies in American Political Development* 19, no. 1 (2005): pp. 1–30. I borrow the concept of the southern veto from Ira Katznelson, Kim Geiger, and Daniel Kryder. "Limiting Liberalism: The Southern Veto in Congress, 1933–1950," *Political Science Quarterly* 108, no. 2 (1993): pp. 283–306.

38. William S. White, *Citadel: The Story of the U.S. Senate* (New York: Harper Bros., 1956), p. 68. For a discussion of southern Democratic dominance in the Senate between 1947 and 1972, see Merle Black and Earl Black, "The South in the Senate: Changing Patterns of Representation on Committees," in *The Disappearing South? Studies in Regional Change and Continuity*, ed. Robert P. Steed, Laurence W. Moreland, and Tod A. Baker (Tuscaloosa: University of Alabama Press, 1990), pp. 5–20.

39. As Jentleson explains, the modern filibuster is the child of accident. It was unintentionally created in 1917, when senators introduced a rule to prevent the filibuster from needlessly delaying the passage of urgent legislation. The new rule allowed senators to call a "cloture" vote to wrap up interminable debate. Fatefully, however, they decided that a two-thirds supermajority vote would be required to invoke cloture (this was later reduced to the three-fifths or sixty-vote threshold of today), apparently unaware how useful this would prove to the southern Democratic faction in the Senate. Southern Democrats soon seized on this innovation and twisted it to their own ends. Taking a rule that had been designed to facilitate the passage of bills, they reinvented as an instrument to block the passage of bills altogether. A Senate supermajority was the perfect instrument in the hands of a white supremacist Senate minority intent on blocking any initiative that would dent their racial authority in the South. Adam Jentleson, *Kill Switch: The Rise of the Modern Senate and the Crippling of American Democracy* (New York: Norton, 2021), pp. 64–67.

40. Ibid., pp. 66–68, 76. Jentleson notes that in the eighty-seven years between the end of Reconstruction and the Civil Rights Act of 1964, the only bills that were torpedoed by filibusters were civil rights bills.

41. On the decision to exclude these workers, see Jill Quadagno, *The Color of Welfare: How Racism Undermined the War on Poverty* (Oxford: Oxford University Press, 1994), pp. 155–58. On the role of southern legislators in this decision, see Jill Quadagno, *The Transformation of Old Age Security: Class and Politics in the American Welfare State* (Chicago: University of Chicago Press, 1988), pp. 115–16; Lee J. Alston and Joseph P. Ferrie, *Southern Paternalism and the American Welfare State: Economics, Politics, and Institutions in the South, 1865–1965* (Cambridge: Cambridge University Press, 1999), pp. 61–70.

42. Robert C. Lieberman, *Shifting the Color Line: Race and the American Welfare State*

(Cambridge, MA: Harvard University Press, 1994), pp. 48–56, Alston and Ferrie, *Southern Paternalism and the American Welfare State*, pp. 70–72; and Eva Bertram, *The Workfare State: Public Assistance Politics from the New Deal to the New Democrats* (Philadelphia: University of Pennsylvania Press, 2015), pp. 16–22.

43. Winifred Bell, *Aid to Dependent Children* (New York: Columbia University Press, 1964), pp. 46, 107, 141.

44. Bell, *Aid to Dependent Children*, pp. 93–110, 126–27.

45. Heinemann, *Depression and New Deal in Virginia*, pp. 132–52; Ronald L. Heinemann, *Harry Byrd of Virginia* (Charlottesville: University Press of Virginia, 1996), pp. 159–83.

46. Dunn, *Dominion of Memories*, 214.

47. Heinemann, *Harry Byrd of Virginia*, pp. 200–202.

48. Quoted in ibid., p. 202.

49. On the rise of southern paternalism and its connection to the idea of the household economy, see Lacy K. Ford, *Deliver Us from Evil: The Slavery Question in the Old South* (Oxford: Oxford University Press, 2009), pp. 144–72. On the practice of southern paternalism after the end of the Civil War, see Alston and Ferrie, *Southern Paternalism and the American Welfare State*.

50. Alston and Ferrie, *Southern Paternalism and the American Welfare State*, pp. 35–39.

51. Quoted in Heinemann, *Harry Byrd of Virginia*, p. 202.

52. Wilkinson, *Harry Byrd and the Changing Face of Virginia Politics*, p. 64.

53. Michael Bowen, *The Roots of Modern Conservatism: Dewey, Taft, and the Battle for the Soul of the Republican Party* (Chapel Hill: University of North Carolina Press, 2011), p. 45.

54. Lee Anderson, *Congress and the Classroom: From the Cold War to "No Child Left Behind"* (University Park: Penn State University Press, 2007), pp. 35–37.

55. Wilkinson, *Harry Byrd and the Changing Face of Virginia Politics*, pp. 113–54; Heinemann, *Harry Byrd of Virginia*, pp. 325–54.

56. Wilkinson, *Harry Byrd and the Changing Face of Virginia Politics*, pp. 129–30; Heinemann, *Harry Byrd of Virginia*, pp. 332–33.

57. Heinemann, *Harry Byrd of Virginia*, pp. 363–64.

58. Iwan W. Morgan, *Deficit Government: Taxing and Spending in Modern America* (Chicago: Ivan R. Dee, 1995), pp. 55–63.

59. On Goldwater's fiscal politics and its overlaps with southern Democratic positions, see Frank Annunziata, "The Revolt against the Welfare State: Goldwater Conservatism and the Election of 1964," *Presidential Studies Quarterly* 10 (1980): pp. 254–65.

60. Clement E. Vose, "Conservatism by Amendment," *Yale Review* 47 (Winter 1957): pp. 176–90.

61. Ibid., pp. 176–77. Up until 1936, a conservative Supreme Court blocked several of Roosevelt's first-term efforts to advance his New Deal agenda on the grounds that it violated the federal government's powers as outlined in the Constitution. Their opposition rested on an exceptionally narrow reading of the so-called interstate commerce clause

empowering Congress to regulate trade across state lines. This changed with the *United States v. Butler* decision of 1936, when the Supreme Court ruled that the federal government had a broad power to tax and spend for the benefit of the general welfare, as specified in Article 1, Section 8 of the Constitution. Although the case, oddly enough, did not authorize Roosevelt to pursue the agricultural program that was in question, it opened the way to a more accommodating jurisprudence and marked a shift in the Court's response to Roosevelt's spending initiatives.

62. Ibid., pp. 177–78. For further detail on this new wave of proposed constitutional amendments from the right, see Russell L. Caplan, *Constitutional Brinksmanship: Amending the Constitution by National Convention* (Oxford: Oxford University Press, 1988), pp. 65–89.

63. Kenneth D. Garbade, *The First Debt Ceiling Crisis* (New York: New York Fed, 2016).

64. The Byrd-Bridges resolution proposed that "the constitution be amended to assure the American people of balanced budgets in the future putting an end to deficit government financing." Senate—Byrd-Bridges Amendment, S.J. Res. 174, July 13, 1954. This amendment would have required the president to draw up an annual estimate of expected revenues and a plan for balancing the budget; Congress would be prevented from adjourning for more than three days until it had approved this budget.

65. Thomas Jefferson, "Thomas Jefferson to John Taylor, November 26, 1798," in *The Writings of Thomas Jefferson*, vol. 4, ed. H.A. Washington (New York: Derby and Jackson, 1859), p. 260.

66. Senate—Byrd-Bridges Amendment, S.J. Res. 126, January 25, 1956. Senate—Curtis Amendment, S.J. Res. 133, February 1, 1956. For a sympathetic appraisal of these amendments, see Robert D. Dresser, "Balancing the Federal Budget: The Proposed Byrd-Bridges Amendment," *American Bar Association Journal* 43, no. 1 (1957): pp. 35–37. On the historical significance of these amendment proposals as precursors to the invigorated balanced budget campaigns of the 1970s onward, see Caplan, *Constitutional Brinksmanship*, pp. 78–79; David E. Kyvig, "Refining or Resisting Modern Government? The Balanced Budget Amendment to the U.S Constitution," *Akron Law Review* 28, no. 2 (1995): pp. 103–104. Caplan identifies the 1936 resolution put forward by Rep. Harold Knutson (H.J. Res. 579) as the first instance of a balanced budget amendment; this was in fact a per capita limit on public debt.

67. See the Research and Policy Committee of the Committee for Economic Development, *Modernizing the Nation's Highways* (New York: Committee for Economic Development, 1956), which lists Buchanan as a "technical advisor" to the Subcommittee on Highways, and James M. Buchanan, *Public Principles of Public Debt: A Defense and Restatement* (Indianapolis: Liberty Fund, 1999), p. xviii. The Committee for Economic Development was active between 1942 and 1964 and for the most part espoused a corporatist or "commercial Keynesian" line on policy issues. Robert M. Collins, "American Corporatism: The Committee for Economic Development, 1942-1964," *Historian* 44, no. 2 (1982): pp. 151–73.

68. Research and Policy Committee, *Modernizing the Nation's Highways*, pp. 11–16.

69. *Highway Revenue Act of 1956, Hearings before the Committee on Ways and Means, House of Representatives, 84th Congress, February 14–17, 20, and 21, 1956*, p. 390.

70. Buchanan, *Public Principles of Public Debt*, p. xix.

71. Ibid.

72. The "new economics" was a term coined by the media to refer to the Keynesian-inspired policy ideas promulgated by the Council of Economic Advisers during the first part of the 1960s. Between January 1961 and November 1964, the CEA operated under the leadership of the American Keynesian and Harvard economics professor Alvin Hansen. During this period, the CEA counted Keynesian economists such as Walter Heller, Kermit Gordon, and James Tobin among its members. On the role and influence of "Kennedy's CEA," see Alice O'Connor, *Poverty Knowledge: Social Science, Social Policy, and the Poor in Twentieth-Century U.S. History* (Princeton, NJ: Princeton University Press, 2001), pp. 140–58. Economists such as Alvin Hansen had been instrumental in popularizing Keynesian ideas in American academia in the 1930s and 1940s but had struggled to exert any policy influence during the Truman and Eisenhower administrations. The economists in "Kennedy's CEA" were determined to legitimize a more activist use of the budget. For many years, Hansen had argued that American legislators should move beyond Keynesian countercyclical policy (which prescribed government deficits during recessions and surpluses in boom years) and instead make permanent use of the deficit as a stimulus to economic growth. Richard A. Musgrave, "U.S. Fiscal Policy, Keynes, and Keynesian Economics," *Journal of Post Keynesian Economics* 10, no. 2 (1987): pp. 175–78. Acting as a "policy entrepreneur" for the CEA, Walter Heller helped school President Kennedy and the general public in the idea that a budget prospectively (if not actually) "balanced" as long as spending was directed toward full employment and the expansion of the economy's productive capacity. Thus, the Kennedy CEA went further than any other government body in demystifying the fetish of balanced budgets. On the novelty of the "new economics" with respect to Keynes's own ideas, see Morgan, *Deficit Government*, pp. 11–12, 86–89.

73. Morgan, *Deficit Government*, pp. 56–63.

74. Buchanan, *Public Principles of Public Debt*, p. 131.

75. The *Baker v. Carr* case arose from a 1959 lawsuit against the state of Tennessee, which like many other southern states was in the habit of manipulating its electoral districts to elevate the votes of conservative rural landowners over those of poorer Blacks and whites living in cities. By bringing redistricting issues under the jurisdiction of the federal courts, the Supreme Court's 1962 ruling in *Baker v. Carr* opened the door to a series of subsequent decisions affirming the "one person, one vote" rule. J. Douglas Smith, *On Democracy's Doorstep: The Inside Story of How the Supreme Court Brought 'One Person, One Vote' to the United States* (New York: Farrar, Straus, and Giroux, 2014), pp. 3–6.

76. James M. Buchanan and Gordon Tullock, *The Calculus of Consent: Logical Foundations of Constitutional Democracy* (Ann Arbor: University of Michigan Press, 1962). The *Baker v. Carr* case was initiated in 1959 and unfolded during the early 1960s, at the time

Buchanan and Tullock were composing *The Calculus of Consent.* The case appears to have informed the book's underlying concern with majority rule. On the history of the *Baker v. Carr* case from 1959 to 1962, see Smith, *On Democracy's Doorstep,* pp. 52–70.

77. Buchanan and Tullock, *The Calculus of Consent,* p. 72.

78. Ibid., p. 194.

79. Southern senators mustered the longest filibuster in Senate history—totaling sixty days—to delay passage of the Civil Rights Act of 1964 and subsequently organized filibusters against the Voting Rights and Fair Housing Acts. Keith M. Finley, *Delaying the Dream: Southern Senators and the Fight against Civil Rights, 1938–1965* (Baton Rouge: Louisiana State University Press, 2008), pp. 233–305. After passage of the Civil Rights Act, however, most southern Democratic stalwarts acknowledged that their remaining filibustering efforts were symbolic. While vowing to resist the Voting Rights Act of 1964, for instance, even Harry Byrd Sr. conceded that "we can't deny the Negroes a basic constitutional right." Quoted in Finley, *Delaying the Dream,* p. 290. Byrd retired from the Senate in 1965, the same year the Voting Rights Act passed, and died the following year.

80. Buchanan and Wagner, *Democracy in Deficit,* pp. 37–38, 49–53. Buchanan and Wagner rightly identify Abba Lerner, exponent of "functional finance," as the most radical critic of balanced budget economics. "In the pristine simplicity of their early formulation, most clearly exposited by Abba Lerner," they write, "Keynesian policy precepts required no substitute for the balanced budget. Functional finance required no such rule at all" (53).

81. Ibid., p. 51. See also p. 169.

82. Leo Panitch and Sam Gindin, *The Making of Global Capitalism: The Political Economy of American Empire* (New York: Verso, 2013), p. 112.

83. Morgan, *Deficit Government,* pp. 102–14, 135–42.

84. Buchanan and Wagner, *Democracy in Deficit,* pp. 23–24, 52.

85. Ibid., pp. 67, 72.

86. Ibid., p. 23. See also pp. 72 and 106.

87. Buchanan and Tullock, *The Calculus of Consent,* pp. 166–68; James M. Buchanan, *The Limits of Liberty: Between Anarchy and Leviathan* (Carmel, IN: Liberty Fund, 1975), p. 201.

88. Buchanan and Wagner, *Democracy in Deficit,* p. 190.

89. Ibid., pp. 183–84.

90. As far as I can tell, there are no previously published accounts of Buchanan's political contribution to the balanced budget amendment campaign. On Buchanan's intellectual contribution, however, see Alasdair Roberts, "No Simple Fix: Fiscal Rules and the Politics of Austerity," *Indiana Journal of Global Legal Studies* 22, no. 2 (2015): pp. 401–31, and Thomas Biebricher, "Neoliberalism and Law: The Case of the Constitutional Balanced Budget Amendment," *German Law Journal* 17, no. 5 (2016): pp. 835–56.

91. "More than anything else I have been involved in, this [book] does have the prospect at least of having some political impact." Letter from James M. Buchanan to Milton Friedman, 30 March 1977, Correspondence Box 8 (Folder "Correspondence—F 1974–1978"), James M. Buchanan Papers.

92. "Nixon Reportedly Says He Is Now a Keynesian," *New York Times*, January 7, 1971.

93. Thomas Byrne Edsall and Mary D. Edsall, *Chain Reaction: The Impact of Race, Rights, and Taxes on American Politics* (New York: Norton, 1992), p. 56; Sean P. Cunningham, *American Politics in the Postwar Sunbelt: Conservative Growth in a Battleground Region* (Cambridge: Cambridge University Press, 2014), pp. 116–17.

94. Kevin M. Kruse, *White Flight: Atlanta and the Making of Modern Conservatism* (Princeton, NJ: Princeton University Press, 2013), pp. 128–30.

95. Kurt Schuparra, *Rise and Triumph of the California Right, 1945–66* (London: Routledge, 1998), pp. 102–106.

96. Matthew D. Lassiter, *The Silent Majority: Suburban Politics in the Sunbelt South* (Princeton, NJ: Princeton University Press, 2007), p. 306. On the other side, Black inner-city residents and other racial minorities were becoming increasingly conscious of their power to impact urban spending during the same period. In his history of the San Francisco municipal bond market, Destin Jenkins has documented the multiple efforts by racial minorities to boycott bond-financed infrastructure spending, which overwhelmingly benefited the white middle class. Destin Jenkins, *The Bonds of Inequality: Debt and the Making of the American City* (Chicago: University of Chicago Press, 2021), pp. 130–49.

97. John Egerton, *The Americanization of Dixie: The Southernization of America* (New York: Harper's Magazine Press, 1974), pp. xx–xxi.

98. Curtis called on Senator Scott to assemble "a good list of witnesses for the hearings," "top people from the business world, the law, the academic world, and some economists and political scientists." Letter from the Honorable Carl T. Curtis (US Senate Washington DC from Nebraska) to the Honorable William S Scott, June 25, 1975. William Lloyd Scott Papers, Collection #C0128, Special Collections Research Center, George Mason University Libraries, Box 95—Committees, Judiciary, 1975, Folder "Constitutional amend—budget."

99. Balancing the Budget: Hearing before the Subcommittee on Constitutional Amendments of the Committee on the Judiciary, United States Senate, Ninety-fourth Congress, First Session, on S.J. Res. 55…S.J. Res. 93…September 23 and October 7, 1975.

100. Balancing the Budget: Hearing before the Subcommittee on Constitutional Amendments of the Committee on the Judiciary, United States Senate, Ninety-fourth Congress, First Session, on S.J. Res. 55…S.J. Res. 93…September 23 and October 7, 1975, pp. 2, 8, 18, 30, 76, 120, 122, 129, 136, 165.

101. "Statement of Dr. James Buchanan" and "Statement Submitted by James M. Buchanan for Hearings before Subcommittee on Constitutional Amendments of the Senate Judiciary Committee, Scheduled for 23 September 1975," Balancing the Budget: Hearing before the Subcommittee on Constitutional Amendments of the Committee on the Judiciary, United States Senate, Ninety-fourth Congress, First Session, on S.J. Res. 55, September 23, 1975, pp. 59–64.

102. Caplan, *Constitutional Brinksmanship*, p. 78.

103. Adam Clymer, "Proposed Convention on Balancing Budget," *New York Times*, February 16, 1979.

104. On the convention as "protest clause," see Caplan, *Constitutional Brinksmanship*, p. 61.

105. Commonwealth of Virginia, General Assembly, House Joint Resolution no. 75, February 23, 1973. For details on subsequent state resolutions and a history of the balanced budget convention campaign, see Iwan W. Morgan, "Unconventional Politics: The Campaign for a Balanced Budget Amendment Constitutional Convention in the 1970s," *Journal of American Studies* 32, no. 3 (1998): pp. 421–45.

106. That senator was James Clark Jr. Charles Mohr, "Tax Union Playing Chief Role in Drive," *New York Times*, May 15, 1979; Isaac Martin, *Rich People's Movements: Grassroots Campaigns to Untax the One Percent* (Oxford: Oxford University Press, 2013), pp. 159–60, 166.

107. Murray N. Rothbard, "Jim Davidson and the Week That Was," *Libertarian Forum* 5, no. 4 (1973): pp. 5, 7.

108. Ibid., p. 7.

109. An early observer of the NTU questioned the sincerity of its support for such left-wing issues as opposing arms spending, noting that "if the NTU isn't boasting of its conservative affiliations," Federal Election Commission records "show that the group had funded only conservative and ultraconservative candidates." Moreover, on "Capitol Hill, NTU has found the most receptive audience among conservatives, most of them Republicans. NTU literature is replete with praise for such supporters of the convention drive as Harry F. Byrd, Jr., Ind-Va., and Rep. Phillip Crane, R-Ill., both of whom scored high marks as penny pinchers in the NTU ratings." Alan Barlow, "National Taxpayers Union: Group Wants to Balance Nation's Checkbook," *Congressional Quarterly*, February 17, 1979, p. 278.

110. Information on the composition of the NTU board has been gleaned from Box 73 National Taxpayers Union (Folder Correspondence—National Taxpayers Union [2 of 2] 1984–1997), James M. Buchanan Papers. Buchanan was appointed to the board of directors after winning the Nobel Memorial Prize for economics in 1986. This box contains numerous examples of letters Buchanan wrote to state senators in the late 1980s and 1990s on behalf of the NTU, pleading with them to retain their state convention resolutions.

111. Kenneth J. Arrow's *Social Choice and Individual Values* (New Haven, CT: Yale University Press, 1951) proved the impossibility of defining public interest, social welfare, or a collective will from a simple aggregation of individual preferences or votes. See note 41 of the previous chapter for further detail on Buchanan's interpretation of Arrow's "impossibility theorem."

112. James M. Buchanan, "Discussion," in *The Constitution and the Budget: Are Constitutional Limits on Tax, Spending, and Budget Powers Desirable at the Federal Level*, ed. W. S. Moore and Rudolph G. Penner (Washington, DC: American Enterprise Institute, 1980), pp. 34–35, 73–74.

113. James Dale Davidson, "The Balanced Budget and Jerry Brown," *Inquiry*, February 4, 1980, pp. 12–15; Harry Flood Byrd Jr., "Letter to the Editor: The Better Path to a Constitutional Amendment," *New York Times*, April 2, 1982.

114. Martin, *Rich People's Movements*, p. 170.

115. On this equivocation in public opinion, see Kyvig, "Refining or Resisting Modern Government?," p. 107; Morgan, *The Age of Deficits*, p. 119.

116. Remarking on the unwelcome scrutiny that followed Governor Jerry Brown's speech, James Dale Davidson is quoted as saying, "We knew that would happen, and Brown's speech was just what we feared." Quoted in Charles Mohr, "Tax Union Playing Chief Role in Drive." See also Martin, *Rich People's Movements*, pp. 176–77.

117. Caplan, *Constitutional Brinksmanship*, pp. 80–81.

118. Cara Johnson, ed., *Transcript of Hearings on the Balanced Federal Budget Resolutions: California Assembly Committee on Ways and Means* (Sacramento, CA: Assembly Publications Office, 1979).

119. Donald Lambro, "The Constitution to the Rescue," *National Review*, August 20, 1982, pp. 1009–1011.

120. On the "coming out" of the NTU and NTLC as antitax organizations, see Martin, *Rich People's Movements*, pp. 166–72.

121. Buchanan's contribution to the drafting process is documented in his 1978 correspondence with Stubblebine. See Correspondence Box 22 S (Folder "Correspondence—S 1978–1979"), James M. Buchanan Papers.

122. Martin, *Rich People's Movements*, p. 171. A copy of the draft is enclosed in Buchanan's correspondence with Stubblebine. See William Craig Stubblebine to Amendment Drafting Committee, A Proposed Constitutional Amendment to Limit Federal Spending, prepared by the Federal Amendment Drafting Committee, Convened by the National Tax Limitation Committee, January 30, 1979, Washington, DC. Correspondence Box 22 S (Folder "Correspondence—S 1978–1979"), James M. Buchanan Papers.

123. This logic was spelled out by Republican senator John Heinz of Philadelphia, who, along with Democratic senator Dick Stone of Florida, first introduced the amendment before the Senate in April 1979. See "News from Senator John Heinz: Press Release," April 5, 1979, in Barr, William: Files, Constitutional Amendment—Balanced Budget (3), Box 3, Ronald Reagan Presidential Library, Digital Library Collections.

124. "Most Congressmen improve their chances of reelection by deficit spending, because it enables them to hand out largess to special constituencies while disguising the costs in the form of borrowing and inflation, which are diffused over the rest of society. Thus politicians have an incentive to increase spending and continue inflationary deficits." James Dale Davidson, "The Balanced Budget Amendment: An End to the 'Good-Will' Theory of Government," *Taxing & Spending* 2, no. 4 (1979): pp. 43 and 42. See also James Dale Davidson, "Requiring a Balanced Budget," *Washington Post*, March 6, 1979; James Dale Davidson, "The Balanced Budget Amendment: A Truly Marginal Reform," in *Beyond the Status Quo: Policy Proposals for America*, ed. David Boaz and Edward H. Crane (Washington, DC: Cato Institute, 1985), pp. 13–28.

125. William Rickenbacker and Lewis K. Uhler, *Taxpayer's Guide to Survival: Constitutional Tax-Limitation* (Loomis, CA: National Tax Limitation Committee, 1977), pp. 6, 12,

14, 15. A summary of this pamphlet was printed in the libertarian magazine *Reason*. See William Rickenbacker and Lewis K. Uhler, "How to Draw the Line on Taxes," *Reason*, June 1978, pp. 47–51. See also Uhler's comments on special interests and the "fiscal constitution" in Lewis K. Uhler, "The Balanced Budget Amendment 'Sensible,'" *Christian Science Monitor*, June 8, 1982. See also Lewis K. Uhler, *Taming the Federal Spending Monster: The Heritage Lectures* (Washington, DC: Heritage Foundation, 1988); Lewis K. Uhler, *Setting Limits: Constitutional Control of Government* (Washington, DC: Regnery Gateway, 1989).

126. Black and Black, "The South in the Senate: Changing Patterns of Representation on Committees," p. 14; Rae, *Southern Democrats*, p. 100.

127. On Gingrich's multiple bids for the Sixth District of Georgia, see Julian E. Zelizer, *Burning Down the House: Newt Gingrich and the Rise of the New Republican Party* (New York: Penguin Books, 2020), pp. 24–38. On Lee Atwater, see Thomas B. Edsall, "GOP Battler Lee Atwater Dies at 40," *Washington Post*, March 30, 1991. Zelizer remarks that "Gingrich and Atwater could have been brothers born to different mothers" given their shared penchant for aggressive smear campaigns and ruthless procedural politics (p. 137). It was Atwater who first introduced Gingrich to Reagan officials in 1981.

128. During his 1980 campaign, Reagan observed that "excessive Federal spending and deficits have become so engrained in government today that a constitutional amendment is necessary to limit spending." Quoted in U.S. Congress, Senate Committee on the Judiciary, *Balanced Budget Constitutional Amendment, Report on S.J. Res. 225, S. Rept. 99–163, 99th Cong., 1st sess.* (Washington, DC: U.S. Government Printing Office, 1985), p. 3. On the wasteful spending that had piled "deficit upon deficit," see U.S. President, Ronald Reagan, "Inaugural Address, January 20, 21," in *Public Papers of the Presidents of the United States* (Washington, DC: U.S. Government Printing Office, 1981), p. 2. For figures on Reagan's budgetary record, see Robert Heilbroner and Peter Bernstein, *The Debt and the Deficit: False Alarms/Real Possibilities* (New York: Norton, 1989), p. 23.

129. Heilbroner and Bernstein, *The Debt and the Deficit*, pp. 23–26.

130. Iwan W. Morgan, *The Age of Deficits* (Lawrence: University Press of Kansas, 2009), pp. 85–86.

131. Lambro, "The Constitution to the Rescue," p. 1011.

132. For an illuminating account of this shift in Republican strategy, see Bruce Bartlett, "'Starve the Beast': Origins and Development of a Budgetary Metaphor," *Independent Review* 12, no. 1 (2007): pp. 5–26.

133. Ronald Reagan, "Address to the Nation on the Economy, February 5," in *Public Papers of the Presidents of the United States* (Washington, DC: U.S. Government Printing Office, 1981), p. 81.

134. James D. Savage, *Balanced Budgets and American Politics* (Ithaca, NY: Cornell University Press, 1990), p. 209.

135. Ibid., p. 207.

136. "Reagan Unwraps His 1983 Budget, without Ribbons," *New York Times*, February 7, 1982; Savage, *Balanced Budgets and American Politics*, p. 211.

137. Quoted in Lambro, "The Constitution to the Rescue," p. 1011.

138. In 1975, Gingrich was among a group of emerging Republican congressmen selected to attend an intensive campaign building workshop in Wisconsin under the direction of New Right impresario Paul Weyrich and his Campaign for a Free Congress. Zelizer, *Burning Down the House*, p. 28. Weyrich immediately saw in Gingrich someone who was prepared to wield power with the requisite political ruthlessness, although he acknowledged that his protégé was a political opportunist rather than a committed ideologue like himself. "I call Newt an experiential conservative, as opposed to a deeply philosophical conservative," Weyrich reflected in a 1995 interview. "Newt has a deep knowledge and so he is somewhat professorial in that respect. But he does not have a deeply held philosophy, say, Biblically-based philosophy as some of us do. And therefore, he is much more negotiable on a lot of issues and, as the old railroad timetables would suggest, 'subject to change without notice.' You know, simply because he arrived at his conclusions based upon what he perceives is happening in the community at large. He is genuinely against the welfare state and genuinely wants to end it because he believes that in his experience, it has been destructive to people. He is not against the welfare state for the same precise reasons that I am." Paul Weyrich, "Interview: The Long March of Newt Gingrich," *Frontline PBS*, November 1995. Elsewhere Weyrich described Gingrich as "the first conservative I have ever known who knows how to use power." Connie Bruck, "The Politics of Perception," *New Yorker*, October 9, 1995, p. 70. For an illuminating discussion of the relationship between Newt Gingrich and the New Right, see Daniel Schlozman and Sam Rosenfeld, "The Long New Right and the World It Made," unpublished paper, American Political Science Association Meetings, August 31, 2018, pp. 60–61. For a book-length study of the alliance between Gingrich and the New Right, and its apotheosis in the Gingrich Revolution of the 1990s, see Nicole Hemmer, *Partisans: The Conservative Revolutionaries Who Remade American Politics in the 1990s* (New York: Basic Books, 2022).

139. Quoted in Ronald Brownstein, *The Second Civil War: How Extreme Partisanship Has Paralyzed Washington and Polarized America* (New York: Penguin Books, 2008), p. 142.

140. On the Conservative Opportunity Society, see Julian E. Zelizer, "Seizing Power: Conservatives and Congress since the 1970s," in *Governing America: The Revival of Political History* (Princeton, NJ: Princeton University Press, 2012), pp. 269–70.

141. Craig Shirley, *Citizen Newt: The Making of a Reagan Conservative* (Nashville, TN: HarperCollins, 2017), p. 79.

142. Ibid., p. 80.

143. On this turning point, see Jacob S. Hacker and Paul Pierson, "Tax Politics and the Struggle over Activist Government," in *The Transformation of American Politics: Activist Government and the Rise of Conservatism*, ed. Theda Skocpol and Paul Pierson (Princeton, NJ: Princeton University Press, 2007), pp. 261–60; James T. Patterson, "Transformative Economic Policies: Tax Cutting, Stimuli, and Bailouts," in *The Presidency of George W. Bush: A First Historical Assessment*, ed. Julian E. Zelizer (Princeton, NJ: Princeton University Press, 2010), p. 117.

144. Newt Gingrich's ambivalent position on fiscal matters, straddling supply-side and Virginia school economics, was already in evidence in the late 1970s. In his successful 1978 campaign for the 6th Congressional District of Atlanta, Gingrich added supply-side tax cuts to his campaign repertoire and was endorsed by Jack Kemp. Zelizer, *Burning Down the House*, p. 33. Gingrich later named Jack Kemp as the spiritual father of the Conservative Opportunity Society, although the group, like Gingrich himself, was considerably more syncretic in its influences. Zelizer, "Seizing Power," pp. 269–70. In its earliest manifestos, the COS advocated supply-side tax cuts but coupled this with a very non-Mundellian call for a balanced budget amendment. Brownstein, *Second Civil War*, pp. 141–43. When Reagan backtracked on some of his first-year tax cuts in 1982, Gingrich stood shoulder to shoulder with Kemp in denouncing the president's betrayal of the "Reagan revolution." Shirley, *Citizen Newt*, pp. 80–81. Yet unlike Kemp, Gingrich also wanted a frontal assault on the "liberal welfare state" and was enraged that Reagan had chosen to close tax loopholes for the wealthy rather than enact drastic spending cuts as a response to spiraling deficits. The strictly Mundellian Kemp always eschewed the austerity politics of balanced budgets; Gingrich, by contrast, was more than willing to brandish the threat of government insolvency as a means of achieving his ends, as evidenced by his threat to vote against a rise in the debt ceiling in 1982. Shirley, *Citizen Newt*, p. 79.

145. Morgan, *The Age of Deficits*, pp. 162–66, 175–76; William C. Berman, *America's Right Turn: From Nixon to Clinton* (Baltimore: Johns Hopkins University Press, 1998), pp. 164–66.

146. Quoted in Berman, *America's Right Turn*, p. 165.

147. Michael Lind, "The Southern Coup," *New Republic* 212, no. 25 (1995): pp. 20–29; Merle Black and Earl Black, *The Rise of Southern Republicans* (Cambridge, MA: Harvard University Press, 2009), p. 5.

148. Although Gingrich and friends insisted that their election victory had given them a mandate to implement the Contract with America, only a partial version of the text was made available to the public prior to the elections and few voters had any knowledge of it. Demetrios Caraley, "Dismantling the Federal Safety Net: Fictions versus Realities," *Political Science Quarterly* 111, no. 2 (1996): pp. 239–40. The first complete text of the contract came out after the November midterm elections of 1994, in the following edition: Ed Gillespie and Bob Schellhas, eds., *Contract with America: The Bold Plan by Rep. Newt Gingrich, Rep. Dick Armey and the House Republicans to Change the Nation* (New York: Times Books, 1994). For background on the Contract with America, see Morgan, *The Age of Deficits*, pp. 178–92; Elizabeth Drew, *Showdown: The Struggle between the Gingrich Congress and the Clinton White House* (New York: Simon & Schuster, 1996), pp. 23–43; and Nicol C. Rae, *Conservative Reformers: The Republican Freshmen and the Lessons of the 104th Congress* (London: Routledge, 1998), pp. 96–130.

149. For a full analysis of the tax expenditures included in the Contract with America and their likely effect on the budget, if implemented, see Philip Harvey, Theodore R. Marmor, and Jerry L. Mashaw, "Gingrich's Time Bomb: The Consequences of the Contract," *American Prospect*, March 22, 1995, pp. 44–52.

150. "In the short run...you have to take Social Security off the table and deal with everything else. And when you finish dealing with everything else, and you've done it right, you will have earned the trust of the American people to deal with Social Security." Quoted in William M. Welch, "Benefit Cuts Proposal under Fire," *USA Today*, December 12, 1994.

151. Quoted in Drew, *Showdown*, p. 27.

152. Quoted in Matthew D. Lassiter, "Big Government and Family Values: Political Culture in the Metropolitan Sunbelt," in *Sunbelt Rising: The Politics of Space, Place, and Region*, ed. Michelle Nickerson and Darren Dochuk (Philadelphia: University of Pennsylvania Press, 2011), p. 106.

153. Peter Overby, "White-Picket Welfare: What Would the Suburbs Be without Federal Money?," *Common Cause Magazine* (Fall 1993): pp. 21–26. Quoted in Lassiter, "Big Government and Family Values," pp. 106–107. For a wider discussion of the role of defense funding in the creation of the Sunbelt suburbs, see Lassiter, "Big Government and Family Values," pp. 86–92.

154. "Taking Speaker's Mantle, Gingrich Vows 'Profound Transformation,'" *Congressional Quarterly Weekly* 52, no. 48 (1994): p. 3523.

155. Dick Williams, *Newt! Leader of the Second American Revolution* (Marietta, GA: Longstreet Press, 1995), p. 211.

156. Louis Jacobson, "Tanks on the Roll," *National Journal* 27, no. 27 (1995): p. 1767.

157. Dan Morgan, "Think Tanks: Corporations' Quiet Weapons," *Washington Post*, January 29, 2000. Citizens for a Sound Economy started out as a front group for big tobacco companies such as Phillip Morris and R. J. Reynolds Co. that were under pressure from public health regulators in the 1980s. By the 1990s, CSE was receiving generous support from the American Petroleum Institute and the Pharmaceutical Research and Manufacturers of America, for whom it staged targeted campaigns against the FDA and climate science. Peter H. Stone, "Grass-Roots Group Rakes in the Green," *National Journal* 27, no. 10 (1995): p. 621. For the names of specific pharmaceutical and oil companies that were donating to CSE, see Jacobson, "Tanks on the Roll" and Morgan, "Think Tanks." For a history of the early links between CSE and the tobacco and oil industries, which traces this influence right up to the Tea Party, see Jeff Nesbit, *Poison Tea: How Big Oil and Big Tobacco Invented the Tea Party* (New York: Macmillan, 2016). While the petroleum and tobacco industries have a history of conflictual relationships with federal regulators, many other corporations, including long-standing members of the Business Roundtable, have called on the services of CSE to ward off threats to their bottom line. Investigative journalists have uncovered relationships between CSE and Microsoft, General Electric, Emerson Electric, and US West. Morgan, "Think Tanks."

158. Louis Jacobson, "Tanks on the Roll"; Stone, "Grass-Roots Group Rakes in the Green."

159. Haynes Johnson and David S. Broder, *The System: The American Way of Politics at the Breaking Point* (Boston: Little, Brown and Company, 1996), pp. 464–75; John B. Judis,

The Paradox of American Democracy: Elites, Special Interests, and the Betrayal of the Public Trust (New York: Pantheon Books, 2000), pp. 212–14.

160. On the historic relationship between the NFIB and the Chamber of Commerce and how this shifted thanks to the NFIB's involvement in the battle against Clinton's health-care reform, see Judis, *The Paradox of American Democracy*, pp. 213–15.

161. As one of CSE's corporate clients remarked, "they touch whole constituencies that my organization doesn't touch." Quoted in Stone, "Grass-Roots Group Rakes in the Green."

162. Nancy MacLean, "'Since We Are Greatly Outnumbered': Why and How the Koch Network Uses Disinformation to Thwart Democracy," in *The Disinformation Age: Politics, Technology, and Disruptive Communication in the United States*, ed. W. Lance Bennett and Steven Livingston (Cambridge: Cambridge University Press, 2021), p. 128. MacLean is referring to the following article by Charles Koch, "The Business Community: Resisting Regulation," *Libertarian Review* 7, no. 7 (1978): pp. 30–35.

163. According to Johnson and Broder, "Citizens for a Sound Economy operatives [worked] closely—and secretly—with Newt Gingrich's Capitol Hill office and with Republican senators." Johnson and Broder, *The System*, p. 466.

164. Louis Jacobson identifies eight former CSE staffers who went on to work for Republican congressmen after the 1994 midterms. Jacobson, "Tanks on the Roll." On CSE's involvement in the legislative battle for the Contract with America, see Stone, "Grass-Roots Group Rakes in the Green."

165. Quoted in Jeff Shear, "The Budget: Who'll Be First to Blink," *National Journal* 27, no. 38 (1995): p. 2336.

166. The first year in which CSE began testifying alongside the NTU and NTLC in favor of the balanced budget amendment was 1989, during the 101st Congress. See the testimonials in *Proposed Constitutional Amendments to Balance the Federal Budget, Floor Action, and Committee Hearings for the 101st Congress: A Legislative History, Volume 4* (Washington, DC: U.S. Government Printing Office, 1994).

167. Wayne Gable, "Statement of Dr Wayne Gable, President, Citizens for a Sound Economy (1989)," in *Proposed Constitutional Amendments to Balance the Federal Budget, Floor Action, and Committee Hearings for the 101st Congress*, p. 493. See also James C. Miller III, "Statement before the Committee on the Budget, US House of Representatives, February 5," in *Why the Balanced Budget Amendment Is Good for Americans: Hearing before the Committee on the Budget, House of Representatives, One Hundred Fifth Congress, First Session, Hearing Held in Washington, DC, February 5, 1997—Volume 4* (Washington, DC: U.S. Government Printing Office, 1997), pp. 143–47.

168. Gable, "Statement of Dr. Wayne Gable," p. 494.

169. Ibid., p. 495.

170. Letter from George Pearson to James M. Buchanan, October 22, 1975, Koch Foundation, 1975-1986, 1997, Box 61, Folder 14, James M. Buchanan Papers.

171. Letter from Charles G. Koch to James M. Buchanan, February 19, 1977, Koch Foundation, 1975-1986, 1997, Box 61, Folder 14, James M. Buchanan Papers.

172. In a letter to Charles Koch, Buchanan recommended Fink as "an entrepreneur, organizer, and coordinator in the sometimes-fuzzy intersection between the academic establishment, the business community, the established think tanks, and the foundations." Letter from James M. Buchanan to Charles Koch, May 24, 1984, Koch Foundation, 1975–1986, 1997, Box 61, Folder 14, James M. Buchanan Papers. For a full list of the George Mason University alumni that went on to work for CSE, see MacLean, "Since We Are Greatly Outnumbered," p. 129.

173. Tom Bethell, "Miller Time: An Interview with James C. Miller III," *Reason*, May 1989, pp. 32–37. James C. Miller III clarifies that he was not supervised by Buchanan. "However, all of us came under Buchanan's influence one way or another—whether indirectly through his colleagues, or during one of the many seminars where we could watch his restless intellect at work." James C. Miller III, "Foreword," in *Public Finance in Democratic Process: Fiscal Institutions and Individual Choice*, by James M. Buchanan (Chapel Hill, NC: University of North Carolina Press, 1987), p. vii. On Miller's stance against antitrust laws, regulation, and consumer protections during the Reagan administration, see Eleanor M. Fox, "Chairman Miller, the Federal Trade Commission, Economics, and Rashomon," *Law and Contemporary Problems* 50, no. 4 (1987): pp. 33–55.

174. On Buchanan's position at CSE, see Jerome Ellig, "The Case for a Tax Limitation/Balanced Budget Amendment, Statement of Dr. Jerome Ellig, Director of Public Policy, Citizens for a Sound Economy," *Balanced Budget Amendments Hearing before the Subcommittee on the Constitution of the Committee on the Judiciary, United States Senate, One Hundred First Congress, First Session, July 27, 1989, Volume 4* (Washington, DC: U.S. Government Printing Office, 1990), p. 34.

175. Alexander Hertel-Fernandez, *State Capture: How Conservative Activists, Big Businesses, and Wealthy Donors Reshaped the American States—and Nation* (Oxford: Oxford University Press, 2019), pp. 28–29. The group initially operated under the auspices of the American Conservative Union but was spun off as an independent organization in 1975.

176. Ibid., pp. 30–31.

177. Ibid., pp. 32–34.

178. Ibid., p. 37. Even then, however, ALEC continued to be involved in issues such as punitive welfare reform bills, school vouchers, and the Parental Rights Amendment, which were shaped by a social conservative agenda to strengthen the private family. Steve Rubin, "Conservative Spotlight: American Legislative Exchange Council," *Human Events*, July 26, 1996, p. 16.

179. Speaking at a 1992 ALEC meeting, President George H. W. Bush remarked that "you at ALEC have done for the amendment, what Rush Limbaugh has done for the art of passionate communication." George H. W. Bush, "Remarks to the Legislative Exchange Council in Colorado Springs, Colorado, August 6, 1992," in *Public Papers of the Presidents of the United States: George Bush, 1992–1993 (Book 2)* (Washington, DC: U.S. Government Printing Office, 1993), p. 1313. On Lewis K. Uhler's involvement in ALEC, see Fritz Pettyjohn, "Lew Uhler's Convention," *Reagan Project*, November 24, 2016. Pettyjohn places

Uhler at an ALEC meeting in 1989 and credits him with pioneering the Article V Convention route to a BBA.

180. Christopher Leonard, *Kochland: The Secret History of Koch Industries and Corporate Power in America* (New York: Simon & Schuster, 2019), pp. 274–75. There is some confusion as to the relationship between ALEC and the so-called Kochtopus of entirely Koch-funded and directed endeavors. As Alex Hertel-Fernandez explains, Koch donations have always primarily gone to the Koch brothers' own closely monitored and controlled organizations. Hertel-Fernandez, *State Capture*, pp. 161–68. Thus while there is a long history of collaboration between ALEC and the corporate arm of Koch Industries dating back to the 1990s, "ALEC is not now, nor has it ever been, part of the Kochs' main network of political organizations" (p. 24).

181. Saturno and Lynch, *A Balanced Budget Constitutional Amendment*, pp. 6, 18–21. In an open letter to Congress solicited by the American Legislative Exchange Council in early 1995, more than two hundred economists signed off on the argument that post-Keynes, America had "lost the moral sense of fiscal responsibility that served to make formal constitutional constraints unnecessary." In an obvious reference to Buchanan, the letter concluded that if we "cannot legislate a change in political morality, we can put formal constitutional constraints into place." Reproduced in "The Balanced Budget Amendment (Senate—March 2, 1995)," *Congressional Record*, 104th Congress, 1st Session, 141(39)—Daily Edition, S3341-S3342. Among those who signed this open letter were public choice economists Gordon Tullock and Richard Tollison. Buchanan expressed his support for the amendment in James M. Buchanan, "Should the Senate Pass Constitutional Amendment? Pro, from Testimony before the Senate Judiciary Committee during January 5, 1995 Hearings on a Balanced Budget Constitutional Amendment," *Congressional Digest* 74, no. 2 (1995): pp. 50, 52.

182. The American Legislative Exchange Council published a model resolution for states in 1995. It continues to promote a modified version of this same resolution today. See "Resolution Calling for a Federal Balanced Budget Amendment," *American Legislative Exchange Council*, January 16, 2016.

183. Morgan, *The Age of Deficits*, pp. 187–88.

184. Richard McGahey, "The Political Economy of Austerity in the United States," *Social Research: An International Quarterly* 80, no. 3 (2013): p. 733.

185. Morgan, *The Age of Deficits*, pp. 188–89.

186. Michael Allen Meeropol, *Surrender: How the Clinton Administration Completed the Reagan Revolution* (Ann Arbor: University of Michigan Press, 2000), pp. 245–47.

187. Ibid., pp. 247–49.

188. Robert Pollin, *Contours of Descent: US Economic Fractures and the Landscape of Global Austerity* (New York: Verso, 2003), pp. 28–29.

189. Flavio Romano, *Clinton and Blair: The Political Economy of the Third Way* (London: Routledge, 2006), p. 67.

190. Pollin, *Contours of Descent*, p. 28.

191. Robert Greenstein, Richard Kogan, and Marion Nichols, *Bearing Most of the Burden: How Deficit Reduction during the 104th Congress Concentrated on Programs for the Poor* (Washington, DC: Center on Budget and Policy Priorities, 1996).

192. For a sobering account of the Democrats' road to welfare reform, and the internal opposition to Clinton's New Democrat agenda from progressive and feminist Democrats, see Felicia Kornbluh and Gwendolyn Mink, *Ensuring Poverty: Welfare Reform in Feminist Perspective* (Philadelphia: University of Pennsylvania Press, 2019), pp. 60–76. On Newt Gingrich's role in determining the eventual shape of the Personal Responsibility Act of 1996, see Brendon O'Connor, *A Political History of the American Welfare System: When Ideas Have Consequences* (Lanham, MD: Rowman & Littlefield, 2004), pp. 205–21. Kornbluh and Mink make clear that Clinton's original plans for welfare reform were only marginally less punitive than those of the Gingrich Republicans.

193. For a history of the Republicans' support for "fiscal federalism" in the form of block grants, see Michael K. Brown, "Ghettos, Fiscal Federalism, and Welfare Reform," in *Race and the Politics of Welfare Reform*, ed. Sanford Schram, Joe Soss, and Richard C. Fording (Ann Arbor: University of Michigan Press, 2003), pp. 47–71. Beginning with Nixon, the fiscal mechanism of the fixed-sum "block grant" was proposed as an alternative to the open-ended matching grant system, under which the federal government undertook to match each dollar of state funding in accordance with caseloads. Although the "block grant" was a Republican proposal, it was driven by the same concern to limit welfare caseloads to the deserving poor that had inspired the old "states' rights" arguments of southern Democrats.

194. Drew, *Showdown*, pp. 85–86.

195. The southern Republican politics of balanced budgets differed only from its southern Democratic forebears in its greater attention to migrants as fiscal threats. The Contract with America made no mention of migration. However, the new Republican leaders of the 104th Congress very quickly integrated the theme into their postelection legislative blitz, inspired by the success of California's Republican governor Pete Wilson in mobilizing the issue to his own electoral advantage. California's Proposition 187 directly tied together the issues of budget imbalance and migration. The ballot initiative, which appeared on the same ticket used to vote in the midterm congressional elections of 1994, proposed to bar undocumented migrants residing in the state from attending public schools or accessing health-care services, except in an emergency, while also compelling schoolteachers and health workers to report suspected violators of the law to authorities. Prop 187 passed by an overwhelming majority, although most of its provisions were subsequently challenged in court and nullified. House Speaker Gingrich capitalized on the experience to set up a Congressional Task Force on Immigration Reform which called for the implementation of even harsher measures at the federal level. Two major pieces of legislation, the Personal Responsibility and Work Opportunity Reconciliation Act and the Illegal Immigration Reform and Immigration Act of 1996—passed with minimal pushback from Democrats—prohibited undocumented migrants from receiving most forms of public assistance or health

care. On Proposition 187 and the Gingrich Congress, see Kitty Calavita, "The New Politics of Immigration: 'Balanced-Budget Conservatism' and the Symbolism of Proposition 187," *Social Problems* 43, no. 3 (1996): pp. 284–305; Andrew Wroe, *The Republican Party and Immigration Politics* (New York: Palgrave Macmillan, 2008); Daniel Martinez HoSang, *Racial Propositions: Ballot Initiatives and the Making of Postwar California* (Berkeley: University of California Press, 2010); Edward D. Berkowitz, *Making Social Welfare Policy in America: Three Case Studies since 1950* (Chicago: University of Chicago Press, 2020); and Daniel Denvir, *All-American Nativism: How the Bipartisan War on Immigrants Explains Politics as We Know It* (New York: Verso, 2020), pp. 53–63. On the Democrats' collusion with both of these bills, see Kornbluh and Mink, *Ensuring Poverty*, pp. 57–89.

196. Ellen Reese, *Backlash against Welfare Mothers: Past and Present* (Berkeley: University of California Press, 2005), pp. 168–69.

197. Reese, *Backlash against Welfare Mothers*, pp. 165–71; Frank Ridzi, *Selling Welfare Reform: Work-First and the New Common Sense of Employment* (New York: NYU Press, 2009), pp. 107–35. Welfare recipients have also been employed as replacements for unionized city workers. See Jamie Peck, *Workfare States* (New York: Guilford Press, 2001); John Krinsky, *Free Labor: Workfare and the Contested Language of Neoliberalism* (Chicago: University of Chicago Press, 2007). On workfare as a way of evading existing labor protections, including minimum wage laws and social insurance protections, see Kornbluh and Mink, *Ensuring Poverty*, p. 84.

198. John E. Schwarz, "The Hidden Side of the Clinton Economy," *Atlantic*, October 1998, pp. 18–21.

199. For an extended presentation of this argument, which moves from the Elizabethan poor laws through early colonial America to the post-Reconstruction period and beyond, see Melinda Cooper, *Family Values: Between Neoliberalism and the New Social Conservatism* (New York: Zone Books, 2017), pp. 67–117.

200. Bell, *Aid to Dependent Children*, pp. 34–35; Suzanne Mettler, *Dividing Citizens: Gender and Federalism in New Deal Public Policy* (Ithaca, NY: Cornell University Press, 1998), pp. 332–41; Reese, *Backlash against Welfare Mothers*, pp. 40–51.

201. Mettler, *Dividing Citizens*, pp. 169–74; Premilla Nadesan, *Welfare Warriors: The Welfare Rights Movement in the United States* (London: Routledge, 2005), pp. 6–8; Gwendolyn Mink, *Welfare's End* (Ithaca, NY: Cornell University Press, 1998), p. 48.

202. Cooper, *Family Values*, pp. 93–96. Having ignored AFDC during its first few decades of existence, the U.S. Supreme Court presided over a full eighteen cases relating to the program between 1968 and 1975, while the lower federal courts issued hundreds of relevant decisions during the same period. The outcome of these decisions was both to federalize control of welfare and to align its provisions with recent changes in family law. In the *King v. Smith* case of 1968, Chief Justice Earl Warren ruled that Alabama's substitute father rule violated the terms of the Social Security Act and was out of touch with family law, which no longer sought to punish extramarital relations and no longer recognized any valid status distinction between legitimate and illegitimate children.

203. Cooper, *Family Values*, pp. 103–106. In some cases, this translated into a form of indentured labor for men also, since biological fathers saddled with unpaid child support debt were enrolled in municipal welfare-to-work programs to pay off their dues. See Noah Zatz, Tia Koonse, Theresa Zhen, Lucero Herrera, Han Lu, Steven Shafer, and Blake Valenta, *Get to Work or Go to Jail: Workplace Rights under Threat* (Los Angeles: UCLA Institute for Research on Labor and Employment, 2016), pp. 7–9.

204. Kornbluh and Mink, *Ensuring Poverty*, pp. 78–79.

205. Christopher Howard, *The Welfare State That Nobody Knows: Debunking Myths about U.S. Social Policy* (Princeton, NJ: Princeton University Press, 2006), pp. 103–106.

206. On Milton Friedman's "negative income tax" and its role in the welfare reform debates of the 1970s, see Marisa Chappell, *The War on Welfare: Family, Poverty and Politics in Modern America* (Philadelphia: University of Pennsylvania Press, 2010), pp. 52–58, 61, 72, 79–87.

207. Howard, *The Welfare State That Nobody Knows*, p. 99.

208. Richard Keith Armey with Matt Kibbe, *Give Us Liberty: A Tea Party Manifesto* (New York: HarperCollins, 2010), pp. 1–2.

209. Ibid., pp. 4, 7–8.

210. Molly E. Reynolds and Phillip A. Wallach, "The Final Fiscal Fight of the Obama Administration—and Its Many Predecessors," *Brookings,* December 8, 2016.

211. During the 111th Congress, the number of threatened filibusters and cloture motions to overcome them rose to an astonishing two per week. Where all previous presidents combined had faced a total of eighty-two filibusters against their nominees, President Obama endured eighty-two between 2009 and 2013. See Thomas E. Mann and Norman J. Ornstein, *It's Even Worse Than It Looks: How the American Constitutional System Collided with the New Politics of Extremism* (New York: Basic Books, 2012), pp. 84–102; Jentleson, *Kill Switch*, pp. 116–19. On McConnell's role in the trivialization of the filibuster and his eventual rift with the Tea Party, see Jentleson, *Kill Switch*, pp. 207–25.

212. Sean M. Theriault, *The Gingrich Senators: The Roots of Partisan Warfare in Congress* (New York: Oxford University Press, 2013).

213. Jane Mayer, *Dark Money* (Melbourne: Scribe, 2016), pp. 162–64. The split seems to have been caused by tensions between Dick Armey and Richard Fink, each of whom accused the other of exploiting the organization to suit their own (or the Kochs') business objectives.

214. Matt Kibbe was appointed president of CSE in June 2004, shortly before it merged with Empower America to form FreedomWorks. Kibbe was appointed president and CEO of FreedomWorks upon its creation that same year. "Matt Kibbe," *SourceWatch* August 4, 2011. Wayne Brough served as chief economist for CSE beginning in the early 1990s before taking up the role of chief economist and vice president of research at FreedomWorks. "Wayne Brough," *Science Corruption*, December 31, 2010.

215. Austin Allen, "Big Think Interview with Dick Armey," *Big Think*, November 11, 2009.

216. "It's a fairly good grounding in preparation for a career in politics, or in office." Ibid.

217. On the relationship between national lobbying groups such as FreedomWorks, local Tea Party organizers, and grassroots members, see Devin Burghart and Leonard Zeskind, *Tea Party Nationalism: Special Report* (Kansas City, MO: Institute for Research and Education on Human Rights, 2010).

218. In January 2010, FreedomWorks brought together sixty Tea Party organizers from two dozen states to prepare for the November midterm elections. It was at this event that FreedomWorks announced a list of sixty-five targeted congressional races. Ibid., 21.

219. Maya Srikrishnan, Jared Pliner, Jennifer Schlesinger, Joshua Goldstein, and Huma Khan, "Which Tea Party Candidates Won?," ABC News, September 25, 2010.

220. As noted by Bryan Gervais and Irwin Morris, it is difficult to compile a straightforward list of Tea Party legislators given the different degrees and markers of affiliation that characterize the relationship of any one member of the House or Senate to the Tea Party. Not all Tea Party–affiliated candidates were endorsed or financed by umbrella organizations such as FreedomWorks, Tea Party Express, or SarahPAC (Sarah Palin's political action committee), and endorsement decisions often depended on the closeness of the electoral race. Some candidates were endorsed by one group and not others. Similarly, not all formal members of the Tea Party Caucus or its later incarnations (the Liberty Caucus or Freedom Caucus) voted consistently with the hardcore bloc of Tea Party Caucus members. For this reason, Gervais and Morris propose a continuum of affiliations to the Tea Party movement. Bryan T. Gervais and Irwin L. Morris, *Reactionary Republicanism: How the Tea Party in the House Paved the Way for Trump's Victory* (Oxford: Oxford University Press, 2018), pp. 31–66. In the case of the debt ceiling showdown of 2011, the final vote on the Balanced Budget Bill of 2011 makes it clear that a hard core of thirty or so members of the Tea Party Caucus, led by Michele Bachmann, were the drivers behind Republican intransigence. See Douglas A. Blackmon and Jennifer Levitz, "Tea Party Sees No Triumph in Compromise," *Wall Street Journal*, August 2, 2011.

221. On the role of FreedomWorks, Americans for Prosperity, and Club for Growth in the debt ceiling showdown, see Mayer, *Dark Money*, pp. 297–98; Vanessa Williamson, "The Tea Party and the Shift to 'Austerity by Gridlock' in the United States," APSA Annual Conference, Chicago, August 29, 2013. For a statement by FreedomWorks urging intransigence on the debt ceiling, with reference to the work of James M. Buchanan, see Wayne T. Brough, "That's $14 Trillion—Trillion with a 'T': Drowning in a Sea of Red Ink," *Freedom-Works Foundation Issue Analysis* 130 (June 2011): pp. 1–14.

222. Charles Babington, "Tea Party Role in Debt Bill Raises Eyebrows," MPR News, July 30, 2011. For a narratival account of the debt ceiling showdown of 2011, see Mann and Ornstein, *It's Even Worse Than It Looks*, pp. 3–30.

223. "WSJ BLOG/MarketBeat: S&P Downgrades U.S. Debt Rating Press Release," Dow Jones Institutional News, August 5, 2011.

224. *Summary of the Budget Control Act of 2011, US House of Representatives, Committee on the Budget, August 3* (Washington, DC: U.S. House of Representatives, 2011).

225. House Speaker John Boehner remarked that he "got 98 percent of what [he] wanted." Scott Pelley, "Boehner: I Got 98 Percent of What I Wanted," CBS News, August 1, 2011. The thirty or so Tea Party Republicans who wanted a balanced budget amendment, however, were still not happy and voted against the bill. Blackmon and Levitz, "Tea Party Sees No Triumph in Compromise."

226. On the lingering aftereffects of the financial crisis, see Barry Z. Cynamon, Steven M. Fazzari, and Mark Setterfield, *After the Great Recession: The Struggle for Economic Recovery and Growth* (Cambridge: Cambridge University Press, 2013).

227. Josh Bivens, "Abolish the Debt Ceiling before It Commits Austerity Again," Economic Policy Institute, September 27, 2021. On the slowness of the recovery, see Josh Bivens, *Why Is Recovery Taking So Long—and Who's to Blame?* (Washington, DC: Economic Policy Institute, 2016).

228. Lawrence H. Summers, "Demand-Side Secular Stagnation," *American Economic Review* 105, no. 5 (2015): pp. 60–65. Summers is borrowing the term "secular stagnation" from the American Keynesian, Alvin Hansen, who was seeking to account for the unexpected return of recession-like conditions in the late 1930s. Alvin Hansen, "Economic Progress and Declining Population Growth," *American Economic Review* 29, no. 1 (1939): pp. 1–15. Hansen described the "essence of secular stagnation" as follows: "sick recoveries which die in their infancy and depressions which feed on themselves and leave a hard and seemingly immovable core of unemployment" (p. 4).

229. Jamie Peck refers to the cascading of federal cuts down to the state and local government as a form of "devolved austerity." Jamie Peck, "Austerity Urbanism: American Cities under Extreme Economy," *City* 16, no. 6 (2012): pp. 626–55; Jamie Peck, "Austere Reason, and the Eschatology of Neoliberalism's End Times," *Comparative European Politics* 11, no. 6 (2013): pp. 713–21. The devolution of austerity is almost automatic within the American system of federalism, given that fully one-third of federal funds flow through state and local governments, most of which are subject to strict statutory or constitutional limits on the ability to issue debt. When the normal flow of funds dries up and no new tax revenues can be found, state and local governments have no option but to slash services.

230. Elizabeth McNichol, *Out of Balance: Cuts in Services Have Been States' Primary Response to Budget Gaps, Harming the Nation's Economy* (Washington, DC: Center on Budget and Policy Priorities, 2012), p. 506; Phil Oliff, Chris Mai, and Vincent Palacios, *States Continue to Feel Recession's Impact* (Washington, DC: Center on Budget and Policy Priorities, 2012), p. 4. According to a report by United for a Fair Economy, more than 110,000 state and local jobs were cut, including 40,000 teachers and 4,000 police officers and firefighters in the two years following September 2007. Mazher Ali, Jeannette Huezo, Brian Miller, Wanjiku Mwangi, and Mike Prokosch, *State of the Dream 2011: Austerity for Whom* (Boston: United for a Fair Economy, 2011), p. 2.

231. "Republicans Exceed Expectations in 2010 State Legislative Elections," National Conference of State Legislatures, November 3, 2010.

232. On the 2010 state-level Republican assault on the public sector and the role

of ALEC and the SNP in coordinating it, see Hertel-Fernandez, *State Capture*, pp. 1 and 179–97.

233. Devin Burghart and Leonard Zeskind, *Tea Party Nationalism: Special Report* (Kansas City, MO: Institute for Research and Education on Human Rights, 2010), pp. 31, 69–72.

234. On "stand-your-ground" laws and the Tea Party state electoral wave of 2010, see Hertel-Fernandez, *State Capture*, pp. 2–3, 55, 58.

235. According to United for a Fair Economy, African Americans are 30 percent more likely than the general workforce to hold public-sector jobs. Latinos, by contrast, are underrepresented in public-sector jobs. Prokosch, *State of the Dream*, pp. 22–23.

236. Thomas Byrne Edsall, *The Age of Austerity: How Scarcity Will Remake American Politics* (New York: Anchor Books, 2012), pp. 118–19.

237. James H. Carr, "The Silent Depression: How Are Minorities Faring in the Economic Downturn, September 23," *Hearing before the Committee on Oversight and Government Reform, House of Representatives, One Hundred Eleventh Congress, First Session, September 23, 2009* (Washington, DC: U.S. Government Printing Office, 2010), pp. 56–163.

238. Gordon Lafer, "The Legislative Attack on American Wages and Labor Standards, 2011–12," *EPI Briefing Paper #364* (Washington, DC: Economy Policy Institute, 2013), p. 41. According to Lafer, model legislation for these cuts was developed by ALEC, NFIB, and the Chamber of Commerce.

239. Ibid., p. 41.

240. Hertel-Fernandez, *State Capture*, p. 197.

241. In 2013, 40.5 percent of Hispanics and 25.8 percent of African Americans had no health insurance, either private or public, compared with 14.8 percent of whites. Thomas C. Buchmueller, Zachary M. Levinson, Helen G. Levy, and Barbara L. Wolfe, "Effect of the Affordable Care Act on Racial and Ethnic Disparities in Health Insurance Coverage," *American Journal of Public Health* 106, no. 8 (2016): pp. 1416–21. A retrospective report by the Commonwealth Fund found that racial and ethnic disparities in access to health care declined significantly after 2013, although progress stalled and in some cases reversed with the election of Trump. After implementation of the ACA, the gap between Black and white adult uninsured rates dropped by 4.1 percentage points, while the coverage gap between Hispanic and white people narrowed by 9.4 points. Although African American working-age adults benefited significantly from Medicaid expansion, they disproportionately resided in the southern and midwestern states that refused to expand their programs. Jesse C. Baumgartner, Sara R. Collins, David C. Radley, and Susan L. Hayes, "How the Affordable Care Act Has Narrowed Racial and Ethnic Disparities in Access to Health Care," Commonwealth Fund, January 16, 2020.

242. Theda Skocpol and Vanessa Williamson draw on observational research and interviews among grassroots Tea Party groups to illuminate supporters' idiosyncratic value judgments with respect to public welfare programs. See Theda Skocpol and Vanessa Williamson, *The Tea Party and the Remaking of Republican Conservatism* (Oxford: Oxford University Press, 2016), pp. 54–68.

243. In a forensic investigation of this claim, Korin Davis and William A. Galston find that Republicans misused data from the Congressional Budget Office to create the impression that Democrats were intending to reduce Medicare benefits. While the ACA did outline a series of budget cuts to Medicare, this would not have involved any decrease in benefits. In fact, the opposite was true. Benefits were set to increase, while savings were to be made with cuts to hospital reimbursement rates and private Medicare Advantage plans. Meanwhile, Tea Party–aligned Republican Paul Ryan's budget proposed the complete repeal of the ACA, while retaining the same cost savings outlined by Obama. Korin Davis and William A. Galston, "Medicare Cuts: What Is the Fight About," *Brookings*, August 15, 2012.

244. Sara Rosenbaum, "The Supreme Court's Medicaid Ruling: 'A Shift in Kind, Not Merely Degree,'" *Health Affairs*, June 28, 2012.

245. Hertel-Fernandez, *State Capture*, p. 197.

246. "Status of State Medicaid Expansion Decisions: Interactive Map," KFF Kaiser Family Foundation, February 24, 2022.

247. Michael de Yoanna, "Why Dick Armey Doesn't Want Tom Tancredo in the Tea Party," 5280.com, March 16, 2010.

248. Skocpol and Williamson, *The Tea Party and the Remaking of Republican Conservatism*, pp. 54–68; Anthony DiMaggio, *The Rise of the Tea Party: Political Discontent and Corporate Media in the Age of Obama* (New York: Monthly Review Press, 2011), pp. 44, 75, 135. According to a CBS News/*New York Times* poll, about half of Tea Party supporters reported that someone in their household received Medicare or Social Security benefits, and 62 percent of those polled believed these programs were "worth the costs…for taxpayers." "National Survey of Tea Party Supporters," April 5–12, 2010.

249. Lisa Disch, "The Tea Party: A 'White Citizenship' Movement?," in *Steep: The Precipitous Rise of the Tea Party*, ed. Laurence Rosenthal and Christine Trost (Berkeley: University of California Press, 2012), pp. 133–51.

250. Samuel L. Popkin, *Crackup: The Republican Implosion and the Future of Presidential Politics* (Oxford: Oxford University Press, 2021), pp. 4, 22–25, 36–39, 44, 53–54. I borrow the term "shadow parties" from Popkin (p. 9).

251. On the Koch network and primary challenges, see Mayer, *Dark Money*, pp. 297–98, and Popkin, *Crackup*, pp. 45, 51, 65.

252. Ed Hornick, "The 'Big Headache': Boehner Backed into Corner by Tea Party, Obama," CNN, July 27, 2011. On Tea Party primary challenge threats against Boehner, see Ronald T. Libby, *Purging the Republican Party: Tea Party Campaigns and Elections* (Lanham, MD: Lexington Books, 2013), pp. 12–13. On Boehner's resignation, see Francine Kiefer, "Meet the Republicans Who Ousted John Boehner, They're Just Getting Started," *Christian Science Monitor*, October 5, 2015.

253. The term "Young Guns" comes from Eric Cantor, Paul Ryan, and Kevin McCarthy, *Young Guns: A New Generation of Conservative Leaders* (New York: Simon & Schuster, 2010). In a stunning display of Tea Party spite, sitting House majority leader Eric Cantor was ousted by a grassroots Tea Party candidate, David Brat, in the 2014 primaries. Cantor was accused

of being too soft on migration. Paul Ryan, too, eventually fell from grace when, as chair of the House Ways and Means Committee, he met with Democrats to help avoid a government shutdown. Kevin McCarthy was blocked by the Freedom Caucus in his bid for Speaker of the House. Ryan Lizza, "Paul Ryan Faces the 'Young Guns' Jinx," *New Yorker*, December 10, 2015.

254. According to the *Washington Post*, "Young Guns" Paul Ryan, Eric Cantor, and Kevin McCarthy had been planning to weaponize the debt ceiling long before the midterm elections of 2010. Lori Montgomery, Paul Kane, Brady Dennis, Alec MacGillis, David Fahrenthold, Rosalind Helderman, Felicia Sonmez, and Dan Balz, "Origins of the Debt Showdown," *Washington Post*, August 6, 2011.

255. Mann and Ornstein, *It's Even Worse Than It Looks*, pp. 5–6. Tax specialist Joseph Thorndike contrasts the first debt ceiling showdown by Senator Harry F. Byrd with the Tea Party showdowns of the 2010s and concludes that Byrd had no intention of actually forcing a default. Joseph Thorndike, "Debt Limit Fights Are All the Same—Except for this One," *Forbes*, October 16, 2016.

256. In an exchange with the *Washington Post*, Rep. Jason Chaffetz of Utah assured reporters that Tea Party freshmen were serious in their resolve to let a default happen. "We weren't kidding around," he said: "We *would* have taken it down." He also claimed that House Speaker Boehner and other so-called moderates had exploited Tea Party radicalism to extract as many concessions as possible from Democrats. Montgomery et al., "Origins of the Debt Showdown." In the right-wing press, Bruce Bartlett warned fellow conservatives of the seriousness of Tea Party threats when it came to the debt ceiling. Bruce Bartlett, "Debt Default: It Can Happen Here," *Fiscal Times*, June 11, 2010. Many of these Republican insurgents, Bartlett observes, had come to understand debt default as an alternative to the balanced budget amendment, a way of ensuring budget balance by force rather than constitutional edict.

257. John Tamny, "Learn to Love a U.S. Default," *Forbes*, May 24, 2010.

258. James M. Buchanan, "The Ethics of Debt Default," in James M. Buchanan, Charles K. Rowley, and Robert D. Tollison, eds., *Deficits* (Oxford: Basil Blackwell, 1987), pp. 367–70.

259. Ibid., p. 373.

260. Ibid., pp. 364–66. From his earliest work, Buchanan distinguished between the "organismic" theory of the state, which subsumes all individual wants within the whole, and an "individualistic" theory, which sees the state as the sum of individual preferences and thereby recognizes the ever-present danger of conflict between the whole and its parts. James M. Buchanan, "The Pure Theory of Government Finance: A Suggested Approach," *Journal of Political Economy* 57, no. 6 (1949): pp. 496–505.

261. As we saw in the previous chapter, Buchanan referred to this process as "internal exit without secession" but also conceded that it amounted to an "alternative form of secession"—fiscal rather than territorial. James M. Buchanan and Roger L. Faith, "Secession and the Limits of Taxation: Toward a Theory of Internal Exit," *American Economic Review* 77, no. 5 (1987): pp. 1023–31.

262. During his 1980 campaign for presidency, Reagan promised to apply the law to all fifty states while restoring to "states and local governments the power that properly belongs

to them." Quoted in Raymond Wolters, *Right Turn: William Bradford Reynolds, the Reagan Administration, and Black Civil Rights* (New York: Taylor & Francis, 1996), p. 30.

263. Atwater confided these thoughts in 1981 to the political scientist Alexander Lamis, who published the interview transcript without revealing Atwater as his source. A full transcript and video recording of the interview can now be found at: Rick Perlstein, "Exclusive: Lee Atwater's Infamous 1981 Interview on the Southern Strategy (Presented by Rick Perlstein)," *Nation*, November 13, 2012, at 15:26–15.51.

264. Ibid., 15.55–16.11.

265. Ibid., 16.27–17.27.

266. Tom McCarthy and Alvin Chang, "The Senate Is Broken: System Empowers White Conservatives, Threatening US Democracy," *Guardian*, March 13, 2021.

267. Jentleson, *Kill Switch*, p. 108. See also David Litt, "The McConnell Filibuster Is Not the Same as the Jim Crow Filibuster—It's Much Worse," *Guardian*, March 25, 2021.

268. *Abbott v. Perez*, 585 U.S. ___ (2018).

269. *Rucho v. Common Cause*, No. 18–422, 588 U.S. ___ (2019). "But the fact that such gerrymandering is 'incompatible with democratic principles'…does not mean that the solution lies with the federal judiciary" (p. 30).

270. *Brnovich v. Democratic National Committee*, 594 U.S. ___ (2021).

271. *Shelby County v. Holder*, 570 U.S. 529 (2013); *Vieth v. Jubelirer*, 541 U.S. 267 (2004).

272. Carol Anderson, *One Person, No Vote: How Voter Suppression Is Destroying Our Democracy* (New York: Bloomsbury, 2018), pp. 62–71, 104–20.

273. Jacob S. Hacker and Paul Pierson, *Let Them Eat Tweets: How the Right Rules in an Age of Extreme Inequality* (New York: Norton, 2020), p. 180.

274. On ALEC's role in voter ID laws and their intent to disenfranchise minorities, see Hertel-Fernandez, *State Capture*, pp. 2–3, 23, 51, 54–55. On the full range of ALEC's efforts at voter suppression, see Elliott Negin, "How the American Legislative Exchange Council Turns Disinformation into Law," Union of Concerned Scientists, June 29, 2022. After 2010, a second wave of state-level voter restrictions was passed following Trump's defeat in the presidential election of 2020. Julia Harte and Clare Trainor, "Where Voting Has Become More Difficult," *Reuters*, November 1, 2022.

275. Alex Keena, Michael Lanter, Anthony J. McGann, and Charles Anthony Smith, *Gerrymandering the States: Partisanship, Race, and the Transformation of American Federalism* (Cambridge: Cambridge University Press, 2021), pp. 105–109.

276. Ibid., p. 3.

277. See, in particular, Michelle Alexander, *The New Jim Crow: Mass Incarceration in the Age of Colorblindness* (New York: New Press, 2020).

CHAPTER FIVE: ABORTING AMERICA

1. Nancy L. Cohen, *Delirium: How the Sexual Counterrevolution Is Polarizing America* (Berkeley, CA: Counterpoint, 2012), p. 335, and Peter Montgomery, "The Tea Party and the

Religious Right Movements: Frenemies with Benefits," in *Steep: The Precipitous Rise of the Tea Party*, ed. Lawrence Rosenthal and Christine Trost (Berkeley: University of California Press, 2012), pp. 16–17.

2. States News Service, "Pence Addresses March for Life 'A Nation That Will Not Stand for Life Will Not Stand for Long,'" *States News Service*, January 23, 2011.

3. Adele M. Stan, "Shutdown Ends, Debt Crisis Averted—But Birth Control Still an Issue," *Rewire News*, October 17, 2013.

4. David N. Bass, "Obama's Abortion Spending Spree," *American Spectator*, December 29, 2008.

5. Janice Shaw Crouse, *A Declaration about America's Fiscal Crisis* (Washington, DC: Concerned Women for America, 2011), pp. 25–26.

6. See John Dombrink, *The Twilight of Social Conservatism: American Culture Wars in the Obama Era* (New York: NYU Press, 2015), pp. 44, 29.

7. Cohen, *Delirium*, pp. 233–37, 315–16.

8. Robert D. Putnam and David E. Campbell, *American Grace: How Religion Divides and Unites Us* (New York: Simon & Schuster, 2012), p. 574. Strikingly, they note that "a preference for mixing religion and politics exceeds a preference for smaller government as a predictor of Tea Party support." With more emphasis on the internal heterogeneity of the movement, Gervais and Morris argue that Tea Party supporters "are distinct from other Americans—and often other Republicans—in one or more of three key areas: fiscal conservatism, racial conservatism, social conservatism." Bryan T. Gervais and Irwin L. Morris, *Reactionary Republicanism: How the Tea Party in the House Paved the Way for Trump's Victory* (Oxford: Oxford University Press, 2018), p. 19. In what follows, I will show how each of these elements merged in Tea Party politics.

9. Montgomery, "The Tea Party and the Religious Right Movements," pp. 249–50.

10. On the participation of the Council for National Policy, see Anne Nelson, *Shadow Network: Media, Money, and the Secret Hub of the Radical Right* (New York: Bloomsbury, 2019), pp. 154–56. On the link between Americans for Prosperity and the religious right, see Adele M. Stan, "Anatomy of the War on Women: How the Koch Brothers Are Funding the Anti-Choice Agenda," *Rewire News*, November 5, 2013.

11. Phyllis Schlafly, "Important Issues for the 2010 Election," *Phyllis Schlafly Report* 43, no. 12 (2010): pp. 1–4. In their study of the Tea Party, Skocpol and Williamson make the perceptive comment that "the fiscal question in the Tea Party imagination is more than just a redistributive matter, more than just a set of worries about taxes and social spending. In the highly emotional telling of many Tea Partiers, the ballooning federal deficit merges into a general sense of coming collapse for America." Theda Skocpol and Vanessa Williamson, *The Tea Party and the Remaking of Republican Conservatism* (Oxford: Oxford University Press, 2016), p. 76.

12. Jim DeMint and J. David Woodard, *Why We Whisper: Restoring Our Right to Say It's Wrong* (Lanham, MD: Rowman & Littlefield, 2008), p. 137. This argument is pervasive on the religious right. A frequently referenced source is John S. Payne, "Factoring Out Abortion," *Human Life Review* 17, no. 2 (1991): pp. 59–64.

13. The association between legalized abortion and national decline was apparent as early as the 1970s. See Bernard N. Nathanson and Richard N. Ostling, *Aborting America* (Toronto: Life Cycle Books, 1979), for a religious conservative view on the nation-destructive impact of abortion. Carol Mason offers a compelling analysis of the right-to-life movement's declinist nationalism. Carol Mason, *Killing for Life: The Apocalyptic Narrative of Pro-Life Politics* (Ithaca, NY: Cornell University Press, 2002), pp. 20–21. See also Lauren Berlant for an extended reflection on the process by which "an entire culture can come to identify with, and as, a fetus." Lauren Berlant, "America, 'Fat,' the Fetus," *Boundary 2* 21, no. 3 (1994): p. 150.

14. The historian Jennifer Donnally has written an illuminating account of the early right-to-life movement and its peculiar interweaving of antitax and anti-abortion sentiments. See Jennifer Donnally, "The Politics of Abortion and the Rise of the New Right," PhD diss., University of North Carolina at Chapel Hill, 2013.

15. See Adele M. Stan, "What Rand Paul and Sharron Angle Have in Common: A Far-Right 'Biblical Law' Political Party," AlterNet, June 15, 2010. But see also James C. Sanford, *Blueprint for Theocracy: The Christian Right's Vision for America* (Providence, RI: Metacomet Books, 2014), pp. 185–91; Julie J. Ingersoll, *Building God's Kingdom: Inside the World of Christian Reconstruction* (Oxford: Oxford University Press, 2015), pp. 207–208.

16. On the multiple connections between Howard Phillips's Constitution Party and the Tea Party, see Sanford, *Blueprint for Theocracy*, pp. 187–91; Ronald P. Formisano, *The Tea Party: A Brief History* (Baltimore: Johns Hopkins University Press, 2012), pp. 51–62; and Sarah Posner and Julie Ingersoll, "Gun Ownership: 'An Obligation to God,'" in *At the Tea Party: The Wing Nuts, Whack Jobs and Whitey-Whiteness of the New Republican Right…and Why We Should Take It Seriously*, ed. Laura Flanders (New York: OR Books, 2010), pp. 116–24.

17. Howard Phillips, "A New Right Perspective," in *The New Right at Harvard*, ed. Howard Phillips (Vienna, VA: Conservative Caucus, 1983), p. 3. On Young Americans for Freedom, see John A. Andrew, *The Other Side of the Sixties: Young Americans for Freedom and the Rise of Conservative Politics* (New Brunswick, NJ: Rutgers University Press, 1997). For a comparative history of Young Americans for Freedom and the New Left, see Rebecca E. Klatch, *A Generation Divided: The New Left, the New Right, and the 1960s* (Berkeley: University of California Press, 1999).

18. Alan F. Charles, "National Legal Program on Health Problems of the Poor: Abortion Law Challenges Growing," *Clearinghouse Review* 3, no. 10 (1970): p. 257.

19. On the fight to secure AFDC and Medicaid-funded birth control and abortion, see Alan F. Charles, "Enforcing Legal Rights to Family Planning and Abortion," *Clearinghouse Review* 6, no. 7 (1972): pp. 422–23. On the battle against parental consent laws, see Joanne B. Stern, "H.R.1: Changes in Family Planning Requirements," *Clearinghouse Review* 6, no. 8 (1972): pp. 476–77.

20. Howard Phillips, "Uncle Sam's Assault against the Family," *Human Events* 34, no. 3 (1974): p. 10.

21. Howard Phillips, "Will Nixon Redeem Anti-Abortion Pledge?," *Human Events* 34, no. 4 (1974): p. 10.

22. See Melinda Cooper, *Family Values: Between Neoliberalism and the New Social Conservatism* (New York: Zone Books, 2017), pp. 25–66.

23. Howard Phillips, "U.S. Social Fabric Threatened by Budget Growth," *Human Events* 35, no. 3 (1975): p. 14.

24. Howard Phillips, "Liberals Receive Campaign Cash from AARP Boss," *Human Events* 34, no. 46 (1974): p. 16.

25. Robert E. Bauman, Petition to the Chairman and Members of the House Subcommittee on Health against Senator Kennedy's Bill, H.R. 21 Government Takeover of Medical Care, Americans against Socialized Medicine, 20 September 1977, Group Research Inc, Records; Box 23, Series 1 Topical, 1955–1996; Rare Book and Manuscript Library, Columbia University Library.

26. M. Stanton Evans, *The Future of Conservatism: From Taft to Reagan and Beyond* (New York: Holt, 1968); Kevin Phillips, "'The Emerging Republican Majority': An Interview with Kevin Phillips," *Human Events* 29, no. 33 (1969): pp. 8–14; Kevin Phillips, *The Emerging Republican Majority* (New Rochelle, NY: Arlington House, 1969); Patrick Buchanan, *Conservative Votes, Liberal Victories: Why the Right Has Failed* (New York: Quadrangle, 1975); William A. Rusher, *The Making of the New Majority Party* (Ottawa: Green Hill, 1975).

27. In *The Long Southern Strategy: How Chasing White Voters in the South Changed American Politics* (Oxford: Oxford University Press, 2019), Angie Maxwell and Todd Shields convincingly argue that the racial and sexual/religious components of Republican Party realignment were inseparable.

28. Kevin Phillips, "How Nixon Will Win," *New York Times*, August 6, 1972.

29. Ibid.

30. Ibid.

31. Linda Greenhouse and Reva B. Siegel, "Before (and after) *Roe v. Wade*: New Questions about Backlash," *Yale Law Journal* 120 (2011): pp. 2028–87.

32. Ibid., pp. 2054–56. Nixon was walking a tightrope: while in his public addresses he borrowed liberally from Catholic rhetoric about the "sanctity of life," he was seeking at the same time to appeal to a much broader swathe of the voting public, who he hoped would see his defense of the unborn as a commitment to social conservatism in general. At the same time, however, opinion polls kept showing that a majority of the American public and a growing number of Catholics were in favor of liberalizing abortion laws. When the *Roe v. Wade* decision was handed down in early 1973 Nixon asked his aides to stay silent on the matter (pp. 2055–59).

33. Phillips, "Will Nixon Redeem Anti-Abortion Pledge?," p. 82.

34. Richard A. Viguerie, *The New Right: We're Ready to Lead* (Falls Church, VA: The Viguerie Company, 1981), pp. 50–51.

35. *Conservative Digest*, October 1980, pp. 11, 17.

36. Viguerie, *The New Right*, p. 56. At a time when both major parties were in flux, New

Right operatives tried their hands at insurrection on both the Democratic and Republican sides before finally settling for an ongoing antagonistic relationship with the GOP. In 1975, at the instigation of William Rusher, the New Right seriously considered the idea of setting up a third party as an escape route from Republican inertia. The scheme was abandoned, however, when their favorite, the renegade Ronald Reagan, declined to join them. Daniel Schlozman and Sam Rosenfeld, "The Long New Right and the World It Made," unpublished paper, American Political Science Association Meetings, August 31, 2018, pp. 35–37. As late as 1978, Paul Weyrich backed a conservative Democrat against the blue-blood Republican George H. W. Bush in the Texas congressional elections, while in the same year Howard Phillips ran as a Democrat against a liberal Republican in the Massachusetts Senate primaries. Daniel K. Williams, *God's Own Party: The Making of the Christian Right* (Oxford: Oxford University Press, 2010), p. 168. Following this, the New Right seems to have determined that the best way to avoid neutralization by the Republican machine was to create ballast to its right. This was an act of conscious mimicry. For years, Howard Phillips averred, liberal progressives had managed to "shape the policies of both the Democratic and Republican parties" by building a network of "extra-partisan institutions" to the left of the Democratic center. Phillips, "A New Right Perspective," p. 6. The New Right was determined to reverse this situation by building an alternative infrastructure to the right, with open doors to the far right.

37. The following biographical information is drawn from Alan Crawford, *Thunder on the Right: The "New Right" and the Politics of Resentment* (New York: Pantheon Books, 1980), pp. 3–41, which covers a broader range of operatives than the well-known New Right four; Michele McKeegan, *Abortion Politics: Mutiny in the Ranks of the Right* (Toronto: Free Press, 1992), pp. 4–10; and Nelson, *Shadow Network*, pp. 24–25.

38. Howard Phillips, ed., *The Next Four Years: A Vision of Victory* (Franklin, TN: Adroit Press, 1992), p. xiii.

39. "I come from a poor district of working-class people," Weyrich recalled, and the "Republican candidates never even bothered to appear in my neighborhood, which was made up of lower middle-class Slavs, Poles, Czechs, Italians and so on." Paul Weyrich, "Family Issues, October 13 1981," in *The New Right at Harvard*, ed. Howard Phillips (Vienna, VA: Conservative Caucus, 1983), p. 20.

40. Crawford, *Thunder on the Right*, p. 246.

41. As late as 1981, Viguerie was upbeat about the prospects of recruiting middle-class Blacks and unionized workers to the cause. Viguerie, *The New Right*, pp. 162–70.

42. Crawford, *Thunder on the Right*, pp. 248–54. For an early insight into the New Right's antilabor activism, see Arch Puddington, "Evolving Threat of the New Right," in *The New Right: Issues and Analyses, Press Profile No. 5* (Oakland, CA: Data Center 1981), pp. 1–5.

43. The National Right to Life Committee was the nation's oldest and largest anti-abortion organization. It was founded under the auspices of the National Conference of Catholic Bishops in 1968. Soon after, it formally separated from the Catholic Church and

made conscious efforts to involve non-Catholic anti-abortion activists. However, the organization continued to be dominated by Catholics and retained close connections to the Catholic Church. See Neil J. Young, *We Gather Together: The Religious Right and the Problem of Interfaith Politics* (Oxford: Oxford University Press, 2016), pp. 118–35.

44. According to Jennifer Donnally, North Carolina Republican senator Jesse Helms told attendees at the Conservative Political Action Conference of February 1975 that the mobilization of evangelicals was a necessary component of Republican Party realignment. Donnally, "The Politics of Abortion and the Rise of the New Right," p. 139. In 1976, Paul Viguerie predicted that the "next real major area of growth for the conservative ideology and (political) philosophy is among evangelical people." Quoted in Jim Wallis and Wes Michaelson, "The Plan to Save America," *Sojourners*, April 1976, p. 11. The New Right finally managed to penetrate the closed circles of Southern Baptists when a member of Howard Phillips's Conservative Caucus, Ed McAteer, secured them an audience with Jerry Falwell. The historic meeting electrified Falwell into action and arrived in the nick of time, a year before the presidential elections of 1980. Immediately after this exchange, Falwell organized a mass voter registration drive among Southern Baptist churchgoers, departing from fundamentalist protocol to urge a vote for Reagan. Outreach to evangelical and Pentecostal preachers soon followed. Williams, *God's Own Party*, p. 172.

45. Williams, *God's Own Party*, p. 3. As Williams explains, conservative Protestants began to look to the GOP as the defender of anticommunism and moral order beginning in the 1940s and made overtures to Eisenhower in the 1950s. However, they did not attain a controlling influence on the party until 1980.

46. Ibid., p. 176.

47. Weyrich, "Family Issues," p. 21.

48. Williams, *God's Own Party*, pp. 76–78.

49. Frances FitzGerald, *The Evangelicals: The Struggle to Shape America* (New York: Simon & Schuster, 2017), pp. 299–300.

50. Daniel K. Williams, "Sex and the Evangelicals: Gender Issues, the Sexual Revolution, and Abortion in the 1960s," in *American Evangelicals and the 1960s*, ed. Axel Schäfer (Madison: University of Wisconsin Press, 2013), pp. 111–12.

51. Seth Dowland, *Family Values and the Rise of the Christian Right* (Philadelphia: University of Pennsylvania Press, 2016), pp. 112–24. For a detailed account of shifting attitudes on abortion among conservative Protestants in the wake of *Roe v. Wade*, see Young, *We Gather Together*, pp. 97–137.

52. Edward E. Plowman, "Is Morality All Right? The New Religious Lobbies Say 'Yes'—with Impact," *Christianity Today*, November 2, 1979, p. 76.

53. Laura Murphy, "An 'Indestructible Right': John Ryan and the Catholic Origins of the U.S. Living Wage Movement, 1906–1938," *Labor Studies in Working-Class History* 6, no. 1 (2009): pp. 57–86; Daniel K. Williams, "The Partisan Trajectory of the American Pro-Life Movement: How a Liberal Catholic Campaign Became a Conservative Evangelical Cause," *Religions* 6, no. 2 (2015): pp. 453–54.

54. John A. Ryan, *A Living Wage: Its Ethical and Economic Aspects* (New York: Macmillan, 1906), pp. 45, 324.

55. Sharon M. Leon, *An Image of God: The Catholic Struggle with Eugenics* (Chicago: University of Chicago Press, 2013), pp. 30–33. Ryan's natural law critique of birth control can be found in John A. Ryan, *Family Limitation; and the Church and Birth Control* (New York: Paulist Press, 1916). Ironically, given Ryan's Catholic critique of eugenics, the term "race suicide" was coined by the eugenicist Edward Alsworth Ross in 1900. Laura L. Lovett, *Conceiving the Future: Pronatalism, Reproduction, and the Family in the United States, 1890–1938* (Chapel Hill: University of North Carolina Press, 2007), pp. 77–108.

56. Leon, *An Image of God*, pp. 1–10, 29–30; Denise Shannon, "Bishops on Birth Control: A Chronicle of Obstruction," *Conscience*, November/December 1991, p. 14. This article is a summary of Maggie Hume and Denise Shannon, *Bishops on Birth Control: A Chronicle of Obstruction* (Washington, DC: Catholics for a Free Choice, 1991).

57. Williams, "The Partisan Trajectory of the American Pro-Life Movement," p. 455.

58. A striking feature of the early twentieth-century eugenics movement was its mainstream respectability among a wide range of progressive reformers, scientists, public health specialists, and economists, including many we would assume today to belong to the left. Thomas C. Leonard, *Illiberal Reformers: Race, Eugenics, and American Economics in the Progressive Era* (Princeton, NJ: Princeton University Press, 2016). The historian Mark Largent contests the importance of the Nuremberg trials in the long-term marginalization of eugenics science. He argues that professional support for eugenic proposals such as compulsory sterilization laws was already waning in the 1930s. Mark Largent, *Breeding Contempt: The History of Coerced Sterilization in the United States* (New Brunswick, NJ: Rutgers University Press, 2011), p. 161. While I accept this reading, I also wish to highlight the special importance of the Nuremberg trials for Catholics. The last state sterilization laws were passed in Georgia in 1937, and most such laws were eventually rolled back. However, the practice of compulsory sterilization continued well into the 1960s, this time outside the state institution for the insane or feeble-minded. The new targets were the poor and the welfare dependent, who could be sterilized without consent or knowledge in hospitals or ordered by the courts to undergo sterilization as a condition of parole. African American and Latina women were the primary targets. Alexandra Minna Stern, *Eugenic Nation: Faults and Frontiers of Better Breeding in Modern America* (Berkeley: University of California Press, 2005).

59. Williams, "The Partisan Trajectory of the American Pro-Life Movement," pp. 454–55.

60. For a widely read example of the genre, see Paul Marx, *The Death Peddlers: War on the Unborn* (Collegeville, MN: St. John's University Press, 1971).

61. Williams, "The Partisan Trajectory of the American Pro-Life Movement," pp. 455–56.

62. Robert G. Weisbord, *Genocide? Birth Control and the Black American* (Westport, CT: Greenwood Press, 1975), pp. 91–109; Simone M. Caron, "Birth Control and the Black

Community in the 1960s: Genocide or Power Politics?," *Journal of Social History* 31, no. 3 (1998): pp. 545–69. Among the many Black Panther texts on birth control and abortion, see Van Keys, "Thoughts for Negroes," *Black Panther* 2, no. 25 (1969): p. 4; Michael Hill, "The Anatomy of Extermination," *Black Panther* 2, no. 18 (1969): p. 7; "And Pharaoh Said," *Black Panther* 2, no. 30 (1969): p. 4; Judi Douglas, "Birth Control," *Black Panther* 4, no. 9 (1970): p. 7; "The Sterilization Bill," *Black Panther* 6, no. 7 (1971): p. 4; and "Concerning Birth Control," *Black Panther* 4, nos. 25–26 (1970): p. 5.

63. Quoted in Caron, "Birth Control and the Black Community in the 1960s," p. 547.

64. Donald T. Critchlow, *Intended Consequences: Birth Control, Abortion, and the Federal Government in Modern America* (Oxford: Oxford University Press, 1999), pp. 150–54.

65. Ibid., pp. 144–46.

66. On the nuance of the Black women's reproductive rights movement, which was simultaneously interested in curbing coercive eugenic measures and enabling sexual freedom, see Jennifer Nelson, *Women of Color and the Reproductive Rights Movement* (New York: NYU Press, 2003), pp. 133–78.

67. On Black feminist opposition to Black nationalist arguments against abortion, see Caron, "Birth Control and the Black Community in the 1960s," pp. 548–49; Dorothy Roberts, *Killing the Black Body: Race, Reproduction, and the Meaning of Liberty* (New York: Vintage Books, 2017), pp. 99–101; and Melissa Murray, "Race-ing *Roe*: Reproductive Justice, Racial Justice, and the Battle for *Roe v. Wade*," *Harvard Law Review* 134, no. 2025 (2021): pp. 2043–45.

68. Interestingly, the Black Panthers' denunciations of abortion as genocide during this period more often referred to the Holocaust than the Black American experience of slavery. See Hill, "The Anatomy of Extermination," comparing the situation of African Americans to the Jews before the Holocaust.

69. Michael Novak, "How Placidly They Support Aborting So Many Black Babies," *Human Life Review* 4, no. 2 (1978): pp. 95–96; John Noonan, "The Meaning of *Dred Scott*," *Human Life Review* 5, no. 4 (1979): pp. 104–12; and John C. Willke, *Abortion and Slavery: History Repeats* (Cincinnati, OH: Hayes Publishing, 1984). Michael Novak's contribution is one of the few to suggest the strategic intent behind the charge of genocide. As he writes: "I can imagine a polemical situation the reverse of the one we have now. Who now defends the rights of unborn black children? Suppose that abortion were perceived as a racist social program disproportionately aimed at blacks. Who then would be accused of genocide?" (p. 96).

70. Williams, "The Partisan Trajectory of the American Pro-Life Movement," pp. 451–75.

71. Williams, *God's Own Party*, pp. 34–49.

72. Michael Lienesch, "Creating Constitutional Conservatism," *Polity* 48, no. 3 (2016): pp. 387–413; Ken I. Kirsch, *Conservatives and the Constitution: Imagining Constitutional Restoration in the Heyday of American Liberalism* (Oxford: Oxford University Press, 2019), pp. 247–96.

73. Dowland, *Family Values*, pp. 23–48; Williams, *God's Own Party*, pp. 70–71.

74. Williams, *God's Own Party*, pp. 38–40.

75. Kimberly J. Morgan, "A Child of the Sixties: The Great Society, the New Right, and the Politics of Federal Child Care," *Journal of Policy History* 13, no. 2 (2001): pp. 215–50.

76. The argument was first made by the supply-side journalist George F. Gilder in *Wealth and Poverty* (New York: Basic Books, 1981), pp. 68–69. It was then popularized on the religious right by Phyllis Schlafly, "American Capitalism = Pro-Family Politics (A Review of *Wealth and Poverty*, by George Gilder)," *Phyllis Schlafly Report* 14, no. 11, section 1 (1981): pp. 1–4.

77. These complaints are pervasive in the evangelical, fundamentalist, and New Right literature of the 1970s. On the importance of the tax issue for religious conservatives, see Robert O. Self, *All in the Family: The Realignment of American Democracy since the 1960s* (New York: Farrar, Straus and Giroux, 2012), pp. 313–14. For an overview of the convergence between religious right and New Right thinking on this matter, see Molly Michelmore, "Creating the Marriage Penalty: Tax Politics, Gender, and Political Realignment in 1970s America," *Journal of Women's History* 30, no. 2 (2018): pp. 150–51. For an insight into right-wing perspectives on the relationship between tax and the family, with contributions from a diversity of religious and nonreligious perspectives, see Carl A. Anderson and William J. Gribbin, eds., *The Family and the Flat Tax* (Washington, DC: American Family Institute, 1984). For an insight into how religious conservatives wove together the issues of tax, inflation, the national debt, and the family, see Tim LaHaye, *The Battle for the Family* (Old Tappan, NJ: Power Books, 1982), pp. 53–102; Jerry Falwell, *Listen, America!* (Camden City, NY: Doubleday, 1980), pp. 59–81 and 130–37; and Onalee McGraw, *The Family, Feminism and the Therapeutic State* (Washington, DC: Heritage Foundation, 1980). Although she was a Catholic, Phyllis Schlafly shared the small-government, antitax sentiments of conservative Protestants. See Phyllis Schlafly, "The Financial Squeeze on the U.S. Worker, Social Security, Welfare, Jobs, Savings," *Phyllis Schlafly Report* 8, no. 7, section 1 (1975): pp. 1–4; Phyllis Schlafly, "How the Libs and the Feds Plan to Spend Your Money," *Phyllis Schlafly Report* 9, no. 10, section 2 (1976): pp. 1–3. On the continuing relevance of the tax issue to religious conservatives, see Richard J. Meagher, "Family Taxes: Conservatives Frame Estate Tax Repeal," *Journal of Policy History* 26, no. 1 (2014): pp. 73–102. On the resurgence of parental rights as an organizing theme in religious right politics, especially as it relates to childhood transition and gender nonconformity, see Max Fox, "The Traffic in Children," *Parapraxis*, December 2022; Sophie Lewis, "On Innocence and Experience," *Tank Magazine* 94 (2023).

78. Williams, *God's Own Party*, pp. 163–64.

79. Axel R. Schäfer, *Piety and Public Funding: Evangelicals and the State in Modern America* (Philadelphia: University of Pennsylvania Press, 2012), pp. 123–62.

80. Sara Dubow notes that the Social Security Board considered unborn children eligible for Aid to Dependent Children payments as of 1941, allowing but not compelling states to extend benefits on this basis. The issue resurfaced in the 1960s and 1970s as women on

welfare sought to extend their coverage to the period of pregnancy via recognition of their unborn children. However, the issue became considerably more complicated after passage of *Roe v. Wade,* since recognition of the welfare rights of the unborn would also have entailed a moral prohibition against abortion. See Sara Dubow, *Ourselves Unborn: A History of the Fetus in Modern America* (Oxford: Oxford University Press, 2013), pp. 62–63. At this point, pro-life Catholic activists turned to the issue of welfare rights for the unborn as a way of prohibiting abortion. With regard to the welfare implications of the human life amendment, the Catholic legal scholar Robert A. Destro wrote that "the protection of unborn life especially must begin from the general idea that preventive measures prevail over reprisals. Therefore, it is a duty of the state to set up social and welfare institutions to protect unborn life" (p. 1347). For Destro, recognition of the welfare rights of the unborn implied a prohibition against abortion since "it is the mother who, by nature, is entrusted with the protection of unborn life," the "chief intention of the state's efforts to protect life should be to awaken—and of necessity—to strengthen the willingness of the future mother to protect unborn life in cases where this willingness has been lost (1348)." Robert A. Destro, "Abortion and the Constitution: The Need for a Life-Protective Amendment," *California Law Review* 63, no. 5 (1975): pp. 1250–351. During this period, pro-life Catholics brought several lawsuits against state welfare departments, calling on them to recognize the AFDC rights of the unborn. See, for example, the case brought against the Virginia Department of Welfare that, included an amicus curiae contribution by Apostolic Administrator of the Catholic Diocese of Richmond Walter F. Sullivan, a pro-life Catholic who was also a strong supporter of welfare rights. *Jane Doe, on Her Own Behalf, and on Behalf of Her Unborn Child and on Behalf of All Others Similarly Situated, Appellee, v. William L. Lukhard, Director of the Department of Welfare and Institutions, Appellant,* 493 F.2d 54 (4th Cir. 1974), U.S. Court of Appeals for the Fourth Circuit—493 F.2d 54 (4th Cir. 1974). Argued Dec. 5, 1973. Decided Feb. 26, 1974.

81. Shannon, "Bishops on Birth Control," pp. 14–17.

82. McKeegan, *Abortion Politics,* p. 63.

83. Shannon, "Bishops on Birth Control," p. 15.

84. Donnally, *The Politics of Abortion and the Rise of the New Right,* p. 133.

85. Ibid., pp. 132–33.

86. Ibid., p. 137.

87. Ibid., p. 165.

88. Ibid., pp. 152, 171. Reagan's comments can be found in Alice Hartle, "Reagan Likes HLA, Gives Views on Abortion, Euthanasia," *National Right to Life News* (December 1975): pp. 1, 14–15.

89. Donnally, *The Politics of Abortion and the Rise of the New Right,* p. 151.

90. Ibid., pp. 167–68.

91. Ibid., pp. 112–14.

92. Crawford, *Thunder on the Right,* p. 38.

93. Following in the footsteps of Mildred Jefferson, a number of other African American women went on to assume prominent positions in the right-to-life movement in

subsequent decades. For discussions of their activism and its complex relationship to religious conservative discourse, see Linda Kintz, *Between Jesus and the Market: The Emotions That Matter in Right-Wing America* (Durham, NC: Duke University Press, 1997), pp. 84–91. For a discussion of Black women's anti-abortion activism and its relationship to the Black conservative tradition, see Louis G. Prisock, *African Americans in Conservative Movements: The Inescapability of Race* (Cham, Switzerland: Palgrave Macmillan, 2018), pp. 95–143.

94. House of Representatives, *Congressional Record* 123 (1977): p. 19,700.

95. Ibid.

96. Ibid., pp. 19,700–701.

97. Senate, *Congressional Record* 123 (1977): p. 21,485.

98. Adam Clymer, "Senate Vote Forbids Using Federal Funds for Most Abortions," *New York Times*, June 30, 1977.

99. Greenhouse and Siegel, "Before (and after) *Roe v. Wade*," pp. 2067–68.

100. Williams, "The Partisan Trajectory of the American Pro-Life Movement," pp. 466–67.

101. The spirit of the progressive anti-abortion movement lives on, however, in the work of self-declared Catholic feminists and socialists, pro-life liberals, and certain strands of feminist anti-racism. Erika Bachiochi, "Where Will the Anti-Abortion Feminist Movement Go Post-Roe?," EPPC, December 10, 2021; Elizabeth Stoker, "Why I'm a Pro-Life Liberal," *Week*, January 12, 2015; "Capitalism," Progressive Anti-Abortion Uprising (2022); and Andrea Smith, "Beyond Pro-Choice versus Pro-Life: Women of Color and Reproductive Justice," *NWSA Journal* 17, no. 1 (2005): pp. 119–40. For an overview of these currents, see Victoria Browne, "Anti-Abortion Feminism: How is This Even a Thing?," *Radical Philosophy*, October 2022.

102. On this point, I follow Mary Ziegler, who argues that between 1890 and 1930, a group of women's rights activists created a unique strain of "eugenic feminism." While several different versions of eugenic feminism can be discerned, they all agreed that the eugenic goal of racial improvement could only be achieved through the political, sexual, and legal liberation of women. Mary Ziegler, "Note, Eugenic Feminism: Mental Hygiene, the Women's Movement, and the Campaign for Eugenic Legal Reform, 1900–1935," *Harvard Journal of Law & Gender* 31 (2008): pp. 211–35.

103. The following detail on Margaret Sanger is drawn from Ziegler, "Note, Eugenic Feminism," and Linda Gordon, *The Moral Property of Women: A History of Birth Control Politics in America* (Chicago: University of Chicago Press, 2007), pp. 134–255.

104. On the equation between slavery and abortion, see Deve Andrusko, "Lessons in Hypocrisy," *National Right to Life News*, August 11, 1993, pp. 2, 14, 26; Cardinal John O'Connor, "A Move to Expand 'Abortion Rights,'" *National Right to Life News*, March 30, 1994, p. 5; Paul Greenberg, "Our Own Roger Taney Retires," *National Right to Life News*, April 14, 1994, p. 7. On the alleged continuing influence of Margaret Sanger's eugenics on the modern-day Planned Parenthood, see Richard D. Glasow, "New Disguise for Planned Parenthood's Old Commitment to Abortion Advocacy," *National Right to Life News*, May 12, 1993, p. 10.

105. One right-to-life figure who made early reference to Margaret Sanger's eugenics was the Catholic Randy Engel, who founded the U.S. Coalition for Life in Pittsburgh in 1972. At the 1970 White House Conference on Youth, Engel identified Sanger as a forerunner of the population control movement while noting that her connections to the eugenics movement were not well known. Randy Engel, "Statement of Randy Engel (Mrs Thomas K. Engel), Demographic Adviser to Women Concerned for the Unborn Child," in *White House Conference on Youth: Hearing before the Subcommittee on Children and Youth of the Committee on Labor and Public Welfare, Ninety-Second Congress, August 2* (Washington, DC: U.S. Government Printing Office, 1971), p. 586.

106. Linda Gordon's groundbreaking historical work on the birth control movement opened the way for more critical appraisals of Margaret Sanger's legacy. Linda Gordon, *Woman's Body, Woman's Right: A Social History of Birth Control in America* (New York: Grossman, 1976). This book is included in the reference list to George Grant's *Grand Illusions: The Legacy of Planned Parenthood* (Franklin, TN: Adroit Press, 1988/1992).

107. Grant, *Grand Illusions*. George Grant helped write the platform for the U.S. Taxpayers Party, which was founded by Howard Phillips in 1992. See Richard Cimino, "Religious Right Agenda Is Basis of New Party," *Tampa Bay Times*, July 20, 1991. At the time, George Grant was vice president of the evangelical Coral Ridge Ministries in the Miami suburb of Coral Ridge. On Grant's connection to the Christian Reconstructionist movement, see Markku Ruotsila, "Christian Reconstructionist Movement," in *Religion and Politics in America: An Encyclopedia of Church and State in American Life (Volume 1)*, ed. Frank J. Smith (Santa Barbara, CA: ABC-Clio, 2016), p. 145.

108. Grant, *Grand Illusions*, p. 133.

109. Ibid., pp. 140, 135.

110. For an unparalleled analysis of this metaphoric constellation and its uses in right-to-life discourse, see Andrea Slane, *A Not So Foreign Affair: Fascism, Sexuality, and the Cultural Rhetoric of American Democracy* (Durham, NC: Duke University Press, 2001), pp. 71–105.

111. Grant, *Grand Illusions*, p. 96. On the equation between socialism and Nazism on the anti–New Deal, anticommunist, and fundamentalist right, Andrea Slane notes that the "consolidation of the conservative image of American democracy as grounded on strict gender roles and monogamous reproductive heterosexuality after 1945 involved the merging of Nazism with Soviet Communism under the common label of 'totalitarianism.' Coined in the 1930s and reinforced by the Nazi-Soviet Pact of 1939, the term drew together elements of Stalinism (which stood in for all communisms) and Nazism, and directly opposed them to the concept of democracy. The melodramatic themes of the destruction of the family and the church continued to be dominant focal points, fanned by the flames of perceived trouble in the American family itself." Slane, *A Not So Foreign Affair*, p. 75.

112. "Republican Party Platform of 1980," American Presidency Project, July 15, 1980.

113. Nelson, *Shadow Network*, pp. 12–16.

114. Williams, *God's Own Party*, pp. 193–94.

115. On the creation of the Council for National Policy, see Russ Bellant, *The Coors Connection: How Coors Family Philanthropy Undermines Democratic Pluralism* (Cambridge, MA: South End Press, 1991), pp. 36–45; Nelson, *Shadow Network*, pp. 20–34. Bellant in particular stresses the council's porousness to the far right. He notes that its origins "were not found in mainstream conservatism or the traditional Republican Party but in the nativist and reactionary circles of the Radical Right, including the John Birch society. The view on the Radical Right that an organization such as the CNP was needed stemmed from their perception that the Council on Foreign Relations—closely identified with the Rockefeller family—was selling out American interests in the pursuit of an imagined left-wing foreign policy agenda" (p. 43). For a list of early members, see Adam Clymer, "Conservatives Gather in Umbrella Council for a National Policy," *New York Times,* May 20, 1981. On Howard Phillips's early role, see Sarah Posner, "Just Who Is the Council for National Policy, and Why Isn't It Paying Taxes?," AlterNet, March 1, 2005,

116. Williams, *God's Own Party,* pp. 199–200, 204.

117. Sidney M. Milkis and Daniel J. Tichenor, *Rivalry and Reform: Presidents, Social Movements, and the Transformation of American Politics* (Chicago: University of Chicago Press, 2018), p. 238.

118. Williams, *God's Own Party,* pp. 197. Bill Peterson and David Broder, "Split in the Senate: Senate Increasingly Divided on 'Social Issues' Timing," *Washington Post,* March 27, 1981.

119. Milkis and Tichenor, *Rivalry and Reform,* pp. 239–40.

120. Sidney Blumenthal, "Righteous Empire," *New Republic* 191 (1984): pp. 18–24.

121. Williams, *God's Own Party,* p. 196.

122. Young, *We Gather Together,* pp. 212–14.

123. "Conservative Leaders Find Administration Officials Undermining Reagan Mandate," *Human Events* 42, no. 5 (1982): pp. 17–18.

124. Ibid., p. 17.

125. Ibid., p. 18.

126. "The New Pork Barrel: How Washington Funds the Left," *Conservative Digest* 8, no. 4 (April 1982): pp. 1–56.

127. "Reagan Grants to Anti-Reagan Groups," ibid., p. 3.

128. Martin Wooster, "Hostile Congress May Scuttle President's New Budget," ibid., pp. 18–19.

129. Fran Griffin Gemma, "Media Proves a Stumbling Block to Conservative Reform," ibid., p. 44.

130. "The Grant Watchers," ibid., pp. 47–49.

131. Bill Peterson, "Abortion Foes Gain Key Federal Posts," *Washington Post,* March 6, 1981.

132. Paul A. Brown and Judie Brown, "White Paper: Tax Payer Dollars (Federal Budget): Programs That Can Be Cut and at the Same Time Do a Great Deal to Advance the Family and Take the U.S. Government out of the Abortion and Anti-Family Business," February

17, 1981, Folder "Human Life Amendment," Box 11, Morton Blackwell Files, Ronald Reagan Library.

133. Ibid., title page.

134. Press Release: "'New Right' Leader, Howard Phillips to Tell 'Unity '81,' 'How to Defund Anti-Life, Anti-Family Organizations,'" Grassroots Pro-life Education Conference, September 11, 1981, Folder "American Life Lobby" (3 of 4), Box 1, Morton Blackwell Files, Ronald Reagan Library.

135. McKeegan, *Abortion Politics*, p. 66.

136. Ibid., p. 72.

137. Ibid., p. 57.

138. Ibid., p. 66.

139. Ibid., p. 75.

140. Howard Phillips, "3 for G.O.P. Eyes (Not Only)," *New York Times*, August 19, 1984.

141. Richard A. Viguerie, *Takeover: The 100-Year War for the Soul of the GOP and How Conservatives Can Finally Win It* (Washington, DC: WND Books, 2014), p. 83.

142. Paul Weyrich became one of Robertson's advisors during this period and lent the resources of his Free Congress Foundation to the campaign. David John Marley, *Pat Robertson: An American Life* (Lanham, MD: Rowman & Littlefield, 2007), pp. 107, 142; David Edwin Harrell Jr., *Pat Robertson: A Life and Legacy* (Grand Rapids, MI: William B. Eerdmans, 2010), p. 92.

143. Williams, *God's Own Party*, pp. 228–31.

144. Harrell, *Pat Robertson*, p. 128; Nina J. Easton, *Gang of Five: Leaders at the Center of the Conservative Crusade* (New York: Simon & Schuster, 2001), p. 212. On the enduring connections between the Christian Coalition and Paul Weyrich's Free Congress Foundation, see the essays collected in Chip Berlet, ed., *Eyes Right! Challenging the Right-Wing Backlash* (Boston: South End Press, 1997).

145. On Reed's early biography, see Williams, *God's Own Party*, pp. 228–29. In contrast to Reed's image as arch mediator during his Christian Coalition years, as a young student he was actively involved in picketing abortion clinics and railed against abortion as "black genocide" in college newspapers.

146. "Robertson Regroups 'Invisible Army' into New Coalition," *Christianity Today* 34, no. 7 (1990): p. 35.

147. Frederick Clarkson, "The Christian Coalition: On the Road to Victory?," *Church and State* 45, no. 1 (1992): p. 4.

148. Ibid.

149. Howard Phillips, "Message for the President," *Review of the News*, January 12, 1983, pp. 55 and 53.

150. Howard Phillips, "Statement of Howard Phillips, Chairman, the Conservative Caucus, Inc.," in *Nomination of David H. Souter to Be Associate Justice of the Supreme Court of the United States: Hearings before the Committee on the Judiciary, United States Senate, One Hundred First Congress, Second Session . . . September 13, 14, 17, 18, and 19, 1990, United States*

Congress, Senate Committee on the Judiciary (Washington, DC: U.S. Government Printing Office, 1991), pp. 890–93.

151. On this ideological and strategic split and the role of Christian Reconstruction within it, see Williams, *God's Own Party*, pp. 224–27.

152. Nelson, *Shadow Network*, pp. 77–99.

153. I am indebted to Schlozman and Rosenfeld for the argument that the Council for National Policy functioned as a system of communicating vases that allowed mainstream Republicans and the far right to intermingle. Schlozman and Rosenfeld, "The Long New Right and the World It Made."

154. For general histories of Clinton's failed health-care bill, see Jacob S. Hacker, *The Road to Nowhere: The Genesis of President Clinton's Plan for Health Security* (Princeton, NJ: Princeton University Press, 1996); Haynes Johnson and David S. Broder, *The System: The American Way of Politics at the Breaking Point* (Boston: Little, Brown and Company, 1996); Theda Skocpol, *Boomerang: Clinton's Health Security Effort and the Turn against Government in U.S. Politics* (New York: Norton, 1996); Kant Patel and Mark E. Rushefsky, *Politics, Power and Policy Making: Case of Health Care Reform in the 1990s* (London: Routledge, 1998); and Paul Starr, *Remedy and Reaction: The Peculiar American Struggle over Health Care Reform* (New Haven, CT: Yale University Press, 2013).

155. On this shift in attitudes among evangelicals and Southern Baptists, see Andrew R. Lewis, *The Rights Turn in Conservative Christian Politics: How Abortion Transformed the Culture Wars* (Cambridge: Cambridge University Press, 2017), pp. 90–92.

156. Lawrence J. McAndrews, *What They Wished For: American Catholics and American Presidents, 1960–2004* (Athens: University of Georgia Press, 2014), p. 307.

157. Broder and Johnson, *The System*, pp. 11–12, 39, 462–63; John B. Judis, *The Paradox of American Democracy: Elites, Special Interests, and the Betrayal of the Public Trust* (New York: Pantheon Books, 2000), p. 212.

158. Wanda Franz, "Pro-Lifers Must Keep Abortion out of Any National Health Plan," *National Right to Life News*, September 14, 1993, p. 3.

159. Dan Balz, "Christian Coalition Launches Effort against Clinton Plan," *Washington Post*, February 16, 1994.

160. Judis, *The Paradox of American Democracy*, p. 211.

161. McAndrews, *What They Wished For*, p. 309.

162. Ibid., p. 311.

163. Ibid., pp. 312–18.

164. Lewis, *The Rights Turn in Conservative Christian Politics*, p. 97.

165. Douglas Johnson, "Clinton Seeks Hyde Amendment Repeal; Wants National Health Plan to Pay for Abortion on Demand," *National Right to Life News*, April 14, 1993, p. 12.

166. Wanda Franz, "Clinton's Health Care Plan: The Latest Step in His Obsession with Abortion Rights," *National Right to Life News*, April 26, 1993, p. 3.

167. Ibid.

168. Franz, "Pro-Lifers Must Keep Abortion out of Any National Health Plan."

169. Richard Doerflinger, "Clinton Determined to Multiply Number of Abortions," *National Right to Life News*, May 12, 1993, p. 20.

170. Ibid.

171. Marian Wallace, "Reform or Ruin? National Health Care," *Family Voice* 16, no. 1 (1994): pp. 4–9. The Family Research Council published similar opinions. See Scott E. Daniels and Gracie S. Hsu, "Whose 'Status Quo'? Making Us Pay for Abortion on Demand as a Fringe Benefit," *Family Research Council*, September 1993; Scott E. Daniels and Gracie S. Hsu, "Liberating Our Children: Abortion, Sex Education, and School-Based Clinics in the Clinton Health Plan," *Family Research Council*, April 1994.

172. Wallace, "Reform or Ruin? National Health Care," p. 3. Although school-based clinics were raised as a possible object of funding in discussions of the Clinton plan, no firm decisions had been taken at the time the bill was shelved. There was a similar lack of specifics concerning the coverage of sexual-health services. See J. I. Rosoff, "The Clinton Health Plan: What Does It Do for Reproductive Health Services?," *Family Planning Perspectives* 26, no. 1 (1994): pp. 39–41.

173. Phyllis Schlafly, "Clinton's Totalitarian Health Plan," *Phyllis Schlafly Report* 27 no. 4 (1993): p. 2. See also Phyllis Schlafly, "Hillary, Health Care, and 'Remolding' Government," *Phyllis Schlafly Report* 26, no. 11 (1993): pp. 1–4.

174. Schlafly, "Clinton's Totalitarian Health Plan," pp. 1–2.

175. Ibid., p. 1.

176. Skocpol, *Boomerang*, pp. 150–53; Slane, *A Not So Foreign Affair*, pp. 87–88, 278–80. For an insight into the phantasmagoria of fears surrounding Hillary Clinton, see Texe Marrs, *Big Sister Is Watching You: Hillary Clinton and the White House Feminists Who Now Control America* (Austin, TX: Living Truth Publishers, 1993). Texe Marrs was a fundamentalist minister and head of Living Truth Ministry in Austin, Texas. These critics often position the white middle-class feminist as exploiting and misleading the naive Black mother. However, for a sharp analysis of the way in which Clinton and others have exploited the Black mother as a redemptive figure of racial reconciliation, see Jennifer C. Nash, *Birthing Black Mothers* (Durham, NC: Duke University Press, 2021), pp. 24–25, 120–21.

177. According to Limbaugh, the term "feminazi" refers to any feminist for whom "the most important thing in life is seeing to it that as many abortions as possible are performed." Rush Limbaugh, *The Way Things Ought to Be* (New York: Pocket Books, 1992), p. 193. Many of these same projections can also be found on the left, of course, which always had a much more frenzied and personal critique of Hillary Clinton than either Bill Clinton or Barack Obama, despite the near identity of their politics.

178. On Anita Hill's harassment claims against Clarence Thomas as a Soviet feminist plot, see ibid., pp. 115–26.

179. "Despite Unanswered Questions, Evangelical Groups Back Thomas," *Christianity Today* 35, no. 12 (1991): pp. 34–35. On the campaign against Joycelyn Elders, see "Can Elders' Nomination Be Stopped?," *Human Events* 53, no. 34 (1993): p. 6. On Elders as a Nazi, see

Paul Greenberg, "The Banality of Evil," *National Right to Life News*, February 3, 1994, p. 12. On Elders as a defender of modern-day slavery, see Andrusko, "Lessons in Hypocrisy," p. 26.

180. Marrs, *Big Sister Is Watching You*, p. 116. On Christian right attacks against Elders, in the midst of the campaign against health-care reform, see Sara Diamond, *Not by Politics Alone: The Enduring Influence of the Christian Right* (New York: Guilford Press, 2000), p. 47.

181. Gerald F. Seib, "Christian Coalition Hopes to Expand by Taking Stands on Taxes, Crime, Health Care, and NAFTA," *Wall Street Journal*, September 7, 1993, p. A18.

182. Ralph Reed, "Casting a Wider Net," *Policy Review* 65 (Summer 1993): pp. 31–35.

183. Ralph Reed, *Active Faith: How Christians Are Changing the Soul of American Politics* (New York: Free Press, 1996), p. 189.

184. "Some conservatives fear we may be raising the white flag on moral issues. They need not be worried. Working other issues—crime, taxes, education—will strengthen our voice in matters of conscience, not weaken it. During the debate on health-care reform, for example, opposition to taxpayer funded abortion interwove with concerns about physician choice and jobs like an unbroken tapestry." Ralph Reed, *After the Revolution* (Dallas, TX: Word Publishing, 1994), p. 232.

185. Ralph Reed, "Conservative Coalition Holds Firm," *Wall Street Journal*, February 13, 1995.

186. Specifically, Reed referred to the Christian Coalition as "the pro-family equivalent of [Newt Gingrich's] conservative opportunity society." Reed, *Active Faith*, p. 198.

187. According to the *Washington Post*, Reed acknowledged that "the shift in tactics, if successful, 'can build up political capital' with business lobbyists and other conservative groups. 'By helping them on issues they care about, they might view us differently.'" David S. Broder, "Christian Coalition, Shifting Tactics, to Lobby against Clinton Budget," *Washington Post*, July 18, 1993.

188. Judis, *The Paradox of American Democracy*, pp. 213–14; Skocpol, *Boomerang*, pp. 134–57; Starr, *Remedy and Reaction*, pp. 112–19.

189. Broder and Johnson, *The System*, p. 466.

190. On Citizens for a Sound Economy and the turn to grassroots organization, see Nancy MacLean, "'Since We Are Greatly Outnumbered': Why and How the Koch Network Uses Disinformation to Thwart Democracy," in *The Disinformation Age: Politics, Technology, and Disruptive Communication in the United States*, ed. W. Lance Bennett and Steven Livingston (Cambridge: Cambridge University Press, 2020), p. 128. On the same issue as addressed by the Christian Coalition, see Skocpol, *Boomerang*, p. 154.

191. Reed, "Conservative Coalition Holds Firm."

192. Broder and Johnson, *The System*, pp. 460–67.

193. See photo image of placard slogans in *National Right to Life News*, August 5, 1994, p. 28.

194. Broder and Johnson, *The System*, p. 467; Skocpol, *Boomerang*, pp. 149–50.

195. Folder 13 "Stop Socialized Medicine Materials," Series 2, Subgroup 1, Record Group 3, Falwell Family Papers, Liberty University Archive, Lynchburg, VA. With slight differences,

the ration card was printed out and disseminated by every group in the Christian Coalition/ Citizens for a Sound Economy alliance.

196. Judis, *The Paradox of American Democracy*, p. 215.

197. Jacob S. Hacker and Paul Pierson, *American Amnesia: How the War on Government Led Us to Forget What Made America Prosper* (New York: Simon & Schuster, 2017), pp. 213–18.

198. After receiving a letter from the USCCB on July 13, 1994, seventy House Democrats announced that they would vote against any health-care bill that included coverage of abortion. McAndrews, *What They Wished For*, p. 317.

199. Clyde Wilcox and Mark J. Rozell, eds., *God at the Grass Roots: The Christian Right in the 1994 Elections* (Lanham, MD: Rowman & Littlefield, 1995); Judith Warner and Max Berley, *Newt Gingrich: Speaker to America* (New York: Signet, 1995), pp. 188–93; David John Marley, *Pat Robertson: An American Life* (Lanham, MD: Rowman & Littlefield, 2007), p. 222; and Reed, *Active Faith*, pp. 197–98. Reed endorsed Gingrich's decision not to foreground abortion and other religious right demands in the Contract with America while reassuring Christian Coalition activists that they would be rewarded for their patience in due course. Williams, *God's Own Party*, p. 236; Diamond, *Not by Politics Alone*, pp. 102–103. In the meantime, the Christian Coalition seized on the Contract with America's demand for a balanced budget and redefined it in essentially moral terms, as a measure to defend the family from the threat of government tax extortion. Reed, *Active Faith*, p. 171.

200. Edward Warsh, "Many Republicans' Votes Came from Those Who Distrust Government," *Washington Post*, November 9, 1994; "Religious Group Sees Role in Election Outcome," *Congressional Quarterly Weekly Report*, November 19, 1994, p. 3364.

201. "Christian Right Helps Work GOP Miracle," *Human Events* 50, no. 44 (1994): p. 7.

202. Quoted in Warner and Berley, *Newt Gingrich*, p. 188.

203. Quoted in Marley, *Pat Robertson*, p. 223.

204. Ibid., p. 224.

205. Ibid., pp. 230–33.

206. Cited in Daniel J. Murphy and George E. Lee, "'Where Do Conservatives Go from Here?' Activists Gather in Washington for 18th Annual CPAC," *Human Events* 51, no. 8 (1991): p. 12.

207. Howard Phillips, Speech by U.S. Taxpayers Party Presidential Nominee, U.S. Taxpayers Convention, New Orleans, Louisiana, C-SPAN, September 5, 1992, 57.01–57.18.

208. Cited in Murphy and Lee, "Where Do Conservatives Go from Here?," p. 13.

209. Eric Holberg, "An Interview with Howard Phillips," *God's Law and Society*, DVD (Murphys, CA: Alliance for Revival and Reformation, 1999).

210. Howard Phillips, Speech by U.S. Taxpayers Party Presidential Nominee, U.S. Taxpayers Convention, 46:14–46.32.

211. Howard Phillips, Speech by U.S. Taxpayers Party Presidential Nominee, U.S. Taxpayers Convention, 25:43–26.08.

212. Howard Phillips and David A. Keene, "Is It Time for Social Conservatives to Abandon the Republican Party?," *Insight on the News* 12, no. 29 (1996): p. 24.

213. Howard Phillips, Campaign Interview, C-SPAN, April 14, 1992, 1:20–1:24.

214. "Interview with Howard Phillips," *Harvard Crimson*, March 5, 1992.

215. Phillips, Campaign Interview, 1:47–2:13.

216. Rousas John Rushdoony, *The Institutes of Biblical Law* (Phillipsburg, NJ: Presbyterian and Reformed Publishing, 1973), pp. 1:550–51; Ingersoll, *Building God's Kingdom*, pp. 23–25.

217. Gary North and Gary DeMar, *Christian Reconstruction: What It Is, What It Isn't* (Tyler, TX: Institute for Christian Economics, 1991), p. 43.

218. Rushdoony, *The Institutes of Biblical Law*.

219. Indeed, Rushdoony claims that secularism represents another form of religion—paganism—that must be considered heretical. Rousas John Rushdoony, *The Roots of Christian Reconstruction* (Vallecito, CA: Ross House Books, 1991), pp. 1112–14.

220. Gary North, "The Intellectual Schizophrenia of the New Christian Right," in *The Failure of the American Baptist Culture: A Symposium*, ed. James B. Jordan (Tyler, TX: Geneva Divinity School, 1982), p. 25.

221. On "losing slowly," see Phillips, "3 for G.O.P. Eyes (Not Only)."

222. Michael J. McVicar, "The Libertarian Theocrats: The Long, Strange History of R. J. Rushdoony and Christian Reconstructionism," *Public Eye* Fall (2007): pp. 3–5.

223. McVicar, "The Libertarian Theocrats," p. 6.

224. Gary North, *An Introduction to Christian Economics* (Nutley, NJ: Craig Press, 1974).

225. See, for instance, Murray N. Rothbard, *What Has Government Done to Our Money?* (Auburn, AL: Ludwig von Mises Institute, 1963).

226. North, *An Introduction to Christian Economics*, p. vii.

227. Ibid., p. 11.

228. Gary North, *Liberating Planet Earth: An Introduction to Biblical Blueprints* (Tyler, TX: Dominion Press, 1987), p. 85.

229. Ibid., p. 84.

230. Ibid., p. 85.

231. Gary North, *Honest Money: The Biblical Blueprint for Money and Banking* (Fort Worth, TX: Dominion Press, 1986), pp. 101–102. On North's catastrophism and its widespread influence on the American far right, both Christian and secular, see Michael J. McVicar, *Christian Reconstruction: R. J. Rushdoony and American Religious Conservatism* (Chapel Hill: University of North Carolina Press, 2015), pp. 186–90.

232. North, *Honest Money*, p. 137.

233. Ibid., p. 141. For North's more recent predictions of default, see Gary North, "The Looming Federal Default: Sooner or Later?," LewRockwell.com, August 6, 2008.

234. The work of Philipp Bagus, Austrian school economist and affiliate of the Mises Institute, is symptomatic of this shift. Bagus takes the generally "deflation friendly" Hayek and von Mises to task for not appreciating the universally beneficial effects of deflation. Philipp Bagus, *In Defense of Deflation* (New York: Springer, 2015). The former supply-sider Bruce Bartlett was one of the few to recognize that for many Tea Party Republicans, forcing

a debt default was the whole point. Bruce Bartlett, "For Many Hard Liners, Debt Default Is the Goal," *New York Times*, October 14, 2013.

235. Ron Paul, "Default Now, or Suffer a More Expensive Crisis Later," *Bloomberg*, July 22, 2011.

236. North, *Honest Money*, p. 102.

237. Sarah Posner, "The Christian Fundamentalism behind Ron Paul's Home-Schooling Curriculum," *Guardian*, April 12, 2013.

238. Julie Ingersoll, "Rand Paul and the Influence of Christian Reconstructionism," *Religion Dispatches*, May 25, 2010.

239. As Julie Ingersoll observes, the "Christian Reconstructionists can be seen as a link between the early-twentieth-century Old Christian Right and the early-twenty-first century resurgence of Southern religious conservatism and the Tea Party." Ingersoll, *Building God's Kingdom*, p. 38.

240. On the split between fundamentalists and evangelicals on the issue of segregation, see Williams, *God's Own Party*, pp. 34–48.

241. Susan Friend Harding, *The Book of Jerry Falwell: Fundamentalist Language and Politics* (Princeton, NJ: Princeton University Press, 2001), p. 112.

242. Williams, *God's Own Party*, pp. 174–75.

243. Nancy D. Wadsworth, *Ambivalent Miracles: Evangelicals and the Politics of Racial Healing* (Charlottesville: University of Virginia Press, 2014), pp. 81–155.

244. Leonard Zeskind, *Blood and Politics: The History of the White Nationalist Movement from the Margins to the Mainstream* (New York: Farrar, Straus and Giroux, 2009), pp. 322–23.

245. Frederick Clarkson, *Eternal Hostility: The Struggle between Theocracy and Democracy* (Monroe, ME: Common Courage Press, 1997), p. 152.

246. Gary North, ed., *The Theology of Christian Resistance* (Tyler, TX: Geneva Divinity School Press, 1983).

247. James Scaminaci, "Chapter 15: The Christian Right and the Formation of the Patriot Militia," Academia.edu, p. 34.

248. During this period, nebulous theories of a new world order were supplanted by the more specific threat of migrants entering the United States from south of the border—the agents, it was feared, of a secretive Mexican plan to reconquer the Southwest. Ibid., pp. 4–5.

249. Clarkson, *Eternal Hostility*, pp. 103–104, 118; Diamond, *Not by Politics Alone*, p. 107.

250. Martin Durham, *The Christian Right, the Far Right and the Boundaries of American Conservatism* (Manchester: Manchester University Press, 2000), p. 180.

251. Scaminaci, "Chapter 15: The Christian Right and the Formation of the Patriot Militia," p. 8.

252. Edward H. Sebesta and Euan Hague, "The US Civil War as a Theological War: Confederate Christian Nationalism and the League of the South," *Canadian Review of American Studies* 32, no. 3 (2002): pp. 253–84. Conservative Southern Presbyterians had advanced the theological war thesis in the wake of the Civil War. For many years, it survived only as

a minor refrain alongside other, better-known "lost cause" apologies for the Confederate South. At the height of the civil rights movement of the 1960s, however, the work of these early Christian apologists of slavery was salvaged from the archive and reissued in new print editions. Rushdoony was quick to incorporate this work into his theological writings, which argued, for example, that the Civil War had defeated a nation of orthodox Christian states and that this nation would have to be reconstructed for God's Kingdom to rule on earth. Other key figures in the revival of this nineteenth-century Presbyterian tradition of apology were the southern agrarian Richard Weaver and Gregg Singer. Rushdoony pays particular attention to the work of the Presbyterian theologian Robert Lewis Dabney (1820–1898), a professor at Union Theological Seminary in Virginia and a Confederate army chaplain.

253. Ibid., p. 267.

254. When asked about Obama's run for presidential office in 2007, then Senator Biden made the following comment: "I mean, you got the first mainstream African American who is articulate and bright and clean and a nice-looking guy. I mean, that's a storybook, man." "Biden's Description of Obama Draws Scrutiny," CNN International, February 9, 2007.

255. Adele M. Stan, "Howard Phillips' World: Could the Constitution Party Pick Up the Pieces of the GOP?," *Mother Jones*, November 3, 2008.

256. Jerome R. Corsi, *Where's the Birth Certificate? The Case That Barack Obama Is Not Eligible to Be President* (Washington, DC: WND Books, 2011), pp. xi, 306–308.

257. Ibid., pp. 42–59. For an insightful commentary on this argument, see Michelle Goldberg, "Jerome Corsi's Where's the Birth Certificate? Why Birthers Won't Die," *Daily Beast*, May 31, 2011.

258. Jerome R Corsi, *The Obama Nation: Leftist Politics and the Cult of Personality* (New York: Simon & Schuster, 2008), p. 240. Corsi is here quoting the website Black Genocide, "Abortion and the Black Community."

259. George Grant, author of *Grand Illusions*, is a Christian Reconstructionist and was a close associate of Howard Phillips during his lifetime. For a recent example of Christian Reconstructionist anti-eugenics, see Gary North, "A Political Alliance of Bastards: The Welfare State and Population Control," *Tea Party Economist*, January 23, 2013. On the entanglement of citizenship and fetal personhood in right-to-life discourse, see Lauren Berlant, who comments that the American pro-life movement has merged "the counter-discourse of minority rights with a revitalized Providential nationalist rhetoric" and thus "composed a magical and horrifying spectacle of amazing vulnerability: the unprotected person, the citizen without a country or future, the fetus unjustly imprisoned in its mother's hostile gulag." Berlant, "America, 'Fat,' the Fetus," p. 151.

260. Nicholas Graham, "'Tea Party' Leader Melts Down on CNN: Obama Is an 'Indonesian Muslim Turned Welfare Thug,'" *Huffington Post*, November 15, 2009.

261. Sasha Abramsky, "When God Laughs, It's Not Funny," *Progressive* 60, no. 10 (1996): pp. 24–25.

262. However, political journalists and public interest scholars closely followed his career, particularly those associated with Group Research Inc. or Political Research Associates. Founded in 1962 by the news journalist Wesley McCune, Group Research Inc. of Washington, DC, followed the activities of the American right up until the mid-1990s. Its archives can be found in the rare book collection of Columbia University Libraries. Political Research Associates was founded in 1981 by Jean Hardisty and Chip Berlet and continues to produce research on the religious, nativist, and neo-Confederate far right. The political journalist Adele M. Stan has been a close follower of Howard Phillips's career.

263. Nelson, *Shadow Network*, p. 157. Dick Armey's FreedomWorks and the Koch-funded Americans for Prosperity were the first to funnel money toward the Tea Party. The CNP executive was concerned about the relative silence of religious conservatives within the existing movement and did not come on board until 2010. Its participation appears to have hinged on the greater amplification of fundamentalist voices by Americans for Prosperity (pp. 154–56).

264. According to Anne Nelson, the collaboration began in the mid-1990s but has become so tight in the last decade that organizations associated with the Kochs and the CNP routinely fund each other. Nelson, *Shadow Network*, pp. 124–29.

265. Heidi Beirich and Mark Potok, "The Council for National Policy: Behind the Curtain," Southern Poverty Law Center, May 17, 2016.

266. Viguerie, *Takeover*, p. 189.

267. Alongside the national broadcaster Fox News, which served as a virtual mouthpiece to the movement in its heyday, the Tea Party message was broadcast across the country by a dense network of local radio stations and news sites built up by the CNP over several decades. This alternative media network is explored in detail by Anne Nelson in *Shadow Network*.

268. Viguerie, *Takeover*, p. 190.

269. Gervais and Morris, *Reactionary Republicanism*, pp. 1–10. See also Rachel M. Blum, *How the Tea Party Captured the GOP: Insurgent Factions in American Politics* (Chicago: University of Chicago Press, 2020).

270. Gervais and Morris, *Reactionary Republicanism*, p. 29. I borrow the term "long new right" from Schlozman and Rosenfeld, who define the New Right as an insurgent project spanning multiple institutions and personae and extending from the mid-twentieth century to today. In their words, "our actors' *approach to politics itself* marks the through-line from the 1950s to the age of Trump," more "than any biographical or institutional continuity" (p. 5). This approach leads them to conclude that "when the Republican Party, as a party, had to decide what to do with the unwanted intruder, Trump, the riddle of a party that decided not to decide, seems altogether less puzzling: the Long New Right hollowed out the Republican Party." Schlozman and Rosenfeld, "The Long New Right and the World It Made," p. 77.

271. Frederick Clarkson, "Dominionism Rising: A Theocratic Movement Hiding in Plain Sight," *Public Eye*, Summer 2016, pp. 12–20.

272. Anne Nelson, "This Powerful Group Groomed Mike Pence for the White House,"

Salon, October 25, 2019. Paul Weyrich described Pence as the candidate "I have been waiting for in terms of leadership." Jason Deparle, "Star of the Right Loses His Base at the Border," *New York Times*, August 29, 2006.

273. Nelson, *Shadow Network*, p. 198.

274. Emma Brown, "Influential Conservative Group: Trump, DeVos Should Dismantle Education Department and Bring God into Classrooms," *Washington Post*, February 15, 2017; Nelson, "This Powerful Group Groomed Mike Pence for the White House."

275. Editorial Board, "Trump Just Won a Battle with Planned Parenthood, Thousands of Women Will Pay," *Washington Post*, August 24, 2019.

276. Nelson, *Shadow Network*, p. 198.

277. *Dobbs v. Jackson Women's Health Organization*, No. 19–1392, 597 U.S (2022).

278. As noted by the Catholic legal scholar Erika Bachiochi in an op-ed response to Dobbs, "constitutional protection of unborn children as equal 'persons' under the law remains the movement's ultimate—if elusive—goal." Erika Bachiochi, "What Makes a Fetus a Person?," *New York Times*, July 1, 2022.

279. Mary Ziegler, *Dollars for Life: The Anti-Abortion Movement and the Fall of the Republican Establishment* (New Haven, CT: Yale University Press, 2022), pp. 9, 11–13.

280. Ibid., 18. The opinion reads, "the word 'person,' as used in the Fourteenth Amendment, does not include the unborn," thus the court "need not resolve the difficult question of when life begins." *Roe v. Wade*, 410 US, 113 (1973).

281. *Roe v. Wade*, 410 US, 156–62 (1973).

282. Mary Ziegler, *After Roe: The Lost History of the Abortion Debate* (Cambridge, MA: Harvard University Press, 2015), pp. 38, 41, 84–85; Prudence Flowers, *The Right-to-Life Movement, the Reagan Administration, and the Politics of Abortion* (Cham, Switzerland: Palgrave, 2018), pp. 63–88.

283. Glen A. Halva-Neubauer and Sara L. Zeigler, "Promoting Fetal Personhood: The Rhetorical and Legislative Strategies of the Pro-Life Movement after *Planned Parenthood v. Casey*," *Feminist Formations* 22, no. 2 (2010): pp. 101–23.

284. Ziegler, *Dollars for Life*, p. 211.

285. Murray, "Race-ing *Roe*." Murray originally predicted that the anti-eugenics argument would be used to overturn *Roe v. Wade*. It turns out that this was not necessary. It seems to me, however, that the argument applies even more forcefully to the religious right's long-standing goal of instating fetal personhood in law. On this point, see Jeannie Suk Gersen, "How Fetal Personhood Emerged as the Next Stage of the Abortion Wars," *New Yorker*, June 5, 2019.

286. "Abortion Bans in Cases of Sex or Race Selection or Genetic Anomaly," Guttmacher Institute, October 1, 2022.

287. Apology by the Indiana House and Senate, Senate Concurrent Resolution, Ind. S. Res. 91, 115th General Assembly, 1st Sess., §1 and §2 (2007).

288. Quoted in Mitch Smith, "Indiana Governor Signs Abortion Bill with Added Restrictions," *New York Times*, March 24, 2016.

289. Justice Clarence Thomas, concurring, *Box v. Planned Parenthood of Indiana and Kentucky, Inc.*, 139 S. Ct. 1780 (2019), p. 2.

290. For rebuttals of the opinion, see Mary Ziegler, "What Clarence Thomas Gets Wrong about the Ties between Abortion and Eugenics," *Washington Post*, May 30, 2019; Dorothy Roberts, "Dorothy Roberts Argues That Justice Clarence Thomas's Box v. Planned Parenthood Concurrence Distorts History," University of Pennsylvania Carey Law School, June 6, 2019. Thomas cites a number of leading historians of eugenics in his opinion. Several of these have publicly refuted his reading. Eli Rosenberg, "Clarence Thomas Tried to Link Abortion to Eugenics: Seven Historians Told the Post He's Wrong," *Washington Post*, May 30, 2019.

291. Thomas, concurring, *Box v. Planned Parenthood*, p. 15. Thomas is quoting from David Dempsey, "Dr. Guttmacher Is the Evangelist of Birth Control," *New York Times Magazine*, February 9, 1969.

292. The dissent was written by Coney Barrett's fellow appeals court judge Easterbrook and cosigned by Coney Barrett, *Planned Parenthood of Indiana and Kentucky, Inc. v. Commissioner of the Indiana State Department of Health*, 917 F.3d 532 (7th Cir. 2018) (2018).

293. Michael Foust, "Abortion Industry Is Guilty of Eugenics, Pence Says: 'Margaret Sanger's Legacy' Continues," *Christian Headlines*, January 24, 2022.

294. Clarence Thomas, "Lecture: Justice Clarence Thomas," Tocqueville Lecture, September 16, 2021, 23.10–24.07.

295. Joseph Serwach, "How Clarence Thomas Found a Catholic Way Home," *Medium*, February 5, 2020.

296. Corey Robin, *The Enigma of Clarence Thomas* (New York: Henry Holt, 2019), pp. 26–32.

297. Thomas, "Lecture," 33.14–33.24.

298. Serwach, "How Clarence Thomas Found a Catholic Way Home."

299. Robin, *The Enigma of Clarence Thomas*, pp. 2–8.

300. Robin argues that in any case the dividing lines between anticapitalist self-determination and capitalist self-sufficiency were always porous in the Black Power movement and cannot so easily be reduced to distinct left and right positions. Robin, *The Enigma of Clarence Thomas*, pp. 90–92.

301. Thomas, "Lecture," 35.13–35.38.

302. Ibid., 36.00–36.13.

303. Suk Gersen, "How Fetal Personhood Emerged as the Next Stage of the Abortion Wars."

304. *Dobbs v. Jackson*, p. 6.

305. Ibid., p. 5.

306. Ibid.

307. Ibid., p. 30n41.

308. Ibid., p. 78.

309. Ibid., p. 2. Feminist scholars have long argued that the privacy right invoked to decide *Roe v. Wade* is not adequate as a specifically feminist justification for legalized abortion. As a consequence, they have attempted to construct an alternative constitutional rationale for abortion that builds on the Equal Protection Clause of the Fourteenth Amendment as it applies to the sex-based rights of women. For a summary of these arguments, see Reva Siegel, "Abortion as a Sex Equality Right: Its Basis in Feminist Theory," in *Mothers in Law: Feminist Theory and the Legal Regulation of Motherhood*, eds. Martha Fineman and Isabel Karpin (New York: Columbia University Press, 1995), pp. 43–72. In the decades after *Roe*, significant progress was made in refining the equal protection framework as a way of challenging sex-based discrimination. Justice Ruth Bader Ginsburg's opinion in *United States v. Virginia* is generally recognized as a turning point in advancing the equal protection framework with respect to laws regulating pregnancy. In *Dobbs v. Jackson Women's Health Organization*, feminist legal scholars Reva Siegel, Serena Mayeri, and Melissa Murray filed an amicus brief that continued in this vein, seeking to demonstrate that Mississippi's ban on abortions after fifteen weeks violated the Equal Protection Clause and thus constituted a form of sex-based discrimination against women. Reva Siegel, Melissa Murray, and Serena Mayeri, "Equal Protection and Abortion: Brief of Equal Protection Constitutional Law Scholars Serena Mayeri, Melissa Murray, and Reva Siegel as Amici Curiae in Support of Respondents in Dobbs v. Jackson Women's Health Organization," *Faculty Scholarship at Penn Carey Law* (2021). Alito is implicitly responding to this amicus brief.

310. *Dobbs v. Jackson*, 2. Alito cites two cases here: *Geduldig v. Aiello*, 417 US 484 (1974), and *Bray v. Alexandria Women's Health Clinic*, 506 US 263 (1993). I confine my analysis to *Geduldig v. Aiello*. For an early and still relevant feminist critique of the use of abstract personhood in this case, see Zillah R. Eisenstein, *The Female Body and the Law* (Berkeley: University of California Press, 1988), pp. 66–69.

311. In *Geduldig v. Aiello*, 417 U.S. 484 (1974), the Supreme Court was tasked to decide whether unfavorable treatment of pregnant women could count as sex discrimination under the Equal Protection Clause. The quote can be found at *Geduldig v. Aiello*, p. 496n20.

312. Laura Briggs presciently argued as much several years before the Dobbs decision. Briggs makes specific reference to the *Geduldig v. Aiello* case and the conservative legal movement's history of deploying abstract sex-neutral personhood to invalidate sex-discrimination cases. Laura Briggs, *How All Politics Became Reproductive Politics: From Welfare Reform to Foreclosure to Trump* (Berkeley: University of California Press, 2018), p. 5. While it was predictable that the *Geduldig v. Aiello* precedent would be used against women, it has also more recently been deployed to deny the specificity of sex discrimination against trans people. Katie R. Eyer, "Transgender Equality and Geduldig 2.0," *Arizona State Law Journal*, forthcoming. This points to the limits of any politics that seeks to transcend essentialist sex categories by ignoring bodies altogether. In my view, the answer can only be a proliferation of sex categories, including trans-sexuation, rather than a subsumption of all bodily differences under the umbrella of gender-neutral personhood. In this regard, see the work of Jay Prosser and Gayle Salamon, among others, who offer a perspective on trans

embodiment at odds with the rampant gender idealism that reigns on the contemporary left. Jay Prosser, *Second Skins: The Body Narratives of Transsexuality* (New York: Columbia University Press, 1998); Gayle Salamon, *Assuming a Body: Transgender and Rhetorics of Materiality* (New York: Columbia University Press, 2010).

313. The clearest exposition of this genealogical logic and its travels across biological, cultural, and religious spheres can be found in Nira Yuval Davis, *Gender and Nation* (Sage: London, 1997).

314. Robin, *The Enigma of Clarence Thomas*, p. 6.

315. Quoted in ibid., p. 27.

316. Quoted in ibid., p. 156.

317. For Thomas's views on interracial relationships, see ibid., p. 27. For his views on integration, see pp. 28, 73–79. To be clear, Thomas also sees institutional segregation as a way of redressing the power relations between Blacks and whites. His defense of racial purity is thus combined with an astute analysis of persistent racial hierarchy in an allegedly postracial context.

318. In a landmark statement of unity published in 1994, prominent American evangelicals and Catholics cited the right to life (hence Catholic natural law) as a key point of convergence. "Evangelicals and Catholics Together: The Christian Mission in the Third Millennium," *First Things*, May 1994. Catholic natural law also underlies Saba Mahmood's plea for a reconciliation between Christianity and Islam via an Aristotelian virtue ethics. Saba Mahmood, *The Politics of Piety: The Islamic Revival and the Feminist Subject* (Princeton, NJ: Princeton University Press, 2011), pp. 118–52.

CONCLUSION

1. "We now face a counterinsurgency without insurgency. A counterrevolution without revolution. The pure form of counterrevolution, without a revolution, as a simple modality of governing at home." Bernard E. Harcourt, *The Counterrevolution: How Our Government Went to War against Its Own Citizens* (New York: Basic Books, 2018), p. 12. Harcourt is specifically talking about the transplantation of U.S. counterinsurgency techniques, first deployed offshore, into homeland policing and surveillance operations.

2. For introductions to modern monetary theory (MMT), see L. Randall Wray, *Modern Money Theory: A Primer on Macroeconomics for Sovereign Monetary Systems* (London: Palgrave, 2012); Stephanie Kelton, *Modern Monetary Theory and the Birth of the People's Economy* (London: John Murray, 2020).

3. MMT has been heavily critiqued by both fellow post-Keynesians and Marxists. See Gerald Epstein, *What's Wrong with Modern Money Theory: A Policy Critique* (London: Palgrave Pivot, 2019), for a post-Keynesian critique of MMT. For prominent Marxist critiques of MMT, see Doug Henwood, "Modern Monetary Theory Isn't Helping," *Jacobin*, February 21, 2019; Paul Mattick, "Money Magic," *Brooklyn Rail*, October 2020; and Michael Roberts, "Modern Monetary Theory: A Marxist Critique," *Class, Race and Corporate Power* 7, no. 1 (2019): pp. 1–15. While the accusations of political naivety make sense at face value, I

suspect that they misread the strategic purpose of MMT as a policy-ready blueprint, with all the necessary simplifications that this genre implies. The biggest weakness of these critiques, however, is their tendency to elide the difference between debt monetization in the service of wage inflation (the specter haunting the 1970s) and debt monetization in the service of asset price inflation (the reality of quantitative easing, or QE). Thus, a recent commentary frames MMT as the "organic ideology of the post-crisis neoliberal state." Jamie Merchant, "The Money Theory of the State: Reflections on Modern Monetary Theory," *Brooklyn Rail*, February 2021. In fact, the debt monetization option entertained by MMT is the reverse of QE, and considerably tamer. While MMT recognizes wage inflation as a limit to debt monetization, recent Federal Reserve policy sees no intrinsic limit to asset price inflation *apart from wage inflation*.

4. For an extended reflection on the possibilities of money creation without private appropriation of wealth, see Alexander Kolokotronis, "Towards an Anarchist Money and Monetary System: An Interview with Nathan Cedric Tankus," *New Politics*, November 5, 2016.

5. Beyond MMT, numerous projects for a People's QE and other democratized versions of monetary finance have been proposed in the years since the Global Financial Crisis. See, for instance, Frank van Lerven, *Sovereign Money Creation: Paving the Way for a Sustainable Recovery* (London: Positive Money, 2013); Frances Coppola, *The Case for People's Quantitative Easing* (London: Polity, 2019); Eric Monnet, *La banque providence: Démocratiser les banques centrales et la monnaie* (Paris: Seuil, 2021); Saule Omarova, "The People's Ledger: How to Democratize Money and Finance the Economy," *Vanderbilt Law Review* 74 (2021): pp. 1231–98.

6. See Isabella M. Weber and Evan Wasner, "Sellers' Inflation, Profits and Conflict: Why Can Large Firms Hike Prices in an Emergency?," Economics Department University of Massachusetts Amherst Working Paper Series 343 (2023); Servaas Storm, "Profit Inflation Is Real," INET Institute for New Economic Thinking, June 15, 2023. Storm provides a systematic comparison of relative wage and profit gains in the 1970s and today.

7. The strategy is implicit in James O'Connor, *The Fiscal Crisis of the State* (New York: St. Martin's Press, 1973), and explicit in London Edinburgh Weekend Return Group, *In and against the State: Discussion Notes for Socialists* (London: Pluto Press, 2021).

8. The group's most recent statement of strategy can be found at Debt Collective, *Can't Pay, Won't Pay: The Case for Economic Disobedience and Debt Abolition* (Chicago: Haymarket Books, 2020).

9. Debt Collective, "Our History and Victories" (2023).

10. "We don't need lower interest rates or less predatory loan terms, we need truly public, socialized finance: public control over public money." Debt Collective, *Can't Pay, Won't Pay*, p. 115. The text references J. W. Mason, "Socialize Finance," *Jacobin*, November 2016.

11. Samir Sonti, "The Crisis of US Labor, Past and Present," *Socialist Register* 122 (2022): pp. 153–54; Sarah Jaffe, "The Radical Organizing That Paved the Way for the LA Teachers' Strike," *Nation*, January 19, 2019.

12. Nelson Lichtenstein, "What's at Stake in the General Motors Strike," *Dissent*, September 20, 2019.

13. Sanford M. Jacoby, *Labor in the Age of Finance: Pensions, Politics, and Corporations from Deindustrialization to Dodd-Frank* (Princeton, NJ: Princeton University Press, 2021), pp. 50–52.

14. Nelson Lichtenstein, "The Largest Strike in the History of American Higher Ed," *Dissent*, November 22, 2022.

15. Ibid.

Index

Bush, George H. W., 33, 79, 96, 154, 169, 171, 246, 268, 271, 274, 275, 288, 335, 337, 343.

Bush, George W., 77, 78, 79, 82, 174, 358; estate tax repeal, 180; presidential cabinet, 95–96; tax cuts, 79–81.

Business Council, 37.

Business revolt of 1970s, 36–37, 44, 117.

Business Roundtable, 37, 38, 42, 117, 125, 147, 148, 154, 159, 161, 179, 195, 340, 347.

BusinessWeek, 36, 124, 130.

Butler, Stuart, 164.

Byrd, Harry Flood, Jr., 250, 266, 268.

Byrd, Harry Flood, Sr., 247, 249–50, 252–53, 255–59, 264, 266, 270–71, 272, 275, 283, 285.

Byrd machine, 252–53.

CALCULUS OF CONSENT (Buchanan and Tullock), 200, 203–204, 206–10, 261, 263.

Calhoun, John C., 224–28, 256, 261, 300, 302.

California, 201, 272; constitutional convention, 269; disability insurance program, 372; fair housing law, 265; house price inflation, 43, 82, 169, 212–13, 382; Proposition 1 of 1973, 218–21; Proposition 4 of 1979 (Gann initiative), 213; Proposition 13 of 1978 (Jarvis-Gann Amendment), 142, 143, 145, 148, 212–14, 216, 217, 220, 230, 237, 238–39, 269; Proposition 58 of 1986, 213; Republican veto power, 213; schools and infrastructure, 230; state and local expenditures, 230; State Democratic Party, 312; State Republican Committee, 312; tax burden on citizens of, 230. *See also* Tax revolt of 1978.

Campbell, David, 305.

Capital gains, 18, 24, 25, 27, 28, 70, 85, 100, 173; economic growth and,

168–69, 174; and family wealth, 91–92; housing as source of, 169; measures of, 170; as proportion of capital income, 30–31; tax treatment of, 32, 37, 41, 60, 73, 78, 80, 81, 104, 166, 167, 168, 171, 172, 178, 184, 277; unrealized, 82, 92, 169; as vector of social mobility, 163; wealth effect of, 169–70, 174. *See also* Asset price appreciation.

Capital income, 30, 41, 57, 65.

Capital in the Twenty-First Century (Piketty), 31.

Carey, Hugh, 48, 51–52.

Carlyle Group, 96.

Carnes, Nicholas, 110.

Carter, Jimmy, 14, 38, 43, 53, 54, 55, 57, 137, 141, 146, 157, 323, 326, 330.

Categorical grants, 214, 333.

Catholic Health Association, 340–41.

Catholics, 122, 166, 306, 310, 312–20, 322, 325–26, 339, 340–43, 356, 359, 367–70, 373–74.

Catholic universalism, 318, 320, 370, 373.

Cato Institute, 176–77, 355.

Central bank independence, 15, 18, 376, 390 n.25.

Central banks, 15, 25, 84, 378

CETA. *See* Comprehensive Employment and Training Act; Comprehensive Employment Training Act.

Chalcedon Report, 358.

Chamber of Commerce, 37, 39, 148, 149, 156, 179, 181, 279, 286, 340, 347.

Chambers, Raymond, 62.

Chandler, Alfred, 87.

Charles G. Koch Foundation, 281.

Cheney, Dick, 79.

Chicago school, 198, 199, 209.

Chicago Stock Exchange, 177.

Childcare, 122, 284, 321.

Christian Coalition, 336, 338, 340, 344–48, 356–57.

Christian Reconstructionism, 307, 315, 330, 337–38, 349–51, 352, 355, 356, 357; and Christian dominionism, 363; on

and spending austerity, 181–82; and supply-side populism, 33–34, 41, 56, 78, 112–13, 131, 139–40, 148, 156; and Tax Cuts and Jobs Act of 2017, 27.
Laffer curve, 33, 183–84.
LaHaye, Tim, 330.
Lauder family, 86, 94.
Laufer, Henry, 94.
LBO. *See* Leveraged buyout.
Leadership Institute, 364.
League of Revolutionary Black Workers, 125.
League of the South, 358, 362.
Legal Services Corporation, 333.
Lehman Brothers, 84.
Leo XIII, Pope, 318.
Lerner, Abba, 247, 259, 260.
Lesher, Richard, 148, 347.
Leveraged buyout, 60, 61–62, 64, 88.
Libertarianism, 12–13, 148, 155, 198–99, 208, 267–68, 280, 304–305, 307, 3 08, 313, 351–52, 355, 361.
Liberty Strategic Capital, 96.
Limbaugh, Rush, 290, 343, 346.
Limited liability companies, 187, 188, 191–93.
Limits of Liberty (Buchanan), 208–10, 211.
Lind, Michael, 108.
Lindsay, John, 120.
Lindsey, Lawrence B., 77–78, 79.
Living Truth Ministry, 343.
Long, Russell, 268, 288.
Los Angeles, California, 70, 214, 216.
Los Angeles Times, 184.
Lott, Trent, 271, 277.
Louisiana, 160, 229, 234.
Lupu, Noam, 110.

MACLEAN, NANCY, 225, 247, 280.
Madison, James, 201.
Malcolm X, 319, 368, 369.
Malpass, David, 27.
Malthusian overpopulation theories, 319.
Managers, professional, 64, 87, 108, 110, 312.

Manhattan, 49, 50, 51, 70, 98, 99, 102.
Mann, Geoff, 11.
Manufacturing sector, 31, 39, 48, 50, 67, 109, 165.
Market exchange, 204–205.
Marriage, 103, 305, 373.
Marrs, Texe, 343, 532 n.176.
Marxism, 10, 268, 377–78.
Maryland, 267.
Mass incarceration, 376. *See also* Criminal justice system.
McAteer, Ed, 330.
McCain-Feingold Act of 2004, 296.
McConnell, Mitch, 289, 300.
McGovern, George, 37, 122, 156, 211, 311–12.
McKinley, William, 104.
Mecklenburg, Marjory, 335.
Meckling, William H., 61, 65.
Medicaid, 52, 245, 246, 273, 277, 293, 294–95, 309, 325, 381.
Medicare, 16, 180, 245, 246, 273, 277, 284, 294, 295–96, 304, 381.
Meese, Edwin, 331.
Mehlman, Ken, 96.
Mehlman Petrzela, Natalia, 144.
Mellon, Andrew, 104, 140.
Mercer, Robert, 94, 181, 194.
Mercer family, 95, 186, 194.
Methodological individualism, 204.
Midterm elections: of 1994, 171, 276–77, 284, 347; of 2010, 182, 290, 295, 303, 307, 357, 361, 362–63.
Migrants, 149, 284, 314; farm laborers, 12; undocumented, 109, 176, 179–80, 293, 358; urban, 45.
Militias, 190, 357.
Mill, John Stuart, 225.
Miller III, James C., 281.
Millionaires' Club, 104.
Mills, Wilbur, 38.
Minnesota Citizens Concerned for Life, 335.
Minority veto, 225–26.
Minsky, Hyman, 71–72.

New York Democratic Party, 51.

New York State Catholic Welfare Committee, 322.

New York Times, 74, 76, 93, 107, 125, 179.

NFIB. *See* National Federation of Independent Business.

Niskanen, William A., 218, 220.

Nixon, Richard, 19, 37, 38, 44–45, 118–23, 133, 156, 207, 264, 284, 308, 321; affirmative action, 119; and "blue-collar" welfarism, 114, 121–22, 125, 140, 189; and the blue-collar worker, 120–21, 138; and budget deficits, 261; and Christian conservatism, 311–13; and gold standard, 13, 21, 309; invasion of Cambodia, 120; Treasury Department under, 34, 42, 137; Watergate scandal, 312.

NLRA. *See* National Labor Relations Act of 1935.

NLRB v. Mackay Radio & Telegraph Co., 159.

Nonaccelerating inflation rate of unemployment, 173.

Norquist, Grover, 78, 80.

North, Gary, 351–54, 355, 357.

North American Free Trade Agreement of 1994, 173.

Northern Trust, 174.

NRLC. *See* National Right to Life Committee.

NTLC. *See* National Tax Limitation Committee.

NTU. *See* National Taxpayers Union.

Nullification, Calhounian, 225, 227, 256, 261, 302.

Nutter, G. Warren, 199, 200.

OATH KEEPERS, 190, 470 nn.427, 428.

Obama, Barack, 112, 180, 186, 190, 288, 290–91, 292, 295, 300, 303, 358–60.

Obamacare. *See* Affordable Care Act.

O'Brien, Rourke L., 230.

Occupational Safety and Health Administration, 149, 155.

Occupy Wall Street, 379.

O'Connor, James, 9.

O'Connor, Sandra Day, 331.

Office of Economic Opportunity, 308, 309, 310, 312, 318, 333.

Office of Management and Budget, 281, 334.

Oil, 93; embargoes, 35; price shock of 1973, 7, 14, 46, 123, 126, 127.

Oklahoma, 182, 188.

Old Guard Republicans, 256, 257, 265, 268, 271.

Old Testament, and free market principles, 352–53.

Olson, Mancur, 199.

Omnibus Budget Reconciliation Act of 1993, 276.

Operation Rescue, 357.

OSHA. *See* Occupational Safety and Health Administration.

PAGE, BENJAMIN I., 95.

Palin, Sarah, 304.

Pareto efficiency, 204.

Pass-through entities, 71, 180, 187, 191–92, 194.

PATCO. *See* Professional Air Traffic Controllers Organization.

Patrimonial power, 102–103.

Paul, Ron, 355; home-schooling curriculum, 355.

Paulson, John, 97.

Peck, Reece, 111–12.

Pence, Mike, 303, 363, 364, 366, 367, 370.

Pennsylvania, 111, 189.

Pension funds, 64, 93, 381.

Peonage systems, 244.

Perkins, Tony, 363.

Permanent capital, 90.

Peroutka, Michael, 358, 362.

Personal Responsibility and Work Opportunity Reconciliation Act of 1996, 285–86.

Personhood: abstract, 372; fetal, 365–66,

Near Futures series design by Julie Fry
Typesetting by Meighan Gale
Printed and bound by Maple Press